D0356201

Printed in Maine, USA

First Printing: September 2012

ISBN (Print edition): 978-0-9817300-4-2

ISBN (ebook edition): 978-0-9817300-3-5

To our infinitely patient spouses.

Foreword

The Critical Path has been an exceptionally well-received podcast. It has an audience of thousands of thoughtful listeners. We believe that the sustenance of any performance is the enthusiasm and engagement of an audience. Our audience has offered us ideas, reinforcement and moral support and this book is meant to give permanence to the words they inspired.

Our goal was to provide the first year's full transcript in a form that can be referenced and annotated and shared. The full year turned out to be too ambitious due to overall length (requiring more than 1000 pages in print form). We chose to exclude the interviews (to be published separately) and removed administrative discussions, banter and ads. As a result there are 31 episodes from June 7th, 2011 through May 30th, 2012, plus an introductory Pipeline interview from April 28th, 2011.

Sometimes spoken language does not translate easily to written language. In this regard we were pleasantly surprised that the language did not require significant rewriting. Some manners of speech were removed and some words were added for clarity [in brackets]. However, we strove to capture the gist of what was spoken to make the text a worthy work of reference.

Acknowledgements

We'd like to thank the following people for their work in making this book:

Ryan Irelan for standing in for Dan in a few of the shows

Duane Bemister and Allwest Reporting Ltd for their excellent work in transcription

Brad Lappin for proofreading and book design

Jory Raphael for The Critical Path show logo

Roger Schutte of J.S. McCarthy Printers for print services

Finally, and most importantly, this work could not have happened without the help from 826 backers who pledged our Kickstarter project.

Sincerely yours,

Horace Dediu
Dan Benjamin

1. @formasymphonic
2. @gustojunk
3. @jeffreymelvin
4. @jwiskowski
5. Abe
6. Erik Ableson
7. Dan Abrams
8. Al Abut
9. Atul Acharya
10. Josh Adams
11. Discover Create Advance
12. Kim Ahlberg
13. Patrick Ainge
14. Ian Bennett Alas
15. Florian Albrecht
16. Michael A. Alderete
17. Aleksandr
18. Alex
19. Gunnar Alexandersson
20. Stefan Alexiev
21. Alistair
22. Thomas Alvarez
23. C Ambrose
24. Amit
25. Carlo Amoretti
26. Li An
27. Suhit Anantula
28. Corrie T. M. Anderson, MD
29. Steve Anderson
30. Pedro Cezar de Andrade
31. André
32. Andrew
33. Anonymous
34. Anonymous
35. Anonymous
36. Anonymous
37. Anonymous
38. Zac Applegate
39. Alex Arena
40. Chris Armstrong
41. Ryan John Armstrong
42. Tom Van Avondt
43. David Avraamides
44. Gabriel Ayuso
45. Abdul Rahman Azhar
46. Ayoub Bacherki
47. Tomislav Bacinger
48. Andrew Bacon
49. John Bafford
50. Dennis Bailey
51. P Thomas Baldwin
52. Mike Ball
53. Al Banfe
54. Matthew Jones, Banxia
55. Neil Barron
56. Yves Bastide
57. Todd Bauer
58. Steven Baughman
59. Derek Beard
60. Luke Bearden
61. Tom Beattie
62. Andy Beaupain
63. Daniel Beck
64. Aaron Beckerman
65. Josh Been
66. Mordechai Beizer
67. Brian Beninger
68. Jeffrey A. Benson
69. Jason Berberich
70. LuAnne Bergeron
71. Noah Berlove
72. Patrick Berry
73. Bertrand Besse
74. E. J. Bezdek
75. Rishi Bhalerao
76. Kiran Bhanushali
77. Vilav Bhatt
78. Reuben Bijl
79. billo
80. billykunz
81. Michael Birenbach
82. Alan Birnbaum
83. Ezer Sembira Biron
84. Carel Bitter
85. Terje Sten Bjerkseth
86. Natasha Blakely
87. Grant Blakeman
88. Dan Boerner
89. Lars Boesen
90. Håkon Bogen
91. Garry Booker
92. Ryan Booker
93. Robert Borkowski
94. Anna Boros
95. Marco Bottaro
96. Michael Bowman
97. Stanil Bozjkov
98. Tony Brassel
99. Cody Brimhall
100. Thomas van den Broek
101. Alex Brooks
102. Rob Brosnan
103. Greg Brown
104. Jason Bruder
105. John Bruesewitz
106. Erik Bryn
107. Jeff Buck
108. Eric Buehrens
109. Paul Kristian Bugge-Asperheim
110. Kirk Burgess
111. Noam Burshtein
112. Joe Butler
113. Ian Byrd
114. Clinton Cairns
115. Brooke Callahan
116. Matthias Camerlinck
117. Jason Campbell
118. Paul Campbell
119. Nuno Filipe Campos
120. Penelope Cansler
121. Dan Capizzi
122. Tobias Carlander
123. Vinny Carpenter
124. Andrew Carroll
125. A. Anthony Castillo
126. Konniam Chan
127. Terence CHAN
128. Trent Chan
129. Andy Chang
130. Gary Chang
131. Chris Chavanne
132. Chris Chen
133. Paul Chen
134. Paul Cheramie
135. Jason Chi
136. Ready Chi
137. Randy "Danger" Chiu
138. Georgi Chobankov
139. Ivor Clarke
140. Kevin Clifton
141. Trevor Cole
142. Peter Coleman
143. Stephen collins
144. S.R. Connors
145. Ryan Cook
146. Aidan Cooper
147. Ken Cooper
148. Les Cooper
149. Tobias Cornvik
150. Jean-François Côté
151. Justin Govonlu, CFA
152. Linda Cowen
153. Martin Coxall
154. Michael Cranston
155. Phil Crawley
156. Aaron Crist
157. Brendon Cromwell
158. Bob Cronk
159. Brian W. Crumley
160. Wayne D.
161. Niels Daalhuizen
162. Michael S. Dahl
163. Ed Dale
164. Nick Dalton
165. Dermot Daly

9

166. Anh Dam
167. David Damore
168. Vitale Daniels
169. Matthias Danner
170. Jonas Amren Dannert
171. Robert Danner
172. Dany
173. dave
174. Jake Davidson
175. Justin Davis
176. Michael K. Dawson
177. Nick Dazé
178. Brant E. DeBow
179. John Debs
180. Michael DeGusta
181. Robert DeLaurentis
182. Toby Delrahim
183. Markus T. Delves
184. Colin Denzel
185. David Deren
186. Christophe Dessimoz
187. Joshua Dickens
188. Chris DiClerico
189. CG diPierro
190. Colin Dismuke
191. George, Miriam, Joaquin, Jacinta, Jayne Diversiev
192. Razvan Dan Dobre
193. Kaloian Doganov
194. Christopher J. Doherty
195. Craig M. Doran
196. Alex Dowson
197. Michael Dragone
198. Pål Anders Dramstad
199. Steven Drost
200. Albert-Olivier Drouart
201. steve dubinsky
202. Ted Duguay
203. Lucien W Dupont
204. Julian Durand
205. Wayne Dyer
206. HR Dynamics
207. Theo van Eeden
208. Amal Ekbal
209. Anders Elfström
210. Fredrik Eliasson
211. Ralph Elliott
212. Philip Elmer-DeWitt
213. Caleb Elston
214. Evan Emolo
215. Morgan Ericsson
216. Erik
217. Jón Helgi Sen Erlendsson
218. George Eves
219. Jeff Bessling (Apple Fanboy)
220. Trevor Fancher
221. Steve Farmer
222. Matt Farrugia
223. Saad Fazil @sfrocks
224. ed fernandez @efernandez
225. Ideh Fesharaki
226. Andy Fisher
227. Richard Fox
228. Scott Francis
229. Tom Fraser
230. Fred
231. Georgerobert Freeman
232. Marc Frei
233. Stefan Freimark
234. Nicholas Friederich
235. Greg Friedman
236. ftlbaby
237. Nico Fuchs
238. Frank Fujimoto
239. John Fullerton
240. Nathan Gaber
241. James Gabler
242. Domingo Gallardo
243. Tomas "Professor Tom" Gallucci
244. Tarun Gangwani
245. James Gardiner
246. Gareth
247. Tom Garshol
248. Robert W. Gates
249. Calin Gavris
250. David Gelphman
251. Yuri Genyk
252. David Gloyn-Cox
253. Cyril Godefroy
254. Mark Godfrey
255. Mircea Goia
256. Lynda L. Gousha
257. David Grady
258. Bobby Grasberger @BGrasberger
259. Glen Gray
260. Darren Grayson
261. Bryan Green
262. Brian Greenbaum
263. Janico Greifenberg
264. Brandon Gribin
265. Jason W. Grzywna
266. George Guerrero
267. Pascal guertin
268. Philippe Guertin
269. Cory Haggart
270. Philip Hakim
271. Maynard Handley
272. Charles Hansen
273. Jared Thomas Hardy
274. Hannes Hauer
275. Tuomas Hautala
276. Kevin Hay
277. Ronald Hayden
278. Bill So - Headnix
279. Christian Heck
280. Esa Helttula
281. Claude Hénault
282. Volker Herminghaus
283. Drew Herrick
284. Jonas Heylen
285. Frederick Hirsch
286. Ben Hobden
287. Michael Höfler
288. Steven Hofman
289. Brandon P. Hollingshead
290. Michael Holmgren
291. Peter Holstein
292. David Holt
293. Michael Honey
294. Harry Hong
295. Christopher Hopp
296. Takashi Hoshino
297. Danny Housseas
298. Sangxia Huang
299. Tom Hubben
300. Nicholas Hudson-Ellis
301. Steven Huey
302. Kon Hui
303. P Huidobro
304. David Hulme
305. Chris Humphreys
306. Alex Hung
307. Bruce W Hunt
308. Kris Hunt
309. Jon Hurd
310. Brenden Hussey
311. Jesse Imbach
312. Imran
313. Matthew Inman
314. LogYourRun for iPhone
315. Jack Irby
316. Aaron Irizarry
317. Johan Israelsson
318. Vlad Ivanovic
319. J.Hwong
320. Frederic Jacobs
321. Morten Jacobsen
322. Simon Jacquier
323. Dániel Jaksi
324. Piyush Jamkhandi
325. Philip Jan
326. Jim Jazwiecki
327. Isaiah Dallas Jefferson, Jr.

328. Jamie Jenkins
329. Duane Jensen
330. jesselperry
331. Fei Jing
332. JLOOP
333. Joe
334. Douglas B Johnson
335. Michael Johnston
336. Derik Jones
337. Nathan Jones
338. Marcos Juarez
339. Marko Jukić
340. Rebekah K
341. Dmitry Kabanov
342. Matthew Kahn
343. Janne Käki
344. Kalyan
345. Arjun Kapoor
346. Dirk Karell
347. Chris Kaschner
348. Sam Kass
349. Rizwan Kassim
350. Darius Katz
351. Anthony Kay
352. Adam Kazwell
353. Kevin M. Keating
354. Keefe
355. Benjamin Kerosky
356. Christian R J Kerr
357. Larry Ketchersid
358. Joefrey Kibuule
359. George Kiersted
360. Daniel Kimerling
361. Grant Klassen
362. Richard Kleim
363. John M Klepetka
364. Matt Klosterman
365. Jerry Knaus
366. Max Velasco Knott
367. Keitaroh Kobayashi
368. R George Komoto
369. Timo Koola
370. Jan Korbel
371. Ville Korpinen
372. KP
373. shane Kramps
374. Stefan Kreutter
375. Ksheerabdhi Krishna
376. Miroslav Kriz
377. Artie Kuhn
378. Ronal Kumar
379. Jeff Kuntz
380. Glenn Kwarcinski
381. Winston Kwon
382. Joe Kyd
383. Christopher Lahey
384. Tim Lahey
385. Trung Lai

386. Jarkko Laine
387. Hillar Lainevool
388. Mayson Lancaster
389. lantinian
390. Casey Laris
391. Seth Larson
392. Bertacchini Laurent
393. Christian Lauritzen
394. Chuck Lay
395. Phong Le
396. Auro Lecci
397. Albert Lee
398. Hoon Lee
399. Leslie R. Lee
400. Mike Lee
401. Paul Tien-Shih Lee
402. Richard S Lee
403. Rob Lee
404. SungMin Chang &
     Wonmin Lee
405. Daryl Lee
406. Alan J. Leeds
407. Jan Lehnardt
408. Duncan Lennox
409. Jay Levy
410. Lukasz Lewandowski
411. Craig Li
412. Jiaqi Li
413. Josh Li
414. Andrew Lim
415. Daan Linden
416. Jim Lindley
417. Charles Lindsay
418. Daniel Lieberman
419. Robert B Liverman
420. Luis Llull
421. Richard Lo
422. Sherman Lo
423. Ian Longley
424. Christopher Loo
425. Mark Lopresto
426. Torsten Louland
427. James Lourie
428. David Love
429. Vaughan Lovegrove
430. Andrew Lovseth
431. Lucy
432. Simon Ly
433. Andy Lyon
434. R MacAndrew
435. Don MacDonald
436. Jonny Mack
437. Rory MacKean
438. Alistair MacLellan
439. Iain K. MacLeod
440. Terri MacMillan
441. Ravi Madala
442. Tom Maes • @tmaes

443. Yanik Magnan
444. Chris Malinowski
445. Brian Maloney
446. Sai Kishore Reddy
     Mamidi
447. David Mana
448. David Mancherje
449. Roberto Mandrioli
450. Tony W. Manino, Jr.
451. Franco Maras
452. Marfil
453. Mark
454. Mark
455. Mark
456. Marcin Markiewicz
457. Nicolas Markwald
458. Tiago G Marques
459. Joachim Mårtensson
460. Niels Martha
461. Hunter Martin
462. Robert Martin
463. James Marwood
464. Jayasimhan Masila-
     mani
465. Jacob Mather
466. Thomas Mauriello
467. Wade Maxfield
468. Stuart Maxwell
469. Jakob Mayr
470. Jeff Mazzone
471. Don McAllister
472. Colin McCrea
473. Sam McDonald
474. William McGregor
475. Peter Mcinerney
476. Matthew Burrow
     McLeod
477. Mohammed Al Medfa
478. Alan Meeus
479. Vivek Meha
480. Devanshu Mehta
481. Bernie Meier
482. Rich Merritt
483. Greg Messerian
484. johan meylaerts
485. Jakob Mikkelsen
486. Jim Miles
487. Aaron M. Miller
488. Chris miller
489. Gerhard Miller
490. J. Scott Miller
491. Walter Milliken
492. Grigori Milov
493. Max Min
494. Dr. Dariush Mir-
     fendereski
495. Brian Mitchell
496. Theresa Mitchell

497. Ronald Tetsuo Miura
498. MJC
499. Romain Moisescot
500. M. Moore
501. Neil Moore
502. Sean Moore
503. David Morrison
504. Christian Moskal
505. Eugene Moy
506. Neven Mrgan
507. Danny Mulligan
508. mummey
509. Nalini K. Muppala
510. Jim Murtha
511. Steve Mydlowski
512. Lucas N.
513. n3mosan
514. Helmut Naughton
515. C.J. Navas
516. Neil
517. Jay Nevans
518. Andrew Newman
519. Mark Newton
520. NewtonRJ
521. Khiem Ngo
522. Jon Nguyen
523. Siyabonga Nhlumayo
524. David Nichols
525. Wesley Nicolas
526. Roberto Nieves
527. Filip Nilsson
528. Tarun Nimmagadda
529. Mark Nunnikhoven
530. Ed Nusbaum
531. Aidan O'Loan
532. Andrew O'Marah
533. Patrick O'Neill
534. Robert Occhialini
535. Ian Ollmann
536. Torje Olsen
537. Tom O'Rourke
538. JC Ortega
539. Claudio Ortolina
540. Günther go Ottendor-
fer
541. Ingomar Otter
542. Dorothy P.
543. Jonathan Paddock
544. Paul Paguyo
545. Erik C. Parker
546. Ketan Patel
547. Rukesh Patel
548. Pete Patron
549. Daniel A Pauw
550. Daniel Pavlides
551. Derek Pearcy
552. Rob Pearson
553. John Davidorff Pell

554. Shawn Petriw
555. Dominic Pettifer
556. Harry F Petty III
557. Ernest N. Prabhakar,
Ph.D.
558. philipp_net
559. JJ Phillip
560. Mark L. Phillips
561. Collin Pieper
562. Pieter ten Pierick
563. Pierre
564. Sam Pierson
565. Kiril Piskunov
566. Eric Platon
567. The team at
Pleisty.com
568. Jonathan Ploudre
569. Eddy Poon
570. Carsten Pötter
571. Michael A. Potts
572. Ben Prata
573. Paul Préfontaine
574. David M. Price
575. Peter Pullicino
576. Brendan Quinn
577. Jonas Rabbe
578. Kevin Rahilly
579. Raja
580. Puni Rajah
581. Ralf
582. Markus Ramstedt
583. Mohammed Rashid
584. Jonathan Rauch
585. George Raynal
586. Charlie Reece
587. Jonathan Reff
588. Gensky Regnus
589. Mark Reich
590. Craig Reidel
591. Carsten Reinhardt
592. Brian Resac
593. Robert Reti
594. Anton Bishop Reut
595. Daniel Reyes
596. Filipe Araújo Ribeiro
597. Jamie Rice
598. Brook Riggio
599. Carl Rigney
600. Nicholas Riley
601. Dan Ritzenthaler
602. Seth Robbins
603. Robert
604. Robbo Robertson
605. Bernardo Rodrigues
606. Victor Rodrigues
607. Ruben D. Rodriguez
608. Roger
609. Mikeal Rogers

610. Mike Rohde
611. Peter Rohde
612. Rollie
613. Daniel Ropp
614. Bernd Rosauer
615. David Rosenfeld
616. A.J. Ross
617. Stephen E. Roulac
618. laurent roullet
619. Maxime Rousseaux-
Bridle
620. David C. Roy
621. Lincoln Rozelle
622. Roman Rubinstein
623. Daniel Rutherford
624. Stephen Ryner Jr.
625. Bernhard S
626. Will S
627. Peter Sahlstrom
628. Hayashi Sakawa
629. Rafik Salama
630. Muhammad Saleem
631. Jeff Samuelson
632. Lincoln-Shaun Sand-
ers
633. Maxwell Santoro
634. Jorge Santos
635. Aditya Saravana
636. Brendan Saricks
637. SBC
638. Andreas Schaefer
639. Markus Schiegl
640. Dirk Schmidt
641. Joseph Schmitt
642. Mike Schneider
643. Eckhard Schnell
644. Damien Schreurs
645. Roger Schutte
646. Marc Schwieterman
647. Scott
648. Adam Searle
649. Etienne Segonzac
650. Peter Seid
651. Joel Selanikio
652. PA Semi
653. Jason Sepp
654. Sam Shafie
655. Matthew Shanley
656. Robert Sharl
657. Gordon Shephard
658. Roger Shepherd
659. Sonny Shetty
660. Clayton Shonkwiler
661. William Shyu
662. Mark Siegal
663. Paulo Sérgio S. Silva
664. Jago Silver
665. Jeff Silverman

666. Jen Simmons
667. Jared Sinclair
668. Michael Skiba
669. Yaphet Smallwood
670. Daniel Smedley
671. Keith Smiley
672. Martin Smith
673. smsag
674. Hank Snider
675. Joakim Sorthe
676. Fraser Speirs
677. Graham Spencer
678. Joshua Spry
679. Brendan Steidle
680. Jonathan Stenger
681. Cole Stewart
682. Guy Stewart
683. Kevin Stewart
684. Mike Stewart
685. Jonathan Sugai
686. Alex Sukalski
687. Stephanie Sullivan
688. Stephen WG Sullivan
689. Bryan Summersett
690. Olivia Sun
691. Sunil
692. Shigeya Suzuki
693. Conny Svensson
694. Jon Sweet
695. Zsolt Szalacsi
696. Lukasz Szymanski
697. Kristian Tapaninaho
698. Calvin Tapley
699. Hilton Tarrant
700. Juan Tascon
701. Pavel Tcholakov
702. Nonprofit Tech
703. Pedro Telles
704. Alberto de Paola Terzaghi
705. Jonathan Theodore
706. Lars T. Therkildsen
707. David Thomas
708. Jim Thomas
709. Kirsi Thum
710. Radu Ticiu
711. J. Tillmann
712. Jens Tillmann
713. Michael Tofias
714. G. L. Tolle
715. Jarrett Tom
716. Michal Tomlein
717. Byron Too
718. Vincent Touquet
719. Larry P. Townsend Jr
720. Alex Tran-Qui
721. Uldis Trapencieris
722. David Truslow
723. Eric Tsai
724. C. Anthony Tucci
725. Peter Tullio
726. Peter Uchytil
727. Maxi Udenio
728. Dmitry Uduman
729. Spencer Underhill
730. Nicolas Untz
731. Esteban Uribe
732. Audun Utengen
733. Bob Van Valzah
734. Antti Vanhanen
735. Eric Varady
736. Pavol Vaškovič
737. Wayne Vaughan
738. Jack Veiga
739. Filip Verhaeghe
740. Thomas Verschoren
741. André Villar
742. Daniel Viney
743. Federico Viticci
744. Derek van Vliet
745. Leif Uwe Vogelsang
746. Chris Volkert
747. Radim Vrška
748. Uwe Wachsmann
749. Thijs van der Wal
750. Matthias Wanke
751. Henrik Wannheden
752. Nick Warren
753. Boyd Waters
754. James Watt
755. Rhys Waywood
756. Chris Weber
757. Julian Wegkamp
758. Tyler Weir
759. Brad West
760. Kwame Weusi-Puryear
761. David E. Wheeler
762. David J. Whelan @djwhelan
763. Julia Whelan
764. Jon Whipple
765. Ann-Marie White
766. Josh White
767. Sam White
768. William Whyte
769. Chris Wiest
770. Arthur James Wilfong
771. Nathan Wilkes
772. Emmett D. Williams Jr.
773. Iain Wilson
774. Shaun Wilson
775. Justin Winchiu
776. Phillip Windsor
777. Matthew Winship
778. Peter Wolanski
779. Jenkin Wong
780. Matt Wong
781. Wai Keong Wong
782. Ming Woo
783. Mike Wren
784. Yan
785. Steve Yang
786. Chet Yeary II
787. Jordan Yee
788. Kevin Yoho
789. K. Young
790. Brad Youtz
791. Daniel Zajork
792. Robert Zangrilli
793. Jim Zellmer
794. Lee B. Ziffer
795. Michael Zoradi

Prelude: The Pipeline

Posted April 28th, 2011, as Pipeline Episode #52

Horace Dediu joins Dan Benjamin to discuss the life of a professional smartphone analyst; how he built Asymco.com to 500,000 readers in only 9 months, curated market intelligence, the language of business, engineering, asymmetry, fearlessness, knowing what you're doing, the post-PC world, and the concept of the disruptive lens.

Dan Benjamin: This is "The Pipeline," an interview show hosted by Dan Benjamin. That's me.

My guest today is Horace Dediu. He is the founder and author of the marketing intelligence site, Asymco.com. He is also an independent analyst and advisor to telecom incumbents and entrants on mobile platform strategy. He's got an amazing history. He's worked for Nokia, and he's got this really, really amazing track record as an analyst. I'm thrilled to have him on the show today. Horace, welcome to the show.

Horace Dediu: Thank you.

Dan: A lot of people know your work from Asymco. They may not know who you are, the man behind Asymco, the man with the ability to come up with these amazing numbers and predictions, but before we get too much into that, tell us, for those who don't know what Asymco.com is, perhaps you could tell us about it.

Horace: It started out as, actually, an app development company, [and] I wanted to have some material to have as content on the website, something that would define the character of the company. I started to write a blog, and that actually became much more interesting than the app development. There's still some of that going on. I don't showcase it, but it's for clients, usually, who are interested in some local work, typically in Finland.

Anyway, I started it as a website that was to meant to demonstrate my competency, and it grew into a very popular place for discussions and debates around mobile strategy and the new world of smartphones and the post-PC era.

It's focused mostly on the marriage of analysis, strategy and some of the technology issues, so it's not news oriented. It's more about in-depth analysis. We try to find out what is the cause and effect of what's happening. A lot of it depends on having data and analysis of all the public information available about the market.

The tagline is "curated market intelligence," and that means we're looking at the markets. We're trying to find the right data to apply to it, and then we have an in-depth discussion, lots and lots of good comments.

Dan: You do more than just that. You're being very modest, because time and time again, you will find insight from looking at pages and pages of numbers. You'll create incredibly insightful... I mean, you'd make Edward Tufte proud. You create these incredibly subtle and smart graphics, and in so many cases...

There's just an article I was reading in *Fortune* this morning about this. Where, again, I read that you tied JP Morgan's Mark Moskowitz for the closest or best iPhone estimate after these numbers that Apple just came out with.

Horace: Well, yeah, there's many threads. One is that we do try to... I try. I shouldn't say "we" because it's actually just me.

I try to speak in a visual language. On Twitter, [my bio says], "I use words as a punctuation to a lyrical tale told by numbers," so the numbers are what I always begin with. I start off with a spreadsheet or a clean sheet of paper, and I think about the data first. That leads me to form a hypothesis, and then I build out the argument. But the data is what really shapes my thinking.

Having spent a lot of time with data and trying to present it to people, I've become, perhaps unconsciously, able to synthesize it in, as you put it, in Edward Tufte's model—although I've never really took his course or anything. I just read the book. But I'm very sensitive [to the visual display of information].

Some people are more visual than others. I know some people prefer to see just the tables and the raw numbers. But even if there's just three numbers, I'd rather see them in a chart. That's what creates in my mind a story.

When you have a lot of numbers and a lot of detail, I want to be creative about how to present it in a compelling way, that people just look at it and instantaneously understand what I'm trying to say. The words come in as punctuation to that. They come in to bring the audience to a point where they can debate it, and they can point to this phrase as saying this, and therefore they can follow up on that.

I've sometimes, actually, [I] just posted a chart saying, "After working so long to get this chart, I don't even want to bother writing about it."

Dan: [laughs] Right.

Horace: I'd say, "This is self-explanatory," but then everybody comes back and says, "Can you explain it?" So, that [would be] a failed experiment. To *me*, that's enough. The numbers speak for themselves. The words are there to punctuate it and accentuate it.

Dan: It's fascinating, though, that that really is the way that you think. It seems like you really do think in this visual language. Can you talk about that? Where did your background in this come from?

Horace: Well, I came from a family where everyone was involved in the sciences in some way, or mathematics. My father is a PhD in math and my mother had a Master's, and they were both professors or teachers. So I grew up in a world of numbers and thinking in a scientific way, and then I went on and did my undergrad in the U.S.

By the way, I'm not a native of America. I'm native of Romania. My family emigrated to the U.S. I spent most of my life there. I'm an ex-pat, living in Finland. I married in Finland and my son was born in Finland, but I'm a U.S. citizen.

Anyway, I went to school in the States, and I was in engineering school. I was very late, in my late 20s [when I] actually thought about doing something in business because I had been in a research lab—a research environment. [I then] moved a little bit into an IT area just to get a bit more experience with "the real world." Then I decided to go to business school, and was fortunate to get accepted to Harvard.

That's where I learned the language. I didn't learn much else, actually. I learned the language of business, but I really think about the world more as an engineer, I think, than as what I might call a professional analyst. [That being] someone who's trained in business, who has a background in perhaps economics, not in engineering. Nothing wrong with that; I'm just saying that my early years were in an environment with a scientific approach to things.

I try to say that also, in my site. That although it's not a pure scientific method—we can't get there quite yet—but I really aspire to bring this information sharing, peer review type methodology, and citation and openness to the discussion of analysis of business.

I find that business is still, in a way… I use the word *"medieval,"* because it's pre-Renaissance. The Renaissance was a period when people realized that it's better to share information rather than protect it. That was in the fields of science, architecture, building things and so on. Newton came out of that process of openness. That hasn't yet been infused in our business thinking.

I know there are good reasons for that, and I'm not naïve about it. I'm just saying, ideally, I'd like to bring a more scientific process to what we call business analysis.

My audience, by the way, if I may ramble on here…

Dan: No, please.

Horace: I think the thing is, that [I know] my audience [only] by looking at the bios of Twitter followers, so I don't know much about them except what they tell me. But it seems that they are very technical people. They're like what I was when I was in my 20s. I was so hungry for pattern recognition about business because I was technically focused, but I wanted to know how the world worked. Knowing the scientific or engineering world didn't really give me a lot of insight in why the company I was working for wasn't successful.

What I try to do, again, is educate that audience without being—what's the word, patronizing?—or without lecturing. I just subtly bring in some theory, what I call "business theory," into the discussion so that they can step back and say, "Hang on. You mean there's *theory* like there's *physics?* There's all these sciences out there, and yet there's nothing like that for business? Could there be such a thing?" I have to hint at it, that yes, there is such a thing and it can be thought that way.

That's my dream. There are others who share my dream, who are in academia in business schools, but their world isn't overlapping very much with the world of technology today. Yet the world of technology is very theory-hungry right now. That's perhaps why the positioning of Asymco has been successful, because there's this interesting overlap between these two spheres.

Dan: Perhaps your background as an engineer maybe gives you... I don't know if an "edge" is the right word, but maybe it is. An edge over the people who are working for, let's say, JP Morgan. You've got an insight, perhaps, because of your much deeper familiarity with engineering. Doesn't that come into play?

Horace: It helps, but it's not the knowledge, I think. It's the way you approach the problem. Also, I think that what I learned through this experiment of blogging... (and I did a bit of it, also, inside Nokia when I was there for eight years. I did it in the last year or so.)

What happens is, when you write, you learn a lot, and when your people actually comment, you learn even more. Many teachers will tell you that teaching is a way to learn.

I see it as, because I am open—in the sense of broadcasting what I do and the way I think—I just expose everything as much as I can.

[For instance,] one thing I was thinking about: When flying, a lot of people who work for companies have these screen protectors that don't let anybody see what's on their computer.

Dan: Right.

Horace: If I'm on a plane, and somebody next to me would look at my computer and ask me what I'm doing, I'd love to share that information with them.

To me, that's the asymmetry in Asymco. The asymmetry of what I do is that I'm looking very hard at how to expose as much as possible—what I'm doing and how I think—so that others can critique it, so that others can teach me where I've made mistakes.

That makes me, frankly, smarter. That, I think, is the key. It's the openness of the process, rather than saying I know more, ([even though I may have had] a background of knowledge that the others may not have had.)

Think about the JP Morgan analyst. He's got only a very small set of people—his peers—and that's all the criticism he's going to get. Sometimes those people, probably for political reasons, won't even raise their objections. [He's] working without any help, in other words, and I'm working with 13,000 people helping me.

I'd love to build on that, and the more I do it, I think, the more I understand and the better off everyone else is.

Dan: It sounds like there's also a degree of fearlessness in the way that you work. And that desire to be open implies that you're not afraid of getting critiqued. You're not afraid of being wrong.

Horace: No. In fact, we only learn when someone tells us we've made a mistake. I don't want to be woken up in the middle of the night by someone telling me, "Hey, you were right yesterday." I want to be woken up in the middle of the night [by someone saying] "Hey, you made a mistake," and then I would rush over and fix things. I'd learn...

Today, I published my own self-criticism of what I felt was wrong with my last earnings forecast. That's where I figured out something about the iPad I didn't know. I made a mistake there.

But in doing so, one big thing I learned is that *nobody* knew what was going on with the iPad. Even those people who said they have secret "Deep Throat" sources in the supply chain telling them what's being built and what's not—it turns out that all that was a masquerade. Nobody knew. Had anyone known, then out of 50 analysts, *one* would have gotten it right. And no one did. So, in a sense, that was a lesson.

There's a lot of these things, subtle things, that happen when you write and you publish, and you invite criticism.

The other thing is that I have an assumption that I don't know what I'm doing; in fact, an assumption that nobody knows what they're doing. I think it was [Wehrner] von Braun (the engineer who designed the Saturn V rocket that took us to the the moon.) He said, famously, "Research is what I'm doing when I don't know what I'm doing." I feel like I don't know what I'm doing, and that's a healthy thing to feel. I think it's what keeps me actually improving and somewhat, maybe, more accurate than others.

Dan: One of the things that we've seen come out of the world of weblogs, of creating unique content like this, is a narrowing of focus. You don't just talk about the mobile industry on Asymco. You talk specifically, or for the most part, about smartphones. Certainly iPads fit into that, and bigger picture things fit into that. Can you talk about that? Why smartphones? Clearly, it's a really hot topic right now, but there's more to it than that.

19

Horace: Actually, smartphones were something of a passion of mine for over a decade. I actually began using a smartphone in 1999. It was a Nokia Communicator—which looks like a brick. Literally. It is the size of a small brick. That product, though, at the time was running a 386 architecture chip. It had a fairly large display, and it ran an operating system named GEOS, which doesn't exist anymore. But it was a real computer and it had a real keyboard, and at the time there was nothing like it. This was in '99.

Palm was also around. Palm was quite a hot product for already a few years, but it wasn't yet a communicating product. It was an isolated... like the iPad, today. It was tethered to a computer.

The thing is that I saw, at the moment when I used that product, I just saw that, "Hey, this is what *all* computers are going to be like." I just didn't know *when*, I didn't know *how*, and I didn't know *who* would make that future happen. So, in fact, I made a semiconscious decision that I was going to figure this out, and I thought I would need to learn a lot to figure it out.

My question was: Whom do I learn from? Do I learn from a startup? Do I learn from a incumbent PC company that makes computers that someday will be this small? Or will I learn from a phone company that's going to make phones that are going to become PCs? I ended up going to a phone company because they were just so far [ahead of] anyone else.

That was Nokia, who was making these things, and they had a roadmap. I actually went there partly because of that logic, partly because the dot com bubble burst and I needed a job. There were a bunch of reasons, but fundamentally, I really thought that this innovation would come from telecom, that a telecom player would disrupt the PC world.

In fact, for many years it looked like that was going to happen. They were successful launching a whole bunch of smartphones. They were selling tens of millions of them before the IT world, or I should say the old-school computer world woke up to this opportunity.

But [the PC] came back with a vengeance. That's the remarkable story of second half of the last decade, which was that it was Apple. Partly it was Microsoft, although they failed... and then Google came. All these people from the West Coast of the United States took by storm an industry that had been fairly well-established in Europe and Asia.

That to me was, frankly, a learning experience. I was wrong that telecom would win, and ever since I've been repeating that story: that the major disruption that happened is that computing companies came and literally took all the money out of telecom. And that's still underway. Many will object to that thesis, but I still believe it's happening and will happen. We just found out today that Apple, in fact, overtook Nokia as the number one in sales of phones in the world.

Dan: It's remarkable.

Horace: Technically, as the most profitable, Apple was already established. They were that in about 2008. But now it looks like they'll be the top selling, not by units, but by value. Again, we're seeing this transition, this transfer of wealth happening from incumbents in telecom to entrants coming from the PC world. And in fact Google, out of all people, also coming in, although they're not yet capturing a lot of profit. They're getting there.

But anyway, this has been a phenomenal decade-long process of learning, and I have to say I got a lot of scars from it because, you see, I was an analyst inside Nokia trying to figure this out. Probably in 2004 I was doing smartphone forecasting, or trying to figure out who would be the platform players, trying to figure out whether...

Dan: You were doing this within Nokia?

Horace: Yeah, within Nokia, it was 2004, it was my job to do these kind of projections like we're seeing from IDC and Gartner. Today, that sort of projecting "by 2015 how many, what will be the share split between the various platforms." But imagine doing that in 2004, you know. There was no Google.

Dan: Yeah.

Horace: I mean, there was no Android, there was no... it was just Windows Mobile, but there were still plenty of [other] players. There was Windows Mobile, there was Palm OS, there was Nokia's Symbian and there were even alternatives like BREW and your Java-based products.

So there were still a... it feels a lot to me like déjà vu because a lot of that was happening a long time ago, although the players have changed. So a lot of people today will say, "Well hang on now, we can project this forward, because we know what's happening, finally." But these guys were nowhere. The Gartners and the IDCs didn't even try to do that in 2005 because there wasn't a definition for them [of a smartphone]; they didn't have customers asking for this [research]. They weren't even analyzing [phones], they were looking at PDAs.

Dan: Right.

Horace: They had IT customers.

Another theme I have is that I think it's too early, even now, to call the long term, because things are changing so rapidly in the space. It is really one of the most dynamic industries I've ever seen, and we're seeing enormous growth, at the same time enormous volatility. There are billions and billions of consumers that haven't been served by this market, and I believe they all will be someday. The phone business grew to be five billion users, but the smartphone business is still under one, and I think it's going to be four, or even five later on, and you can't guess what that's going to look like.

Dan: A lot of people are describing 2011 and really anything forward, perhaps even going back a few years, as the Post-PC world. Now, is it a term that really seemed to start, although I was certainly seeing it, but it certainly started when the iPad was frequently described as a post-PC device. What does that mean? What is that better... more important question, what does that mean to you as somebody who is really looking at this, and the PC industry as well?

Horace: Yeah, it's a charged term, and a lot of people take issue with it. They are very defensive about it because they make a living out of PCs, and they grew up with it, and it's a very precious thing to them, and I respect that.

But I'd point out a couple of things. First of all, it's not, it shouldn't be called post-PC, it should be called post-microcomputer. Unfortunately, there's nothing catchy about that word, but the PC to many sounds like Windows [and hence] that this is all about killing Windows or killing Microsoft, and it isn't necessarily that. It isn't either about killing anything because...

One phrase I use is that "the Stone Age didn't end because we stopped using stones," or the Iron Age for that matter. We're still using a lot of the technological eras that came before the current era. Steve Jobs used this phrase that PCs are trucks. That's not great. From my point of view, I think that's again a little bit divisive as a comment. I think it's important to just say we're going to just move consumption of computing to new contexts.

So, for example, an iPad will not replace what you do on the desktop, not for a long time, but at the same time you're going to use it in places where you don't use a computer, and not even a laptop, not even a notebook. You're going to use it in niches of time or niches of space that currently are unoccupied by computers. So in that sense it expands consumption of computing.

For me the post-PC era is about creating more opportunities for using these computers, and over time those new devices will actually grow up to be more and more powerful and will eventually vacuum up some of the consumption from the old era, just like happened with PCs and minicomputers, and the minicomputers took share away from mainframes. But they're all still around to this day. So minis became servers and mainframes became clouds, but it's still the same idea of centralized and departmental computing. Now I think micro-computing is going to be branching off into really truly mobile computing and then portable computing and then fixed computing.

Unfortunately, we are settled with these old terms like "PC" which have a huge number of connotations. It has a Windows connotation, it has all these livelihoods attached to it that people get defensive. I still see it as a growing thing, as a new thing, as an improvement on new dimensions.

Dan: Fascinating, though, to hear this perspective because when I hear you talk about it, and all of these topics really, it really makes it sound so simple and straightforward, and that's, I think, a really unique approach. Is this the approach that you take when you're dealing with all these numbers and looking at these different factors? Do you just simplify and simplify and simplify?

Horace: Yeah, tell a story. I mean, it sounds corny and somewhat impossible to really advise someone with something like that, but it's just a simple thing. You have to invoke personal history, you have to invoke how people... Don't be combative.

One thing I should say on my side is that I've been very lucky that I have a commenting option which some, [for example John Gruber] don't. And I respect that, but I struggle with this question of comments because I wanted it to be a reflection on what I do, and I was afraid that we're going to get a lot of abuse. but it hasn't happened. The reason I think it hasn't happened is because I don't put forward just opinion, I put forward thoughtful things, hopefully. People respond in kind. I police the site in the sense that I will delete abusive comments. I only have to delete about a dozen out of over 13,000, so that really means to me, a lot, that this is a way to compose, and, what is it to behave online as a writer that you need to make sure that you create good quality and that good quality content is amplified by good quality comments. That's been a wonderful experience. I really hope it can continue this way.

Dan: Well, Horace, I really appreciate you being on the show today. Thank you so much.

Horace: Well, thank you for the opportunity and I really enjoyed it.

The Five-Year Plan

Posted June 7th, 2011, as The Critical Path Episode #1

Horace Dediu and Dan Benjamin try to weigh the strategic implications of Apple's WWDC announcements. We take a look at the impact on RIM, operators, Google and Apple's flirtation with Twitter.

Dan: Now, we've been planning to do this show and talking about it for a while, and I know both you and I like to really plan things out before we just jump in and do them. But coming from yesterday's WWDC announcements and the keynote, there's just so much to talk about and so many great things, we just thought, you know what, we just got to strike right now while the iron's hot.

Horace: Right, right. So yes, this is one of those things where you have to seize the moment. So much happened that there's too much material to talk about and actually it has a short half-life. We need to get going before it fades from people's memories. Although I think we can certainly bring some of the topics back a few weeks from now, there's no better time than now to get it over with.

Dan: No, that's very true. I think it's such a unique time right now for mobile, and this is something that you and I talked about. If people haven't heard it, there was a Pipeline a few weeks ago—we'll put that in the show notes—where you and I talked about what you do at Asymco—and mobile in general—but just seeing what's going on in the space right now, it's just amazing.

And WWDC I think really put an exclamation point on that yesterday.

Horace: Right. So this is what I take away from the show. I mean, I almost tweeted this, but I didn't. It didn't feel perfect. It said "Apple went from being Apple Computer to Apple Inc."

Dan: Right.

Horace: And now it is, suddenly, Apple Devices. I think, [it doesn't] have the poetic ring to it, but it's basically: Apple, not just Computer, but rather as the Computer not being that relevant at all. You know, the famous phrase that Steve Jobs said, that we are *demoting* the PC, and he did it in a way to show how it [moved] to the same line [as the other devices] and it made sense in his graphic.

But the idea deserved [to be] the big theme of the show: That now the world is about mobile computing. One could say post-PC, but even that doesn't quite encompass it. One should just abandon the PC concept altogether. And so I think that—one thing I wrote, maybe the first thing I wrote—was that if you think about mobile computing without the cloud, it's really an incomplete concept. You have the tethering problem, that you have to go back to the computer at some point, and so the devices aren't truly independent unless they are depending on the cloud to synchronize and to backup and to do all those sharing functions.

Dan: Right.

Horace: So I really think that this is when Apple finally accepted that, or may have accepted, but it finally implemented that in a way that only Apple can deliver. And so now we're at this next phase of the post-PC era where the child abandons the links to the parent.

And I think that the main story is that we have this cloud-plus-mobile combination that really is the fuller picture of mobility and ubiquity. So there are a lot of implications here we need to think about. For example, what's going to happen with respect to bandwidth, with respect to the fact that you need or you may never have enough bandwidth with 3G to satisfy the needs of documents and media in the cloud. And so more and more this will be dependent on WiFi. And I think there's some issues there. But one thing at a time.

I think the things I've drilled down into—some of the stats that we received and what I wrote already in the blog today—is how these numbers about the app downloads are just phenomenal relative to the song downloads, they're nearly the same number now—14, 15 billion.

Dan: Which comes out ahead, the app downloads or—I haven't compared the two.

Horace: Right. So, actually I plotted the data more than nine months ago, and at the time it looked like the curve of cumulative app downloads was going straight up and the curve for cumulative song downloads was flattening out. And clearly it was evident that there would be a crossover. And the question was, how soon? And I think I had actually predicted that by the end of 2010 it would have happened. But it wasn't quite there yet.

So now we're at the point where 15 billion songs have been downloaded and 14 billion apps have been downloaded. So they are 1 billion apart. But again, the slope of the curve for apps is far more vertical, so the crossover is imminent. And the other things to measure from that data (which actually Apple teases. slight bits and fragments of data are released.) For example, we can obtain data about the price point, because they mention how much developers are paid.

Dan: Right.

Horace: $2.5 billion. Now, we know that an app that's sold has 30 percent going to Apple, 70 percent going to developers. So we can measure, relatively speaking, how much money Apple got out of the whole thing and therefore how much the whole pie was.

We can also get figures about the pricing of each application. Because we say 2.5 billion divided by 14 billion apps gives us X in terms of price per app. So that's called the average selling price. And of course, that includes free. So now that number is about 25 cents per app, including free again, and it's slightly down from a year ago when it was 29 cents. But from that number we can then estimate how much Apple uses. Because they say they want to break even. So we can take the 30 percent of the pie that Apple keeps and ask: If they spent all that money keeping a store open, what is the budget for the iTunes franchise?

We can do the same for songs, because songs, we know roughly that Apple pays out 90 percent and they keep about 10 percent. But if we combine the two properties and decide, well that means that to keep lights on at iTunes, it takes X billion dollars. So it's amazing to be able to deduce that data, which allows us then to say what a competitor would have to ante up to participate in such an ecosystem.

Dan: Right.

Horace: They may not do all of the same things that Apple does or on the same scale. Nevertheless, this demonstrates this is a very capital-intensive business, much more so than people imagine. And I think also this is one of the key secrets that Google had in achieving its dominance, in that their data centers are extremely expensive things and few players can really walk into that business.

In fact, they kept secret for a long time how many servers they needed to run their operations. That was a trade secret. So in this case, we're getting a hint from Apple about how big the business is, on the cost side. So clearly there's a lot to think about there, and I think… the other point that this brings up is that all these costs are really not offset by increased income. So one reason perhaps why the market doesn't like what's happening with Apple or this new event is that they see these as increased costs that Apple has to bear while there's no significant new device income that they see.

So in other words, the cost of doing business seems to be going up. I don't necessarily agree with that because what we have also is a very high-margin business that's actually being expanded and sustained with this strategy, and that these data centers essentially act as a protective moat around the iPhone business. So other than having to fight on lower price points, they say, "Well, we're going to enhance the experience with our cloud strategy and allow consumers to have an integrated, smooth and pleasant experience"—which is what Apple is known for—without having to reduce prices, although the cost may slightly increase. It's an ongoing discussion we have to have with the reader on what is the final impact of this strategy. But it looks good to me.

Dan: It seems something that for most companies, competitors especially, they have to be looking at these same kind of numbers too.

Horace: Yes, and I've pointed out not only the cost, the fact that if you were Samsung today and you said, "Well, in order for us to be competitive what have we had to do so far? We've had to make devices that look and feel like an Apple device, and fortunately Google has made the software available." [Prior to that] they only had Microsoft to give them an operating system, or maybe Symbian, although Symbian was already not competitive a few years ago.

But then Google stepped in and came up with a salvation. Android was every phone vendor's lifeboat, as Apple was beginning to dominate the industry. So now the question for them is: "Right, we've dodged a bullet by having an alternative to the iPhone with Google as a supplier, but what are we going to do about this new experience of media and data synchronization?"

Dan: Right, is it enough just to have this?

Horace: Well, that's the problem: Google may have the components necessary to deliver similar experiences, but it's not going to be an integrated whole as Apple offers. So, again, Apple is ahead by maybe two, three years now, in showing how smoothly it's integrated. Again, people argued that Apple is late to the game because they didn't have the components, but Apple doesn't deliver just components.

They deliver the whole experience, and when that experience is integrated, now suddenly that's the new benchmark against which the modular solutions are going to be compared. So we have a new high-water mark, and a new definition of where Google needs to go. And they're a fast follower. I fully believe they're able to react to this, but it may give a few more years for Apple to continue to be seen as the best in class.

Dan: So how do you think then Google responds to this? I mean, right now. It's 2011, it's June. WWDC is underway. Does Google respond right away? Do they wait? What do you think is going to happen?

Horace: Well, it depends a lot on whether they feel it's a threat. You see, the problem with a competitive response is it only is effective as long as the competitor feels that there's a threat there. Then the mechanical part of the response kicks in, which may or may not be effective. But fundamentally, management has to say, "We need to do something."

The problem with the iPad is that when you go back a year ago, there were a lot of competitors who looked at the iPad and didn't see a threat. You know, 90 percent of the commentary about the iPad was that it was not going to be a successful product and that it was a solution looking for a problem.

So there was a period of probably five to six months during which Apple had absolutely nothing to worry about, because there simply wasn't a response mechanism. And although Google did finally begin to address that by adapting Android into a large-screen format, competitive with the iPad, which is still now under development. They still haven't released what I would call a market-ready version of Android for tablets. There are versions, of course, but I wouldn't say that they're polished enough because they're not even releasing the source code. So, in that sense, Apple had a one-year lead because they simply weren't perceived as a threat.

Now the question is, is this cloud going to be seen by Samsung and LG and Motorola as a clear and present danger to their core business and thus pressure Google to say, "We need to have an equivalent functionality from your side." Again, that discussion is going to take time. People have to feel the pressure. By the way, the trigger to the iPad response was actually when the iPad began to sell, which actually took one or two quarters. People said "Holy cow, it's not a flop, it's actually selling in the millions."

Dan: Right.

Horace: And it actually takes market analysts to measure the market. It takes Apple to announce their quarterly results. It takes the pain of the retail and the sales force to communicate back to their head office saying, "Hey, this is really happening." If management doesn't have an instinct for it, they need data. And data often takes months to finally validate and get it to be the state of accurate belief.

So, you know, these are the mysteries of analysis. I think one of the indications—what I'm seeing already, by the way—the first signal is always the reaction of the stock market. The stock market reacted negatively to the news [of iCould] and at first I didn't know why, because I don't understand how the market behaves. But then I read some of the comments.

The comment I read was from an analyst saying that there's no new hardware. And that seems a rather simplistic view of the market, because, again, as Steve Job said, hardware is the brain and the sinews of the product, but the software is its heart and soul. And so the question [becomes] "I only saw heart and soul here, where's the body?" *Obviously*, the body is going to come out of this.

But the problem I see is that maybe the [stock] market is the first hint of what competitors are also seeing and feeling and they're sort of probably saying that this isn't that relevant. "I'm not going to feel pain from this for a long time." So I don't think we'll see a competitive response anytime soon.

Dan: Yes.

Horace: [Not] a panic situation, "Oh my God, we're really in trouble now."

Dan: I'm curious to know what you think about the industry as a whole, not just the Google reaction to this, but some of the outliers. I mean, iMessage was released and that's something that is a direct response, I think, to what's going on with RIM, with BlackBerry.

Horace: Right. So, and not only that, but RIM itself provided a [direct response]. [It offered] an alternative to the SMS business model, and although RIM shared its revenue from BBM with the operators, BBM was a nice, palatable, digestible messaging solution for operators. Whereas iMessenger is more a institutionalized version of WhatsApp [Messenger] and other messaging solutions built by third parties over IP.

I mean, we've had great numbers from early on from some of these app solutions, and the problem is that now there are multiple people being touched by it. So the app developers may have a hard time now really differentiating their solutions. The BBM solution is suddenly no longer a differentiator for RIM.

Dan: Right.

Horace: And finally, SMS and the operators are going to have a hard time unless Apple comes to them and says, "Just push the iPhone more and you're going to make up the difference on the fact that you're going to get high ARPU (average revenue per user) from data services through the iPhone."

So more and more of what Apple is offering to operators is saying: "We'll just get people to use mobile broadband, and that's how you benefit." Although, longer term that may not actually be a good story for an operator because that tends to commoditize over time. The pricing, as we've seen actually in the Nordic countries where you reach 100 percent penetration of 3G, prices begin to rapidly collapse. We're not seeing that in most markets because still many people are trying to move up to smartphones and data plans.

You know, I was actually in two or three Walmarts over the last few days, I try to do my own little research—

Dan: Reconnaissance work.

Horace: Yes. I noticed that the shelf space was overwhelmingly now allocated to smart devices. They might be selling bundled voice-only products with minutes of prepaid, but as far as getting a contract phone, the smart devices were vastly outnumbering the voice-oriented devices, and that was not true probably one year ago.

Dan: Right.

Horace: And so, when I spoke with the sales person there, I asked him "Do you believe that we're going to see only smartphones on your shelf here?" And he said that yes, it's only a matter of operators being able to sell data services to everyone. I tweeted about it, saying that he seemed to have more vision than most people in the industry because he's able to see that we're moving to a data-oriented service and device.

Dan: Right.

Horace: Of course many of them are Android, but that's where the future is going.

Dan: It's fascinating that that's such a great way to kind of go into the trenches, almost, and see what people are seeing firsthand. Not by going to Apple or going to, you know, Verizon, but going to somewhere—

Horace: Well, I do it in a very limited way, but many times what you'll read in terms of what analysts are doing as research is they do actually call twenty, thirty stores and try to get that information firsthand from the sales people. It's one methodology. It has limitations, but it's actually very valid.

So, the other story is that BlackBerry was also getting significantly less exposure and less shelf space, and I think in Europe we're seeing that happening with Symbian, that Symbian is literally becoming the bottom shelf on an operator's phone display. So once that happens, it's a slippery slope.

All these trends are all converging and I think what Apple did yesterday was to kind of point in the direction that's saying, we've been improving these products for four or five years now, and we've reached the point where the performance improvement is going to happen in a new dimension. It used to be that the performance of an iPod was measured by the capacity of the hard drive. Then it became on the screen and the quality of sensors or the quality of input method, and these were all innovations in the last three years.

Now Apple is saying, as bandwidth becomes available we're going to actually integrate what's in the cloud so that you have a more cohesive experience.

I've struggled with the question of what is Apple's next frontier of improvement, because once a product becomes more than good enough, it's in very big trouble. You become very vulnerable if you're just improving [along the same dimension]. This is why BlackBerry is in trouble. You cannot make email and messaging better than they were a few years ago. And so unless they redefine the basis of competition they're vulnerable to someone else doing that for them.

So Apple has the same dilemma, that four, five years after the iPhone launched, it has to somehow redefine the market. I also pointed out that when the iPhone launched in 2007, January, Steve Jobs stood up and said, "We are five years ahead" of the competition in terms of what our software can do. And that five years is up January 2012. So we're six months away from that five years.

Now, of course, the product has improved, but so has Android come in and improved arguably—I mean, it's catching up faster and faster. So the gap is probably very narrow. Some would argue it's still broad, but I'm going to take the point of view, let's say, that it's a one-year gap.

Now, Apple could say [essentially], "Now we're going to redefine the product." So my point when I made that comment a few weeks or so ago, it was that we should see a redefinition of what the iPhone is by 2012.

And I think this is a hint of that. I mean, I didn't know at the time which direction they might go—new input method, new definition of service, new definition of price, perhaps portfolio strategy, penetration strategy—so it allows them to serve lower price points and consumers in emerging markets and prepaid and all these things.

These are innovations you can do. They're not technological innovations, they're business-model innovations. So that could have happened. But I think what Apple just showed is that we're going to innovate along a dimension that's under-served, and that happens to be the integration of the network services.

This is only a hint, because there's so much more they can do, and I'm not trying to be a visionary, but these things are fairly clear if you just read them.

Dan: I think you're being a little bit modest. I don't think a lot of us, even those of us who are thinking about this every day, see it quite as clearly as you do. So it's really refreshing to hear you break it down so simply.

But do you think, then, speaking to that under-served segment, I mean is that—you know, we are going to be caught up in a lot of ways on the Android side with what Apple is doing with iOS and the iPhone—you know, a lot of people had this sort of "Aww" reaction when they said that iOS 5 isn't going to be available till fall. Like that, for a lot of people was this huge bummer.

And I feel like there's kind of two ways to look at this. One is, you know, for the developers out there, that's almost not enough time for them to—if they're just getting the iOS 5 data now in June of 2011, they're just getting it, fall—I would say that's enough time. It's enough time.

But I don't feel like Apple would cater to them, it never has before, and say, "Oh, we're doing this to give you enough time." I feel like they feel there's a lot more that they need to do.

Do you see that as a bad thing? Is fall, is that too long, is that too late?

Horace: No. Again, we've seen this before. There's been a lot of these, not delays, but maybe timing issues that have occurred over the years. But they're quickly forgotten. Come the fall nobody will remember what happened in June and whether there was a big delay or not. Everyone will be talking about just how phenomenally long the lines are for the new product.

But I think Apple is just moving at the best speed they can possibly move. There is only so much you can do as an organization to get things done, and Apple is tremendously efficient. If you look at any of these numbers about how many people actually are employed by Apple, given the budgets we know for their R&D and SG&A [Selling, General & Administrative Expenses], which are public information, we can calculate roughly how many headcount they have. And those numbers aren't growing as fast as their business is growing.

They can't hire people as fast the business is growing because they're growing at 70 to 90 percent—the top and the bottom lines are growing at those rates respectively. So you can't really double your organization every year with quality hires. So there's that constraint that they need to grow their people organically while the business is growing exponentially. So there's going to be limits to how fast they can really improve things.

The other thing is that there are problems with production issues and timing of launches and windows of opportunity and technology standards as such as we've seen with CDMA. A lot of people thought that the argument for or against Verizon was based on politics, and to some degree it was, but to some degree it was also based on the fact that Apple couldn't dilute its efforts on multiple standards. It was still learning the business, and it was still learning the distribution business, which is why it couldn't grow broadly with operators right out of the gate. It's still only four years into this business, and no vendor that you compare Apple to in the phone space has entered in such a limited time.

HTC's been at it for over a decade. You know, they were making PDAs before then, so they had a lot of experience also integrating product. So their HTC is considered the newcomer, right? But they've had more experience than Apple building phones.

Same with RIM. RIM is also a smartphone-focused company, but they've been at it for much longer than Apple has. So it's amazing what [Apple has] been able to do in such a limited time.

So to say that the fifth generation of the product is going to take a couple months longer, because also it's integrating multiple network standards and because it's going to be globally launched, I think it's not a bad performance at all.

Yes, I mean, there's so many ways you can look at this resource, production, strategy, pricing. What are the constraints that Apple has to face? And the more you know about how product is built, the more you're impressed by their performance. And I think that they're doing an amazing job.

Dan: Do you feel, then, that iOS 5 coming out in the fall, that's absolutely tied into the iPhone 5 also coming out in the fall simultaneous? Is that what you predict?

Horace: I think it makes sense more from a marketing point of view and it makes sense also that they try to coordinate. I don't think that the iPhone—obviously iPhone 5 has been pre-announced, so there aren't constraints on the hardware, that you need a new piece of hardware to run this—but I'm sure it's going to run better on an iPhone 5 or 4S that we're going to see.

So, no, I don't think the two are linked. I think the software roadmap and the hardware roadmap are loosely connected, and I think the software development is rushing as fast as it can.

The hardware guys have a different constraint. They need to work out, "How do we ramp up the product? Are we going to hit the right window in terms of holiday sales? Do we have the right suppliers available to feed into this new assembly process?" That is what strikes me.

I've tried to analyze, also, just how steep the ramp has to be. Every year the product has to sell twice as many as the year before. How fast can you go from zero to maximum production volume? If that ramp is vertical, it really is mission impossible. You can't see going from zero to 50 million units [in one quarter], especially a high-end product like this. That has not been done before. They're pushing the envelope in new things like the thinness of it, the components themselves, the fact that you have much thinner screens and the different binding technologies for the screens.

It's just staggering when you start to think of how do you serve hundreds of millions of people—and by the way, this has been maybe one of these sound-barrier type problems. That beyond a certain point it doesn't look like they can actually continue with a yearly cycle. They just can't go and ramp up the production, have it running for six to nine months, then have to shut it down and start up a new production because there's a new model that's completely different. And yo-yo this up and down, each time doubling the amplitude.

When you think about it, it just—you know, from a phone manufacturing point of view, no one has done that before. The only answers have been that you do a portfolio strategy, overlap products, so that when one starts to fade another one is ramping up, and so you have some evenness in your output.

All of these are production issues, which is what Tim Cook is probably sweating on.

So what I've always assumed, again, is that after the four or five years or iterations of this basic product, that it has to somehow be redefined as a portfolio or as some kind of a different product. And because Apple integrates everything, if you think about it this way, you say, "Okay, they can't ramp with infinite, so they have to do a portfolio, but that means X about the software, that means Y about the market, that means Z about the user."

And only Apple will look at all of these things, put them together and say, "Can we make it an integrated approach that everybody's satisfied and everything works just right?" And if they can't do one of those three or four things, then they just stick to the plan and say, "We'll give up share or we'll give up and not do the wrong thing, until such time as we can integrate all these things."

And that's the difference between Apple and other companies. Others may just compromise and say, "We can't let that money sit on the table, let's go ahead and build what we can." So, that's—I think partly the—what's the word? The exceptionalism of Apple, is that they really are so product focused that they'll let the market actually get away from them while they figure it out. And it's worked for them so far.

Dan: So you've really got this thing figured out. You know, you don't admit it, but you really do.

Horace: I don't think I do.

Dan: I think you do.

Horace: No, I can't accept that. There's so much I don't know. The more you learn, the more you realize how little you know. But there is—what I'd like to do to make myself comfortable with this is to get data and try to actually see it and point to something as evidence, and yes, I may have some intuitions, but a lot of these things are speculative and, you know, I don't feel comfortable saying I know it until there's some evidence.

So I search for it all the time. I try to find every kind of proxy for evidence that I can. Sometimes you don't get it. Sometimes you go down the wrong path, and fortunately I have readers who will point that out to me and help me out. But yes, it's an interesting puzzle.

Dan: What else do you think isn't getting enough attention yesterday from the keynote? They covered—I guess they said, I think there were ten features of line they talked about. Ten features of iOS that they talked about out of hundreds. And a lot of the things that are getting attention, I mean some of them we've touched on here, but is there a subtext? Is there something else we should be taking out from this that maybe we're not really aware of?

Horace: Yes, I'd have to go through and actually look at those fine print on those slides, where they had these clouds of words, where they showed all these things that they didn't talk about, and try to find if there's something in there that is less evident. But, you know—two hundred, three hundred—whatever numbers they're putting out there, they're all significant.

One thing I should say about this event is that I'm still digesting it. I try to go watch the full presentation and so far I've actually not gotten through it all, and I try to take notes and once I find something that I need to explore further, I may pause and then do that for a while, as I did with the app data. So I should say that I don't quite yet have under my belt what the cloud implications are, especially on the music, which was at the end of the show.

I think some of the implications, like you said: in the telecom sector, the implication on messaging, John Gruber's comment that operators

35

didn't know about this coming (not a surprise frankly). They didn't know the iPod touch was coming, when that came right after the iPhone. I remember the CEO of AT&T saying that he had no idea that the iPod touch was going to be competing against the iPhone essentially.

So that's a huge implication. We need to really think about that. It's one of those things that probably people will be able to sort of become comfortable with and think that, "Well, it only works between iOS devices, so it doesn't really threaten the whole SMS franchise." But again, you know, wait long enough and you're just going to manage decline. You're not going to see growth.

Dan: I mean, if it's going to save me ten or fifteen bucks a month to go from an unlimited texting plan—which is preposterously priced anyway—to, "Oh, I only send and receive ten texts a month now to people who are not, you know, who are not on iOS devices, I can go down to the bear minimum. I can go down to nothing."

Horace: Yes, that's again what John said. You know, SMS is an artificial type of messaging, that is not well integrated to our computer-based lifestyles, right? I mean, it's anachronistic in a way, and exorbitantly priced for what it delivers. But it is ubiquitous.

But yes, I'm trying to go back to your original question and trying to think through some of the implications of all these APIs and just the PC-free aspect of it. It was one out of ten things, but cutting the cord: As long as the iPad discussion has been ongoing, the argument against it being a PC-competing product or there being a post-PC era has been that it needs to be connected to a PC to be alive.

Dan: Right.

Horace: And this is something that's come up over and... I can guarantee that if you wrote a story about the post-PC era, the first comment in your comments would be that this is not a post-PC product because it still needs a PC. And, yes, you could argue against it saying, "Well, you know, PCs co-existed with every other form of computing that preceded it, so we still have mainframes and mini-computers and, you know, post-PC does not mean no PC."

But, still, now we finally have yet another argument taken off the table against this era because these devices truly are autonomous, and there's been no technical reason why they couldn't have been so. Anyone arguing these points should have been assuming that they'll fix it at some point, right? Yet still the show-me attitude is, "I'm not going to believe it till I see it."

So now we have a truly—and the devil's in the details. It isn't trivially easy to do. Technically, yes, in theory, yes, but practically you have all of these dependencies about synchronization and dealing with setting up things and dealing with updates and all these other things that were done by iTunes. So now finally we are in that era and, again, Android may have solved some of these pieces already.

But Apple does it in an integrated way, and now we are at the dream.

By the way, just as a footnote here: Microsoft, when they entered the phone market, which was with Windows Mobile back in 2002 or '03, actually promised over-the-air OS updates. I remember this was a big, frightening thing for Nokia at the time because Nokia could not deliver such a thing. Microsoft promised, but they couldn't actually deliver it.

They attempted to do one or two updates over the air with their original operator partner, which I think was Orange at the time, but it didn't work very well. And even now with with Windows Phone we're seeing problems even pushing updates through the regular, connected-device model. Lots of problems are cropping up, bricked devices, all kinds of bad experiences.

That's Microsoft trying to do a far smaller job, on far fewer products, than Apple is. Or far fewer, I should say, installed base. More SKUs but fewer units. So you see, it's quite tough to do very well. And again, the jury may still be out whether all of these dreams and promises that Apple just highlighted will come true. But if they do, then there's no more [of] this post-PC skepticism. So I think that's a profound thing that we will have to really let sink in. Maybe it'll be simmering in the background of our consciousness for a long time until suddenly, boom, we realize that we're in the future, and one year hence we'll look back and say, "Ah, this was the trigger point that caused this change to happen."

I'm a big fan of history, because it's like living in multiple universes. Going back in time and thinking how things were like [before]. Even back when you were there—and you've forgotten it and [are] feeling it again—just gives you a sense, "Wow, look how much progress we've made."

[For example] three, four years ago operators were a different thing than they are today. So how can we project forward three years from now, what will be the dynamic?

And by the way, again, the hints are that different parts of the world move at different speeds. So you can actually see hints of where things are [going by looking at different places]. Just like those places which today don't have mobile broadband.

Case in point: India. People feel that the iPhone doesn't work in India. [It doesn't work] in India because there aren't really that many reasons to pay for broadband-based devices, right? The product is expensive. But it's expensive because it gives you value in the broadband. If you don't have broadband, then the whole product doesn't make sense, right?

So the same thing happened in China maybe two years ago. They were in the same situation, not having 3G. [In contrast] the Nordic countries of Europe have saturated broadband, mobile broadband, and what's happening there is a good clue of what's going to happen as far as pricing and what I call pricing innovation and new models of getting consumers to sign up for these things.

[And there the] iPhone is doing well. It's not dominant. You still have Android, plenty of Android to go around. But it doesn't mean also that Android is dominant. So, there's a nice mix of operating systems, and it's a dynamic marketplace as far as operators themselves, rivals, you know, trying to compete for your business. And consumers are doing very well.

Dan: It's a fascinating industry and how quickly things can change, just based on some announcements for an update to software that runs on a phone. That literally they can disrupt in this way.

Horace: Yes, that's the big word, right, disrupt.

Dan: Right.

Horace: You know, that's been the undercurrent of a lot of the things that I've written about: That a newcomer can come in and take the money right out of the pocket of the incumbents. It's just an amazing story because the incumbent has all the advantages.

Not only in the fact that they're big, but they're actually having the most important advantage, which is knowledge. They have information about the market, they have information about how to get things done. And the new guy—even if he has the resources—has no information, has no access, is not trusted, is not valued and has everything working against them.

And to come in and actually just completely destroy the value of these existing vendors…

The story is now, by the way […] that Apple's cash will soon be larger in value than the market value of all of its mobile phone competitors.

Dan: Wow.

Horace: So it could theoretically buy them all. It could buy the whole industry with pocket money, without leverage. Of course it's illegal—well, not illegal—but they would be resisted by the authorities, prices will change dramatically if they make a bid. These are not practical options.

But in theory what we're observing is that a guy came in and essentially beggared the whole industry and that, to me, is one of the most poetic things I've seen. (And also, by the way, behind those devices, there's all these service providers, like operators themselves, and we would have to measure their value at some point in the future. I don't think that's going to go much higher, if at all.) So now the question will be, ten years down the road what's going to happen to the service-side of the business.

So on one hand we have the disruption of [the] PC industry and the computing industry, we're seeing that Wintel is worth less than Apple, and so that disruption has already happened. The phone-business disruption is underway, and so we have potentially also service-level disruption into the future.

How could one company be responsible for all that? And then there's the media side of things as well, media disruptions that are happening with or without Apple, because the technology is changing there so rapidly. So these things are becoming more co-dependent than less, right? So we're seeing that computing changes are affecting the telecom business and vice versa.

Mobile computing to me is a convergence—I hate that word. The *convergence* word has been overused, but it's the fact that there are two disruptions happening simultaneously: The phone business and the computing business are on a collision course. And it's not that one or the other will win. What will happen is both will lose and essentially a new model will emerge. One that actually Apple is defining right now, and that's just phenomenal.

Synchronized failure

Posted June 17th, 2011, as The Critical Path Episode #2

Horace Dediu and Dan Benjamin discuss how smartphone pioneers Nokia and RIM falter while the market is booming.

Dan: Today, Horace, we're going to be talking about how and perhaps why great companies fail and in particular we're going to be starting with Nokia.

Horace: Yes, Nokia—and RIM.

Dan: And RIM.

Horace: Just announced another bad quarter. Nokia preceded them with a warning, and it all looks very bad, and sad. And I think what I wanted to do now, given this timing, is to reflect on what are the causes for great companies to fail. These are two great companies, and [there's] no mistaking that. I mean, they were innovators and drivers of phenomenal growth and disruption in their own time.

Dan: Just a few years ago, these two companies were—to say they were at the top of their game is an understatement. They were at the top of the industry. They were running the show.

Horace: Right. So you think about it, and Nokia came from nowhere, in fact, back in the '90s. They were a severely over-the-hill conglomerate that had been in various areas. There was sort of a joke that they used to be in the rubber boot business, and they were also in the paper business, and cables, and televisions, and all kinds—it was truly a '70s-era conglomerate that was way past its prime in the '90s.

And it recovered, and went on to take on the giant Motorola, which was the inventor of the mobile phone, among other inventions in its history. But at the time, that was the most important growth market. And Nokia went and basically took their profits away, and grew the whole industry, and it's certainly a fascinating story, what the causes of the success were.

And then we can contrast those with the causes of its failure. And again, same thing with RIM. RIM came, starting as not much more than a pager company, becoming a mobile phone vendor in the early 2000s, and went on to capture vast amounts of the North American phone business, in terms of profits, if not volumes.

And yet again here we see a great company like that suddenly looking, as they say, a going concern issue, in the sense that people are actually forecasting its demise.

So I just want to step back and reflect on how great companies fail. And I think that we can start by putting aside some of the theories that are most commonly cited.

The first, I think, is that it's a failure of management. And what's interesting is there are a couple of ways you can disprove that, but one thing I just thought of was that if you go back in history and look at how great companies failed decades ago, nobody cites management, because nobody remembers who was in charge.

Dan: Right.

Horace: People may remember Digital Equipment Corporation and Ken Olsen. But if you go back [to remember] their contemporaries like, Data General or Honeywell or Prime or some of their other competitors in the mini-computer market, no one can cite who ran those companies and therefore blame those managers for failing. And certainly I'm not an expert in history, but there are plenty of historical failures that I think if you were to look up their Wiki pages, you would not find out who ran the company. But we're familiar with management today, and familiarity, I think, breeds contempt. And so it comes easy to blame whoever is in charge.

The other way you can disprove the theory is by simply pointing out that the same people who you're blaming today for failure you were praising a few years ago for brilliance.

Dan: Right.

Horace: And so the way to think about that is, if you ascribe failure to a person, then you have to also say what about them made them fail? And normally human nature would [be to] say, well, they just became foolish. And there is a problem there, because knowing what we know about humans, we know that they don't become foolish overnight. People just tend to be pretty much the same, intellectually speaking, their whole life.

So do they just suddenly flip a bit and go from smart to stupid overnight? And there is all kinds of absurdities about that theory that you can then say, "Well, how did that happen?" And that's why I think that's another reason against blaming management as a cause in general.

The next reason, a third one, if I may, is that companies tend to fail in unison. As we see here, Nokia and RIM together, but they're not the only ones—LG is in trouble as well. And management there is being blamed as well, by the way. And then we can go back in history a little bit and look at Siemens and Sony Ericsson. Several Asian companies have come and gone as well. And once again, how did they all manage to fail together? And you can blame a person for failing, but how can you suggest that they all colluded to fail at the same time?

So there are three good reasons why management failure is not a good way to describe, in general, company failure. But it's a controversial topic. Whenever I bring this up on my site, I always get a lot of comments that say, "No, no, no. They really did screw up." Yes, you can always find fault with the decision making. But in a broader scope, what's happening is far deeper. And these companies all did the best thing—the best they could, given their circumstances.

And many times…

You know, it was just today that an article in the Finnish press said that Olli-Pekka Kallasvuo, the last CEO of Nokia, regrets nothing. And I'm sure you can go back and ask the ex-CEO of Motorola, and he regrets nothing too, because they can't see having made any mistakes.

So if it's not a failure of individuals, there has to be something else we can point at. And I'll just use Nokia as an example here, because I'm more familiar with their day-to-day decision making for the last few years. And if you look at the daily process of decision making, you see that companies tend to just follow a best-practice rulebook. They listen to their customers, they build products using the best processes known [and taught] in engineering management courses everywhere in the world. They actually hire very bright people. They have plenty of tests to filter out bad ones. They improve their work force through training—that's well-known and understood as being the best way to get these people to improve their skills and so on.

So [paradoxically] the answer is that actually failure comes from the combination of all of these best practices. Because what they all do is point you into a direction of sustaining your core business. You're just going to make it better. But what happens typically when you fail is that the business changes. And it changes in unpredictable ways. You have a competitor that comes in, as Nokia themselves did, and takes the business away from you, and you are not motivated to respond to them. So in the case—you know, sort of the elephant in the room here—is Apple, that came in and somehow took the candy away. And that's where we need to sort of step back and say what specific decisions were made by Nokia which ignored the threat from the iPhone?

And what I would point out is that they listened very carefully to their customers. So their *customers* actually aren't the *consumers*. The *customer* is the operator and distributor who buys the product in bulk. These are their best customers. They might listen to consumers, but that would be a conversation had in the background. But in the foreground, there is conversation with the operator and the operator would have told them, "Look, we're building out these networks, these are very expensive things to build, we need products to sustain our business." And that primarily was a voice business that was transitioning to a data business. And so what normally a salesperson would communicate back to the management would be that, "Look, we have to make these products sustain the operator business." And that means more improvements along these dimensions of value that operators care for. Am I making sense so far?

Dan: Absolutely. I'm, as usual, quite enjoying listening to you talk about it. How, then—is there any way to predict that one of these companies is going to fail? Like, when—I think for a lot of us in the Apple community, you know, Mac fans, when they announced the iPhone, there are a lot of us who were saying, "Man, this thing is going to takeover. This isn't just for us geeks in this room right now with Steve, who is announcing it. This is going to be really big." I mean, does that show up on Nokia's radar?

Horace: Well, that's the amazing story—that people are motivated to ignore it. Even though the mass media glorifies and hypes it up, and there is so much buzz, and it's an echo-chamber effect happening with blogs and everything else. But months after the product was announced, there was barely a ripple of interest [at Nokia]. I would say in fact that [ignoring the iPhone] was institutionalized to the point where no one was even assigned to pay attention to it. Typically, you have someone whose job it is to pay attention to a competitor. There wasn't such an interest at the time, in 2007. No one was assigned to follow Apple as a competitor inside Nokia.

Dan: And it wasn't—I mean, it wasn't just Nokia. I remember there was a famous quote from Palm's CEO, Ed Colligan.

Horace: Yes.

Dan: And this is back in, you know, I think maybe toward the end of '06.

Horace: Yes.

Dan: And there was a famous quote that he says, you know, "They're not just going to walk in."

Horace: Right. That's a famous one.

Dan: Yes.

Horace: And Microsoft's Steve Ballmer actually also laughing at the product when it was announced.

Dan: Right.

Horace: So, yeah, there is this tendency of the people who are incumbent to laugh at and scorn an incomer. Going back to Gandhi's famous quote, "First they laugh at you, then they fight you, and then you win." It's the classic asymmetric struggle. And so let's try to get a little bit more focused on what the steps involved were. So, when Nokia would observe the iPhone, the first instinct was to say that, "Well, it's a 'version 1 product.' It's not going to work well because we know. We've launched plenty of these things, and they're unlikely to function properly, and there will be bugs, and, you know, it's hard to get operators to support it, and it's hard to get *many* operators to support it." So it's likely that RIM and

Nokia as well would look at this thing and say, "Well, let's wait and see what happens."

And so what happened with Nokia and the iPhone is that also they were—remember there were a lot of critics that said that [the iPhone would fail because it] didn't have the [physical] keyboard. And that maybe people would wait until they also launched a voice-oriented product like an iPhone mini or a nano. That there would have to be a portfolio. That Apple wasn't behaving as a normal phone vendor would behave. That they didn't have a portfolio strategy. That they didn't attack mass distribution. That they didn't really threaten the incumbents in a painful way. That there wasn't this immediate feeling of threat.—But if you go back and ask, "Why didn't Nokia actually build the iPhone?" the answer would be "Because the operators told them not to." They said build a voice product, not a computer with a voice app.

Because if you think about the iPhone, it's really an iPod touch with an app, an extra app on the screen that has a phone icon on it. It's not any different internally. Yes, it has the 3G chipset.

Dan: Right. Right.

Horace: And so does the iPad itself, and the iPad could make phone calls. But they chose not to put a phone app on it. So the problem was that, from Nokia's point of view, they would need to build a voice product and try to put computing functionality in an application framework on top of it. And if they were to throw away that approach and start with a clean sheet of paper…

In fact, they did, with Maemo, which was not very well known, but it was an attempt at making a computer slate-like, small tablet-type device. It did not have voice functionality in it because, again, there were discussions with operators, and there is a subtle steering away from that with respect to, "Well, we're not going to subsidize it. We don't like something about it. We're not sure how the consumer relationship would work." And these discussions tend to force you away from doing the right thing.

So, in fact, you can also say that RIM was partially drawn into this discussion with operators. Pulling them away from what the consumer probably would be willing to do, and even unable to copy the iPhone quickly enough because it wasn't seen as a threat (to their core business). And the conversation always goes back to your top customers, and they would always take your eye off the ball. That's really, I think, the fundamental [cause] in what's driving a lot of company failure. Listening too closely to their best customers. And when the iPhone came, it was—again, not targeting their best customers. Notice it came in usually with the second-tier [operator] in any market. It didn't actually go in for head-to-head battle [with established vendors in top markets]. It grew slowly.

And that's what really ends up slowly, it's—the boiling frog analogy or something like that. It happens so slowly and gradually that by the time you're able to react...

And RIM is reacting by buying QNX and trying to implement a true modern operating system—they should have done that in 2007. By now, there would be plenty of product in the pipeline and they would be essentially at feature parity, let's say, with an Android-type product. So, in fact, RIM has a timing issue and they just didn't see the urgency of it all. And maybe now it's too late.

Dan: So how does a company like HTC fit into this picture?

Horace: Well, HTC didn't have its own platform to deal with so they're far more agile. They had simply at the time, when they were competing also with smartphones—before the iPhone—they were using Windows Mobile. And Windows Mobile was a very popular licensed platform with hundreds and hundreds of licensees.

And HTC was the most dominant of them because they were actually the earliest and the quickest and the most competent integrator of mobile phones. And that goes back to the fact that they were the ODM [original design manufacturer] hired by Compaq to make the iPAQ, the first popular PDA running Microsoft's PDA OS. Pocket PC, it was called.

Dan: Right.

Horace: And so their experience in engineering leadership allowed them to very quickly take off-the-shelf components and put them together in desirable packages. And HTC out-executed everyone else. They had at one point 80 percent of the Windows Mobile market. They suffered greatly when Windows Mobile was deprecated and the switchover was happening to Windows Phone, and so HTC dropped quickly—stepped off the gas with Windows Mobile—but then had to retool for Android. And they did that also quickly because of their agility.

So they are a very good engineering company and, as a result, they're able to stay with the trends in licensed operating systems. The challenge for HTC would be vis-à-vis, let's say, a Samsung or an LG, which do the same thing, but not as quickly, will be issues with differentiation.

So HTC has done well, but they haven't been disruptive in the sense that they haven't gone and taken away what the big boys had. They've been playing in a small niche and growing it nicely, and essentially actually creating their own brand. Maybe in another few years they will be disruptive. It would take quite a few years, though, because they would need to do so with someone else's operating system. And it's more likely that profits will accrue to the operating system supplier rather than to the handset vendor. They're in the wrong part of the value chain, if we look far forward enough.

So it's a good company, it's just not a disruptive one. And that's—I think that that's to their credit, actually—because they've managed to, you know, withstand this disruption, in a way.

Dan: So where does that really leave things, then, today? You know, it's 2011. The iPhone is clearly successful. They did walk in. And these other companies—RIM, Nokia—are stunned and clearly unprepared for what's ahead.

Horace: Right. So the problem is that historically in the mobile-phone business there hasn't been much opportunity to recover. So, what we've seen is that companies tend to reach a pinnacle, and then there is a decline, and then there is usually not a recovery. Some people point to the fact that Apple[as a computer company] did recover, so why can't someone else? You know, Apple recovered from the '90s. But that's quite a rare thing. And you need to be very, very innovative. You need to actually—when Apple recovered, they did on the basis of a new product, something completely different: the iPod. And they didn't just make the Mac suddenly once again a dominant platform.

Dan: Right.

Horace: They had to really say, "We're going to let go of that, or we'll maintain that business, but we're going to move into new businesses." So for someone to say that a mobile phone vendor will recover, they would have to do superhuman feats. They would have to somehow say, "Okay, we lost everything. Now, we're going to build it all back up again, against a whole new set of competitors that are competing on a different basis."

And that's the challenge, I think. That's just a huge, huge historic fact. You can't overcome that statistic.

Dan: It's almost like if you're running, you can't afford to even trip up a little bit. You've just got to… You've got to maintain that speed, and you can't stop.

Horace: Exactly. So there are some oddities about the phone business, right? Because you have to go through these channels. You have to go through these distributors, which amplify what's happening. If you are with them and they are working with you, they get you volumes far higher than you'd get alone. That's why channels exist. A wonderful amplifier. On the other hand, they amplify on the negative as well, because if they withdraw support, you have a much harder time getting back in.

This is the gating factor of a distributor. They have huge, concentrated power, because you can't reach out to customers directly. So Apple has been actually unique in its approach to all of its markets—having its own stores, having its own distribution. It's able to, sort of, dampen down this amplification factor. But still, it's a tough business because of that reason, because of the constant concentration of power in the value chain above where the devices sit.

Your first question, though, was, where do we go from here? And again, I would say that there is still potential for entrants to come in. Not necessarily coming from hardware side. I see innovation coming in from services and from what we call now *apps*, which are really the front end to services, the interface to services. And one could imagine Amazon as a mobile phone entrant, although they would just put out a platform.

Dan: Right.

Horace: Facebook is another contender. Perhaps Baidu could come in, especially regionally, where they're strong. Keep in mind that all these [recent] entrants took away the business from the phone incumbents, right. We're talking about Apple, Google, and to a much lesser degree, if any, Microsoft—came as software companies or, as in Apple's case, an integrated software/hardware company. But [they're all] from a different industry, from the computing industry, and they clashed with the telecom industry and basically took a large chunk of it. And so now when you have to envision the next generation coming in, they're probably going to come in also from another industry. And that I consider to be the service-based social media—I don't know how to cluster them but, you know, Amazon is essentially a media distributor.

Dan: Right.

Horace: Facebook is, you know, is an advertiser with social media as its medium. And then we have, of course, also other search providers such as Google and Baidu. And those disruptors will come in and redefine where value is captured.

You know, a few years ago, not even ten, perhaps, you bought a phone on the basis of which operator was running it. So you didn't know… You remember in the voice era, people didn't know if they'd bought a Kyocera or a Samsung? They said, "I got a Verizon phone."

Dan: Right.

Horace: Right. Or an AT&T phone. And that brand value, the brand essentially…

Dan: That's a great point.

Horace: …pointed out where the value was. Consumers' minds were working very, very well at that point, right? I mean, you *knew* Verizon was capturing the value because that's what consumers perceived. So as we move to the data era, now we have much more interest in the brand of the device. So BlackBerry was the first to establish a device brand in the United States and now we have more and more—obviously the iPhone established that brand, and people buy an iPhone first, and then, "Is it a Verizon iPhone or is it an AT&T iPhone?" You can have that discussion now.

But still, that's where the money moved, right? Higher up in the value chain, if you will. And then the next level above that is the platform. And that's where we're now seeing Android come in and [causing us to ask] "Is it an Android phone or an iOS phone." So the discussion on the iPhone moves a little bit higher, saying, "Okay, it's about iOS. I'm part of an ecosystem. Maybe iCloud will be part of that discussion." So now Apple is able to keep up with that shift, right? You know they've branded iOS. It's only recently that's happened, right? And now they're branding cloud—iCloud. Messaging, iMessaging. And so on. So you see that happening. And of course Google has done that already. That's their basis of competition. So we're moving up the stack.

And then what happens after that? Once the platform commoditizes, in a way, it's those vendors on top of it [that thrive]? So who sits on top of a platform are [the] app vendors. And that means an experience. That means something else. Will you buy a phone because it offers you Angry Birds? Not likely. But there might be a Facebook-oriented phone, or it might be—well, I wouldn't say necessarily that's the brand—but there might be something around social that does job-to-be-done [theory], that you're hiring the phone to do. It's to stay in touch with your family or your friends. In the same vein, you might be buying a media device that's branded Amazon, like you do now, a tablet reader. You can apply the same logic, by the way, to the book industry. I mean, here it is, you know, Amazon capturing the value of a century-old industry in the thing called a Kindle. And so people consume books more and more through that device as opposed to thinking of it even as an Android store.

So again, of these maneuvering of branding and so on, it's really a symptom of something deeper that's happening, which is moving the capture of value up the value chain, and I've sort of said this in a very ambiguous way, but I believe that apps will increasingly be the focus of profit-capture in the industry. And how that may happen, I don't know. Nobody knew five years ago iPhone would exist. So it's just some trend you need to keep your eye on.

Dan: Now, you wrote earlier in the week about the significance of Apple selling unlocked iPhones in the U.S. And I know it's a little bit of a tangent here, but I'm wondering if that's something you could address. Because I feel like it kind of does fit into this conversation.

Horace: It's funny. Yes, it does fit, because it's a distribution question.

Dan: Right.

Horace: Apple has had sort of an obstacle in its path to world domination, and that has been these operators. And at least in the phone business, and even in the computer business, they couldn't get—think about the fact they don't actually have an enterprise business because they didn't tolerate going through VARs (value-added resellers), or they didn't tolerate going through resellers and integrators, and all these people who essentially end up dictating what you should do. They just don't want to be beholden to anyone but the consumer. No intermediaries. Steve Jobs famously called them "orifices."

Dan: Right.

Horace: So whether they're operators or VARs or even retailers selling Macs, we don't want to bother. We want to go direct. So, in the case of retail, they just abandoned their whole—don't forget when they launched the Apple stores, there were a lot of Mac resellers, Mac vendors, Mac shops, that were upset about it. In fact, probably they're all gone now.

Dan: Yes.

Horace: Or most. Except for a handful, right?

Dan: Yes, I was going to say, that used to be the place to go. That was where all the other Mac geeks hung out. And those things are a relic. They're just from a bygone era.

Horace: They're still around internationally because Apple hasn't gotten their stores everywhere in the world. They're very well saturating the United States, but it's a tough thing to break [into] internationally, and it's retail in general is actually very hard to export as a concept. Ask Walmart about that.

But the thing is that—what this implies, is that—Apple looks at the distribution question and they either say, "How can we control them rather than vice-versa?" Or, "How can we actually become the distributor ourselves?" So in retail, they essentially abandoned their partners, quote-unquote. And then they went direct. Now, they can't do that in the phone business because there are just far too many points of sale, right? You can't put a store everywhere, in the Philippines and Indonesia and everywhere else that people buy phones. And secondly, because ultimately the power resides also with the service provider. They have this problem of divvying up the value, if you will.

So what Apple has to do is, I think, in the case of the iPhone, it's almost had to kind of bite their lip and go forward and go ahead and work with these vendors, and compromise, in a way. And there are many things they didn't compromise on, but they did compromise on, for example, pricing. You know, pricing is subsidized, and it's obscure. And I don't think it's the way Apple should do it, or would like to do it. And you don't see that same pricing illusion happening with the iPad.

But because of these constraints… they can't go and make these complicated, subtle and lengthy deals happen with hundreds of operators. They're just slowly able to get more and more operators, and they're probably working as fast as they can, but there will always be obstacles. DoCoMo, for example, just said no to the iPhone—the largest operator in Japan. Verizon, obviously, is a long story in the U.S. China—long, long

50

story there trying to get the dominant operator in China. Vodafone is probably holding out in many territories.

So because of the politics, Apple cannot go as fast as it wishes. So how you alleviate that pressure is, you open up gray channels. Now, of course, that's probably not what Apple would want you to know. Or maybe they don't even acknowledge that that's really their strategy internally. But by allowing unlocked phones—and they've done that in Hong Kong, for example—it essentially relieves the pressure of demand in a particular region. So in the U.K., for example, you could buy an unlocked phone., but you had to stand in line typically (so that channel was not big enough to serve the whole of Europe.)

But if you were traveling in London, or you know someone who is, you tell them, "Could you please just get me an iPhone? Or as many as you can." But all of these are really awkward ways of distributing product. I think it's a slight bias on my part that I think the United States is actually a far bigger market. I've had pushback on some of this in my blog, saying, "No, no. U.K. is plenty big to serve the gray market of Europe and North Africa." There is a convenience factor, there is a pricing issue that the U.S. tends to have lower VAT in the form of sales tax than Europe does. And Hong Kong is great, but it's still a fairly narrow footprint for trying to get really [large] volume sales through there. So I really believe that this unlocking business is more than just nice to have for Americans. I think it's probably also relieving pressure and applying pressure also on the operators in markets where Apple doesn't have a relationship.

Dan: So where do things go from here? I mean, you said these guys can't recover. Does this spell doom, then? I mean, are we seeing the end of Nokia and RIM and everything else?

Horace: It's sad, yes. I'm afraid history would indicate that. And, you know, I didn't know how to frame the discussion on Nokia for a long time because I have such a long history with them and I know so many people still affected by that.

There is always the possibility… You can always think of a way out. Like in the case of Apple, there was that miracle of Steve Jobs coming back. And you'd think that was the key. And I think probably they are kicking around ideas. They use this word "disruption" a lot internally now, and you hear it from Stephen Elop himself. But just the odds are very bad. And it would have to come with a new product, a new concept. It could be something in the service area. Maybe they could—(but it's unlikely) use maps as leverage, for example, as they do have this maps business, with NAVTEQ.

I don't put out any hypothesis, any guesses here, but I think there may be [a] 10 percent chance that they can do this. In the case of RIM, starting from a clean sheet of paper with QNX, that's going to be a 2012 story. I don't know how that can turn into a business as big as what they're giving up. Of course they're still growing, it's just they're really losing share. They're growing 18 percent in a quarter, last quarter, year on year. And that's not a bad story. That's units, by the way, in terms of value it's a lot less than that.

Dan: Right. Right.

Horace: But still, you know, as someone wrote a wonderful phrase saying that platforms live on momentum. Once the momentum disappears, it's a vicious cycle versus a virtuous one. It just goes very quickly downward. And so we see the platform dying on BlackBerry, as we saw the platform die on Symbian. And that's just because of [a] momentum issue.

But, yeah, I think RIM maybe is a bit more agile. Maybe RIM can do something. They were an engineering-minded company, which actually is a shame thinking that, you know, they could have engineered their way out of this probably if they started early enough. I'm sorry, I don't have a silver-bullet solution for either one of these companies.

Dan: Mm-hmm.

Horace: And no one would have foreseen in [the] 1990s how Apple got out of its predicament. Because, again, what they did was completely unforeseeable.

Dan: And you don't think anything unforeseen like that could happen over there? I mean, look at J.C. Penney getting Apple's guy.

Horace: Yes.

Dan: You know? I mean, that's something that you just see the response of the market to that announcement.

Horace: That's an interesting story, right? But, again, many execs have left [Apple] and taken positions like [Jon] Rubinstein at Palm, and less well-known individuals have gone to careers in startups and other places, and there is no guarantee, in fact, often there is a very bad history of the alumnus of Apple turning around failing companies.

Or creating great new ones. Because it, again, goes back to the first phase of our discussion today which was that if you can't blame management for failure, consistently, it's unlikely you can actually say management caused the success. Many times, management I see as important, you know, [is] just as important as having good salespeople, just as important as having good engineers.

Dan: Right.

Horace: Just as important as having great designers. They're just a piece of the machine, and the machine itself is just guided by—sometimes by management but often by the winds blowing in the macro environment. And that's really why I don't think that the solution to a turnaround for Nokia or RIM will be in management change. It may be a precondition but it's not going to be a sufficient precondition. And, again, Motorola. Great new management.

Sanjay [Jha] is brilliant and everyone knows that. Didn't mean that they've done a complete turnaround. There is not that much optimism around Motorola. So, again, we don't have a great deal of evidence to support any of these hypotheses, that management is the key to surviving or creating disruptions.

Steve Jobs is an amazing person. But I would give credit to a lot of his organization as well—or equally so. But I think there is this question of what did they do that was crazy, and what did they do that was against the grain, and what did they do that everyone said was a bad idea? That's when you see genius. And I think that's really maybe what Steve Jobs brought, and I hope they can institutionalize.

Dan: It's a great discussion. There is so many—well, there is so many different ways to look at this, and this is an interesting one. But it kind of paints that grim picture of, you know, they didn't see this coming. They didn't react fast enough.

Horace: Yes.

Dan: And now it's over. Is this—is that kind of thing unique, though, to the mobile industry, do you think?

Horace: No. It's just the thing with disruption theory that it actually applies almost to every industry. And it is a sad discussion, I have to say. It's almost disheartening.

Dan: Yes.

Horace: That you think that, "Boy, you know, it's inevitable. It's like we're all going to die someday. Why bother?"

But there is a flip side to it, you know: It's entropy. But you can and should see this also as the key to growth, that you can be a disruptor yourself. And something can be created out of nothing. Small guys can win against giants.

When a big guy fails, the thinking ought not to be, "Well, it's inevitable." The thinking ought to be, "How [can] we once again pull ourselves up by our bootstraps and become a disruptor again?" So anyone who is preaching this theory as a management consulting-type practice normally focuses on how a large client or company is able to spot signals of disruption and act early enough, et cetera.

But it's still extremely hard, even if you have all the schooling in it. And in a way, it's almost poetic. It's almost subliminal. You have to spot these things, but then you have to act very much on instinct. If you don't have data you work on pure intuition. And that's leadership. That's magical. So, I don't have… Again it's almost like going to ask a guru on the mountain. And he tells you to look inside yourself, or some nonsense like that. And it's completely inscrutable.

53

But, in fact, many times that's exactly what you need to do. You really need to look inside, and say that we just have to be crazy enough to think that we can change things.

Dan: It seems to me that Apple, unlike some of these other companies we've been talking about today, Apple seems to be very tuned in and I wouldn't say paranoid or nervous, but very aware of what its competitors are doing and always trying to react and respond to that. Even if it's not instantaneously, with some degree of speed, I mean, notifications is one example of something that's been—you know, you could be honest—say, pretty poorly implemented in iOS. You know, it's an acceptable solution, but nobody is saying that it was a great one. And that was something that Android has. It was something that WebOS had. Both of those implementations, in my opinion—having used both of those phones—were superior. I'm not saying they're perfect, but they were superior. And now, with iOS 5, we've got a whole notification system. That's their response to it. Now, that might be a bad example of the way that they respond. But it seems like Apple is constantly, constantly trying to push the envelope, trying to do something better.

Horace: Right.

Dan: One-upping themselves, almost.

Horace: Yes, you're right. I think Apple does these massive quantum leaps, and then these tiny refinements and constant polishing and improvements. So 90 percent of what you'll see coming out of Apple seems derivative or seems like they're just bringing in features that others have had for a long time, and integrating those features, and... well, they're not unique. Every company is watching, and watching their competitors, and trying to bring the best of the improvements as long as they can get away with it.

The question is, really, are they copying business models, though? Are they copying—figuring out where the value is, where the puck is going?—and all these other things which I think are the more important strategic things? I mean, execution is about running a tight ship. But where is the ship going? And that's where I think you can be reactive or you can be proactive. Some companies think that they can execute very well and they can always just say, "Well, we'll just follow another ship."

Sometimes, though, the ship starts to fly, and then you're in trouble. I think Apple is good at both, good at following and they only fold things in when they're good and ready. But then they sometimes—they just completely say that being on a ship, this is the wrong thing altogether and, you know, let's make an airplane.

It's Good to be King

Posted July 3rd, 2011 as The Critical Path Episode #3

Horace Dediu and Dan Benjamin discuss the power of cash to control supply chains in the post-PC era and how Apple is challenging conventional wisdom about its value to shareholders.

Dan: The topic that we're thinking about today, another one of your excellent topic ideas, is cash.

Horace: Yes, cash is one of the things that I've written about a lot because obviously Apple's accumulated a huge amount of it, and it's something that is so big that it kind of has its own gravity zone. It attracts comments. It attracts attention. It attracts speculation.

The problem is that a lot of people who might comment on Apple technically, or even on the marketing level, may not be aware of what cash is all about in terms of as an asset, and what is so magical about it and why we don't discuss other things like headcount or real estate.

But what I'd like to start out with is… you know, cash is a funny thing for a company. I mean, for consumers or people, for individuals, cash is a sign of wealth.

Dan: Right, you always want to have cash.

Horace: Right.

Dan: There's no such thing as having too much cash or having bad cash, and I think for people who don't understand the business side of things—I'm kind of raising my hand here in some cases—why is that bad? Why is not? Of course, Apple has cash. Of course, why wouldn't they? Why wouldn't they have as much as possible?

Horace: Right. So the thing is, with companies, too much cash is actually not a good thing in the sense that it's not maximizing the utilization of the capital. So capital for a firm is all the assets it has available. It tends to be seen as inefficiency when you have too much cash. Usually cash is something you have on hand to make sure you don't run out. A way to think of it is like in a chess game, it's like the king. The king is usually a useless piece during the game.

Dan: Right.

Horace: Until maybe the end game, when the king actually may do some offensive moves. But the thing is also if you run out of cash, it's like the king dies and the whole game is over. So it has very little power in itself, but it's something you can't live without. And so, by definition, a company goes out of business when its cash balance goes to zero. Doesn't matter how much it has in accounts receivable, doesn't matter how much it has in sales. If a company cannot pay its immediate debts, which by the way typically is payroll...

Dan: Right.

Horace: You have to shut it down or have some kind of fire sale to raise that cash. So, in effect, cash is one of these things that in large quantities is useless, more or less, but in small quantities is fatal.

So I think the discussion on Apple is more like, well, they've gone through this near-death experience and a lot of people think there's been a philosophy of hoarding. You know, it happens with many people who go through this in life, "refugee mentality" sometimes that's called... where you're always just a little bit nervous about survival. And so you tend to have a bigger buffer.

So the main question should be, though, how long can you go on like that? Because the buffer has gotten so big and it's now—let's see, the latest number is, to be precise, 65.7 or 65.8billion [dollars].

We should probably now dive in a bit deeper, into what this cash is actually used for.

Technically, cash includes obviously what you might put in the bank. But also short-term equities like stocks or bonds or things you may hold that have a short-term maturity. And so technically speaking, that doesn't add up to 65 billion.

Cash and cash equivalents for Apple are about 15.9 billion and short-term securities are 13 billion. But then they have long-term marketable securities, which are 36 billion. So this long-term part of the balance sheet is often not included in what people quote as cash. But the difference for Apple is that these long-term [assets] are really the same instruments as the short-term [ones] with the longer maturity. So for example, you might have bonds with a longer date for maturity.

So I like to lump it altogether because I think they're just as liquid, the long and the short. Though an accountant may disagree with that. So we're looking at a huge number, 65.7. I don't know if any company has ever held that much, which is not a bank. Certainly a few technology companies have come close. I think Microsoft did, but I think they were around 50 at one point, and they've been trying to get rid of that cash through dividends.

Now, the question is again, what can you possibly do with 65.7 billion? And by the way, that's growing every quarter, probably another five or so billion is being added, depending on the quarter. Usually Christmas quarter is a little bit higher. But it tends to have a very steep and increasingly steeper slope, this curve of cash.

Dan: Right.

Horace: So we're looking at possibly a hundred billion dollars within another few quarters. I'm not going to be precise about that, but it could be less than two years that we'd be looking at that.

So that's a scary number in some ways, because you can't spend it all. And we can get into the pros and cons of alternative ways of getting rid of the money. But one thing I should say first of all is that that money doesn't actually belong to Apple. Nothing belongs to Apple. Apple belongs itself to shareholders. So that money belongs to the shareholders right now, and it's not a question of [management] blowing it on something. They have a fiduciary responsibility, management does, of spending it in the interests of the company or giving it back if they can't find good interest for the money.

So there's this big question of, when these numbers are so big, just what kind of judgment you are using in making a decision. A lot of people get very emotional about getting it back or finding a good use for it.

Dan: I just still, you know, you think about it from the consumer standpoint and you think, having this has to put them in a great position, though, to spend that. I mean, why not start their own mobile cell phone company, essentially, or buy one of the big ones.

Horace: Right

Dan: And just own it, and say, "You know what, we'll buy one in Europe, we'll buy one over here," and they're just done. I mean, it seems like this puts them in a position of power and it almost feels like they're waiting for something.

Horace: Yes.

Dan: They're waiting to pounce or something like that.

Horace: Right. So that gets into the question of acquisition as one of the most likely scenarios. And so what would you buy? I mean, trouble is that there are few companies worth 65 billion. To put it bluntly, there's nothing they can buy with all that money at once.

In fact, you can go on various financial websites and try to do your own stock-picking search and try to rank companies by market cap and then you'll quickly see that the number of companies above $100 billion market cap are less than 20 probably.

So it's not easy to spend it on one thing. Now, the suggestion that you buy a technology company, therefore, is not an option. There are many small ones, but there isn't really [a] mega-acquisition that's foreseeable. Buying an operator comes up a lot, because then indeed that's consistent with Apple's integration logic. That they could own the experience for— and delivering experience as to consumers.

The problem there is, though, if you buy one operator you end up in a confrontation with the rest of the operators because you suddenly bought into your distribution network. You become a competitor to your channel. So [there's] this notion of channel conflict.

So what's likely to happen, and it has happened also with other phone vendors that have dabbled in—not necessarily acquired, but dabbled in—financing, for example, vendor financing their own operator/ customer. They've advanced them money to buy their phones, and whenever that happens the other operators tend to boycott you because you've given an unfair advantage to a competitor. So the challenge for Apple or anyone else who is a supplier to the operators is that you make an overture to one and then the others essentially block you out. So the problem for Apple would be that even if they bought one operator in the United States, for example, they would end up being shunned worldwide as a threat.

Dan: All right.

Horace: And so this is the problem. They can't buy them all. The market value of all the operators, and there are literally hundreds, at least 500 operators worldwide. That's something also they can't afford, nor would they ever be permitted to, obviously.

I've also pointed out that the amount of cash they have is nearly— not there yet—but nearly enough to buy all their competitors in the phone business because those competitors have all sort of collapsed in value lately and that 100 billion, that certainly will be very nearly [worth] the whole pile. But again, there, you have issues with why would you do such a thing, and it's not really practical and it's not valuable to Apple to do these things.

So, unfortunately, when you go through, it's a process of elimination. You sort of say, "Oh, operators are not a good idea because of channel conflict. Competitors are not a good idea for various reasons—why not just beat them in the marketplace." There's no value in acquiring a failing company. By the way, this is all putting aside the most important notion, which is that when you do buy something you tend to mess it up. It's a natural phenomenon that occurs extremely frequently.

Dan: Now, is Apple guilty of this? What have they bought and messed up? Shake?

Horace: I can't really recall—I mean, they bought NeXT, and that was like a reverse acquisition.

Dan: Right. People might say Shake. I guess it's sort of like an animation/editing-type thing that would plug in with Final Cut Pro for video effects and things like that.

Horace: That was probably—you know, these are such small companies that they're not really acquired for their business. They're acquired for their talent. They're acquired for either intellectual property assets or the team itself. So even the acquisition they made in chip design, what was the name? I can't remember it just now, but that team may or may not have been part of the building of the A4 chip.

Dan: Right. I'm trying to remember the name. I can't remember it either [P.A. Semi].

Horace: Yes, but they actually—there were rumors that the team was disbanded and people had left and there was a lot of bitterness about that going badly. So we don't know for sure.

But the problem is that Apple hasn't bought a mega company that's kind of been—except for NeXT—that has been designed to drive growth. Usually, you consolidate to save costs and create "synergies," or you buy something like Microsoft did with Skype, to drive growth because you're unable to find it on your own.

So the problem has been that Apple hasn't needed to find growth through acquisition. They've bought little pieces of property, essentially to enhance their own R&D efforts. But the classic failures, and there are so many I can't even recall, but academics have studied this for decades and the verdict is unanimous, that acquisitions destroy value in general. So the motivations seem to always be there, however, and they keep happening, but I think Apple has been actually fairly lucky in not getting drawn into that.

So again, we have here a phenomenon where we can't find something to buy. Even if we bought it, it probably would be for the wrong reasons and it would end up getting messed up or destroyed in the process. The value would be destroyed.

So really, this becomes a real problem, because all that money is earning practically zero. Something like tens of millions of dollars a quarter in terms of interest rate, which is pitiful. And the typical asset that Apple [does] own, which is its people and its intellectual property, is used to generate massive returns for shareholders, right? That's why the sales double every year. So it's essentially the 80 percent or so of the balance sheet is actually very, very, very efficient in generating cash, but its cash is not very efficient in generating cash. In fact, it's extremely inefficient.

The CFO, [Peter] Oppenheimer, I think he was asked a lot during the recession about that pile of cash, which at the time was closer to 40 [billion dollars], and people worried that that was in jeopardy because interest rates were going to zero, number one; and somehow devaluation could happen regardless of where the money was located—whether it was in dollars or Euros. So Oppenheimer said that he's very concerned about capital preservation. So all hands were on deck at the time to make sure that he bought assets.

I forgot to mention that, at the time, if they had put their money in equities and equities were collapsing, then their cash would actually be collapsing. So they had to be careful to either put it really in nonvolatile assets, bonds. [But] people were even worried that bonds would collapse. Everything was collapsing. So that cash was being discounted by people saying that they're not going to have it.

Fortunately, they went through that and they reported on it and they said, "Look, we actually managed to not lose any money, with the equity collapses." So in fact they did a very good job. Oppenheimer should be congratulated that they survived. Think of it this way, by the way: He's now one of the world's biggest fund managers.

Dan: Right.

Horace: He's having to manage a hundred billion dollars, almost, and few people have that responsibility. I bet he has a very small team, relatively speaking, to do that with.

So anyway, there's all of these pitfalls.

We can talk about two alternatives of how to return money. One is to pay a dividend, which is [the] traditional way of [returning] retained earnings to shareholders. Or to buy back shares.

Now, the first problem with dividends is that you get taxed on the dividend once you receive it as a shareholder. So the company has paid tax on it already, because there's a tax on earnings. The money that's leftover is what goes into the cash pile, and now you're saying you're going to give it to the shareholder and he has to declare it as personal income and pay personal income tax. So that's called double taxation, and the government specifically knows and is aware of that effect, and that's a way to discourage dividends. Dividends are only paid out really by utility companies or companies in a late stage in life, which aren't growing. They're value-driven companies.

So growth companies, if they pay a dividend, it's usually a sign of terminal illness, which is in fact what Microsoft had to go through a few years ago when they couldn't find opportunities for this cash. So it's a really negative signal. People think, "Oh, it's great, it's going to drive the stock price," but I think people [could also] run away saying, "Oh, look, it's no longer a growth company. So dividends are not a great signal. Dividends are not a really good way of creating value for shareholders because you get this double taxation.

And there's another sinister problem. Much of that money that Apple has been able to stash away is actually offshore, meaning that they earn profits from their business outside the United States. For example you've seen the growth they've had in international markets has been phenomenal lately with the iPhone. So the iPhone is much stronger than the Mac is internationally, right? So China and Europe and so on have caused it to accumulate all this money.

Typically, Apple wouldn't pay tax in the United States for any of that income outside of the United States.

Dan: Right.

Horace: There might be some local taxes, but there's a very curious tax regime, where money outside the United States doesn't get hit as badly as money inside the United States. So what Apple would have to do is repatriate that money in order to give it back, and repatriating that money actually would incur a penalty, a huge penalty because that money was not taxed in the first place. So now there's all this talk about extending a tax holiday because there's literally trillions of dollars outside of the United States that's not being brought back in because the companies don't want to pay this tax. And people debate about it politically and so on, whether they deserve to have this holiday or not.

I'm not going to judge that, but the problem is that, again, we're not looking at $60 billion if it comes all back in. It's going to probably get a huge haircut on the way in. So, again, Apple has to deal with this question of, "Am I doing the best thing for shareholders by bringing it back in just to give it back to them."

Then there's finally this question of, what do you do with trying to buy shares back? And the problem with share buybacks is that they have a very poor history of actually creating shareholder value. When you buy back shares, theoretically you're reducing the pool of available shares and therefore the value per share should increase proportionately. But you know, markets are weird, right? They never really react the way you expect.

Motorola, actually, I remember recently looking at their financials, and Motorola during the RAZR period was making a lot of money and, in fact, built up a huge cash pile and then they bought back shares in order to get rid of the cash.

Dan: Right.

Horace: But their share tanked anyway. I mean, it collapsed very rapidly, and then they found themselves in very precarious situation because they didn't have enough cash to capitalize the spin-off of Motorola Mobility. They were in a crisis situation during the recession, trying to also do a spin-off while at the same time their stock had been so badly beaten up. So it did no good at all to buy back those shares for Motorola, and I'm sure we can go through history and find examples of the same phenomenon.

So, although you don't get at the same tax penalty—the double taxation—there's still questions of whether you're actually doing anything to create shareholder value. So you turn to one more option and it doesn't look good.

So this is where we have to go back and really ask the deeper question of, how can Apple use capital as muscle to improve its core business? And that's where I think we need to really think creatively, and I think

61

Apple is probably thinking also this way because they haven't done anything else.

Dan: So I think you've kind of convinced me that maybe all this cash is bad and that they should probably get rid of it, but before we kind of get into one of the other topics you told me before this show you wanted to talk about, one question I have for you is, do they have to spend all of it? In other words, do they have to make sure that it's all gone? Do they want to have zero? What's the ideal? Because it's good to have some, right?

Horace: It's good to have some, of course. You need some. I mean, there's working capital—cash on hand—to make sure you cover periods of seasonality, periods of economic slowdowns, saving up for a rainy day. You know, certainly there's a big amount you need, but it's probably an order of magnitude [less]. Meaning they could probably get away with having only five to ten billion on hand, and that would be actually a very rich position.

As a financier one would look at this question and say, "There's inefficiency in this model." But as a strategy thinker, I actually think that… I'm sort of in agreement with you that I think the option value of this cash is something people don't actually put their finger on. Option value means that I've always got that there and I can use it at any time, and that in itself is valuable.

Dan: Right.

Horace: And that value actually forces many competitors to do probably suboptimal things. We just saw Apple spend money on IP patents. They have the power to essentially force competitors to [do the same, or] they would force them out of an option, for example. Or they might use it as they did with their suppliers, to fund manufacturing and fund the tooling for new screens or new memories. And essentially what they've done is not vendor financing, but supplier financing.

So they've taken the money and given it to their suppliers as a loan, essentially, saying: "Here, you buy this equipment with this money. Yes, you own it after you pay us back, but we have dibs on the first year or two or production." In so doing they've essentially assured themselves capacity, but also assured that no one else gets that capacity.

Dan: Right.

Horace: So that is something they've used in the past for memory chips during the iPod era, and they're now using it as leverage for the screen technology for the larger screens that they have in the iPad. Actually, pretty much Apple has a monopsony—there's a word for this—a single buyer versus a single seller.

So the thing is that now they're the sole buyer and as a result they have inordinate power. And so I think what you have to think of is that there is probably a few tens of billions of dollars that actually could be used as this kind of leverage into the supply chain, and maybe that will scale up and then people will start to really see the patterns.

So it's possible that that's the plan. I've even suggested that Apple could do more in ensuring—or re-architecting—the supply chain, because what's really not good enough about Apple today is their inability to meet demand. So they can't really make enough of the products.

Dan: Right. This is exactly what—as I was listening to you say this— I was starting to think: Where could they improve? What's something they could improve on? They already know how to make cool stuff. They already know how to market it. What about that, what about the assembly line, what about actually meeting the demand? You know, they outsource almost everything essentially to China. Basically the Chinese are building a lot of this stuff. Would they bring that in-house? Would they have their own operations over there? I mean, is maybe that what they're gearing up for, is some kind of really big potentially overseas assembly operation?

Horace: Actually, I kind of toyed with this idea back since the summer, where I kind of wondered if Apple should go back into controlling or owning manufacturing, because that's what's not good enough about the value chain right now. I've come to realize that ownership is not the only means of control, right? So we have this ability to exercise control through financing only, so that you don't have to be an equity holder. And that's probably what they're actually doing.

So in a sense I had kind of a hint of the right answer, but I'm asking myself, "Where further can this go?" Because a couple things are telling. One is that the market is far bigger than we can imagine. Right now there's 200 million iOS devices, but there's 5 billion, 5.3 billion, phone users in the world. And I believe that not only will that number grow, but also that most of those will be smartphone users.

So there may come a point where—in fact, this is actually easily foreseen—that there will be a market for a billion smartphones a year. Not necessarily iPhones, but a billion smartphones a year. And within the next three, four years, which I would say is within a couple of cycles of new generation iPhones coming out.

Which, by the way, knowing what I do about product development, that means they have to be thinking now about that generation of product that's going to be selling into a market of a billion units. And they have to be thinking about how much production can they get out of this design, which will meet their marketshare assumptions. If they may be 20 percent, for example, then you're looking at selling 200 million iPhones in 2014, let's say or '15. So that's not that long from now, given the cycle time of product development. Those products are probably right now in conceptualizing stage. But you have to think about the whole go-to-market strategy, the whole distribution strategy, the manufacturing, all of that is interconnected. It's not just designers who are looking at this now. You have to design for all of those criteria.

So my question would be, "Okay, now if you can foresee a billion unit market and you can foresee a marketshare within that market, how are you going to deliver 200 million units?" Like I mentioned in another episode, if you're looking at a 12-month product lifecycle—you're going to have a new generation comes out every 12 months—then you have to worry about how are you going to ramp up from zero to 200 million or whatever the run rate may be for 200 million a year.

So it really is—these numbers are staggering, and I think Apple should be even more ambitious, should be looking beyond the 20 percent. You know, they have almost 20 now, so why not grow? Why not go into the low end [of the market]. And I think that's possible, and it's something that they need to engineer and plan for. Everything has to be coordinated.

So my question would be, "Well, if the bottleneck is that you don't have enough production capacity, what can you do with capital, of which you have plenty, to solve the capacity, of which you have little?" So this is to me one of these obvious things. That, hey! there's nothing else that's more important and more valuable to you, because this is the very thing that constrains you. So you have to focus that capital on the production question.

And how to do that beyond what we've already experienced, which like I said, is financing, which is great, but that only partly solves the problem. I don't know the answer, but I think that they need to be very creative.

From my own experience, I've seen things at Nokia, and Nokia was having a very interesting architecture for manufacturing, where they have multiple plants in multiple regions. So there would be an European plant or—maybe more than one. There'd be a North American, maybe manufacturing in Mexico, and then there'd be an Asian site or two, serving those markets. So that when you're dealing with low-cost product it doesn't make sense to ship things around and have it centralized. It makes sense to distribute, and that gets you to the billion units a year.

So I wonder if, architecturally speaking, Apple would be better served by having distributed [manufacturing]. Now, what we've heard also is that they're moving to Brazil with iPad. That makes sense on the tactical level because Brazil happens to have a very onerous tax regime for imports, and it makes sense that they have somehow an easy way of addressing the Latin American market. And Brazil is just the biggest part of that. So I don't know if that's a part of an architectural decision they made.

Let's step a moment back and say if it's an iPhone that sells for $600, approximately $200 of that—although it's maybe closer to 180 as volume grows—but 180 to 200 of that is the materials that go into it, right? The components. And what people assume when they think about manufacturing is that there's a huge additional cost for producing and marketing and all these other things that are attached. But in fact I would guess that on an average phone—I'm not talking about the iPhone—on an average phone the labor component of the cost is single digit dollars. So we're looking two to three dollars for a cheap phone, probably up to five to eight dollars I'd say for a smartphone.

So there isn't that much labor involved. The reason for that is it's mostly an automated process. These are machines that are used to build the phone. The components come in on strips of paper. There's a machine that takes them off the strip of paper and then puts them on the circuit board or puts the boards together into a sub-assembly, and then that moves on to another robot that fuses that with the casing, and so on. Because these are such small parts, a human couldn't possibly have the dexterity to work with them.

But where there is human labor involved is usually toward the end of the process, where things get screwed together a little bit, where things are packaged, where things are tested. Especially tested. There have to be certain automated tests, but there's also visual tests and looking whether the fit and finish is good enough and so on. And then there's packaging and the actual shipping of the product and the trucks have to be driven and so on.

So that's, roughly speaking, the process. Now, Apple may have a much more complex, more labor-intensive process because their products do tend to be a little bit more mechanically challenging, let's say.

Dan: Right.

Horace: But nevertheless, for as long as I can remember, the entire industry has been squeezing labor out of this process. So that's why it's not so much a labor question. You can think of these as really being lines of robots. And those are fairly mobile. Labor is difficult to move, but you can take an assembly line and then move it someplace else fairly quickly, and they can probably scale. So you can have a plant that runs 10 lines and you can have a plant that runs one line. And so you can position these things.

The problems are much more complex with respect to logistics of things feeding into the plant and feeding out of the plant. So it's not so trivial as sort of just dropping a couple of containers in Mexico and you have a factory. Some things you can do that with, but not phones at this time, and certainly not iPhones.

Dan: Right.

Horace: So I think that Apple is doing the best they can with respect to [manufacturing]. It may make sense that they're doing it in a centralized fashion today, with Foxconn, but I'm still wondering if they can't get a little bit clever about it. Whether they can't really re-architect...

If you were to ask Jony Ives and Tim Cook to brainstorm on this, I'd love to have them think about how can we build a phone, a future generation iPhone, that keeps in mind all of these questions and is designed to be manufactured in a distributed, localized fashion, which allows perhaps new economics to emerge. And that to me is one of these open questions, and I think it would be lovely if Apple could do something like that because we would have not only great distribution, but we would have potentially less dependency on one manufacturer and all the political costs that go along with that.

Dan: So if you're financial—I know you're not—but if you're a financial analyst, is this something that gives you pause, should you as a consumer perhaps be concerned and say, "Man, they've just got too much cash, we don't know what we're going to do with it, this doesn't look good for them in the long term."

Horace: Well, it's hard to say. I mean, I'm not nervous. I do have some shares I own, but I don't feel very nervous about it, actually. I think it's in good hands. Like I said, if they did things with it to theoretically please shareholders, I don't think it's going to really change the stock price that much. Heck, you know, they're selling twice as many phones as they did last year and the stock hasn't doubled—well, maybe it has—but we're not seeing the multiples that we're used to seeing on Apple. So the stock is fairly cheap on a multiple basis. So the stock is not reacting to growth in the traditional way you might expect.

I don't think the stock will react to a share buyback very—I don't think it will react even positively necessarily. There's a lot of mystery about how stocks behave, and I think probably the company understands this and says, "Look, we're just going to drive the top and the bottom line and that's how we serve shareholders. We're going to grow the business. And, yeah, we've got the spare cash, we'll just keep it around until we find something useful." I think they're going to use it as leverage, they're going to use it in interesting ways.

There's been a lot of speculation about buying media assets or getting into a new business, communications.

Dan: Movies.

Horace: Movies, yeah. To me these are not really likely things, but I'm not a—I can't make with confidence a recommendation of what they should buy. But I would just say that if they can solve this production issue, I think that would be a very big win.

Dan: I mean, maybe they just buy one of these companies in China and say, all right, you know, keep it in the family and then they go and buy Pixar and then they spend a lot of money on this new campus, and they hire some more people to fill it. Aren't they just sort of chipping away, piece by piece, at that fortune?

Horace: Yes, but they're able to do that out of—I mean, as far as hiring people and building campuses—they can do that out of existing cash flow. They don't have to dip into the till. So, you know, they'll make payments on land and make payments to contractors and hire new people, just on the amount of money coming in every quarter. So they've done that with respect to their stores. I mean, they've built what, 300 stores without having to dip into cash? Every quarter they probably allocate a certain amount to building stores or buying data centers.

So the problem is really, now you've got to have some kind of huge leap, some non-linear kind of step function that you go from zero to 50 billion, that's just gone over night. That's where I'm wondering what they could possibly buy. I mean, you can look at all kinds of statistics about how many engineers would it take, you know, could you hire to spend that money.

Dan: Right, right.

Horace: There aren't enough in the world. Or you could look at it and say, "What if they stopped…"—and this was a funny exercise. What if they stopped completely making any money or even having any sales, how long could the company run. Because you know their SG&A [Selling, General and Administrative expenses] and you know their R&D expenditures. You can project that they're going to be in business for eight to ten years if they sold nothing. That's just like keeping all those people employed: Hey, we're going to go for a whole new category of product, shutdown everything else. You give them eight years to come up with something like that.

So that's also improbable, but it shows you the magnitude of the problem that, or the magnitude of the value they've created. But it's an amazing number and it's a struggle to really think creatively about how to spend it.

Dan: In your knowledge, has there ever been another company in a similar situation? Obviously not quite with this much cash, but in a situation like this where they just have way, way, way too much and then they've resolved it somehow positively?

Horace: Two companies come to mind. Obviously, one is Microsoft, and the other is Cisco. I think both being technology companies makes them somewhat comparable. Microsoft did accumulate an enormous cash pile, which they made the decision in the '90s to give back to the shareholder. They pretty much realized that there was nothing they could buy or they couldn't spend it in any rational way.

Again, the stock has gone completely flatline since, like, 2000. So there's been no discernible shareholder value. What would have happened if they hadn't spent the money—or given it back? Would the stock have fallen? I don't know, but there hasn't been a huge cheerleading going on about that strategy.

Cisco, on the other hand, has also been acquisitive. They acquire many companies. They acquire typically smaller companies. But we've seen lately with Cisco a slowing down in that strategy. They've tried to expand into consumer business, and as you know, they've shut down the Flip camera effort and they've pulled back from that strategy, although historically they've bought a lot of other assets in enterprise and communications.

So Cisco is kind of a mixed report card. I mean, they've done fairly well with acquisitions, but they've had their misses as well. And, yes, they are a company, however, that hasn't seen shareholder value created in the last few years because of that cash. I mean, it hasn't really caused the company to explode in value.

Dan: Right.

Horace: So, again, if that's the criteria by which you measure the value of the cash, that it can somehow be put to work, neither scenario, acquisition—or in the case of Microsoft—dividends, has done that.

By the way, Microsoft has also done acquisitions, various large-dollar-figure acquisitions. They famously failed to acquire Yahoo!, but they've gotten Skype and a few other things. I don't recall all of them. Curious, you know, there is even companies which have relatively high cash going after acquisitions, like Dell buying consulting firms, and HP as well. So, you know, these companies are in a state of not too much cash, they're in the state of no growth and failure of their core business, so they're going into trying to become something else, trying to become an IBM.

Dan: Right.

Horace: And not so much—they're in a state of distress or, you could say, disruption, or being disrupted. So they're searching blindly, if you will, for an outlet. That is not a good comparable for Apple, unfortunately, because Apple is growing. So you have a company that's growing very quickly, which actually Microsoft wasn't growing that quickly. I mean, they were growing during the last decade, but not that quickly, and yet they went to a strategy of dividends.

So we have a couple of weird things about Apple that again are not fitting any kind of example I can think of. Having the world's large cash pile, being one of the fastest growing companies with 90 percent growth, and so therefore it's just hitting on all cylinders and its core assets are just enormously valuable assets because they're returning hugely to the shareholder. And you have this huge lump of cash that isn't returning anything—but you can't as a shareholder complain because they are just growing so fast, right? So [do you] bother with that underperforming asset?

And the management is also known as being extremely competent, whereas in many cases people get nervous about the cash because they know that management may be not so competent and may be actually blowing it on things which actually suited their egos rather than doing anything useful. Well, you don't see that with Apple. There might be egos, but not with respect to acquisitions, right?

Dan: Right.

Horace: They're not going around saying I'm great because I bought so and so.

Again, there's no precedent I can point to right now, and none has ever been presented to me in the blog or anywhere else, nor in the media, that I've seen that's credible as a good strategy for this.

I come back to this question of what is missing. And what they really need is not growth, is not consolidation, is not that they're slowing and therefore need synergies or that they need growth by finding new markets or finding new—well, I shouldn't say new markets—but new business models to go into. These are not things that Apple needs. These are not things that are failing inside the company.

What it does need is simple meeting of demand, and that's really why I see this great opportunity to put that money to work on the thing that they need most. The problem is that you can't really practically implement that, but then again, we don't have all the visibility, [the]knowledge of all these details that they do. And some of these questions are geopolitical in nature. They're not just questions about the practicalities of building assembly lines or hiring people or scaling things and engineering questions and process management and so on. These are sometimes questions around politics and what capital needs to be expended politically in order to move sites and build plants and who knows what else.

It's very likely, by the way, that in order for Apple to have good presence in China, as a vendor there with the operators—let's not forget that of the [Chinese] operators, the largest is a government entity, and in order for them to get concessions from them, the need to access the market—they may need in fact to grant manufacturing concessions. So, for example, it may be that Foxconn has been blessed by the government there saying, "Look, Apple will work with you alone."

So we don't know this. This is just speculation. But if there are things you can point to in China, like the location of the stores and the presence of iconic landmarks in the middle of [Shanghai], these aren't things you can typically even buy, no matter how much money you have. So sometimes you have to spend political capital as well.

So I'm just saying that we don't know all of the details. These are just hints that there might be a lot of unknowables or that there are a lot of things that are constraining them. Yes, it's an interesting puzzle.

Dan: So where does that leave us? Where do we want to wrap up for this week?

Horace: Well, I think, as usual, we go through these exercises and try to solve a puzzle, but sometimes we—you know, frequently we end up with more questions than answers. That's what I like about this, is that it's a continuous challenge and we have the ability to get feedback and get the smartest people in the world to come back and criticize and improve our thinking.

So as usual, I'd love to get feedback from our audience and then we can take the thinking further. Because I really think what's being learned about Apple is actually very important to many other companies.

One thing I should state here is that, as we say in the introduction, we're looking at everything through Apple as a lens.

Dan: Right.

Horace: And therefore, I think, what Apple is doing now is setting the best practices for many companies, not just in technology. The question of how to deal with cash is one of these questions. Probably by doing nothing they're actually essentially contradicting some of the long-held beliefs about what's the right thing to do. And they may prove us all wrong, but they also they may be proven right in showing that actually, look, "Bam" or "Boom," whatever Jobs will say. You know, suddenly you've got the checkmate move now…

Dan: Right.

Acquisitions

Posted August 16th, 2011 as The Critical Path Episode #4

Ryan Irelan speaks with Horace Dediu about Google's planned acquisition of Motorola Mobility and the potential ramifications for competitors.

Ryan: So, Horace, I have been keeping up to date on the latest happenings this week. And there has been a lot going on in the mobile space. So the big thing, of course, is Google acquiring Motorola Mobility. So I guess first we probably should talk about what happened, and then maybe jump into what that means. There has been a lot of articles written about it. I know you've written about it at Asymco.com. And I know that Florian Mueller has written about it as well. But I guess we would need to kind of navigate these waters. Because it seems like as the hours go on, there is more and more being unpacked out of this whole situation. And it seems to be becoming a bit more complex than maybe it was at first glance.

Horace: Yeah. I think a lot of people jumped to conclusions, myself included. But as it's settling in for the last 24 hours I think there's a lot more subtlety and. perhaps, the story is a bit more complex than we first thought. There are two themes, primarily.

I think, one: Is Google going to be a new device maker? Or takeover where Motorola was. And two: Is this an IP story exclusively?

And I think it's probably both, in fact, and that's where I'm trying—I am struggling, because you need to do a lot of due diligence on both of the value of the IP, which, by the way, is almost impossible to do. As a bystander, you have to have a serious deep dive into the value of those patents—which of those can be exercised in defense—or offense, if you will—versus some patents which might actually be already pooled into resources that are available for licensing on an unencumbered basis. I won't get into that. I think Florian Mueller is the authority on this. I'd like to talk about the first option, which is, what does it mean for Google to be a device-maker?

First, I think that is not entirely out of the question. What we've seen, in fact, in the press release—what passes for a press release in Google is a blog post—is that they didn't talk about IP, except in the last paragraph, saying, "Oh, by the way, we're going to protect Android with this." They mostly talk about innovation and what's great about Motorola, and all that. But [explicitly] there is no indication that they are going to abandon the core business.

The other fact that lends itself to this hypothesis is that—or rumor, not necessarily a fact—is Om Malik's piece that Motorola was actually getting a bid from Microsoft as well. But Microsoft didn't want the device business. And, therefore, their bid was not as interesting to Motorola because Motorola wanted to keep going as a device company. Because there are 19,000 people there. And obviously management wants to have a role going forward and so on. So Microsoft's bid was partly disadvantaged by this insistence on the IP being the core.

So I believe there is some validity to the notion of Google being interested in the device business. And I'd like to explore that on this show, and we can also get into some of the other questions. I've just written a post and [it's] just came out in the *Harvard Business Review* blog. I explore the causes that led to Google getting into this relationship, which I think are really mistakes on their part. Or missteps, or mis-assumptions.

Ryan: Sure. So what led up to this, then? Stepping all the way back, are we talking about—is this all been borne out of this, the bidding that happened for the, was it the Nortel patents?

Horace: Nortel, yeah.

Ryan: Yeah.

Horace: Well, actually, I'd like to step back even further.

Ryan: Okay.

Horace: I think we need to step back to 2005, actually.

Ryan: Okay.

Horace: When Android was acquired by Google. There's a couple of things that historically—today's a different world, but the fact is that the roots of the decision-making are actually that old. Google acquired Android at a time when the dominant operating system was Symbian. RIM was actually an up-and-coming company. And Microsoft was the disruptor in the business, meaning Microsoft was coming in with a radical business plan. The radical plan was that they were going to license an operating system so that every manufacturer of phones could use Windows Mobile. In fact, Microsoft entered into that market as a licensor of operating systems, in 2003. They had developed the product, or began developing the product, in 2000. It was an open secret, because they actually talked about it. Its codename was Stinger. It was an operating system that was based on Windows CE. It was already running in Pocket PCs, which were, you know, sort of the copy, if you will, of the Palm in terms of being a PDA. But it was based on the different operating system, had touch as their interface, with a stylus.

And so this goes way back. And so Microsoft was coming in from 2003 to 2005, really taking a lot of share in the smartphone space, which, granted, at the time was a lot smaller. And Symbian was dominant, and there was Palm OS as an alternative. There were also the same mix of giant companies and small companies, software-based, and integrated companies, and so on. And there were even app stores and there were app aggregators, and everything that we see today was still going on back then. I know this because I was in Nokia at the time. [It was] actually my job to analyze this. So we were measuring all these numbers and projecting them forward years and years ahead.

So what was interesting in 2005 was that the acquisition happened and the logic of it was, if you read between the lines— and it's been corroborated by several people who were there— that Google felt threatened by Microsoft. They felt threatened because you could easily see the disruptive potential of a Windows mobile, [meaning] that they would eventually be the new Windows of the mobile world, which meant— stepping back even a bit further you realize that devices are not like PCs in one crucial way, and that is they are far more integrated and it's far easier for that integrator to decide to flip on and off certain features and on and off certain access to APIs. And in that sense, it wasn't regulated—

As you know, Microsoft had to deal with antitrust regulations that forced their hand, and it forced them to open up all their APIs, so that they couldn't actually block Google from being on the desktop.

Had they not lost the case with the [United States] Justice Department, it may have very well turned out that Google wouldn't exist today because then we would be running Microsoft's vision of the future.

So Google is alive partly because on the desktop, or on Windows, Microsoft was not allowed to block them. But what happens on the device is that you can easily block things. And no one has yet regulated [mobile] to the degree that the desktop is regulated. So in fact the scenario in 2005 was clear for Google: If Microsoft wins [mobile], then [Google is] going to be essentially at the mercy of Microsoft. Not necessarily [in the sense that they're] going to be blocked, but [that they] have to make sure that this does not happen. So by buying Android the idea was that [it would be] a Linux-based operating system, open source, [and that] by giving it away, they would ensure that those licensees who are now beholden to Microsoft—and we're talking about the same suspects today, Samsung, HTC, a lot of ODMs [original device manufacturers] in China and in Taiwan—Sony Ericsson took the license, Motorola took the license for Windows Mobile. The only one who didn't, actually, was Nokia. It was the only one that was holding out and saying no to Microsoft.

So Microsoft had won all these design wins, basically. They were in every device practically. The number of SKUs [stock keeping units] or the number of products that were running Windows Mobile at its peak were numbering in the thousands. [Microsoft had] more prolific Windows Mobile licensing going on than even Android is today.

So clearly this was disruptive, and Google was very nervous. So the whole objective of Android was a defense against the hegemony and the monopoly of Microsoft in mobility, [wherein it] would be a lot easier for them to block Google on the device than it was on the desktop. So, you know, everybody thought that mobile was going to be big, and that was not a debatable topic. It's just a question of who wins the platform game.

Keep in mind that while all this was going on, we at Nokia were like, "But they're ignoring us. The fact is, we *can* beat Microsoft." In fact, Nokia did beat Microsoft because Windows Mobile didn't actually disrupt the market. And even RIM outsold Windows Mobile. And the reason for that was that Microsoft's approach was saying, "We provide the operating system, you provide a bunch of other things, including hardware, and together we put it all together in a complex interlocking product." Sort of PC 2.0.

However, in 2004 and '05, it was still very hard to put the pieces together in a way that you end up with a smooth experience, which is why when Apple came in, in 2007, with an iPhone, it was just such a bombshell. Because it was so well integrated, and yet it had all the power of a small computer. And suddenly it was a watershed event. The realization was, for me at least, that integrated is the way to go forward.

And [this was realized] at this late stage in the game, in 2007. But Google and Microsoft in their fundamental DNA do not believe in integrated products. They believed at the time, and I think still do to a large extent, that modular would win. That eventually you're going to commoditize the hardware and the software is going to be the focus of innovation and profit capture. This is their belief. [They] made this decision that that's a clear decision, and clear path forward.

So the point, then, is that at the time, in 2005, when the core decision was made to enter into the mobile space, as a system software provider, that they would launch something which would itself be disruptive to Microsoft. Microsoft was coming in saying, "Software is the key value here, and we're going to own that layer and we're going to commoditize the hardware." Instead, Google said, "We're also going to commoditize the software, meaning the system software, the operating system that sits on top of the hardware, and give that away for free. And thus the value will be moved above that in the stack where services lie, which is where we [Google] provide all of our products."

You can argue that Android was a defensive move, a moat, if you will, a protection for their core services. And it would prevent Microsoft from having a blocking power over their services.

And my contention is that, in fact, they were in error about the timing of this commoditization transition. That, in fact, value today is still being captured predominantly by the hardware. And the hardware keeps improving and keeps moving in new directions that you cannot foresee, as it did with touch in 2007. And now we may have even further innovation in terms of input methods. And as new innovations come in, then you have to integrate them and redefine the product every time it happens. So the problem was that they thought the world would freeze in a PC[-like configuration]—in terms of technology but also in terms of business model and business integration—as of 2005.

Way too early. So 2007 comes, iPhone changes the game again, and what Google does is they reorient Android from being a defense against Microsoft to it being a defense against the iPhone becoming a hegemony. So Google, although their services run on the iPhone, they are *again* nervous about Apple at some point pulling the plug and saying, "Okay, Google is no longer welcome on our platform."

Which could happen, I have to admit. Now, the point is that [Google] said, "Okay, we're going to then release the virus of Android and make sure that does not happen." But the problem is that they use a modular approach to fight against an integrated product, whereas the disruptive model they had originally in 2005 was, "Let's use a modular approach to fight against another modular approach, but let's be disruptive on price." In other words, go free.

And here [against iPhone], they're trying to say that they're going to have a free product that grows in a viral fashion with licensees, fighting against the integrated product, smooth and easy to use. That's a different battle.

Ryan: Yeah.

Horace: That's a different battle, and that's why I think there's a mismatch because Google is running into all kinds of obstacles, some foreseeable, some unforeseeable. For example, fragmentation—the needs of the community or the ecosystem are at odds with the needs of Google. [For instance, the original equipment manufacturers] don't want to constantly have to change the software in the phones. They'd rathe we buy the cellular phones. [But] Google's incentives and Samsung's incentives are at different ends.

That's just the tip of the iceberg. There's a lot of problems underneath that. I'm not introducing anything new here. But what I'm saying is that the overall picture is that Android is actually not quite fitting what the market demands, which is smooth integration; a uniform, addressable market that developers can write to; a uniform app experience. There has been a need to have consistency across different versions of the operating system.

And of course now the move to tablets, where you want to be able to transition the software seamlessly between these two domains, and that's not the case with Android. So Android again was caught a little bit unawares by the iPad. The iPad was dismissed even by Google's management as being nothing more than a large iPod touch back in April, 2010.

Ryan: Right.

Horace: Meaning that they weren't really in a panic situation. And so they had to have a crash development effort once it was proven that the product was actually a success. And we're still feeling the effects of that because [the version of Android nicknamed] Honeycomb isn't quite baked yet.

But these are side stories. The big story is that Google looks at the world as modular. Now here is the bombshell from yesterday: Here they come in, and then they tell the world that they're going to keep [Motorola] running, and at the same time going to license the same building blocks that are used in that business to its competitors...

You know, I personally have experienced the pitfalls of that, because in Symbian that was exactly the logic. You had one company called Nokia that actually had, not a majority, but the largest interest in Symbian, and could dictate terms. [Nokia was] also licensing Symbian to its nominal partners. That just didn't work, in spite of Chinese walls—you know, Chinese walls are this notion that you prevent leaks of information inside of your own organization. And that's just really, really difficult to do—even if you could legally prove that that's being done, there is no trust. There is very little trust from the other vendors.

So there was never that much enthusiasm for licensing Symbian, even though, we had people not only in the ecosystem of Symbian, but that had equity. [The OEMs] actually owned shares in Symbian, Inc. They had paid money to be part of a business. And that's not the case with the Open Handset Alliance [a Google-led Android consortium]. There is no commitment from the device maker to be committing resources to maintaining the core operating system.

So, it's got a lot of things that looked to me, having been there, unworkable.

Ryan: Right.

Horace: The other thing, by the way—sorry in just going on about this—but the other thing is that the time frames here sound extremely suspicious. It's been confirmed, or sources say, that the negotiations began pretty much after the Nortel deal went down. And...

Ryan: So that was within the last five weeks or so.

Horace: Yeah, that's what Om says. I find that credible, actually, because it did look like they were quite upset about the Nortel deal.

On the other hand, having been also exposed a little bit to the M&A [mergers and acquisitions] world, things don't happen at that pace for anything like above a few million dollars worth of value. Right? We're talking 12.5 billion [dollars], a significant premium. And it happens in five weeks. Five weeks is not even time to set up meetings. I mean, five weeks, you've got to have a due-diligence team to come—flies in, gets access to all the documents, goes through and pores over all the documents to prove that there is nothing, like there is no skeletons in the closet, the company isn't fudging on its reports, and then they go in and they would scrutinize the IP. They would have to go through 20,000 patents one by one, and assess [the total] value.

Ryan: Yeah, there's no time in five weeks to do that.

Horace: There is absolutely no time. So, obviously, also Nortel may have had somewhat of a rush bidding process [and] those guys didn't go in there with the usual due diligence. But, still, [Motorola is] an operating company, not a bankrupt one, that's probably already [had] a lot of hashing of its assets. Here we have an operating company, 19,000 employees, being assessed as what its value is to Google in a matter of weeks.

Ryan: Right.

Horace: And also rumor has it that Andy Rubin, the most important player in this saga, is actually only invited to the meetings late in the game. Whatever that means, I don't know. But my point is simply that there are a lot of things here that don't seem to make sense and I'm struggling with a lot of these open questions about what the point of this is. And what were they really thinking? Are we seeing a shift, like I said, from the 2005 mentality and the mentality that Microsoft still holds to this day, which is that software is going to commoditize hardware?

Ryan: You kind of went back to the history, back to 2005, when Google purchased Android. And how that kind of led up to, you know, some of the decisions that Google has made. And that this five-week window between when Google lost out on those Nortel patents—with some oddly, you know, numbered bids—to yesterday when it was announced that they had acquired Motorola Mobility. And you know, we're talking about how that five-week window is barely enough time to do due diligence, and probably not for the size of the acquisition.

Horace: Right. So all these are pieces of a puzzle, right? So we don't quite know what the picture looks like. But the key question for me is, did Google change what they think of as the way the value is captured in this business?

I've been critical of Android for a number of reasons. One is that I don't think it benefits Google all that much. I mean, protecting the core business is not as interesting as actually building new [businesses]. Right? So, in one way, I feel like Google ought to be innovating, not so much on ways of protecting search but rather thinking about social.

In fact, when I wrote about when Eric Schmidt left [as CEO], I asked, "Why did he leave?" I wasn't very kind. I said, "Why was he fired?" But basically the question is really about why does a CEO leave when the company is doing well? And the answer, to me, was that they haven't done the things which really threatened them. I mean, to deal with disruption. [Google is] dealing with Facebook coming in and just capturing the eyeballs that normally would have gone to Google had they done something other than protecting the core.

So I am critical of Android because I think it keeps Google from being Google enough. You know, if they think about commoditization, why do they want to be plumbing suppliers? [Android] is low-level. It's not in the cloud, which is what Google is all about. Here you are selling system software based on Linux, which is a 20-year-old kernel. And somehow this is innovation for you? Come on. If you really don't believe in the value of these components, then move around them. Don't be fearful of encroachment and all of these machinations of Microsoft.

Ryan: So are you saying that everything from 2005 up to this point has been a defensive move by Google in the mobile space?

Horace: Well, not everything, but in mobile, certainly. I think Google's idea is that "Our innovation in mobile is to commoditize the operating system so that we can allow our services—which are really not that different than they are on the desktop—[to prosper]."

But you need to ask what is it about mobile that makes Google more powerful as a business. And you could answer it in multiple ways. (And of course they've tried a couple of ideas.) I think you could do a lot with maps. You could do a lot with social. So mobility ought to be sustaining to Google's core. And yet they treat it as something of a threat, and they try to address the problem as "How can we not lose," rather than "How we can win?"

So that's really my criticism of Android. Because I do think highly of the company. I think it's one of the most disruptive companies and one of the most innovative companies in terms of business-model innovation. And I just don't think Android is up to their standard, frankly.

[I am conscious] that I might be blind to the potential of Android as the disruptor. I struggled with that because, yes, it's coming in and it's changing the economics of devices, but I still think an integrated player can also do the same things. And the way you test the disruption is that if you enter, do the incumbents feel motivated to fight you, or do they feel motivated to flee somewhere else, to higher ground. And so what we're seeing with Apple and Microsoft is that they absolutely felt threatened by Android and they absolutely felt like they were going to respond as violently as possible to an existential threat.

That is not a typical disruptive impulse. The disruptor comes in and it becomes completely benign in the eyes of an incumbent because it's just not [seen as] a threat. And that's in fact how Apple took the business. They were dismissed by everyone for two years as they got a foothold in the market.

So, you see, that's the essential thing. That Android doesn't feel disruptive to me. It's only got one out of five things on the check list. One thing it has is price—lower pricing. But it doesn't make profits, which is another indicator. It isn't invisible to incumbents, so they are motivated to respond. And it also has this IP issue hanging over it, so it's not truly innovative in that sense, because if they copied significant portions it's not really all that innovative.

But, anyway, I don't want to get into a battle about what is or isn't innovation.

So now we can finally talk about the deal because, I think, if you look at the background, you look at the actual execution, and then you ask yourself, "Well, what is it going forward?" And the thing with Motorola is that it went through a near-death crisis when the RAZR imploded. And that caused their headcount to go down by two-thirds. I mean, we talk about 19,000 [today] but I think this company used to be 100,000.

Ryan: Wow.

Horace: Yes, they were a bit bloated, to be honest. But the fact is that they lost a huge number of people. Granted, some of those have gone to the other Motorola—[Solutions]. But there was a huge amount of drama during this decline. One thing is that a corporate raider, Carl Icahn, came in and said, "Okay, I'm going to unlock value," because the stock price had collapsed.

"I'm going to unlock value by doing a management takeover. I'm going to get rid of the current management." So he did that, effectively. He bought five percent or more of the company. And then he put one of his people on the board, and then he forced a management change. And so, sure enough, the former CEO, [Edward] Zander, left. They recruited a very bright guy, Sanjay [Jha] from Qualcomm—who everybody respected as the guy who really knew the business—and essentially set forth on the path of splitting the company up. Because it was worth less as the sum of its parts, they spun off the government business and the radio business. They still make walkie-talkies, you know, for example.

Ryan: Right.

Horace: And then they took the other assets out, those include the mobile-phone business and the set-top box business. And I don't know if there is anything really substantially other than that. And of course the patents that go along with that. And that became [Motorola] Mobility, Inc., MMI—not MOT, as the stock ticker was called—and so MMI was actually founded as a new business in January [of] this year. That's brand new.

Ryan: So there was some talk about how Google was, you know, this was an important acquisition because of the set-top box work that Motorola does. But that's actually—is that a different company, then?

Horace: No, no. That's part of MMI.

Ryan: Oh, it is. Okay.

Horace: Yeah. So those are the two things that went into MMI, which is the set-top plus the phone.

Ryan: Okay.

Horace: So, a couple of things also, by the way, which are intangibles in there. One is the Motorola brand, globally known, historic value, all kinds of good things about that.

But you're right. I mean, the set-top box is one of these things that you ask, "Okay, can you leverage that in some way?" That's a long story. We should have a show just about the future of television and why I think that that's really not a good play there.

Ryan: Right. Is that not important to Google, or not?

Horace: It might be. It might be actually, you know. That's one of these things that's kind of a hot-potato issue now. What can you use if you're in the technology business to kind of, as I say, disrupt television? You know, television has remained unchanged since its inception, and is still almost exactly the same business model, exactly the same distribution, exactly the same production, exactly the same content types.

Ryan: Right.

Horace: So there hasn't been almost any innovation except for reality shows. Literally, since the beginning. So it's fascinating to me that it has withstood everything that's been thrown at it, including, PVRs, VCRs, DVDs, every technology you can imagine in terms of screens, all of these things have been applied to the TV business, and it hasn't changed its business models. [The] only thing that's really innovative now is YouTube. But we'll get to that perhaps in another show.

Ryan: Yeah, absolutely.

Horace: But my point is Motorola is valuable for many reasons, and I think that it would be a complete disaster if it was shut down, [which is] what Google could do, let's say, if they said: "Okay, back to Plan A, back to commoditization, back to the idea that Android is the only thing that matters and forget hardware. Let's make sure we get those patents, apply them for whatever they're worth, go have a massive battle in the courts."

If that happens I would think the logical thing would be spin-off, yet again, a chunk of Motorola and call it Motorola Mobile Phones. Keep the patents but spin-off that division. I don't know how much that would be worth, given that it doesn't make money today, and it's sort of a marginal player, and it kind of had to go through Google. Who knows? It's just one of these things that's imponderable.

Ryan: So, Motorola could—I mean, Google could keep operating Motorola as it is and just—and essentially just have, just use, the patents that they acquired as part of the purchase.

Horace: Yeah. What did Google buy? Did it buy a phone business? An IP pile? Or both?

I think I'm leaning to say it's both right now, even though the two—those two entities—are actually somewhat at odds with each other. Here's what I mean, by the way: If you're going to nurture the IP and say it's all about the IP—it's all about protecting Android—what you're saying, basically, is that we're going to enhance the value of the ecosystem. If you're going to enhance the value of the ecosystem, it necessarily means you're going to enhance the value of Samsung and HTC. You're going to make them wealthy, healthy and happy. Great. However, as soon as you do that, you're also going to put stress on your other asset, which is Motorola, the device business.

So, if, under the same roof, you have an organization that says, "Our mission in life is to make our competitors happy," and you have another organization which feels the pain of that, at some point, somebody's going to have to call time out. This is not working because these guys are going to be fighting each other all the time.

Ryan: And you have a post at Asymco.com that you wrote yesterday called "The perils of licensing to your competitors."

Horace: Yes. And this goes into the history of Symbian and why that didn't work out.

Ryan: Right.

Horace: And that was essentially the same setup. Although Symbian was incorporated as a separate business, the ownership structure was basically that Nokia had more or less a lot of the control.

Anyway, the thing is that I'm suspicious that this is workable as you have these as two separate strategies. Well, call them businesses. It's about two separate strategies that are somewhat asymmetric or even in competition with each other. And I just don't like incoherent strategy. It doesn't tend to work. You want to have clarity. You want to have simplicity. Even in that space—I mean, Apple's strategies are always simple. And that's why often they're successful.

So, anyway, it just looks weird, and I... I don't know where we are going with this, but basically I struggle with how this can all be done as a juggling act. I struggle with the value of the independent businesses as a Plan A or Plan B. I even struggle with the notion that IP is actually a killer, a sort of a weapon of mass destruction. Because as Florian Mueller points out, some of those are encumbered patents. Some of them are not. And it's not clear that that they deterring anybody from actually attacking Motorola in the first place. It's being sued by both Microsoft and Apple, violently. So why would buying that [entity] protect you since [the entity is] actually under attack?

So, I don't know. I'm not going to dive into the legal dispute here, I'm not an expert. But I just think it's not a clear-cut case, for either this being an IP play or this being a device play.

Going back to the 2005 history, is Google really changing its business model? To be honest—given five weeks, given all these things we know—I don't think they know. I think the big secret here is: I don't think Google knows what it wants to do yet. This is the "emperor has no clothes" hypothesis, that Google is actually just randomly moving around chasing ghosts. And I don't mean to be—I'm very sensitive to calling people fools here—but it just doesn't look like…

Ryan: But from the information that you're seeing, that's—

Horace: Yeah, it's reactionary.

Ryan: That's a conclusion that someone can easily come to.

Horace: Yeah, it's reactionary. It's not proactive, it's not strategic-minded, it's not playing chess by looking five steps ahead. It's playing chess by looking one step ahead. And that's just not a very good game.

And by the way, there is another overarching theme here. The mobile space is going absolute bonkers. It's going crazy. And I've called this out, as you know, on my blog many times, saying that anybody who tries to predict this five years ahead is absolutely insane. I can't predict this thing one quarter ahead. And you know, people publish forecasts. I mean, Android could cease to exist, literally, in two years, or less, because of some missteps that [could] happen or some weird deals that get done and, somebody gets fired and—boom!—it's gone.

Ryan: And especially with all of the patent warring going on. You don't know how that's going to turn out in court.

Horace: Yeah, I mean, how committed…

Ryan: Of course.

Horace: …really can Google be?

Ryan: Right.

Horace: I mean, you're dealing with fairly low capital investment here, and so things can go up, especially when you have management [that] seems to be a little bit—not irrational, but a little bit, you know, bidding pi on things. That's not a sign of—that's not—you know, I don't want to, again, call these guys a little bit flaky, but I think it's just…

Ryan: It's kind of strange. It's a little strange.

Horace: It is strange. And you know, there is genius in insanity. Sometimes you've got to respect that. but sometimes you've got to ask yourself , "Well, is this really just plain insanity?"

Ryan: Okay, we're going forward, you know—it's only been basically a day, as of this recording, since this whole deal went down. But we've talked about the history back to 2005 of Google's acquisition of—or purchase of—Android. And how the steps, the history of that, and how that's led to where they are today. We talked about the—you know, how odd it is that there's only been this five-week window, you know, that's been reported from, I guess, anonymous sources, or essentially what are rumors that it's only been five weeks since they started courting Motorola as an acquisition. So, where do you—I mean, you're probably not in the prediction business, but where do you see this going, and what are you going to be looking for in the coming days? I assume that more information is going to start coming out. One of the things that I thought was interesting, and that maybe will play a role, is this, and I don't remember the exact term: Is it, like, an acquisition-cancellation fee or something like that?

Horace: Yeah. Yeah. It's the breakup fee.

Ryan: The breakup fee. And it's high for this.

Horace: It's remarkable, 2.5 billion [dollars]. It's not—it's unprecedented in terms of [the] proportion of the actual deal value. I mean, it's —what is it?—20-some percent? So, I am not an expert, again, on M&A, or the way the deals are made, but just from reading whatever has been commented on this, it does seem extraordinary.

I've heard of breakup fees in the millions, or even hundreds of millions, but never in the billions. And so, it does also add yet another wrinkle to the story, another piece to the puzzle, that something doesn't sound right. It may be that because it was rushed, it may be because there wasn't enough diligence, it may be just Google's hand was forced.

Here the other funny thing is that right the day before this deal went down, Sanjay, CEO of Motorola, makes a comment maybe they're going to sue other Android license holders. If I was conspiracy-minded, I would say, well…

Ryan: That would be the last ditch effort by Google to seal the deal.

Horace: That, basically, Sanjay was just firing a shot across their bows, saying, "Hey, let's close it now."

Ryan: Right.

Horace: And, you know, it's just publicly rattling the sabers, and scaring the bejeezus out of Samsung or whoever else is in the firing line.

So, I don't know. I don't know. We can't know these things. But the thing is that it does look weird from many angles, which speaks of a bit of desperation. And I don't want to say that it means it's the end of anything. It's just that the management feels a little bit stressed out, and sometimes you act in ways that are suboptimal. And, again, I think Google is a solid business. And the stock market only gave them a three percent haircut, which isn't a big deal, maybe even ended up being a lot less than that. Twelve billion is a portion of—I forget how much—20, 30 percent of their existing cash. But they make it up in a couple of quarters in terms of new cash. So it's like spending your holiday money.

Ryan: Right.

Horace: As an individual, it's like spending a couple of thousand dollars on an impulse buy. It's not going to be the end of the world if it fails for them. The real problem of Google is, if you ask me, it's Facebook. It's big stuff. It's whether their search is valuable, whether the apps are going to be the real interface for accessing services versus a browser.

That is the fundamental existential threat. If you're going to channel viewers via apps, vis-à-vis browsers, that's a fundamental trauma for Google. So, in the big scope, it's not make or break for Google. But if you just look at it as a mobility issue, and the impact on Samsung and HTC and anyone else, it could be catastrophic, though. This is where you go back to some of these comments.

Early on, I was saying, "If you're a device maker, you should not license. You should do everything you can to build your own operating system." And it sounded crazy at the time. I had a story called, "Android is the pursuit of the weakest players." Something to that effect, that Android's pursuit is really of the weakest handset makers, and by that I meant that Android appeals first to the most desperate. In fact, it appealed to Motorola first. It appealed to then Samsung and HTC. [I received comments,] "How can you call these people desperate? These are very successful companies now." Well, they weren't successful in the way that they were getting the highest margins. They weren't successful because they had very limited smartphone portfolios. Motorola and Samsung were almost out of the business of smartphones because they'd been depending on Microsoft. And you saw Windows Mobile implode. So these guys were desperate. And of course Android was a lifeline.

And for that reason, now, they're even more desperate because they suddenly lost financially the support of Google and they're being sued on one side by Apple and Microsoft. Microsoft has its hand out, saying, "You need to pay me," (they put the price on the licensing of Android to be about equal to the price of licensing Windows Mobile, or Windows Phone.) Fascinating if true, if true. They're saying, "You can come with us. Get a great operating system! Get a unique experience vis-à-vis the iPhone! Get indemnification so you won't get sued! And get the support of the ecosystem we're going to build!" This is what Nokia took.

And, by the way, the others did as well. Let's be clear that Samsung did license Windows Phone and Windows Mobile. There are [Windows] phones on sale from Samsung and HTC. And they both publicly declared their commitment to that platform. But they haven't put a lot of wood behind the arrow. They haven't really committed in terms of portfolio.

So, Microsoft comes and says they're going to tax Android to an equal value as would be buying a Windows Phone [license]. So they're really making it hard to stay with Android. And that's the pull that Microsoft gives, and the push is Apple as well, saying, "You're infringing on us as well. And by the way, we're not going to grant you a license because that's not what we do. We want you to just to be out of the market." And that's how Apple is playing the game because they just are really pissed off with Google.

You have Apple pushing and then Microsoft pulling. It's like they're on the same team because it would be beneficial to both of them if Android was put out of the picture. Then Apple would get a competitor in

Microsoft which they can deal with. I think they believe they can. The-devil-you-know kind of thing. And they know the reason they can deal with [Microsoft] is that it's not viral. You can't get Windows Phone to spread like Android's spreading because you need to sign a contract.

Ryan: Yeah. And it's expensive.

Horace: You need to have a deal. It is expensive. You're not going to get every ODM, every Chinese back-room operation building Windows Phones because they're going to need to sign on the dotted line and say they won't hack it, and they won't do things to it, and so on. That was the Windows Mobile model. And I think Apple would have been comfortable with Windows Mobile. I think they know how to compete with that. And they're probably not against competition per se. They just think Android is an unfair competitor.

So, anyway. That's just my take on that.

HP's Innovation Antibodies

Posted August 23rd, 2011 as The Critical Path Episode #5

Horace and Ryan discuss HP's departure from the PC business, the end of the Touch-Pad, buying your way into innovation, and what it takes to compete and survive in the post-PC era.

Ryan: Okay, Horace, when we talked last week we were talking pretty much only about the Google acquisition of Motorola Mobility, which in and of itself was a huge piece of news. But last week something happened here with HP. They decided that they were going to get out of the PC business, and they also decided to stop making and selling the TouchPad, which is obviously a big deal considering that have they been in the market for just a couple months maybe.

Horace: Right. So a couple of footnotes on that. One is that they haven't really made a decision on anything. They've only said that it's up in the air, which is actually a worse thing to do because it freezes everything. It freezes the market, it boosts competitors because they're going to rush into their accounts now and pound the table saying, "You know, you're better off with Dell, you never know what HP is going to do." And until they actually execute a trade on whatever assets they are selling, even if they keep them, they call it a non—I forget the exact word, something like a non-event. If nothing happens, then they're still basically sacrificing a huge amount of momentum.

So having said that, this is why the market basically just slammed HP. They lost 25 percent of their market value in a couple of days.

The other thing is, on the TouchPad, they're actually putting WebOS in purgatory as well.

Ryan: And they had a fire sale on the TouchPad this week.

Horace: Right. Let's not forget that actually it's not just the Touch-Pad. That got a lot of press because of the price, but also that they were planning on selling phones as well. They had a whole portfolio of new WebOS devices. And that was the Pre and its successors and the Pre was really where the core of Palm was, right? Palm was mostly focused on smartphones and when they were acquired there was no TouchPad. The TouchPad came only as a branch of the WebOS-product family.

So it's interesting that all of that got swept away. I mean, not just the TouchPad, but also the smartphone business that was in contention. And also the fact that WebOS was nominally going to power a lot of other devices that HP sells, including their printers, to somehow enable them to be more intelligent or more network-centric or something about the UI. We're not quite sure what they had in mind.

So all of that is in jeopardy, and it beggars belief. Of course, one of the great hypotheses out there, which actually John Gruber picked up on and is a very good hypothesis, is that it's all about the background, the resume of the CEO [Leo Apotheker], and that he came from the SAP background and therefore he's just going to remake HP into another SAP.

I like that hypothesis because it's actually very, very credible. One would hope, however, if you are in the CEO position that you are able to have multiple hats on and that you're able to conform yourself to the company, rather than being just a uni-dimensional person, and that's typically what one expects from a high-powered CEO.

So it would be even more tragic if HP's board managed to hire a guy who had tunnel vision about the company and couldn't imagine doing anything else.

So it doesn't look good no matter how you look at it.

I'd like to step back a little bit and say, "What's happening overall? What's the big picture and what led to this," and not try to define it only with these tiny tactical things that are happening. Even who the CEO is shouldn't really matter because I think there are fundamental tectonic forces acting on the industry, that no matter who would be there I think they would have been forced into some similar decision.

Ryan: So last week on Asymco.com you wrote up a post where you argued that this change, like you said, isn't sudden, it doesn't have to do just with this CEO and his desire to turn HP into SAP. You're saying that this thing has been going on for ten years and we're just now seeing really the big shift here?

Horace: Yes. Without going and rehashing the whole history of the PC, the fact is that even by 2000 it was pretty clear that the PC business was not a great business. It was low-margin, even then, and there were many, many clones. There was a period of time in the mid-'90s when it looked like it was all going to be clones and white-labeled companies selling mail-order PCs, that would rule the industry.

What happened with Dell and, later, with HP is that they went back to branding. They actually said, "There's value in the brand," and partly it was because Dell offered support, plus it offered customization and fairly low prices, while being all of those things. And [then] HP came and said "We're going to offer support and we're going to offer enterprise-grade quality product."

So by 2000 the industry had consolidated around some larger players, rather than being really fragmented. Of course, there was still fragmentation at the low end, but there was significant consolidation happening at the high end. That's when Compaq was acquired by HP. So the logic around 2001 was that we have these two major players targeting enterprise and it would make sense that they would be consolidated and thus overheads would be slashed and we could get a slight increase in the margin, which was single digits—very low single digits.

So the idea behind that—and this was Carly Fiorina's idea [when she was CEO of HP]—was that consolidation at this point in time was the way to go forward with the industry. Notice that nobody's talking at that time about innovation. What we consider innovation today would be new form factors. The Tablet PC was out there. It wasn't really embraced, but there wasn't anyone saying, "Well, we need to really innovate either on the product side or on the business-model side." Or even crazy ideas like game PCs or something about turning PCs into something completely different, like positioned or monetized around the different value proposition than what they had.

That wasn't really being debated. iMac came out, it was sort of innovative in that it put everything in one box. It was an integrated product, so you didn't have these boxes to wire up together, but that was about it. And the PC industry halfheartedly tried to copy some of that, but basically it was the same exact product that was around since the late '80s.

So into that stepped this merger, this mega-merger [of HP and Compaq]. Twenty-plus billion dollars worth. And it was heavily contested. The heir to the Hewlett empire—one of the sons of the founders—deeply argued, or was deeply against the deal. And his argument was that there's no synergy here and the company would be better off basically splitting off the printer division, which was very profitable, from the PC division and not so much adding more weight to the baggage.

In any case, it was ugly. It was a boardroom fight, and Hewlett lost, and what happened is Carly's plan got put into action. But three years later already it looked like it was a failure. There was a long piece I read recently that was originally written in 2004, looking back on that merger and saying, "None of the value that was promised was delivered."

So what I did then is I looked up the time frame when this was happening and I realized that the launch of the iPod was literally a month [after the merger]. So the two things actually happened simultaneously and at the time all the attention was on the HP-Compaq merger and there was almost nothing interesting about the iPod.

Now we fast forward ten years and you see what happened.

So from a strategic point of view, HP made a great gamble and a great mistake, whereas Apple made a small gamble and initially a small success that became a great success, and that begat not just the iPod but the iPhone and then the iPad. And all the things that followed were because they started down that road at that point in time.

There were efforts by HP to fold mobility inside its portfolio, but they were all halfhearted. And we can get into the discussion of why management had no incentives to really pour energy into that business. It was not an interesting business. And it wasn't just HP: Dell also tried to do something there, Toshiba tried as well.

So a lot of the PC vendors—partly because they were also in a relationship with Microsoft, which was a supplier of software, and which couldn't really move into new directions, into really embracing mobility, which turned out to be a disruptive—had they embraced it early enough, they may have been a contender today.

So that ties into the whole question: What about the iPad now? Is that a disruptive product and will it come in and upset the PC world? And if it is the post-PC product, why is it that a late comer, even a PC vendor today (a Lenovo for example as the inheritor of the IBM PC), why can't they do iPads instead? We can talk to that point, that, in fact, it's not going to be in their advantage to do so for various reasons.

Ryan: So where does this leave us then with HP and… obviously this has an impact—right?—on Apple and the iPad, and one of the things I've been talking about is whether, you know, is this the end of the competition in the tablet market? Are people going to be scared away by this? Because suddenly, you know, I mean HP has—I know that they haven't really said what they're going to do, but they have kind of thrown up the white flag on this TouchPad.

Horace: Right. So the problem is that TouchPad is now an orphan, and of course it's a disaster on many levels. They're getting rid of inventory at a fire-sale price of $99—some people are suggesting that this might actually disrupt the value proposition of Android as well because people are going to say, "Well, if that goes for 99 [dollars], shouldn't I wait until the Android Galaxy Tab, whatever, is going to be $99," and thus it could freeze the market for competitors.

I'm not so sure. I think people understand that this is a fire sale, that this is a liquidation deal. So I don't think the perception of what value is in the tablet has changed that much. But what I would say is that we should probably deconstruct some of the myths in the iPad world.

I mean, the problem with the iPad as a product is that it's neither a PC and isn't sold or bought or hired to do the same things; nor is it really an iPhone or Android or smartphone of any kind, which has associated with it typically a different channel—a carrier channel, which subsidizes the product, which pushes it aggressively, which seeds the market with enormous volumes. So it sits in the middle. Operators are having difficulty selling this product, partly because it's too big to sell in the store which is not set up for it.

If you think about the retail layout of an operator, it's oriented towards small products lined up on a wall. Tablets are sold more like PCs on a flat table and you need to see a bunch of them next to each other and lift them and play with them. It doesn't make sense to have a tablet device be a plastic mock-up that does nothing. They all would look the same. What differentiates them is when you touch them and you see how they feel.

So that's the trouble with an operator. They can't put up a hundred tablets in their store. They would maybe have room for a handful. And that's not the way people want to shop for them. They want to shop for them in a big-box-retailer-type environment, right? Like a Best Buy or like an Apple Store, which is bigger, anyway.

So, that's one problem. The other problem is that operators like to sell service plans, and for most people who buy iPads maybe the 3G is slightly more popular, but the fact is they don't actually turn on the 3G functionality. It's considered option value. It's something there if they need it. Most people would not like the idea of buying an iPad with a two-year commitment because they know they won't use it. In fact, tests prove that people don't use that feature that much. It's not truly a highly mobile device that depends on the network. It tends to sit in one place—at home, for example. It's sort of like an in-between, right? If we can imagine, in between a laptop and a phone.

So there are issues with point of sale. There's issues with monetization. There are issues with how to incentives buyers, and it's almost as if the Apple Store is the perfect way to sell it and the perfect way to show-case it, and the way the Apple infrastructure works is the perfect way to market the product.

So that's one reason why if someone makes an iPad clone, like a TouchPad or a Galaxy Tab, they're going to necessarily run the same game plan as Android phones ran. And it's just not going to go very well through operators. And it feels more like an iPod. An iPod touch, perhaps. A bigger iPod touch, which is in fact what the early criticism of the product was.

Ryan: So they won't have the, they won't basically... when you're saying it won't be the same game plan, is that they won't have like Verizon, employees in the Verizon Stores pushing this tablet like they would, you know, the Android phones? And I think we talked about this—I think I talked about this with John Gruber on his show—is that you have a lot of... there's probably a lot of kind of back-room incentives for pushing some of these Android devices, and once you get out of that...

Horace: Absolutely.

Ryan: Once you get out of that, which is kind of like a fixed channel of sales in some way, you're actually having to compete in the normal box-store marketplace, which is where... you know, I guess maybe Apple doesn't really compete because they have their own stores. But, still, I mean you're having to compete outside the realm of these wireless carriers, which is a much different game.

Horace: Yes. If you follow the money, you realize that a carrier stands to gain revenue of about two, three thousand [dollars] from a customer that buys a smartphone under the current subsidized model in most Western markets. If that's the case, that's sort of the lifetime ARPU, average revenue per user. You follow that money, you realize that there's a big pie to split and you can take some of that money up front and give it to the device vendor. You can take some of that money and give it the storekeeper and the sales person to push the product. You can spend some more on advertising.

So that's typically what happens with smartphones today. The economics allow you to create these push and pull effects. That's not so true on the tablets, which I think Apple knew this all along, which is why they didn't try to stuff it into the same channel. And they also marketed it separately, differently. And in price, keep in mind that the iPad—when you look at the financial statements—the iPad is priced (so-called average selling price) about the same as an iPhone. They're about 630 to 650 dollars per unit. It's a very capable product on one hand, large screen, sort of computer-like, and then you have a phone-type product [on the other end]. And yet they cost the same as far as Apple's charging price is concerned.

Ryan: Right.

Horace: So what this implies, again, is that they really thought this through, that [the iPad] doesn't hold up well in the subsidy model. And this is also what caused all the consternation with competitors, that they just couldn't come in at a lower price because they couldn't bring in subsidies.

It reminds me also of how the market about a year ago was trying to introduce, through the operator channel, netbooks, especially in Europe. The idea was that you buy a netbook with either a dongle that had a SIM card in it or it would be an integrated device that had the [cellular-data] capability. And even Nokia got into the business of selling these mini-laptops through operators.

It didn't take off. There were some initial sales which caused everybody to pile in, but it didn't really go very far. And for the same reason, that people don't want to buy computing from a service provider that they know is overcharging them.

So putting that aside, what's happening in terms of the dynamics of post-PC is that you see all of these effects of distribution: How do you sell the product? How do you price the product? What are the intangible ways of attaching users to the product? Like we talk about the app store model versus the traditional software sales model. The effect of the enterprise when the PC took off—the enterprise was actually the early adopter and the consumer was the late adopter. We're seeing the reverse happening in the post-PC era, where the early adopters are consumers and enterprises are reluctant to adopt these things. Of if they do adopt them, they are doing so reluctantly.

So we have a lot of asymmetries here. Players who have tuned themselves have optimized their business—they've optimized their employees and their channels and everything around the PC model—are having trouble adapting to this. So it's not just the bits and pieces that go into the product. It's not just the fact that HP looks at this thing and says, "Ah, it's just a PC." Or even Microsoft who looks at it and says, "It's just a PC with a thinner form factor."

The problem is, it doesn't sell the same way. You cannot sell it the same way. You cannot hire it for the same jobs. People, if they try it and say, "We want to make a PC out of this," they get frustrated and they all complain everywhere online, saying, "This is not a proper PC. It won't work."

So really what makes the post-PC era, I believe, disruptive is the asymmetry of business models, asymmetry of channel, asymmetry of processes necessary inside the company to even get the product built to the right level of smoothness and quality. If you followed that logic, you realize that you run into these massive obstacles—as an HP or as a Toshiba—and you say, "I can't get software into this thing because Microsoft won't give me the software I need or because Google won't give me the software I need or as quickly as I need it to make an integrated smooth experience that appeals to consumers, which, by the way, I cannot reach because I don't have a channel to consumers. You know, I'm used to selling to enterprise."

So you see how anyone thinking through the problem would run into these walls. [They] might have a plan to overcome those, but it just keeps getting harder and harder. It's almost like the sound barrier. It seems the closer you get to it the harder and more energy you need to overcome it.

So this is why one of the hypotheses I have is that what makes the post-PC really interesting is that it really doesn't lend itself to the embracing of the incumbents of the PC era, and that includes Microsoft as well. They're always trying to cram it into their current business models. HP just basically tried to ingest this thing and threw up.

Ryan: So do you think, then, Microsoft's idea of creating one massive operating system that will then be able to be deployed on different devises, is that part of this old way of thinking and kind of cram—

Horace: Absolutely. They would look at [the iPad] and say, "Oh, this is just another extension of Windows. A tablet is nothing but an extension of a PC. Everything's a PC." They even have all these funny names. They don't like the word "tablet" internally or externally when communicating. They call them "slates" because they already had a tablet. The Tablet PC was a ten-year-old idea in form factor. It was really a convertible PC.

Ryan: It's the big screen with the big stylus and essentially it ran a— pretty much a regular Windows, right?

Horace: Exactly, exactly.

Ryan: Yes.

Horace: It was just sensitive to a different type of mouse, which was a stylus.

But that didn't work because when they were using this thing it didn't feel right to use a stylus. The software didn't feel right. Everything was too small to be used while standing and moving, or even sitting in a different posture. It just wouldn't work.

So there's a lot of reasons why that didn't take off, the convertible model. But internally they still called that a tablet, and then what they call slates is something of the iPad generation. And then they have these different names. I forget. They have like five, six different names for all the form factors, and to their mind they're all PCs. And so all they have to do is make Windows work on all of them.

But again, to me, you see the subtlety is that it's not about technology, it's not about APIs, it's not ecosystems. These are all valid issues, but it doesn't cover the core of the problem, which is what about the use case, and that's usability in general. But what about the selling model? What about convincing buyers to buy these things? Ultimately, how do you reach the customer? It turns out that each input method begat a new channel, a new platform, a new everything.

This is the amazing thing: If you look back to every innovation that basically kickstarted every wave of growth for Apple, it's been an input method that begat a new platform. So the mouse made the movement from a cursor interface to a bitmap UI [which came] with the original Mac. But that forced them to use a new operating system. And so when Windows followed in 1995 with Windows 95, they also had to adopt a new operating system. They couldn't really live on DOS anymore.

So, really, the mouse enabled a new platform evolution, right? And when Apple then launched the scroll wheel they introduced a new way to interact with a device, which was more touch oriented and that eventually led them to develop a touch UI. But the touch UI of the iPhone was the quantum leap, that [created a] need for a new—completely new—platform as well, which is iOS, and then that also launched Android a few years later.

So the point is that if there's enough of a gap between the old input method and the new input method, you really have to re-architect the operating system and the user interface. But that typically also implies a whole new ecosystem, and as I point out, a whole new way of selling things. So a new economic—or a new business—model.

And that's really the challenge for anyone. If you are a technologist and you look at [this problem, you'd ask,] "Why can't they just get it to work?" It turns out that there's much more to it than technology and user experience. It's also this whole question of market access.

94

Ryan: Obviously fixing the market access is probably one of the hardest. You know, arguably, that maybe the only way to compete—to get to the point where market access even matters is that, you know, obviously you need to recognize how things have changed and that a tablet isn't a PC. But also maybe that you need to control both hardware and software to deliver the best experience.

I mean… But I guess I wonder if you have those but you're still missing market access, I'm thinking of—I guess Microsoft is an obvious example, right? You know, in terms of producing hardware and software, I'm thinking of—what do they do? Their biggest success was the Xbox, and then I guess maybe a moderate success for at least a couple years was the Zune, but other than that, they don't really have…

Horace: Yes. And, arguably, neither of those actually created real value for shareholders because remember…

Ryan: They were a loss, right?

Horace: …they caused losses for a long time. In fact, Xbox probably, if you sum up all the losses and all the gains, it's still a net negative. And it may take still years for them to officially break even.

But that's a technical discussion. The fact is that for Microsoft, the bulk of their revenues—Windows and Office—are still sold the same way they were in the '80s. And there's been no business-model innovation from them with respect to how to sell software. And Google came in basically with a notion that they could disrupt this by giving software away online and monetizing it through advertising. And that's still something that Microsoft probably couldn't do. They couldn't put enough effort into Bing, because that would really be disruptive to their core business. They really followed the logic of what Google was doing [but stopped short.]

Now, in a way, Bing is a defensive move. It's not really offensive as much because they're just trying to block Google a bit and trying to capture a little bit of the crumbs off of the table. But they really needed to think, "How do we compete? Not head to head against Google, but undermine them with yet another innovation in the business model?"

But, anyway, this is getting a little bit off the topic. The thing is that, in the context of HP, what I would point out is that these companies are gigantic companies that are built on these existing business models, [and] could not absorb the changes that were happening. And this is why we're seeing these abrupt, illogical—irrational, if you will—inexplicable reversals.

So, HP saw the writing on the wall.

Ryan: Yes.

Horace: They saw this coming, and they decided to spend one or two billion to get the assets necessary to survive this transition. But you can see how hard it is to internalize that. And you see how it immediately gets rejected.

There's a phrase I like to use: the corporate antibodies. These are things inside the company—as an organism, if you will—these are entities, be they people or budgets or processes or rules in binders. These are things which are designed to eat up innovation. To eat up changes to the core business.

I don't mean eat up innovation because they're stupid, but they see this newcomer, this entrant, as a pathogen—as something that's damaging the organism—and so they act, sometimes even collude, to destroy it. And they're paid good money to do that. Their incentives are all very clear: Please do that. And they go to their boss every year and get a raise because they've done that.

That's the fundamental thing you have to understand: It's that no matter how much the CEO has that vision, if the organization underneath has not been properly incentivized to absorb the change—and it's almost impossible to really build that kind of structure, it's almost schizophrenic to do so, right, to accept this intruder that's trying to take away your core business and build a career around it, right? I mean as an individual...

Ryan: Right.

Horace:...salespersons, everybody. Everybody in the company looks at this thing as a pathogen. And so [when a disruptive idea emerges] the corporate antibodies are immediately stimulated and they go in and they eat up this innovation. That's how I see it. And it's something you can't deal with unless you take that threat—and, of course, opportunity at the same time—take it and you place it in an autonomous way.

The way to handle this acquisition, or any acquisition that's potentially seen as a pathogen, is to give it perfect autonomy and then basically build walls around it so that it's protected. Then the only real gatekeeper to that investment should be the CEOs themselves.

So the CEO has to stand guard over this group of people and basically shoot anyone who comes near. And that's the trouble. This is where we go back to the hypothesis that Gruber put forward, which is that this guy wasn't the guy. He couldn't have done it. He couldn't have done it because he could not have stood guard over this little embryonic property. And the pathogens were let loose and, indeed, they would normally have killed it and that's what happened.

So I think you'll see this over and over again. I'm sure even at Apple, unless—if you go back the folklore on this is long and I'm not qualified to speak of this—but basically what I've heard is that the Mac itself was seen at Apple in the old days as such a disruptive thing. And that's why the politics and all the recriminations that occurred, and there was a very difficult birthing process to get the [Mac] born. And part of that also ate up the company internally during the '90s, that they couldn't really innovate because anything that was brought in was chewed up before it could possibly reach maturity.

It happened at Nokia. I could go on and on. You know, in Nokia the problem was, "What do we do with Linux and the future of mobile operating systems?" And there were teams inside the company, working mostly in the research groups, that said, "We can make a mobile Linux. In a matter of months we can build a phone that would work with Linux." And, you know, that worked fine if they were allowed to be in the labs. But as soon as they tried to commercialize it, immediately people jumped on them and then dragged it down. [It was] only through some executive [who] could run interference and protect it [that the effort survived]. But that executive was not the CEO.

So as long as that executive was sufficient, let's say, in good standing, then that project would go forward. In fact, Linux efforts at Nokia emerged as Maemo. But they were not on a phone, they were on a tablet, a mini tablet-type device. It was a half-hearted attempt at doing an evolution of the operating system. That eventually became Meego and then finally Meego was killed.

So it's one of these tragedies that you can see how—if it was organized differently… When I run through this in my mind, over and over again I ask, "Yes, but at what point would this still have been killed" because it would need again this type of champion at the very highest levels, someone who could endure the birthing process for a long, long period of time—the gestation, I should say—the gestation for a long period of time. That type of person is so rare as a CEO, which I think is part of the mystique and magic of Steve Jobs, is that he's the only one that we know of that is able to do these types of schizophrenic things, like maintain sustaining business and disruption within the same organization.

Ryan: And also be able to think far enough ahead where, you know, I think—I read somewhere that Apple is mostly working right now on their next disruptive thing.

Horace: In fact, I wrote this in my blog as well.

Ryan: It was you that maybe I read it.

Horace: I feel that if you look at the cyclicality of things and you say, "It took ten years for Apple to really emerge as the post-PC champion, where HP didn't begin ten years ago, they were trying to become bigger at that business and ten years ago they were just consolidating." I would say that, "Well, by now Apple ought to be, therefore, thinking about the next thing beyond the iPhone era. And, you know, that may be seen as a fanboyish comment, but I think it's just a simple plot on the chart. Ask: "How long do these things last? Is a five-year cycle typical for web things?" Five years seems to be the cycle time. But for hardware, especially integrated with software like this in systems logic, ten years is a more likely wave of disruptions. Things go up and down.

So, I think that, if anything, Apple ought to be right now gestating the next thing, because it does take so long. And you know, the iPhone is four years old, and if we believe that the era will last ten years, then they ought to be starting now, maybe even seeding some new products out there. I think the iPad is such a product, that maybe even something new may come down the pike.

Now, keep in mind, by the way, that none of those companies—HPs and Nokias and Microsoft—they're not without resources or vision. They actually have huge numbers of researchers working inside the companies. These are the best and brightest, often in secluded laboratories, that are given free reign to invent things. And sometimes they write academic papers. I actually used to work in such an institution called GTE Laboratories, which is now part of Verizon. And our job was to think outside the box and do all these things.

That actually turns out to be not all that hard. These people are actually fairly modestly paid, they're usually coming from academia, very, very bright, Ph.D. and so on. But then the step of getting out of the lab and becoming a product... That's where things get rough.

Steve Jobs has the vision. Well, I'm sure every CEO has lots of... You know, they probably go through a review, where all the greatest inventions are presented to them. So it's not that they don't see these things coming. MP3 players were around, tablet computers again, styluses, all kinds of input methods in the labs. All these visualization [options], all this gesturing. We saw it in the movies.

I mean, you know, what was the movie where there was this person doing this kind of waving their arms around? I forget it. Anyway, the thing is that these things are in our imaginations already. So people try to implement prototypes and so on, but we don't get to the point where we launch a product. And not only just launch it as a kind of an afterthought, but launch it with all the company behind it and all i's dotted and all the t's crossed and the marketing strategy and positioning.— Everything works.

That's how Apple does it. They don't launch until not only is the product perfect, but they've figured out how to interface it into the whole web of interdependencies that exist in the real world.

That, to me, is... When I speak of innovation and successful innovators, it's the ones who actually get that done, who ship not just the product, but ship the whole ecosystem, a whole interdependency.

That's where Apple, I think, stands alone right now. Unfortunately, I wish it weren't so, because then we would have a lot more innovation going on.

Ryan: What about our topic from the last show, which is where we talked about Google and Motorola Mobility. Do you think that puts them maybe in this space with Apple?

Horace: Well, I think that's the dream. I think that's their ambition now. And it's a worthy ambition. I'm not sure the way it's being done is the right way. I mean, with an acquisition and all the politics and everything that goes with that.

You know, I think if—again, we don't know for sure, but—if their goal is not just IP in this acquisition, if they really want to become a player as an integrated vendor, then it is a worthy goal. But I just don't know if that's the right way. Again, let's not forget that this took ten years for Apple to get to this point, with the iPad becoming a real threat to an industry that was 20 years old.

So, it's one of these things that you have to say, "This has to be almost organic, it cannot be a big bang. It cannot be a thing you buy with money."

A famous quote…I think Jobs once said that many people think technology can be purchased. Meaning, you can write a check and get technology or get innovation. It doesn't work that way, unfortunately.

I think he was referring to the creative process vis-à-vis the technological-innovation process, and I think he said creative people in Hollywood think they can buy technology, and technology people think that the creative process was people sitting around drinking beer and writing jokes. Both are wrong.

I mean, the creative process, exemplified by Pixar, is a lot of blood, sweat and tears, and the technology process is a lot of blood, sweat and tears. A lot of creativity goes on in both. A lot of very deep thinking has to happen in both as well. So they're a lot more alike than they are different. It's just that the two worlds never really talk very much.

Anyway, that's a separate topic. But, again, here's the magic and I try to deconstruct it and say, "It's not really magic, it's something that anybody can do if you had the right mentality and I think that the Jobsian approach is something that other people can do." It's almost like there's a secret formula to it. But there is a formula. And the problem is that most people think it's just the person, and I think it is more than that.

The analogy that comes to mind is that in the Middle Ages people thought very differently than the way we think today, right? It was a world of myths and prejudice and persecution. Then came the Renaissance. In the Renaissance suddenly everybody thought differently. In fact, what happened is there were a few people and they were the painters and the thinkers of the era, they [came to be] called Renaissance men. And they invented a new way of thinking. And in fact we are all Renaissance men today. We are able to think in objective ways. We are secular, mostly, and we have a view of the world that's rational and says that there are causes and effects.

We are all like that today. And the problem is that as far as innovation is concerned, there are again [today] one or two of these Renaissance men running around—like Steve Jobs—and we all look to them as saying that they're somewhat near to magician. But I don't believe that. I believe that in a few decades, maybe sooner, we'll all be Steve Jobs.

We have to just learn to think like that. So the problem is that they won't tell us how they think, right? They're secretive. As was the case in the Renaissance. Those masters did not teach others how to do their art because it was a very valuable thing to be able to make these wonderful paintings or be a navigator that could get you from point A to point B without dying. All of these were secrets. And the scientific revolution was actually about *publishing* secrets. We're not yet at that stage with business thinking, that we take some ideas that are really, really revolutionary [and publish them]. We still keep them as secretes, because they're trade secrets, they're things which make us money.

And so the idea is, how can we possibly, *through a learning process*, transfer the knowledge that's in the heads of some of these magicians.

That's really to me what motivates me in doing what I do, because I try to deconstruct the magic.

I don't know how we got on this topic.

Ryan: No, it's fascinating. I think that this is a great topic. This is fascinating to me. I love tying it into the Renaissance period. I think that's quite a…

Horace: Yes, that's another thing we could do for a whole show.

Ryan: Right.

Horace: We could talk about Newton and then we could talk about the scientific method, I think, which is the best invention ever because it allows us to actually make more inventions.

These are some of the things that run around in my head—to try to think of how to actually do this analysis that I do on my site. It's really nothing more than a slight experiment in that direction because I'm saying, "Okay, I'm going to lay bare some of these myths and maybe introduce people to some of these topics that may not be [for] a typical audience."

There's a lot of things like that that are really actually interwoven with what I do in my site. But I don't want to bore people with philosophy right now.

Ryan: You certainly won't bore me. I find all of this fascinating because, you know, when you break it down—and I know that you do this at Asymco.com—this is more than just chatter about technology and it's more than just a horse-race type of discussion. There's really a lot more to this.

I'm fascinated by the idea of, you know, maybe Steve Jobs being one of the Renaissance men running around today trying to change the way that we think and the way that we approach problems in our lives. And again, I don't want to get too philosophical with it either. Do you think where we are right now, because I'm thinking about, like, who can come in and possibly at this point in time compete with Apple and this momentum that they have? Are we in a period of no competition and where it's going to take a little bit of time for some of these other companies? Maybe it's Google, maybe they come in and it takes them a little time to get up to speed and start to think like maybe Steve Jobs does.

Horace: I don't want to say that it's... Again, I do want to see others doing the same thing, because we would have much more richness of product to play with. But the problem is that if you see the evidence of this spark—of coming at the problem the right way—instead of using crude, blunt instruments like,acquisitions and things like that [instead of trying] to really be innovative. That's the trouble.

Google is a very innovative company in the sense that they really had a tremendous business-model innovation with the idea of giving stuff away and making money through another means. That really is very disruptive, I think mostly to Microsoft, though it's going to take time.

The trouble is that they themselves are being out-innovated, in a way, by what I consider social media's model—the model of capturing people's intentions and what's in their heads, which is what search is about.

The great thing about search is that people tell you what they want, and that's what every advertiser in the world wants to know: "[Tell me] what people want, and I'll give it to them."

Well, search is the best way we know of for finding out what people want. But perhaps their wants aren't always what they say they want. That's where social media comes in. When you say, "I want to buy a new pair of shoes" and you get served up ads for shoes, that's one thing.

But what if the person is actually looking for shoes because they want to go on a date and because that date is really about fulfilling some emotional hole in their life. The point is that the social media will get you that answer. What is it really that the shoe is hired to do?

And then you can serve up different solutions to the show-buying question. You can say: "Well, you're going on a date. How about box of chocolates or how about this and that to help you in your quest?"

Then the advertiser's actually digging far, far deeper into the psyche of the buyer. And that's where I think the innovation has to be going on, in terms of what the business of Google is, rather than plumbing, which is what we talked last week: Buying the plumbing that allows someone to see shoe ads.

Experiments are going on, obviously, with Facebook and Twitter and other things. People are trying to get to the bottom of what people want and what are they thinking, and then serving that up.

That's where I don't see the act 2 from Google. Act 1 is well understood, but there's no follow-up. Where's the next big thing? Whereas, again, we saw the transition happen so that Apple is a serial disrupter, they did the iPod and then they did the iPhone, on and on. That's not happening with Google, which is why, by the way, their stock has gone nowhere for, like, five years.

Ryan: That sounds familiar. It sounds like Microsoft.

Horace: Yes, yes, and that's the problem, is they think that they're so highly innovative because everybody in the company is so smart and everybody can spend a day out of their week doing crazy things. But they're tinkering. They're tinkering with technology. They're tinkering with the tools they have available on their workbench. But the real innovation is when you say, "You know what? A workbench isn't the way to go, we need to go sailing on a lake to figure this out."

That's what I mean by thinking out of the box, and I just don't see that ability from that company to be pathologically, for lack of a better word, disruptive. And what I'm looking for is these kinds of companies.

By the way, Apple is not the first. Microsoft was a serial disruptor in the '90s because they were able to [repeatedly] bring low-price innovation. Basically, they took almost every software business that was out there and they disrupted it by putting it on a PC [first], and then making it nearly free, very cheap. So whether it was networking or whether it was corporate messaging or whether it was any number of communications, any number of productivity tools, they just slammed the price on everything. That was innovative in a way because you figure out how to make money from that [lower price].

So they did that and they had their run, but then when software itself was not the way to make money anymore they needed to integrate it with something else, either the network or the device. [That's when] they ran into walls.

Sony, before that… In the '70s and maybe a part of the '80s, Sony was a machine. They just kept innovating when they were making consumer electronics. They started with this transistor radio and then they moved on to all kinds of tape recorders and VCRs and new screen technologies. So you had the Trinitron and all of these amazing, amazing things that sustained huge margins for them. So Sony was known as a serial disrupter back then.

We could probably go back even decades earlier. HP back in the '50s, and so on. So these are great stories and they last for decades sometimes. Typically, one of the problems is that sometimes the person who is in charge leaves. And that causes an end. But, you know, I don't think that needs to happen.

Again, it's like Michelangelo running the studio. He makes beautiful paintings, he dies and suddenly you no longer have great paintings. Why can't somebody learn that?

So I think it's still possible that we can all absorb this knowledge. And sadly, again, it seems to take forever. And all I'm doing is documenting success and failures. Success and failure. Maybe you'll see a pattern, and that's why last week we had two great stories to tell with Motorola and now HP.

Black Boxes
Posted September 14th, 2011 as The Critical Path Episode #6

Horace and Dan tackle corporate valuation and hypothesize whether amateur bloggers know more about Apple than professional analysts. We also look at the ancient economic history of Windows and how that history still shapes it today.

Dan: I remember when people were first talking about the mobile industry. This was back when most people did not have smartphones. People who really saw back then where things were going, and we're talking about mobile, I remember somebody that had just joined up with some mobile startup of some kind, and I'm, like, "Really?" And they were like, "Oh, this is where it's all going to be at." And you think about it now, I mean, look at where things are in the smartphone. That's where most of the news is it seems like today. Most of the news surrounds mobile and mobile platforms.

Horace: It is an amazing growth story. I mean, I was actually on the phone with *Newsweek* about half an hour ago, actually, on this story.

Dan: Nice. Of course you were. They're lucky to have you.

Horace: I do get a lot of requests from the media to talk about the industry, which is, again, reflective of the boom that's happening.

Dan: Right.

Horace: But, you know, the thing that strikes me is that we're in a tough economic era, if you will. I mean, we have scandal after crisis. And now Europe is on the precipice, and just awful news for, it seems, years on end. And yet inside all of this bad news, there is this amazing supernova of growth. And I have to say I'm an optimist. This helps me a lot because, you know, if I think back even at periods when great companies were born, companies which you see flourish today, they were not good times. They were not times of economic boom. I would argue that, for example, Apple and Microsoft—contemporaries, right?—both were born at a time when there was stagnation. It was the '70s, the late '70s: bad economic time.

And yet innovation flourished. The Depression era brought us all kinds of innovations. Like radio. And of course war is a great source of innovation, though we don't want to see that happen. But usually times of great stress and great pressure bring out the best in people. So I'm glad to be in this time, actually, because I see this great flourishing going on…

You have to balance your thinking. I get a lot of questions on the blog and on various forums where people say, "Yes, it sounds great, Apple's story is great, smartphone story is great. But what about these macro issues? What about the crisis that's about to blow up in place X or Y?" So

I usually cannot predict that. But I can predict or, at least I think I can predict, the evolution of the technology or the evolution of the markets. And you might see some drag, some friction happening from these other forces. But I still think the story is a very good story, so it's interesting.

Because when you talk about this with people in the media—as I was saying, not just *Newsweek* but many others globally that have contacted me—this is a common theme, and because I know their audience is not focused on smartphones, they're not focused on technology in general, I try to spin it in this way of saying, "This is something that should give us all hope." I try to give that spin to it. Because it's more. It's bigger than just these developer events. It's about society. It's about where we are going as a civilization.

Anyway. Well, we have to pick a topic to talk about. This is all very good.

Dan: How do you pick a topic? Because so much has happened.

Horace: Well, let me give you some thoughts. I had thought about—because things have happened, right, while we've been off the air—one thing that's happened is actually quarterly data from Apple.

Dan: Right.

Horace: One thing that's happened, also, it's like there's been a lot of gyrations in the stock market. So one of the things I kept thinking over and over again is, "How do we actually discuss this question of how the market perceives Apple and whether that actually is a big disconnect from how a market analyst would see Apple." There are various ways of analyzing a company. There is one from the market point of view, which is what I tend to do. There's another one from a financial point of view, which is what a Wall Street analyst would do. And there's another one from sort of a competitive or operational point of view, which is what an analyst hired by a company would be doing. I've done that in the past.

And [each] of these three perspectives comes up with a different answer. So I'd be curious to sit back and ask the question, "Well, how does the market—the financial market—see Apple and how do they put a value on that?" That's actually reflected in the voting that happens every day and the millions of votes that are cast every day by investors. And there is this question, "Well, what are they seeing that we're not seeing? Or, what are we seeing that they're not seeing?" And I'd like to explore that at some point and maybe introduce also to the audience, if they're not familiar with that, how to value companies and how companies are valued by their financials.

Dan: Let's hear that.

Horace: So that's one topic.

Dan: No, that's a great topic, and I'll tell you why: Everybody is always talking about the stock market, and how they are so volatile and responsive, dramatically, to all of these things. And you're like, "Well, you know, to me as a consumer…" and we'll pick Apple because we always talk about Apple anyway, that's our lens, right?

Horace: Mm-hmm.

Dan: You know, like, Apple comes out with some announcements in the morning, and to me they're still the cool company they were at 6 AM. They're still the same cool company at 6 PM. And, like, oh, you know, they had a good quarter, they had a bad quarter, whatever. Like, I still like my iPhone.

And so consumers are often surprised or, in my case, frequently puzzled by, the way that analysts view a company, especially [the] financial side of things, and why the market may say, "Oh, don't buy Apple right now." And you're, like, "Why? They're cool. You know?" Like, from the simple consumer standpoint, right?

Horace: Yeah. It gets even worse that that because what you have is analysts now more or less agreeing in the consensus that Apple is a good company to buy. But the market itself, the people who actually transact or buy or sell, are not agreeing with that consensus. And that's the weird disconnect, actually—that informed opinion and uninformed opinion agree, basically, on the inherent value. And yet it seems not to be reflected.

Dan: Yeah.

Horace: So the basics are fairly straightforward. And, actually, it took me a while to get my head around this. Because, as I said, I came from an engineering background, and I wasn't studying even economics in college, and it was not a topic I ever bothered with. So it took me a while to understand how stock markets work and so on. And this may be again commonly understood by others, but I'm just going to say it anyway: A company is basically a black box. It's just a machine that is designed to spit out money. It's a great machine to have. I mean, I just see it as a black box that throws out cash.

Now sometimes, unfortunately, the machine doesn't work, and doesn't throw anything out, or sometimes it actually runs out of cash and you've got to put some in, which is the worst case. And when nobody puts any money in, it collapses. So we talked about this a little bit when we talked about the cash and Apple. So that particular quantity of cash inside the company is the critical limit to whether it exists or not.

But [a company is] designed for one purpose, and that's to throw this money out. And often what happens is, you know, Apple is throwing the money. But it isn't quite landing in the owner's lap. It actually goes back in the company, and just sits in a big pile.

So the question is, then, let's say if you were to ask an engineer, a technically minded person, "Well, here is a box that supposedly throws out money. How much would you pay for it?" That's the whole discussion about what the value of the company is. So to answer that question, you begin with, "Well, how much money is in it?" Well, that's easy. We know how much money [there is]. We can open the box and look at the pile inside. We know that. That's easy. That's called a book value. That's the assets. If you take away any liabilities… there's another weird thing, that sometimes a company owes money to another box.

Dan: Right.

Horace: But let's ignore that for a moment. If you have this black box you can open it up and see how much money is in it. Okay. With that, then, you have book value. And then you say, "Well, if it is spitting out money, then how frequently and how much is the stream that comes out?" And then you can just add that up and, if it keeps doing that for the next 20 years or whatever, you can take all that money that will come out, then assume an interest rate, and bring it to the present (that's called discounting.)

So this box plus all the future money that will come out of, it is worth this much. So then, as an investor, you ask yourself, "Do I want to own this box?" Of course, you'll only own a part of it. You own a tiny share, like a slice. A minuscule part. But, still, it's a business you own as a shareholder. And then maybe the way you make money is not that you wait for the cash to land in your lap, but you hope to sell it to somebody else later on.

That's really the whole story of Wall Street: deciding what the box is worth and deciding when you want to buy it and when you want to get rid of it. And that makes fortunes, and makes tragedy as well.

So what's interesting, then, is if you formulate this way, the black box and the cash flow—that's called cash flow, what comes out of it although, again, typically it stays in—if it goes out, it's taxable. So you've got all kinds of issues there. But that's the basic fundamental question.

So if you were naïve enough, like I was, to put this in a spreadsheet and then plot out what does this box actually spit out, and what are the things that make it generate money, then you can actually create a spreadsheet and plan…

Dan: Why is that naïve?

Horace: Well, it's naïve because it seems simple at first. Then you have to say, "Well, how many iPhones are you going to sell?"

Dan: Right.

Horace: And how many iPads? And so on. But the problem is that there is a lot of complexity to that. When I started it, the reason I was doing it was because the iPhone was being accounted for in a weird way. It was accounted for as a subscription. And this was because they had some regulation in effect where a product that is changing… This came into place because of shenanigans that Enron was doing, you know, years ago.

They were accounting for things in the future as the present, and the product that they were selling was actually going to change over time. They were told, or everybody was told, if your product is going to change in the future, you should account for it as subscriptions. [For example,] you're saying you've got $600 for an iPhone sold. You say you got $100 and then another $100 next year, and another $100, and so on. It was actually a different schedule, but still, that's the idea.

So the problem was this weird accounting. So I was trying to figure out… well, some analysts were writing about next quarter, or the one after. And their numbers seemed to be lower than what I knew the company already had already received as income. Because they were just going to account for it in the next period. In other words, I was seeing that some analysts were not doing their homework. So I decided to do it myself, just so that I could call them out and sort of laugh at them, and say, "Well, look, you know, obviously you're wrong on this." So that's how I began modeling Apple. Because I felt that there wasn't a good model out there that you could rely on. And I can understand why some analysts might be lazy about it, because they're using probably a cookie-cutter system or program to analyze all kinds of companies. And the iPhone—they had to do it in a standard way and not in the way that it actually was being accounted for. As a result, they were getting errors in their forecasts. So anyway I did it myself.

So once I did that, it just grew and grew as a project because there were so many details and I was learning as I was going along. I was learning how to analyze the financial statements, and everything from how to deal with taxes and so on. But bottom line is it's like any hobby: You tend to get absorbed by it.

But the point is, though, that when you look at this black box, there's so much money in it, and it seems to be ready to put out a lot more because the opportunity is huge, and then you say, "Well, it's worth a lot more than it seems to be." So you buy it and you wait for it to grow in value.

So what's happened lately is that people are—you know, it's not lately… It's been like a process of many years that market analysts and technology people have been looking at this and saying, "Wow, this is a huge amount of money [that's going to]
come out of Apple." And yet the market doesn't react. So people buy the box, if you will. They buy the shares and then they don't go up. And they're frustrated. And they get rid of them. And then they see the whole market tanking, and all that.

So you have to have this faith in the long term. Because sometimes the markets are not efficient. Sometimes they don't take all the information that's out there and absorb it or process it. And thus you get this kind of opportunity, if you will. I don't know if I have a particular story to tell, but I've been doing these analyses, and on my site I try to measure the delta between the opportunity and the actual price.

And you can get a handle on it by something called the P/E ratio: What is the price versus the earnings that [a company] just got. And this is a rule of thumb. There is nothing magical about a P/E ratio. But the earnings [for Apple] were getting so big and the price was holding steady that the ratio became very low, lower than comparable companies.

And so you could then ask the question, "Well, is everybody being treated the same way as Apple? Or is it sectored—technology companies in general being discounted below what they're worth? Is there some funk in the industry that people just say, 'Throw the whole lot out, they're worthless.'" And in some ways you can get a feeling that there is, in fact, a discounting going on. But at the same time, what happens in good years, when the economy grows, those very same companies tend to get overly valued. And then they tend to have an amplification effect. So it's amplified downwards, and it's amplified upwards.

And so Apple is kind of like the canaries in a coal mine. They get hit hard. But maybe canaries are not a good analogy because there is no upside to a canary. Anyway, the idea is that when times are good there is another measure called "beta," which measures this effect.

I'm just trying to get at the bottom of this, and fortunately I've had help from a fellow who was actually nearby here, in Helsinki, who is a financial expert. Actually, he's been trained in finance, unlike me. And he's been doing some number-crunching and also digging. His name is Dirk Schmidt, and he's now getting his name on the articles. And he's contributing by writing as well.

Anyway, the point being that now we're collaborating a bit more, trying to get to the bottom of this. What surprises me a little bit is that there isn't that much discussion going on around this. I would have loved to just copy/paste the results of this analysis from somewhere else.

Dan: Yeah.

Horace: But it doesn't seem to be anywhere. If it is maybe it's in some kind of hedge fund secret publication, that is eyes-only and all that. But it's not happening in the forums that are public. So, anyway, maybe it's also too boring for most people. It isn't exactly an exciting topic. But it's one of the things that I like to sometimes take a stab at: understand value versus price. Price is what it is, but value is what it could be.

Dan: Is this the kind of thing, though, that regular—maybe this is even too generous of a word, but amateur—investors like me, people who are thinking about doing this, should we follow this kind of information when we're making decisions? Or should we just say, "Follow the old, like,

Fool.com (I am familiar with this) recommendation, which is invest in the companies that you like, that you use, or what?

Horace: Well, no, I don't expect people to go through this. But I think there are degrees of interest and degrees of competency, or degrees of willingness to tolerate this minutiae. But I should say that I'm not by any means an expert. Like I said, there are people who inspired me. For example, a blogger out of Venezuela whose name is Deagol. He's a blogger who has been doing this for many years, and he has a far more complex and sophisticated model. But he doesn't write frequently, maybe has a few posts per quarter.

But there are people who are very deep into this. There are others—four or five amateur bloggers who are strictly focused on analysis of Apple's financials. There's a bulletin board, Apple investor, and so on. There are many places where people can debate. But I think if you don't have the time and you don't bookmark these places and go every day, the best advice is to do your own research by sampling the product as much as you can. And then maybe going to the stores and seeing if they're busy, reading a couple of articles, and just making a decision on your own. That's what I call the uninformed opinion. But that's actually very intuitive, and a very good opinion, typically, as far as picking winners. And you know, it's hard not to be bullish on Apple when you go into their stores, right? If you have a chance to visit an Apple Store it's almost always busy.

Dan: Oh, yeah.

Horace: And that to me is testament enough. And what I'm trying to find out is more precision and also trying to see if the disconnect is something that… Are we missing something that so-called Wall Street knows?

By the way, the other angle of this is that I've had conversations with people who actually are fund managers. These are people who are paid to invest other people's money. And they tend to have lots of money to invest. And so I've had the opportunity to actually talk with them about Apple. They solicit and engage in these conversations with amateurs like myself, or experts from the industry because they want to get opinions. And sometimes [because] they question you, you get an idea of their point of view as well. So you learn something. And I appreciate that.

Some of these are hedge fund managers, some of them are what you might call mutual fund, or investment fund, managers. What I get overall is the picture that they don't know anymore than we do. "The market" is not particularly more informed than we are. In fact, they shouldn't be. If they are more informed, it's insider knowledge, which is actually illegal, and therefore they should only be informed as much as the public information that's available. And with the Internet, we pretty much get access to all of that instantaneously. So they have no advantage in information than an amateur would.

In fact, the amateur, if they're focused on one company, gets to see actually more of it because that fund manager tends to have to cover a lot of companies. And so they're usually splitting their time and their attention among way too many things. That's why sometimes the accuracy of an amateur is higher than the accuracy of a professional analyst. In that sense, I don't think that there is… You know, a lot of people ascribe to the analyst community or to the fund managers or the hedge funds some ulterior motives or some conspiracy, that they're colluding or they're manipulating. I don't see that at all. There is a lot of opinion out there. There are a lot of questions and, frankly, nobody knows what's going on. The fact is, the market is not manipulable, especially something as big as Apple. Small-cap or thinly-traded stocks, very likely. And I'm sure I'm going to get a deluge of people pointing out how much manipulation actually happens, but still, overall, a company of the size of Apple, trading volumes that we're looking at—tens and tens of millions of shares traded, billions of dollars every day—it's very hard to make a dent in that, even if you're phenomenally wealthy.

So, I tend to be simply saying that the market and the buyers and sellers of these shares are not all that—I think that we're reaching a tipping point in which amateurs and people like yourself who are actually so highly tuned in to what's going on, who are watching every single tweet…

Dan: Right.

Horace: …who are watching every single keynote of not just Apple, but all of its competitors and just being completely obsessed about it—they know more than the guy who is managing a billion dollars worth of Apple. I think that's where we are right now. And does that mean that we have an advantage? I don't know. I just think that the Internet has caused this democratization of financial information and knowledge, which is probably a good thing.

So that's just my take on the financial markets. Maybe we can go back to this topic later and sort of dig into it a bit more, if we had more specific questions.

Dan: Yeah.

Horace: But it's something I wanted to touch on because I think it's such an important part of what's going on and how we perceive Apple.

Dan: So what else do you—I mean, that's a big topic. But like you said, the specifics—maybe we'll get some good feedback.

Horace: Yeah, you know, we're having to do this live now and without a script. So there is a lot of questions—I'm sure I could ask myself some. But the other thing maybe we could touch on in this show is what we just saw yesterday, Windows 8.

Dan: Yeah.

Horace: I'm not the one to actually critique it. It's something that can have lots of ink spilled about—that I'm not qualified to do. But what I would say struck me about it was that—and this, again, is not something new—we kind of knew what they were going for here, they were going for merging of their old Windows and the new Windows UI that's touch-oriented, which is Metro, the experience that was first released with Windows Phone. And I think my concern is if I look at this in terms of the theory of innovation, that I've often spoken about, what is Microsoft actually doing here? And my interpretation is that you need to follow not just the technology but look at the money. And look at the way Microsoft makes money and what this product says about that.

I have maintained that as devices become the predominant computing platform, a lot of things have changed. A lot of industries have been turned inside out, disrupted, if you will. So we had telecom. We've had the handset vendors. But now the question is finally, "What about the PC?" And I think here the debate is really that back in the day when the PC cost $3,000, in 1985, for example, DOS cost $30. And so the amount of money you spent on the operating system was tiny. In fact, negligible. Now as time went on and the price of the hardware dropped to $300, how much is a Windows license? Well, we don't know exactly. It depends a lot on what kind of deal Microsoft is offering OEMs [original equipment manufacturers]. But I've heard up to $40. And there was a discount during the netbook bubble, if you will. Netbook makers couldn't afford $40 on a $300 product, so they were actually pressuring Microsoft by licensing Linux or installing Linux on their laptops, or these netbooks. In fact, for a while, Linux was the predominant way you would get a netbook in the first few months or years.

And Microsoft responded very rapidly to that threat by dropping the price of XP so that it became under $20. And so they dropped it just to the point where it's barely tolerable to a device-maker [so] they could still put it on the shelf for that $300, let's say.

So it's a curious thing that if the price of the hardware drops below a certain threshold, it becomes very hard to justify what's called the software BOM, or bill of materials. Because that becomes the most expensive component. You know, if you think about a $300 tablet, for example, it's not going to have a great screen but it's unlikely that the screen is worth more than $40, $50. So you have this dilemma for a device maker. "Can I make this product and be profitable with a good margin? And be competitive, at $300, let's say?" But Microsoft wants $40 for the software. What do you do? What do you do? Again, you get into this back-and-forth with Microsoft and they're forced to lower their prices. And so the question I have for Windows 8 is, how are they going to price it to the OEMs? Because at some point—this again goes back to an investor question—what is the market's reaction to Microsoft Windows 8? Positive or negative? Because is this going to impact the ASP, the average selling price, of Windows itself?

And people are less tolerant, not just for paying for [an] operating system on devices, but even for applications. You can see how Apple positioned iWork components at $20 apiece. These are Numbers, Pages and Keynote. Each individually is now $20. And these are analogous to the Office suite. So they've unbundled Office. And then they offered it for very, very low prices.

So, again, how does the device—if you get an app store model for the Windows 8—how are you going to price Office if you're going to sell it through the app store? Are you going to go to the app store and, say, have one option to buy Office Profession for $490, or whatever? That's going to be more than the device is worth.

Dan: Right.

Horace: People would be very reluctant to impulse buy Office. So again what we're seeing here, with the device, is a pressure on Microsoft's core business. Forget about whether they're doing the right thing architecturally or as far as the user experience. What I'm asking is, "What's this going to do to the economics of Microsoft?" And I'm sure I'm not the first. And, usual disclaimers. I'm sure they thought about this. But I would be very nervous as an investor because there are these unknowns. I'm sure Microsoft strategy is driven a lot by this.

You see they're cramming too much into it. When people argue that it needs to have a user experience, and it needs backward compatibility, it needs the enterprise, it needs all these things. And so you smash it together... I argue that they put it together like this because of the economics. Because they'd have to be able to charge $40, and they're going to say to their OEMs, "Look, this is a PC, it's just a different from factor. All devices are PCs at the end of the day, with Moore's Law and everything."

Dan: Right.

Horace: And so let's make sure we maintain our core business model of $40 per PC. That's the Microsoft tax, you know. It sounds negative to say that it's a tax. It's a price, though. That's what they charge. Value or not, that's the price.

So that's where I'm questioning, strategically, what this is going to do to their business. And by the way, just one more data point: As far as Windows Phone is concerned—which is not full Windows, not the whole enchilada, it's just, quote-unquote, a mobile OS—that [price] is only $15, according to some sources. And that's what they're actually trying to get from Android in IP licensing. So basically they're offering their OEMs an option: "You can go with us, with Windows Phone for $15, or you can pay us $15 if you're using Android, and you get nothing but Android. Whereas we give you X, Y and Z." So that's been their entire mobile OS strategy.

Dan: Right.

Horace: But notice the price point. It has to be $15 because the phone business does not sustain a $40 bill of materials for software. And if the tablet… And I point out also in my data that an iPad and an iPhone, as far as Apple is concerned, are priced about the same, $650. If you take the number of units sold and the amount they report as income for those two product lines, you get almost the same number. The margins are different. iPhone is more profitable. The iPad is about 30 percent estimated [gross margin], and the iPhone is about 50 percent estimated. Obviously, the iPhone has got subsidies and therefore they can charge more. But bottom line is, hardware-wise, this is the going rate, and so if you're a competitor, you've got to look at that and say "I've got to target that price because the channel is going to bear that price." So you're going to target $600 for an iPad equivalent, and so on, and so on.

But you work out what you need to get in the door and all these things. I mean, you end up with this bill of materials that you need to put together, and then suddenly Microsoft shows up and says, "Oh, I need $40 more for my part."

So, it's tough. It's a tough business. I'm not sure how it's going to play out. I think, ultimately, this trend—this migration to mobility—is undermining a core Microsoft business model. And they've tried to get away from it. Let's be honest. They've moved into devices and they tried that business, although the volumes they're going to get on devices to be even moving the needle on their Windows and Office, I mean, they would have to be selling hundreds of millions of $15 licenses to get near the Windows business, right? So it's not likely to happen anytime soon. So that business won't pick up the slack.

At the same time they've gone into services, and they're trying to do things in the cloud, and selling not the software but access to the software. These again are not yet big enough. Some enterprise buyers are going that route, but it's not big enough to offset the decline that's likely to happen.

So Microsoft isn't standing still, but they're fighting an increasing current that's going against them, and I think that's what mobility is doing to them.

Dan: Do you see their direction—their recent direction of this new OS, and all of these new announcements—is this the kind of thing that developers should be getting excited about? Should consumers be getting excited about this? Aside from their longer term, I mean, is this the kind of thing they need to be doing to really revitalize everything?

Horace: Well, you know, I think Microsoft has been a little bit surprised by the events of the last four years, first by the iPhone and secondly by the iPad. And they have really reacted very—I would say commendably—to these threats by, I think, turning things quite quickly.

Now, the problem is that it still will need iteration and we're not sure if it's actually built along the user experience necessary.

Dan: Right. We don't know that yet.

Horace: We don't know that. So the thing is, if you're a developer or consumer... I think first of all as a consumer, generally, I don't expect people to try to figure out what the product is. They're just going to go into Best Buy and look at it and decide yes or no. I think the enterprises, however, which are a large part of Microsoft's customers, are, I think— and again, I'm not an expert, I don't follow Microsoft 100 percent—but I get some signals that they tend to not buy every new version of Windows. They tend to amortize or buy something and let it penetrate slowly, and then drain out of the organization slowly. So it took a long time for XP to replace 2000. It took a long time—well, Vista never made it. So it took some time for 7 to takeover XP, and XP still has a large installed base.

So the question is, as 7 is growing, how long will it be before 8? I really don't think 8 is going to make a big impact. I think it will probably be 9 [that will]. So I'm thinking mid-2012 or in the teens that we'll see true adoption of this new paradigm that Microsoft is pushing. In the meantime, [most] will still be on 7, the bulk of users. But enterprises are going to be looking at this thing in all kinds of weird ways because, of all people, the enterprises are the ones who are not all that excited about change. They're not all that excited about having to retrain. And what's in it for them? What is the value? Microsoft as a brand is a productivity thing. It's a productivity job that they're hired to do. So how can you prove that this is going to make my workforce more productive by using touch on the tablet? I'm not quite sure. I mean, I'd have to rebuild all the apps I'm using, or the applications, I should say.

Dan: Right.

Horace: That these are not—although they claim to be— finger-friendly on the old UI, it's not going to work. Let's be honest Steve Jobs was right about filing your fingers.

Dan: Yeah.

Horace: So there are a lot of issues here with the enterprise, which is their core business. But this is where I give them credit, because they do need to move these people forward. It's just they hold you back. Platforms are great, because you build all of this loyalty. But at the same time they hold you back because then you've got to drag all these people forward and unless you can be somewhat harsh about it, and earn the bad reputation of being not a good player, which is the idea of firing your customers and moving forward.

There was a great story I was reading a couple of years ago in a book called *Breaking Windows*. It was about how Windows was litigated by the Clinton administration and all these antitrust trials. But one of the things that was interesting in that story was how Microsoft understood early on in early '90s just how important it was to be able to have independence from your customers, in a way. So, what happened was that when they had the DOS and Windows early versions... Actually, DOS already had a killer app with Lotus 1-2-3. And the problem was that Lotus was getting kind of cocky. And so when they moved to Windows, Microsoft found that Lotus guys weren't too excited about porting to Windows.

Dan: Mm-hmm.

Horace: So it was like saying, "Hold on. Who's controlling whom right now?" That was actually one of the main reasons why they got into Office as a business. It wasn't because they wanted to create this huge empire. It's because they wanted independence for the killer app that was driving usage of their product. So they actually bought Office by acquiring pieces. They acquired Word, they acquired several components that made up Office. They bundled it, lowered the price as a bundle vis-à-vis the independent components, and put Lotus out of business. It was almost like an afterthought that Lotus was crushed. And it was done because they needed to have the core apps under their control, because they wanted to move the platform forward. So they knew that in the '90s. But the problem is when you get bigger and bigger and bigger, and you've got a billion users, how do you fire them all? You can't. You've got to work your way very slowly through that.

Dan: Yeah.

Horace: And so now their so-called partners... I mean, they're developers. They're the people who build these apps, and you have to make sure that you don't piss them off. You have to build a lot of these VAR [value-added reseller] relationships, and these are people who sell your product. So these people are as much a burden as they are... or [as much] a liability as they are an asset because you will have to pull them kicking and screaming into the future. I'd like to think that Microsoft is very smart and wise about things. But the problem always is that once you are too big, it's hard to maneuver.

And it takes not just courage, it takes really this kind of value destruction to make a greater value in the future and sometimes you wonder about the courage of management. That's where leadership comes into play. That's where you ask yourself, "Is this the right team?" So, in some ways, I can see how internally they would have debated and said, "Look, we need to go Metro 100 percent." And then somebody came back and said, "No, you can't do that because we're going to lose everybody. We are going to migrate people slowly." So I see Windows 8 as kind of a halfway step, a hybrid. They want to go to all-electric cars, but right now they've got to have a hybrid car. And, you know, maybe that's a great analogy, because hybrids are great cars.

Dan: Yeah.

Horace: But still, you know, this is kind of a kludge. That's how I see it, Windows 8.

Dan: But when has it not been?

Horace: Yeah.

Dan: I mean, since going—… looking back at Windows, since Windows 3…

Horace: In truth, you know, I'm an old Unix guy. And, yeah, I think you are as well, right?

Dan: Yeah, definitely.

Horace: Listening to some of the other podcasts you mentioned that. And, you know, I cut my teeth on Unix back in the '80s, even.

Dan: Yeah.

Horace: And, yeah, we always looked back then at Windows as a kludge. I mean, it was built on really rocky—sorry, not rocky—shaky foundations: DOS. It was, you know, wrong number of bits. All kinds of wrongness. And yet they were successful because sometimes markets don't value elegance. They value things that just work and are distributed and get into the right hands. And so they bulldozed their way through, even though they weren't very clean.

And the problem is that you get cocky and say, "Hey, it was kludgy then, it's kludgy now, we know, we're going to keep hacking it and hacking it and hacking." And they kind of ran into a wall with that. I think with Vista. And probably the point of pivot for Microsoft was actually probably even Windows 2000. And what I call the pivot is this idea that a product reaches the point of being more than good enough.

Now, the thing is, what was the basis of competition for Windows in the '90s? When I ask that question [I mean] "What is it that you would look for in the next version?" And people think, "Oh, it was more features, or it was more…"No, the thing you looked for in every new version of Windows in the '90s was that it would crash less.

Dan: Right. That was the future you prayed for.

Horace: Yeah. Fewer blue screens. And that was the killer feature, and it was only when 2000 came into being, and 2000 was important because it was actually using the NT kernel, and they finally moved NT into consumer or, I should say, desktop. And that was a lot more reliable as a kernel than what was before. And I think that's actually when Windows kind of became good enough, because if you're thinking operating system theory, the most important function of an operating system is to keep the system operating. It is not to crash. It is what mainframes figured out in the '60s. It's what was on the desktop workstations in the '80s and '90s, and it wasn't on the desktop in terms of a PC, even a Mac, until the last decade, right, 2000s?

Dan: Yeah.

Horace: So as far as consumer—or I should say end-user based operating systems, end-user targeted operating systems—that pivotal point occurred in the Windows world with Windows 2000 and in the Mac world or Apple world it happened with OS X.

But that's important. If it became good enough and not crashing, then the basis of competition has to change to something else. And so what happened was, in the case of Apple, OS X kept improving, but the focus, the product, where you devote all your energy, they went to being more around portables, right? They integrated deeper into what made them successful. The fact that they were in an integrated company.

So OS X took the path of becoming a smaller computer. Or, I should say, Apple decided that the roadmap of their evolution was going to be small. And that meant learning all about [being small.] I mean, Apple invented a lot of the things we take for granted in laptops. The fundamental design, the palm rest. They were the first with a lot of the screen technologies, the trackball first and the trackpad, and all these other things. They were doing these in large volumes. And learning.

Now, the thing with Windows that, once it peaked in 2000, I would say, from a reliability point of view—although again, everything is relative—[at that point] they had to ask themselves, "Where do we go from here?" And what Microsoft, I think, started to do is, they piled stuff into Windows. It just became bloated and bloated, and bigger and bigger, because they had to say, "There's a good reason for you to get another version, because it's got this, this—it's got X, Y and Z."

Dan: Right. But you're never losing A, B and C. It's always there.

Horace: Yeah. It's always—there is legacy plus. Legacy plus.

Dan: Right.

Horace: And they hit a wall. Frankly, there is no one that can look at the current new version, version 8, and say that this is a complete rethinking of that logic. [They did not say] "No, enough is enough." But I'm sure if you ask the experts, who always are free and quick with an opinion, they would have said, "Oh, no, we want more." Experts always will ask for more. It takes courage to say no to the experts, and listen to the not-so-powerful users.

But I still don't think they listen enough. Again, if you study computer science, you realize that there isn't really anything more you can do to a kernel that hasn't been done 20 years ago. This is why Linux is taking over in terms of devices, and the Unix kernel and the Linux kernel, which are somewhat historically related.

I think that logic is from 1968 or '69, when Unix was born. It's very old technology. But it's because that is all it needs to be. Keeping processes running and balancing resources was figured out in the '60s, and since then it's all been a question of where does the value move. It was clear to me in the '90s that what was happening to Unix back then was a sign it was declining, in a way, but it was because it was already good enough. No one could make money from it. And so, anyway, that's a long story.

But that's how I see Windows today. It's having an existential crisis. Because the value proposition of Windows, that it keeps your computer from crashing and allows you to experience things on top of it, then you don't really need a new version of it every two years. And I think, implicitly, companies and people are only upgrading because frankly their computer died and they need a new computer.

Dan: Right.

Horace: And it happens to ship with the newest version. They're not out there clamoring for a new operating system. And even in the Mac world I think that the thing that makes it better in the Mac world is that it's almost free, right? The software is so cheap that you don't mind—you know, and installation is fairly painless. Migration Assistant and all that stuff makes it easy. But in the Windows world it's a very painful process. And people don't do it because they want to. It's because they have to.

There are so many other constituents, like I said. VARs, developers. And then you have OEMs. They're going to have to look hard at this product and decide. Of course, being a monopoly, Microsoft can say, "Well, there's only this option. You can't put XP on anymore." They tried. They had to extend the life of XP multiple times because there was so much resistance to Vista. And Vista was so bloated that it wouldn't fit on these small computers, these tiny laptops. So now we'll have to see how that moves forward.

But to me, the [Windows 8] story isn't one of enthusiasm or anticipation of greatness. I only ask myself if they can hold on. Because I think the concept is very much an end-of-life concept.

Dan: Well, I wonder. When regular people, consumers, look at this, and they think, "What should I invest in right now?" Not from the standpoint of financial investments in the stock market, but technology, I mean, I would say Mac, Apple. Right? And that seems to be the common thinking. But there is still plenty of people who are getting new Windows PCs for home, and certainly in the corporate world it's just going and going and going. I mean, is that—isn't that enough to sustain them, and what should we as consumers think…

Horace: As I was saying to this reporter, or journalist, in the tech business, in the device business in particular, it's up or out. In other words, if you're not growing, you have a death spiral. There is no middle ground. It's either all positive or all negative. Because what happens when you stop growing you lose all of these other people who used to be your friends, right?

Dan: Yeah.

Horace: You lose the VARs and the developers and then you lose some of the larger accounts. And then it's a corrosive process. And the corrosion actually gets worse as it progresses. That's the challenge. Microsoft has to keep growing. And the problem with growth is that of course you've got several real markets which are saturated and are sluggish and are not interested in growing. I think the latest numbers for IDC [International Data Corporation] show, for example, that the PC market is not only slowing down globally but if you look at developed markets it's actually shrinking. And some of that is attributed to macro issues, but some of it is actually obviously from these tablet disruptors.

But Microsoft has traditionally also sought a source of growth in emerging markets. But there again—is this newfangled operating system that has a schizophrenic user experience, that has all these strings attached to it, and all these pricing concerns—is that something that is going to set China on fire in terms of growth? Where, if not there? Africa? I don't know. Maybe there is something out there. But this is not a product that speaks to me that says, "Hey—boom!—low end. This is about a now competition with non-consumption. We're going to takeover these great non-consuming markets."

It doesn't have that feeling either. So, that's where growth turns negative. And I'm not predicting anything here. I'm just saying that I get a feeling that this isn't a story for Microsoft that says, it's a clear "buy" signal—everybody pile into this new platform. [Or] if you've got kids, teach them right away, no matter how old they are, to program for it. I wouldn't do that.

I would say there is lots of opportunity in apps and devices and mobile, and those aren't Microsoft strongholds right now. So that's where I think they're struggling even more. And I think maybe on another show we'll have to get into just exactly Windows Phone fits in the history of Windows Mobile. Which is fascinating—how that happened and what they were thinking, at what point in time. Windows Mobile traces its roots to about 1994. Windows CE, which is its kernel...

Dan: Ah, right.

Horace: ...CE. CE stands for Consumer Electronics. Did you know that?

Dan: Now that you say it I remember that, but that's crazy.

Horace: It was built to be embedded in televisions, or set-top boxes, or even maybe your stereo or something that people back then thought was relevant. So that traces its roots all the way there. There was a clear decision made by Bill Gates to enter into that market.

Automobiles, by the way, was another opportunity they looked for. And so what happened was a fork in the road. They went that way, and then what happened... to this day we're still using Windows CE, or they're using Windows CE inside of Windows 7. They haven't had to change it. But at the same time the whole business has been completely gutted and changed in terms of what it is. And they're still saying, "Hey, $15 a pop. That's our price."

Genericized Trademarks

Posted September 21st, 2011 as The Critical Path Episode #7

Horace and Dan look at brand theory and decide it should not be left to the experts. Also, we ask what jobs products are hired to do and tie that to the meaning imparted in the brand and the visual imagery associated with it.

Horace: So, just to get right into it, I had an idea of what to say and it's on the topic of brands and branding.

Dan: I love this topic.

Horace: And it's one that I think deserves quite a bit of attention because it's something that it's again very well known as a concept but not well understood as a real business phenomenon. So here's the thinking.

I'm going to approach this from my perspective, which isn't necessarily the academically correct one.

Dan: Okay.

Horace: It's not something you're going to read about on Wikipedia or any reference manual on what a brand is. And I came to this through my own discovery process, and what I like to do is just convey what I figured out, in a language that perhaps you can understand, because I too am not from that field. I'm not from the world of advertising or brand management or consumer products—non-technical consumer products—which is where most of the theory developed.

So from them it comes out sounding very abstract and very, I think, from a technical-minded person's point of view, it sounds, frankly, fluffy. So here's how I would think about it.

It took me a long time. I should say, it took me probably a decade to understand what a brand is because, again, I thought of it as most people do, that it's actually the name of something that is usually promoted through advertising and makes it famous. It's just a well-known name, right? So Coca-Cola is a brand because it's famous.

But it turns out that it's nothing to do with fame.

So let me point out that a brand is typically *a name that has meaning*. Note that it's not just a name. A name by itself would be a trademark and anybody can register one. The difference is that it has *meaning*. So the question is, "How do you build the meaning that goes with it?"

So, for example, if you think back and ask what is the history of a good brand? Like maybe you think of Coca-Cola.

Dan: Sure.

Horace: Coca-Cola is a century-old brand. If you go back in history, there were contemporary brands a hundred years ago that we don't know about. Now, they may have been famous in their time, but they're no longer meaningful to us, partly because they haven't been promoted, but partly because what they stand for is not meaningful anymore, right? So we have products in those years that have disappeared from our use, right? Whereas Coca-Cola has been maintained, and it's that maintenance that is really where the heavy lifting goes. They have had to work really hard, and Coca-Cola's probably the most brand-oriented company because there's nothing else there but the brand, right? I mean, it has to be maintained constantly.

So that's one thing about brands, is that they can go up and down in value, and that value is primarily in what it means. I became aware of this while I was actually writing and becoming more visible online. There comes a point when you realize that you yourself are branded at some point. Whenever you gain any kind of audience you become a brand automatically because people impart meaning into your name. So you're not just Dan Benjamin, you're suddenly "that Dan Benjamin," that means something to somebody. Maybe, hopefully millions.

So it is with people who are so-called celebrities. I mean, they're a person but then there's their persona and their presence and what that means, what that brand means.

That's kind of just as a background.

So it's interesting to me how to build a brand and how to create this meaning. Because sometimes the meaning can turn negative, so a brand can—they call it tarnishing, which is interesting because there's no sort of antonym to tarnished branding. What is it instead, is it a shiny brand? I mean, it's a good brand or a bad brand. But the idea is that it's possible, very quickly, to turn something which is very positive into something very negative, and I'm sure people try to prevent it and also perhaps tarnish or damage other people's brands in a competitive fashion.

Dan: Right.

Horace: So here's some thoughts. The theory goes that there are different types of brands. There's aspirational or referential or, you know, functional. But what I'd like to think of mostly is *what a good brand is*. What it's positioned on—meaning that it's related to something that it's hired to do.

So in other words, it's kind of like a functional brand. [In contrast] if you have a brand that is aspirational, typically—let's say a luxury brand—you just want to tell people you possess it and that's really what you hire the brand for. You want it to speak for you: that you have good taste, how much money you have, or what have you.

[Consider] Apple. A lot of people think that it conveys luxury or aspiration or premium. But many people just hire it to get the job done, and many people actually hire it to become creative with the tools they give you.

So it means obviously different things to different people, but what I would point out is that the functional meaning of the brand—and how do you build [that], what it's hired for—is really the key of making a successful brand.

So one thought I had was [thinking] of the framework of disruption, that products over time get better and better, and unfortunately they have a tendency to get even better than they need to be. In which case they're vulnerable. And in this sense, also, you can think about a brand. A brand in the early days is associated with a product that isn't necessarily good enough. So you have the idea of a brand through whose meaning you're trying to narrow the gap between a person's intent and the person's decision to actually purchase something.

Let's [take] the early days of a product that didn't work so well. Let's say electric razors, okay, or even just plain disposable razors. Disposable razors didn't compete effectively vis-à-vis the razors you would buy with the blade separately and you would assemble together. Wilkinson Sword made a brand of blades that you would put inside of a razor and then you would shave. And then came disposable razors, various brands—Bic and Gillette... And the problem was that those new brands were struggling against something as prestigious as Wilkinson and, yet, they were coming up the trajectory and getting better all the time.

The problem is that for someone who is now Gillette, for example, who has built first the single blade and then the double blade and then triple and quadruple and so on, they get to the point where they're actually more than good enough. So during the ascent the brand Gillette makes you think, "Well, do I really need two blades? I mean, they've proven to me that they actually work, so now I'm going to use the fact that it's a good brand to convince myself to buy the next generation product."

So you get up this trajectory using the brand to pull people along. But the challenge is that once you get to be too good the brand actually doesn't help you at all because you start to think, "Well, I really don't need five blades. I was satisfied with four. What value is it to me that Gillette has five blades?"

That's kind of the framework I'd to like to put forward, and maybe it helps us think through what the Apple brand is and what competitor brands are all about. Because I think the Apple brand has been very carefully cultivated. It has been managed and it's very meaningful, and I think the problem with a lot of competitor brands is that they're tied to a product or to something whose meaning has evaporated over time. So, in the sense that Microsoft perhaps may be associated with Windows, if it's Windows that is no longer relevant, then the question is again for Microsoft: Where is the value in their brand? And they were extremely confident with that brand for many, many years because they attached the Windows name to everything and they were getting a lot of good feedback about the value—

Dan: Everything is Windows that they do now.

Horace: Yes.

Dan: Everything.

Horace: In Windows Live there's nothing Windows about Live.

Dan: Right.

Horace: Or Windows Mobile, there's nothing Windows about the mobile experience that they're selling. And now, of course, the Windows that they put forward with the Metro interface actually doesn't even have windows anymore. I think that somebody pointed out that it's no longer just this notion of overlapping Windows. That's how Apple pioneered the new metaphor.

So, maybe they shouldn't call it Windows. They should be calling it Tiles. So you see what I mean. But it's a problem that sometimes the brand can work against you. So, now, I'm struggling with this also in terms of what the meaning of my own brand is or when I build something. Or you have "5by5" and what is that trying to do, and how do you manage that and do you want to actually stray off of the brand, because people then pigeonhole you and they say, "Okay, this means that." And it's a positive thing and you get nervous about diluting it and you think, "Oh, should I get involved in the new business associated with that." Let's say 5by5 conferences or something like that.

Dan: Right, sure.

Horace: Is that going to hurt you because "That's not what I thought the brand was all about?"

This is a struggle for anyone, I think, who has the responsibility and power over brand. We have to really be careful with it, and I struggle sometimes thinking what happened with Nokia, with Symbian for example. I think the real problem, when they broke with that past—which was a necessary thing—but when they broke with that past the brand had a huge violence done to it.

And the reason I think that is is because in the minds of the buyers—and I think in the case of Nokia the buyers aren't just the consumer, there's also all these other people who are buying and selling the product to consumers, to intermediaries—to them, this idea of Nokia stepping back and not being an independent company as much as it used to be, [this idea] suffered in a lot of people's minds, and you can't put a number on that.

You can't actually put a spreadsheet together and calculate what the impact of that is. It's deeply psychological, and I think this is where you have to someone—not a magician, but someone who is extremely sensitive to notions about value of a brand—that is in charge of it. And the trouble with large corporations is that typically there's a lot of rotation in and out of job positions and in and out of the company, and there's no one who is custodian of something that has such a deep bond with the buyers.

So that relationship is not something you can put in a box and hand over to someone else. That's where I think there are these huge struggles with brands fading and suddenly you wake up one day as a company and you realize that nobody respects you anymore.

Again, this is another thing that I feel that somehow Apple has some special powers to maintain this. There's an awareness, —even if it's not vocalized, even if it's not codified or even if it's not written down—that there's an internal process of maintaining this.

I'm reminded of one episode where supposedly Apple had needed an icon for one of the keyboard keys. It's currently the Command key, and initially it was the Apple key and had a little Apple logo on it. And Steve Jobs supposedly killed that idea because he said they are trivializing the brand by putting it on the keyboard.

Dan: How did they respond to that then? Is that why they changed it? I mean, is it—and why were they triv… I mean, explain that.

Horace: Well, so the problem…

Dan: Because I've heard this. I've heard this but it's never exposed.

Horace: So the idea was that you overexpose it and, to them, the Apple brand and the logo are part of the same image. If you commoditize something, if you overexpose it, it becomes less meaningful, right? We take words all the time and we end up destroying them by overusing them, right? I mean, words like "awe," from which comes awesome. And we will use "awesome" so much that we can't use the word "awe" anymore. "I'm in awe of something" sounds meaningless.

So there are a lot of words in the English language, which, because of our vernacular habits, become completely useless. Sometimes people of minorities actually take a word which is derogatory and put it on themselves. That is to enhance its value, and that's also the same phenomenon [in reverse].

But you have to be careful because what happens in society is one thing, but there's also this notion of taking something like "Xerox" or "vacuum." In the U.K. vacuuming is called "hoovering." So the Hoover brand has become genericized.

Dan: Right.

Horace: So to have a genericized trademark which is also a brand is very, very destructive. So Xerox…

Dan: That's actually a bad thing.

127

Horace: It is a bad thing because, essentially, you can no longer use it yourself, and it becomes, you know, googling something, right? This is a modern equivalent. Googling something. The companies actually try to stop this.

Dan: Really? Because you would think, you would think…

Horace: But you lose control over it, too, you see. I see what your point is. There's no such thing as bad publicity, but it is in this case because you lose control over it and then people can spin it out in all kinds of directions. Not to mention, it ends up being embedded in the language and if it is a trademark it means that it should have a "TM" next to it and it should not be misused.

I'm not an expert and I'm not going to necessarily agree with this hypothesis, but that's how the thinking goes: that you need to control these things.

So in the idea of Apple, I think if you look at where the Apple logo shows up on an Apple product, it's very carefully placed. I think on the desktop there's only one place, which is up in the corner. And then there's usually one place on the product itself, the front of the Mac or the back of the laptop or whatever.

Dan: Right.

Horace: And that's it. It cannot be overused.

By the way, what is the biggest brand in the world right now? In my opinion, it's "Made in China." Those words appear on more products than anything else.

Also one of the most ubiquitous symbols in the world, which is actually something of an issue, is the American flag. Now, the American flag is so commonly used on all kinds of products that it kind of becomes trivialized. I'm sensitive to this because, you know, I live also in Finland, and in Finland you cannot display the flag just whenever you feel like it. There are only certain days of the year when you're allowed to show the flag.

Dan: No kidding.

Horace: They're special days, holidays.

Dan: So people, I guess, they don't put bumper stickers with the flag.

Horace: No, it's considered an extremely disrespectful thing. You can't fly it at night and so on. There's one occasion—where, if there's a building and someone in that building dies—you're allowed to fly the flag that day. Once. It's that important.

So it's something that, again, it depends on the law. I mean, I think the U.S. actually has laws like this. There's also a law in the U.S. about how to dispose of a flag. I don't know if you know this.

Dan: Right.

Horace: You're not allowed to throw it away. You're supposed to burn it, actually. Or deposit it in a place where it gets taken care of that way. So the burning has to be ritualized, not just in protest.

So there's all kinds of rules, right? I'm just pointing these out, and it's funny how when you intersect some of these theories with some of the business thinking that goes in, it's funny because these are independent threads of thought. So you have the thinking around branding, right? It's usually in the hands of brand managers or people who are studying these things and theories. And there are people in engineering and there are people in marketing, and if there's no integration between these teams it's not clear how you actually think about the whole problem.

So this topic came up because I was writing about the evolution of operating systems and whether we can measure operating system cycle times as a proxy for whether they're nearing an end of life, the thinking being that if an operating system is being delayed a lot, it tends to indicate that the platform is on shaky ground. So I tried to find data to back this up, and I had to go back in history and find out, to measure the speed of change of an operating system. So I was using a proxy, using basically a version-numbering system.

You know, when you look at multiple operating systems you have to have a common measure of how fast they evolve. And you assume that the marketing people chose a numbering scheme that's also consistent with the engineering team, that's also consistent with what the market needs, et cetera.

The problem was that for Windows, technology-wise, there's been so many threads of Windows in history, where they move from 16 to 32 byte, and then they changed from the DOS to the NT kernel, and then they had so many different patches that went on. And the question is really, "Is that still Windows? Can we measure it as one thing?" And the only thing that ties it together is the brand.

So you have people who decide at Microsoft what do to with the technology. Then they give these things version numbers. Then they have other people in marketing who say, "Well, this is what the market demands in terms of improvements in the product line." And you have other people who think, "Well, we need to make sure that we maintain the branding of Windows because it means something, it's meaningful to users, they need to make sure that they upgrade along this line."

So you have all these three threads, and it's very hard to reconcile them. I think Apple here, again, had an interesting pivot because there are two threads of Mac OS. There was the old Mac OS that sort of died when NeXTSTEP was used—or OS X was used to replace it, although, they were living side by side for a few years. So System 9, that was the last version, and…

Dan: I think with X they had started calling it OS 9.

Horace: Right, yes. Well, Mac OS 9. Then they became OS X, which was Mac OS X. The "X," though, signified to me sort of a difference in the branding. And so there was meaning being imparted, saying, "This is a break…" Somehow the "Mac" was maintained as a historic thing, maybe as a crutch, and then forward-looking this "X"—which actually stands for 10—and then the versions actually are 10.1, 10.2, 10.3, and so on.

So there's all this debate about me not being fair to the Windows history because I'm taking that thread of history saying, "Well, now it's 8, so what was 7? What was 6? What was 5? What was 4?" And back in those years of 4, 5 and 6 they didn't use numbers, they used something like XP or 2000 or ME. So which one is which?

Whereas, you know, in Mac's world you had this clean break, and so what do you measure off of? So that actually brought me to think about branding because these operating systems… You know, with the brand you're actually communicating things, trying to make it meaningful. I'm trying, still struggling with this, how to make a good definition of what the brand means. You know, what Mac OS X means now, given the fact that also it's now iOS, which is based on the same thing as OS X as a kernel, and then you have all these new layers on top.

But technically speaking, people might argue that this is still OS X. But, in fact, by branding it iOS—which they only did it two to three years ago, right?—by branding it iOS they made that decision to communicate that it is a different thing.

When I was in Nokia, one thing that was debated was, "Do we market Symbian," because actually it was a separate company and so Nokia created another brand called Series 60, which was the user-interface layer on top of Symbian. And they started calling it S60 rather than Series [60], and there was an internal naming convention, but they never really got so far as to say, "Well this is a product, the Nokia XYZ phone is a Series 60 product." They didn't focus on that branding of the platform or the operating system beneath it because it would have clashed with their idea of what the value of the device was.

So you get into all kinds of things trying to figure this out. In the end, what ended up happening with Nokia was that they didn't put any emphasis at all on the platform side from a consumer's point of view. So no one felt that their attachment was to the platform. Their attachment was redirected towards the device. But devices have a short shelf life. So there's this whole problem [where] now there's no loyalty to the platform itself. In fact, most people didn't even know that they had a platform product at all. And because you don't have that meaning in it, you also don't think about investing in it. You don't think about adding applications to it. Of course, lots of technical people did know these things, but they're always a minority.

So I've been also thinking about Android, because Android is another funny thing. The trademark of Android belongs to Google. Droid, on the other hand, belongs to Verizon.

Dan: Right.

Horace: So some people get it wrong when they say, "Which Droid do you have?" referring to any Android device. You can't say that because Android is only referring to Android devices.

But that trademark belongs to Google, and if you don't license the Android operating system from Google and just download or FTP the code and build your own or build it as a genericized Android, you cannot actually call it an Android product. So, in that sense, the product that Amazon may launch will not be rightfully called Android unless it actually is a bona fide Android license, and I don't think it will be because they're probably going to put their store on it and their services.

So we're going to get into a lot of problems with branding of Android because, again, Android-like is probably a better way of saying it, but it's still not quite what we're seeing coming out of new forks of Android.

And by the way, Android at the core is Linux, right? So it's not fair to say that Google invented most of what's in there, right? I mean, it's Java plus Linux. So that part is open source anyway, and they don't really own that code, to be honest. I mean, it's shared. So it's going to be an interesting evolution of that platform.

Just today I was reading in the Korean press that HTC actually confirmed that they will be doing their own OS and that Bada… Yesterday or the day before Samsung mentioned that they would take Bada into open source. Bada is not an Android-like product, but it's still interesting how that story is evolving about the Asian [market], particularly Asian vendors moving into their own OS or their own platform development.

This also follows Baidu [and] Alibaba, which are service-oriented companies—rather than device vendors—making their own platforms.

Dan: Right.

Horace: So it's an interesting story there.

Dan: It's fascinating to me because when you analyze it this way it's almost like, yeah, very much I guess this is true. The engineer's analysis and breakdown of a brand and what it means, and do you think that companies are very cognizant of this kind of perspective that you're sharing with us now? Do you think they see it this way or is it cloudier for them?

Horace: You know, it's very hard because if it was possible to codify brand theory in a way, in a language that people would understand, then it would be much more commonly debated, discussed, dissected.

Dan: Yeah.

Horace: Analysis on brands is done by specialists and their language, the language they speak, sounds extremely foreign to everyone else. So I don't think that it has crossed this chasm from being something of an archaic thing—or at least something being very abstract—to something being well understood and debated.

You don't have to be an engineer to talk about technology or at least to talk about technology business. Lots of people who are bloggers are not engineers, right? But we don't have the debate [there] that goes on about branding. You would sound very silly if you tried because you'd start using these phrases about psychology, really, not so much about hard, quantifiable questions.

I don't claim to have the answer, but I just came to this simple question of, "What is the grammar? What is the meaning? What is the value and how to measure these things?" And thinking all the time about the impact that the brand may have on the business. It's so subtle. It's so hard to even explain it to someone. It's almost like it's a feeling, and you have to think very deeply about it.

The other thing that's interesting is how it interweaves with the job-to-be-done [theory]. I mentioned this idea that you should position the brand on a job, and I don't know if we ever went into the whole discussion of job-to-be-done theory, of how to define and categorize products. But it's very much that Clay Christensen, who came up with a lot of these things, at least he assembled a lot of these things, these theories together...

One of his latest papers—actually, I'm looking at it here—it's called "Integrating Around a Job to be Done." He ties together the notion that brand, job-to-be-done [theory], and integration are interrelated. So the idea that we talk about whether you're integrated or modular, whether you should be doing one thing at one time and another thing at another time, that value chains evolve... Talking about job-to-be-done [theory], the products are hired to do things sometimes different than what you think you are actually building. People buy different things than what you're selling. That's the basic dilemma there.

Dan: All right.

Horace: So that's integrated, that these three things—and the last one being the theory of branding—that these three things are actually, possibly, interrelated. So when you build the brand you need to be aware of the job-to-be-done [theory] and you need to be aware of whether you should be integrated or modular in your approach, overall, as an architecture for your business. Because it turns out that I can't do the paper justice in a quick chat, but I think it's worth looking at this offline. I can send later a reference to how to find it.

But this is where I think the leading edge is right now, in terms of theory development around branding, and it's not these [traditional] experts who are looking at it this way, are not coming from the traditional area where brand management took place. I think it needs fresh eyes, it needs fresh thinking, and that's what I'm trying to educate myself about.

Dan: It seems like, you know, you'll often hear people talk about how valuable the brand is and protecting the brand, and I was just talking with somebody yesterday about how—you probably remember this—I feel like it was within the last year when GAP changed their logo, and how that affected the perception of the brand as well. They changed it and it sucked, and then they kind of put it out for the design community, "Oh, design our brand for us." And then they of course went back to the old brand.

People didn't say, "Well, I'm not going to go to the GAP anymore, I'm not going to buy clothes from the GAP because they changed their logo," but it sounds like [what] you're saying is that the perception of a brand—and paying attention to it and the potential damage it can have to a brand when even just using its name in that way—becomes destructive.

I mean, these sound like things that a company should be especially aware of and cognizant of.

Horace: Exactly.

Dan: Do you think they are?

Horace: No, that's the problem. I think we're just pushing right now into areas where people are not even putting their resources into understanding and managing.

By the way, a logo is extremely important because it's the visual representation of the brand. And I don't want to belittle that at all. It's just like saying, "Well, it's just a picture." It's not. It has so much meaning, and that's where you can't screw up. Actually, my dilemma is that I don't have a logo. I'm toying with some ideas, but I need a professional to look at this. So I'm embarrassed by the fact that I'm talking about logos and yet I don't have one.

Dan: Right.

Horace: But I do respect that. So I do respect the idea of the logo. What happens is that people put so much meaning into that, and when they look at it it invokes a notion. People get as excited or as violent reaction to the change in the logo as they might to the change of a company's name.

But, you see, these are important things. And sometimes when you see people playing around with these formulations, it's also indicative of some kind of other crisis, that something isn't quite right with the company when they go and they feel the need to make these changes.

There's a famous pictogram or infographic or something like that about the history of Coca-Cola versus Pepsi as logos, from a hundred-years-or-so perspective, of how the Coca-Cola logo changed—and it didn't. It actually looked almost exactly the same, whereas Pepsi-Cola changed like twenty, thirty times.

Dan: What about that? What about changing the logo? I mean, you know, you look at the classic logos—obviously, you have Coke, you have Pepsi, you look at AT&T, whether people liked the death star or not.

Horace: Starbucks changed and also that was controversial, yes.

Dan: Yeah, but I mean, then you look at something like Nike, who's one of the most memorable, most simple logos out there. It's almost never changed once they decided what it was really going to look like a few years in. It's pretty much stayed the same, with such minor little changes over the years.

Horace: But you have to ask these questions about what are they changing. So something may be changed simply because it looks old-fashioned, and their brand needs to be modern, or they need to think of themselves and say, Well, we're a soft drink for young people. If we have a logo that looks like something from the last century, we're not hip anymore."

Again, there are deeper things at work here, and I think that you can't just—you have to ask, "Well, why not change the name? Is Pepsi-Cola Pepsi? What does that mean?" It had something to do with digestion at some point in time, right? Just like Coca-Cola once had something to do with cocaine. True story, by the way.

Dan: They deny that. They deny that.

Horace: Well, maybe I'm not up to date.

Dan: No, I've heard the same thing. I've heard the same thing that you're saying.

Horace: But these were tonics. These were called tonics, and they're still called tonics in some maybe old-fashioned way of speaking. But they were called tonics because they were things you took in the morning to either get you over a hangover or [to give] you a boost. Like [how] we use coffee today, to give you that kind of kick in the morning. And oftentimes these were sold by quacks [as having] curative purposes and were just basically loaded with stimulants.

So there's nothing unusual because that was normal at the time, to take a tonic in the morning. They evolved into being "soft drinks." Okay, I again am probably stepping over boundaries here in terms of my competence, but the idea is that that meant something back then and that resulted in Coca-Cola and Pepsi-Cola as brands and names.

So now people, over time, decided to reposition these things because the meaning is changing, what it's hired to do is changing. Once refrigeration came into use things were no longer about getting a boost to your glucose level. It was more about being refreshed or something like that.

So, they had to change, obviously. But the question is, when you try to change something—like the GAP or Starbucks or Netflix—and you're trying to do it because you have problems in your business and you think that's going to give you the necessary boost, again, the symptom is not that that's broken. It's something else that's broken and you're using this as a patch. So I would be very wary of that.

I think here we're getting into this dilemma of Windows. I mean, I'm back to Windows. If the metaphor has changed and it's no longer Windows. Or even deeper than that, Microsoft. Microsoft: It's about software. They invented the software business. But if it turns out that they need to be in hardware…

It leads into this dilemma of, "What do you do about the name and the brand image when times are changing."

Dan: They are changing. So what kind of advice, then, do you have to throw down to the companies out there? Because you know what? I think the big ones, I think the people are listening. I think the big companies listen to this show.

Horace: Great. Not that I need more pressure. Now we're going live and next thing I know…

Dan: Weekly live, and now, you know, Microsoft's top execs are waiting for your advice here.

Horace: Not to disclaim it, but I think we're dealing in the realm, still, of entertainment. Serious discussion requires a lot more investigation of the data. Obviously, we can't do that. That's what the blog is for. Ideally the blog leads to yet more private discussions or some community involvement in solving these puzzles.

So I cannot say right now exactly what the answers are. But I think the beginning of a discussion, at least, should be in understanding these jobs to be done and not understanding so much the image of what you're trying to convey. In other words, don't sweat too much the representation first, but rather what is the underlying meaning you're trying to convey.

I would argue that if you understand the job to be done, you actually understand the product you need to build, and once you understand the product, then the way it actually should be presented becomes more clear and [is] communicated.

Some companies actually go about this the opposite way. You might actually start off with writing the tag line to the product. You know, "Product X, it makes you feel good," or something like that. Less generically, maybe "For those days when you're down." And then from that line you start to think about the product.

Now, in a consumer-oriented company you might want to just develop it that way. But in a technology company you've got to start with a deeper point of reference, more about, "What am I trying to achieve with

135

the product?" I think the Apple theory of development, if there is such a thing, would probably be that you have this conversation that happens: "What do we not like about the world around this? What is it that we need to fix that would make our lives better?"

Supposedly this is what went on in building the iPhone:

"What do we hate?"

"We hate our phones."

"Why do we hate them?"

"Because they have lousy interfaces, they don't do anything except voice, badly. And text once in a while."

So people thought about that problem and then it evolved into thinking about, Well, we need to make a little computer."

In a sense, there are plenty of opportunities around us worldwide that you have to solve using this conversation, this dialogue, this inquisition. And then from that you say, "Aha! Now we understand the job we're trying to solve." The product people can go off and do it, but the communications people can now build the brand in the imagery and all that stuff. That can happen in parallel. They don't need to know what the product will end up looking like, because they know what the product will be hired to do and you build the imagery accordingly.

So that's the thing. You actually speed things up by doing it in parallel. You also save a lot of trouble because you don't need to invite the communications people to every single engineering meeting so that they're up to date in what's happening. You have to have this cohesive view of that it is the product is hired to do, and that extends also to services.

If I were to ask, "What's the job that 5by5 is hired to do? I mean, what is it? Is it education? Is it entertainment? And if it is entertainment, is it about particular contexts? Are you trying to make sure that people have an uninterrupted period of time to listen? Or can it be broken up in pieces? Is it something you do while you exercise? Is it something you do while you drive? Is it taking on radio? Is it taking on television or is it taking on [web] surfing as competitors?"

All these things you have to think about, and then if you do understand deeply that the job is, let's say, entertaining people who are really hungry for knowledge. Then the product you generate entertainment with is not trivial but it is thoughtful. Then you can communicate that. And it becomes instantaneous when you just think of the phrase that actually describes it, and then you can pass that on to production people and say, "This is what we're going for." And then they go off and build a product. They have a huge amount of enthusiasm because they finally know what they're targeting, and that's what I think drives engineering people to greatness.

136

So that is why I think Apple does things better, probably. I don't know for sure. I'm not an insider in any way. I think they have this conversation and they decide very clearly what they're going after. It's a tough bet to make, because you know that if you bet wrong, you set all this machinery in motion and at the end maybe you've targeted the wrong thing and so companies don't like that approach, typically. It's very risky. They would rather sort of just muddle along, see what happens, put something out, if it doesn't work try something else, and in so doing you probably are better off with a portfolio, so, "Let's do a dozen things at once because one of them may hit and the others won't."

All that ends up completely clogging up your communications. You cannot say what you are anymore, and the comms people are just as smart at any company as they might be at Apple. It's just that they don't have a clear message on what they should be communicating. So it ends up coming out poorly and then you blame them, but it's not their fault.

So, you know, if I were to give advice, it would be: Just focus on the job first and things will flow from that.

Dan: I think everybody in these companies, they should be listening to you. I think I need to just sit down with you for a day and let you beat up the brand, tell me what to do right.

Horace: Well, again, I don't think I have answers. What I would like to offer instead is: Here are the tools by which you should go forward and self-analyze. I would say this also to anyone who would like to hire me, I mean—one great story, and this again comes from Christensen.

He was asked at a seminar, I was present at the time, "What are your rules for making a great business." He said they're the same rules as making a great family. If anyone asks you—where did you go to parenting school? how did you learn to be such a great parent?—it's not that there's particular rules about it, and everyone who has a rule book on parenting probably knows right away to throw it out. It's just the things you do everyday and you guide it by a particular philosophy—and some people call it morals or a moral compass, but others may call it different things. It's cultural, it varies. But it's still things which guide you and say, "This is wrong and this is right, and I believe in education, I believe my child should have opportunity to be…"

But at the end of the day you're having to do day-by-day, hour-by-hour, the best you can. And at the end, hopefully, you have a wonderful family, and similarly you might just one day wake up and find you have a wonderful business.

Unfortunately, you can't codify this. What is helpful, though, is to give you the tools by which you can self-analyze, the tools by which you can actually start to think: "I'm at the crossroads, which way should I go?" But I don't think it's quite so simple.

I'm afraid I'm not giving you a very good answer here, but it is partly process, it is partly intuition—and that you just gain over the years.

By the way, the teaching method that everyone uses in business thinking is really just storytelling, and that's what I do with you, right? I mean, we just love to tell the stories of what happened in the past, tell stories of good and bad, and these are the things which actually convey these rules, if you will, these fables, these wonderful anecdotes. They convey these lessons. Because we don't have the right formulas yet to say that this is how [things should be done.] Because if we did, frankly, then we wouldn't need managers. We could just have a computer run the company.

Dan: I think some of the companies seem like they have tried that.

Horace: I think Google is probably the closest to getting to that, because they really believe that if you're so data-driven, you have so much data you can put a lot of faith in it, then it does begin to sort of lead you.

I worry a bit about that because I think that the data you tend to have doesn't really tell you everything you need to know. Sometimes you need to step outside of the comfort zone. But when you do have terabytes of data—think about what they know, think about how much information they have. You stand in the meeting and you say, "Well, look, my intuition tells me what we should ignore all that." Then you've got some other people saying, "Come on, look at the evidence! This is the way we should go."

What is it that Steve Jobs said? You can only connect dots about the past. You can't connect them about the future. Data about the future doesn't exist. Data about the past is only good if there's a sort of continuation of the past. But the job of the manager is to realize when that stops: "When is the world going to change dramatically for us?" This pivot point, I think, that can never be replaced by a computer. That is pure guts, and even if you train a computer to recognize patterns of change, I think they still will need a courageous type to throw the dice.

Dan: This has been so fun to think of it in these terms. Seriously, if you're listening to this right now, you know how they say six degrees of separation? You've got to tell people in the big ways, to listen to this, shake things up.

Horace: Well, I don't know. I can't say much to that, but I would say that the problem... If I may, just another few minutes...

Dan: Of course.

Horace: ...just talk about the process of the way companies are usually trying to get problems solved with someone helping, right? And if you think about the consulting business, that's how it's structured, that you bring in somebody who has fresh eyes, hopefully, and you present them the problem. It's an amazing story that actually management consulting exists at all, because if you think that the people who know most about what the company is doing and how it should work and what all the constraints are and what the competitors are, are people in that company.

The thing is when consultants are hired it's usually because companies don't think their own people are good enough to solve their own problems, right? And that's always a little bit depressing to me. The first thing that the consultant does is canvasses opinion. They go and speak to as many people as they can, which actually creates great billing because you have so much time you spend doing that, and basically all they're doing is trying to get up to speed with what the company is doing, which is, again, something that the insiders already know.

So the consulting process is really, to me, symptomatic of a lack of faith in one's own resources and a lack of imagination, if you will. Because if you hire the person to give you a new direction, why didn't you think of it yourself?

So I'm being very harsh and critical of consulting, but you can kind of see how fresh vision or fresh eyes are helpful. So if I was engaged with a company, probably my objective would be not to listen to anything they had, [and instead] rely as much as possible on public information, because the public information is not going to get polluted with bias that the company may have internally.

I think the other way that you can shake things up is to think of the consulting not as a problem-solving engagement, but rather as an educational engagement. We go there to teach the management how to think for themselves. They should hire you as a teacher, not so much as a puzzle solver. Because the puzzle solving is something… there are far better people in your company who know how to solve that puzzle.

This is a little bit—what I maybe call asymmetric or an approach that is a little bit disruptive: You rethink of yourself from being a consultant to being more of an educator. And that has all kinds of wrong connotations, but I'm sorry, I'm going to have to still use that phrase, because I think it's correct.

People dismiss corporate training and all the other stuff as being time wasteful and a boondoggle. But, really, at the end of the day, we don't get anywhere without learning. So I don't know what else to call it except education.

So that's a simple formula. You just tell people and you teach through example and anecdote and storytelling. And you engage the audience to tell their stores, and then you say, "By the way, have we seen a pattern here?" You know, humans are great at pattern recognition. Hell, we see patterns where there are none. You know, like faces on the moon or in the clouds.

So we're very good at that, and one can just try to say, "Okay, now I've taught you, go off and fix your own problems."

In Memory of Robert Boyle
Posted September 28th, 2011 as The Critical Path Episode #8

Horace and Dan talk about why CEOs are paid so much and what analysis has come to mean in equities research and the value of cross-pollination between the camps that form around technology companies.

Horace: We had change of leadership at HP, and it's funny how that came on the back of a change of leadership at Yahoo! and a change of leadership at a bunch of places. Going back to last year's Nokia [change], and Eric Schmidt has left [as Google CEO], and of course Steve Jobs has left his job, and we had some turnover at [the] Microsoft top level, but not the CEO.

Actually, that got me to think a little bit about what's going on with CEOs in general, tech CEOs in particular. But it's one thing, by the way, that intersects this thinking: A lot of people got upset during the financial crisis about how much executives were paid, especially in the banking sector. But in general, tech people don't get blamed for being overly paid. But you do have a certain sense that there's a big gap between the pay of top executives and the average worker.

What I started to think about was, given all these turnover in the executives, it's a funny phenomenon to me in the first place that we have executives treated in such a deferential manner. They're given so much. Not just compensation, but they're given so much responsibility and so much is placed on their shoulders. You see, the thing is, it's a free market, right? If companies felt that they could get away with paying a lot less, I'm sure there are plenty of candidates they could pick from. The question really ought to be… It's not that the CEOs are forcing anyone to pay them, right? I mean, yes, once they're in power they might have some influence in that regard, but a board is supposed to oversee this.

So a board, or whoever hires a CEO—when [Leo] Apotheker left [HP], he had only been on the job 11 months, and yet he walked away with 20 plus million at least. It's a parachute that they get paid for leaving.

Who negotiated these things? I mean, these are standard terms. And how is that possible? Why does this happen? You can't blame the CEO. He got the best deal he could get. The question is, really, "Why did anybody on the board actually agree to the terms, as they did?"

So one thing I want to point out is that along our conversations so far I've made the claim that in many ways management isn't really "responsible" entirely for the failure of a company. [But conversely] nor should they be rewarded entirely because of the success of a company. Now, that frame of thinking is a little bit incomplete.

141

What I mean is that there isn't [an] if-and-only-if relationship. In other words, if the company succeeds it's because of management and only because of management. So I'm saying management contributes but is not the exclusive cause of failure or success.

So the problem is, there isn't this perfect relationship of cause and effect. What I'm trying to point out is that many times companies are faced with disruptive change and, actually—no matter who's in charge—they would tend to fail because their hands are tied. They have to deal with forces beyond their control… In fact, they cannot change a company fast enough to the threat that's being faced. And secondly, the company's business model is so fragile or so much under threat that they can't go and replace it quickly enough.

So, that's why typically these companies fail. We're seeing that in real time now with RIM and Nokia, as I mentioned before.

Looping back on the question of compensation, what you're seeing with compensation is the fact that the boards in general—I think society, in general, [and] markets, if you will—are placing a huge weight on these individuals and they really treat them as all-powerful magicians, that can pull things out of their hats and make things happen, and when they don't succeed, well, you know, they're fired but their given a nice compensation because they had opportunity costs.

So my point is, though, that the problem with CEO compensation is that we believe them to be magicians when they really aren't. And the realization that you don't need to have a magician as a governor of an enterprise is what's going to change the relationship between society, let's say, and these people in charge. This is really the fundamental problem, I think, with the way companies are governed, because it's a non-scientific method being applied, because it's very much driven by gut instinct. [In essence] you have to trust at some point, that you're going to put all of your hopes and dreams with this person.

Imagine if society was run that way. Well, maybe politics is a lot like that. But it seems to me like we have a long way to go to really rationalize this. And once management becomes much more predictable, much more scientific, then we can step back from affording individuals so much credit and so much responsibility for failure and success.

So that's kind of my only really novel thought of the day about CEOs. But I think the debate is a little bit gone off into populism or gone off into the wrong direction and we should be thinking really about how to better govern companies. And better tools.

Dan: These guys, they just need to get you in there for a week. All these companies should say, "Get Horace in there." Just give you a desk and a place to set up base, and they just have you go around and kick things into shape.

That's what I predict. I predict a year from now you won't be able to do the show anymore because you'll just be spending a week at a different company every week, 52 weeks a year, no breaks. I'm just saying. Going on record.

Horace: Well, I appreciate that, but I don't know. To be honest, I don't know if I'm really breaking any new ground here. I think there's quite a lot of people that thought about this. Actually, again, I often don't give credit enough to those who have come before or are even contemporary thinkers on the subject, because the scholarship necessary to really defend a lot of these theories is done, the heavy lifting is done by researchers.

Dan: The segue is that you have a book that you might like to recommend.

Horace: I'm not a big consumer of business books, but there's one book I think has been more influential than others, and that's the works of Clay Christensen. He started off with *Innovator's Dilemma* in, I think, ''97, '98, and then followed up with *Innovator's Solution*. You know, I think *The Solution* is a better book because it actually prescribes an answer or a set of answers, rather than just being descriptive, which was the first book. And being prescriptive you also include the descriptive part by necessity. So I think the second book embodies a lot of the first as well.

So that's what influences really almost all of the things I talk about. I mean, job-to-be-done theory, modularity versus integration, whether a company is over-serving or not. All these phrases and thoughts came from Christensen. And I should say that he was my professor. I was in his class in my first year at business school in 1994, and then I took him second year as well for some optional classes. Unfortunately, he had to leave because he had to stand in for the dean, who had just left.

Anyway, the point is that we go way back. You know, at first I didn't really "get" the book. The book came out after I graduated, and I didn't really get it until I was actually experiencing what he was talking about. This is really the most important thing. That this theory is, in a way, it's entertaining. It's valuable just to read on its own, but until it affects you personally you don't quite internalize it, I think.

It affected me in 2004 when we were at Nokia and tried to think through how to make the company shift gears. You know, I brought his theory into the company and I tried very hard to push it through the powers that be, and I faced—like one of the chapters would say, that you're going to have resistance and the reasons are X, Y and Z—I faced all those things and I said, "Wow, this is really deep and very correct."

So, going back and iterating over time I got deeper into it and I became, let's say, a devoted disciple of it. Sometimes you may disagree, even. You know, with anything so fundamental in terms of theory—of a new theory being developed—sometimes the authors themselves have to adjust it as they go along because all theories need to be tested. Sometime there might be disagreement with the author about things. And in fact there are schools of thought branching off and people are testing it in different ways. And to this day it's probably, in my opinion—and it's a humble opinion because I really don't have a lot of data points in terms of theory, there's a lot of business books out there, and I haven't read them all—but my humble opinion is that it is in fact the most important book out there in terms of business theory, if maybe not the only one. I can't say that for sure, but most theories are very very shallow compared to what this one offers, and it's been tested a lot.

So, I'm just giving out an endorsement of this book that I really feel is as important as any seminal work in the new field of science. In fact, this castle where we were staying [last week] was the birth place of Henry Boyle, who is the founder of chemistry. It was pretty cosmic to be in the same place where the father of chemistry was born. In fact, he invented the word *analysis*, which is amazing.

That got me thinking also about what it is. What analysis has become as far as business, and maybe we can touch on that topic in the next few minutes. But I want to give you some time if you want to mention any other thoughts you may have that we can talk about.

Dan: Well, there's so many things. I mean, first of all, it's my job just to try to keep up with you here. But, no, I think, there's so many [potential topics]. Well, you mentioned earlier how many things have happened just since the last show. I guess we worried that maybe we wouldn't have enough to cover on a week-to-week basis, but just look at what's gone on in the last week. Look at just what happened today.

I don't know if you were paying attention to the announcements that Amazon had this morning, but there was an article that you may have mentioned or linked to on Twitter that was on AllThingsD, saying the iPhone has an 89 percent retention rate, which is something I wanted to get your take on.

There was another article, probably because it talks about you, that you would probably not have mentioned, but a friend of the show, Phillip Elmer-DeWitt, writing over on Fortune, says that Apple and Wall Street, six-quarters of lousy estimates. And it says [paraphrasing], "For as long as we've been tracking them, the bloggers"—and he's talking about you—"have trounced the pros."

Horace: That's exactly what I wanted to bring up, because I left it hanging with you on this question of analysis. I was thinking on my way back yesterday, last night, I was walking a little bit from the bus that took me home, and I was thinking because I had been reading during the day. There was this announcement from JP Morgan Asia—not [an] announcement, it was sort of a note written by an analyst working for JP Morgan in Asia—that there had been a 25 percent cut in iPad production. Then there was a dispute about whether that was significant, if that was true. People confirmed it, that it was true, but then the question was about significance, and then JP Morgan's analysts in New York said, "We don't agree with the conclusions of our colleagues in Asia."

The analyst in Asia had been… his job was mostly to follow the supply chain. You know, the folks building the components that go into the products Apple makes. The New York analysts were following Apple directly and they would see things in a different way. That's normal. I think disagreement is actually very healthy.

But what troubled me more was that analysts, as far as these sell-side analysts [go], what they get headlines from and I think gets a lot of attention is investigation of non-public information or digging… I mean, the problem I have with supply-chain analysis, if I may say this word in that respect—which I don't think is proper—but the idea of picking up data points. There are two problems.

Number one, you are getting probably too far away from the actual business to understand what the impact is. These are second or third levels away from the product that's shipping in the stores. So, supply-chain analysis has a huge elasticity… what changes at one end doesn't necessarily reflect in the other end because there's so many other inventories in-between.

But the second real problem is one of motives. I mean, anyone who speaks about this to an analyst over beer somewhere in Taiwan or who knows where, what are their motives? I believe, and I think that the SEC would argue similarly, that if you are contractually bound not to reveal information, then when you get that information it's actually inside info, even though you haven't actually broken any contract yourself, right?

So the problem is that I'm suspicious. I'm not accusing anyone here of breaking any laws, but I'm just suggesting that I don't know what the motives of such a person who would want to reveal information that their employer, their contracts and so on [are] working on. I found myself very despondent. "Has analysis come to this? Has analysis of a company come to the point of how much information can we extract from someone who doesn't have perhaps the right motives to release it?"

You know, people call it all kinds of euphemisms: "Chatter," and saying that these are rumors, or saying "my sources" [or] "unidentified sources" are saying this and that. And journalism has historically had rules about publishing information like this. So these rules have broken down over time.

I think the problem with analysis is that you really need to add value by thinking through the implications of something like this, because data is all around you. I'm not painting all analysts this way. I just think that too much emphasis is being placed on bits of data which actually turn out to be probably of dubious value and motives.

That's got me thinking, the fact that I was in the birthplace of the father of the word *analysis*, and birth of chemistry, and other things which enrich us today. And so I'm maybe a little bit disappointed that that debate hasn't risen to the right level as far as how to evaluate businesses today.

That's by example. Hopefully I can push a little bit in the right direction and say that we need to really apply all of our intelligence and skills to making this work of a higher quality. And one thing I've begun doing, actually, is I've decided to branch out and apply it as much as I can. If I'm going to start looking at other companies than Apple, [then] using the same methodology of research.

Dan: How do you pick those companies?

Horace: Well, the usual suspects are the first that come to mind. I want to do Google and I want to do Microsoft. And I want to be able to speak with the same confidence about them as I do about Apple, because I've studied their financials and I've studied their management. Sometimes they come up, but I don't have every data point in my mind, or even in my own collection of files, to say with authority that I believe absolutely for sure Apple is succeeding in operating in a better way, for example.

One of my collaborators in the site is Dirk Schmidt, and he has begun doing more comparative analysis. So Apple's peer group of technology companies are all being compared. We're comparing things now, and that requires huge data sets. So what I'm trying to do is expand breadth and depth in all of these new directions.

Ultimately, maybe we need to bring in more help to do that, because there just isn't enough time for me to do it, for he and I to do these things. So what we might end up with is, for example, an expert who can write about the company and do all… You know, every quarter when the earnings come, that they actually update their data sets and then we all combine them and publish together. That would be a dream of mine. It's essentially what other big houses do, right? They have a team of analysts, each one specializing in a particular company or set of companies or industries.

Anyway, this is the evolution of a concept of analysis, of sourcing analysis from intelligent people who are willing to contribute on a volunteer basis and will do so because it enhances their knowledge firstly and, secondly, their reputation. And they become basically, if not celebrities, at least brands online that can be valued and monetized in some way later on.

Dan: So when can we expect this kind of analysis to start?

Horace: I can't make promises, unfortunately. A lot of these things end up just filling up blank spaces of time.

Dan: Right.

Horace: And if you don't have the space of time, then you can't deliver. But the good news is that what used to take weeks and months of research can be done in hours now. We have all these companies' financials and you don't have to go to the library for that. You'd get it online and it's usually in the format that you can consume, it's downloadable. It's Excel and you can copy/paste that into your own tools. So I'm confident that we can [do this.] I'm going to start looking at doing some time series.

Again, the main thing is that I like to get these things going back significant time frames, right? Because I want to see patterns, recognize patterns. So I want to pull in all the financials for Microsoft going back a significant number of years, pre-iPhone, let's say. iPhone era is 2007, so a little before then.

By the way, the problem also is that these businesses change, so the line items in the income statement change and so you want to be making sure you have [an] apples-to-apples comparison.

Anyway, there's a bound, you can't go back 20 years, but we'll try to pull in some data. And then start to look at it the same way we look at Apple. Look at, for example, growth, and look at profitability by segment. I mean, some of these things we know intuitively about Microsoft. When I was speaking about Windows, we know Windows is an enormously profitable business and we know that the online business is not profitable. But exactly how much and how do we do compare and contrast with say, for example, Apple, which is our framework right now. And I'd like to do the same for Google. I'd like to take Google apart and say, "This is where the money comes from."

Imagine a chart which is—like my famous, not so famous maybe, but this is a standard chart I do—which is a stacked-area chart, which shows, for example, all the product lines of Apple. Because it's stacked the whole thing together is all of the product lines. It's the whole sales of the company.

Imagine if you did that for Microsoft or Google. In Apple's case you have significant color differences between the Mac and the iPhone and the iPod and the iPad. But if you did the same thing for Google what would it look like? Would it be monochromatic because it's one thing that gets all the income and there's invisible Android [and] invisible services. I have an idea in my mind of what this chart would look like, but I'm thinking now it's time to do it, time to actually put it together. And then we could do a nice posting showing, "Well, here's three [companies]." And when you look at them the same way, with the same sort of color palette and then we say, "Here's what these three companies actually look like." With your own eyes you'll be able to see who's diversified, who's growing faster, who's doing a good job at balancing multiple business models.

This is where the value of what I do expands beyond being just an Apple and mobile site.

So, these are things I'm working on. I don't know how we got on this subject.

Dan: I think we got on it because you, as one of the bloggers Phillip Elmer-DeWitt was talking about, again and again getting it right.

Horace: What I'm wondering, for example, is—because I don't have time to pay attention to every technology out there in terms of what people are saying about it, I try to keep up via Twitter with people who are in the Microsoft world, and I try to keep up with the Google world as well—but I'd like to finally become, myself, aware of this in a deep way. I do wonder sometimes if there aren't really people like myself or John [Gruber] or Phillip, who are as deep in their respective companies. Is there someone out there who's the absolute zealot for Amazon? Who's going to know, who has millions of people listening to his every word about what's happening with Amazon? Or Microsoft?

I could imagine maybe there being a lot of zealots about Google, but I don't know whether we're living in a bubble of analysis that's only really been done for Apple. Hopefully, by doing this I'll bump into these people and so we can finally figure out and share. Because these worlds need to mingle. We need to mingle together and figure things out together. Not as camps which say, "Well I'm in the Apple camp and I don't want anything to do with the Google camp."

I don't want to invite that sort of division. I want to have a discourse between them, that we can establish at least the same vocabulary. So we could say, for example, we're going to discuss it as a financial thing. Many people who come to my site whenever I discuss Google will probably argue the case of openness. Or they'll argue the technical value of Google technologies, which is fine. But if my argument is about the financials, I'd want to see an equal argument coming from that side as well.

So people tend to just talk past each other. You have people who argue that Apple is successful because of its profitability, other people argue that Google is successful because of marketshare or overall number of users. But let's just set the framework to be the same, let's talk about the same things. If it is about business-model evolution and disruption, we should all talk the same language and not try to be dogmatic.

That's just part of the thinking. Yes, this is all in the framework of analysis, and where can it go from here. I think my site and what I do has been an experiment in not just sourcing of the data but public relay of the data and the publishing of everything and the invitation of review of everything in a public way. I mean, these [professional] analysts that we talk about that are debating these things, we're only hearing secondhand. They aren't able to Tweet—or maybe they are—but I don't know if they are doing it. They're not able to discuss hypotheses. They're not typically putting out their… I can't link to these reports. These reports are not online. How can you be a member of the human race today, as an author of anything that you call analysis and not have a URL associated with your work, not having an ability to publicly discuss these matters?

I'm not saying that they don't want to. It's probably because of their organizations that don't let them, because they have all these walls that they built around these products. These walls are there to protect some source of income. But you're not getting smarter standing behind walls. You need to get out there and become part of a community, and I'm sure they would argue, "Well, there's an internal community." But that's a very small community compared to what's in the world out there. And, yes, you're going to take a lot of lumps with that as you're going to get beat up. And you're going to get a lot of noise as well, but unless and until we get to the point where business can be analyzed in a collaborative fashion…

I don't know if Apple is the only galaxy in this universe where there are actually people discussing these things and we have Phillip at *Fortune* collating or collecting this data, putting it one place so people can then actually see a score and performance, at least hold it up and say who's done well and who hasn't.

I don't know if such a thing exists for Microsoft. Are there forty, fifty analysts of Microsoft's performance every quarter, debating online who's done well, who hasn't? Maybe there are. Maybe there's one for Google as well. I just don't know.

I'd love to hear back about that and say, "If it isn't, let's build it, let's do that. Let's become good at knowing all these other companies as well as we know Apple, and then we can speak with authority and we won't be called blind or the "F" word about what we do." So that's all I'm saying.

Dan: A lot to think about.

Horace: I wish we could have talked about moving the ball forward. I just had this thing with the CEOs, which I don't think…

Dan: I think it's great. It's insightful. This is what people tune in for. This is exactly what people tune in for.

Horace: Yes. This has been more like a wish list. You know, dreaming on my part, saying I wish we could do this, I wish we could do that. I tend not to just do that and wish, I intend to actually do something about it and I will write and publish. But maybe it's a call to action. You know, it's a call to action out there to people, to communicate, saying, "Look, you're missing [out] on this community, or you can tune in to this or that." That's partly what I hope from getting the word out there.

I think there are people out there who do this, who have an ear towards that audience or towards that community, and are careful to be aware of what's happening in various camps. Technically, that's a very smart thing to do, right? You wouldn't want to be a developer and say, "I will not listen to anything that's happening in the technology area." If you're coding in Objective-C, you don't put your fingers in your ears whenever you hear Java, right?

So I would say that we need to be the same way about the analysis of the business of Apple and the business of devices and not just point and laugh. And sometimes you do laugh anyway, but it better be funny.

Getting to Know You

Posted October 5th, 2011 as The Critical Path Episode #9

Dan and Horace talk about some of the more profound implications of "intelligent assistance" in personal devices, both in terms of business models and in terms of industry dynamics. Getting assistance is an implied bargain we all make as Internet citizens, but what do we pay for that assistance?

Dan: How are you?

Horace: Good. I'm recovered from yesterday, but I haven't quite absorbed everything yet. And there's so much to read.

Dan: For those who don't know yet what Horace is talking about, yesterday was October 4th, 2011, the iPhone 4S was announced at a special Apple event. And here we are. It's not quite 24 hours later, and there is so much to talk about here that's not specific… We're not talking about, like, hardware and things like that. But you're talking about industry-wide stuff.

Horace: Right. So to try to put things in the perspective of what's happening strategically, what's happening competitively, and trying to see the patterns behind these announcements. It's more about where people are going and where companies are going, where companies are changing strategies, if they are changing.

Dan: Right.

Horace: And I think it's actually interesting that there is quite a bit happening—given the rapid-fire announcements we're hearing every other week almost—that there is a strategic shift happening. We've seen management changes at HP, we've seen management changes even at Google. Something dramatic, I think, is happening with Amazon, in terms of what they're doing with the Kindle product.

Dan: Right.

Horace: What I tend to do also in times like this is I go back in history and look at what happened when another strategic shift—which we see the benefit of today—how was that received? So I'm analyzing the analysts. I'm analyzing the market and how it behaves in response to these events.

You know, when there is a keynote event, Apple posts it on iTunes.

Dan: Right.

Horace: The latest one is uploaded now, and I'm going to watch it. But you can go back and look at all the other events. So if you go back in your iTunes podcast history for Apple events, you'll see that they started at about 2007, with the iPhone actually. I think that was the first one that

151

they uploaded. And what I did is, I went back and I looked at every date that there was such an event, and I tried to understand what happened to the stock market. Because there is this interesting effect where typically there is a sell-off on the day of a major Apple announcement. So I was trying to see if there is any correlation between the significance of that event and the drop in value in Apple shares.

Dan: Right.

Horace: Unfortunately it's not clear-cut. The iPhone itself led to a significant rise in the share price—and I think that's probably the most profound event—but at the same time it was easily perceived. It was easily understood as important.

Other things aren't so clear. iCloud, I think, is a fundamental shift. Now, with Siri. This is a fundamental shift. I think markets will discount that.

Dan: No, it does take time. And you're certainly the kind of person who has a different perspective, I think, than most. You're willing to sort of hang back and look at things, and, you know, people joke that you always come out with a chart for it. But those charts, those things take a lot of time.

Horace: Well, you have to have data, and you have to go fetch it, and hopefully it's available. But, you know, things are a lot easier than they used to be. I mean, this used to require a department. It used to require a team.

Dan: Right.

Horace: And now we can do it individually. We can do it all with our computers at home, and we have all this wonderful public access to information through the Internet. That's where I am. And I'm also having to read in real time what other people are writing because I don't want to dismiss that.

Dan: Right.

Horace: So there is a pattern. I've been watching this space for about two, three years, if not more, and there is a pattern of disappointment. Usually, before the disappointment, there is a pattern of excessive expectations. And then there is a deflation. And then there is a recovery, when people realize what's happened. And, usually, it goes up afterwards, in terms of sentiment, and the company's value if you want to measure that as a stock price.

But you have to strip away other factors like the macroeconomic conditions in 2008, for example. A lot of important things were happening with the iPhone. But everything was collapsing. That was actually an interesting time in 2008.

Anyway, do you have any kind of open questions you'd like to tackle?

Dan: Well, I do. A lot of people right now, Horace, are focusing on… They're looking at kind of two things right now. If they're super-geeks, they're saying, "Oh, cool, you know, we get a new camera, we get iOS 5, we get, you know, twice the performance." They're very much focused on the hardware of the iPhone 4S, for example. Yesterday on the show, you were talking about some of—and you touched on it here somewhat—the longer-ranging implications of what I guess you would call a digital-personal assistant, Siri, who you were going to be asking questions to and giving information. And the example, of course, that was used… I guess it was Phil Schiller up there, who was saying to Siri, the personal assistant that's come on the new iOS 5 for the iPhone 4S, you say, "Oh, when I'm done with work, remind me to call my wife." Well, there is the implication of what that actually means, but there has been a lot of discussion, a lot of speculation, that it isn't just your iPhone that knows this. It's actually the services that Apple provides, and you were talking about [how] we're starting to get a feeling for what actually is going on in that big data center in North Carolina. That's what I want to talk about now, about the whole… You did talk about that on the show yesterday. But that's such an important topic, and you were saying that this is how Apple is actually attacking—I think it was even your word —"attacking" Google or "going up against" Google. I'd love to hear more of what you think about that.

Horace: Right. This is just a little bit embryonic as a thought, but I believe that with the iPhone, and with devices in general, we're seeing a complete shift in the way we users are being productized. And I made this point that there's an old adage from advertising, that "If you're not buying something, you're the thing being sold." And these are like clichés now. But, indeed, that's how Google operates. That's what drives Facebook. That's what drives Twitter. That's what drives even Amazon, in a way, because, through affinity algorithms they are able to sell you things, so essentially you are a product to them as well.

And so the logic of a lot of what the Internet is doing—the Internet's primary fuel for growth—is the knowledge about the user. It's that knowledge that's being productized and used to create commerce in the form of sales of some kind that ultimately drives the value of the whole Internet. And this is quite a profound idea. We think of [the Internet] as a public service. We think of it as a benefit. And it is a benefit.

[But there's a] tradeoff we are making, as users, in that we are saying, "I will grant you a peek into my world in exchange for access to all this wonderful information, and all these other services that this web offers."

And, you know, it's nothing new. I think humans have—or, we should say, citizens—have had a dialogue like this with government for a long time. The question of, "What am I offered in exchange for information about myself that I'm willing to share?" The census is the first time that information about people has been bartered with governments. And the census began in, I believe, 18th century, not in the U.S., but in Europe. There was a bargain struck: "You tell me about yourself and, in exchange, I'm going to offer you more government services."

Later on it happened with taxation. It happened with service in [the] Armed Forces, that people were essentially giving up things and getting something in return. And that's been going on for centuries. Now we're at the point where we're doing this bartering—this trading—with commercial entities, not with governments. We're saying things about ourselves and being offered a bargain in return.

The problem I see, though, is that because of the very rapid change happening in technology and bandwidth—in the power of the device, the power of the data itself growing exponentially—that it's changing quite a bit the dynamics of power. Of where the power resides, I should say. You know, the evolution of value chains. So without getting too bogged down in the verbiage and the buzzwords, what it boils down to, I think, is that these devices with their sensors and the pervasiveness, and the constant companionship they offer...

Dan: Right.

Horace: ...It's always with you. It's always on. It's always broadcasting something, and it's always absorbing something from you, whether it's your location, whether it's your communications. All manner of things. Because these things have sensors on them that computers never had. So all of that is going and being fed into a massive database somewhere. So mapping, for example.

You know, Apple got into some kind of a controversy with the fact that there were files on the device which were available to snoopers which would tell something about where your location had been, approximately. Why was Apple collecting this? Everybody was all upset about it. Well, they were collecting it because they were building a mountain of knowledge. That's what I call it. A mountain, a huge amount of data.

Dan: Yeah.

Horace: They were using it to improve their mapping data and to improve their coverage data for operators. And Google was doing the same thing. So all these little signals are being all captured and accumulated, and databases are being built. And Google has been doing it longer than anyone. What I think is happening is that the game is—I don't want to trivialize it, call it a game—but basically the platform issue isn't so much that the device and the software are the locus of value.

In other words, the debate has been, "Well, you make money on hardware. You make money on software. You make money with the hardware, but in fact invest in software." And all these debates about [the appropriateness of] business models of modularity versus integration versus... Your Samsung and Nokia model versus your Apple model versus your Microsoft/Google model, and all these things.

154

I think that's actually only part of the picture. The real picture is what happens with the data that's being collected through these platforms, through these devices, that's being then assembled and managed and massaged, and sold through a data center that captures it. So, the cloud.

Dan: Right.

Horace: So I think when you couple the device with the cloud, it becomes an interesting dynamic. And I call this a meta-platform. It's the end-to-end engine of knowledge capture and commerce. And now Apple is going to be in the messaging business with iMessage.

Dan: Right. Yeah.

Horace: It's going to be in the mapping business. It is already in the ad business. It's now going to be in the personal-assistant business. And by the way, this would be interesting discussion to go off on the side: This is the beginning of the device as a personal assistant. You know, it's going to be a bad one at first.

Dan: Right.

Horace: But that's great, because...

Dan: But this is the first time it seems like it might actually work. It might actually do what people want.

Horace: Normally, I would be very skeptical because I've seen— we've seen AI [artificial intelligence] and we've seen language recognition and understanding. These have been Holy Grails for such a long time. Decades, right? And the AI business going back to the '60s. And they've always failed. And now, the only reason we give it any credence at all is because Apple is doing it, and Apple usually doesn't fire stuff out that is half-baked.

We just give them the benefit of the doubt. But, you know, it could fail. We don't know. But if it even is slightly good, it's probably going to be good in small domains. Just asking simple questions. But over time, it's going to get better. And it's going to get better because it's going to collect more knowledge, right? It's going to get smarter. The more it's used, the smarter it gets.

So while that's happening, my expectation is that the device will become suddenly something new. And I've always expected that the iPhone at age 5 needs to be redefined in terms of what what it is. It has to go through a fundamental shift in not just positioning but the job it's hired to do.

Dan: Right. And different...

Horace: Because if it doesn't, it's going to be commoditized by me-too products.

Dan: And not apparently... not apparently by changing the form factor. Not that way, but by changing its role in your life, in a way.

Horace: Of course. That goes without saying. I think form factor is not an innovation at this point already. That would be only a question of appealing to vanity, or appealing to some other reasons to buy a phone other than making it useful. It's about also doing all kinds of aspirational things. But in this case, I think that for the larger picture, where Apple needs to be competitive against low-end disruption, and competitive against new market disruptions that are inevitable, I think Apple needs to redefine what the goal is, while protecting its low end.

And it's doing that by essentially... One of the other stories that I think is under-reported is that Apple now, finally, has a portfolio of phones. They have three, with variants. So, we're looking already at a price point from zero up to several hundred, depending on whether you want your product unlocked. And so, every hundred dollars, we have an iPhone for you. And that happened with the iPod. The iPod started at $49, and it was interesting that at a point in time you could lay out the entire portfolio of iPods and from $50 up to $500. There was a product at every $50, or maybe it was $100. I don't recall. But it was basically very, very reliable that [price range].

So the question for you was, "Which iPod should I get?" The answer would be, "Well, how much money do you have?" Because there was one for you. I think that's happening with the iPhone, and it's something that is not quite yet absorbed as a notion.

But, anyway, the point being that after five years the iPhone finally now is on a new trajectory of being not good enough. Not only is it not good enough as a computer—and I think perhaps it never will be because of the screen [size] issue, and that maybe is a job that the iPad will be given—but over time I think the iPhone will get better at that. Never good enough, but I think it's going to try to improve.

But now it's not good enough on the notion of being a personal assistant. And we're going to have to see how that evolves. You might end up using the iPhone on the desktop along with your computer. So when you don't want to look things up you push a button and you say, "Hey, can you look this up for me?" Just like you would a real assistant. Just like you would ask someone who helps you in the office, "Hey, can you just book this meeting for me?"

It actually would be faster to do that than to open up the application that you need to book this thing. I think especially these small jobs that you would love to have an assistant for, [Siri] will just lubricate your life. And this new job to be done, that they're assigning to the iPhone, is really exciting, and it might give them enough room to grow at the high end of the business for still quite some time. And that's going to be an interesting dynamic. Because, again, how asymmetric is that to existing competitors? What do you need to make that happen?

And now we go back to the original question of this meta-platform. Very few companies can put this together. Very few companies could even put a phone together, right? In having their own platform, right? So you have to have your own platform, your own hardware people, your own distribution, which is hard to build on the global scale, and that's hard enough for the Samsungs of the world to do. Right? They've tried and many times failed. It's hard for Microsoft to do because they're not yet doing hardware. So they're relying on partners.

So what I'm saying is that here is Apple stepping up, doing these things, and then it's also saying, "We're going to build a coupled system where you need both a large back end and a very powerful front end." And this is going to solve deep problems that people have. And in so doing, they're going to get to know you better. And in getting to know you better, they're going to probably offer you things that you didn't think you needed yet. This is the whole question: We don't know if they will. But I suspect, like with Genius on iTunes, I think they're gaining all this knowledge about how people consume media. They're learning so much.

You know, I began composing this tweet as we began this show. I was thinking about algorithms. The algorithms that Google depends on for its existence—and it does depend on algorithms, right?—They are fundamentally statistics-based, right? They get a lot of data.

Dan: Right.

Horace: And they do a lot of correlations to determine how to place ads and so on.

It's interesting. So then you have another class of algorithms that Amazon uses, which are affinity analysis. So they're looking at patterns of consumption. Then you have Apple stepping in and saying, "We're bringing in artificial intelligence as our algorithmic foundation, if you will." And it's interesting that they're the ones coming up with this. Of course, that's not to say the others don't use AI or Apple doesn't use affinity or statistics. But fundamentally, I think there's this clustering of competencies that, as an old comp-sci guy, I'm finding fascinating, that this is happening. And I would love to explore this further.

And the other one out there is Facebook. I mean, Facebook, I don't know if they have an algorithmic approach. I suppose it would be some kind of a database analysis, because in Facebook, you tell it pretty much everything it wants to know. Facebook doesn't require a lot of inference because you're just giving the data. But they might need to do some interesting analysis as well.

But all of these businesses are predicated on the notion of getting to know you. And that knowledge will be sold. Or used internally to offer you upgrades or offer you better products. And that's what I'm thinking, again: This requires certain abilities and certain money and resources and priorities and strategies. All these things. And you ask yourself, "Who has those things, and who doesn't? Who is going to get them, and how are they going to fill in the gaps?" Facebook, for example: It has excellent-quality data. But it doesn't have as much control over the front end of the business, right?

So, case in point. You know, you may have read the rumors or the innuendo that Facebook doesn't yet have an iPad app.

Dan: Right. And there has been discussions about this, that there is some kind of hidden war between...

Horace: But why? You know, this is the tip of the iceberg. Why does Facebook feel that this is such a politically important question? Why are they playing games with HP, or whomever? Why do they hire a guy to write it, and the guy quit because he felt frustrated that they weren't launching this thing.

Dan: Never coming out, yeah.

Horace: It's a fascinating little microcosm of what's happening because here you have... I mean, why not just build an app? Because it's so important. That app is the way they're going to capture information from people who are on the new platform and the new domain. And that is becoming a focal point for Facebook as a strategic question. And I think Facebook, there's been rumors about them getting into the device business, or the platform business. I think WebOS being for sale—that's another interesting hot potato there, that WebOS is not going to be acquired because somebody wants to be in the platform licensing business, it's going to be acquired because they're going to be able to control this whole meta-platform question. My initial guess was it was going to be Amazon as the frontrunner there, and I thought Facebook would make a bid, although Facebook may just not be a mature-enough company to be putting all of these things together. I don't know. This is speculative.

I would not bet that WebOS would be bought by a Samsung or any of the device guys. I think this is one of these assets that is going to get plugged into a meta-platform-coupled system.

So these are the major trends and questions that, I think, the community of analysts out there ought to be looking at. Because it's going to be in three or four years from now, I think these is going to be the grand game that will be played out for the Internet as a whole, that the Internet becomes divided into these device/back-end ecosystems, and it's a really mysterious thing. The more I think about it, the more amazed I am that it could get to that point. But everything is pointing in that directionSo, anyway, there's a lot to think about here.

Dan: Yes.

Horace: And I apologize. I'm just rambling because the thing with these questions that are algorithms—are server farms and clouds, are devices, platforms—are they all really interrelated? And business models and this sort of data mining that's happening... The more I think about it, I think there is something there.

Dan: And you think—what you're saying is that this is all very, very carefully planned, very carefully engineered, very carefully... This isn't something that happened by accident.

Horace: No, no, no.

Dan: They didn't say, "Hey, let's launch some fun new services, this will be fun for every..." No, you're saying this is calculated.

Horace: No, this is the sort of Jobsian thing that they thought about back in 2005, and now they're finally executing on it. This is a five-year plan. This is where you buy Siri and you ask, "Why do we buy Siri?" We don't need voice recognition in the product. We know that sucks. No, we want an intelligent assistant. And why do we want an intelligent assistant? We need an intelligent assistant to understand what the users want.

And the whole game that is played with maps, with who owns that data: People get into lawsuits over these things, and they become very bitter lawsuits, as happened between—I forget the name, but the company that sued Google for being kicked out of Motorola's location services. And you see when you peel back a little bit the cover over this—peel back the mask—just how important these data sets are. And how Andy Rubin will say it's a stop-ship issue. We will stop the Droid if that product is on it, right? That you hold up the entire business on that question of who is going to capture location data.

Dan: Right. Right.

Horace: That's how important these things are. And you can bet that not just Apple, but all these other players, have been thinking about this for years and years. And architectural issues. I mean, this is not just a business discussion, this is a very deep technical issue. Architecturally, what's happening with messages? What's happening with notifications? What's happening at the low level that you enable the pipes to be built between people and databases, and you make sure that that does not impact the quality of service, that it doesn't impact the battery life, that it doesn't impact the the latency, and all the usability of the product.

So I think this has been a very, very careful—and it's not, again—not that Apple just figured this out. I think everybody knows this, and everybody is applying enormous resources and talent and people, Ph.Ds, and all these smart people looking at this thing day and night. And I'm surprised a little bit that it doesn't get a lot of discussion because it seems to me that this is really where the crux of the matter is.

Dan: It almost sounds like you're saying—or maybe you are saying—that these devices where the consumers are really focusing, and saying, "Wow, cool, new toys," the reality is the devices are simply a gateway for what Apple and these other companies really place the value on.

Horace: Yes. And I call that *getting to know you*. Getting to know you is where they will capture most of the value. Yes, of course, Apple is wildly profitable with selling the device itself. And selling the lust, and responding to people's inner feelings of passion for gadgets. But I think they would be foolish to rely upon that long term. And I think they know that. Because the other players are assuming that that's going to commoditize at some point, and that they're going to be basically sucking the data and getting to know you.

Dan: Right.

Horace: Through a plethora of devices out there. I don't want to trivialize it by saying, "Yes, you are the product," but that's really what it's all about. And I think *you as a product* is what the Internet is all about because that's where the money comes from if you follow the money, and ask, "Why is all this money going into the Internet where we're paying almost nothing for anything on it?" We're paying very little, of course, for accessing the bandwidth itself, but that's just paying for the plant, the physical plant of the wires and things that need to be drawn to the house. Or the cellular, or whatever plant we're using.

But, fundamentally, the investment that goes in all the hiring, all these engineers to write all these clever software, that's given away. Well, hang on. How can you just give everything away? Where is the money? So anyone who is a big fan of Google—and I am one—I think one needs to realize that the Google business model is about getting to know you. And selling that knowledge. And that's reality. I don't judge it. It's just the way it is. So I think it's what Facebook is all about, it's what Twitter is all about, it's what Yahoo! is all about, it's what Baidu is all about, it's what Alibaba is all about. And soon it's going to be what Apple is all about. Because if Apple doesn't play this game, they will essentially be a shiny-toy company. And as much value as that is in the near term, longer term I think they need to be [in getting to know you]—and this is why the servers are there.

Dan: Right.

Horace: This is why you have North Carolina, which is a multi-, multi-year commitment. And that's what I'm guessing right now, because it's been out there. It's been a mystery for as long as that news has come out, and everybody who has done the back-of-the-envelope exercise about what the value of that data center would be, well, it doesn't add up. It doesn't add up that it's just a place to store your files or to serve up apps or to serve up media. You don't need that much capacity. You don't need that thing. And it's not the only one. They have multiple centers, not as big, but they've claimed that they've got several. This is their fourth one or something like that.

So, I would answer that question today by saying it's about getting to know you. It's about compiling that huge amount of data.

Dan: Right.

Horace: And that's the reality.

Dan: So where… What should people be thinking about now when they go to run out to buy these phones?

Horace: Well, I mean, you know, I don't—again, this may sound a little bit doomsday, you know, and all that…

Dan: Yeah, you were sounding kind of doomsday yesterday, so I want to get your take on it.

Horace: Well, let me be clear, again. I said in the beginning that we've been making these bargains as users for a long time. We've been making these bargains with our governments. We've been making these bargains with advertisers and all sorts of media.

Dan: Right.

Horace: Filling out sweepstakes tickets, doing all kinds of silly things in order to get almost negligible benefit.

So I'm not judging. Again, this is something people—if they feel that it's an acceptable bargain—to be entertained in exchange for giving up all of your private knowledge, or private information—fine, then, that's your decision. I'm only saying that from a business-model point of view, the Internet enables that to be done on an exponentially larger scale, and I think that as a user and device owner you make that bargain. And I'd be happy to do it, frankly. I mean, I think the improvement in my life of having a personal assistant is worth telling Apple a little bit about what I like to eat or something like that.

Dan: Right.

Horace: Besides, anyway, the data is aggregated, and it's somewhat obfuscated in terms of the identity. But you're contributing something to the knowledge of consumer behavior. And, again, this will become a political question, I think, in a few years. This is going to be in front of every legislature in the world. To what degree is this permissible? And then some will overreact and will stop permitting this to happen. And then maybe the device business will just—poof—disappear. Because that means there is no more money to feed the whole innovation cycle. That happens sometimes. You know, technologies are legislated out of existence.

It may be seen as such a dangerous thing as atomic bombs were once. I mean, they still are. But these things are doomsday issues for some. But I'm just thinking through this and this is the sort of thought that comes from watching this evolution that we've seen in the last couple of weeks with Amazon and Apple now. And let's see what happens. I don't have any specific advice to anyone buying except decide whether it's a good product for you, and if it helps you, and so on.

Dan: You know, people always refer back to Google's statement of "Don't be evil," and when you look at it and when you describe it the way that you're describing it, here we are seeing lots of our favorite companies, the companies that we use the most. I mean, as a consumer and a computer user and a geek, you know, here on my desk I've got a handful. I mean, we've got a little studio. But even so, I've got a handful of Macs. Use Google constantly. Chrome is my current browser of choice, until Safari 5.1 works out some kinks. I mean, Google and Apple are two of my favorite companies. Should we be worried about that? Should we be worried about them being evil and how can we use an iPhone going forward without worrying about it?

Horace: Well, evil is a judgment word, and I don't like judgments. In Myers-Briggs I came out as being someone who is—what's the opposite of judging?—perceiving. I think it's interesting that although Google says, "Don't be evil," Eric Schmidt also said, "Well, there is no such thing as privacy. Get over it." So they don't see what they do as evil. So whatever they define as evil is something else, right? So I don't want to call anything good or evil. I would just simply say, "Buyer beware." And more importantly, if you are a fan—an advocate or whatever you want to call yourself—of a technology or a company, be very cognizant of the way they make money and understand whether in fact that corresponds to your idea of being good or bad.

There is no such thing as a perfectly good company and there is no such thing as a perfectly evil company. Because obviously they wouldn't probably stay in business either way. Somebody is going to judge you evil no matter what you do, and somebody is going to judge you good no matter what you do, as well. But I think that I'm not an advocate or I'm not even qualified to discuss privacy issues. But I would simply say that this is the reality and a bargain we're making being a member of this thing we call the Internet. It is a bargain that we made.

It assumes being part of a state, a state that taxes you, the state that conscripts you, a state that knows a lot about you. And that was a bargain that we felt worth making. And I'm not just speaking of the United States or western Europe, I'm speaking of practically every boundary today in the modern world that has followed these principles. And so citizenship has with it some costs. And so, again, being a citizen of the Internet will have costs with it. And you need to be aware of that, and being ignorant of the "law" doesn't make it not apply to you. So being ignorant of the fact that you are the product on the Internet doesn't—shouldn't—allow you to say, "I want to ban this practice." You see what I'm saying?

Dan: No, I totally do.

Horace: It's just a fact of life for me. It's like if you're a parent, and you realize that after you've had a kid that life changes. It's no longer about your notion of freedom, your notion of happiness, it's completely different. Well, maybe I'm just trying to shift people's perception of what it means to be a good Internet citizen, and... Get used to it, and be cognizant, and be aware of how that impacts you. Opt in or opt out, be aware of privacy. Lots of people have fallen into traps as newbies, right? We've all seen the jokes for years and years about AOL first, and then Facebook, people just saying stupid things online and not realizing that it becomes permanent record. And, you know, it's going to come back and haunt you someday.

That's just part of growing up. Part of growing up as a citizen on the Internet involves understanding that you are the product, understanding that if you're using location services somebody is going to know something about you, even if not necessarily you as the individual, but rather you as an aggregate. A member of an aggregate. So, on and on and on it goes.

I mean, we've become, as citizens—as I said—aware of our roles and responsibilities as part of society, and we need to do the same about our roles and responsibilities as a member of the Internet. And I came at it from purely a business-analysis point of view—realizing that the businesses that we treasure and value have this side to them which may not be so palatable. But it's a necessity for them. They have to do these things because that's where the puck is going, if you will.

Dan: Mm-hmm. That's not too depressing, really.

Horace: Well, for me there is no word such as "depression." I mean, it's just knowledge or not knowledge.

Dan: You take all your intuition and judgment out. I love that. So at the end of the day, is it really that bad? I mean, is it really that bad? So let's say Apple knows everything about what I buy. I'm going to, hypothetically... Google, Apple, Amazon, the three of them, they know everything about what I buy, they know where I live, they know my wife's phone number. They know where I'm going to go get a haircut and when. I mean, why is that bad? Doesn't it just make my experience online, and my experience overall, better? So—I mean, there are a lot of people who would say, just, "So what? Who cares? Why is this such a bad thing?"

Horace: Yeah, exactly.

Dan: Who cares?

Horace: We don't need to wear tinfoil hats. So I would agree with you that that's part of the bargain. You can opt out. You can can avoid having all of these data...

Dan: In many countries, maybe perhaps yours, I don't know, but in many countries it's well known that if you walk out your door and you walk down the street, it's likely—if not certain—that you're being video-taped, that you're being recorded. And not just a still picture, but live video of you as you sit at a restaurant, as you walk down the street, as you drive your car. You know...

Horace: That's the case in the U,K., right?

Dan: Yeah.

Horace: I mean, they have I don't know how many cameras per citizen. It's really a huge concentration, and that's again a bargain that a citizen of the United Kingdom has made with his government, that in exchange for a feeling of safety that there will be surveillance state. And that anytime they are outside of their home, that they are being—what is the word, not *surveyed*—observed.

Again, it's a bargain you make. If you don't like it, tough. It's just the way society has voted already. [Likewise] having a credit card, having any driver's license. So there are people who are considered extremists, where they think that they'll just drop out of this world and won't have any of these things, won't have an address, even, and all that. It makes it very tough to live that way. And that's again something we're willing to tolerate. Again, being in a democracy, though, if ever it gets to stepping over a boundary, an undefined boundary, people may react through legislation, and stopping things. The problem is that that's a very blunt instrument. Legislation tends to do as much damage as heal problems. Unfortunately, that's reality as well.

And so, legislating technology is always fraught with peril. But that's how we live. So, again, I don't know how we ended up on this topic as starting with a nice discussion about an iPhone 4S, but that's, to me, that's really the logical conclusion of the evolution of devices in general.

Dan: Yeah.

Horace: And one thing: I don't know if I stressed this last time as well, but the thing is that you have to appreciate also is that there are few companies who can do this. You can't just join this club. My perception is that Apple has applied for membership, and... maybe I'll leave it at that. And we'll analyze this further. Unfortunately, there is so little data, public data about what the data is, even, we don't know even what is being captured and how, and for what means...

Dan: Right. Right.

Horace: ...that we can't really analyze things. And this is where we have to use our keen sense of observation, pattern recognition when we don't have data. And then we have to collect collectively, actually pull together as many anecdotes as possible. And people should write posts and blogs and so on, observing things like this and saying, "Hang on, now. As citizens, we can work together and collect knowledge about what others are collecting about us." Right?

And then we can actually become aware more of what's happening and make judgments on it. Again, I'm stunned, hearing myself here talk about these subjects, because these sound like pretty political subjects, and I'm apolitical. But they are what the analysis leads me to talk about because that's what I see happening. And I come to it from an outsider's point of view, because again I didn't cut my teeth in the industry on Internet business models, which is what Google has, and Yahoo! and so on. These are advertiser models. And coming at it from the outside, maybe I over-exaggerate some of the observations I make because they sound so fresh and novel, whereas people would be like, "Yeah, yeah, big deal. That was, like, interesting in 1997."

But I still see this as interesting because now, with the device model, we're getting into a whole new control point issue, a whole new coupling of models, and a whole new dynamic of competition. So who knows where it's going to go. I would say that…In fact what I will try to do is, I'll try to codify this framework that I'm thinking, maybe sort of create a sort of language, if you will: What is a customer? What is a trajectory? What is an improvement? In this model, right? And then we'll apply it to all kinds of different… we'll test it. We'll test it with Yahoo!, we'll test it with eBay, for example. Crazy things. Throw at it everything you can and say, "Okay, does it actually fit these models of why certain companies are succeeding and why some are failing?" And then maybe it will become robust. But that's a nice project for the next six months.

Dan: And I'm very interested in the 4S. Two reasons. Well, iOS 5 is interesting because of the cloud. I'd love to see how that plays out, and I've been dying for the cloud. I want to get rid of as many hard drives on my desktop as possible. I want to move things into the cloud.

Dan: Right.

Horace: I'm a fan of Google Docs. I want to move my data there, although there are some limits to that because I don't find analysis easy on a web spreadsheet. But still, over time, I'm moving my data sets. I can share them more easily, so I love that aspect of Google.

Just to turn the tables a little bit on myself here, don't forget that what I do as a blogger is, I want to get the word out to as many people as possible, and I couldn't do this if we didn't have this open Internet, if we didn't have Google saying, "Sure, sure, upload everything and share. Yeah, we'll get to peek at it, but so what?" I want everybody to peek at it.

So, I tend to be more about openness in terms of sharing, right? So that works for me. And let's not forget that I—as a blogger, and podcaster—I get to see some data about my audience as well. And another thing that I should say is that when you are a producer of a site, or where you are actually publishing and having an audience, you realize also the power of the data that you're obtaining about your audience. And it's all pretty benign stuff. I mean, just your log file, right? Telling you who visited. I mean, these are things which are not controversial and are 1990s vintage. But you then realize through Google stats, and Google's own Analytics, that there is a vast amount of stuff you could learn from that. And, again, there are experts who do nothing but this all day long. I think they're called, SEO—or that's just for search, or I don't know what—I don't even know the titles of these people who are experts at reading analytics. But there are many of them.

And so I'm aware of the knowledge that can be obtained, even if you're a very, very unsophisticated producer.

So, the iPhone 4S, I think, is interesting. Like I said, number one, because of the cloud. Although that's not just the 4S, that's going to be available to other devices. The second thing is Siri. And I think Siri is—I want to study that under the microscope, and not in its performance, which I think will be, you know, subjective—I want to study it as what is it possible for it to become? What is its potential?

Because it isn't positioned as a dictation system, that it helps you transcribe or remove the keyboard. It actually wants to assist you. And not just assist you with stuff that a concierge might assist you with, like getting tickets or things like that. It tries to actually make your life better. And that is a very powerful job that a lot of people have [for hire], that they want done. I think it's the natural evolution of productivity tools like spreadsheets and Office and all these other things that allowed us to get rid of layers of helpers and work, right?

And having people who did your slides, or having people who typed memos or having people who manned mail rooms, people who were in business as facilitators and helpers. And they disappeared. They disappeared because of the PC. They disappeared because… You know, middle management disappeared because of PCs as well. All these people were disintermediated.

I should ask myself: What is the iPhone going to end up doing to people or to other pieces of software that we hire to help us? And what will it do to Google? Will we actually prefer to search by asking questions of our little assistant that's always with us? And because what we *really* need to know is not, "Please, show me the top 100 hits that match a keyword." [Instead, it's] "I want to buy X, or I want to find a restaurant." And that knowledge, by the way, is going to be funneled through Apple, not through Google. At some point you have to realize that the query, which is where the meat of the matter is, the query is going to go through an Apple server, and that's what Amazon wants, as well, with respect to their device. So that goes back to this whole discussion of the meta-platform.

Now, how is Apple going to find the answer? Maybe they'll use Google, but Google won't benefit if Apple asks the question. Right? So very interesting stuff. I'd love to see it, play with it, and figure out and think and observe. It's going to take years for this thing to reach its natural conclusion. But I think there will be reactions before then. I think there will be a lot of scrambling around and trying to figure out how to deliver this also on Android and perhaps others as well.

And there will be patent fights, like there are now. Then there will be asset grabs, assets like whoever is an expert in AI suddenly will have their salary tripled. And that's just another wave of innovation. Because that's where the value is.

The Means of Production

Posted October 19th, 2011 as The Critical Path Episode #10

Dan and Horace talk about Apple's quarter with an eye toward the operational commitments being made. We cover the cost of store openings, data-center purchases and machinery used in manufacturing iOS devices. By tracking capital expenses we can get a clue about where Apple wants to go.

Dan: …This was a big earnings call for Apple.

Horace: Yeah. So I was hoping to spend time on that, if we can.

Dan: Yeah. A great topic.

Horace: Okay. Then, we'll dig in, as necessary, and bring out some interesting new research that I've been doing the last few weeks, that might color, might enhance, the quality here. So as I was saying, the event: I call it an event because to me it's entertaining. I look forward to this as much as people might look forward to a product launch.

The thing with earnings is, they're very predictable. So they're always happening the same time every year, pretty much, and you have the usual celebrities going on stage. You have Tim Cook, you have Peter Oppenheimer. You have some people in the audience who you might have heard of that are asking questions and so on. So it's a fun thing.

And then what I like doing is tweeting about it in real time. Now, at the same time I'm doing that, I'm also updating the spreadsheet which has my data and my forecasts.

Dan: Right.

Horace: So I'm trying to populate it, and people are asking me questions in real time. I'm back on Twitter, and I'm trying to answer them, and I'm trying to be at least unique in my insights and try to come up with something appropriate to say when something has happened.

I don't like to do news stuff. I like to sort of come up with impromptu analysis. What is the takeaway on this particular nugget? And one nugget, for example, could be that they mentioned how much cash was now on the balance sheet, and then also how much of it is overseas.

And just try to keep up with that flow. So in that spirit, here's a couple of things that I think were probably not picked up as the main headlines.

So, first, the interesting thing about the cash, for example, is it went up by $5.4 billion which actually is a modest amount by Apple standards. Now, it's not modest because they had a slower quarter than usual, it's modest because they spent a lot of it. They actually had cash flow over $10 billion. Cash flow is not always directly a function of what's happening in the quarter, because sometimes you pay bills and sometimes you buy things that are one-offs. So in this case they bought the Nortel patents. But they sometimes pay for things. Like they had to pay Nokia a certain amount last quarter, that was a royalty payment for their patents. And in the end they ended up with 5.4 [billion] added.

Sometimes the amount added is higher than you might expect, and that typically happens in the Christmas quarter where they get a huge amount of money, and they don't pay as much (the bills).

Anyway, the thing is that a lot of that money is offshore, as I mentioned. And we'll see what happens to it. Tim Cook was very comfortable talking about the cash. He said he's not religious about it. He's not committed to any particular strategy, he's just thinking about it all the time and weighing all the options. So he came across a lot less dogmatic about it.

Dan: Right. Right.

Horace: A lot of people assumed that they have some kind of religion about cash. But he said no.

And, of course, the big topic was what happened to the iPhone. I wrote a post today doing my usual self-critique of the performance in my estimates. Last quarter, meaning the second quarter, I made a huge mistake on the downside because I had expected the iPhone to drop off dramatically, because that's what it typically does in the fourth quarter. But instead it actually shot up. And so my error was 35 percent on the iPhone. And if you get the iPhone [estimate] wrong, you get everything wrong. The top line and the bottom line are so dependent on the iPhone that you're going to have a bad performance. As a result, I gave myself a C grade for my last quarter.

Dan: Oh, you're too hard on yourself.

Horace: Well, you have to [be]. You don't learn if you just pat yourself on the back every time. I had to ask, "Why did I get it wrong?" And I answered it in one way. And then that made me hesitant about taking the next quarter because I said, "If it doesn't go down as expected, there is no more cyclicality." Maybe it's going to keep going [up] because all these new factors are coming into play: They have so much more distribution, they are selling multiple SKUs. So I thought, "Well, maybe next quarter," and I actually presented my dilemma in writing. I said: "Well, it could be high or it could be low. I'm going to split the difference. I have low confidence in my number."

By the way, the same thing happened in the second quarter with respect to the iPad. The iPad went through a transition. Remember when iPad 1 was switched out to iPad 2 and nobody really knew how to forecast the iPad. And people were guessing 9 million [units], and when they came in at 4 everybody said, "Oh, what a tragedy. They missed on the iPad." Well, nobody knew how the iPad was going to ramp up, and nobody knew what the transition would be, how that would be affected.

And so we've seen that before on the iPad. We've seen it on the iPhone. And, again, I wrote that today in terms of showing how you always have a down quarter prior to a product launch.

Now, what I want to get into more is why that happens. Why does Apple do this? Or are they forced to do this? Is this something they volunteer to do? And so on.

Dan: Right. Right.

Horace: And to answer that question, you actually have to think a little bit like Tim Cook. Operationally, what does it take to get a product shipping in high volumes at a certain point in time? And I alluded to this early on, in one of our first shows, where I said that ramping things up and down is very, very difficult because you have to set up the factories, you have to set up the supplier network, you have to get all these parts together at the right time. And in order for you to switch out to a new product, a completely new type of phone, you're going to probably replace a lot of machinery, replace a lot of your processes. You have to test everything, make sure it runs smoothly, and then once you flip the switch, you've got to have things coming out in the tens of millions, right?

That's hard to do when every year you're doubling. So the volume that you have to output is twice as much every year. And that's really challenging, and if you're going to do that, you need to be able to probably shut things down and start them up again very quickly.

Dan: Right.

Horace: And so I didn't have at the time—like, when I proposed that this is what was happening—I didn't have any data to back that up except the actual volume of shipments and the knowledge that operations is hard and manufacturing is very hard.

But, now, the last couple of weeks I started to look at a part of the Apple financials which is not often scrutinized, and that's the balance sheet. That's where you have the reporting of what they actually own, in terms of not just cash, which is, as we talked about, the bulk of the assets of [technology] companies. But the thing is that they are owning a lot of other things.

They own basically three classes of assets: They have property. They have land and buildings. That's sometimes called "plant." They have their stores, which they don't own but they own the improvements to the stores. The so-called…

Dan: What do you mean when you say they don't own them? What does that mean?

Horace: Well, they lease them. So most of their stores are in properties that they don't own. So in a mall…

Dan: Right. So you're saying they don't own the building, they're leasing the space in a mall, or they're leasing a space in a shopping center.

Horace: Exactly. Almost all retail is built on that principle, unless you're a Walmart or something, where you have a big box sitting on your land. You typically rent that from somebody who has the box. So Apple has followed that in the more traditional sense.

And I'm sure even in their biggest stores, the flagship stores—like the one in New York or Shanghai or London—they are also properties that somebody else owns. They get a long-term lease, and then they fix it up. They beautify it. They make it all pretty and Apple-like.

I mean, consider that they're about to open in Grand Central Station. You can be sure that they don't own any part of Grand Central. So that's how Apple stores are [treated] as property.

But the inside of the store, whatever they're putting in—in terms of not just renovations, but even the equipment, the tables, the infrastructure, that stuff—for tax reasons, they're allowed to depreciate it. They say, "We are making an improvement to a property," and you're allowed to say that that's worth so much, and you can take that off the books, which makes an impact in terms of depreciation which allows them to pay slightly lower taxes.

So, for that reason, that shows up as what's called "leasehold improvements." And that's a line under the PP&E [Property, Plant and Equipment] asset that they have.

So we have buildings and land, leasehold improvements, and the third category called, "machinery, equipment and software." That's [sometimes] just called "machinery and equipment." That's usually big pieces of equipment that companies own. If you're a factory, if you're an industrial company, you're going to own these things, depreciate them, but you're going to use them as the *instruments of production*. These are the things that you're incentivized to invest in. And that's where you get a deduction in terms of taxes, right? So even if you're a small business, if you buy a computer, that's part of that asset class.

So, it's interesting to observe what happens to that. What's amazing is that as a company that's modern in a sense, that is building intangible things like software and building also services—of course [Apple] sells hardware, but it contracts the manufacturing, it sub-contracts that… Apple is not known as a company that is really bending the metal itself.

Also they have their own chips, but that's a fab-less thing, meaning that the fabrication, the *fab*, is done by someone else and they just send the design to them, and then they build those.

So the modern way of thinking about almost all devices and computing equipment, and everything else, is that you separate the manufacturing from the design and marketing. And the manufacturing is outsourced or contracted out. And indeed that's what Apple does.

But the amazing story here is that when you look at that machinery and equipment line in Apple's assets, it's a huge number. I mean, it's really enormous. If you add all the PP&E, it adds up to over ten billion in value today.

Dan: Wow.

Horace: Actually, that was even the quarter past. I think it's even higher by probably at least another billion and a half this past quarter.

So, it's not so much that it has *some* of these assets. The question is, *how much* and do they signify anything by their scale? So I went through each of these lines—as I mentioned, there's three of them—and tried to actually understand how to analyze these things. I'm not an accountant. Actually, accounting was the worst subject in terms of my schooling—I did very poorly, and it's an abstract thing for me—but I went back and tried to understand these lines in the balance sheet, and I tried to tie them to something that I knew, something that was a proxy of what's going on.

For example, if you look at the leasehold improvements, if you look at fixing up stores, you can ask the question: How many stores were opened after that money was spent? And if you try to match the two, you'd see that, indeed, as they spent more money, more stores opened. And if they spent less money in a particular period, then fewer stores opened. So, sure enough, there was a correlation between the change in spending in leasehold improvements and stores.

So I said, "Well, this is a good analytical tool. You can find out things about how much stores cost to build." They also each year, give a forecast. They tell their shareholders in the 10-K. They say, "We will be spending this much on capital expenses next year." And that includes so much for leasehold improvement. And so you see in 2010 they made a projection that in 2011 they would spend X amount on store openings. And then you can realize that that means something about how many stores will be opened. And if you can tell that about stores, can you tell something about the other asset classes and what they mean?

So, it's a long story, but hopefully I'm not boring everyone with this. But when I looked at leasehold [improvements], I got some idea about how much stores actually cost to build out. And there is some noise in that, because some of them are being renovated. And there's not just new stores opening, but old ones being renovated. And that's part of the cost. And it turned out that, assuming it's only new stores, an average store today costs about $9 million to build out, which is a huge cost.

Dan: Oh, yeah.

Horace: And some people took issue with that number because they couldn't see how you could spend that much. But let's not forget that that includes your average mall store, but it also includes a lot of what they call flagship stores. So you have a combination of flagship and regular, which turns out to be about $9 million or so. And of course there is some renovation in there as well, so maybe it's a million less or so.

So that was… As a technique that was interesting. You know, there's a good topic of discussion just about how much do stores cost, what is their commitment? What are the competitive implications? Because if you're Sony, Samsung, Nokia, even Microsoft, and you want to say, "Heck, these guys at Apple did a fantastic job with stores, let's do that ourselves." Well, you look at the costs and you realize it's a $2 billion commitment over a couple of years. And you realize that you can't open them quickly because there aren't enough people who know how to do that, and you don't have the locations if you don't open up quickly enough. So there is a certain limit to how fast you can do this. Even Apple can't open things too quickly. It took them forever to go international, and even there they're very, very thin. That commitment is really very hard to make.

So that's an interesting discussion. Then you start to look at the other item, which is plant and property. There isn't much again that Apple owns. I mean, they own their campus buildings, although some, I'm sure, they lease. But their main campus is probably owned by them. And then they buy some new stuff. So that's where you see a change happening in that value. So, when they bought the HP campus in Cupertino, that showed up as a spike in the PP&E, in particular in the property and buildings line.

And what's also in there is the property they purchased in North Carolina. Now, going back and reading the news reports from 2009, you can time the moment when Apple made that commitment because that was a politically interesting thing for lots of people in North Carolina. It affected the local budgets and so on. So that was public knowledge, that they committed to spend a certain amount of money. And so you back that out, and you figure out how much campuses cost, how much for data centers. As far as the infrastructure or the physical plant, that's how much that costs. Again, you put those out and you realize the timing is consistent. So things are paid for and they are put on the books in the time frame you would expect those assets to actually become property of Apple. So all that is great, and I was very pleased that that was working.

And then I took the same technique to machinery and equipment, and there the challenge is that if you look at the change from quarter to quarter, they're spending and spending and spending. And it's growing and growing. But can we tell what that's being spent on?

It could be a bunch of things. It could be server equipment for the data centers. It could be stuff for the Mac. It could be stuff for all those

CNC machines, the numerically controlled machines that they have for milling. The unibody…

Dan: Right. The unibody… Well, pretty much all their laptops now.

Horace: Yes. When they launched the unibody Mac in 2008, they made a big deal to show videos of those machines working, and they all looked very, very impressive with lasers and drill bits and, looking like, old-school machine-shop equipment that was all automated, and people were remarking that that stuff was normally not used for manufacturing in large scale. It was used for prototypes, or it was used for a small batches of pieces maybe in manufacturing aircraft or something. Because those are aluminum billets. And people were saying, "Well, to make enough Macs, you'd have to buy thousands of these machines." And that was, like, "Wow, imagine the order that Apple had to place in order to get…"

Dan: Right.

Horace: But what you have to understand is that when you start to think about the iPhone and the iPad and the iPod touch, the device side of the business, it is the same problem of getting the equipment you need to make these parts exactly how Apple needs them. The glass they need, in terms of having it be thin enough, and having it binding to the touch-panel beneath that. To have everything be to such close tolerances that they demand, Apple would have to require custom-built equipment. And there is no way that Foxconn is going to front the money for that because they're working on thin margins.

And so it all fits. When you put this together, you realize that Apple has to do this. You realize that Apple has to do this in a huge scale. And then you realize what it costs because you have the data from the balance sheet. And then you realize when it actually went into operation because you see these huge spikes that happen coincidental—or, rather, I should say—one or two quarters prior to production coming on stream. In other words, Apple would have to place these orders with these toolmakers and say, "Please deliver to me 1,000 machines that make special cases for iPhones or special glass screens for the iPhone. I want them in China set up and running before I flip the switch to start production on the iPhone 4 or 4S."

So it's obvious to me that once you look at these numbers that we're dealing with billions of dollars of commitment and equipment, that these have to be scheduled well in advance and that you have to make the call on how many units. Because if you say, "Oops, it turns out that demand was twice as much, or half as much," you end up with factories full of machines that don't do anything or that you need another factory on top of the one you already built. And that kind of commitment only Apple needs to deal with because they're dealing with the huge volumes.

I mean, Android is much bigger than iOS, but there is no single Android manufacturer that has to deal with the numbers or volumes that Apple does.

Now, before I continue, let me just point out that Nokia has the same problem, but they don't build products in volume of this kind of spec. They usually build cheaper phones which are plastic-based, which are easier to manufacture and lower-priced. And, yes, they can make 400 million of those, and they own their own factories. And here is the funny thing: If you look at Nokia's CapEx [capital expenditures]—how much they spend on their factories, and they actually own their factories—they don't spend nearly as much as Apple does.

That's a bombshell to me, Apple's expenditure on equipment. Some of it, yes, is for the servers, but there is no way you can pay that much for servers. It would tell me that Apple spends as much on servers as Google does. And we know they don't need to do that yet.

So Apple is spending a huge amount on equipment, more than Nokia is spending. In fact the other way to calibrate the number is that it's on the order of about half of what Samsung spent as a whole on its CapEx. And Samsung is an old-school industrial manufacturer, right? They even build ships. They even build TVs. They have fabrication of their own chips, and all of those things are extremely expensive. And yet with all of that focus on manufacturing that Samsung has, Apple is spending half of that on machinery to build its phones. It's an unbelievable number. I'm still working through calibrating this versus all the other companies that are in this space, to try to make sure that this is absolutely confirmed, that this is on equipment [destined] for placement in factories.

But once you get that all figured out, then you have something really powerful because you can go back and see *when* things are being spent, and *what* the result is. In other words, you can see that Tim Cook is making commitments *when* to buy things and therefore he knows *how much* volumes are going to come out.

So, in other words, this goes back to the primary thesis I had in the beginning, that the iPhone isn't driven by demand, it's driven by supply. And that supply is very carefully orchestrated and planned in advance, not just in commitments of suppliers in terms of getting chips and getting memory and getting all the things they need, but also in terms of the equipment that needs to go into these factories. And that's a commitment which, by the way, also has implications for competitors. If Apple buys all the CNC equipment in the world—there are only a few companies that make that equipment—if Apple buys it all, there just won't be anyone who can make a unibody aluminum laptop.

Dan: Right.

Horace: Perhaps that's why we're not seeing any in the marketplace. It's just that they can't. There is no one who will sell them the machines anymore because that production of machinery has been allocated to Apple for years and years going forward. And that's like sucking up the oxygen in the value network. It's not just components, it's the equipment that's used to put the components together.

Dan: Right.

Horace: That's the monopoly of Apple now.

So what I'd like to do next is to take these numbers about equipment spending and try to build a very detailed picture of each generation of phone that's been shipped so far, and plot how much they probably produced, how much they spent to get that production in terms of CapEx. If I get a good, highly tuned model then I'll be able to be more predictive about things because, as I said, the CapEx expenditure happens in a quarter or two quarters prior to when the phones are shipping.

And then you get into this whole question, "Well, what about the 4 and the 4S?" You see, if you look at these huge numbers, then you see it makes a lot of sense to keep the production going at least from some of the components, like what they call the mechanical part of the phone— the case and the skin and all that stuff. It used to be that these actually were moving parts, but no more.

But those pieces now, you see how they're carried from 4 to 4S. It's because that equipment doesn't have to be repurchased, and also, by the way, if you're running three shifts, the equipment probably depreciates over a two-year schedule or a three-year schedule, not the usual five. So Apple is optimizing also its cost structure, its depreciation schedule. So if they run the 4 and the 4S as a two-year project, or even longer… And by the way, this is why it makes sense to keep the older models around, because they've got the tooling there and they'll just keep the line running. The equipment could have just already been depreciated, and they'll just turn down the volume, but it's still there, pumping out. And it's basically free for them to keep putting out 3GSes. The margins on those will be phenomenal, which is why it allows them to sell at a lower price point.

So we're going into this analysis from a very gut-level, this-makes-sense type of thing to going to be detailed with numbers and try to show correlation between expenditure and output.

Dan: It's amazing, though, how many of these factors are things that fall, at least from my standpoint, as somebody even who is very interested in this kind of stuff, you don't even think about that when they come out with, you know, an announcement and they talk about form factor and things that a lot of us say, "You know, the form factor should change. It should change." But behind the scenes, Apple is making a really, really big decision by changing something even as small as the size of the mute switch, for example.

Horace: Yeah. This is all Tim Cook, you know. I think this is why the company is so much different now than it used to be, because when you get to big numbers—and let's not forget the company has been doubling and doubling and doubling again. That's exponential growth. It's been doing that for at least half a decade. You see it in the stock price, although it doesn't quite keep up with that. But still, you see it in a lot of the factors. And you kind of get used to it: "Oh, yeah. It's a hundred billion dollars a year company. Oh, yeah, it's the biggest company in the world in terms of market cap. Yeah, it's the biggest single manufacturer of smartphones." [You] get used to that.

But you realize how much is involved in getting that actually operational. The design part, yes, that's something we can get our heads around because we can think that, "Okay, just have a design cycle. And they've got designers and they've got people thinking hard." And then the market side of things, we can get our heads around that as well because we know how many people are buying these things, and what's happening there.

But to understand the operational side: There is the old adage that amateurs like to talk strategy but professionals talk logistics. And this is in terms of a military. But in terms of business and in particular this unique Apple-like business model which is a broadly integrated model...

And by the way, here is another little nugget:

If you think about what these line items tell you in the PP&E, it's kind of an almost-cosmic thing. Take the leasehold [improvements]. What does it really represent strategically? You're talking about Apple owning *forward* from where it is in the value chain, *forward* into the distribution of the product. So they own the stores and hence the relationship with the customer. That commitment of several billions of dollars, an ongoing commitment and long-term commitment, was made essentially so that Apple would expand from its core forward, if you will, *forward* into the value chain.

Then you look at the other line in the PP&E, and that's this M&E [Maintenance & Engineering], and you realize what they're doing is they're extending *backward*. They're extending into their manufacturing, which I've argued they should be going there, because that is not good enough. It needs to become better by [their] getting involved with it. They're going to be improving it in the dimension that matters to them.

Dan: Right.

Horace: Which means volume and quality at this moment in time. They've got to get those right. And they need to serve a billion customers at some point in time. They're not going to do it by just outsourcing everything. So, again, they zigged when everybody was zagging. They went into manufacturing. When you strip away the fact that their supplier and their contract manufacturer basically is nothing more than labor at this point. [The bona fide manufacturer] doesn't own the means of production—the manufacturer in the classic sense, right? Foxconn doesn't own the equipment, doesn't own the components and raw materials. All they own, quote-unquote, is labor. So it's really outsourcing labor only. And that itself is fungible. They could potentially automate that part…

Dan: Right.

Horace: …if Apple wanted to invest even further and clean up some of the issues with labor practices. So then you've got two out of the three are about moving forward and backward in the value chain, and integrating even further what was already an integrated company in terms of hardware and software. Right? So they're going into the channel and distribution. And they're going back into production.

And then there's the A5 chips and everything else, actually getting into designing the components themselves. And the battery technology. No, let's not even go there.

But there is a third item, which is the [real estate]. And that's the data centers. There is another extension of the core business. What they're doing there is moving laterally into a new value chain and saying they're going to be in the service business. They're going to know something about you.

Like we talked in the last show, Siri and these other enhancements to the phone which look like they're sustaining the phone. They're making the phones better, more valuable to the consumer, but at the same time tying them closer to Apple. But also letting Apple know more, which allows them either to build better products or to somehow monetize that knowledge at some point in the future. Again, we're seeing with these three lines in the balance sheet an extraordinary strategic thesis of integrating and creating points of control and points of new value for the company.

I always come back to the question of competitiveness and ask, "Who can do the same thing?" I mean, certainly there are people who have the means, but do they have the commitment, the alignment with business models, the alignment with competencies that they have to have internally. These things you don't just hire people for overnight. These things need time to build.

And you know, this has been debatable. And people have come back and said, "Well, certainly Google can do Siri, and they bought Motorola in order to be more integrated into the hardware side, perhaps. And certainly Amazon can do a lot on the server side." But no one does everything, right? Some of these competitors are moving in the direction where Apple is. But no one has gone all the way. I think that's what made Samsung great in operations and production, but they're not really in software.

Dan: Mm-hmm.

Horace: And, certainly, they're not in retail. They're going through channels and so on.

So you see that's where I think [this balance-sheet analysis] goes from being truly fine-grained to being a birds-eye view of the strategy. And as an analyst you have to be flexible and be able to go deep, and also pull back and see things from a 30,000-foot perspective. And that's really been exciting. And I don't know where it's going to lead me. But every week it seems that it takes me in a new direction, and you know I really enjoy doing this.

Dan: It's amazing how much information somebody like you can actually glean from this kind of... In some senses raw data would also imply data... The way you put this together. So I'm glad there are people like you around.

Horace: Obsessed about this.

Dan: Yeah, yeah. So that we don't have to.

Horace: The other thing is that I haven't spent a lot of time now, post-earnings, to look at how the other analysts have been interpreting the data. The thing I notice, of course, is that it seemed like a miss. It seemed like we all were too high in our expectations. Again, as I said, we were sort of given a head fake. We all looked the wrong way as Apple threw this curveball at us with last quarter's 140 percent growth. You know, 140 percent is astronomical for the product as late in its life as the iPhone 4 was, and we all thought then the game had changed. And sure enough it didn't. And so we went down this quarter.

But, to me, the game isn't about getting to be the first in a certain ranking. Winning an analysis is being able to write down the formula that gives the best consistent results. It's like in engineering or math, when you're supposed to solve a problem and show your work. And even if you don't get the right answer, if you have followed the right process, you will get credit for that. And of course you may have made a mistake along the way in your calculation, and you should get a penalty for that, but overall, it shows that you know what's going on and you understand how the business runs.

Really, for me, I think there isn't enough introspection or analysis of the methods themselves that analysts are bringing to bear. I try all the time to understand how I do things, and also understand maybe how others are doing things. And it's very hard when they don't tell you. They don't tell you what process they use to come to these numbers, or if they do, it's fragmentary.

So one thing I think [that] is not going to work with Apple is things like doing channel checks and trying to find out non-public information and tips and tricks, that would get you some piece of data that somehow will tell you what's going to happen in the next quarter. No one predicted what happened to the iPad in [the] Q1-Q2, transition. No one predicted what happened in the last quarter as far as iPhones. Some…

Dan: Well, when you say "No one," I mean, do you think that people internally at Apple were saying, "This is going to be big, this is what we anticipated." Or do you think this exceeded their expectations?

Horace: I think Apple knows very well where they are…

Dan: Yeah.

Horace: …and where they're going. I think in fact, because of the constraints on production, they have to have this mapped out a year or two in advance. So I think right now they know how many iPhone 5s they're going to manufacture. Never mind the 4S.

Dan: Yeah.

Horace: The 4S was planned long ago. They're just now turning the crank. And because there are limits to what they can build, that's how many will be sold. The primary thesis is that this is supply-constrained, not demand-constrained.

Dan: Yeah.

Horace: Demand is infinite. At least for the next few years. But, you know, one thing I should say about Apple's knowledge and what they share is—this was a footnote in my last post—when Tim Cook went on-stage at the 4S launch, he said, "We just sold 250 million iOS devices," and was proud of that fact, and everybody applauded. If someone was quick on the uptake, they'd go back to their data set and then say, "Well, hang on. How many did they ship at the end of Q2?"

If you take all the iOS devices and add them up, it turns out it was 222 million. And that meant that as of early October, when they made that announcement, Apple would have had to ship another 26 million or so. So the question was, "Is that what your model tells you about this quarter?"

In fact, this came up in my blog and, to the credit of my readers, they said, "Did you notice that? If that's true, then what does that say about the iPhone shipments?" And sure enough, I went and looked it up. I went back to my model and put in, "What would iPhone be?" And I had to shave off 13 million units to make it fit into 250 million for the last quarter.

Now, why didn't I just go out and say, "Hang on, warning, warning. Apple just leaked to us this very important piece of data that they're not going to ship as many phones as we think"? Well, because you never know when they say something like that, like 250 million [devices], whether they meant that it just happened end of the quarter or it happened some time in the middle of the quarter and they wanted a nice round number to talk about, 250 million. And, you know, had there been 260, would they have said 260? It doesn't sound quite the same.

But it turns out, sometimes, this is where the curveball happens. Sometimes they give you numbers that are low-ball and sometimes they give you numbers that are spot-on. And you ought to be paying attention and go back and stop the presses.

Here is where I think, again, we all failed as analysts because there should have been immediately a lot of articles after that event not talking about the disappointment in the 4S, but talking about the growth rate in the iPhone is going to be 20-plus percent, not 80 percent or whatever everybody had dialed in.

And, again, I sort of half knew, but I just pulled back from making that call there and saying, This is a material number. This is material to the stock and to everything else. They just spilled the beans."

By the way, Apple has done that once before. And it was actually a warning about that quarter when they were thin on the iPads, and they had given two days prior to earnings… There was a legal document that had leaked as a part of a case they were in trial with, that they had filed with the court. They had stated how many they had sold of each particular type of device. And there was consistency in terms of iPhones, but the iPad looked weak. And I ran the story about that, and I ran it in my blog, and I said, "Look, it looks like the iPad is going to be really weak this quarter because if we believe that the moment when they made the submission to the court, if that was accurate as of that moment, which was only a few days prior, then they did not ship the numbers that we think they shipped."

And that turned out to be the right call. I adjusted my number on the iPad and it was correct when they published it. So sometimes they give you numbers which are under what really happens, and sometimes they give you exactly the right number. And you've got to use your judgment, whether you go with one or the other. And in this case—I think because there wasn't a lot of discussion about that 250 million—I think most people just either didn't latch on to it or they dismissed it as being just a marketing number.

Dan: And it's really going to be interesting to watch, really. What happens over the next year, I think, is going to be very telling. What do you think? I mean, you know, we're coming up on the holiday season. Those numbers are usually really, really big. But a year from now, you almost feel like you need that year to see what an Apple without Steve Jobs is going to be like, and how the perception of that is, the public perception in that, the market in general. You need that year, right?

Horace: Yeah. So, things are measured in years, as far as these commitments, when you start to look at the numbers. Because you think about budgets, and you think about the time scale, and the process of opening stores, building data centers. The data center in North Carolina, the commitment was made in 2009 to spend at least a billion dollars acquiring the property. And then, of course, more to outfit that and bring it into use, and also then even more money to keep it running.

At the time when they made that commitment, the iPhone was just two years old and barely had 20 million units sold. And they sell 20 million in one quarter today. So we're looking at a commitment they were making two, three years ago to support this fledgling business, which was mobile computing, with a data center that was bigger than anything else in the world. And so that's why I believe that they're really looking at things on a different time scale.

Same thing with the stores. The commitment was made in 2001—or '02 or '03, I forget exactly, but it was early on, ten years ago. And they're still working through that plan because clearly it's not over. There is a lot more they can do internationally there.

And so I have to say the reason I feel that is not a high-risk proposition for Apple to do these commitments is because I know that the market is enormous. And this is another analytical technique, this is the top-down approach. You realize that there are five billion people on the planet who use phones and that they're probably going to move to smartphones. And if Apple even gets 20 percent of that market, it's a commitment to build more phones than anyone else.

And that's why you have to say, if you were either Steve Jobs or Tim Cook, back in the day, "We're going to make a commitment to be in the phone business and mobile computing, and we're going to change the PC to be a tablet. That's a ten-year commitment. That's X billions of dollars. That's tens of thousands of people. That's new campuses. That's all these other things they have to do." And those commitments were made early on and now they're just executing.

So, absolutely, this year I would take that and double it, and say two years, three years down the road, we're going to see the impact of Siri, we're going to see the impact of artificial intelligence in devices. We're going to see the impact of emerging markets and lower price points for phones, smartphones in particular.

We're going to see whether Tim Cook was right yesterday, saying that the tablet market is going to be bigger than the PC market. Indeed, it's got that potential. So any one of these bets is a world-changing bet. It's the vast, vast impact. And, you know, it's not just about Apple. I think Apple kind of forges ahead, but they can't carry all the weight. So there will be plenty of others in there as well.

But there is no more interesting time, I think, if you're a technology fan or computer guy or whatever you want to call it. This is one of the most interesting times since the 1970s when PCs were first put together. And to see the transition to mobile and pervasive and cloud and all of the dreams that computer scientists have had for decades.

I'm just very, very excited about this.

Dan: Well, you know, again, I'll say it again. I'm glad I have a guy like you to straighten all this out, and help it make sense to the rest of us. You're a useful person. .

Horace: Thank you. I try. But my point is that you have to have this flexible mind-frame, right? Or frame of mind, so that you begin with looking at it and saying, "Oh, the future is so bright, I have to wear shades."

Dan: Right.

Horace: That's one point of view.

The other point of view is, "Let's look at it from [the] bottom up and let's see what this means in reality. Let's put the nuts and bolts together and analyze this, not just as entertainment but try to actually be adding some value to the public knowledge, to others who might want to help put the puzzle together and so on. And that's all I'm doing.

The fact is that we can't rely on the companies to tell us because they have reasons to keep everything secret. And, you know, the more we know as consumers and ecosystem participants, the more we can benefit by building new businesses that are going to take advantage of these infrastructures that are being built. So that's really, I think, of practical value.

I think, of course, there is an entertainment value. That's great. And I think that that analysis as entertainment is the best business model that you can imagine for analysis. Because it really makes you think hard about how to make it engaging and thus clearer for everyone. That's why I like doing this in the way I'm doing it with you here.

Dan: Yeah.

Horace: Overall, I think this is a useful technique or a useful profession for people. And I think anyone can do this. Certainly any engineering graduate can do this.

Dan: Yeah. Any of them. Anyone. All they have to do is just pick up a pen and a pencil, calculator, and start punching in numbers.

Horace: No, I believe that. It may sound—what is the word? Exaggerating. But I do believe that people ought to get excited and do it, and try it. And go ahead and send me questions. I love replying to puzzles like this. And in so doing, sometimes, you're exasperated and say, "Well, you know, you should just look this up yourself." But at the same time, it forces you to go back and remember it again, look at it again. It's that teacher's gift that the teacher gets to learn more than the student. And that's wonderful.

The Thermonuclear Option

Posted October 26th, 2011 as The Critical Path Episode #11

Dan and Horace talk about patents and litigation as a means of defending innovation. We go way back to the beginning of the last century and talk how patent wars have played out in the past and how they affected the fortunes and fates of innovators.

Dan: Hi, Horace, how are you? It's been an interesting week or so, huh?

Horace: Gosh, you know, I just barely remember one or two days because it's been… Today, for example, we had the Nokia news with their new Windows Phone, or their first Windows Phones. I've actually got a couple of calls from reporters to talk about that. And then there has been the news from—obviously from the Apple universe, with more market-share data coming in. Or I should say more competitor data coming in. And Apple's numbers are still being digested, I think. And of course then we have the bombshells from Netflix. We had bombshells from Amazon in terms of earnings yesterday, which were quite a big miss. I tend to not pay too much attention to the delta between what analysts project and what happens because often we've seen analysts be ultra-conservative or ultra-optimistic in some cases. But this case, I mean, the miss was… The guess was 24 cents and they came in at 14. That's a big percent.

Dan: The link that I have here is on Bloomberg and the headline is, "Netflix declines most since 2004 after losing 800,000 U.S. subscribers."

Horace: Well, that's Netflix. I'm talking about Amazon.

Dan: Oh, Amazon. Right.

Horace: Yeah. The Netflix story is also an interesting one. The problem I have, by the way, with both of these companies, and I've spoken to the question of the [Kindle] Fire, as whether it's disruptive or not. I've mentioned what I believe is the issue with television businesses in general, when they try to disrupt by using the existing content pool, or the set of content that's out there that's being produced for the current TV value network. And I think that that's where the problem lies.

And I've tweeted that. The tweet I wrote yesterday was that when you think about disruption of the TV, if your idea requires content deals—this is the key phrase, *content deals needed*—if your idea requires that, then you're doing it wrong, because the problem is the content. The problem is the dependence on something which itself depends on the thing you're trying to disrupt, which is the intermediary distribution model. And whenever you're going to have pressure from that target of yours on the content people, they're going to withdraw support to you. And that's what Netflix is experiencing.

A lot of these problems they have with pricing, and the defections that follow, is because the content people said, "We can't offer you this discount anymore," or "We can't offer you this value proposition anymore because we're getting our arms twisted by our existing customers, which are 90 percent or more of our business."

Dan: Right.

Horace: So, anyway, I won't dwell on that now, I think. What I wanted to talk about, actually, is something else that came up, which was the news flow—constant news flow from the Steve Jobs bio.

Dan: Oh, yeah.

Horace: The thing that caught my eye was this rant he had against Android. And what he said... Obviously, there were two episodes that were quoted. One was that he said something to the effect that, "I won't stand for this." And telling Eric Schmidt in a coffee shop, that he doesn't want his money, he just wants him to stop. And then later on he said "I'm willing to spend all of Apple's money to right this wrong. And I'm willing to go thermonuclear on this."

Of course, there is a lot of emotion involved. But what worries me, firstly, you shouldn't read too much into this because obviously he's in a state of an interview and not really making a statement about his strategy. But clearly he was really angry with this. And what I wanted to explore is what he meant by "thermonuclear."

Dan: Yeah, what... Well, let me read the quote here.

Horace: Yes.

Dan: Because I was hoping that you would want to talk about this. So here is the quote:

"I will spend my last dying breath if I need to, and I will spend every penny of Apple's $40 billion in the bank to right this wrong. I'm going to destroy Android because it's a stolen product. I am willing to go thermonuclear war on this."

Horace: Right.

Dan: And then subsequently it says this is what happened at the café: Jobs told Schmidt that he wasn't interested in settling a lawsuit. "I don't want your money. If you offer me $5 billion, I won't want it. I've got plenty of money. I want you to stop using our ideas in Android, that's all I want."

Horace: Okay. Right. That's how I recall. So there is a private interview, and then there was the conversation with Schmidt.

Now, let's step back a moment. These are very catchy words and they're very good headlines. But I think that there is something more that we need to think about, and that is that Apple has been really trying to compete with Android. First of all, with its products. Second, with the litigation and the IP issues, right? And both sides have been arming to the teeth with intellectual property. And I mentioned the fact that you can see it in Apple's balance sheet that they have actually had a huge rise in their intangible assets related to acquisition of intellectual property, and I'm sure if we looked at Google's balance sheet we would also see that, plus they have acquired Motorola.

But here's where I want to step back a moment and [there are] a couple of things that I want to mention. One is that IP wars are nothing new. In fact, patent wars have been around for more than a hundred years. I'm going to give an illustration of that, where there was another tremendous technology and an industry was born, and it was tied up in litigation for years and years. But also people who are new to IP should understand that it is not about cataclysm. It's often a negotiating tool. Apple is particular because they don't take money, as Jobs said. They don't settle for compensation. Often, that is in fact the end state: The way you resolve these things is somebody writes a check. Or you pool resources and you split the money with other people. Apple doesn't work this way. They really are not looking for money, they're looking for blocking people out of their market, what they feel is theirs.

So, I'm struggling a little bit trying to think of how to tell the narrative here. But I want to give this example now. And it's an interesting one because it may tell us what we can and cannot expect from this.

So, I wanted to talk about the history of aviation. This is the invention of flying machines. And what's not well known, I think, is that that industry was born through a huge patent war. In fact, the very notion of what was the first airplane wasn't defined by what we think of as proof of flight because there were many people flying in different types of machines at the time. What really defined and is recognized, at least in America, as being the first flight was actually because those people who flew the first time and built the instrument patented it. It's the patent that actually says that this is the first.

Dan: Interesting.

Horace: A court had to decide that. At the same time, keep in mind that for the last century many people have claimed from different countries that we French, let's say, or we Russians, or we Brazilians were the first to fly. When I grew up, for example, I didn't know that the first flyers were Americans. It never occurred to me. It was not taught in school. So, clearly, there is something going on here. When you start to read about the industry, you realize that the Wright brothers, their patent was not a flying machine but the *controls* that allow a flying machine to be controlled. Gliders existed. Powered flight existed. But people couldn't make the machine go in the direction they wanted it to go. So usually it crashed. But that meant they *were* up in the air for a while, right? So the point is that the Wright brothers said: "Look, if you turn the wings in a certain way, warp them, then we can control movement in one dimension and if you have these planes and these little mini wings in front of the plane, you can control movement in another direction. And then if you have a rudder, you control it in the third direction, which is the three dimensions, the three axes of control."

And they wrote a patent, and were granted this patent, and then they went to court because by the time the patent was issued and all this was happening, people had developed alternative flying machines that weren't actually exactly the same as the Wright Flyer. [Glenn] Curtis was one of the first to invent a different machine that had slightly different controls, or tried to work around the Wrights' patents. And they went to court and they stayed in court for a decade.

Now, the punch line here is this, that we don't fly today in Wright aircraft. In fact, there is no Wright aircraft company. There is something with that name in the company name, but they make parts for aircraft. So the [Wrights'] legacy is clearly very obscure now. And what is important to remember is that what happened to the Wright brothers is not a good story. For as long as they lived—one died fairly young because of typhoid fever, but the other lived on until the late '40s. And so throughout the rest of their lives they never saw—they got some royalty income, they sold some shares in companies over the years—but there wasn't the legacy left in terms of a business legacy. They were inventors but they weren't really innovators. They didn't build a useful product. The few planes that were manufactured with their name on it went to the Army, and they crashed. They weren't actually very reliable as practical aircraft.

And here is one of the tragedies of this story: The first flight took place in 1903. And World War I began in 1914. So, 11 years later. And the U.S. joined that conflict in 1917.

By the time the U.S. joined World War I, there were no American aircraft companies to supply American pilots with aircraft. In other words, there was no Army Air Corps with American planes because there was no U.S. aircraft industry twelve, thirteen, fourteen years after the Wright brothers. All the aircraft that were used in World War I—we know all these famous... the Red Baron and the dogfighting that began in that conflict.

Dan: Right.

Horace: All the planes used in that conflict were European airplanes, and they were very advanced for the time. And there were no such things in the United States. Because of the litigation that was taking place, the entire industry basically went offshore. And all the innovation that happened, all the records that were being set, all the improvements and engines and controls and all the thinking and ideas on how to make things faster, putting the engine in front rather than behind—called the tractor engine rather than a pusher engine—those innovations came in Europe.

And it took until the late '30s for America to finally create iconic aircraft that we can be proud of. That's an amazing story to me because here is the invention taking place in one nation, but the development taking place outside of it.

And here is, by the way, an interesting side story. The very reason you have an industry at all is that the conflict, the war, was actually driving the innovation by about 1914 or so. But prior to that, the only way you could sell an aircraft was because some daredevil would take it up and have an air show. So the very first way you could make money from airplanes was not transporting anything, they weren't good enough for that. They weren't good enough for military use—even the military would only look to them as observation tools. They would fly up and look at the enemy and come back and report. That was the only extent that the army could see any value.

So, in fact, air shows... That's what the Wright brothers were fighting over for more than a decade. [They claimed] that anybody who had an air show had to pay them royalties. So obviously it stifled everything.

But they're heroes. They were the first to scientifically understand how flight can be controlled. But because they weren't innovators in a business sense, they didn't really allow an industry to emerge. Not only did they not create it, they didn't allow it to emerge.

So this is a cautionary tale. What I hope is that whoever invents something allows the invention to turn into an industry, an innovation. In fact, strangely, that's what Apple did with the innovation of the user experience, both with the Mac and with the iPhone, in that the innovation was copied by others. Somehow they didn't really benefit, but they stayed alive. And yet, you know, vast wealth was created. And the whole world benefited.

And it sounds unfair, but the way you deal with that as a business is that you cannot go to market with the idea that you're going to protect everything completely airtight. What you have to think about is: "I want to take the best customers with this innovation and let the world move ahead with my ideas, but let my competitors benefit with the lower-quality customers." I think perhaps that's what's happening. And it would be dangerous, in my opinion, to try to stop Android all together.

They need to force Android... I'm not suggesting not to litigate. What I'm suggesting is that it would be strategically a mistake to *depend* on that litigation. The way they should fight, I believe, is by making the next thing after the iPhone. Making the iPhone itself obsolete. And in so doing, creating yet another gap to the competitors that are rapidly trying to copy them.

But, hopefully, over time those initial adopters of Android would perhaps migrate also to the next thing that you're building. And I don't know if I'm being particularly clear in my message here, but my concern

189

in something like [a] statement of thermonuclear war is that you might [be tempted] to say, "You can't build anything with a touch interface." That would not be the right way to go forward for Apple.

This may be a little bit controversial. I'm not advocating a defensive strategy but, in a sense, that the best defense is a good offense. The best way is to move forward or the best way to protect yourself is to move forward, and seed the ground that you've conquered already by just finding more ground to take over. Eventually, I think that's a better strategy. And it's going to force you to constantly keep fighting for new customers, for new growth, rather than trying to fight a defensive battle which bogs you down. [In a defensive battle,] by the time you win, it's actually not worth fighting anymore because it's a commodity business.

So I don't know if that's actually [a] very good story. But that's what came to my mind when I heard this thermonuclear option. And I kept thinking back to other stories in history. I think even if you go back and study Thomas Edison and the electrification story. He made no money from General Electric. He sold his shares in disgust. If you go back and read the history of television, who invented television? Who actually benefited from television? Two different groups of people. Same thing with radio. And the same thing with telegraph, and all these other great inventions. The problem, I think generally, is that inventors are a different class of people than those who actually know how to build businesses. It's very rare to have both in the same person. I mean, Steve Jobs did actually put his name on a lot of patents, and I think he has tried to cross these two worlds. But I think the genius more was in the adaptation of the invention, not so much in the actual, "This is a new cool way of doing something." You have to have both, hopefully within your same organization. And that's a rare thing.

Dan: So do you think that the actions that Steve Jobs actually took... Again, you mentioned at the beginning of this that this was a quote. It was in an interview. He probably was feeling a little bit angry about it. But do you think that the actions he's taken, or potential actions that he has taken that we haven't seen yet, are things … I mean, what…

Horace: No, I think cooler heads prevailed. First of all, when he launched the iPhone, I remember distinctly how he said, we invented this thing, it's got all these cool UI, and this was in January, 2007. And then he said, "Boy, have we patented it!" It was very clear. He said it and he put up a slide saying "Over 200 patents filed."

Dan: Yeah.

Horace: And he was signaling at the time. He said, "Look, this isn't going to be a rerun of the Windows world. We really feel we invented something here and we're going to protect it, and we're going to go to the mat with this." So I think even from the very beginning he knew—and they knew—they were on to something.

But I'm just cautioning against relying on that. I think a lesser company would have said, "Okay, now we've got this great thing called the iPhone. We think we're going to get 20 years out of this, and so we're going to fight it all the way." I think that that would just be a huge mistake.

I think they need to try to protect themselves. Again, use litigation as kind of a way to protect your flanks, so that you don't get blindsided. But you also plough ahead, and you move to the next thing and the next thing.

And the reason you also need to protect your flanks is, as you plough ahead, you want to expand a little bit to the sides. Meaning, you want to suck up some of the customers that maybe would not be your early adopters, and you want to make sure that you have a solid base. And that base would be eroded by companies that are coming in with me-too products. So in a sense you have to have this two-front strategy. In front, plough ahead, but at the same time backfill and protect. And that's where I think that obviously there is evidence that they're doing that, that they are moving ahead, and they did so with the iPad, and I think that we might see more coming in. Obviously, the Siri thing is a really important new vector. But the…

Dan: Which everyone else is downplaying, by the way.

Horace: Who?

Dan: Everyone else is downplaying, you know. I wanted to hear your comment on that.

Horace: I can't judge or measure these feelings.

Dan: Well, you heard the quote coming from the Android folks, the Google folks, saying that nobody wants to talk to your phone. Nobody wants to do it.

Horace: That [may be their] official line. I don't buy that, really, that they're really dismissive of that. I think historically you could that when Steve Ballmer laughs at the iPhone that, really, they did not think much of it. But I think Google guys are smarter than that. And I think there are smart people at Microsoft as well. It's just that, you know, somehow, does management get it? And that might take a little while. But I think in the case of Siri, this is one of these things that's a quantum leap, meaning that it is going from zero to 100 in like an instant, rather than sort of in a gradual [way.]

So in order for someone to catch up there, there'll have to be yet another patent war and, I mean, they'll—you know, they'll have to hire lots of people who know AI. And I think we spoke about this last time, but basically the algorithmic approach of Siri is very, very orthogonal to the algorithmic approach of Google in terms of what makes a smart system because I think Google acts more on a statistical data source, statistical analysis. That's really Google's core. And the artificial intelligence that

Siri is built on is much more heuristics. And these are different ways of approaching the same problem, but if it turns out that Google's approach—for example, for natural language recognition or translation or any number of other things they've been working on—if they find that that approach has a dead end with respect to solving these other problems that Siri solves, then they'd have to somehow retool.

But it's not something impossible. Ideas are very fluid, very liquid, and smart people also are free to move around.

Put it another way: Competition for me is another weird thing that I think needs to be discussed in a different way. Competition is always praised. People say, "Competition, we love competition. Even Cook says "We love competition except when it's not fair."

Dan: Right.

Horace: And my thinking is actually, well, that's paying lip service. No good business, no disruptive business, has competition. If you have a business plan, when you make a pitch, people always ask, "Well, what about the competition?" And you're supposed to have a slide that talks about the competition. And if you don't, it sounds like you're not completely aware of what's going on. But again, that's just paying lip service. All the real great businesses that have ever been created have had no competition whatsoever.

When you look at them in the proper light—like, you might look at Walmart or eBay or Google, even—and you ask, "What were they when they started? Did they have competition?" What was the competition to Google? AltaVista? Well, it wasn't because it wasn't just about search. It was the way you make money, the way you scale, they way you operate, all the little pieces that made the business what it was. Nobody could do it quite like Google did.

Also, you can say that scale itself is a competitive barrier. And another way to put it: If you're really small, and you're starting out with a startup, and you think you have competition, again, you're doing it wrong. Because what you need to have is only non-consumption as competition. If your competition is bigger than you, they're going to beat you. If they are symmetric [competitors], right? Then they're going to beat you. It's no doubt about that. In the head-to-head fight, the biggest wins. If your competition is much smaller than you, then you always win. So these things are not [quiescent], they cannot exist long-term. The competitive landscape is fluid, it is dynamic. And a company that proposes to enter a market with a certain competitive field will find itself either completely destroyed or completely dominant, not too long after it gets started.

Dan: Right.

Horace: So, in other words, competition is really only interesting if it's unfair. It's the exact opposite of what people say: "I like competition unless it's not fair." Unfair competition is the only way to go. Unfair competition means that you figured out a business model where your competitors are just delighted that you're in there. They're delighted that you're taking customers away. That's the sort of environment you want. You want to build a business where people say, "I'm glad that he came in. I'm an incumbent, I'm glad that this company came in and took these customers away from me because they were a pain in the ass, these customers of mine."

That, to me, is one of the issues, around competition and symmetry. Because when you think Apple has competition with respect to iOS, then there is something seriously wrong. They ought to be in the business where there is none. None in the exact definition of what you are building value upon, and what customers are hiring you to do. In that sense, I get very nervous even when doing marketshare analysis because you're assuming implicitly that these companies are competing.

Dan: Yeah.

Horace: But they really aren't. They're really all in a different world, and there is a slight overlap in customers, but it doesn't mean that one can substitute for the other. You see what I mean?

Dan: I do.

Horace: This isn't a very well thought-out conversation, but I wanted to touch on this and maybe I'll write about it more clearly. But that's what I came up with in thinking about this thermonuclear thing. And like I said, I think cooler heads have prevailed. So your question was, "Did Steve do something to back up his words?"

Dan: Right.

Horace: We should probably have some experts chime in on this. Like, Florian Mueller, or someone who watches this space very closely. But litigation is a complicated story. Yes, they may have hundreds of patents. But first, they're not all issued. Secondly, they may not be strong enough to really throw at this. So you find that sometimes they are successful in asserting a patent that is obscure, or doesn't seem to have anything to do with the core value of the product. But that just happens to be one that works, right? So, they're going to pull something that was actually filed before the iPhone, had nothing to do with the iPhone, and somehow that is enough to bring HTC to a point where they're potentially out of the market.

Dan: Yeah.

Horace: So even if you say your strategy is to litigate, you've got to go back and really do a huge amount of trial and error. And the cycle time is very long. Say you try something and it fails. You find out it fails years later. So, I don't know what he meant by thermonuclear war. But I hope it wasn't litigation. And I hope that they thought through that this isn't actually a strategy. Fighting and defending a territory like this is not proper strategy. I think maybe they were a little bit surprised—who knows? I can't really... I don't want to speculate. I think a lot of it was a feeling of betrayal. A lot of this was emotion.

Dan: Yeah, I think the betrayal thing has got to be big because, you know, I mean, Schmidt's sitting there on the Apple board. He knows what Apple is working on. And meanwhile, they're working on this. I mean, if they had come out with it independently, in the sense of nobody was sitting on Apple's board, nobody was watching all of this stuff develop week after week, and month after month, year after year, potentially because you even heard—I don't know if you watched the video that Apple released, in celebration of Steve Jobs, where there were some anecdotes shared of what goes on in the boardroom. And they made it very clear that demos of products are given in these board meetings well in advance. They didn't say how far in advance, but certainly months if not more in advance.

So you have to know that the iPhone was showing up in the boardroom before anybody saw it as first it was announced.

Horace: So, yes, obviously Schmidt had advanced knowledge. We also know that the first prototypes of Android phones looked like Black-Berrys.

Dan: Yeah.

Horace: And therefore they quickly adapted. But on the other hand, let's assume that Schmidt had not been on the board. Wouldn't Android still have emerged? Perhaps it would have emerged later. Perhaps it would have taken another six or nine or twelve months. But...

Dan: But that's a huge difference in time—at the rate that these cell phones come out, at the rate that things change—I mean, six months is huge.

Horace: Possibly. But let's not also forget what triggered Steve's rant. I think it was mentioned that it was when HTC shipped the (first Android) phone. And in fact that HTC phone was, I think, in late 2008. It was actually the Nexus 1. Or maybe it wasn't because right before the Nexus 1 there was another HTC phone that had the first real Android—the very first implementation of a good touch UI. But still, I think Android was announced months—only a couple of months after the iPhone launch. iPhone launched in, I think, June, 2007. I think it was September or so that the Open Handset Alliance was launched. That was just an alliance. But, again, shouldn't Apple have gone ballistic at that point? They waited until the product was shipping. So I think partly they thought, "Oh, well, this is just another one of those dreams that Google has." And they're not going to execute. And sure enough, they executed, and they executed quickly.

Dan: Right.

Horace: And then they got product out, and then suddenly it was a real threat. And my point is simply this: It's extremely improbable that you won't get people copying you. Everything gets copied, down to the design, the look and feel, the accessories. I remember seeing how Samsung went so far as to copy the power brick that goes with the charger of their Samsung phones, and so on. And lots of people will copy the industrial design. So I think Apple should have known that anything and everything will be copied. You can't fight it all. You have to think of another way. You have to think of how to capture the customers. And by the way, this goes back to our discussion about brand. At some point, you have to rely on the fact that people will want to have the real thing. The copies are actually almost a compliment, they're drawing more attention to the original. You only get that, though, if you constantly innovate and you're constantly in the forefront. Yeah, it's hard. Yeah, it's painful. But that's the nature of this business.

And by the way, another way to protect yourself is to grow big enough so that you suck up all the oxygen out of the value network, so that even though others can copy you, they can't do it in scale. They can't do the volumes you can get out of these aluminum type of products and so on. And you're always two, three steps ahead.

And that's really the answer to this puzzle. It's never going to be about going to war. I think that is just probably a misdirection, actually, from Steve Jobs to say that. It may scare a lot of people. But, you know, I just hope that's not their real strategy. And I don't think it is.

I don't know what else I can say, really. It's an ugly business. One other thing I just thought of is that if you look at some of the other companies that have been enormously successful in non-technology areas—what is so innovative about a Walmart, what is so innovative about Toyota that can't be copied?

It turns out that it's not the way Walmart does its store designs. Anybody can copy that. It's the fact that they have so many of them, and that the logistics are done a certain way and that the buying of product on such scale gives them some cost advantages. But what about Toyota? Again, same thing, people copied the Toyota production method, which allows them to make cars with high quality, high volume and just in time, and a minimum inventory and so on. A lot of people copy.

But that hasn't meant that Toyota has lost its prominent position and its brand value. A lot of competitors, their game improved but GM and others still failed, ultimately. In Europe there's still plenty of pain around automobiles as an industry. So in other words, the great stories, the great company stories, are much more about the innovator solidifying their position, entrenching themselves through continuous innovation, and scale itself.

Whereas I think companies that rely on defense—defense would be someone litigating—even Microsoft, you could argue, is a little hampered by the fact that they don't know where to go with Windows, and as a result they're playing too much defense. And that's a sign of a company in distress.

So, again, I would look for these weak signals, that if Apple is not moving the ball forward and rather trying to play defense, that would be a bad sign. I really think that these statements that are coming through the biography—these are probably not representative and are not nuanced enough as I think Steve Jobs would actually think. You'd think a lot of thoughts, and then probably balance them out from being bipolar to something in the middle. So, anyway, that's just my hope, I guess.

Dan: I think it's a reasonable hope. I think people—if he had really been planning on doing some of the things that he's been saying, maybe we would have seen it. So I think you're right in that you say cooler heads did prevail. I think going forward, though, it's just very interesting because we've... I don't believe we've ever really had a deep—other than what we've touched on today—ever had a really deep conversation here about things like patents and whether they are beneficial or detrimental to innovation. Can you talk more about that?

Horace: So that's what I wanted to do, the historic perspective, because patents have been around with us for two hundred, three hundred—at least 200 years in the United States.

Dan: Yeah.

Horace: That was one of the first things, first laws that Congress passed. And they were very, very important during the Industrial era. And I think that there are a lot of people saying that patents are broken, and that they shouldn't be applied to software, or they shouldn't be applied to business methods.

I think the system is much more resilient than it's made out to be. The real problem is that the time it takes to settle things is so long, and so, when you depend on litigation, it actually ends up being very costly—and that penalizes the small guy. But it also was designed to defend or protect the small guy. If you go and read Wikipedia about the story of the Wright brothers, and how people tried to worked around the patents, people tried to actually wait it out until the patent would expire. And just tie things up in courts. And how it destroyed—shattered—people's relationships, lives, even health, and all of these things, all the drama, was 100 years ago exactly in the same spirit, and [with] the same consequences. And yet we ended up getting aviation as an industry and, yes, some fortunes were lost and some were made.

But there is another story I can give. It's not a particularly evocative one, but it's also speaking of World War I. Another instrument that was obviously an innovation in that war had to do with firearms. The rifles that soldiers used were bolt-action reloading rifles. And that was something that was invented in the 1880s by a German company. Or several mechanisms were actually being invented at the same time, and I don't know if you may have heard of the Mauser rifle, which was this rifle that the Germans had invented and they had sold them to the Spanish so that in the Spanish-American War, the Spaniards in Cuba had these rifles and the Americans didn't. [The Americans] had to load the bullets slowly and as a result they were getting a lot of casualties.

And so Teddy Roosevelt, when he was a witness to this, made it a priority when he came into office to have the American Army develop a repeating rifle the way the Germans had it.

At the time there weren't American companies who were doing this. It was actually a government-owned facility, an armory, whose job it was to create the battle rifle of the American Army. And Springfield in Massachusetts was where it was located. And it was called the Springfield Armory. And those people were asked, "Please make a rifle for the U.S. Army that can compete with this thing from Germany called a Mauser." And they did as quickly as they could. It turns out, though, that that rifle which was created, the model 1903, was infringing on the German patent. And the Mauser company in Germany eventually figured out that, maybe they should get royalties for this. So they sued the American government because that's who owned this rifle, and had created it. And they said, "You owe us royalties for these rifles." And there was a lot of politics involved, and Congress didn't want to admit it, and so on, and fought it and fought it. But, in fact, the courts had jurisdiction on this, not Congress. And it just dragged out. And it dragged out through the beginning of World War I. And here is the curious thing. Obviously, Germany is at war with the United States. And [a German company] is suing the United States government for royalties on rifles that they're shooting at them with.

Now, here is the odd thing. Congress stepped in and said, "That property, the patent, is now our property because we're at war... We're fighting with the patent owner. And property of anyone [we're at war with] in the United States is appropriated." So they could appropriate the ships and factories German companies had left in America. They could appropriate them and say, "These are our things now because we're at war. That's the law."

So during the war they said, "We don't owe you anything because we're at war." But the war ended. And sure enough, Mauser came back afterward and said, "Now you still owe us." And in fact the case settled in favor of the German company, and in the 1920s the U.S. government paid a big royalty check to a German company that invented the action used in the U.S. rifle used in war to fight the Germans.

And so patent war literally spills over into physical war, and yet it's still settled with a check years after the conflict. And this is a story that isn't particularly evocative. Like I said, it is just a curiosity. But this patent system has been so resilient that not only has it stood the test of time, it has stood conflict between nations and the property rights associated with patents are very robust. I'm not an expert and I can't say whether it's being abused too much, or whether there is a degree of value here that's shifted over the last few decades when we've moved on beyond these physical mechanisms to something more ephemeral.

But I still think that it's not quite as broken as it's made out to be. You have to read up a little bit on the history and what the world would be like if we didn't have that.

Speaking of firearms, maybe just one more little anecdote. This notion of patents did not exist in the Soviet Union, obviously because property rights didn't exist in the Soviet Union. So, if you were an inventor, you might get your name associated with the product. But it isn't something that you could earn anything from. And whatever you called it, if it was a patent, it was only existing within the borders of the Soviet Union or the Warsaw Pact. And that actually applies to one of the most famous firearms in history, which was the Kalashnikov. The Kalashnikov was not patented. And it was specifically not patented because they they wanted to export these things, and let local people build and use these very disruptive instruments, the AK-47. And it was... It became a really sore point once the Soviet Union was dissolved, that not only did Kalashnikov not receive royalties, but the company and all the other people in Russia who were building these things felt suddenly the world owes them something for this. And then they began to litigate and stop the manufacturing abroad of this firearm. They even sued the Americans because they were buying these rifles from, I forget which other third country, to equip the Iraqi Army.

So the Iraqi army is being equipped with American-purchased firearms that were of a Russian design that was not patented, and yet the Russians would like to get some money for that, please. That's how things work in this world.

Basic things, like a 60-, 70-year-old mechanical design, are the subject of international politically motivated disputes, not to mention the telecom industry and the patent wars that have been waged in that industry. They are beyond the scope of what I can even talk about. But people have built ways of dealing with this in terms of patent pools, so that companies would contribute their patents into a pool and then everyone who tries to make a product in that category would have to pay royalty into the pool, and then the royalties would be split out by the pool owners.

Basically, it's like forming a joint ownership and then individual companies would be compensated based on the share they had of the patents. This is, for example, what happens with 3G network technologies, and Qualcomm has a share and Nokia has a share. And then they have to be licensed in so-called "FRAND," which is reasonably—I forget what the acronym stands for [fair, reasonable, and non-discriminatory terms] , but the pricing should be reasonable and they should be offered to everyone equally.

But what I was saying is that, in fact, these patent pools require so much coordination that governments sometimes step in and say, "You've been bickering so long that it's causing us a problem with the whole industry, and we're not able to move forward. We're not going to force you, but we strongly recommend that you get together, pool your patents, stop fighting and split out the money as we go forward. I think I read once that that's what Google expects to happen with smartphone patents. That all the patents will be acquired by some major players who had the means to do so, and then they will be pooled, and then anybody who wants to be in the game has to essentially pay royalties into the pool, and then they would get back whatever they had as a share of that whole thing.

The problem with that is that it again favors the incumbents, and if you're small you have to pay a tax to participate. And it also, in a perverse way, stifles innovation because then you can't move the ball in any direction without having to deal with these issues.

So, it's an unfortunate thing, but I don't see any other way around it. I think the alternative, like I pointed out, is that you end up with a system that doesn't reward enterprise at all. And that's the problem. It's an ugly solution, but it's the only solution we have.

So, I'm not dogmatic about this. I've read a lot about patents, they're just one side of intellectual property, and copyrights is another. And copyrights are in fact a bad... See, the thing that I think patents have in their favor versus copyrights is that patents have a far shorter life. Copyrights have been really perverted because what happens with copyrights is that expiration date has been extended to essentially be infinite. And that's been purely because of the content-industry incumbents insisting on it, and somehow they get their way no matter what. And so the famous story is that Disney would always extend the copyright back to making sure that Mickey Mouse was under copyright, and they could not let that expire.

Dan: Right.

Horace: And I think that's been confirmed. I don't think that's really just an urban legend. But that process of extension of copyright, I think the Europeans have actually called an end to that. And some things are beginning to come out of copyright from the 1950s, perhaps. But that really is perverted because I think that was not the intention of the original copyright writers—an instrument of protection. It was meant to have a limited life and the public would benefit from having it out of copyright. And that simply is no longer the case. Patents at least still survive. It's just because business cycles or the company lifetimes are so short now that 12 years—or whatever the patent's lifetime—ends up being nearly infinity. The famous problem with this is that knowledge is growing exponentially and so the data and value is growing exponentially, the half-life is really very short. So maybe it's not really that much of a relief to have an expiration date.

I feel a little bit out of my depth here because I'm not an expert on this stuff. But I want to talk about mostly is that these are not good instruments of strategy. Strategy is much more about avoiding conflict and making sure that you actually welcome participation, and building your business so that the real competition is non-consumption, meaning that people are not using the product or the innovation and therefore you really ought to convince the buyers to adopt it rather than the competitors to stay away. And that's really, to me, the best kind of business out there.

Oh, there is one thing I would love to talk about, actually. I just remembered. It's been said, and I haven't tracked down the actual original source, that Steve Jobs was deeply influenced by Clay Christensen's *Innovator's Dilemma*.

Dan: Hmm.

Horace: That's an amazing story in itself because I've always wondered whether he had an innate sense about being disruptive, or whether he got it from a book. I think it's both. I think he had the sense, and the book crystallized his ideas much more. Because when you see it explained, it actually makes more sense than what you just feel, and it gives your feelings that much more power. So that's an interesting little anecdote. And if it's true, then supposedly it's the only business book that he recommended or he even read, probably, and thought important enough to mention. By the way, overarching all this discussion is that the thinking within that series of books [*The Innovator's Dilemma* and *The Innovator's Solution*] is what I believe Apple embodies. And I didn't want to say that Apple's success is because of the books. Clearly it's not. But what I really like is the idea that somehow there was an influence exerted by this material, and we're seeing a hint of it. It's never mentioned by name. They don't even use the vocabulary of the book, or these phrases that are evocative of disruption. But they do seem to live the life and act in that spirit. And it's really gratifying to see that.

Back to the Future

Posted November 2nd, 2011 as The Critical Path Episode #12

Dan and Horace talk about the tension between relying on data and using intuition to make strategy decisions. We also apply this dual approach to think through the next evolution of user interaction and the jobs we might hire mobile computers to do for us.

Horace: So I wanted to follow up with two things. First, the subject matter in general I wanted to talk about is the future. The reason is that I've been invited to give a talk next week in London. Actually, more than one. But one topic I have been asked to look at is, "What does it all mean given that we have this data that I've published?" And in terms of what I write, I don't like to make predictions. I don't make…

Dan: Yes, you are about facts and figures.

Horace: Yes, but on the other hand, what I try to do is tell people, "You go figure out the future based on this." Because I think that the prediction business is… In my opinion, there's more intuition involved, and that intuition requires a lot of domain knowledge. It requires a lot of in-depth knowledge, stuff that isn't public. So in your business, whatever your business may be, you need to take that information that I publish and then look at it and cast it in your own light, and think through what the implications are. Whether that may be, for example, deciding on investments, or if simply you want to read the blog to figure out whether you want to buy or sell some equity, or if your business might be as a developer and you want to invest in a platform. I don't want to give advice and say, "This is going to win and this is going to lose," because, frankly, I don't know what your definition of winning and losing is.

Sometimes people say, for example, "This platform is not going to be relevant." Let's say iOS is not going to be relevant because Android is going to be dominant. Let's say that's the thesis. Well, by what measure is "relevance"? For example, if we look back only a couple of years, iOS was zero marketshare. Now it's actually, depending on your measure of the market, five percent at best, given the number of phones out there. And on smartphones it's another thing. But that varies by country, that varies by definition of smartphone.

So if someone were to say that iOS won't be relevant, I would say, "Well, it's never been relevant, if your definition of 'relevant' is "marketshare dominant." And so, generally, I'm reluctant to do that. But I've been asked to do it anyways, so I had to go and think a little bit harder about what it is that I could say about the future.

For one thing there is this question of how much do you rely on data and how much do you rely on intuition. And a lot of people because I'm so data-oriented, think that I would vote for data as the basis of decision-making. But it turns out that I don't think that way. In fact, I've never made a decision in my own life about what I would do next, or what I should concentrate on, based on data. It's always been an intuitive decision.

Dan: Right.

Horace: Doing things like a podcast, doing things like a blog, if I had relied on data or expert opinions, they would have all told me that this is not a good idea because of the stats and the odds are so stacked against you. You are not going to be getting any traffic, you are not going to be visible, especially talking about something as overexposed as Apple. So that has never been the way I decide things.

Also, I believe that what you need to do in order to make great things happen, great inventions… You know, as we use in the intro to the show, "What does it mean to be great?" Greatness never comes from data-driven analysis. The data only speaks of the past and if you want to invent the future and redefine it, you can say almost that whatever we did before, we shall throw it away. And so the data only acts to convince you what not to do.

But here is the paradox: On the other hand, intuition is never useful without having an understanding of what has happened before. If your intuition is to build a touch-screen device and you don't know that iPad has existed or how well it has done, or what it's market impact has been, then you'd be foolish. Obviously. So the simplest counterargument to ignoring data is that you won't know what has worked and what hasn't worked, and you are just going to be blind, completely blind.

So there is what I call the analyst's paradox, or you could say the strategist's paradox, that you can't act on the basis of history and you can't act without knowledge of history. So I think of it more as, having information and data helps you think about all the options you have. And more importantly, it lets you see patterns, which is why the core of the decision-making should be pattern recognition, should be looking at, "What is the bigger picture? What is the causality for what has happened in the past? And can we make use of that knowledge going forward?"

So just to give this example about what's next, what's the big thing that's coming up—is there a revolution coming, for example, in user experiences? And I just go back in history. If you look at the details of what happened in the phone business, for example, and you look at it far back enough with enough richness of data, you recognize that there are these pivotal events—we call them *disruptions*—which changed the economics of the businesses involved, which typically meant that incumbents fell from favor and lost most of their profits to newcomers and entrants. For example, if we go back to the launch of iPhone in January 2007, Steve Jobs stood up there and said, we've been involved in three major revolutions of what he called revolutionary technologies for computer interfaces. The first was the mouse, then came the click wheel, and now we introduce touch, or multi-touch.

Now, what I did in looking at that, I said, well, if you think about that pattern and when these things occurred, positioned on each of these technological innovations were platforms as well, and therefore ecosystems and therefore business models. And by the way, there are things that Apple would not mention that still were pivotal, for example, the mini keyboard on the BlackBerry was pivotal as an input method.

Dan: Right.

Horace: It generated a richness of messaging, email, but also SMS, that even now is running its course outside of the United States mostly. But it's running its course in disrupting several ways of communication, doing away with whatever people used to do as far as sending notes to each other.

And so we had these pivotal events, and now the question is, "If you see that pattern, what's common about these?" These are all input methods. One was a pointer that you actually maneuvered on the screen with a proxy of a device. Then we went to a more direct form of interaction with the device based on a rapid-scrolling motion. Then we went to a keyboard input on a device using your thumbs: That was a big difference from using all your fingers. And then we've had touch using one or two fingers—multi-touch—allowing you to do a lot of the things the keyboards could do, a lot of the things that scroll wheels could do, and a lot of the things that a pointer could do, and yet you could do these things not as well, perhaps, but you could do them well enough and they could all fit into the same very tiny package. What's happening, then, is improvement in the things we can do on devices based on input method.

And the output has also improved. We've gone to better screens, but they are all still bitmapped screens of various sizes.

So then the question is, if you ask me what the future is, I would answer simply, "It's going to be another input method," because every big change since the 1980s has been input methods. So that's how I would answer that question, that the next revolution will be based on the new input method that is going to be more natural, easy to use, accessible by more people.

Of course, naturally, we could debate what they may be. They could be touch-less gestures, it could be motion, it could be face recognition. But I think voice is an obvious one, too. And I've sort of been very skeptical about voice as an input because we know how inaccurate it can be. But, then again, touch was inaccurate initially. You weren't very good at typing with it, and people complained that they couldn't type on the glass screen, and the autocorrect is obviously full of errors, comically so sometimes. But there we are. Everybody is doing touch screens now. All those complaints about the limitations of the interface pale in comparison to the benefits we get and so, more or less, everyone has committed to that new user interface.

Again, going back in history, people always rejected the new input method because it wasn't as good as something it replaced. People who preferred command-line interfaces were power users. They didn't like the fact that you had to use a mouse to get things done. It slowed you down.

So, anyway, it's going to be a new method. It's more than likely to be worse at some things than what we are used to right now, and the consequences of it will be that there will be new winners and losers. There will be new platforms, there will be new ecosystems. If you are making your bets today on multi-touch being around forever, I have bad news. It's not. That's really the only advice I can give right now.

Now, the next question will be when? Again, we go back to history. How long did these platforms take from the first realization of that input method? How long did it take to incubate? How long did it take to be commercialized? How long did it take to reach some mass market? How long did it take, therefore, to commoditize, and so on?

What happens is, if you look at that again over a time frame of decades, you see that the time frame seems to be shrinking. What used to take twenty years started taking only ten. The iPod lasted with a scroll wheel from 2001 approximately until the iPod touch launched, although you can still get it on a scroll-wheel device today. The bulk of the value now has migrated to touch. So you could say that that was about a seven-year cycle. The mouse was probably closer to fifteen years or maybe even longer, twenty. I don't know how to measure the end of that.

But then you realize that touch has only been around for four or five years and, in fact, 2012 will be when we will have the five-year anniversary of the iPhone.

Dan: That's hard to believe, isn't it? Five years.

Horace: To me, it's a blink of an eye.

Dan: Yes.

Horace: I was noting that, again, during that launch event—I went back and watched some of it on YouTube to refresh my memory—during the launch event Steve Jobs said that, "We are five years ahead of the competition." And five years is going to be up in January. So I've always said that expect something new in 2012 just because five years is a nice round number. I mean, it could be four, it could be seven, we don't know, but the thing is that these things are finite. And so my best guess would be that after five years something new has to come because this cycle time is shrinking, right? Seven years was the last one and now it's five or so. And so I would expect something to happen dramatically. So that would be my explanation of what to look for.

I am not a technology expert, so I am not going to say absolutely, "Artificial-intelligence interfaces are the future." I will say only that it's likely that they will be disruptive and a change in the market due to the new input method that happens to come along after five years, most likely. And then it's up to you to figure out what the relevance and importance and consequence of that may be.

You know, if you push me and push me and push me, I'll maybe blurt out something about the fact that I believe an integrated player will probably benefit more because they will be able to take that new technology and build a complete system around it, as opposed to waiting for it to mature so that its modular enough so that it can be plugged in into an open API, et cetera, and that therefore it's more likely that the early phase of that new disruption will be beneficial to an integrated company, which is why it always seems like Apple seems to win these early battles.

The DNA of Apple is that they will only build integrated solutions and they are not going to license. They are going to just build it, and they will lead and others will follow and they will get upset about it. But it's inevitable. And so on. So, yes, I would be more sure that Apple will be the first to do it in a commercially viable way and that they will commercialize something which has been in the labs for decades.

And so, again, Siri fits into that pattern. And sometimes, you know, it's thrown at you and you see it coming, but you still don't get it. You kind of swing and miss because it's not what you expected. It's not, "Well, I was thinking about input methods, that it would be something else." But suddenly you realize that there it is.

But if you have the pattern in your mind, you sort of test it and say, "Yeah, it fits along a lot of these criteria, and so that would be my prediction there."

And, again, there's a lot of consequences because things are happening so quickly that the old technology—the old input method of touch—has now maybe reached half life in terms of value, of wealth creation because the next half will be harder to get.

So I published this week a chart, which I called the mobile phone landscape, and it shows the whole market in one shot, where you can see both smart and non-smart devices. And I color-coded it. The blue area is non-smart devices and it is very big. It looks like an ocean. And then you have the smartphones, but I broke them into proprietary, integrated solutions, which are Apple, RIM, and Nokia still, before the switchover to Windows Phone. Then we have in the middle the Android world, which, since 2008, more or less if you were licensing an OS, it was all Android. Prior to then there was a lot of Windows Mobile. So I cut it off at 2008 and made it clear that we are talking about Android. And those are all color-coded.

The green area was the integrated, the brown area was the Android, and then the blue. So you can think of this way: The green area is where the most profits occur. It's like the fertile part of the business.

Dan: Right.

Horace: And the brown area is like you have solid ground under you, but you are not yet making a lot of money. The companies in the brown area, except for Samsung, are actually struggling. And even Samsung is finding it difficult to somehow maintain the momentum. In other words, there's volatility in that world. It's a little bit slippery.

And then the blue area is the ocean of opportunity. But at the same time, that is now only two big companies that are left. Samsung still makes non-smart devices, and Nokia. Pretty much everybody else has been squeezed out and they've either abandoned being in that market and [gone] to smartphones exclusively, like Motorola and Sony Ericsson are going in that direction, Motorola having been acquired by Google. I doubt that Google is going to make dumb phones. They may make RAZR, maybe continue to use that brand, but they will use it on smartphones. And Sony Ericsson is about to get bought by Sony and I doubt that Sony is going to want to be in that business either. They are still losing money, by the way.

So that just leaves these two giant companies, Samsung and Nokia, and a bunch of others. And "others" are ZTE, and Huawei, but then there is a lot of smaller companies using off-the-shelf chipsets from a company called MediaTek, and they are sold under a variety of brands, but it's a high-turnover market where there is a lot of volume but not a lot of value.

My point is simply that the dynamics of the non-smart market have gone from a fairly diverse set of competitors to really two big ones and a whole bunch of small ones. And the big ones are actually trying to get into the smart business as quickly as they can.

So what does this have to do with anything? Well, the point is that if you think about this migration... what I was saying about the input methods. If we are about to enter a new era where voice is suddenly a disruptive input method, it might be more interesting to address this non-consumption market, this vast blue ocean through a different UI because the device you are going to be carrying is not going to need as big a screen or as big a processor or as big a memory. It might need memory, but what I am saying is that you don't have a localized-computer concept. It may make more sense, for example to address the market of people who really... Let's be honest, these are not people who want to learn interfaces. They have voice as a primary usage model.

So once the market reaches 50 percent smartphones, the next half are people who are not going to wanting to bother so much about learning new things or paying a lot of money for this new thing. So it might actually be an interesting disruption because it's going to come in at the low end of the market, and it's going to attract the non-consumption part, not so much that it's going to convert existing smartphone power users. Right?

Siri is going to be a nice addition to that. It's going to be sustaining to the smartphone world as it is today, but it might get disruptive to the dumb phones because you could imagine Siri being infused or implemented in a very cheap phone without much of a screen on it, right? It would just need a microphone and a data connection and a very tiny screen saying, "Here is what your question is and here is my answer," and [then] "Accept or not." And so it is an interesting thought that, the implication of the input-model disruption theory is that it might be a low-end approach to dealing with a large, vastly unaddressed market, which is still today about 80 to 70 percent of the phones being sold being sold worldwide, of which there are over 1.3 billion every year, and still growing.

So that's kind of been the way I've been thinking through the next week's presentation. But I've got only ten minutes to deliver it.

Dan: Wow.

Horace: It's not going to be easy.

Dan: Well, you talk about interfaces for one thing, and you think about—and I've talked about this on a couple of different shows so I don't want to repeat myself too much—but you think about how interacting with the iPhone, when you look at it today and you got to this point pretty effectively too. It becomes almost an obvious way to interact with a phone, and that's how you know that something is good. That's how you know that something is great. When it seems like, "Of course, this is what we needed. It seems obvious now that this is the best way to do it." Do you really feel like voice could supplant that? Do you think that people would prefer talking to their phones as opposed to typing on them?

I'm not talking about what Apple… Is this a preferable thing? I am sure there are people out there, people with handicaps or vision impairments or things like that who are going to say, "Of course, I'd love to talk to this." And then when you think about driving…

Horace: The fact is that there are billions of people who are using phones who are not literate.

Dan: That's an amazing point. Amazing. I didn't even think about that. But then you think about the convenience of doing things when you are driving, which is one of the reasons I love Siri. I wish Siri could be set up to just listen all the time. I know that there would be a problem with that, and they had problems in the past with having things that are just always listening, and they get commands you didn't intend for them, or they don't hear the things that you do intend for them to hear. But the future is certainly going to be that as a interface. Because what do all human beings… For the most part, how do they communicate? For the most part, through language. There is spoken communication. It's natural. It's the first, maybe second way that your kids learn to communicate. If you don't teach them sign language then they pretty much learn to listen to you and to talk to you.

But do you think we'll get to that point where Siri or whatever will just replace everything? That will be the way that people talk?

Horace: No, no, no. Again, when you have a disruption, it tends not to replace but rather complement initially, and eventually migrate more and more usage out of the old paradigm into the new. But in so doing, it impoverishes the old. It sucks out the profits from the old and thus makes that industry contract and wither and lose talent and attention and everything else. But it still stays alive. We still have mainframes and we still have legacy computing systems.

The point is, though, that the new paradigm is worse in many critical ways, but it is better in new important ways as well, and it tends to have a foothold with these new, better things. So one thing that computers aren't very good at today, I say, is that they are not good companions, they are not things that we think of as a helper or an assistant, or they are not easily personified. And the thing is that the vast bulk of humanity is not interested in learning complex and abstract ways of interacting with devices. So the logic would be—the disruptive logic here—that the thing that a new, ubiquitous or always-with-you-and-always-on device becomes better at, and the job you hire it to do, is to be your companion.

So we have half the formula already because the computers now have become more personal by becoming always with us. But they are not really a companion in the sense of helping us when we have to struggle through them to get things useful out of them. So that's really where the new product will say, "Well, I'm not going to be a good browsing machine, I'm not going to be a good email machine, I'm not going to be a good app interface, but I'm going to help you get things done." I don't necessarily think that may happen or that will be a killer, but I suspect that that's how things like this get born and thrive, because they are going to have a foothold with this new unique job to be done, and they'll be so good and so addictive that people will say, "Yeah, okay, I'll buy it for that reason," and then, "By the way, in the next version, could you fix that email thing?" Or, "Can you get a little bit better browser."

So this new product that comes out, and doesn't even have a screen, let's say… Let's say it's just a Bluetooth headset. The guy is making plenty of money with it, and the next thing he does is he adds a little screen. Then he adds a bigger screen. Then he adds in those things that by now have become commodities already because the old paradigm made them. So the old paradigm of touch—because it got mainstream, prices collapsed and so now it become ubiquitous and commoditized and suddenly they can easily pick that up off the shelf.

I'll give you the example of RIM. When RIM started out, they started with a pager, as a user metaphor. So it was a keyboard device without much of a screen at all, and it used, actually, the pager network as its signaling and its data channel. Then, around mid-2000s, they decided to make a phone. So they had been doing data for a long time. I remember a particular phrase made by one of the CEOs, I forget which one. He said, "It's a lot easier for us to add voice to this thing, this pager thing we built, than for the phone guys to add the data services that we've built."

For him, voice was a commodity, but for the voice guys—meaning the phone guys—this data product was extremely complicated. It was very hairy and very ugly and nobody could figure out how to do it right because, although people could do email, they couldn't do in this really instantaneous way that RIM worked [out] because they had their own network, they had their own infrastructure to build this.

So those were early days. But you see the point is that they started out by solving a problem that seemed like phone people didn't care or didn't want, or nobody asked for it. And then they said, "By now it's matured enough and, by the way, people ask to also make phone calls from their BlackBerries." And the original BlackBerries had terrible voice quality. They had terrible accessories. Even the look of it and the size of it and the battery life, and everything was awful, but that didn't matter because they did email and voice was secondary. And so they just got better and better at voice and eventually they added screens to make them into more capable quasi-Internet products. And by the time the iPhone came, BlackBerry was the dominant interface. BlackBerry was the dominant form factor, so much so that everybody was copying them, including Nokia, including HTC, including Samsung. Motorola had the Motorola Q and Samsung had the Samsung Blackjack. In fact, the first Google prototypes looked like Blackberries. Again, for the reason that they had defined the dominant user experience. And they had done it by starting out with something that was absolutely crummy and uninteresting.

So that's where, I would think, we would see the next idea. You replay again. Here we go again with the iPhone, terrible voice quality, lousy network, lousy battery life, you name it. You know, everything about it was lousy, except it had a killer browser and it was really, really smooth and easy to use, and people flocked to it. And eventually they got better and they built all those other things in that everyone said are absolutely essential. But it turned out not to be so essential.

You know, remember multitasking. Remember all the scandals about quality and who knows what. They just got added on later.

So the problem is, again, that it has to repeat itself yet again, and so we have to ask, "Who is going to do the next thing?" And that's where you have to ask, "What are the motivations of the companies involved?"

Who is making the bets? Who is doing what?" And you just have to keep a close eye on the industry.

I have to say, Siri sounds and fits a lot of this paradigm shifting stuff. It just fits all of it. And let's hope that they take it in the right direction. Because if they keep it as a sustaining thing, then that's going to make the iPhone happy for a while. But if somebody in their garage today looks at Siri and says, "Hey, I know how to do cool algorithms like that. I've studied computer science and I've studied AI and I've got a bunch of friends who know how to do that too. We can get VC money and build servers and all these other things, and then we are going to pair up with somebody out of China to make this stupid phone that doesn't have anything on it but our own voice-based interface." And they go off running into China with it, and then they serve these markets that would love a cheap phone that acts as your companion.

And so the incumbents are going to look at it and say, "Hmm, that's not a problem." We'll just do what we do. And then those guys, like RIM did before them, and Apple did before them, will just make that product better and better, and then it suddenly shows up as a credible threat.

The smart, big companies would look at this and say, "Okay, stop everything. We are going to pivot our business around this because it is so important. We see voice coming this way. We are going to go buy up that garage company, we are going to buy up all the garage companies that are doing the same thing, and then we're going to make sure that we set them up and give them freedom to innovate, and we're going to create a big firewall so that our core business doesn't kill them."

And we talked about this before, about how companies kill innovation. And so you have to have this management that is absolutely psychotic about it. And then they let that thing grow.

And I think Apple has a lot of that DNA because you hear historic examples of how the Mac unit was set up as a "pirate unit." And how even today I think the iPad is probably a disrupter to the Mac and, yet, they nurture it rather than kill it as Microsoft did with their tablet effort.

So does Apple have it? Yes. There's a lot of good evidence that they are doing the right things. It is just that it is so hard to pull it off every single time, and this is where you've got to have faith.

So now we go back to the original thesis: Is it about data? This is the paradox. I have a ton of data but all of this discussion we are having is based on inference and intuition and putting it all together, looking at the pattern and saying, "I have *faith*. At the end of the day, my call is going to be based on faith. I have faith that Apple can pull this off, so I am going to make the bet in that direction." Or, "I have faith that Google can pull it off," if that's your inclination, and then you go make that bet. But at the end of the day, take that leap with the basis of that knowledge. But it's still going to be a leap of faith.

Dan: It seems like the kind of leap, though, that is willing to be made or needs to be made.

Horace: Yes. All companies have to face this at some point, and everybody in their life has to go through and make decisions, and that's why great things happen. I think it's just because people at the end of the day make bets. I can't think of great bets being made strictly on data because then you are just fighting the last war, but you can't also be ignorant of what the last war was. So you have to have both, and that's how I think about the future.

Dan: Because you said you didn't like to make predictions, really, but if you had to look ten years from now—I mean I know it's kind of difficult and impossible—but I'd be curious to know: What do you think things will look like ten years from now? Will people be walking down the street, seemingly talking to themselves, issuing instructions to an unseen assistant somewhere that is maybe making phone calls, setting reminders? You see that a little bit, at least, in the Apple commercials for TV for Siri and for the iPhone. I do it. I see people doing it. How prevalent will this be? Will this simply be in five, ten years—maybe more—just the way? People just talk to stuff and it just does stuff. I mean, is that the future?

Because we've all talked about *Minority Report*, and we've all read the trivia about the movie where—and I think I was talking to Marco [Arment] earlier in the week about this too—where Tom Cruise, after a few minutes in… maybe it was *Merlin*. I'm sorry to whoever it was I was talking to about this if I'm getting it wrong—where after a few minutes of doing that scene where he was moving his hands around, moving stuff around on this super giant Microsoft Connect-type, multi-touch-sort of screen, he would have to take breaks and sit down and rest because that's not a normal way for people to move around and interact.

Horace: You're right. I mean, using your whole body to interact with a computer is a huge waste of energy.

Dan: It's fun for playing a game where you are doing karate moves or dance moves, or making a dog roll around on the ground, but that's certainly not the way that you want to work.

Horace: No, but the way I would think about it is that the computer is improving to the point where we get into some of these science-fiction scenarios. The science fiction is good because you start with a clean sheet of paper and try to imagine the future. That's a nice way of thinking it through and what I would argue is that this voice interface was actually in *2001: A Space Odyssey*. That was probably the most influential science-fiction movie with respect to artificial intelligence because it dealt with this sentient-type of computer, and the purpose of that computer was to help the crew manage a spacecraft which was very complex.

The thing that I like about that metaphor, or that use case, is that that's indeed what computers ought to do, but with our lives, managing our lives and helping us deal with the things we don't want to deal with. So get things out of the way, the things which cause friction, pain, irritation. And that's where I think the next leap...

Computers initially helped us to be more productive. Then they helped us become entertained with the media-displaying and discovery process. Then they helped us with the Internet, they helped us become a little bit smarter, at least being able to find things, not having to look things up and not being as ignorant.

It also had the opposite effect as well, sort of amplifying some ignorance and amplifying some biases and so on. But that's because information was accessible, so the web made information possible. And as we mentioned, as we talked about in a previous episode, it also became a relationship that we've had to have with the Internet because it gives us free information, but in exchange we give it information which it then collects and sells on to someone else. That's the trade.

But that's just one more step in an evolution. Because as the computer gets better and better, the next step that would make sense will be to help me get stuff done. I don't want to search for something, I want you to tell me what I need to have in the first place.

So the idea of the computer [would be] not as just a resource or a better entertainer or a better office assistant. Make it a companion. *Companion* has many meanings. What I mean is, make it like an assistant that is with you and also maybe helps you solve some problems. People may hire an assistant to do all kinds of things. And that's what I mean. It's like very basic competency in terms of helping you. Very basic competency, but still a huge leap forward from what it used to be.

It was a tool, now it becomes a bit more conscious of your needs. And that's simply a natural thing. We can go back to the '60s again— when *2001* was filmed and written—to think about, well, obviously there's another few steps after that when computers become even more important in our lives, but these are still very small steps forward, and it's all logical and it's all something that we could have foreseen as an evolution.

Now your question was: How common is it going to be?

Dan: Yeah.

Horace: I think in a couple of years it will be very common for us to ask questions of the computer using voice, but we are not going to use it to replace typing or book writing or complex tasks—complex creative tasks. It will be a lubricant. It will allow our lives to be a little bit easier, just like all the machines we hire to do things in our lives. We don't have to sweep, we can use vacuum cleaners. And then we have Roomba, which actually vacuums for us. We don't even have to turn things on.

Then we have things like cars. They aren't driving themselves yet, but that's another issue, another day's discussion about the fact that the problem is with roads, not with cars.

And so we have all these machines we've built, and infrastructure we've built, to make our lives easier but also allows to focus on the things which we are best at. As a parent, you can probably appreciate this. That you realize one day you are involved in complex problem solving and you are doing all this intellectual work and you are a "knowledge worker." And the next thing you realize is that you are wiping poop and being nothing really more than a chauffeur. And so this is our life. We are so flexible, we can do all these things, but even in the intellectual pursuits we can do away with the dreary stuff and have a computer take care of it. That's all it is.

You know, Steve Jobs had another one of these quotes [about computers]: "It's a bicycle for the mind." It gives you much better efficiency in doing things, which are what the mind does. It makes it more efficient and lets it do things with less effort and more speed.

That's really the way forward. And you can take that metaphor and just keep running it because it really has a lot of legs behind it. It's really, really a great metaphor.

The Innovation Anomalies
Posted November 16th, 2011 as The Critical Path Episode #13

Dan and Horace talk about innovations in emerging countries related to mobile service and how that might foreshadow changes in the developed world. We also discuss why some industries seem to be exempt from disruptive innovation and suggest that there are boundaries societies set to value redefinition.

Horace: So what's happening overall? First of all, we think about the phone business, and I measure that, and I sort of plot that out, and give everybody a perspective. But that's not the whole phone business. You have the services that operators provide and that's actually a bigger business in terms of revenue. Not as big in terms of profits, but it is very, very big because there are so many consumers and they each pay on a monthly basis. Or prepay. And that pile of money is about a trillion dollars a year.

Dan: Wow.

Horace: So that's kind of to give you an order of magnitude. So a trillion dollars is spent by people on mobile service, and the phone is something in addition to that. The interesting thing is about 57 percent of that is voice today. So let's say roughly 60. Messaging, which is really text, SMS, is about 16 percent. And the rest is data.

But what's interesting is, of course, data has been growing. And that's really what the smartphone enables. But the challenge for [mobile operators] is that voice and messaging are declining. And not just as a percentage. Also, as a result, the whole industry is either [showing] no growth or negative growth. And they feel this pain. It's no longer something that they panic about because it's with them. It's something they have to manage at this time.

So, it gives you perspective on it because maybe someday I'll be able to actually correlate and show how value is transferring from the traditional services that were telecom, to devices as the means by which you capture profits, and perhaps [to] additional innovative business models that we're seeing from additional service providers.

By the way, this is another interesting acronym operators use in the business called OTT, or "over the top." What that indicates is all these services that don't show up on your phone bill. Over the top means, and this is a funny word, but over the top means, "Pay directly to the service provider." So Amazon could be considered over the top. Google is over the top. Apple's App Store: All the apps and all the advertising that happens within that framework is over the top. So they really see the world as kind of *them* and *us*, where *us* is services we deploy through our network

215

based on call centers, or on-site, on-premises servers, and integration with the billing systems.

And it's a pity, really, in a way, that that needs to be so. But that's how they see the world. And that's really what they're concerned about: How to remain relevant with these old PTT [Post, Telephone and Telegraph] players.

But let me just put that aside for a moment and mention some other interesting stats I picked up. So we have the division between over the top and below the top. And then we have a division between emerging markets and developed markets. And there, there are some really striking contrasts as well. For example, churn. When you have prepaid, the churn is so much more of a concern because you have people swapping SIMs a lot. And it's come to the point, where, for example in India, 30 percent of users change operators every three months. That's an amazing number.

Dan: Yeah.

Horace: It means you have 100 percent turnover a year at least. So every user is guaranteed to disappear off of your customer list once a year. Of course you'll get back, or get others in, but it's a huge turnover. In fact, the trend in those markets is to have what's called "dual-SIM devices." So either you have two SIMs or very easy to swap SIMs. Literally, you push a button and you swap your SIM out and then you put another one in. So you send one text message, you take the SIM out to put another in, and send another text message. Literally, that quickly. And the reason for that is, again, prepaid. It's indicative of the innovation that's happening because now, in order to retain customers, they're going towards what are called top-up plans. So how do you get people to stick with you and be loyal to your prepaid program? They have things like top-up surprises. You're automatically entered into a lottery and you win prizes, or extra things like extra minutes or extra texts, if you top up. And they run ad campaigns, and then they're using minutes and messages also as rewards for other loyalty programs. Or, if you are at a bank, or you fly an airline, or you rent a car, you get these packages of minutes as rewards.

And so operators are selling minute/text credits to other people to offer as gifts, or loyalty programs.

Another thing is mobile payments. In some countries, like in Africa... There it's extremely common to the point where I'm told 12 percent of the Kenyan GDP is exchanged through mobile payments. People are paying each other, paying for merchandise, doing a lot of these transfers. It's a system called M-Pesa. And that's another staggering thing. Because if you think about it, when I've been talking about the future of smartphones and the fact that if you go through an inflection point, that means that the second half of the late adopters of the platform are going to be harder and harder to get. Those late adopters, you're going to have to be very innovative about packaging the device and the service together in a way to attract them. And we haven't seen a lot of innovation happening there. Since the iPhone launched, the data plans and the service plans have been very, very static. The idea is to grab as much as you can of the non-consuming voice users.

But if you want to see what will happen—what can happen if you look at these emerging markets and you see all the incentives and all the creative ways that people have to attract those of lower income—that might be an indicator of what's going to happen, even in other economies. So you might have very innovative pricing plans, making minutes and other things much more liquid, so that users are expected to switch and change—churn a lot more. And I'm sure operators want to avoid that. But at the same time, there is a vibrant economy around that. These are growing faster in developing countries than they are in the developed world.

The other amazing story was, for example, how well BlackBerry is doing in these markets.

Dan: Hmm.

Horace: In Saudi Arabia—or perhaps it was Dubai or Abu Dhabi, I don't remember exactly the country, but somewhere in the Arabian peninsula—BBM is so huge that it's the normal way of communicating between major sectors of society. Partly because it's taboo to do it any other way. It may not actually be appropriate for you to speak with someone, but messaging them is perfectly acceptable as long as you can find their BBM ID. Then you're basically in conversation mode.

So people are taking up the service enormously, and engaging at 90 percent rates. But at the same time they're seeing a 70 percent decrease in messaging revenues from traditional SMS. So as soon as people switch to BBM, poof go the text revenues. And again, remember that the whole industry, it's 16 percent of the whole trillion dollars today. Sixteen percent of that is text messaging. And you're seeing in limited markets how when a disruptive technology of free messaging—or, let's say fixed-price messaging, like we see with BlackBerry—really affects the economics.

So I think there is a lot to learn from these examples. And another thing that was interesting was that people are actually being offered different types of service discounts in some regions, and what people do is change the SIM during those hours. So let's say between 6 PM and midnight, one operator is having a sale. So since people carry a SIM for every one of the operators, they just pop that in, top it up and then play online or whatever it is they do in terms of communications during that period. So they tell each other and they tell all their friends and everybody swaps their SIMs at the same time.

This to me is very refreshing. This is actually the proper way to think about these services, not that it's something that you're locked into for two years, but you're locked into for two minutes because that's the minimum time you're willing to keep your SIM in. And if you go to a future where the SIM itself becomes virtual, which is what the device people want, then the swapping can be done at a wholesale level.

A lot of innovation can still happen. That, to me, is the interesting thing about a trillion dollars at play, well beyond what people are currently valuing devices [at], well beyond what they're valuing software [at]. This is service. And that trillion dollars is very much in play because of the disruption of data that's happening, that's enabling a lot of these things to be virtualized, to be essentially liquid. In other words, it can easily be fungible and tradable and exchangeable.

And this may be all obvious to some people who are in that business, but I don't see that leaking out, and I don't see a debate going on in the community that would be reading up on either Apple or Android. Discussing some of these implications, that to me is really something we should probably spend more time thinking about.

Horace: I also recently spoke to Samsung Securities clients. That means fund managers. They are the people who are usually blamed for being the hidden hand behind a lot of the market's big moves because they seem to be secretive. They're the biggest buyers, biggest institutions out there. But it's great to sometimes sit down and listen to what they say.

Mostly, they get to ask the questions, but by knowing what they're asking you get some insight into what their thinking is. And they are usually well informed. It's their job to understand what makes companies work well, and so there are a lot of questions about Apple, but there were questions about other players in the industry as well. My thesis was on the future of smartphones. And I used Siri as a proxy for the change in user experiences that we might see coming. I had written a blog about this, suggesting that there are revolutionary user interfaces that come every few years, which tend to not only change how we use computers but, because of that change, changes what we hire the computer to do.

Dan: Right.

Horace: And that tends to create new platforms, that tends to create disruption, and it tends to actually destroy the livelihood of the incumbents. I've talked to this before. We had gone through the mouse era, then the click-wheel/thumb keyboard era, and now we're in the middle of the touch/multi-touch era as an input method, which has had a tremendous impact on the telco industry: firstly, on the handset vendors, but increasingly also on the service providers. But now the question really, for me, is how quickly has that already begun to be commodity business? How quickly is it racing toward this point of ubiquity?

And I take the position that it's predictable, that you can track this data, and that's what I do. And it's pointing to a certain point. So given that, can we predict anything about the future?

So that was what I was talking about, and I think that maybe it's a little bit too far ahead for most people to think about this as an investment strategy. But the idea that you get into this super-platform as a way you build value in the future. It's not device-centric or cloud-centric, but rather it has to be both. It limits the certain number of players that will be in the game.

I don't want to just suggest that this is over the heads of the audience, but I think it's safe to say most people hadn't thought of it this way, that this Siri could actually enable a huge change in people's behavior, and thus in the platform game. And there is usually more impatience for that. Investors want to know more practical things: What's going to happen near term? And then it gets difficult because you're trying to argue about things much more mundane, like CapEx spending and what we might see from Apple in terms of new products. There is a lot of expectation around television and what I would consider sustaining improvements to iOS, and sustaining the path that Apple has been on.

What I am puzzling over in my mind, however, is really, "When is Apple going to change this thing they created to really once again revolutionize user experiences and move on to the next big thing," because I think Android is an example of how quickly that can be copied.

And I also got to play with some devices. I'm not a reviewer, but it is interesting to see a ZTE $100 Android phone, and then to see also some of the Samsung devices that are very large-screen devices, like the Samsung Note, which is enormous. It's like a mini-tablet. But it's also a phone, and it has a stylus, of all things. So they're going back to the idea that you use it for note-taking. So it's like a mini-notepad. It's a tough proposition. I think, as Jobs would say, "If you've got a stylus you're doing it wrong."

Dan: Yeah. You've already failed.

Horace: The big question in my mind... This is proliferating so much. I have the numbers now for the third quarter as far as the market-share of all the platforms. What was missing was Bada and Windows Mobile. And Gartner published that data, and once you have those last two pieces, then you can actually back into what Android did because you know the overall number.

You have a pretty big difference between sell-in and sell-through already showing up in Android, because of the data that came in from one analyst as far as sell-in, or the shipment data. That came from one analyst. And then Gartner provides what they considered to be the estimate of sell-through, or end-user purchases, and there seems to be a fairly big gap between these two numbers. And most of that seems to be in this category of "other," because we know how much Nokia did, and how much RIM did, and how much Apple did with the iPhone. So we know roughly whether there was extra inventory—in fact, they drew down inventory. Nokia had more in inventory the previous quarter, so they basically sold through more than they sold in. You see what I mean?

Dan: Yeah.

Horace: So that means that they drew down inventory, and Apple maintains a pretty steady number in that case. But if you add it all up—and if you believe those two other analysis independently—it does appear like there is as much as ten million Android out there that might be sitting on shelves, which is significant, I think. Ten million is a big number, whether it's a little bit of a channel stuffing or whether there is just an enormous amount of growth in Android. And there is certainly growth there, well over 50 percent of the market in terms of smartphones today. And I would say they're about 17 percent of the whole phone business in terms of all phones sold. Android itself is powering 17 percent of that market. Apple is only about 4 percent.

Horace: The other thing I wanted to talk about: Can operators themselves be disrupted? Because if you think about it, there is that trillion dollars at stake. But not all of it can disappear because, firstly, the operators will always be doing the heavy lifting. They have to provide a network. They have to upgrade the network. They have to spend a lot of money. Otherwise, we're going to run out of bandwidth. And they tend to appeal to governments to ease up on regulation or allow for consolidation, or approve the sale of more spectrum. That becomes a political discussion.

But for me the fundamental question is: Can that industry itself be replaced by something altogether different? A new way of communicating that isn't based so much on these public resources, public-spectrum resources? And the so-called unregulated spectrum, which is what's driving WiFi, and has limits.

Whenever we think about disruption, it brings up the question of, are there industries where this does not happen, where disruption has never happened, or where disruption is forbidden.? There are plenty of examples of disruption. Almost every industry has gone through a disruption. But there are examples of industries which haven't and one could call these anomalies. These are the exceptions.

And they are a notable few. So perhaps mobile operators as a whole might be one such thing. Before I go into the causes, let me go through a couple of examples. And then maybe we'll see a pattern with these examples, because it may tell us why.

One thing that hasn't changed, broadly speaking, is healthcare, the industry of providing health maintenance. Another is the education industry. More or less, it's been a hundred years, and no matter where you are in the world it's been unchanging. Higher education has been more dynamic, but the basic education (K–12) has remained in what I consider to be its agricultural-era roots.

We also have utilities in general, but in particular energy. Then there's electricity, the provision of power. That has not changed fundamentally—its business plan or business model, or the way it operates—for a hundred years, ever since it was conceived in Edison's era.

In contrast, telecom did go through several transitions as we went from telegraphy to telephony and now to mobility—although there have been some giant government or government-sponsored corporations that have maintained hegemony through this period. There has been still quite a bit of deregulation happening, and quite a bit of dynamism, and I think a lot of the brands that are new in mobile telephony today didn't all get rooted in fixed phones, or fixed communications. So I wouldn't put telecom in with that group quite as quickly. It is changing much more slowly than one would hope.

So it's interesting when you look at these anomalies, these exceptions. I would add even one more. That's air travel. It hasn't been a hundred years, but air travel hasn't changed, I would say at all, since the 1950s. One can point to different things but, remember, my definition of change is disruptive change. Any sustaining improvement, where it got better in the definition of what good is, that doesn't count. Planes did get faster. But in many ways it has gotten worse because of what we expect from airlines has changed, and they haven't met those needs.

So, they are not more flexible, they are not more convenient. They have become cheaper to some degree, but that's because they've made it more crowded and made it more uncomfortable. Fundamentally, I think air travel's business model—where you have airlines, airports, aircraft, the companies involved, the way that they make money—none of that has changed. We've had innovation in terms of low costs, but it's always been a zero-sum game. And usually the low-cost players are simply a spin-off of the incumbents. There have been companies going out of business, but many times they just get reborn again. There's a zombie effect. They die and then get reborn, and there are no real entrants coming in with completely different asymmetric models.

There are nuances and differences in-between all of these industries. You can't really say that there is anything in common between airlines and utilities. One thing that's in common is—you may have noticed already—that there is a lot of regulation in all of these. In some cases, it's actually a government provision that the government hands out a monopoly. There is that sense of entitlement or that sense of grant.

And usually, in exchange for that, you have to account for yourself. You have to make sure that you do things the "right" way. Where "right" means you're accountable to the public good. I'm not saying there is anything wrong with that, but there is this implicit coupling between deliberate definition of what is good and what is not good, and that does not change. And someone sets that. Perhaps they set it with a consensus of the public, perhaps not. Perhaps it involves all the mechanisms of democ-

221

racy. Perhaps it doesn't. But at the end of the day, there has to be this decision about what's right and what's wrong. The players themselves don't decide what's right and wrong.

So that's one thing that's common. We all agree education is important. We all agree healthcare is important. We all agree utilities are important. We all agree transportation is important. And we get around for a hundred years saying exactly why it's important. We don't change any of that. But whenever people put their heads together and study this from a disruptive point of view, you realize that always when an industry disrupts, the guys who come in and redefine the rules don't know what's right and wrong. They come in and completely redefine what the value judgment is, and they do it mostly out of ignorance. They don't actually maliciously want to say, "Oh, I want to screw these guys." No, they come in and say, "Look, I see things from a different perspective. I'm coming in as a novice." You know, we're podcasting here. We're not going around saying, "We're going to kill NBC or anything like that." We just say, "Hey, this is fun, I like doing this. I'm going to follow my instinct. I'm going to do what I like to do. If I get fuel to keep going, I'm going to keep going." And that's always the case. So there isn't a notion even of competition. You just do what you instinctively feel is the right thing to do.

But often when you look at these networks of value that are rigid, and haven't been changed, they actually block—effectively block—anyone from coming in and redefining the value proposition. So what I concluded, and maybe it's a bit provocative, is that the incumbents make innovation illegal. It comes via government mandate: Thou shalt not innovate.

So one case in point, and it may sound absurd, but let's ask: How would you fix air travel? Well, how did we fix land travel? Land travel was also [in medieval times] under government mandate. Back in the days of kings, you had no right to travel first of all, and if you did, you had to have armed guards because the countryside was lawless. So if you wanted to get rid of the lawlessness, you had to establish a turnpike system that was policed and thus guaranteed safe passage. But that was provided by the quote-unquote government at the time. So for a long time, the idea of land travel was a government mandate.

But over time technology allowed that to rapidly evolve, first with canals, then with railroads, then with self-propelled vehicles. And as that happened, people themselves were able to take care of themselves in terms of travel. This cannot happen in air travel. The equivalent proposition for air travel is that we all become pilots. We talk about flying cars. The problem with flying cars is not a technological problem. It's an air-traffic problem. And it's really a problem of airports.

Think about also going back 150 years when you didn't have the automobile. You had railways, and that was a network. It had network properties. You also had terminals in those networks, called "railway sta-
222

tions." And you couldn't think outside that box. You had to somehow figure out a way of developing a new network, where you didn't end up driving on rails. We ended up driving on roads. And roads had to be built, and gas stations had to be built, and a completely new network had to be built. So in terms of air travel, what we would need is not airports.

We would need to have millions of airports. So that every place would be a place of starting a journey and ending a journey. So the natural progression would be going from large airports to small airports to smaller and smaller [ones]. Then we should go from airlines to air taxis, at least, right? Maybe you'll have a regulated piloting profession, continue to have that, but at least we don't have to be put into a certain size flying package anymore. Maybe we could have a lot more flexibility in terms of the way people are allowed to travel.

But a lot of these things run into all kinds of obstacles. Because of the energy involved, airplanes are dangerous products. Of course, cars are dangerous too. They can be considered weapons if used in a violent manner. So can airplanes, and they're a lot more dangerous because, obviously, they have a huge amount of kinetic energy associated with them.

So the government steps in and says, "No. There is so much kinetic energy involved in this transportation system that you cannot allow it to go into the hands of those who don't have the right credentials. Just like there is too much power involved in healthcare, we cannot allow nurses to practice medicine beyond a certain threshold." And it would make sense for the disruption in healthcare to happen by doctors becoming less and less focused on the mundane, and letting the low end of healthcare be taken over by nurses. And by the way, [Clay] Christensen has talked to this, and he's written books about this. What would it take to disrupt healthcare? What would it take to disrupt education?

And these books are out there. *The Innovator's Prescription* is one, and *Disrupting Class* is another. And people are going forward trying to implement the ideas within. But when you think about it, stepping outside the box is really bumping up against the very question of what is value, of what is allowable by law, and what is in the public good, because sometimes people say, "Absolutely not!" Should someone be allowed to self-diagnose for disease? If you have intelligent enough equipment, you might make it foolproof that you can detect or even fix certain health problems. If you had the right equipment. But then you have the FDA stipulating, "No. First of all, the equipment has to be rated a certain way. Secondly, it has to be administered by a professional. That professional has to be certified."

So if someone has a heart attack, you cannot apply the shocks necessary to defibrillate a heart unless you're an emergency medical technician. Why couldn't we just wear a strap around our chest that automatically detects heart problems?

Technology people couldn't imagine that the government could step in and say, "You can't have a wireless mouse. A wireless mouse requires radio frequencies, and there's laws against that."

All of these [technologies] we take for granted, they did go through some government checks and balances. But the problem is that the governments do draw lines, and in fact they not only do so in one state, they tend to do so globally. You can't say that practicing medicine is something that's regulated only in the United States. It's regulated worldwide. There's a consensus, and all the professionals get together and agree, "This is the right thing to do." Same with air travel. You don't have civilian pilots running around in China with their own homemade airplanes, right? There is somehow an unquestionable agreement that that's beyond the ability of individuals to do. Or even if they could do it, they shouldn't be allowed to do it.

So whenever someone asks me how to fix air travel, my answer is, "You've got to fix airports first. Or the whole network has to change." If someone wants to talk about flying cars, I'd say, "Well, what are you going to do about a million airports?" If you want to talk about fixing the automobile as the means of transport, the problem there isn't just that we change the power plant to try to become green. The question is: Can you do something about the roads? Because maybe the fact that we have congestion, that we have roads, that we have all these other systems in place, is that point-to-point travel is problematic.

So you might say that it makes sense for us to form convoys of cars that are intelligent, and they tend to cluster, and we go from circuit switch to packet switch as we did with voice. All these things make a lot of sense architecturally speaking. But you realize that the constraints are, in fact, the roads, not the cars.

So that's where I see the dilemma there, that you push innovation far enough and it bumps up against a wall, a barrier that is unquestionable. And this is why at the end of the day you have industries that go for a hundred years without any innovations. This is why we have problems on the global scale in terms of energy, in terms of the way we find and extract and consume energy. It's because the problem isn't that we're greedy as consumers. The problem is that we don't have the systems by which we can permit innovation to happen. And that's really cosmic when you think about it.

If we could each have a power plant in our home, and someone would allow us to do this, I'm sure entrepreneurs will come and say, "We'll give you free power if you'll tell us how you use it." What would the Google of energy look like? The Google of energy would say, "Hey, we give you Internet for free, and all the knowledge of the world for free, in exchange for you letting us know something about yourself." Why not apply that to energy? Or transportation? Why not the airline of the future—you fly for free but you get to tell the airline your deepest secrets?

That would really be marketable. But you can't do that. Not even network operators can do that. Network operators have petabytes of data about what you do on that network, but they can't sell it. They cannot sell that because it would be illegal. So, in other words, they have to charge all these ridiculous rates and then they have to go spend all the money in CapEx and then lobby Congress. But they're not permitted to because, again, there are fundamental legacy concepts at work about who owns what, and how value is defined in the communications network, as well as a transportation network. And those core definitions—you pay for bits to be transported or you pay for vehicles to be carrying people. They cannot change because that's the definition of the value. If, on the other hand, someone—an innovator—says, "I want to redefine the business proposition, that it's not the transport or carriage of bits." Then that should not be the thing you regulate. It's information or meta-data that's much more important.

In the future we're going to be concerned with learning systems and intelligent systems, where it's the intelligence that matters, not the actual carriage. So these changes need to happen and be allowed to happen for real innovation to occur. Stepping back far enough, it's not about bickering, about social goods, or socialism versus capitalism. It's not about these age-old divisive politics. It's more about what are the real values we're debating? Can we innovate by stepping out of those divisions and looking at questions about integration, modularity, and so on? And maybe people have thought about it, but they just step back from that: "Looks like the abyss. It looks like—holy cow!—we cannot predict what might happen." And so we don't even allow the experiments to take place.

You can't help reach these conclusions if you think about, truly, what are the causes and the way innovation happens. Just stepping back a little bit, in the context of Apple, we're hearing that Steve Jobs wanted to start his own network.

Dan: Right. He wanted to use the unregistered WiFi space.

Horace: That's a natural thing for an innovator to do. They would have this conversation: "What do we hate? We hate our phones. Why do we hate them? Because they have lousy interfaces. Okay, we fixed the interface, but then we realize we can't monetize it, why? Because we've got to get permissions from the network operator."

So you ask again the question, "Why do we need their permission? Because they have the regulated spectrum. Why do we need the regulated spectrum? Because it's the only way to get ubiquity. So why do we need ubiquity? Well because then you can have a nationwide network. Why do we need…" You know, it goes on. It's like having a dialogue with a three-year-old asking "Why? every three seconds.

But that's exactly what an innovator does. They come to a dead end at some point and say, "The numbers will never add up. I could create a network which is provisioned by every Apple Store in the world—they'll have an antenna on the roof, and then I can do a mesh network with every iPhone transmitting passing through signals from another iPhone."

All these wonderful ideas are out there, technologically speaking. But at the end of the day, you run into the regulator wall, and you say, "It doesn't scale globally. It doesn't even scale nation-wide. I'll never get anyone to work with me if I want to inter-operate, or drop into a secondary mode." Let's say that's the primary mode, or we drop into sort of a roaming onto a network when you have no option. And they won't let you on. Because you're not playing by their rules.

So, ultimately, you run into these walls and you give up, and then you go comply with the rules. If there ever was a dialogue by Apple, I'm sure it wouldn't have lasted more than a few months. And they would have said, "There is nothing we can do at this time. Maybe we'll have to wait 20 years." That's how an entrant would look at the world. If people were to ask, somewhat jokingly, "Why doesn't Apple get into the automobile business, or into the TV business," then you run into several significant barriers that do not let you do the right thing. If you were a critic of the company, it's because they couldn't do things their own way. And they don't compromise and just try to fix TV the way it is now. They're not going to do that. They're going to fix TV to be the right thing. TV is going to be a big discussion because you have all of these obstacles, like I mentioned. They're far easier than dealing with energy policy, or dealing with healthcare. But still, the value networks are deeply, deeply interdependent right now, with a value model that doesn't work anymore.

You see it everywhere. You see this problem everywhere. Whenever you see an industry in crisis, or that doesn't seem to have any money being made, and everybody is frustrated, that's a strong signal that there are some invisible barriers going up. And innovators are just not permitted to enter.

Dan: Invisible barriers.

Horace: Invisible barriers. The anomalies. The limits to innovation.

Who's Paying for My Lunch?

Posted December 21st, 2011 as The Critical Path Episode #18

Dan and Horace ponder why some companies are more mysterious than others. We ask whether transparency and simplicity of business models is a sign of strength or weakness. We compare the measurement, creation and capture of value, and why we should celebrate the mortality of businesses.

Horace: Google is a topic I like to talk about with people who are in the industry, who know something about Google from a different angle. So if I go to conferences, it's one of the things I like to bring up because I think it's one of these things that people look at it from different angles and see different things. And if you see all of the perspectives, it's kind of like the elephant in the room. Is that the right analogy? You know, the blind men trying to figure out what an elephant looks like by touch. I'm really bad with that.

Dan: No, that's the right one. For people who haven't heard that, they've got guys—I don't know what the real story is—but blind guys and they all walk over to an elephant and one guy is touching the trunk, one guy is touching a leg, another guy is touching the ear, and they all are describing something completely different as to what an elephant is. I think that's perfect for what you're talking about.

Horace: But Google is in so many areas and it's such a different thing to so many different people. It's not just search or index search, it's all these things. And I don't know if anybody, even inside Google, knows what it is. But I like to get these perspectives.

We are part of a community that analyzes Apple. Apple is one of the most scrutinized and analyzed companies on the planet, partly because it is so visible as a brand and it attracts so much attention. So you have the positive reenforcement… Once you analyze something you get a lot of feedback, you get a lot of positive feedback that compels you to do more. But also it is very easy, in my opinion. to at least get started. It seems easy saying, "If I can just guess the next thing, I'm in business of predicting Apple."

But I see it from the other perspective of how hard the company is to analyze on the basis of what are its products lines, what does its income statement look like, how simple is its business model. In the case of Apple, all of these are positives, all of these are good quantities. So you have a limited number of products. Tim Cook said that everything that Apple makes fits on the kitchen table. Indeed, if you put all the products next to each other they would probably not cover that much more surface area than the typical table.

They have four or five units that report individually. So you have the iPhone business and you have the Mac business and you have the iPod business, et cetera. So those are simple things. They make things that cost them a certain amount and then they sell them for a profit, and that's very simple. There are no magic tricks about losing money on one thing and making it up on another thing. In other companies you have to try to look at all these tangents. That doesn't happen with Apple, it's very simple.

It has big piles of cash which everybody can understand. It doesn't do financial engineering. It doesn't try to leverage this or stuff channels or do things which are difficult to tease apart when you try to analyze what they are doing here. There is none of that. There is no mystery. Apple is easy.

When you try to apply that to other companies, you realize how difficult it is. I mean, even something like Microsoft. There are all kinds of mysteries about Microsoft. Where do the costs go? I mean, if you look at mobile, which Microsoft used to report independently—right now it's part of something called entertainment—but mobile used to have certain numbers for its sales. But you wouldn't know the cost structures because when they were developing things. Most of the costs are in R&D, but those are buried in what Windows was doing. And you'd be looking at cost structures with respect to sales and marketing. So the whole business ran as if it was nothing more than a sales organization. So you were looking at profitability: Did they actually spend more in sales and marketing than they got in through license fees? And so the R&D didn't appear in that equation. Or, if it did, it wasn't reported.

So given that, how would you look at a Google? Or Facebook? There is no community of analysts scrutinizing them as amateurs. There might be people who are professionals doing this, as amateurs, as people who are publishing and getting a lot of feedback publicly. That doesn't happen for many companies. Maybe there are some BlackBerry people, and there might be some Google people, but they tend to be technology-oriented. They're not looking at the whole business, at the whole ecosystem/dreaming up strategies, and offering free advice to Google on how they should run their business. Everybody gives free advice to Apple.

So that's one of the things that makes Google somewhat mysterious and I'd like to get this feedback.

Anyway, I'm talking to Om [Malik] about it. And the way I put it to him, I said, "It's very much like Kremlinology." Now, for our younger listeners, back in the old days when we had the Cold War, the U.S. adversary at the time was the Soviet Union, and a lot of people were trying to scrutinize and analyze what's happening there. And they came out with this word called "Kremlinology," which is the idea of being able to understand what's happening inside the Kremlin, the seat of power [in the Soviet Union].

And the way you would do it, for example, is you would watch when they were having a military parade, which happened once a year, and you would look at the viewing stand of the leadership and try to figure out what the political situation was by seeing who was standing next to whom.

Dan: That was how they knew the pecking order of what was going on.

Horace: Or they would try to tease out from a statement being made on TV about some meeting of the Politburo, and they would try to understand what the coded language was and who was in power and who wasn't in power.

Even if a tragedy happened, let's say Chernobyl or an airplane crash, what were the signals that the country was sending and the leadership was sending and the military in power.

Actually, we are seeing that now with the North Koreans. The trouble is North Korea doesn't let you have any of that. It doesn't give you hints, there is no public communication whatsoever, so it's actually even harder.

But the whole point is that analysis, when you are given so little data, is almost comical. I mean, it sounds absurd that you could do an analysis on a country on the basis of once a year seeing a bunch of people standing on a podium. And yet that's what people were forced to do.

And that's the thing that strikes me also about Google, and that's why I use the analogies. Here is the company that has more information than any other. They are very proud of that. They have this information about the world which they index. And, in fact, they say that it grows exponentially. It doubles every 18 months, or something like that. And they are saying that this is the key to the universe and the world and everything else. But the amount of information that they release is not just little, it's actually less than what most other companies release?

Dan: Why is that? Why is there such a difference?

Horace: Well, this is the paradox, in a way. Let's take, for example, yesterday. They released that they have a certain rate of activation of Android, and you know that they know everything about Androids: How many there are, where they are, who is selling—which vendor, which operator—where the activation took place, how long the device was in use. They know all that. They have a huge amount of data and who knows what else they are privy to.

I would imagine Apple has a huge amount of information as well, but Apple publishes its sales data because they make money from the sale, and it's material to their shareholders to tell the world how many phones were sold. They chose to do that. They said, "This is material and important and we should do this." Other companies don't.

Samsung, the second largest vendor of phones in the world, doesn't even tell the world how many phones it sells, never mind how many smartphones.

Google doesn't tell the world how many Androids were sold. It tells activation rate, which is like saying, "Occasionally, we are going to give you the first derivative of the function that you are trying to figure out." And sometimes they even give you the second derivative by saying the rate of growth in activations. But what you care about is how many units have been sold.

Dan: Right.

Horace: And nobody tells you that. Not even the vendors themselves tell you that. So if Samsung doesn't tell you, you have to guess from a bunch of other data-capture opportunities like retail, or if you are doing sampling, or if you are doing various other analytic tools that are expensive and therefore need to be sold and are therefore not public. So that's why we only have fragments of data. When we are looking as private individuals we cannot get that for free.

I'm trying to put it together. I've actually been working on it today, sort of looking at all the public statements that Google has made about the activation rate and making assumptions—interpolating—trying to figure out how that matches to the actual data they have given. They have given a few data points about the installed base. They said when they crossed 200 million, or when they crossed 100 million units. I've put those all in the data chart and table, trying to see exactly how the shape of the growth of the product is.

Why couldn't Google just have a website, like they do on so many other things? You can find out what a search term's popularity is, so you can find out all these details about what the public behavior is. And yet they don't tell the very basic things, like how many Android phones were sold in a particular month or a particular quarter. Do it sort of like Apple does. No, that's not something you are allowed to know. I don't know why.

Dan: Why, though? Yeah, that's the real question. Why? Why not? Who does it... I certainly understand that there is a degree of interest in keeping privacy when it comes to certain sales figures, numbers, things like that—especially for smaller privately held companies, sure—but when you're dealing with a company like Google, why not share that information?

Amazon, famously, will not share—and I think you and I have talked about this. They won't share their sales numbers specifically unless they are really good, and only very occasionally. Why not share that? What's your theory? I mean you've got to have a theory.

Horace: I wish I knew. Because the problem is I don't think it hurts them to say this. It actually helps because they do clearly want to signal that the ecosystem and the platform is strong, and they want to break out the versions in a pie chart. They say this is the number of units running what version of the OS, which is fascinating because you have a quantity whose total you don't know, but you know what the subsets are, and so developers supposedly can get an idea of the pie.

I can imagine there might be some legal issues, that they are afraid of giving too much information in case they are sued, although I think a court can get that information. If the litigation happens, then they can subpoena that and it may be held privately.

But I draw no conclusion from this other than it's a paradox and somewhat of an irony that the company with the most information reveals almost none of it.

Which actually comes to another point, that information, like time, is money. And the problem is that openness is the idea that we are sharing, but Google doesn't share what is valuable. It only shares what isn't valuable to itself. And in this case, if they don't share that data then it's obviously very valuable to them somehow. I don't know where that value might be, but that's why when I talk to people like Om, or I go to conferences and so on, I try to say, "What have you heard about Google?" I'm trying to find out what's happening and what their decision process is like. What are they thinking about strategically, because it seems odd that they do things like an acquisition of Motorola. It seems odd that they don't yet have a business model for Android beyond, apparently, a good defense.

But I don't know what's happening there and it's one of those mysteries I'm trying to get to the bottom of. And as I said, because Apple is selling stuff, that stuff gets measured because it has value in itself. But stuff like Android is not sold, therefore there is no transaction, there is contract. There is nothing but some bits that go over wires. There is no financial transaction as a result of most of what Google does. And therefore we don't have the ability to scrutinize it, at least from the angle of financial or follow-the-money type of analysis.

I wrote a story on Business Insider that they invited me to do, and I approached the question. It was an open question, like, "Can you chime in on the question of Android versus iPhone?" It was the broadest question you can have, and I chose this idea that you can measure one and the other one you cannot measure. You can measure the value of iPhone because you can follow its numbers and you can see what it does to the stock price, you can see what it does to the bottom line. But Android you can't. You can't measure anything about it. We don't have data on units, we don't have data on value created. We know that there is secondary or tertiary value. We know that vendors are getting some value out of it. We know consumers are getting some value out of it, but Google isn't getting direct value and certainly their shareholders seem not to be getting direct value of any kind from it, because throughout its rise and exponential growth, the share price has gone nowhere for Google.

So as a shareholder you must be saying, "Fantastic that we are seeing this great growth in Android, but where is my money?"

I don't want to make fun of the thing but, the fact is, how many years, how many decades do you need to wait? And that was my conclusion of the article. A lot of comments came back saying that because you are not measuring value doesn't mean there isn't. And I completely concede on that. It's not about whether value was created, but whether value was captured and by whom. And if it isn't Google shareholders, then why are they doing it, and how long can you get away with that?

Just on this point also, one thing came up in the last few days, a simple question about why is the iPhone so expensive in Brazil. Let's see. How much exactly is it? I built a simple five-line table to get the data from Brazil and I compared it to the data from Finland and the data from the U.S., which are easily obtained because you can go to an Apple store and look up the prices—and then you know the conversion rates and you know the tax rates—and you can work out if they are overcharging or not. And why would they be? And are they doing it more for some products and not for others?

So we did that as an exercise by email with this other person in Brazil, and I thought now that I've done all this work I might as well write a post about it. So I wrote a post and I thought, "There are some interesting oddities about these two markets, maybe people can send in more information about their local pricing and we can compare them to other countries," and then I wrote that in the last paragraph of the post. Then people started sending emails and putting up comments in the site stating prices in Switzerland and Germany and Norway and Trinidad and Tobago. And I started to type all this into my big spreadsheet. Then somebody on Twitter said, "Why don't you put it up on Google Docs?" I said, "Great idea," and I did. And then I tweeted that and updated the blog posts and the next thing you know there's 40 countries for which people added the data themselves.

So here we have an example where I can crowdsource, and I can get detailed knowledge about the pricing, and whether there is any oddity, or what is the strategy of pricing internationally for Apple. Some of these prices come from Apple directly because they sell through their stores and therefore they have control over that, to the extent that the operator deals allow them to. But we could start to really look at this problem, and the data is out there.

But what if you were to ask this question about Google. Right? Here I am using Google Docs. The irony, right? I am using Google's own tools to study Apple, and I can't use Google's tools to study Google, because what am I going to study about Google in terms of their finances? What am I going to study? I am going to find out what the pricing of their ads are? How am I going to crowdsource that information?

Dan: Yes.

Horace: Perhaps it is possible. Perhaps. But it seems enormously complicated, especially since most people who are buying these ads are not really the users of Google.

In a weird way, and I am just forming this idea in my mind, it's a little weird. My thinking is this: I am a big user of Google. I use it every day, multiple times. I use search. My email is with them. As I said, I use Google Docs a lot for my own data and to share it, and I'll increase my usage of that. I really am fond of a lot of their products.

The problem is, though, as a user of the product, I don't pay for it, right? Because they don't have a price for them, it's free. On the other hand, obviously, they should be making money from me some other way. I really don't know how because I don't consume their ads, I've never clicked on their ads. So maybe they are monitoring my usage somewhere and they have this huge file on me and they absolutely know everything about me and they can sell it to advertisers. But that doesn't help the advertisers because I haven't clicked on anything that they have ever put in front of me. And I can assure you that most of the time I don't even see their ads because I have AdBlock on.

So the question in my mind is this: How do you follow the money on Google? I am a big user of Google's services—I'm obviously a beneficiary of Google's products—and yet I don't contribute back. I feel like I'm cheating in a way. I feel like Google is transferring value to me but I am not giving any back, and therefore there must be someone out there that's giving Google a lot of value and probably not taking a lot back. It's as if Google is taxing that person and giving me the money because their cost structure is benefitting me, whereas the revenue is coming from somewhere else.

Dan: Yes.

Horace: So I sort of formulated this hypothesis that perhaps what Google is doing is taking advantage of people who don't use their sophisticated tools which, frankly, are not easy to use. Google email is one thing as a user, but trying to create your own domains and trying to manage Google email… it's a lot easier than it used to be, but it's not for everyone. And then there are a lot of other things like Google Docs, which are not easy to use. And even search: It is really hard to be very good at search unless you are searching very trivial things. You need to understand the process of formulating a good query and so on.

And what I am struck by is that there are billions of people out there using Google but they are not gaining that much benefit from Google services that are "free." And so the controversial notion I have in my mind is that it is like they are taking from the poor and giving to the rich. Because a lot of the people who are big users of Google are intellectually rich. They are smart people. They are people who know how to make the

233

best out of the tools available from Google. That's why you have a lot of people who are fans of Google being nerdy, or they are of a class person who really dives deep into their stuff. They are the people who actually take value out of Google, in net. Google's biggest fans are those who actually bleed it the most, if you think of it that way, as a transfer-of-value question.

And the people who actually don't use Google's R&D very much, are those people who actually click on a lot of stuff, the less educated-type of users. Google, in that sense, is a tax on the poor and subsidy for the rich. It's a regressive tax. I feel weird about it in many ways because it is this contrast between those who are really knowledgeable and are able to draw huge amount of value out of Google but don't give anything back. It feels strange to me.

Compare that with Apple. The biggest fans are those who actually spend the most money on the company. If you were to ask who the biggest fans are, it's those who are spending thousands of dollars a year on Apple products. And those who don't like Apple are usually not spending any money on Apple products.

But those who don't like Google actually use Google products a lot. That's the weird thing about it. So a lot of it is upside down. I'm sure it's going to get shot full of holes, this idea, but it is something that I am trying to play with in my mind—understand the economics—because we just have so little to go on.

Dan: This is a fascinating topic.

Horace: I'd love to get other opinions on this. I mean, if someone could really think through the whole value proposition of Google. How do you work out a way of thinking, "Where does it go from here?"

John [Gruber] posted a recent comment that the better it gets, the worse it gets. The better Google gets at what it does, the more it is likely to pollute your world with ads.

Dan: Yes.

Horace: And so where does that lead? Because if that's a trend, what does that lead to? Perfection for Google is really a nightmare for everyone else.

I hate to pick on them because, like I said, I really love their products. I wish they could deliver them to me for free, but somehow that strikes me as, "There's no such thing as a free lunch." This is an old law. The TINSTAAFL law. TINSTAAFL is the initials for "There is no such thing as a free lunch." And if you take that as your premise, who is paying for my lunch?

Dan: We are. You are.

Horace: How am I paying for my lunch if I don't see ads? You see what I mean? How am I contributing? As a big user of Google, how am I contributing to the benefit and welfare of Google's shareholders? Because if they are not happy, ultimately the company cannot succeed. Because Google shareholders, at some point, will rebel.

At some point the owners of the company are going to say, "Enough is enough." This has always been my question. And this is a paradox. Again, I'm not saying that from that anomaly—from the weirdness of my behavior—we can draw conclusions about the company, but it is one data point. I don't have many and I'd love to get more, but it's another thing to think about.

You can study the same thing. Follow the money. Assume the conservation of value or whatever you want to call it. You know, what happens at Yahoo!? Who pays for Yahoo!? Or who paid for AOL? And how? And all these companies have hit a wall at some point because it looks like that didn't work out, that there was not value for the long-term.

And in the universe where search may be replaced by apps—we've gone over this before—but basically at some point these other things which they built that haven't got a price tag associated with them, like Android, like Google Docs, how do they benefit the shareholder? Ultimately, that has to be answered.

And so it's a hard business to analyze. I really find it difficult to start even to peel back the first layers and see, "If you do this, then this happens." What is the causality here? If they spend more on improving and innovating in these complex areas like social, how does that benefit everyone?

You'd think that it somehow goes through the income statement because of ads or something like that, but it's really complicated and it's very elastic. It is as if their action and the income statement are connected by a huge rubber band. You wiggle one end and nothing happens at the other whereas, in the case of Apple, it is very rigid. It's like a metal rod. What they do on the input is visible on the output.

They don't buy stuff just for fun or because it is hip. It is like they really think about it and it seems to be working out for them.

Dan: It's a great topic.

Horace: Yes.

Dan: Is this what your sit-down with Om was like? Pretty much?

Horace: Not that much. I think I was thinking more about my own business or my own life more than anything because I was telling him what I do, and I went off on this question of what is Google doing and I got a little bit upset about the fact that I wasn't getting very far in analyzing Google. He kind of chuckled, like you did, and he said, "Look, I don't have any better insight than that, and it is just a big a mystery." And that's what I am getting a lot of. No one has come up to me and said, "I've got it all figured out. I've got these guys figured out." Some have theories and say, "No, Google is all about this." But that's clearly shown to be not a complete theory because you can find a lot of examples where that doesn't work.

Telecom is one thing, but the other theory, the sort of meta theory... I think we talked about this when the Motorola deal came up and I said maybe what the real analysis is here is that Google doesn't know themselves what they are doing. They are really nothing more than a discovery process and they are always going through a learning process. And that actually fits a lot of the facts. That is the only thing that universally fits, but it's not a comfortable conclusion because that means if they don't know, you don't know. You are just saying, "We're all clueless." The blind leading the blind.

But there is that academic feel to them to some degree. There are folks there who are running the show who really haven't had much of a history before Google, haven't really failed before Google. If you see some of the other names out there who have been there, a few gray hairs, they have been burned more than once, and you tend to learn from that. And I think that Google management is fairly young.

So, again, it sounds a little bit biased and I hate to come across that way. I just want to say how much I appreciate what they do. I just wish I could understand it.

Dan: Do you think we ever will? Do you think they will ever change that? Do you think they will open things up somewhere?

Horace: Not likely.

Dan: Because Microsoft—really, as you mentioned in the beginning—they never have.

Horace: They haven't satisfied the shareholders for a long time. They have had several philosophical transitions, or you could say value-system changes, value models, or profit algorithms that have been modified.

One is in the case of the Internet. I think they embraced it very quickly after ignoring it for a long time. Famously, when Bill Gates wrote his first book *The Road Ahead*—it was published I think in '97—it didn't mention the Internet once. He talked about the information superhighway, but his notion was purely based on the dial-up services available at the time.

Dan: Right. Right.

Horace: And within two years they did a complete 180 on that. He wrote a famous memo where basically he said, "I want every single product, every single product manager, everybody has to be convincing me tomorrow how they are going to make use of the Internet and embed that into their product."

Then they've gone through the crisis they had with the government, the antitrust investigation, and they really were very antagonistic, and I think they flipped a bit and they said, "We are going to turn that attitude around completely." That's a value thing. "We are going to be more open. We are going to be more inclusive." It may or may not have been perfect execution on that, but I think they did actually come to realize that it is going to hurt them if they don't.

Of course, Apple has flipped a couple of times, but mostly it's been due to management change. Remarkably, I think Microsoft has had consistency in terms of their management hasn't really changed that much.

And so I think that they have gone through a maturing process. I don't see how really Google has gone through that yet, and sometimes companies never make it through one transition. They really are a one-trick pony. We're seeing that happening to RIM in real time.

Nokia, by the way, I'm a little bit familiar with them. They are a very old company who has gone through near-death experiences and has had to change what it does deeply without being bought out. So they used to be in a completely different industry, more than once. And that's more typical of non-American companies because once they hit bottom, no one comes in and buys them out or decides to flip it and do some kind of leveraged buy-out and whatever tricks that financiers have to try to squeeze some value out of depleted assets.

If you don't have that, then you say, "We've got nowhere else to go. We're going to have to rebuild from scratch." And that happens more frequently in older economies or countries.

But in the case of Google, I really don't know where the next phase will come from. I hear a lot of criticism of Apple that this or that is coming to an end, and that's very good criticism. You should be critical of iPod. You should be critical of the iPhone. It has reached its turning point, its peak moment, and these things are good. Hardware products are good because it's easy to measure life and vigorous competition. But I haven't heard anyone going around, "Oh, search has hit a peak." Or maybe I have heard one or two times. But it's not like repeated and re-cited as a mantra that, "Obviously, search is not going to stick around." That would be a very provocative thing to say, that there is no future for search. But I guarantee, just like there is not a future for anything, that there is no future for search.

You can argue about when Windows peaked, or not, but as a percentage of all the devices in use in the planet, Windows is going quite quickly down because they are not on [mobile] devices to any degree. And yet no one is saying, "When are we going to see the next thing after search, the next thing that Google has to skate towards."

Social is out there, but no one has really quite figured out that it is really a replacement, and that's where I think the discussion is not happening. When Steve Jobs said that he sees people spending more time in front of apps to get things done—they don't search for a restaurant, they pick up Yelp or they pick up some app that is focused on that problem. Now, when he said that, a lot of people laughed. They said, "Search absolutely is the best way to find anything. It's more flexible, it's more powerful." But it still has this constraint of interaction. And so it goes on and on. People argue that they can still hold on and that Chrome is something that's going to help them and Android is going to help them. But I am of the opinion that we need to put in a lot more effort—and I'm not the one to do it. Like I said, I don't understand it very well. We could put a lot more effort into understanding the disruption cycle of search: How long did it take [to get to this point]? How long will it last? [We need to] understand what they need to do.

The assumption that underlines everything that Apple does is that they will either get disrupted or self-disrupt because everything they do has a finite life that is really discussed with respect to Windows, with respect to search, with respect to enterprise. Oracle just had a pretty lousy quarter. And no one is saying enterprise software is actually going to go away, but I can assure with hand on heart that it will, that there will be no enterprise software business, that there will be no enterprise *anything* business because it will be all consumerized. It will be all very much the same.

Just like we don't have a separate car for going to work as we do for having fun. Or maybe some people do. But the notion of enterprise being different, and software bits don't work the same way there, or Internet doesn't work the same way there. It's just an anachronism.

So it takes time and the prediction isn't useful unless you give a time frame. In that sense I don't see value in my prediction, value in saying, "It's over." What I need to say is when, and that is something that requires heavy-duty analysis. Someone needs to step up and do it. But if you ask Gartner, if you ask any of these incumbents, or those who serve incumbents, they say, "No, this is actually perpetual. Everything is going to go on forever." And that's all I'm trying to say, that all the data points to that not being the case in history, and that's all I do is talk about how things fail.

Dan: But in a positive way.

Horace: In a positive way because from death comes birth. I mean from death comes new life.

Here's one interesting thought. I think it was something Chomsky said. He was criticizing capitalism and he was criticizing the corporation as a concept. He said corporations are not like people but they are like super-people. They have some benefits that people have and yet we give them powers that no people could ever have. And he's right in general.

One of the powers that he said they have is that they are immortal. And I thought the opposite. Corporations are much more mortal than people. Name any corporation that actually lives as much as a person does, especially a technology corporation. They are barely middle-aged right now in the best scenario.

In fact, imagine a world in which the corporations did not ever die. We would be employed or having to deal with corporations from the 19th, 18th, 17th century. We would still have the East India Company as a monopolist.

Dan: Right.

Horace: You would have the companies that were running steamships and transportation companies that were built around each technology of steam or sail. Still around, with us today flying airplanes. That does not happen. The companies tend to die as technology changes because they are disrupted by it.

That's the problem. Technology is changing even faster and so the mortality rate—the infant mortality rate, you could even say—of companies is higher than ever. And so if you want to study how companies are born and what makes a great company, you have to understand how they die. You have to understand, forensically, that what makes a company successful is the flip side of what makes a company fail. And almost no one likes to write about that.

But the first step is to understand that they do fail, and to underline the fact that all companies must in fact fail, because otherwise new ones won't come around, and those who do survive into middle age tend to have to change themselves. They go through a crisis and they become something else in later life. For example IBM [which just turned 100]. You know, you can see that happening with any brand beyond a certain age.

Some companies do live a hundred years, but they arc extremely rare, and usually you wouldn't recognize them. They have gone through multiple rebirths and all you really have is the brand.

So that's what I am saying: Mortality is actually a sign of good health in an innovation space, that mortality is the heartbeat of innovation and nothing to be sad about in terms of companies because they are not people in that way.

Below the (belt)line

Posted January 4th, 2012 as The Critical Path Episode #20

Horace and Dan begin a journey through the financial carnival that is Hollywood and talk about the wonders they encounter.

Horace: So one thing I wanted to talk about… Actually, we've been doing a series now, I suppose, a sequence of shows about the entertainment industry. And it's a funny thing for me. As I said before, this is not something that comes naturally to me, and it's not something that I've spent any time with prior to this year. I remember when I was in business school I was marveling at so many things. This and that industry were being introduced to me, and I had not thought about manufacturing all that much. I had not thought about banking or consulting or service industries in general. I was pretty much an engineer, and I thought I understood the engineering part, but then didn't understand the business part of engineering. And that was what I was hoping to get out of school.

But I was getting exposed to so many more things. But there was always one thing that was a mystery, even after I got out of there, and that was the business side of entertainment: the way Hollywood makes money. Of course, I use "Hollywood" in the broad sense because I'm including the television part of that, and also perhaps some of the music and other performing arts that are monetized.

And whenever I see something mysterious I marvel at it. I think it's fascinating. I think it's something I'd like to learn more about. So I was always puzzled. How does it exactly work? I was getting little bits and pieces of information about people. I knew someone who actually had been a producer, and I was… Everybody gets excited about anything to do with Hollywood, right? I mean, you have this association with stardom. And people are naturally attracted to that. I wasn't so much a fan of the product, not because I have anything against it, it's just that it's hard for me to enjoy the escapism of it. I'm more interested in product, which tends to be data or, I should say, a documentary-type format.

I hate to say this, but I kind of have a problem with suspension of disbelief in general. I think as I get older I'm finding it harder and harder. Whenever I see something I tend to think about how it works, not allowing myself to escape into it, which is a problem.

But I was interested by the mechanical aspect of movies and film, and how money is being made in that regard. This is a long preamble, but my point is that to this day I find it mysterious. So recently I began to try to understand it in a more rigorous way. And the path I follow whenever I try to explore something new, is I start with some fundamentals, some categorization, some way of getting a handle on it. And I think financially it's interesting to start with the numbers, and start with following the money.

Dan: Right.

Horace: So here is what I have learned. I wanted to talk about what I've learned. And it's incomplete. I've forewarned everyone. It's incomplete. There is a lot of gaps. But at least I think I understand a little bit about the production side of the business. I'm having a hard time knowing where to jump in. Let's use movies as the product. And we can see how that changes when you go to TV, for example.

Dan: Okay.

Horace: A movie is not a business in the same sense... Even the movie studio is not a business which we typically analyze. Let's say if you analyze Apple, you understand it's a bunch of product lines, and these product lines have a margin, and you'll have a certain growth rate. Things in Hollywood, and movies in particular, are projects. So the accounting is project-oriented. You put a team together, it works together on something, and then it breaks apart. There is no continuity. Everybody is a free agent, more or less. And they are assembled like a construction crew. You can think of it as building a house or building. You account for it in the same way. A lot of it is physical, a lot of it does involve hard physical labor because these sets are complicated, and unless you're doing a lot of graphics that's done in computers now, there is still quite a bit of heavy lifting required.

So it's project-oriented. And these projects are fairly complex things. Once the project is done, there is a whole bunch of other things that happen in terms of marketing the product and getting it into the theaters and getting it monetized and getting it sold to consumers. So I don't want to get into that yet. I'm going to assume that the boundary is what happens when a movie is built, as a house gets built. What is involved in that? And how do we think about the cost structure of movies?

The reason this is hard is because [the information is] not something that is public. We don't know these budgets. I've been able to find five movies whose budgets have been either leaked or have been published due to litigation. It's eye-opening because this is where the money trail begins.

You start with how much money is put together to build this thing, and then we get into some of the creative accounting that happens once you build it, how you sell it. And the sales process, and who gets how much money out of that. That's where there's a lot of controversy right now—has been for a long time, actually—about the fact that movies don't make money. That once the movie is made, people tend to have their hooks in it, but the movie itself is declared to be a loss-making business, so that people who are expecting to get a cut of the profits never do because there are no profits. And that becomes controversial because people are getting robbed—creative people who have contributed and are assuming they will get paid in terms of equity in the film never get anything out of it. And this began in the '80s. But we'll get to that in another show because it's going to take so much time.

So I want to focus now on this question of production costs. By the way, the reason I want to study this is because in the last few shows we've been asking, "Can this be democratized?" Can we see a future where people like you and me who are now creating content for distribution through various means, that content is very cheap to make compared to, let's say, having a movie studio or having even a radio station, right?

Dan: Right.

Horace: So these things have already gotten cheaper for audio, for music production. You have GarageBand or you can use other tools. You can even shoot video. But somehow people—and this has come out in the feedback from the shows, in my comments in my blog—people are saying, "Yes, but it's different for Hollywood. It's different for film. It's different for TV. You cannot democratize that content." There is always this exceptionalism about this particular medium.

So I took that as a challenge. That's why I began to look at this again, and I said, "What is it that's so hard? Why is this not something that can be done on a low budget?" And only by studying the data can we get a clue. And so here is are numbers for you.

Movies nowadays, if they're blckbuster-caliber, they're expected to have budgets about $100 million or more. And that's a staggering amount of money if you think about it.

Dan: It really is.

Horace: Sometimes the studios will publish this information and will state the budget for the movie. And often these are suspicious. There is actually a nice list of about 3,500 movie budgets I found online. I have scanned through all 3,500 of these, and the budgets I see are typically rounded off to the nearest 10 million. To me that sounds a little bit suspicious because you know the budget didn't come in with that level of precision. So I'm not quite sure those are quite accurate. But it gives you an idea, and I think again as we peel back the layers of this onion, you'll see how much of this industry relies on deception. And that's why I'm putting a big caveat here, that these numbers are actually quite approximate.

But these numbers are enormous. So a movie takes $100 million, let's say. I have the numbers here. For example, *Spider-Man*…

Dan: Mm-hmm. The first movie, the Tobey Maguire movie? Or…

Horace: Actually, the second one.

Dan: The second one, okay.

Horace: *Spider-Man 2* was $200 million.

Dan: Wow.

Horace: *Terminator 3*, which is a bit old now, it's about ten years old, $167 million. And then we have *Sahara*, which was not a great movie, but it came in at $160, and the details of that came through litigation. *Lara Croft: Tomb Raider*, $118 million. And something called *Unbreakable*, which was $73.2.

Dan: Did you see that movie, *Unbreakable*? Bruce Willis.

Horace: No, I haven't.

Dan: It's not a bad movie.

Horace: No, and actually I haven't seen any of these except T-3, I think.

Dan: You mentioned to me in chat offline, privately, that you don't really see movies. You're not a movie fan.

Horace: No. Like I said, I have trouble justifying spending two hours watching it, and I don't really get a lot out of it.

Dan: And yet you're still fascinated by this industry.

Horace: Well, yeah. I'm fascinated by a lot of things.

Dan: But usually people, you know, focus on something that they like and have an interest in, aside from just the, "It's interesting to me."

Horace: Well, to me, I could be interested in aircraft, and I don't need to be a pilot. You know, I don't need to fly everything.

Dan: That's true.

Horace: It's technically interesting.

Dan: Very true.

Horace: So you have these movies varying in budget from $70 million, which is *Unbreakable*—$73 million—to about $200 million. So that's only a sample of five. Not many. But let's see what we can get out of this.

The interesting thing, and I learned this from someone in the TV business, is that there is distinction in that budget between two major categories of cost, and that's called "below the line" and "above the line." This term is actually used in accounting in some other ways related to whether the expenses of something are affecting that particular period of time when they're being accounted for. But this is nothing to do with the Hollywood definition of below the line and above the line.

Dan: Right.

Horace: Below-the-line accounting, or below-the-line budget, in a Hollywood production, means people involved in the mechanical aspect of production. Meaning, that these are people typically who are operating the equipment, people who are building the sets or tearing them down, people who are either in cinematography, photography, makeup and so on. These are people who are actually doing the hard jobs.

Typically, and I would say almost universally, they are unionized. And they get a certain rate per hour.

Dan: Right.

Horace: But they get paid whether the movie is successful or not. They get paid because they are really basically hourly workers.

Now, that's below the line. There are a lot of other costs. You have, for example, insurance and other things which are attached to that cost structure, but that's all the lump of costs which are basically fixed, and they don't really change depending on the idea of the film, as opposed to above the line.

Above the line is what the creative people are paid. So they are typically the screenplay authors, the story itself if there are rights involved, the producers, people who are essentially management and who organize things and make sure that things get done, but they have ultimate responsibility. So there is management and artistic people are lumped into this, above the line. The director, obviously. And of course the cast. Now, the cast itself is very asymmetric. You have the lead, if there is a lead—typically there is a lead—getting paid the lion's share. And then you have supporting cast, one or two supporting actors, and then a whole bunch of extras. And they get paid, like, 20 percent [of casting costs]. So it's like 80/20 in terms of what the cast is paid.

It varies dramatically, and this is where you start to look at the films side by side. A movie can be positioned very much around the rights to Spider-Man as the franchise, a very big part of the cost structure. So there, for example, the story rights and screenplay cost $30 million, whereas the lead actor only received $17 million, including perks.

On the other hand, in *Terminator 3* the franchise depends on the lead actor, which was Schwarzenegger. And so he received $31 million, whereas [here] the story was still significant, it was a $20 million payment for that, probably again because of legacy issues. But you can compare that, for example, to *Lara Croft*, which is a franchise built on another character. That only cost $4 million to license that character and the story that went along with that.

Some of the movies are built using a lot of special effects that require outdoor shooting, and those end up being really expensive in below-the-line costs. Other movies depend very much on the star quality of the lead and [the other] actors. For example, *Unbreakable* had $20 million below-the-line budget and above the line was $47 million, of which $22 million went to the lead actor. So you can see how it depends very much on how you position the movie, whether it's really driven by the story, or the actor, or sometimes the director.

Many times if the director is very good he'll put in people who are relatively unknown, and they'll save a lot of money because they don't need the star quality to attract people. They're attracted by the name

"Spielberg," or they're attracted by knowing something about the franchise being very, very attractive. *Indiana Jones*, for example. It gets tricky when the franchise goes through sequels and so the star starts out as unknown and over time because they become famous, they can negotiate much higher fees for themselves. So you go from being paid $3 million on your first show, or movie, and then you end up with $30 million by the fifth version of that movie.

And this actually also happens a lot in TV. In pilots and initial seasons of a show, the lead actors will get very little money. But once the show builds up a lot of momentum because you've got to keep those people as the face of the show, then they end up negotiating higher and higher contracts.

So that's above the line. The above-the-line part of the business, or the cost structure, ends up being very flexible as the business grows. And so for that reason you have to think very carefully about where the value is.

There is one other component to this cost, which is neither above nor below the line: postproduction. It's increasingly more important because that's where the visual effects is done, typically. Also, that's where music is categorized, you know, in terms of where the cost for the music rights are. And anything else that's done in editing.

So a lot of that work used to be small, but now it's growing. For example in *Spider-Man 2*, postproduction was more expensive than the production, the below-the-line production. What's interesting also, if you think about cost structures, is Pixar. Pixar, since they don't have any of this physical work needed to set up the shooting, there is zero—really, zero—production costs. And very minimal above the line because it's just getting the actors to say the lines. So there is the voice recording of the actors' voices. That's not very expensive. We don't have broken-down figures, by the way. We do know because they do release the overall budgets, that the budgets are actually keeping up with the major Hollywood productions. So, for example, the latest film—which was *Cars 2*, I think— was around $180 million from Pixar.

So it's an interesting question: What did they spend that money on? Because they don't have production, or they don't have below-the-line costs. They don't have that much in terms of talent. Sure, they have a director. But the story isn't something that they had to buy, right? They usually work off a story that is very much written in-house. And maybe was even conceived of years ago. I think Pixar famously said that their first five movies they had sketched the stories on a napkin in a restaurant and said, "We want a story about toys, or we want a story about fish, and we want a story about cars." So they had these very simple ideas, and then they developed the story through the production process.

Now, that means that they have very few of these traditional costs. But they had a lot more of what's typically postproduction. So of that $180 million, my guess would be at least $150 million of that was spent on people sitting and animating the movie. It gets expensive because this is a time-consuming process. So you take the salary of all the production staff... If you go look at the end of a Pixar movie and try to see how many minutes it takes to show the credits, literally it goes on and on and on. They have to have a little mini-movie to show next to the credits because it literally takes ten minutes.

And in those credits, they list thousands of people, it seems like thousands of people. Maybe it's hundreds. But it's so many people that worked for 18 months, sometimes two or more years, and all of these salaries added up to $180 million.

So that's why those movies are expensive. They're polishing and polishing and polishing what is basically a very simple idea executed very well. So a very different structure [than movies with actors]. It doesn't change the bottom line. It doesn't change the cost overall. But what they seem to be changing is that they are more reliable, they're more consistent, and probably they meet targets a lot easier versus the volatility and the unknowns that happen in producing movies where you have sets and you are over budget all the time.

So there is a lot of risk associated with [filming live action]. Pixar is relatively low risk. So when you're writing that big check for them, as Disney does, you know what you're getting. And that really improves your economics.

I don't know if there is a punch line to this, but I've looked at the numbers and what I'm getting is that this is a structure that is not typically sustainable. It's grown over time. The cost structure has grown tremendously. A lot of the people involved haven't changed. The studios haven't changed. Yes, the stars come in and out, but basically the model has been unchanging, except it's inflating all the time.

At the same time, the audience is shrinking in the theaters, and they're trying to get more and more revenue from other sources—from DVD, from distribution through other means. But economically, if you follow the money, costs are going up but income isn't going up very much. And therefore you have a potential crisis. So the real question, I think, is, does this system of making movies for $100 million that require three times that in terms of revenues to be truly breakeven, even for the studio to break even... The studio typically takes 30 to 40 percent of gross. And so they need to get that, they need a $200 million movie to sell at around $600 million in revenue to break even, even as a studio.

It's really challenging to me to see how this can be scaled going forward. And what I began reading, also, is why a lot of the funny things that happened in terms of accounting for these products, how that's changing. There are people who are exposing some of the methods that are being used to obfuscate what's actually happening. And I'm starting to feel a little uncomfortable because the answers are not pleasant. The answers seem to be pointing to an interesting—how do I say it?—there is not deception, necessarily, but there is a decreasing opacity of what's really going on in terms of where the value in the business is.

And [then there's] distribution versus the creative part of the business. Is the product more important than the distribution? And that's where I'm going next. But what I'd like to get some feedback on is, if you are in the industry—if you are in this business—how much of what happens in terms of accounting practice, in terms of understanding where the value is, in terms of understanding what the job to be done is... How much of that is actually a topic of open discussion, and how much of it is completely ignored? The reason I ask this is because whenever I see a debate in the technology press about media, there is usually asserted a conspiracy that there are bad guys who are in the industry, who are either organized as RIAA or MPAA, that are trying to infringe upon people's rights.

Dan: Right.

Horace: And so there is always this them-and-us attitude between technology people and content people. And then there is a lot of conspiracy theory. There is a lot of blaming of individuals, assuming that there is malice. And at the same time, I think there isn't any debate about where does the money come from and where does it go. Is the industry itself—if there is a surplus of profits in the industry—is Hollywood actually just sucking up all this value and stashing it away, or carrying it off in suitcases to Mexico?

Whenever you get into this magnitude of capital, there has to be conservation of capital. Where does the capital go? Are these studios who are sucking in more and more supposedly illicit profits, are they just blowing it on extravagant things, or are they ploughing it back into movies which are increasingly more and more expensive?

Is anyone happy in Hollywood with the way things are? Are they all just smoking cigars and rubbing their hands together gleefully? Or are they actually pissed off at the world because things aren't working out the way they used to work out?

I suspect more and more that Hollywood is actually under a lot of stress right now and that they're not happy. And the technology industry—which blames them for doing all these bad things—is seen as the bad guy because they're taking away the growth that they have been expecting.

So both sides are talking past each other. I suspect that there is something related to disruption happening. What I'm curious is how much of the dialogue that needs to happen is happening. But I haven't seen the kind of debate about where the industry is going fundamentally through disruption, through technology, vis-à-vis fingerpointing and blaming one another for what's happening.

I suspect that, as typically happens, there is no one at fault per se. There is just the stress of change that's uncomfortable. And I'm trying to find out how this could probably evolve. Again, my hypothesis is that this is going to happen through a drastic reduction in the cost structure, a drastic reduction in the expectation of profitability, but also the expectation of distribution of this product.

It's where I've been coming from.

Dan: It's very interesting, and I think it's really cool that you're turning your gaze to this. This all seems connected, though, to what we've been talking about in the last few shows, as you mentioned, but your bigger examination, I think, of maybe where Apple is headed and what's going on with entertainment in general. And it sounds like what you're saying to me is that this industry must change.

Horace: Right. So here is where it gets interesting. And I have so many thoughts that I have trouble completing them all. These samples which I mentioned, the $70 to $200 million projects, are probably profitable in the sense that they gave money back to the the people who financed them. They actually probably broke even. Again, there is the paper profit and there is the actual profit. I suspect that they've done rather well. But when you look at that list of all greatest films of all time—3,500 films—and you look at some of the ones which actually had the greatest box office returns, or the greatest box office income, relative to their budgets, there are some really spectacular standouts. There have been several movies that have grossed enormous numbers, even though they cost almost nothing to make. They were virally successful. I'm trying to think of the name right now. *The Full Monty* comes to mind.

Dan: Okay.

Horace: This was a hit—I don't know how many years ago. But it was a very small production that just exploded. There was that other one where it looked like it was made like a homemade type movie, it was scary [*Blair Witch Project*]. But these low-budget productions… Again, some of the budgets are, like I said, fictitious, but they're still an order of magnitude lower than a classic production in Hollywood. And so what's interesting is that you can have a huge hit from a very small amount of money. The problem is predictability there.

The other question, though, is if you can spend and you can build a movie for under a million dollars, and I'm sure you can, the challenge for the builder of that movie is that they need to then find distribution for that movie. Historically, that's been the problem. The avenues to the customer are controlled by institutions. They're controlled by either those who distribute to theaters—which are the large houses—there are also problems of getting DVDs in the hands of people, and then there are problems of getting the rights sold to those who might actually want to broadcast or sell the movie.

So there are these gatekeepers to these channels. And I think that the truly disruptive approach would be that someone says, "We can make a movie for a very low budget. Even with very advanced visual effects." You can substitute all the stunt work, which has enormous costs associated with it. It's not just the stuntmen, but you've got to deal with insurance issues, you've got to deal with all kinds of regulations. You've got to deal with where you can shoot and fees and... It's amazing when you look at these budget line items how expensive things are.

That's why a lot of people are going to visual effects, not because they look better or they are more believable. In fact, they don't and aren't. I think they look very artificial to me. But they do it because the costs are so much cheaper. Even if they're not cheap, like I said, with Pixar, or *Spider-Man*. Visual effects in *Spider-Man* cost... I think it was $60 million or more.

These things still are more reliable, predictable. People sitting in cubicles are a lot easier to deal with than people who are having to blow things up.

So that's happening already. There is this flow away from the physical more towards the virtual. But that's where we get excited because we know, as technology people, we know Moore's Law. We know that that stuff can easily and very rapidly go to zero. And has been happening. So I've seen examples on the Internet or on YouTube where people have, on their own time and with their own equipment, built brilliant visual effects—almost what you might call Hollywood-quality, science-fiction-like material.

And that stuff is going to get better and better. That's where the disruption happens. Right now, the way that person gets a benefit from it is that they might get hired into working for a major studio or a production company that builds these special effects. So people are using their own time and their own effort to build a brand for themselves. It's like a blogger writing their heart out and then getting hired by the *New York Times*, and then getting a salary as the payoff. You know, even writers like this— the person who wrote Sh*t My Dad Says [on Twitter]...

Dan: Right.

Horace: Sorry for the profanity there. The person who wrote that ended up being employed by a studio to make a show about the very thing he invented.

Dan: Right.

Horace: But they didn't write Angry Birds and become a billionaire. They just wrote Angry Birds and then got hired to be a programmer. You see?

Dan: Yeah.

Horace: It's a crazy idea when you come from the tech world to see how badly treated creative people are. [They] get nothing. [They] may get some very small residual upside. But really it's about getting a fee. The the show gets cancelled—and you get fired—because they screwed up in executing the implementation of your idea. Because you're just a small part of [what needs to be built]. To me, whenever I compare and contrast the app and the developer world, which I think is just as creative as the people who are doing material for movies and film and TV...

Dan: Yeah.

Horace: ...you see the disparate reward schemes. The only people in Hollywood who seem to be getting super, super-rich, are those who have been essentially vested into the system for a long time. You have to struggle even if you're a writer or an actor. You know the right people, you get in—you have a lucky break or two. You persist and persist and you continue to stay lucky. And eventually you become part of the machine. And at that moment, when you're vested, you put all your energy into sustaining that. You don't really work at disrupting it or changing it. You are a made man.

It's really a very curious phenomenon. In technology, people build something and only turn around and destroy it and build something new. There is always this innovation process which throws away the old and builds the new, whereas that doesn't happen in the system that we see in Hollywood. When you start to look at the accounting practices and you start to look...

I don't want to be judgmental, but you do get this impression that there isn't honesty, that it's all an illusion, that the most creative people are the accountants. There are all these clichés about it. And I'm always puzzled by why. Why is this so? Why has it become this way? How long has it been this way? And a lot of people are warning [creative people], "Stay away from [Hollywood]. Don't do that. It's a trap. Don't do that. Get away from it. It's not good."

All of that happens. Why is that? Why is that? To me, the answer is always because there is no innovation. Because the system is designed to prevent innovation or, if it accepts it, it only accepts a sustaining innovation, where the focus is on the preservation of the existing business model. And the business model is distribution. It's not production. Production is, again, there is a cost side to be minimized. Yes, you have to pay off the talent. But the studios are in the business of distributing stuff. That's the machinery. That is what cannot change.

We have great stories over time, and you have Sony coming in, buying into the system.

Dan: Mm-hmm.

Horace: Sony didn't come into this business [to change it]. They had been making a piece of the value chain. They made the players, the end terminals. And then they said, "We understand that we need to integrate backward." The way to do that is to buy pieces of the value chain, so they bought backwards into the value chain. But they were completely co-opted by the system. They didn't go in to say, "We're going to use these new properties of distribution and the catalogs we got with Sony Music to give stuff for free." That would have been a very disruptive thing. They could have offered everything: "All-you-can-eat entertainment if you buy our slightly higher-priced hardware." They did no such thing. In fact, they completely flipped the equation around and they said, "We will do whatever we can to sustain Hollywood and to sustain the movie and the music businesses, to the extent that we'll impose draconian DRM [Digital Rights Management] on our devices."

Dan: Mm-hmm.

Horace: "And we're going to protect that thing which actually is rotten, and we're going to dismantle the cool thing which was the technology." That is the crisis that they faced long ago in their strategy, and I think partly unraveled with Apple and the iPod coming in and saying, "No, the value is here. The value is where the thing touches the human hand." And it's not even in the creative. The creative guys are getting screwed as everyone else is. The problem is that it's in the distribution that value is basically absorbed today. But there is the question of how much value is that adding given that we have the Internet.

I believe it's going to take time. This will happen, this disruption will happen. I'm just trying to figure out exactly what is a roadmap to that.

And by looking at the data, by looking at these numbers which, again, are not open, we don't have visibility, but we can try to get these fragments and put them together, and we can get a clue where things might go.

Dan: Do you want to speculate? Do you want to...

Horace: This is the criticism that I get: The assumption is that you cannot get quality. Quality entertainment costs money. That's the fundamental assumption. And I believe that that's not true. I believe quality entertainment is as cheap as quality writing. There is no formula for making a great movie cheaply.

But I do have another formula. Here is how to make a great newspaper cheaply. Here is how to make a great musical experience cheaply. Here is even how to make theater, as I spoke about with Hoon Lee [in The Critical Path Episode #15], here is how to make theater cheaply.

Plenty of people do it entirely out of the goodness of their hearts. So when you follow the logic, the assumption always becomes, "It's a $200 million price point to get a good movie reliably." And the answer to that is, "Well, maybe not. Maybe you can make ..." As I said, Pixar gets $180 million and they do it reliably. But I think the disruption that may need to happen is that you'll have a Pixar 2, or a Pixar n+1, where it's actually done at a huge discount to the current [model].

So if you can make a Pixar-quality movie for $10 million... Here is where we get into a good debate because you say, "Look, that takes 500 people two years to do, and you can't get rid of the people. You can't—even if you have faster computers—you're not going to get a movie out faster than that." And you do need all these people because you have all of these details in the characterization, in the way that you make the really high-quality performance look live, look alive, look compelling.

I cannot argue against that. The only question is, does technology help? Can you get an intelligent system in place that will accelerate that development process? And this is controversial. But this is the question of... those people who are employed doing this, perhaps their salaries are very high and it might make sense to perhaps offshore some of that. And I don't say that that's necessarily what you need to do, but there are questions about whether it really does require $180 million to make an animated movie.

So one has to look at this under a microscope. And I'm not the one to do it. But you have to think about that. And I'm sure people are doing this. They're thinking about how to make great movies less expensively. And they'll probably be predominantly done inside of a computer. They're not going to be done with actors being paid tens of millions of dollars along with stuntmen and all that. So that's what's happening. The cost pressures are very strong.

The other thing that I would look is innovation in terms of financing. Right now, the idea is that the studios need to open their checkbook, write these huge checks, make sure the production happens, and then they get rewarded for that. That equation of taking a big risk with a lot of money forces the quality to actually go down. This is why they're doing more and more cookie-cutter type of movies. They're doing more and more Spider-Man or whatever comic book character we can possibly dredge up.

That's because they know the formula works, right? They're all about predictability. When the numbers are so big, you get more and more risk aversion. And so, again, is this unsustainable? How far can you go? What is *Spider-Man 20* going to cost? And why would you go see it?

The other side of it is, can you flip it and ask creative people to think of how can you make a low-cost movie that's very good quality? But also, can we get it financed by people who normally are not in that business?

And this is where it gets interesting because I've heard that there are a lot of people now who are typically advertising or brand-oriented people. You remember product placement has become a big part of…

Dan: Annoyingly so, right?

Horace: Annoyingly so.

Dan: Now, if you said that was the reason you don't watch movies, I would have understood that immediately. It's getting worse and worse and worse.

Horace: Well, to me, of course, it jumps out at me if I ever see it. I used to be a big James Bond fan. But now when you go see it today, it's basically a Sony commercial. And it just completely sticks in your craw. But what I would point out, though, is that if someone can come to the table with… Let's say it's a $5 million movie about vampires. We're going to bring the… not A-listers.

By the way, do you know what the whole listing thing is, A-, B-, C-listers? This is actually another thing I discovered a while back. "An A-list actor," that's not just the term thrown around. There actually is such a list, and the list is compiled and it's calculated by several metrics. [It measures] whether the star is bankable. Can you actually quantify how much money that person's presence in the franchise is worth? And bankability is not just because they are famous. Bankability also goes deeper in terms of, do they have a personality that projects well in the promotion of the movie? Can you have them in interviews and they won't embarrass you? Are they able to articulate well? Are they funny? Are they presentable?

So there could be people who are very, very good actors, but they aren't bankable. That's why foreign actors have trouble in the United States. Because they're not bankable in the same way, in a promotional way.

But anyway, you get these A-listers and B and C, and then you make a movie and you start to calculate things. "We have a certain budget, we're going to pull this level of talent into it." But the question is, where is the money going to come from? Traditionally, again, the people who put up the money are the distributors, those who have access to the market, because the assumption is that's where the value is. But if you upend that, if you completely reverse that question of where the money comes from, and where the value comes from, you can get really creative.

It could be a sponsor. I wish it weren't. I don't want to see a vampire movie sponsored by some drinks company. But, again, this is where innovation happens, where people start to think, "Who can benefit from the movie?" It could be, for example, something to do with tourism. If you wanted to have a movie set in a particular location, and the financing comes from the people who would benefit from visitors to that location. So there's all kinds of ideas.

Dan: Mm-hmm.

Horace: It could be even technology companies that come in and say, "We need content to distribute to our devices." So if Apple, for example, or Google, were to say, "We want to get into the production business because we want to create..." HBO did this, by the way. And HBO is not the traditional player in the game, but they came in and began to produce content because they wanted to have something original that cost less in total for them, and it differentiated them. So an HBO original production is something that really put them on the map. So you have here a player who's typically far further down the chain getting into production, and I would imagine someone even further down the chain like your Apple, Google, Microsoft—whatever—comes in and says, "We're going to produce."

What I would prefer to see is that they provide a platform for other people to stand on, like in the app world, and say, "You become a producer if you have minimum requirements in terms of quality, but you can actually deliver content."

It's the same story in TV, by the way. All of this discussion we've had was about movies, but I think TV production has also gone through a crisis. There is also below the line, above the line. There is also the question of technology that has changed the economics. There is also the question of reality [TV] as a format that has changed the economics as well. So all of these are happening to some degree, and I just imagine that... Unfortunately, I don't have the data to plot this, but what I imagine in my mind is that there is a progression and an end point where we see this collapsing or we see a crisis happening.

The other thing you have to think about is the final question of what people are used to consuming. Here is where another exception is thrown, another objection comes up. There is the fact that people are used to blockbusters, they don't want to see something that feels weird, is the wrong format, is unusual, is different, and so on.

Dan: Right.

Horace: It's [tautological] it is what it is because that's what it is. Well, the problem there is, again, that the way it is now is not the way it's always been. It's gotten to this point through a period of innovation, through a period of experimentation. The definition of what a Hollywood movie is is the result of a process. A blockbuster, in fact, was invented in the '70s—the summer blockbuster in particular. Prior to that there was no such thing. Summer was a dead time, when no movies were shown in the summertime. No good movies.

Dan: Mm-hmm.

Horace: It was all about whether it was a holiday movie or not. And that all changed with *Jaws*. And later with *Star Wars*. And they established this consistency about creating huge hits for summer viewing. You can go to Wikipedia and look up *blockbuster* and there are great stories there. But that's just one example of it. But the whole idea of how you package this stuff, the idea of sequels, the idea of computer movies, think about that. We have so many computer-generated movies now, but that was a very novel thing when it first came out. Even animation itself—*Cinderella*, which was the first animated movie—was a huge risk for Walt Disney. Most people thought that would be a flop. And that established that genre

CGI was also established as a genre. So now the question is, can we establish a new genre? There is nothing wrong with being small in the beginning. You have to think creatively and you have to try things: a low-budget movie, financed in a curious and interesting way, sold through a curious and interesting channel. Perhaps getting the audience built virally [online], so that you don't actually have to pay anyone to deliver that audience to you. All of these things can happen. And I would imagine even that the leadership in making it happen might—and this is where courage needs to be—it might happen from Hollywood insiders.

If someone will step out—either a director, a great director, or one who has the deep pockets, or Tom Hanks, or someone of that caliber—actually takes a leadership position and says, "I think I'm better off bypassing the system" they'll be blacklisted. They will have the wrath of the whole system upon them. But perhaps they feel that they can live with that. That's tough. That's hard to imagine. Most of the disruptions happen from complete outsiders who are too naïve to know what they're facing. They're just doing it. They just did it because they thought it was cool, and let's see what happens there.

Again, this debate is going to continue for a long, long time.

Dan: Yeah.

Horace: But you know, what I'd like to do in our next show, perhaps, is try to figure out exactly the causality for a lot of what passes as creative accounting. Like I mentioned earlier, this notion that no one is telling the truth here and that there is so much deception going on, and mistrust of the industry from outside the industry. But within the industry itself, what's actually driving that? It's a very, very curious question. I think you need to ask "why" five times before you really understand the cause of such a thing. Right now, we're just at the first "why," and the answer typically is, "They're just bad people." I don't think that's the case.

Dan: It's an interesting examination. I'd love to do it for the next show.

Horace: I mean, it's one of those things that... As you said, we are outsiders in this game, and I'm not even a consumer of it. And maybe that's what you need to be able to step back and be unattached, unemotionally attached. To sort of think it through. You know, there is a saying about sausages. This was a saying by [Otto von] Bismarck—that those admire the sausage and the law should never see how they're made. So those who enjoy Hollywood, who enjoy movies, are not the good people to analyze it. Because I think they get too attached to believing that this is a good product. The fact is that it could be a lot more. It could be a lot better, could be a lot more interesting, a lot more innovative. And I get the sense that this is one of those things that's going to happen, that disruption will happen in the next five years, at most.

Dan: So the industry as we know it is...

Horace: It's the last domino to fall. Like I said, we've seen print, we've seen music, we've seen magazines, maybe. And many of the media types out there have suffered. And now it's only a question of when, not if. We're still debating "" with respect to the visual media. And I can't for the life of me see why we should draw an exception for that. And that's why I'm trying to think through how that will happen. And just today I tweeted, "Why is it that movie prices are all the same? Why is it that if you watch a lousy movie or an unpopular movie, you have to pay the same ticket price as if you watch a good movie?" And almost all theaters are priced the same way. There is a lot of strangeness about pricing. Pricing is very important because pricing is the signal by which markets identify quality, and identify where investment should happen. In other words, they're not doing it through that price, they're using other metrics, like volume of purchases for defining quality. So why not be able to actually implement something like that? And there is an interesting discussion on that. It was in *The Atlantic*—and one can even see that as a symptom of something deeper in this industry that is really not right—that is really ripe for dramatic change.

Dan: Yeah.

Horace: More of that coming.

Dan: Well, I'm looking forward to the next show.

Horace: Yeah, this is all so—it's not easy to put it in a narrative that's clean, that flows nicely. I don't know enough and it seems incomplete. But let's muddle through it. Let's muddle through it together. Let's figure it out.

Dan: If this is muddling through, I think we're doing pretty good.

Horace: A lot of what you heard today has come from people who have sent me information, who have spoken with me. And of course anything that's public I try to absorb as well. Like, these budgets are indirectly via Wikipedia, of all places. There is a book out there by a man—his last name is Epstein. He has a book called *The Hollywood Economist*. I've actually ordered the next version of it, which is going to come out at the end of June, so I haven't read it yet. I decided to wait until the next version. He's an investigative journalist who has dug up a lot of this material. I think he's focused more on telling the story of the mysteries of Hollywood. I'm very hopeful that he has more about the causality in there.

I've heard him speak also at a podcast for a show on NPR. We'll get some of these links for you. But it's almost like he's tilting at windows. There are so few people who are exploring this—and they have to be trained as investigators. No one is analyzing this in the way we might study a technology or a technology company—that we may get the annual reports and we may pore over them. Or we get the quarterlies and we get the data and we put up spreadsheets and we debate our assumptions. There seems to be a veil across the whole industry. Nothing leaks out. They're almost bound by a code of secrecy that they cannot reveal even the most basic questions of how much things are worth, and where the value is, and who's getting paid and who isn't.

And it only comes out through litigation, or investigation. It's a pity. This is a huge industry. It's crucial to the economy in general. I think it's a cultural product that the whole world is hungry for. And it's mysterious also that it hasn't been duplicated outside the United States. There have been many attempts. But, again, I hope that through our conversation here we can get to the bottom of it. We can get more information flowing out of this. And not for the purpose of destroying it, but rather for the purpose of building something greater.

Negative Costs
Posted January 11th, 2012 as The Critical Path Episode #21

We continue our discussion of the creative side of Hollywood accounting, Dan and Horace take on the way income from movies is distributed and why no movies ever make money. The observations sharpen focus on the overarching influence distribution has on the creative process.

Dan: Horace, how are you?

Horace: I am very well, Dan. Thanks for asking.

Dan: This is not our first show since the New Year, though, is it?

Horace: No, we've had one and it's been a great one actually. It was on what I call "Below the belt(line)," which is a take on the "below the line" accounting term used in Hollywood production accounting. So we dove a little bit into the way to account for, and therefore to think about, how Hollywood produces movies and, indirectly, how TV is produced as well.

And the great thing about the show for me was the feedback. I had a huge amount of it, not just comments but also direct emails from people who were in the industry, and I managed to get a few conversations going. And so that's great, I feel like I've learned a lot. In fact, I think I will follow up with some of those conversations in terms of having interviews with people who can share more and who have seen it from the inside.

Today I wanted to go with a second episode in this line because what we talked about last time was the costs. I think it's a good starting point. Now we have to talk about the revenues—how is money made and where does it go?—which I think tells the other half of the story.

And the third half of the story will be on some of the bigger implications of... In fact, there's pieces which we cannot even get into—things like development, which is what happens before production even begins. We need to think about also the implications of this model that Hollywood uses for the creative process, the way they monetize creativity vis-à-vis the way technology people monetize creativity. And I think technology people are really a mirror image of what happens in the other arts, and the ideation process—the way people think of new ideas—and the way they commit those ideas to product, and the way those products then become valuable. A very similar process happens with the other media types. And now with apps becoming a media in themselves, I'd love to contrast these two universes.

It's fascinating. I've gone down that road a little bit in my mind and I think it's absolutely fascinating because you can really compare. If you are listening right now and you are in the world of development—software development—count yourself among the lucky ones because there are so many other people who are creative who are not being compensated well for their work.

So if that's okay with you, I'd like to sort of plunge right in.

Dan: Yes.

Horace: So, again, as I said in the last episode if you didn't catch it, a lot of the facts that are being discussed or that we are discussing now are based on leaks. They are not public information. Either leaks because someone broke a confidentiality agreement, or because they were actually part of a lawsuit. So whatever we have, we weren't meant to have. If the industry were to have its way, there would be zero information about how it works.

Having said that, we get a very limited sample. Out of thousands of movies, we only get to see the financials of literally a handful. And for that reason I must disclaim a little bit, that the conclusions we draw may not be accurate. But still, with these small glimpses into the industry we can still tell an interesting story.

So what I did last time is I went over—and I also put on my blog— the data from five movie productions. One of the feedbacks was that a lot of that data seems incomplete, seems inaccurate—seems, not false, but you are getting a partial view. That's because, again, this is not a transparent process.

What I am turning now to look at is some of the data that has come out about what happens once the movie is in the can and it's distributed. So we had the production costs, and like I said, there is some development cost before production, which we can get to perhaps in the third show. Then there is the production itself, which is literally like a construction project. It's accounted as a project and a lot of the way construction works is the way movie production works. Literally, you've got people who are carpenters coming in and you've got people who are architects coming in, and you've got a lot of chaos for a long time. Sometimes you are over-budget and things run longer. And it's dirty and it's smelly and it's all those ugly things.

Then after that is done, the movie is complete and now it is time to sell it, and the selling is the distribution process. It's advertised and marketed by what we know of as the movie companies, the studios. Studios used to do everything in the value chain. They would do the production themselves in factory-like lots. The production was done indoors in the famous lots of Hollywood, and then they would be selling these things through their theaters. So it's like they owned the retail chain as well. And so there really was complete vertical integration.

That ended in about the late '40s because Congress intervened and said—or was it the Supreme Court? I forget exactly—but it was declared infringing on antitrust law. And so the split was made between theaters

260

and distribution. Eventually production also became outsourced, mostly. Not exclusively, but there is a lot of outsourcing of production. So once the movie is made, it becomes a corporation of its own. And there are complex reasons why that is. We will get into some of the accounting issues, but basically there are tax implications and other reasons why the movie stands as a separate corporation. And then once it is set up that way and marketed, then the money starts to come in.

Now, of course it first comes in from theatrical release, which means movie theaters. But then there are all these other releases: television, non-theatrical, foreign—which actually are considered separate from initial release in the U.S.—pay TV, video cassettes, and then merchandizing revenues, and various other royalties that might come from the franchise.

What's interesting, though, is that all these pools of money are being built up. You can visualize it as a container where money is pouring in, but at the same time... Remember when we had the discussion about cash and how companies can be seen as a black box?

Dan: Right.

Horace: The difference is that [typical] companies are designed to make money. A movie black box is not designed to make money. It's a design where money comes in and money comes back out, but what is left inside the box is usually something negative. It's a debt. I'll explain that a little bit. Let's assume that money starts flowing in from all these revenue sources like I said. The first thing that happens is you have to pay out the expenses of this company. Now, the number one expense of a movie is a fee to the distributor. And remember, the distributor is the original financier. This is the studio who decided to make the movie in the first place, and they paid a lot of money to the production company. And they paid out for the talent and all that other stuff that had to be paid up front, and now they are taking a fee back out of the movie.

Now, here is the magical thing that happens. That fee doesn't go against their expenses. It's like you've got 100 million dollars to make a movie and you start to receive, let's say, 30 million in the first month or so. And you don't write down that the 100 million dollars is now 70 million dollars that the movie owes me. No. That money is kind of like a tip. It's a commission for having sold the movie. It has nothing to do with paying off the movie. The movie's costs are buried in the company that is the holding company for the movie, and that's actually called a negative cost. It's not negative because, as a value, negative is less than zero; it's negative because it's called the cost of the negative, of the film negative. Back in the day when you had film—I guess you still do—you'd have the negative. So the negative cost was like, "How much did it cost me to build that original movie in a can." And that's put in there as negative cost, and added to that is the interest rate.

I really hope I'm not losing everyone here.

Dan: I think it's interesting. I think it's real interesting. It's the same thing we talked about before. I don't think people approach it this way. So this is educational.

Horace: It was an eye-opener for me, and it took me a while to get it. So I am hoping that if I tell it to you, you'll get it. But I think it's hard to get. You may have to listen to it twice and look at the data. And I hope to again visualize this in some way on my site.

But the point is, why did this become an issue? It becomes an issue because some people are given the contract, or negotiate a contract where they are told that you get a certain amount of money. Like you do if you build a software company, you get a little bit of salary and you get a bunch of equity. Well, in the case of moviemaking, the equity tends to be like, "After we pay off the expenses, you are going to get a cut of the profits of this movie." And what has happened historically is that people have fallen for this as a trap. There is never any money that comes out of the moviemaking process. There is never profit in a movie.

And this is where people outside the industry are appalled and shocked that movies which are fantastically successful—iconic movies, classics—end up being declared as money losers. And the person who took a deal where they're going to get a percent of profit gets nothing. And a lot of people have fallen into that trap. Obviously, those who fell into the trap were from outside the industry because no one in the industry would take a percentage of net. You'd take a percentage of gross if you can or, if not, you'd just get paid up front.

I think five percent of movies ultimately do make money. It may take decades to get there. So even if they do make money you won't see anything for a very long time.

So this came out and people were so upset that they sued, and so these lawsuits entered into the consciousness of people about how the moviemaking business works. And we've had these scandals. I can give a couple of examples, but I think the most commonly cited is *Forrest Gump*. *Forrest Gump* was a huge hit. It was probably number one that year, but the original author of the concept of the story—it may have been a book actually...

Dan: Yes, it was a book.

Horace: He never got any money out of the movie.

Dan: None?

Horace: Practically none.

Dan: No kidding.

Horace: And what happened is he had written a sequel as a book and he refused to have it licensed for a movie because he said he cannot consciously throw good money after bad. He feels that he destroyed value with that. Of course, he is being somewhat cynical... He really was

262

robbed. And the robbery took place in broad daylight because everyone in the industry... He should have gotten good advice, I suppose, because it seems like everyone knows that this is how the game is played.

And it wasn't the first. In the '80s there was another one. It was *Coming to America*, I think it was called, with Eddy Murphy. So this was a movie where the guy who came up with the story was actually a writer.

Dan: You are talking about *Coming to America*.

Horace: Yes.

Dan: Okay.

Horace: Same story. The original concept came from somebody and he was robbed of that idea.

So this is where people get all upset, but I'm trying to figure out... When you look at the way the actual accounting is done, you get to see an actual understanding of why it is done this way.

So I am going to give you an example. This particular example is *Harry Potter and the Order of the Phoenix*, and I'm going to put up a link here. Again, this was a document that was leaked out to the world. This movie was released in July 2007, and we have a report of that movie's financial performance to date, as of September 30th, 2009. "Cumulative to Date"—so 2007 to 2009—and "The 12 Months Ended 2009," these are two columns and we are going to publish this.

And you can see the major line items where how much money came in. So, for example, at the end of 2009—actually around September 2009, two years into the movie—the movie had received total gross revenues of $612 million. And that's broken out also into line items "Domestic," "Foreign," "PayTV," "Video" and so on.

Immediately, the next line after that saying all the gross income, the next thing is the distribution fee. The distribution fee is what was paid back out to, in this case, Warner Bros, who was the distributor. And they received about $212 million out of the 612. So not everything, but they got, I think, a standard rate of about thirty-five, forty percent of gross paid directly to the studio. So over time, that adds up.

After all that, what they are left with is about 400 million, and you have a bunch of expenses. Now, these are the ongoing expense of continuing to show the movie. For example, physical costs like prints—making copies of it—dubbing subtitles when you have to do internationalization, advertising, ongoing advertising, taxes, duties, and so on. So keep in mind then the studio gets paid before taxes here, right? So this is not about getting a cut of profit. It's a fee. I think of it as a commission, "Thanks for helping us out. Thanks for the distributor, thanks for the sales guy to go out in the field and sell this for us."

At the end, what happened over this two-year period, all these fees and essentially all these extra costs ended up being about $200 million more. So out of the 400 that was left after having paid the studio and all the expenses, we are down to 200 now.

Here is where it gets weird though. You'd think that now you have profit. But that is still not profit because what happens is you have to count against this negative cost. This negative cost was the original cost of production that is buried in this movie. Even though, again, the studio gets its 35 percent, they don't use it to write-off the cost of production. That cost of production sits inside the movie and that's sitting in there as the huge number of $373 million, which is phenomenal because the movie didn't even cost that much. There is a bunch of stuff that's been added to it, like interest: $57 million of interest. So they're burying all their expenses. These are not sitting on the books of the studio. The studio just dumps it into this container which is called a movie and it just sits there as a liability until the movie pays it off, essentially, and then whoever has a claim on that movie gets to be paid.

So two years into *Harry Potter and the Order of the Phoenix*, we are at a negative balance on the movie of $167 million. That's, again, after it received $612 million. It's extremely important that when you hear box office numbers, or even gross-revenue numbers, you have to understand that it is completely meaningless. All of these players have to be paid, meaning that the studio has to be paid, a lot of these expenses have to be paid, and the movie itself has a huge liability of production costs. Only after all of that is paid off can you say that the movie actually generated profit. And from whatever is left, anyone who has a claim on the movie because they were given this net of profit available, that is when they get paid.

Some movies will actually be useful and valuable for decades. Some of the most iconic films like *Dr. No*, it is still making money. And I'm sure if you were a composer, if you were an actor, if you were a writer who worked on the original and you got net on that movie, you are still—or your family is still—getting money from that 30 years later. So in some ways that's a good thing. But in most cases if you expect to be paid from a hit movie, you won't get paid. You need to demand upfront fees.

And it gets ugly because actually you can sign a deal with the studio and say, "Okay, I'll accept this but you need to tell me in advance the chances that I might get to that point," and they'll probably break out some of their assumptions for you. The problem is they can write a contract with someone else after they wrote your contract. A new star, a new person comes into the movie who actually gets ahead of you and will get the money before you do, and you never knew that [when you signed]. So let's say they changed the cast and they bring in Schwarzenegger, or the latest star out there, and they suddenly have a claim on the movie of $30 million and you suddenly are at the end of the queue and you'll never see your money because they get in line in front of you. So that's actually a practice that is very frowned upon because then you signed the contract with information that was no longer valid.

So the takeaway here is that the process of Hollywood is really about getting these fees rather than getting equity. It's about getting either paid up front or getting a percentage of gross. But this is very hard to negotiate, in general, unless you are an A-list actor. And the studio themselves don't really own the movie in the way that they don't create a liability that they try to erase with revenue. And so when they say they had a great year—this was a criticism leveled at the studios because how can they say they had a great year on the movie that's losing money?—it is because of the fee structure. They are just getting 35 percent off the top. It's a very steady stream of income.

Eventually, when you add up all these streams of income, even if the movies don't make money, they're a good story for shareholders. Of course, they sunk a lot of money [into them] as well, but that's the way this accounting system works.

It's unbelievable.

Dan: Again, this is something we talked about just a little bit last week. This is something that you don't really think... I mean, we are deeply entrenched in this. This isn't going to change and even though it is sort of unbelievable and—you think about the volume of money there and it doesn't have to be that way—that's the way it is, and we don't see any external force, right now, really coming in to change this or disrupt it.

Horace: Right. I guess you are bringing up the valid point of why are we doing this at all, this analysis.

A couple of things come to mind. One is that if you move towards a model where risk-taking and financing is done differently, and that is done because of distribution... Let's not forget that the money being paid out is a royalty for distribution. That's really where you need to focus your attention very closely, that your analysis is on this question of distribution. It's because distribution is so important that all of this works the way it does. So the question is, technologically speaking, distribution has been disrupted, or the change in distribution has been the cause of disruption to a lot of other industries. So the question will be for movies... Again, the feedback you are always going to get is that things are different in this case, that there is no potential for change of distribution going forward.

Technologically, what we have seen is bandwidth has actually solved a lot of these problems over time. I remember even myself being fooled a bit in 2006, for example. I didn't think that streaming or the emergence of YouTube or the emergence of downloadable music, downloadable video—even at the early days of iTunes—that you could download some bits of video. They weren't yet doing movies but they were doing MTV-type music videos and they were doing some shorts. I remember some of the first video content were Disney cartoons. And that was interesting, it was all novelty in 2006, and here we are only five years later and we are doing movies as if there's nothing to it.

Not only Apple, but everyone else can do movies now. And yet the product hasn't changed and suddenly it's available in a much more over the top (as they say in network terminology). It's over the top. It's not through the network infrastructure, it's basically IP bits and it's layered on top of whatever the network carrier cares about.

My point is that given what we know about Moore's Law and the network effects and all the other things that technology people are keenly aware of, will these things undermine—by sheer weight of bandwidth, sheer weight of megahertz or gigahertz—will they undermine some of these business arrangements that have been built up over a hundred years?

Notice how, interestingly, technology has been embraced by the movie industry. They have somewhat opposed video tape and then DVD—although less DVD because it wasn't a recordable medium—but they have been reluctant adopters of new media because these cause some disturbance, but not a disruption. And the reason they have been embraced is because they actually could continue their business model. Nowadays, actually, theater revenue is about 18 percent of overall movie revenue. So the industry is definitely making the bulk of its money from technology that didn't exist 30 years ago.

Dan: So I don't know how far back you've looked at that particular number, but that's kind of interesting to me. So you say people going to the movie theater today, 2012, 18 percent, that's the total amount that's been made by human beings physically going to a movie theater.

Horace: By year. This latest data point I had is 2003, actually. It's quite old. But in 2003 if you took all the income that was flowing into studios, if you traced it back it came from outside of the theater. So, roughly, let's say 80 percent was from non-theatrical forums.

Dan: That's amazing.

Horace: It is, and most people never even see those numbers. They only look at the theater data. Even that isn't all that interesting. Don't forget there's also foreign theater, which is broken out separately. There is also opening-weekend data. People are so obsessed with the theater data they just look at that opening-weekend number and then decide whether the movie is successful or not. Many times, the bulk of the money will come from these secondary or tertiary sources of income.

And what I'm pointing out is that there have been technologies invented that have actually improved the finances of movie studios. They've been sustaining. That's the word to think about, is they've "sustained" the industry, and that's why it is still alive today.

What I'm saying is that the Internet is yet another one of these technologies that they could embrace and say, "That's going to sustain the exact same thing we've been doing for a hundred years. In fact, it's probably going to amplify it because it is going to make movies even more valuable and make movie distribution even more valuable, and therefore we are sitting in the middle with even more money flowing through us."

They may not keep so much of it, but things tend to amplify. Movies are costing $200 million when they used to cost $100 million or $50 million.

Of course, it's actually not so simple. Distribution is changing, filmmaking is becoming more expensive at the high end and much cheaper at the low end, and the middle is getting squeezed out. So if you were to segment movies by cost, you would see polarization—very low or very high—that's affecting a lot of the economics.

But one of the things in terms of feedback I've received is that no one in the industry is really feeling great about this. No one is thinking that this is a good time to be in the business. Everyone is feeling like they are making less money now than they used to. So although it seems like more money is flowing through the system, less of it is staying in people's pockets and is basically all being churned. So why is this happening? Is this a symptom?

This is where it gets interesting. My hypothesis is that these are symptoms of the pressure that the industry is under. No one is happy: The movie insiders aren't happy with the situation; consumers are finding things to be formulaic and repetitive and there is less creativity; a lot of critics are complaining, saying we are not seeing great product out there.

Prices tend to go up and so people complain about that. More people stay home, buy home-theater systems and do time shifting and dilation [of content]—which affect the economics—and make themselves more comfortable with the product even though it is not as good as it used to be. They deal with it by changing their consumption patterns. They change the convenience: "I'm not going to put up with a lousy movie by traveling and sitting in the theater, I'm going to put up with it at home [where I can take the edge off the downside]."

This is what is happening, and these are the symptoms. They are symptoms of pressure because of lack of innovation. The innovation isn't in 3D movies. They're the same thing.

To me, movie innovation is that the movie is redefined by principally what job it is hired to do. Meaning, the movie is distributed in new ways so that the connection between the consumer and the creator... And I don't mean the producer. I'm saying the actual artistic talent that's at the core of the thing that drives the emotions of the consumer, which is what the consumer wants to feel. That relationship needs to be closer and tighter.

As we've seen with the integration of electronics into being not just hardware, but software and services and emotion and brand, the movie value chain needs to reintegrate. The Hollywood model that I spoke of, of the '40s, needs to be built again in an integrated way. But in this case it is not the studio that sits on top of it and dictates terms, but rather it is closer to wherever the locus, the focus, the center of gravity of creativity is. And that may be in the mind of the producer [i.e., management]. Or in the mind of the director. Or in the mind of the artists, the writers or the actors. And that shift of power has to happen.

That is where distribution really is the key. If distribution is no longer the bottleneck between the emotion feeler and the emotion riser—if disintermediation is an outcome—[then] they get closer together and innovation can happen again.

This is the ideal view and I'm only saying that you have to understand the system as it is and what causes it in order for you to be able to even foresee how it might become. And that's what this exercise is about.

Dan: So you said that you got some contacts from people in the industry.

Horace: Yes. Folks everywhere from the value chain. I have someone from the theater industry, who is working in the theater business; someone from the writing side of the business, or development; some folks who have actually seen the cost structures themselves; someone who works in production. They have sent me some signals, and some of them I can speak with publicly and some privately only. But what I hope to do is reveal more and more. So now we get into more iteration: The core principles of costs and revenue division is what I'm trying to set the foundation with in these two shows.

And then what I jokingly call the third half, which is where we get into some of the contrasts. What I'd love to do, for example, is to build a model and put yourself in the shoes of a developer today, as you are, and then think, "Imagine if I had to go through this pain in order to have my creative idea reach the customer."

One example is just looking at the cycle time. How long does it take for an idea to pop into your head and for you to launch an app, a website, a web service, even a hardware product. What is the typical cycle time?

Software guys tend to be finding the hardware game to be far too slow. Right?

Dan: Right.

Horace: But when you think, "How long does it take for a movie to go from idea to blockbuster," it's shocking. The numbers are unbelievable.

Dan: You are just saying it's a very, very, very long time.

Horace: It's sometimes measured in decades.

Dan: I always hear about that. You'll hear about some movie that... Let's say you read a book and somebody options the book to turn it into a movie, and you are like, "Oh, good, they are doing something with it." Then you'll read maybe it will go into preproduction early 2015. You're like, "2015? Forget about that." Why does it take so long?

Horace: Well, I'll give you an example which I think is a good case study. You know the movie *Mamma Mia*.

Dan: Sure, sure. The musical thing.

Horace: That was out a couple of years ago as a movie. The interesting thing is that it is based on music composed in the '70s. ABBA's songs were out in the '70s, and what happened around that time was that a woman who was a producer of Broadway musicals became enchanted by the music. Let's say during the late '70s early '80s. She then decided that the quality of that music would make for a good musical, that she could develop it into a musical.

So she lobbied the two guys in ABBA who had the rights to the music. She lobbied them in the '80s to make a musical out of their songs and she created the story at that time. And the story was—spoiler alert here—that a woman who is in her 20s is getting married and she doesn't know who her father was. She was conceived in the late '60s, maybe early '70s. Therefore her mother was part of that culture in the late '70s where people were...

Dan: Free love, right?

Horace: Free love. Let's give it that broad stroke. So she's trying to figure out who here father was before getting married which, presumably, given the fact that she's probably in her 20s, would have to be late 80s if she was conceived in the '60s, or early 90s if she was conceived in the '70s.

So [the producer] was planning on launching this Broadway production around that time when the story would have been resonating. There would be a hippie father and a hippie mother who had a love child and now the love child is trying to find out who her father was and all the intrigue that follows [told through music contemporary to the mother's fun times]. This was the story. The most important part of the story is this context, this feeling, because the music had this feeling about it that was very '70s.

So the thing is that she finally succeeded to persuade the owners of the music—by the late '80s, I believe—to make this musical in the '90s. And it had a great run in the musical theaters: London, New York, and then on to Las Vegas. And they milked it for billions of dollars. It was a very successful musical.

And then, naturally, you make it into a movie. But that took another ten years. So the movie is in the movie theaters in 2007 or '08. Basically, in late 2000s there is a movie about a girl, and it's set as contemporary. You don't see the movie shot as if it was the '80s. The movie is shot as if it was today, more or less. Although they didn't really make it explicit that it is contemporary. But it would have felt weird if it wasn't. And yet this woman is supposed to have hippie parents. She must be 40 then. That's the weird thing [about the movie, not the character or the actor].

So if you get into trying to analyze the time structure of this production, it took twenty years to reach the screen from the music. Or even longer, 30 years. That's the time frame we are talking about. So I dare not think how long it would take to do some of these comic books, or these characters that are comic franchises. Probably they've been thinking about it for a long, long time. Contrast that with, an idea for a web service. If you spent even two years time thinking about development, you know that it's going to be obsolete. Because everything is going to change under you. [So] the creative side of the industry is so non-creative in terms of technology, right?

Dan: Yes.

Horace: Ironically, [movies] are comfortable in a 30-year cycle time. People aren't saying this is tragic. And that's what amazes me: How the cycle time, and therefore costs... Time is money. All of these things end up expensive. This is someone's life. If that producer spent a significant portion of her time trying to get this idea to that stage, it means that she really spent her whole career working on one show. Imagine the risk involved, and imagine the investment and the hope. Everything needs to work. Imagine if all your life as a developer was spent on one app, one site. How much would you want returned to you because it was an investment of a lifetime?

So all these things end up really costing, and because society and inflation and everything else gets more expensive over time, you have this ballooning effect of cost structures and expectations, and thus potentially an explosive downside as well.

So I don't know. I'm just an observer. I'm just pointing out these weird things. And coming from a technology perspective, it's even more striking than if you are a lay person because it is striking that it could be so much better.

I think we are cut from the same cloth. If you are the creative person, technologically speaking—a designer if you will or even a developer—your impulse is the same. Your thought process is the same. And yet as a developer you can bring it to market, you can benefit personally from it.

Consider the guy who has a concept for a sitcom versus the guy who has a concept for Angry Birds. The guy in Angry Birds is going to become a multimillionaire, and the guy who has a show concept is going to get a cubicle job for being a writer on the TV show.

And it just seems unfair to me. I feel that it is not so much that the developer is getting too good a deal, it's quite the opposite. I just feel that the writing community, the acting community—not the superstars, but the people who are as good, I think, as the superstars—they don't get anything out of life, even though they deserve it.

So that's my point. And it just seems like the system is unfair in that way.

Academically speaking, a lot of people have studied the long tail. The premise being that if you have a distribution disruption, the long tail is no longer so long or, rather, people who are in the long tail can make some money. But people have observed that with the Internet the blockbuster phenomenon hasn't changed—in fact sometimes it's amplified—that there are still very few who capture all the value.

But I am unconvinced still. That's simply because I think there's a hybrid system underway, that some of the properties being sold are sold through multiple channels, and so you are combining both in looking to value and saying, "Yes, blockbusters are still blockbusters." But I think there is still a lot of opportunity in the middle of this distribution of value to still create interesting new content.

It's going to be an ongoing debate, and personally I want to get involved by trying to create stuff. Obviously, we are doing this right now. We are doing a talk show, and I think the writing part, and the non-visual forms of production, if you will, are indeed being democratized. And now I'd like to think about what I can do in video as well.

Dan: Taking this one on. Knocking it down.

Horace: Yes. From my perspective, if you can't implement something, you are not really understanding it. So in that sense it's eating your own dog food, right? If you believe in disruption, can you try to be disruptive? If you know the method, you should practice as well as preach. So it's just common sense, but I think there are some interesting experiments we can work on this year, and maybe I shouldn't say it now, but I am looking at potentially doing something with a new form of video. We can combine what we are doing now, for example, with some visuals and, ultimately, you know, also doing something live, a form of live presentations.

Dan: Exciting stuff.

Horace: So I'd love to think it through. I haven't really practiced this very much, but I would like to think through some of these economics. Some people talk about the economics of app building, or the economics of web services, and so on. And if you think about the budgets involved in movies, and how it breaks down and who captures what, I have to say that there is probably a huge opportunity there.

The flip side is things like financing. When you get to such big numbers then it is very hard for small people to play the game.

Consider it this way: The venture-capital industry emerged since the 1950s. It's one of the best inventions in finance because prior to venture capital, you couldn't fund technology unless you were a large corporation. So if you think back before VCs, how did technology get funded? It was because large companies—like RCA, General Electric, some of the original names in radio and TV—they would fund certain development. Or it was the government doing it through defense industries. And so there wasn't the startup phenomenon until people found a way to package $5 million for someone small.

I mean, if you were an entrepreneur and you did have an idea for either technology or non-tech, you had to know somebody. It was either friends or family that were your only sources of possible funding, capital. No banks would lend to you obviously.

So the thing is that the VC industry was an amazing invention. But it is still very much a provincial one. It is [mostly] the west coast of the United States, a little bit on the east coast of the United States, and maybe a little bit in Europe. But it hasn't yet been able to scale that much. It is interesting why that is. But be that as it may, the fact is that as far as technology [is concerned], you have the possibility to go to the capital markets and get some money to get your idea started.

But you can't yet, as a creative person, go and say, "I have a great movie idea, is there a VC who would fund me?" In the music industry that's what the role of a music label or a studio is, to act essentially as a VC. And they look at deals and then they think about what are the chances of this being a hit, and therefore to probably subsidize all the losers with the winners. So certainly there is an element of risk. But it is such a tight, small group of people who make decisions,

Imagine if all the VCs were really just a dozen people and all the technology ideas would have to be funneled through them. So the problem is that those people would reach mythical value and mythical importance in the industry because they are the ones who have the keen sense or ability to decide the winners and losers. You would have inefficiencies simply because the human decision process is so concentrated, and certainly there wouldn't be enough debate or enough people placing enough bets all over the place in terms of what should be funded.

So this is another approach to this problem: By looking at the financials, or where the source of money comes, why is it then that Hollywood has not created a venture-capital industry? In other words, a new financing method where a creative person, like a developer in Silicon Valley, could go and say, "I have a project in mind, let me pitch it to you with some slides." Or, "Give me some seed money to do a prototype and once we see if the prototype is successful we can go to the next phase." It doesn't work that way.

You ought to be able to answer the fundamental question of what's wrong [with Hollywood] by answering why there are no financing possibilities? Is it because the risks are too high? No, I think it goes back to the distribution question, because even if you have a great concept, the guy who funds you is the one who is going to sell it.

You see? There is this fundamental dilemma there. So they are the gatekeeper and the financier. I haven't thought through the implications of this, but you can see already that there's something wrong with this picture.

Dan: Yes.

Horace: And, again, if you throw away the distribution power, or you devalue the distribution power, could a new financing method emerge? Because suddenly you decouple these things and suddenly capital markets are open to you. Maybe hedge funds will get set up to finance movies, or maybe you will have VCs, or friends and family, or you will have angel [investors] for movies and for other forms of creative work.

Since the economics are similar—the risk and reward, the fact that you do have a blockbuster versus a lot of failures—all of the dynamics are exactly the same. The processes of creativity and the processes of selling the product of creativity are extremely similar between technology and other media. So that's why I think this is really the big story, and we'll see whether it develops or not.

Asymconf

Posted January 18th, 2012 as The Critical Path Episode #22

Horace announces Asymconf and takes an archaeological expedition into the ancient history of personal computing so we can understand the distant future.

Horace: It's been an interesting couple of days here. I got a hold of some new data and I wrote it up, and it's just getting a huge amount of traffic, and a huge amount of comments to look through, and I even posted it as a video.

Dan: You're talking about [the post] "The rise and fall of personal computing"?

Horace: Yes, but the problem is, it's been changing. It's getting error corrections. It's extending—extending in multiple dimensions. I'm getting more company-platform data. I wanted to make this a subject for the show, that I go into some of this particular data set, and talk about some of the profound implications that are coming out of it. It's the first time that I've been able to get this sort of archaeologically significant data. Normally, [tech-business] analysis is done on a very short time frame. I mean, we're looking at quarters. People like to maybe do a year once in a while, look at the whole history of a year. But it's very hard to even get a whole year, like what happened in 2011. Very few people publish that type of information.

What I'm doing in this set is looking at 35 to 37 years of data about the computing industry because it goes back that far. We don't even have mobility as a type of computing. But 35 years—it's almost like doing archaeology—trying to find out how many units did sell of a particular product in the particular year? And an interesting thing to me is that that data is almost forgotten. It becomes the job of an historian to find it.

Fortunately, some people did a lot of work ahead of me. There are snapshots in time, and I went back and filled out a lot of the detail. Once you start, people give you much more data.

The good thing about is that this is the sort of data you only do once a year, the resolution of the data is one year.

But it really is a fascinating story. With the data I have now, I'm more comfortable talking about some of the historic perspectives in the transition between eras of computing and how that affects not just the company that you work for, but your career. It's a very interesting story when you look at a perspective of multiple decades. And I point out in my post that this time frame, although it looks astronomically long—35 years—it's less than the typical career of one person. If you were 20 when you

275

started and you work for 35 years, you'll be 55 by the time this reaches its current state.

So within that 35 years we've seen multiple eras. And within each era, we've seen multiple dominant companies. So no single company has actually maintained what I call a position of prosperity longer than about 10 years. And so if you bet your career on one company, or one platform—that has such a limited lifespan, what are you going to do the rest of the time? You need to constantly think about the disruptive impact on yourself and your career, on your tooling of how you approach your own life in terms of your skills and what you want to learn. Because the time scales involved are long by the journalism of the day, but they're really quite short from a biological lifespan of the people involved.

So, I think we'll get into that today. The other thing I want to talk about is—we're going to go live today with a new show, a new conference I'm actually going to put on.

Dan: And this is big news.

Horace: Well, I hope. So what we're planning on doing is having an event that will be what we call "Asymco live." Or, the Asymco experience is live, face to face. And the idea is that we want to actually create an asymmetric conference, where the audience will be very much the people who solve the problems. And the concept is, those who come are there to teach the presenters, although the presenters will be there to also give their point of view and coordinate and do a lot of the framing of the problem. I think we want to attract an audience that wants to solve the problem themselves and can contribute. Meaning, I think, like the way I run my site, which is a place where I have 10,000 of the best teachers in the world teaching me about this market. And I, of course, give back what I know as much as I can.

So that's the context. I've been thinking about it, and I think having an event where we do this live will be beneficial to moving this problem-solving process forward a little bit more quickly. Because the online process has limitations in terms of communications, bandwidth and so on.

If we do something live, we have concentrated minds—we have one place, one time, we have visuals that we can do in animated form. We have, of course, the network effect of having so many people communicating at the same time with each other.

So, just to mention it right now, the name of the event is"Asymconf." And there is a URL, Asymconf.com, where you can go and register your interest in this event. It's scheduled to take place April 13th. And it's going to take place in Amsterdam.

I have four topics that I want to cover in this live format. Before I jump into that, let me just explain about what I envision happening. This sounds vague: How do we get an audience to participate? I am drawing upon a method that's been used to teach for over 100 years, both in our law schools and in business schools, and that's the case method. The case method is in use because we don't have good axiomatic [canonical] textbooks… like in engineering or medicine or other forms of science. We cannot tell students, "This is the truth and this is the basic ways things work." Business and law is open to interpretation.

For that reason, law schools have developed a case method and business schools have copied that. And the case method [means] you read up on the subject in advance, but you debate the topic and, in so doing, you learn from your peers, and you tend to think about the problem in different ways. I think that's exactly what's happening inside the Asymco experience. We have the topic put forward as a blog post, and then we have hopefully hundreds of people debating it.

And as I said, there is a slowness to that process online, and I think we can speed it up. In the case method you're going to have the audience, or a subset of the audience… It depends how big the audience is going to be, but we're going to have a subset of people on stage or in some configuration that can be directed by the presenter. I don't want to say that they're the speaker. They're just giving an initial kickoff to the topic, and then we're going to pass the mike around, basically, or everybody will have a mike so they can contribute their opinions.

And it implies a little bit that we should have an audience that's composed of people who have a willingness and desire to contribute. Again, this is something we haven't done before. Hopefully that will happen. But the idea is that you come there with your life experience, you come there with your background—hopefully we'll have a diverse set of backgrounds. We're going to have people from the arts, people from design, people from engineering, people from many countries. It only works when you have a rich, diverse background of people. And everybody brings their opinion, and then we have a discussion, and we're going to probably record and synthesize that as well for others afterwards. But the idea would be to come to some new point of view on these problems. Again, this is what I think happens online. And it's been working out very well.

So the four topics I wanted to put forward right now are: We're going to look at what is disruption and how can you harness it. I'll use as a sample the data I've been putting forward about the mobile space, and maybe we'll talk about this new data as well, computing and mobile together. That will frame the whole discussion, "What is disruption?" Readers or listeners that have been tuning in for a long time will have heard bits and pieces of [this], but we're going to be doing it in a more structured way. That will probably take an hour or so.

Then we're going to look again at the entertainment industry, applying this lens of disruption to entertainment. And we want to think about the future of that. Again, this has been something of a theme throughout the last few shows as well. But make it rigorous: What is the case study of

Hollywood as an industry? You know, is it susceptible to or is it immune from disruption?

One of the new topics which I haven't yet spoken about or even written about is applying the theory to Wall Street. This is something that's very charged politically right now with the Occupy movement, and we've had plenty of criticism of the mechanism of Wall Street. I'd like to take a run at that. I think there is quite a bit of evidence to show that, in fact, Wall Street is running almost on empty in terms of innovation. It's not clear that there has been any innovation in that sphere since perhaps even the 1950s.

And the question about what is a job to be done: What is Wall Street hired to do by society, or by their customers, in fact? And have they exceeded this notion of being good enough? And, in that case, what are the consequences? It's quite a profound topic. It doesn't get looked at this way as an industry, and I think it's a worthwhile thing to do.

Finally, I want to take a run at education. In general, the problem has been that education, like healthcare… These are institutions that are not scrutinized through this lens of disruption. [Clay] Christensen has written about it. And he's got a book out called *Disrupting Class*, and he applies the framework there.

We want to step that forward a little bit and look at exactly our own experiences with this event, asking, "Are we actually changing the way teaching happens?" We're going to look at things like Khan Academy, which is a way of teaching using video, and the University of Phoenix, which is an online university as well. And look at examples like that. Are we learning using the metaphor of theater? And what are the implications if you blend narrative with teaching?

So that sounds a little bit perhaps vague at this moment, but this will be fleshed out a bit more. Really, at this moment we want to have an idea of who might be interested, and that's why I'm speaking about it now. Practically speaking, it's a one-day event, but there will be opportunities to socialize. We're going to have interactive technology, of course, and we're going to have some interesting tools. And an app that will be used wirelessly throughout the event showing presentation and the data-sets that we're going to be discussing will be on this iPad application that will be wirelessly streamed to displays, thus allowing people to interact naturally with the data.

It's going to be really exciting, and hopefully we're going to break ground on some new topics.

That's Asymconf, and I'm really excited about it.

Dan: Congratulations. I think it's going to be great. Hugeness.

Horace: Yeah. So, anyway, Amsterdam. I could talk for an hour about it, about the history of Amsterdam. In fact, one of the interesting things is why is Amsterdam what it is? Why was Amsterdam this magnificent city with canals, and how it came to be this way. And there is a richness of history there. Probably we'll talk about this during the event. But I really want to bring disruption theory to Amsterdam itself because what happened there is magical.

Amsterdam was the Hong Kong and New York of its day, put together. It was the most vibrant city at a time before either the French or the Spanish or the British empires were really world powers. Amsterdam, through its fleets, was able to dominate world economies. And it did so because it was disrupting, in a way. It was one of the first Enlightenment products.

And there are amazing stories there. I'm reading a book about some of the history behind the wealth of nations and how these things happen. And it's a great story there in itself.

But I don't want to do that now. I want to instead talk about this data I am working with because it's fresh in my mind. I think there are some interesting takeaways [for an audience that's] technology oriented. I think that getting this perspective out there is exciting.

So to recap, I stumbled upon a data set which showed the history of various platforms, like ancient history of sales of certain computers, like TRS-80s and Atari, and NeXT was there, and Apple II, and the early PC, which was mostly IBM, with a little bit of Compaq in the beginning. The history of personal computing starts in 1975. Both Microsoft and Apple were started, I believe, in 1976. So, there was a period of time when the PC was brand new. And it's fascinating to see what happened, how many players were in the space at the same time. Was there a lot of rivalry in the industry? How long did it take before things consolidated?

This is a hot topic today. We're always asking, "Is Android going to be dominant? Will there be another Windows-like environment for mobility?" What were the conditions back then? And can we trace all of these events all the way to the present, and in-between can we see what happened, not just with these individual companies? And everybody thinks that we entered this long period when Microsoft was dominant, and the PC was dominant, and nothing else happened. Well, it turns out there was still a lot of rivalry, there was still a lot of turnover happening within the companies that were in the PC world.

We had companies like Packard-Bell, companies like NEC. IBM itself came and went, it disappeared after a while because they sold off [their computer division] to Lenovo. Compaq was sold to HP. There were companies that were in and out of the space, in terms of being in the top five. We had Toshiba for a while, we had Fujitsu. And so a lot of these interesting episodes occurred.

So we have this drama of turnover of companies. No single company stayed in the top five for a long time. The second drama is that we had also this tremendous growth. My charts are on the log scale because everything is happening ten times more every few years. So, we have this phenomenal growth happening overall in the size of the market. And then in the late 2000s, we have the emergence of mobility. These two worlds are not usually compared or overlaid. You usually have analysts following mobility, and then you have analysts following PCs. So the two never meet. But here, I'm putting them together and you can see the patterns, right?

By the way, it's interesting that when the PC emerged, nobody was looking at the computing market and asking how much will these new microcomputers be competing with mainframes or minicomputers. There were analysts studying minicomputers, and there were analysts studying the mainframe market, and it was a hobby to look at these microcomputers. And so, again, had one put these together, we would have seen some interesting patterns. Of course, you could not measure units because there were very few of the large computers sold. But you could have looked at sales, you could have looked at consumption, you could have looked at a lot of things. The early '80s would have been the right time to predict the future of computing becoming a PC-dominated world, and I'm willing to bet that did not happen. It was still in its infancy and considered to be toy-like, relative to the big iron of the day.

Fast forward to today, and you see the same pattern of rejection of the notion that a tablet or a smartphone could be a real computer. And yet, when you see it all represented in these charts, in these log charts, it's clear to see the same dynamic industry structure emerging in the last few years. And the numbers are what tell the story because the orders of magnitude… How big is the iPhone, how big is Android, how big is the iPad relative to the PC market? And when you put them on the same scale, you realize that they're within the same order of magnitude.

And the growth is so rapid that you can easily see how in a few years they will be much bigger than the PC industry. And that's really a fascinating story. Is there a limit, and what is the trajectory likely to look like? You have a certain type of growth, but it can't go on forever because you can't go selling a billion of these a year, not anytime soon. And you can't sell ten billion either, right? So the numbers of orders of magnitude above where we are is limited.

And so all of this comes by staring at the data. And I've started to look at it in different ways. And I think that's really a fascinating story. The era is visible. You can see it with your own eyes.

The second question is, can you predict from the patterns of the past the lifecycle of platforms? Or the lifecycle of companies when they are in their prosperity zone? When they are at the top of their game, in the top five, growing rapidly and hence creating shareholder value?

And there is also a sad story because when you look at it on this scale, you realize that nothing lasted for a very long time. Things happen very

280

quickly, and you have a very steep ascent and then a steep decline. And you can see the data for 2011 versus 2010. You can see Symbian, you can see RIM. You can see the decline already beginning. And as soon as they crest, as soon as you have this peaking effect visible, you can see how share prices collapse. You can see how the market automatically discounts everything.

And within all this there is this continuing thread of Apple. Apple is a line drawn throughout the charts. And it's the only one that spans from the very inception of computing to the present day. And when you look at the numbers, if you add the [mobile] devices to the computers, you see that Apple actually now is in the highest spot. So it's actually the most prosperous and the oldest of the players in the game.

Now, it's a little bit incorrect to say that Apple should be in all this because I'm trying to track the top five. And it wasn't necessarily in the top five every single year of its existence. However, it is the only thread that I can draw amongst all of these companies. I could have cut off some part of it, but it would have looked awkward to have two different Apple lines. It's a small caveat, but it's about storytelling, and we want to look at patterns and not be pedantic.

One thing that came back to me was, for example, what about Unix? What about Linux? What about workstations? And there is so much detail and richness that I cannot fit into the data, I have to somehow put things in "other." But it's an amazing, almost, flashback. A lot of people saying, "Wow, this is my life. I'm looking at one chart and this is the story of my life. I remember as a kid being on this platform. I remember growing up with this. I remember going to school with this."

I don't know if it's ever been done this way, because the idea of overlaying mobile on top of what, typically, people think about the web world... You know, they think about the Internet era, they think about the early PC era, and then they think about the mobile era. And it's three different things. And here we are seeing it all in one place.

Dan: TRS-80, Apple][, Atari ST, Amiga, Commodore—they're all there.

Horace: Right. Those are all there, and then the PC is a proxy for the Wintel, although it's different versions of Windows—DOS era, and Windows era. And then every version of Windows in-between.

But this is the sales... The data we have is the sales that are tracked by market research firms like Gartner. And they would add up all the known sales from all the known PC vendors. That's the PCs. So I can't break it down any further. And even if I did, I'd go for dozens to 50 lines, which would be completely impossible to see a pattern through.

It gives a wonderful story, and when you see it this way, you see things going up and down. You see that these lines don't run for 35 years. They run for five years or ten years. And you see how there is a clustering of activity early and then late. And then you see gaps in the middle, and then you ask the question, "What happened here? What happened in this decade?" And then when you look at post-PC, the current era You see what's going to happen, what we have seen already happening.

And so there is some interesting patterns. There are very few companies that last for a long time at the top. Whether you are a platform company or whether you are licensing a platform, there are problems of what I call longevity and prosperity. Longevity meaning, "How long are you in the game?" And prosperity is how high up you are in terms of ranking among peers and in terms of growth and sales.

So these patterns emerge. You need to ask yourself, "What is it going to look like in five years?"

It may seem like an infinity, five years, but it's not. We all live much longer than that. Our children do and, obviously, everything around us is geared towards institutions lasting decades. So here we have a technology space with attention deficit syndrome and we don't think about the long term.

There is one more thing. There are implications for investors. If you're thinking about investing or owning any of the shares of these companies, or even if you're a VC, or you want to put money behind the platform—even if you're a developer and you want to get behind a platform. These are very important questions. There are real commitments you need to make. And so when you look at it on this scale, you start to ask things like, "What matters most?" Is it being around long enough to survive even though you have ups and downs, or is it that you just want to have a short but spectacular existence?

These are the things that come out. For example, one of the things that struck me was that whenever you deal with analysis of companies—and I've written about this also with respect to how analysts are seeing the growth of Apple—they tend to project a future which seems to be that growth is going to slow down, that the growth will go towards what's called reversion to mean—that it will go down to the same level that the industry grows.

But if you study these patterns, the data about growth in computing, you determine that there is no such thing as steady state. There is no such thing as a company that settles down to having a long and comfortable life. Either it grows phenomenally quickly, or it collapses phenomenally quickly. There is no in-between. If you took those lines that you see on the chart, and ask, "What is it going to look like in the forward," and you draw a horizontal line, thinking that it's just going to be steady-state, then you know it's going to be wrong. You know from looking at this history that things are going to go up and they're going to go down.

That in itself is a very valuable lesson when you think about investing your time, your money, your energy. It's about understanding that these things are highly volatile. You need to be able to change yourself rapidly and your commitments rapidly, and it's about embracing disruption. It's not fighting it. It's not ignoring it and saying it doesn't exist, which is what most people do. It's embracing it. And that's really the lesson that this data shows. I've always said that anecdotally I remember these things. I remember how much change happened. Now I have the data. Now I can actually show a picture. And it's public data. It just has never been put together, I think, in this way.

Dan: Well, it's really fascinating. And I totally hear what people are saying when they say "This is my life," because you see all these computers and these systems on here that you remember, but seeing them overlaid this way, and seeing how you have these really impactful time periods,

How did you decide what to put on this chart?

Horace: Partly, it's what's available. The challenge is putting it in a way that tells a story, that doesn't deceive, that doesn't mislead, and yet you balance these needs for being accurate with the needs for being clear. And sometimes being accurate is actually being too accurate because you clutter this up. If you have a hundred lines, you will see nothing but noise. So we as humans cannot perceive this noise. And if you want where to say, "Okay, we'll just analyze it through a different layer," then you abstract it so much that people don't know what you're talking about. So I'm just looking at the distribution of growth rates of this or that. And then you put up a chart that shows this second-level abstraction of a fundamental fact. So I want to stay as close as possible to the actuals, right? And make a visual. And this is where sometimes you still stumble. You still make errors. And this is where people come and help you.

For example, NeXT. NeXT is great to put there because it is a significant influencer on the market [since] it went on to be Mac OS X. But the problem is that it actually doesn't fit because it was so small it wasn't in the top 5, which is nominally what I'm trying to do. So you have to struggle with, "Do I leave NeXT in or take it out," because technically it shouldn't be there. Or do I leave Apple in during the '90s, when it wasn't one of the top 5 vendors—or even today, globally, it isn't one of the top 5. But it's a thread that runs throughout the whole storyline. So you want to talk about Apple and saying, "Look, it's survived." And with [mobile] devices now, it actually is number 1. And so there are a lot of tradeoffs you have to go through.

But the big picture, the big questions—that's where I want to see the debate. And when I ask, "Is the cycle time of disruption increasing," what does this mean? Does this mean that, for example, in the case of Apple and iPhone… If you look at iPhone alone, in isolation, it looks like a line that's going straight up. Android is going up even faster. But it's not a single company, right?

So you have the iPhone going straight up, and then you ask yourself, "Well, what are the analysts saying about next year? They're saying it's going to go up 28 percent." And you try to think about what would that look like on this chart? It means it's not going straight up. It's going to go suddenly at 90 degrees. And there is no precedent for that. So you have to say, "Well, from historic pattern recognition alone, the iPhone trajectory is likely to go up in the parabolic curve. It's going to go up and then come back down." And what they're saying is that next year it's going to already start coming down. It's unlikely. It's unlikely, given what we know. So there is a way to disprove 90 percent of the assumptions out there already. Just on the historic reference. Can it happen? Sure. Lots of things can happen. It's just not likely.

And so, studying the iPhone, or studying the iPad... When they started the very first data point of the iPhone, the very first data point of the iPad and the very first data point of Android... in other words, the first year in the market wasn't at the order of magnitude of one million. It was in the order of magnitude of 10 million. So already it's on a part of the chart which is beyond what we've seen historically.

So you can see that the iPad today is bigger than the whole PC market was ten years ago. Or you can see, going back a little bit in time, just how high up it is relative to what the history was. And furthermore, again, you see the trajectory. You see how it's going to bump up against the PC world. And you see how the PC world is also flattened out. You see how, if you take the Mac out of the equation, which is now separate in terms of a platform... you look at the PC/Windows Wintel world, you see how it has already peaked.

And this isn't a topic of discussion every day. Yes, people talk about it in terms of it being a post-PC era. But look at this curve. Look at the derivative of this curve. It has reached zero. That means it's an inflection point. That means it's over. So all of these things are self-evident when you put it down on paper, and whenever you do these types of discussions—what is the iPhone going to ship next year, what is the future?—you see dozens of reports, Deloitte & Touche, Ericcson, everyone's writing these reports and using all kinds of sophisticated language to tell you a story.

I just look at these charts and ridiculous things like saying it's going to double again next year don't sound so ridiculous anymore. It seems that everybody's pulling their punches and saying, "Let's be conservative." And conservatism ends up looking radical when you look at the data. The only normality is exponential growth. The only normal thing that can happen is exponential growth or exponential decline.

So that is the lesson, for at least this industry, this technology industry, which is the driver of growth for a lot of other industries as well.

Dan: Right.

Horace: And again, we're going to go back to the question of what happens when this monster, this force that's irresistible, meets other supposedly immovable objects like entertainment? What happens when it moves against education, or Wall Street? The fuel behind this industry, the Internet, that has turbo-charged it, the amount of investment, the amount of value creation of this industry is so big, orders of magnitude. Consider Google. The fact is that the information that's fueling Google, the information that's fueling the computers that we use to process all of that information is doubling. It's exponential. And yet the things, the obstacles supposedly against it, the obstacles of copyright law, the obstacles of institutions that have fossilized a hundred years ago, when they meet this force... We're in the middle of this political discussion about copyright and SOPA [Stop Online Piracy Act] and the potential for litigation against this industry.

I get a huge amount of confidence by looking at this data because I say no matter how we misallocate resources in terms of preventing these things, the force is enormous. This is a force that just cannot be stopped. So it really gives you confidence. It gives you comfort, and it gives you the motivation to say, "Yes we can." I'm willing to dedicate myself to this endeavor. I'm going to keep working on this project even though I hear a lot of noise about this not being viable, or having all these threats to it. So that's what I hope to do with this.

Dan: Good stuff. It's fascinating. You know, I think when people see this... No, let me take a step back. This is kind of a technical question. How do you generate this kind of stuff? I mean, what are you putting the data into? What is it? What application are you using? Because I'm sure people look at this and think, "Man, you know, Edward Tufte, he would be proud of this." Are you following a methodology? How do you come up with it? How do you decide, you know, how to focus on which data?

Horace: To be honest, I think it's a creative process. It's not something that you can actually be specific about it. You know, if you ask a writer, an actor, How do you do what you do?" And you have a particular process. Even though it's data, to me it's paint on a canvas. I think of it in terms of what is the story. And you iterate. You iterate enormously. So whenever anybody asks me about the tool, I tell them it's Numbers. Or it could have been Excel, but Numbers is a lot prettier. It's a lot clumsier, to be sure, and especially with large data it's very slow. And then people are almost critical of my choice there as far as no real analyst would use Numbers.

But because I put presentation first—as I say, if I can't make it look enticing and engaging, and draw people in with it—it doesn't matter how fast I am with pivot tables.

Dan: Right.

Horace: What matters is that it's entertaining. You know, again, I use that word with a high level of respect. It has to be engaging. The tree in the forest: If there is no one there to hear it, does it make a noise? And if no one is there to read this, then it has had no impact.

So with that in mind, I very much think about the story. I think about the composition. And you don't see it until you prototype, and so I start with the data. I have it in the back of my mind: "I think this might work as a bar chart, or it might work as a line chart." So I very easily quickly try these out. And once you've practiced a few hundred times, you immediately get an idea of, "Yeah, I know this is going to work and this is not going to work." And then there is a huge amount of polishing. And this is where I don't even recognize it because you just do it without blinking. Suddenly three hours have gone by, and all you've been trying to do is to get the right colors in there.

You know, again, I think people who are in the creative arts, they practice and practice and practice, and they refine and refine. And so it's the same process I use. It's not that... In the beginning, I was sloppy. I would just do the standard default bar chart. Everybody does it. In Excel, you barely know how to do it because it's not easy, so you do it once and that's it, you're done, you copy and paste that. But as you get more and more proficient with the tools, you realize that there are little subtle things you can do to make it better.

Then you have the danger of doing too much. You can do too much decoration. You don't want 3D. You don't want shading. You don't want opacity. You want to have cleanliness, you want to have good color palettes. I haven't been trained in design and I haven't been trained in the visual arts in any way. But you get a good sense of what works and what doesn't, and you get good feedback. And you just improve. In that sense, you just stare at it and you iterate. So, you say, "Okay, I see this chart." But then you know instinctively that it needs to be a log chart. And then you ask yourself, "How do I make sure that people know it's a log chart?" Because a log chart can be deceiving if you don't pay attention to the axis. It looks like these things are linear in fact when they're exponential. And people don't realize that changes at the top realms, being a lot more than changes at the bottom.

So then you have to ask yourself, "What do I put in the title? How do I label the axis? Do I do gridlines that actually show the gradation?" And there are tradeoffs. If you do that you make noise in the chart and clutter it up. And again, Tufte and others have spoken to these topics. I read Tufte decades ago, and I sort of... It's in the back of my mind. But I don't actually go through and do a checklist and see, "Did I do this or not that?" It's purely instinctive. And as I stare at it, I see that it works better this way or that way.

And there are flops. Sometimes I put out bar charts that, looking back on them, I say, "No, that wouldn't have been a good chart." And

286

then all kinds of problems, limitations. Can you get the labels on there? Can you get the labels so that they don't actually overlap the lines? And it is very much a process of editing, revision, taste, experience, and all of that baked in. So if someone asks me again, "What do you use as a tool?" I say it's Numbers, but I almost feel sorry for them because they're going to go out, get it, try it, and it will be like crap. And I say, "Yeah, it's Numbers, plus 20 years of practice."

So I don't want to discourage people from trying. I think they ought to definitely try it. The same charting tools are available in all of Apple's iWork [applications]. So once you know one, you can reuse it.

And it's easy to move from one tool to another. So I can make Keynotes with it, and so on. But I still struggle. And as I said, we're actually working on a tool to go even a step further. Because what's missing is the animation part. What's missing is that the story should be told in the narrative. It should be told as a function of time. So this is one reason, for example, I did this video on this latest post [because] I wanted to actually capture some of the dynamic nature of these charts. Because sometimes it's too noisy to show it. And then again, Hans Rosling is a pioneer in this. I use his motion charts. Very good stuff. Still not perfect, and we can do better. There are a lot of ways to visualize things.

And when you do things live, in front of a live audience, you get the feedback instantaneously. And you get people gasping when you see these things. And I think there is a drama to it. There is as much a drama as there is in the presentation of a great story on a motion picture, a theater. There is so many great dramas here. And when you tie them in with the words that touch people, then it becomes a performing art. And it becomes a next thing that I think should be recognized as, if not art, at least craft. At least the presentation of material that is technically data-oriented, but yet it touches people. That's important to me.

So, that's what I hope to get better at.

Spidey Sense

We talk about Apple's fourth quarter, Horace's trip to California and his visit to The Colbert Report. It's all leading up to a fusion of entertainment and technology to create something never seen before, something wonderful.

Horace: [Apple reported earnings for Q1 2011].

The numbers were… People keep thinking up new superlatives every quarter about how well they are doing. I try to predict that. So when you predict it and you get pretty close to what you predict, you can't use those words. If you foresaw that happening, you can't say, "Oh, they were just amazing." The expectation for me was pretty much in line with what happened. I had my [prediction] published. They are actually aggregated by Philip Elmer-DeWitt at Fortune/CNN.com.

So PED, as he's called, aggregates the data every quarter from over 40 analysts, including what are so-called unaffiliated bloggers and writers like myself. And then we have the so-called professionals who are the ones who publish their results typically to a private audience in the form of sell-side analyst research.

You can go to his blog, it's called Fortune 2.0, and see some of the latest results. I need to publish my own self-critique of how well I did, or how poorly I did. I've been doing that for a couple of quarters and I give myself a grade.

So one thing I am hoping to do with Philip is to publish every quarter a scorecard, or a grade report for all the analysts individually, and as part of a group, so we can get into that discussion of how well people did on the basis of a metric that everybody understands.

So I am going to be writing up what I did. But basically, Apple came in pretty close to what I expected. I was a little bit under. What happened is that most people were far under, far lower than what was delivered, so there was a lot of the congratulations and there was a lot of this surprise, true or not, about the performance.

The fact is, though, that they grew the business at nearly 100% again this quarter. And that's a pattern that's actually not particularly surprising, it's been going on for a while. And the culprit is, as usual, the iPhone. The iPhone delivered 37-million-plus units, which is about double what it was last year. The only thing that was surprising was that in Q3 they were not doubling. That product increased about 25 to 30 percent. I forget exactly. But that was considered a big shock and, indeed, I was, and everyone else was, expecting a bit more. But that was a dip due to the [iPhone] transition, so now it has sort of bounced back with vigor and we've got the above-three-figure growth rate.

But to be fair, that's what also happened in Q2. Q2 iPhone grew at 120 percent. So this massive growth is not a new phenomenon. We've been seeing this consistently on a yearly basis, ever since the product launched. It's been almost doubling every year. And that's pretty much my thesis as far as the products and Apple itself growing, this doubling that's happening.

So they did well on all the other products as well. Even the iPod, which has been declining lately, has declined a little bit less than expected. But it is still declining. It's not a re-surging product, and we'll see what happens with it later.

Bottom line is the company is doing phenomenally well. It grew its cash reserves to nearly a hundred billion, about 97 billion. We talked about this last quarter, what does that number mean and where do we go from there. That hasn't been answered yet, though Tim Cook is saying that they are they are having discussions on this. It isn't something that is a sacred, religious principle—not to get rid of the cash somehow—but they haven't made a decision.

So 97 billion. The prediction I had about this time last year, given what we knew then, was that it would be about 100 billion by the end of 2011 and it came in within three percent of that. So that's a pretty good prediction.

The other thing that's happened is they have retaken the number one spot in marketshare. Now, we don't know for sure what Samsung shipped in terms of smartphones. They have stopped reporting that information for over a year now, or about a year.

Dan: Why?

Horace: Nobody knows. They are second and probably this year they will actually reach the number one spot, the most-selling brand in terms of mobile phones. They will probably overtake Nokia. And yet, we have a situation where they do not even tell the world how many phones they sell. Not just no notion of how many smartphones or tablets, but no notion of how many phones altogether. They've been releasing very funny-worded statements about growth rate. They have been saying "about 30 percent" or "high 20s" or "low 10s" or referring to growth from the previous quarter, not from the previous year. So they are giving us an idea of growth, but relative to something which we don't know itself what the number was.

So if we don't know last quarter, multiplying it by 33 percent, [means] you are amplifying the error as you go along. So then the job goes to analysts to figure it out. [They] try to sample their various supply chains or their various distribution chains to figure out what an actual number is. But it is tough to get subcategories. It's tough to find out exactly how many smartphones. And what you end up with is a bunch of estimates. So we've seen anything from low 30s to high 30s (millions) of units of smartphones.

And the other problem is that when they report this number, they include tablets, they include Bada, and they include Android, and they include Windows Phone. So you are not really sure…

Dan: Not sure what you are getting there.

Horace: Yes, exactly. So we are not really comparing iPhone to Samsung's mobile division with operating systems. It's this kind of vagueness that bothers me.

By the way, in contrast, not only does Apple tell us how many phones they shipped and how many iPads they shipped, they tell us how much revenue was generated from that sale. We can therefore calculate the average selling price, so we have this idea of how much they actually received per unit, and we get a notion also of their overall profitability. We then try to figure out how much the profitability of the iPhone is. [I am] getting a rough estimate of 50 to 60 percent. People vary their estimates there, but nevertheless we know it is very high. We don't have any notion from Samsung about how many units, how much sales was generated. Well, we sort of do. They give sales for their telecommunications unit, which sells a bunch of other things other than phones, but we also don't know clearly the profitability on the smartphone versus non-smart.

And I'll contrast it further with Nokia. Nokia is actually very, very good about reporting this information. They give a breakdown by smart and non-smart, but they also give a breakdown of what the average price of the smart devices is, and therefore we can get an estimate of how profitable that business is.

While we are on Nokia for a minute… When they reported their numbers they said that they had sold up to a million Windows Phones. So whereas they sold something like—I wish I had it in front of me right now, but let's say about 12,–13 million; I could be wrong, it could be 16, 17—but somewhere in the teens of millions of smartphones. Of those you can assume that about a million were Windows Phones.

The problem is that they gave that estimate as of now, which was late January. It wasn't a number of Windows Phones sold in the quarter. So you have to back up a little bit and say that maybe they only sold about 650,000, maybe 700,000 during the quarter. And that's where we start to build up a picture of how Windows Phone is doing. There are analysts out there who are suggesting what their shipments were. So, again, we are getting a picture now of the platform game.

Android, there are some interesting mysteries there as well, because if you add up some of the other companies that have reported Android numbers—Motorola was down, Sony Ericsson was down, LG hasn't reported yet. Estimates vary again for Android, but it probably was at 70 to

80 million total units. So that is still comfortably above—doubling actually—what the iPhone delivered. Nevertheless, in the U.S. it seems that they lost share. There is clear data from AT&T and Verizon about how many units of smart devices they sold and how many of those were iPhones, and clearly there has been a bit of sea change in terms of the split between the two.

So I am giving just a very rough sketch of the market, some of the noteworthy events that happened in the quarter, but you must go to my site to really read up on the details. I am not really prepared on this show to dig into the data.

Overall, I think it was a fantastic performance but, again, not unexpected. One of the interesting aspects of the conference call, by the way, was that they said they hadn't sold any [of the iPhone 4S] into China. China had not launched the 4S yet. So probably in China it was like it was in the U.S. in Q3. There was a lull in sales and they should be picking up now in the first quarter. It's also Chinese New Year, typically gift-giving season. So if anything, I would predict that Q1 will be flat with Q4, meaning that we will see maybe even a slight increase in volumes in Q1. This is a phenomenon that started occurring once they moved into China because we have this second holiday quarter, if you will, that follows the Christmas quarter. And that's been actually driving growth quite a bit for Apple.

Dan: How do you think Apple must feel about China in general? I've been reading a lot of this. A lot of people writing articles about China is the next frontier for Apple, and it's something I've been meaning to talk to you about and it hasn't really come up in conversation. Do you have any predictions or thought on this?

Horace: I think it is absolutely true that they have been focusing. So Apple doesn't go in an opportunistic way, they go in a deliberate way when it comes to expanding their market. They have been seeding the ground, if you will, with deals, with political discussions about having a presence in China. Because you cannot get a significant presence in China without this kind of wheeling and dealing.

So I will touch upon a couple of hints I have received. One is that the employment of so many people in China for the purpose of manufacturing, that gets a lot of attention, but let's not forget that Foxconn—still, probably 75 percent or more of their employees are working on non-Apple products. Nevertheless, there is still a significant number at 25 percent assigned to Apple. Given that there are over a million people employed by that company, we are looking at hundreds of thousands probably working on Apple stuff.

That employment itself is politically charged. I am not even going to touch the sensationalist view of labor issues in China, but the basic question of whether you are manufacturing in one town on the coast or whether you are manufacturing in the center of the country, that is a political discussion that has to happen because the problem in China is migrant labor. A lot of these issues about workers being unhappy comes from the fact they are away from their families, and they are away from families, because manufacturing is taking place usually away from where there is idle labor. They have been [manufacturing] in cities around the coastlines and the reason that was happening was there was concentration of expertise, but also concentration of suppliers, concentration of communications in terms of roads and rail that allowed this engine to run.

What happened over the last decade, I would guess, is that China has expanded their road network, they expanded their rail network so that they can actually allow manufacturing to take place in some of the inland cities, and those are very large population centers from where people had to migrate in order to work.

So what happened during the last few years is that we have seen plants being established closer to the center or away from the traditional manufacturing zones. That decision about keeping those employees happy by bringing the work close to them, that has to be taken by Foxconn, by the Chinese government, and by Apple together because these are disruptive events in many ways. You have to maintain production while this is happening, so it is something you schedule a long time in advance.

So one of the aspects, I think, that you need to think about in terms of Apple's commitment to that country is that they have committed to ramp production, do all the right things they need to get the product shipped and done, but also to keep the labor satisfied and to keep the government satisfied so that these workers are not going to be rebellious and so on.

So they are very focused. And getting these concessions also allows them to have things like placement of stores in great locations. To get the Shanghai store where it is, it's not just because you were able to write a large check. You have to have a lot of political clout to be able to get that kind of placement. And the decisions about getting in the carriers themselves has to be negotiated through a very Byzantine process.

Dan: And this is something very specific to China that they would need experts on and people there, and it's a long process, too. This isn't something that you just…

Horace: Exactly. You can't say, "They did great this quarter because they finally launched the product." That product launch took years and years of work. It's clear to me, given all the facts, that Apple's presence in China is not one of just being an outsider coming to sell the product. It's about actually integrating deeply into the fabric of the nation in terms of relationships. Everything in China runs on relationships, and they have been building these relationships for a long time. And in order to do that, they must have had a commitment. I would say three, four years ago, they must have green-lighted the idea "We need to be in China in a serious way and we are going to start making that happen now, in 2006 and the pay-off may come four or five years later."

Again, I don't know the exact magnitude. It could be two years, it could be three years. But we've seen rumors about meetings between Tim Cook and operators there happening long, long ago. So this is all coming now to fruition, and you are seeing the vastness of scale that you can get as a result.

Now, the interesting thing is that when people then ask what are they doing about India, Brazil and Russia, the other members of the so-called BRIC group [Brazil, Russia, India and China], which are the fastest growing economies outside of the western economies.

The answer is they are getting to them in their own time. They are, I think, building the relationships they need to build in Brazil, they are doing what they need to do in India and you'll see the benefit of that two or three years from now, maybe four years from now. In the case of India it could be five years from now.

Dan: You are almost saying that where things are with China today, this is what, looking ahead three to five years, we will be talking about in relation to India and some of these other countries.

Horace: Exactly. People are accusing Apple of ignoring X or Y country and they are saying, "Well, obviously they don't care about us here in India."

Dan: Right. You hear that a lot. You hear that a lot.

Horace: The caring starts early and you can't say that. Once the pipeline is full and you've got every relationship built… I was at Nokia, and Nokia built these relationships over decades so that they were able to have hundreds of operators buying their product, and hundreds of consumers aware of the brand, and all these other things that had to happen. It didn't happen overnight. You can't just pick up the phone or send a sales guy down there. This is political, it's relationship-driven, it's trust-driven. People have to know who you are. And that is being built, piece by piece. They couldn't have started the iPhone with a global launch. Remember they started with one operator in the United States, AT&T, and then it took a couple of months to get another operator in Europe. And when they did, they did these weird exclusives. But that is just for getting started.

If they had built relationships with 500 operators they couldn't have delivered all the product that was necessary to put in front of customers. So it's a process and I would just say you have to wait. And also the other thing is that they have to tailor their product to some degree. It sounds like they are delivering the same product globally but there will be aspects, I believe, that will address these BRIC opportunities, as you can imagine because you have cost issues. And I've always been hinting that the product iPhone today may not survive, it may be completely redefined. My guess it will be rebranded for a low-end solution. So there will be something else, and my guess would be iPod will get that role. That the rebranding of the iPod will be about the low-end phones in other countries.

But, again, this very speculative. I don't like to get into this game at all.

Dan: That's the most like a prediction I've ever heard you make.

Horace: It would be as close as I can get to that. But my point is simply that iPhone, as it exists today, don't expect that. A lot of people say, "Obviously, it is going to run out of steam because it's going at a six, seven hundred dollar ASP [Average Selling Price]."

And by the way, I also published data which shows the ASP of all of Apple's products.

If you go back to this, it's called Price Competition in my blog, and you can see how the price of the Mac, the iPhone, the iPad, and the iPod attract what Apple receives in average sale price. This is not necessarily what the consumer pays. But it is what Apple receives. And they have been receiving the same price for these four products consistently.

The iPad is fairly new, but the others have been around for a long time, and you can see the pattern. You can see that they haven't ever changed that price, not in a fundamental way. It's varied up and down a little bit by a single digit percentage-wise. And the Mac itself has eroded slightly downward, but that's because their costs have also dropped.

But in that diagram you see that Apple doesn't play games with pricing. Pricing, once it is established, it's almost like this is the product. The price is the signal. The price is something they put a stake in the ground and say, "This product exists around this price." It's a Mac, that means it's a thousand dollars. Or a MacBook, let's say, is a minimum of a thousand dollars and it doesn't make sense for them to move that point. If you launch something else, it's going to be called something else and it's going to be around a different price point. So it's almost like the brand is attached to a price point.

The iPhone is what it is, but it is $600. If you say that, it means that there will never be a low end with that product. In a way they bracket it by building variance with more memory and they keep the older product around and you get that ratchet effect down. But the average remains unchanged. That's what is amazing if you look at the pricing history.

So what I would suggest is that if they needed something at a $100 price point, it doesn't make sense to launch a bunch of hundred dollar iPhones and then compensate with a bunch of $1000 iPhones to make up the difference in getting the average to remain constant. What I would imagine instead is they would simply reposition the iPod, which is already at $170 or so—reposition it as a communicating device. That just makes sense to me. Or launch something new around it.

That would be the next category for Apple, if you will. I think they are being very, very careful. These prices aren't chosen arbitrarily. They are not chosen as a reaction to anything else. They are not chosen because Samsung places their product at that price point. It's almost like a design question. Treat it as a design question. What does the customer expect to get, what are they hiring this for? And that is the price. That is it.

So we will see. That's is my thesis on that. But that's why I say let's not get ahead of ourselves in terms of predicting the iPhone as saying, "Well, it's at one point and it will never move from that point." The answer will be that there will be something else as a different point, and that's how they are going to take care of the BRIC opportunity.

And the margins will change, obviously. A lot of things have to change. Keeping in mind that that is an integrated company, that means integration all the way to the price. All the way. So from the user experience to the hardware and guts to the price, it's all the same question. It's all one thing. It has to resonate exactly together in that particular configuration.

So that's a slight tangent on the quarter, but I think that we will see opportunities and growth because, again, doubling every year, at some point you reach saturation, everyone who has the money can buy the product and distribution has been maximized and all that. So that's a quick recap of what I observed. A couple of other things may come to mind as we go on.

But the other thing I want to talk about is I went to speak at Macworld. I had a very small role in a track of MacIT, and I spoke about the history of computing as I published this chart that grew rather popular which I showed what the PC era looks like when you overlay mobile devices on that.

Dan: Which is absolutely fascinating.

Horace: Yeah, and it is done on a log scale so you can see patterns easier. When everything grows exponentially it's hard to see what happened there in historic terms. So I actually had the history of this happening back to the 1970s, before the Apple][launched and what was happening in the sort of prehistoric era of personal computing.

So I talked through that and I tried to explain to a live audience just how it is unlikely that you see the trajectories that we are on right now with mobile devices and with Android and iPhone. Historically these things have a trajectory where, on a log scale, they go up and then maybe they go down, but the cycle time, the width of that curve would be about a decade. So people who predict that things are just going to go straight down next year, or flatten out, if you were to plot this on the same log graph, it would look very unusual. It would look almost as if something catastrophic happened. It is unlikely that that will happen to established platforms like this.

You can go back again and see companies like Amiga and Commodore and some of the vendors out there that fell out of favor. Even in the PC we had quite a few names disappear. Compaq, that was acquired, and then there were companies like NEC, Toshiba and so on that at one time were in the top five, and then they fell out of the top five. But even when they did, there was this gradualness about it. So there is no such thing as a discontinuity that people are predicting when they say this. And again, this continuity, on the scale I'm dealing with, is a yearly analysis. So year by year.

So in one sense what this helps you do is temper down your expectations in terms of change—dramatic change—happening with companies that are at this level of performance, that you have exponential growth, that have minimum marketshare, which means tens of millions of units. When you get that level you shouldn't predict discontinuities. It's just not likely to happen.

Anyway, that was my talk. And then, what is interesting, I also visited with some companies. The interesting thing that I came away with after I toured some of these companies—I won't mention names, but they are in the social media and you can guess who they are—is that really one of the biggest problems they have is talent, obtaining people. And they are all growing really fast, but there isn't enough capacity in the number of people that are qualified to work there.

I said, "Who is your competition then? Is your competition another brand that we are aware of that is somehow hotter than you are?" It was clear to me that the labor pool, this talent pool was not going to the HPs or the old brands that are already in decline. The question I was asking was, "Are they competing with the hot brands." And the answer was no. Interestingly enough, they said the most difficult competition they have is with no-name startups. Meaning that people who were graduating were coming out from a degree program in computer science straight into launching their own startups. This hasn't happened since the dot-com era.

What's happening is that they know that their skill is in such high demand that they have that option value of always going into a real job. So, in the meantime, "Why don't I just exercise the ability to try something starting new." And also there's a lot of capital that is sloshing around, a lot of access to VC capital that allows people to have the crazy dream of launching a startup, no experience, with no track record, and nothing but a piece of paper with a diploma on it.

So that is interesting to me because it gives me the flavor of this place being just completely in a boom era. We are seeing a phenomenal growth happening with new names, new brands, but also potentially new disruptors that are right now under the surface, invisible. This is all good. There is always the danger of overshooting in terms of saturating and so on, bubbles and all that. But at the same time, what I am observing—again, this is my only spidey sense out there sensing this—is that we are seeing an opportunity of a new type of business because of Web 2.0.

Technically speaking, there's been that revolution. But what is happening is that it takes less effort and less money to start a business today than ever before with apps, with devices, and with the Internet and broadband. It allows people to connect talent—which at this point means programming talent—to consumers and get an audience very very quickly.

Case in point, even my own blog, my experience has been that it is relatively inexpensive, not in terms of time but inexpensive in terms of capital. If you have time, and most young people do, that's great, because now you don't need a hundred million dollars. You don't need even 1 million dollars.

One thing that struck me... If you remember back in the day when the iPhone and App Store launched, that the VCs were offering these huge funds, a hundred million dollar fund for app developers. Well, it turns out that app developers don't need that much capital. You don't need a lot of capital to set up a website or a web service. It's interesting how that is playing out in terms of the dynamics and the constraints on growth for some of the companies that are now really the hottest names in the business. It was a good experience to learn that.

The other thing I did was, after San Francisco, I went back to the East Coast and I spent a little time in New York on Monday and Tuesday. I went there to visit some of the people who I had conversation with: Hoon Lee, who was one of the guests on the show, and a future guest on the show, was my host as well, and took me around and showed me a couple of things. And one of the things he showed me was *The Colbert Report* in production.

Dan: Very cool.

Horace: His name is Dan Abrams, he's going to be on the show in the future and I owe him a lot for doing this, but he—more than just showing me around—he and I had enough time to chat about the business. He's a writer and producer, independent at this time. And I'm starting to finally...

Remember, the stories we were doing with Hollywood and all that is still crystallizing, it is still congealing. I'm reading the book *The Hollywood Economist 2.0* by Jay Epstein. I highly recommend it. You really need to read that book to understand some of the business models of Hollywood.

It's anecdotal. It's a journalistic-style book, so it is mostly about experiences or interesting events and stories and snippets of information that this author has been able to collect.

I am analyzing a lot of data and I'll be publishing next week a lot of data about the industry that when you take a view of the world strictly through the data without coloring it with anecdote, it tells you one story. And then when you get the anecdotes which are very valuable, and they are consistent with your data and the patterns you are observing in data, then you have a much more powerful story altogether.

You could see where people gossip or tell stories, but somebody who is unattached to the environment comes in and observes... To use an analogy, you've got people in the ground. They are sniffing and talking and spying, if you will. Intelligence gathering. And then you've got a plane flying over it at Mach 3, or a spy satellite, taking high-resolution pictures. Each one has qualities of its own, but put together is where you get good intelligence. Put together is where you start to get the really good picture. And that is what I am doing right now, I am flying the satellite over and taking pictures and I am getting some interesting pictures.

So my underground training was going to the [*Colbert Report*] show. And it's a fascinating thing for me. A lot of people may know already about it, but for me, I was completely new to this phenomenon. I had seen the show, *Colbert Report*, but I wasn't a devoted fan and I don't watch TV every day so that is not going to penetrate very deeply to me. But I did get to see the show being taped, and it's unbelievable.

When I thought about it afterwards, though, and I thought about myself in the experience... You know, I'm sure people go there and they see a show. It is also a live show as well as a recorded show, so you are part of the studio audience. But it is a show, it's entertainment and they handle you as the audience, very carefully because you actually contribute to the feeling of the show, because they want to get the laughs, they want to get the enthusiasm. And Stephen himself feeds off of that, and they definitely want you to react so he can get a good performance. So there is that critical element, the integration of the entertainer and the audience. Very much what theater is all about. Anyone who works in theater says the audience is half the performance.

So seeing that and being part of it was really energizing. But at the same time you can take a step out of yourself and suspend it a little bit and then think of what the process is, the process of the show itself. This is a show that they do four times a week, so it is extremely highly productive. The amount of output they create in a half-hour show every day is phenomenal. It's all scripted, it's not live like we are doing now. It's more of a product. It is really polished. They work on it very hard. They work all day long with 20 people or so at least involved in the writing and editing and production.

Dan: Every show takes hundreds of man hours to do.

Horace: Exactly. Hundreds of man hours. Stephen Colbert comes in the morning at 9:00 and goes home at 10:00. That's his work day. It's an extremely tough day. So even as presenter, you might think he gets given the lines but, no, he needs to be an active participant. So is everybody else in there. And after we were done with it… We began at six o'clock. Everyone was assembling for the show and about an hour later they brought us into the room where the filming takes place and then we left about forty, forty-five minutes afterwards. There were some breaks in the shooting.

But after that, the editing begins. They have about two hours to do the editing and get the show ready for broadcast. And even during that time, Stephen Colbert and the crew would be rushing off to work on the editing. So their day was not over.

Besides being impressed by the quality, the dedication, the details of the creative process, I am also impressed with—I hate to say this, but in a way it's true —it's a factory. I also saw it as a process for production and in a way it's like there are certain raw materials coming in—talented young people—and there's basically the show itself, which is hired to get laughs, and of course also to get advertisers. And that process is what you think about, and you think about cycle time. You think about issues like you would in a factory, and you realize that they have taken this television show and made it into a highly efficient production machine, a laugh-production machine. And that was also, for me, very impressive because you think of serendipity of performance, the serendipity of artistic output, but yet here they've turned it into a repeatable process.

And this goes to the heart of a lot of what Hollywood is about. In fact, a lot of what Apple is about. They have been able to productize, in the case of Apple, sparks of innovation, sparks of design and sparks of insight into the consumer. At the same time, Hollywood may productize the essential entertainment: Drama and comedy are the most common genres in the world and they have been the same genres for thousands of years. When the Greeks were around writing the first plays they had exactly the same methods Colbert used. And yet today we are seeing a highly refined production process.

It is not for everyone. When you do it in a mass market way there is going to be a lot of homogenization, there's a generic nature to it. But yet, but yet, I have to say it's something that needs to be admired. It needs to be understood. It needs to be probably understood by people who are not in the industry. It needs to be understood by people who are in our industry, technology. We need to understand the creative process.

And I tweeted, "Those who make software need to know how art is made." And vice versa. The two worlds are in a collision course and they are going to, not necessarily break each other or one another, or one will not win, they will fuse. They will fuse to something new that isn't recognizable to either at this moment. So this what I'm trying to figure out: What will emerge from this?

So having the conversations, speaking and cross-pollinating the two industries which, frankly, are quite antagonistic and separate and not understanding each other.

But there is so much you can learn from that. There is so much you can see that's similar. As I was saying, the dedication that you need to get it right, that you need to ship product. Real artists ship, right? That's a saying that Jobs uttered, but it actually came from Hollywood. Real artists weren't people who stared at their navels, they were people who shipped a product, a commercial product that got paid for. That's what was considered a virtue and that's what Hollywood essentially—to the envy of everyone—managed to do successfully. And that process is something we can learn.

At the same time, I think that the industry of television, Hollywood in general, has a lot to learn about technology. There is a lot to be learned about how to reach customers, how to understand jobs-to-be-done [theory], how to understand creating experiences and other things which are actually completely novel. I think apps are a medium. They may not be identical to anything that's been created as an art form before, but they are an interesting new way of expressing things. It is an interesting way of consuming things and so on. So there is a lot to be learned by both sides and it needs to be done with a sense of mutual respect because this isn't the engineer laughing at the arts major, or the arts major laughing at the engineer and calling them names, right? This is not the time for that.

So I came away with a deep sense of respect, but also an incredible opportunity, a vision, that what's happening in show biz is going to affect a lot of what we do.

In one of my conversations back in California, we talked about our histories and I said what I had been doing and I mentioned how I was ten years too early in pretty much everything I was doing. I was doing research in the late '80s, early '90s at GTE Laboratories. I was doing research in something called information retrieval, which turned out to be search. Search became commercially interesting ten years later.

In the late '90s I was working on ebooks. That became commercially interesting ten years later with, of all things, the Kindle. And then they asked me, "So what are you doing now?" I said, "Well, I am studying entertainment." So let that just be a little hint there that I really think that in ten years from now there will be something new. You can call it disruption, you can call it something negative if you want to.

There are people writing things like, "Let's kill Hollywood." I am not much into the conflict side of things, but I think there is a lot to learn from Hollywood, and that's what I intend to do.

And I am learning right now, doing what essentially amounts to producing content, if you will, and the more I do, the better I get.

Dan: Very cool. So what should we be doing then as listeners? What should we be thinking about?

Horace: Well, help us by sharing your stories. I've had great feedback. When I wrote the stories in the podcast on Hollywood, "Below the (belt)line," remember that show, I think the numbers showed that to be extremely popular, right? And we had follow-up shows and I'm getting a huge amount of feedback from that. I am getting a lot of people writing in with their stories. I've had people from Hollywood who are involved deeply in the business—being union members, being life-long dedicated professionals in the industry—explaining to me where I am wrong about it.

That's great. I love to hear that. It is something we need to continue the discussion on. I think we need to have this two-way discussion rather than antagonize one another.

The thing that I like to see is this participation by people who are from outside the industry and inside the industry which, by the way, again, is what I'm trying to do with my conference. So that's just one of the ways that you can engage. It isn't free, unfortunately. It may require travel and admittance and all that. But physical presence is always a lot more expensive. Just ask Amazon.

Only the Freshest Mountain Dew
Posted February 17th, 2012 as The Critical Path Episode #25

We take a look at Mountain Lion as evidence that Apple is cross-pollinating its product lines. We look at the Apple Stores as a service brand and Horace tips his hand ever so slightly about Asymconf.

Dan: Hi, Horace, how are you?

Horace: Hey, hi, Dan. I'm very good. How are you?

Dan: It's good. You know, we don't really do news and stuff on this show per se. But, you know, I wanted to mention for those who don't know that Apple announced Mountain Lion yesterday. I know you've probably got an agenda for this show, and maybe this is part of it. But before we go into that, I'm curious. Seeing more and more iOSification of OS. It's not even called Mac OS X. It's now just OS X. So we've dropped the Mac.

Horace: Yeah.

Dan: So what's your take on this? Can we jump right in and talk about this first?

Horace: I think it's a good topic. One, I think for me… Again, I don't hyper-analyze. I don't get into the product side of things.

Dan: Right.

Horace: But I do try to look at what is signaled by the company in terms of the way it may change its strategy, or it may change some of its operations, as a result of these product announcements.

So one thing that I think is interesting is that this is a pretty fast cycle that we're witnessing here. I had done a retrospective analysis of the speed of software or major software upgrades as far as operating systems are concerned. And the observation is that they tend to get longer and longer over time. So a platform that is about ten years old, or longer, tends to have a cumulative delay in its release cycle. I've plotted it into a circular spider chart, where you can see this turning of the platform, this cycle increasing over time. The spiral goes outward, in other words.

Whereas in a fresh platform, you have far tighter turning radius. So things are happening much more quickly.

Dan: Yeah.

Horace: The military analogy is that you're turning inside of an opponent. And as a result, you have a better firing angle on them. It's not particularly relevant as a competitive issue, but it does signify that in a fresh platform, you're tending to go up the trajectory more quickly. You intend to improve more quickly.

So what's this got to do with Mountain Lion? Well, Mountain Lion seems to be coming very quickly on the heels of Snow Leopard. And I think… I haven't measured it yet, but someone noted to me over Twitter that it seemed like Apple was accelerating again with OS X. And that's great.

I think the reason that they're doing it, by the way, is because they're simplifying it. In many ways, they're re-architecting it. They're cleaning it up, and then they're adding a lot of the knowledge—what I call the DNA—of a mobile version of OS X, or iOS, into the desktop version. That is cross-pollination. It allows them, probably, to rejuvenate and re-build from a new perspective the platform. I think that's really the story today, although again it's very tentative, very early. That we're seeing a shifting of gears happening within the desktop OS from Apple.

As a result, I think that's a good, positive thing. I've seen one or two mentions by Apple in the past where they've said, "We're re-architecting deep inside of…" I remember, actually, once being at the WWDC, and it was the "State of the Mac" speech given by Bertrand [Serlet]. And he was talking then about how they were rebuilding the foundations of a skyscraper. That was the analogy he used.

And, you know, even back then—and I think it's about almost four years ago—they were thinking probably about what we're seeing today. And they were folding at the time—I remember I was struck by one thing—they were folding in some of the iOS QuickTime features. And they were thinking already about what have they learned with iOS in terms of media playback. And simplifying QuickTime as a result.

It seems like they're taking stuff out, but it's essentially just cleaning up. And I see it as a continuation of that trajectory that they've been on. And so now we'll be able to put more data behind a model, and look at it again.

And so the iOSification, for me, is not just the look and feel, or some of the app-like behaviors, or the commerce model with the App Store, but it's also the fact of cycle times, the fact of simplifying the entire de-sign, which is what iOS has taught them to do, I think.

And that's probably also why, competitively, what Microsoft suffers is their inability to learn from the mobile. The mobile experience at Micro-soft has been essentially an independent effort that initially was based around Windows CE, which was not the same kernel. It was based on a trajectory to enter into telecom as a strategic interest, not as a way to learn about new software. In fact, probably they weren't speaking to each other, technologically speaking—the two efforts were completely inde-pendent. And so they didn't learn from Windows Mobile. I mean, you didn't see any influence in Windows proper which, at the time, was mov-ing from XP to Vista. And you didn't see any Windows Mobile-ness about it.

Dan: Right. Right.

Horace: [Today] potentially they might bring Metro into the Windows world. But that is the sort of thing where, again, politically speaking—and I have to step back and say this is somewhat of a controversial topic that somewhat politics comes into play—the group inside Microsoft that holds the most power is the Windows technology team. Because that's where the money is, ultimately. That's what drives a lot of the business. Of course, Office does as well but, I mean, vis-à-vis other OSes, potential OSes, it's Windows.

Whereas in Apple, they've given free reign to iOS. As a result it's actually gotten a lot bigger. And I just posted some data which shows that iOS outsold all the Macs ever sold. So in 2011, there were more iOS devices shipped than all the Macs in the history of the Macs, over 28 years. So in one year you've outsold 28 years' worth of the Mac. And that means the power base, if you will, politically and economically within the organization, resides within the iOS group. And therefore they can influence easily and say, "This is the path forward." And when you turn it around and ask, "What is the power base of Microsoft, where there has been no traction in mobile?" the Mobile guys don't seem to have anything to stand behind and say, "Well, you know, our way is the best way." Why should anybody believe them?

So that's why I think that you see this disruption that happens with mobility. That if you let it happen within your own organization—so that you let the mobile guys influence the legacy, and that allows within an organization like Apple—it allows them to grow and evolve a lot more quickly, and even bring the desktop world forward.

Dan: Right.

Horace: This extends also into companies which aren't necessarily selling platforms. If you're just a plain-old operating company, and you have legacy… [An] IT organization which has legacy. And then you have a fledgling mobile unit, or people who are trying to deploy on the mobile platform. Again, where is the power base? If a decision comes up, where do we invest resources? You have 90 percent of the staffing, 90 percent of the budgets, and 90 percent of the revenues comes from desktop, how are you going to get any kind of positive feedback from those folks as mobility happens?

So you have to think that this disruption, the mobility aspect of things, really has been changing as much the industry and all of what it touches, as the microcomputer changed the IT industry away from centralized computing. Which, again, that is something I lived through. So it's déjà vu.

Dan: Yeah. That's a really interesting way to set it up and using that term "déjà vu," I mean, really this kind of thing is just showing how the approach of each of these—the different companies that you've mentioned, and what the trends are—and it really does seem like companies (Microsoft, Apple) are going in these very different directions. Is there… Do you think that, like, has Apple got it right? Do they know something? You know because their approach is different?

You know, it's simplification of things, minimizing of things. Even the names of the applications within the update are simplified. And John Gruber mentioned this in his article—instead of iCal, it's just Calendar. That's the same name as on iOS.

Horace: It's affecting their marketing in the sense of how they're positioning, how they're cleaning things up. I think that's indicative of an internal-review process, where they're asking themselves questions about names, pricing. We've already seen OS X drop in price, radically.

Economically, you might say that's a huge revenue source. That actually is almost pure profit. It's a fixed cost. And then, periodically, you get a huge windfall. But they thought deeply about it and said, "We want to move people more rapidly. That's more important than gaining that windfall for that one quarter. We want to move people to this new platform because it actually has a halo effect, or it has some knock-on effect onto the mobile space. Or that it's going to impact our strategy with respect to cloud, where we actually believe that long term the value lies." And all these other things that they're doing.

So you're seeing a lot of [actions] which sound suboptimal, but they're doing them because they have longer-term plans and [they're] trying to think through the right thing to do. And that's another remarkable—and, I think, almost miraculous—thing that happens. They're vetoing the economic basis of decision making and sticking to the question of what is the right thing to do by the measure of platforms. Or cohesiveness, integrated experiences. And they just basically have to have a faith, long term, that it pays off.

So as you point out, you have Calendar. And the changes they've made in media. The changes they've made in productivity and in messaging, which I think are valid. It's very frustrating and slow for me, the process of migrating away from iChat and moving into something more modern. Sometimes these things take way too long.

And even FaceTime didn't have the impact it should because it wasn't properly put together with all of the other bits and pieces. Now we're finally seeing FaceTime merging with iChat, merging with the mobile messaging. And in fact sort of embracing and extending SMS as well.

Dan: Yeah. Yeah.

Horace: When iMessage came to the iPhone, I [thought], "This is great." I haven't used SMS for a long, long time. And then usually with someone who is not using an iPhone, which I don't have many friends who don't.

But the thing is that already works wonders for me. But now it's on the Mac as well, and that's almost been screaming as a need. And yet you sit and twiddle your thumbs and you wait and finally, it happens. And so that's the way it works. And when it does happen, you're hopeful yet again that this is going to be a watershed event, but then again you might find out that this is something just not right, and you have to wait a bit longer. Right now we're using Skype to do this call. But one day we hope to have the ability to do this over a protocol from Apple, which would be potentially more useful that we could actually do it, maybe, in a mobile way.

Dan: Yeah. So do you plan on installing it and trying it out? Well, before I get to that… It's fascinating to me, just to further your last point, how Apple—and I think this is intentional—they are trying to blur the lines—and I think this is where you were going, trying to blur the lines between not their operating systems, not between OS X and iOS, although I think they're maybe working at unification eventually, maybe. But they're trying to blur the lines with the way that people think of them as being separate. They're trying to connect those two things in more and more obvious ways. Not through the unification of an interface yet, but through the way that you think of devices, that now I can communicate seamlessly using Messages on the Mac, and iMessage on iOS. But there is now one way to communicate with everybody. And wherever you are, it will figure that out. If you're on your phone you get the message there, if you're on your Mac you get the message there. There is now just one protocol, as you say, for connecting these different devices and communicating across the board. And Apple is the one that's providing this infrastructure. This, in a way I think, is what they're trying to do very much with iCloud and more and more from what Steve Jobs had said, and their direction, it's clear they're going… They want iCloud to be that cornerstone. They want that to be the center point for everything.

Horace: Oh, yeah. I'm desperate for it too. iCloud working the way… For example, I mean, what I do when I travel is, I have to take with me a laptop. But that's not my main computer. My main computer is my desktop. And I know Dropbox…

Dan: Yeah, yeah.

Horace: …is sort of an interesting option there. But what I need to do, basically, is copy files from one computer to the other in order to make sure that they're synchronized. And it's just an administrative task that is pointless. I mean, you could use a shared drive. You could use all these other things. But in my particular circumstances, it makes sense that I just need to remember to do that, and then dump them back when I'm home.

And that's just something that needs to disappear from my life. What needs to happen is everything needs to be in the cloud, as far as files. The file system should just be something of an abstraction from our lives. And

I think that's where they've been going. But, again, these things just take time. And I'm waiting patiently for that to happen.

And by the way, the other thing is that the Mac is growing quite rapidly relative to the industry, but it's nowhere near as big as the iOS world. So what's interesting, when I charted the growth in the Mac... Usually platforms have an inflection point where they go from having very rapid growth to slowing down. And then they plateau. But what happened with the Mac is, it plateaued for a while, but then it started to pick up again. They had a second inflection point, starting another growth phase late in its life. Part of it is halo effect. What happened is, the device business starting with the iPod caused this massive boost in the brand, and along with the Apple Stores, led people into having a Mac experience again.

And this is where some very unprecedented dynamics are happening. Like I said, the idea appears to be a very late in its life platform becoming fresh and young again because it's getting the DNA from a donor, if you will—from an entrant that is new and thinking freshly. And so that's what we're witnessing, and that's what I'm taking away from this announcement. And again, it's not, I think, a particularly novel idea that I'm saying here, that this isn't something that only Mountain-fresh Lion is bringing this idea forward. It's more that it's been going on for a while, but we're seeing an acceleration of that trend. And Mountain Dew Lion—Mountain Lion...

Dan: Yeah, we'll dissect the thing for sure.

Horace: Yeah.

Dan: It's interesting to hear your take on it from the standpoint of coming from you who spends so much time thinking about the mobile side of things, and thinking about Apple from a very different perspective, maybe, than somebody like John Siracura, or Marco [Arment], or [John] Gruber. So it's great to get your take on things like this.

Horace: So the other thing I wanted to talk about, and this is something that's come up because I had a call from someone at the *New York Times* that wanted to pick my brain on one of the topics that I published, and that's on the Apple Stores. This is something that people are starting to discuss because Apple Stores are now doing phenomenally well. They have always been, but now it's sort of become an enormous story.

The numbers are just staggering. And when I was having this conversation with the reporter, I was thinking, "How do you tell the story?" And there's obviously data that I published. And what the data is showing... What's quirky about it is that although the number of stores is increasing, we can take away that variable by saying, "All the data we have we divide by stores." So we can take, for example, revenue and profit and employees. And all of those numbers we can divide by the number of stores to normalize. So we're not looking at the natural organic growth of the franchise, we're looking at it as if it was static.

And the interesting thing that I observed with the data is that the number of employees is growing per store. And now it's over 100 on average. And these aren't big places. If you think about how big an Apple Store is… Of course there is some huge ones, but, I mean, the average Apple Store is not that big. It's a mall store. Even the New York Fifth Avenue one. It's striking how small it is. It's just a tiny room. Compared to some mega-stores like some department stores, or even a Wal-Mart, these are small stores.

And they have over 100 employees, which I think is again off the charts in terms of what other stores that size-per-square-foot basis have.

But the reason why they're adding more employees is because they're adding a lot more visitors. So this is what the interesting thing is. It looks like the employee-per-store number is increasing, which sounds inefficient. But at the same time, they're doing it because the number of visitors is increasing. So what they're trying to do is make sure the visitors coming in don't have to wait longer than necessary, and that there is essentially a sufficient quality of service for the foot traffic.

And don't forget those extra employees cost money. But it's all easily paid for because the foot traffic brings in a lot more money. But what's interesting is that the way they created the incentives for these stores is that those people aren't salespeople. The employee in an Apple store is not there to sell. The employee in an Apple store is there to serve. They're service-oriented. That makes sense, by the way. If you increase foot traffic into any other store… If you increase foot traffic into a Walmart, you're not going to hire more people. The merchandise sells—you may need a couple of more cashiers. But there are only people who stock the shelves and who check you out. There's nothing else to do [for an employee] in a Walmart. Whereas in Apple stores, the idea is that more traffic means more service. They're there really as a service. So the whole concept of the Apple Store, you have to rethink it now, that it's really a service concept.

And yes, you have the Genius Bar. We thought the Genius Bar was a necessary evil, in a way. If you're in retail, you think of it that way. You think, "We're here to sell merchandise, but we're going to have a bunch of helpers. People who are in the help desk." That's how you might think about it.

Or if you're a Geek Squad in a Best Buy, that may be an extra profit center for you. But they have to be justified that way.

But in Apple, the thing is that the Genius Bar is really a symptom of something else—of something that the store is hired to do by the company. The stores are hired by the company to create a high level of service for the whole brand. This is what I finally got [from] thinking through the data, and it doesn't pop out at you. You have to say, "Look at the weird data that's coming up, like this notion of how many employees they have."

And then it drops out of that, the question of efficiencies, that the dollars per employee are phenomenal. There's hundreds of thousands of dollars a year. I mean, I think it was something like $460,000 of revenue per employee at an Apple Store.

Dan: Oh, wow.

Horace: These people aren't paid enormously well. They're probably paid average or a bit, maybe above-average retail. But that number—I remember a couple of years ago, a McKinsey consultant would bring in supposedly over half a million dollars. Maybe now it's a lot more. But there was a time when I remember that was a golden number: half a million dollars in revenue [per employee]. Here we have a retail employee bringing nearly that much. And it's an unbelievable number even if you're a technology company and you're measuring the performance per employee in terms of an engineering employee.

But they're doing it because I think they're trying to ensure that the store provides a good-quality experience. By the way, here's another magical number: The total traffic measured, as they call "visitors," was over 323 million last year in all Apple Stores.

Dan: Wow.

Horace: Now, that's actually higher than the population of the United States. The population of the United States is about 303 million. So you can think of it as pouring the U.S. and Canada through an Apple Store's front door over a period of a year.

It's an amazing story there., just that number. Of course, some of the stores are outside the U.S. But the vast majority are in the U.S. So we're seeing some enormous numbers. Apple used to cite things like, "In the last quarter we had the population of New York and Oregon." They would give some states. They would say two, three states ran through our stores last quarter. And now I'm saying on a yearly basis we had the United States plus Canada running through their stores.

Dan: That's just crazy.

Horace: It's unbelievable. And that's where you get these phenomenal numbers. So you take the number of visitors and revenues, and you can calculate that each visit generated $50 in income for an Apple Store.

Dan: Wow.

Horace: So then you put it this way: The population of the United States plus the population of Canada walked through an Apple Store during the last year and everyone dropped $50 on the desk. That's how big the numbers are. Man, woman, child—they all walked into that store.

Dan: That's amazing.

Horace: So that's the sort of numbers we're dealing with. And then this business is nothing more than a footnote in most analysis of Apple. The Apple Stores: What do they do? They might improve margins, right? Many were critical of [the stores] from the beginning. A lot of failures happened from technology companies doing this. Dell even tried it. Gateway was doing it when Apple started. And it was a disaster. It was an unmitigated disaster. And now we're hearing that even Amazon wants to do stores.

And then Microsoft, of course, has been trying to do stores. And Sony has been trying to do stores. I very strongly doubt that they're going to see anything near the impact that Apple has had.

They're doing a lot in the stores. If you observe them also in terms of throughput, in terms of dealing with these questions about how to check out people, they've reengineered the whole experience quite a bit.

Dan: Let me throw something else out to you, then. How can Apple screw this up? I mean, are they at a point where success is ensured or guaranteed? And if so, that's great, but if not, if we're in the real world, is there a way this can not continue? Will we still be seeing these kinds of numbers and this kind of success in ten years or five years?

Horace: The answer I always give to that question, (and it does come up a lot) is as long as they're innovative, as long as they're not afraid to break some of the major principles they have as sacred... There are some which you may not touch, like the value system of the company, doing the right thing.

But there are a lot of things you can break rules on. For example, you shouldn't hold sacred things like even the iPhone, the idea of what it is. And you should always plan to cannibalize your products. "Cannibalize," by the way, gets misused a lot. It's when you try to destroy your own products, not a competitor's product. You don't cannibalize a competitor, you compete. Cannibalization is about eating your own. It's not eating some other species. We don't cannibalize cows when we eat burgers.

So the point is that you need to cannibalize, meaning that you need to take care of your own products as if they are on a finite life. And you don't hold them sacred. So the way I would provocatively answer this is, I hope that today job number one at Apple is the destruction of the iPhone. And I make it a little bit provocative because it's more about the proper replacement of that product, and the idea that you need to think beyond what is the next thing beyond the iPhone. The iPhone is a fantastic idea. But it isn't going to be the end of user interfaces. It's not going to be the end of the sensors that we have available to tell what we want to a computer. We've been telling what we want our computers to do with a keyboard, then we've been telling them with a mouse, and we've been telling them now with finger touch. And voice, we're adding voice. But there's a lot more. They should be reading our minds. They should be

311

reading our gestures. They should be reading our intonation of voice. We should be able to communicate to these machines as if we're communicating to other people.

And people are much better at picking up what other people want to say. So, all of that is going to lead to new innovations, I think Apple should be the one building them. And in so doing, every new generation that will have a new user interface, my hypothesis is that it will create a new platform that will orphan an old platform, and you need to be prepared to do that, and Apple is the company to do that.

Failure for Apple is simply stopping doing that, is simply stopping being willing to sacrifice its own creations. That's what most companies find extremely hard to do because they have an economic incentive not to do it. You have vested interests—people, management, and employees, who treat this novel thing, this new thing, as an antibody that needs to be destroyed. Organizationally, companies aren't able to do that unless this new thing is somehow sustaining and coordinating with the existing world.

Again, I talk about the Mac in its 28th year. And the fact that iOS overtook that. But the fact is that that Mac is not the same Mac that it was in 1984. Even within the Mac there were generations and there has been a lot of orphaning going on, a lot of cannibalizing, if you will. Obviously, the operating system has changed and the entire job to be done has changed for the product. So in that sense I think Apple has already been exhibiting [cannibalization], even before the current 2.0 era of Apple, the device Apple.

But that's in the DNA. Whether it's Steve Jobs or not, the DNA of the company is about constant reinvention, and [reinvention] of everything internally, except some core principles. There are some core moral compass-type decisions. What is the right thing to do? Those things should not change. But you should change pretty much everything else.

If you were to look for a signal of something screwing up at Apple, if you will, I would look for things like sustaining the iPhone after ten years. iPod has already been led out to pasture. And it's less than ten years old, or it just got over ten years old last fall. But it's already something that we don't think much about.

But I remember what happened when that quarter happened, where we had no growth, year on year, on the iPod. Wall Street just ripped the company to pieces, even though the iPhone was probably just emerging. And the Mac was going [over to] Intel architecture, and a lot of things were happening.

But 40 percent of the stock price value of Apple disappeared because it didn't grow year on year on the iPod.

Dan: Yeah.

Horace: And so that's the world voting and condemning you for moving in the right direction. And you get nothing but absolute negativity from that. Of course, internally, you're going to have even far more of this type of negative behavior. So that's where you have to stay focused and have leadership. That's where leadership comes in saying, "We're going to say no to the iPod. We're going to build something new."

So I think the iPhone will probably have to go through a transition like that. And the Mac is going through that transition as we speak because the iPad is going to replace it. We may not like the idea, but it's happening. This Mountain Dew is all about that, right? So that's a weak signal, but still, I see change.

You saw that also on Final Cut, when they may do things which users dislike. That to me is a positive sign. A sign that they're willing to break…

Dan: Right. Take chances, take risks.

Horace: Take chances. Iconoclastic, that kind of thing. It gives you short-term pain, and if you see short-term pain happening, that's a good sign. Don't ignore a lot of the anguish when that happens because a lot of the people who are most affected by it are the smartest, because they're the most avid users, they're most tuned into what's happening. And that's where you get a lot of negativity from the blogosphere, the people who are actually technophiles. They tend to be more negative about short-term pain. And yet I always think that whenever a blogger cries, a cash register rings.

Dan: That's great. No, I think it's fascinating, though, because you have to… I think Apple has to be thinking about this all the time. Look back at the way that Toyota was, and how they quickly became, relatively speaking, very quickly became the number one car company. Was it Toyota or Honda that had this saying that their main focus is, "How do we keep from being number two?" You know, that was constantly their goal. I'm sure that I'm paraphrasing and misquoting, but that was sort of the internal philosophy of, "Okay, don't focus on being number one, and don't coast. Look what happened to the American automobile companies. We can't do that."

Horace: Yeah. The Japanese got it in many ways. And I don't recall either. I think Honda was probably more happy with being number two than Toyota. But still, the idea was that: "Let's focus on what matters."

By the way, they did take a long time. The car industry did go through that disruption with Japan taking a leading role. But it did happen over a long period of time. They did start in the '60s.

But yeah, that's the thing. It's humility. A lot of the advice I give is paraphrasing Clay Christensen. These tend to be moral discussions. You end up saying this is virtue and this is sin. Virtue being humility and willingness to learn, and doing these things which parents tell their children to do. It's nothing really technical. I'm not appealing to you to be clever.

I'm appealing to you to be more emotional. And thinking about it with your heart. Doing the right thing isn't what your head says, but what your soul says.

So a lot of this advice ends up being, essentially, this kind of fuzzy stuff that nobody really takes seriously but in fact really is the core of all civilization. So we touch on this once in a while. It isn't rocket science. It's more about being aligned with what your parents told you.

So, yeah. That's the advice.

Zeitgeist

Posted February 22nd, 2012 as The Critical Path Episode #26

Act I: An analysis of the manufacturing cost structure for iPhones. Act II: The $10 billion App Store economy and how to quantify value of apps per iPhone. Act III: Like GM and IBM, rather than seeing it as the exception, Apple may be the rule that defines an era.

Horace: A couple of things that I want to touch on. One is, we had this piece from ABC last night about manufacturing processes at Apple—or, I should say, at Foxconn.

Also I did a story last weekend on some of the numbers from the App Store. What's interesting is that in the last conference call Tim Cook revealed this new number, this payout to developers reaching four billion dollars. And the amount that was paid during the fourth quarter, which was several hundred million. This is new granularity we've never had before. This allowed me to dig into some of the numbers that... By the way, also, they have the 25-billion-download counter that also came up last week, that allows us to now get some new insight into just exactly what the economics of the iTunes ecosystem is like. I'd like to delve into that a little bit.

But that's what I have in mind. Anything you want to add?

Dan: Well, I think the first thing that you pointed out, the visit inside Foxconn, that's something I think a lot of our listeners are really keen on. But really, everything you mentioned—and I think it's great—I would love to hear about this. So where do we dive in?

Horace: Here's the thing with manufacturing. It used to be, back a hundred years ago, that understanding how that works was what every business person had to know. Nowadays, understanding or knowing how manufacturing is done is quite rare. It's still taught in business schools. It's still one of the requirements, I believe. It's called "operations" sometimes: basic fundamentals of how to measure and how to optimize manufacturing. There's been a lot of innovation happening in that area. From about the mid-20th century there's been continuous improvement in some of these metrics of productivity. We've seen innovation in "just in time manufacturing," which was an American idea, but it was mostly put into practice by the Japanese, so the Toyota process, which is very efficient, very lean.

Total quality—this notion of quality in general—comes from manufacturing, because the idea was to eliminate the sources of failure in a production line. And if you take that thinking forward, you can actually apply it in multiple areas in your business.

So the point is that you can spend a lot of time thinking about manufacturing. And I don't spend a lot of time thinking about it. But I know enough to get an idea of the importance that that discipline has to Apple's business today. And so I've been thinking about it. I've been...

Dan: Now, you have visited the Foxconn factory yourself and spent about a week there...

Horace: No, no, no. I haven't—

Dan: ...masquerading as an employee. Building iPhones.

Horace: No, I haven't. What I have done is I've visited a Nokia factory many years ago where I've been able to see production of smartphones.

Dan: Where was that? Was that in...

Horace: Oh, that was in [Salo] Finland. There was, or is still, a plant that does do that work here in Finland, and I think they're going to shut it down. They just made announcements a few weeks ago that all Nokia's manufacturing in Europe will be shut down, which they used to have it here plus in Germany. The German plant got moved to Romania. The Romanian plant then got shut down, and now they're going to shut down Finland as well.

The U.S. phones used to be made in Mexico. But now I think that also is going to move to Asia, if it hasn't already.

I've seen one plant. It isn't a huge sample. But what impressed me most was that it is very much a robotic process, meaning you have machines which put these things together and then you have people at the end of the production line doing some highly delicate operations. It can't [all] be quite automated. Usually it involved the putting-together of the final casing, and screwing some bits and pieces together, and then quality assurance, and then, finally, packaging—putting things in boxes.

These last few steps were at the end of the line, and they involved probably a dozen people. It wasn't a very labor-intensive thing I saw.

However, what we saw from Foxconn is very different. And this is where I'm trying to get a picture. My assumption had been that the Foxconn production process for iPhones was similar to what I've seen at Nokia. But it doesn't look like that to me. So I've been thinking about, "Well, how do we measure these things?" And the interesting thing is the ABC piece threw out a lot of data, actually. The numbers may have been put in for effect. They're things like it takes so many people and it takes so much time to do something.

And yet, if you understand how to measure processes, these numbers are extremely important. They may not give you the whole picture, but they give you a pretty good picture of what's happening.

So let me explain. One of the things I first noticed was not in the report I saw online, but it was in the slideshow that was put out a day earlier. It was a promotional piece for the segment that was going to air later that day.

There was this slideshow, and it showed some photos and then some interesting points. One thing it said that grabbed me immediately was that it takes 24 hours to make an iPhone.

Dan: From start to finish.

Horace: Yeah. So assuming that the parts show up at a loading dock somewhere, and people say, "Okay, now, iPhone with a certain ID number is now being built." So what happens is they assemble the pieces, they get put together. And somehow, 24 hours later, it's a finished product going back out of the loading dock into trucks and to a customer.

This is an important number, 24 hours. They also added even more for good measure. They added another datum which said that between six and eight hours of that are spent in what they call a "burning" process, which actually they meant "burn-in," I believe.

Dan: Right.

Horace: What I think that meant was that's when the software is installed. And everything is tested electronically. So all the possible configurations that could cause failure are tested. And that's a completely automatic process.

So let's take an average between six and eight. That means for seven hours out of the 24, no human hand is touching this thing. What happens in the meantime? Does that phone then get picked up by somebody and handled? Because once they are handled by a human, you can start to run the clock on that human's time. And that human time has a value which ABC spilled the beans on and said that the starting wage was $1.78 per hour.

Dan: Hmm.

Horace: Now maybe on average it's a bit higher because not everybody has a starting wage. But let's start with that lower boundary. And now let's say all of those hours—17 hours left over after the burn-in process—all of those hours are spent by somebody doing something to that phone. That's a human being, that's labor input.

And that gives you an upper bound. That really says that $1.78 times 17 hours' worth of labor is what it takes to build an iPhone, assuming that the robotic part of that that's not accounted for as manufacturing costs. There's ways of expensing that, but I'm not going to get into that. We're going to try and figure out what is the exact variable labor time that comes into play.

So that gives you an idea that actually you're getting about $30, if all those hours are spent by some human being.

Dan: Right.

Horace: But that means that it's not waiting. It's not just sitting on a shelf somewhere. There are pictures in the same slideshow that do show phones sitting on a shelf. They're in batches that probably get carried between buildings or they get carried between rooms. And there is this idle time that the device isn't being handled or being processed, which means that—again, out of that 17 hours that we're left with—probably not all of it is handled by humans all the time. So that $30 becomes an interesting upper bound.

I also came at it also from another point of view. What is it the phone costs? It's $650 when it's sold. The bill of materials, which is the cost of hardware components, we know to be about $200 from teardown analysis. So that leaves so much that needs to be spent on manufacturing, on transportation, warehousing, on inventory—even warranty expense has to be accounted for as a variable expense.

I'm trying to figure out how do we narrow this down to an actual cost of manufacturing.

By the way, people do estimate this. There is iSupply, which does the teardowns, did estimate in their reports. They say $8 to manufacture. And I think that was another interesting data point because here we have one assumption it's $30, another one that it's $8. So can we get even something in-between?

So I took another run at it, and this time what I set is more data points that came out of this report. One was that there was 141 steps in making an iPhone. Again, the reporters aren't specific about what are those steps involved. Are those human steps and robotic steps? If you coupled the statement with the film that they're showing, they're showing these rows and rows of people that are working on the phone. And what's interesting is that statement of 141 came because they were walking up and down this line. So the reporter is asking, and that person is saying, "There are 141 steps here." So that I took to mean that there's 141 people in that line and that, basically, to keep things smooth, probably each one does a bit of work and it's a fixed amount of time that they spend on this. In fact, they all spend the same amount of time.

And the other clue came because they were saying that there was this robotic voice that came across the PA system and said something to these people, and I think what it was telling them, what would make sense, is that, "Move to the next unit. Put down what you were doing and then move it to the next person." And this makes sense. It's kind of like the clock cycle, like in the computer. You have a clock cycle that says "Execute the next instruction."

And so it makes sense that they would break the work up into segments that each took roughly the same amount of time. So a person does a little bit of polishing, stops if they're done early, waits for the buzzer, hands it off, puts it back on the line, and it moves to the next station and that person picks it up and then does the next step to it. And each step is designed to take about the same amount of time.

So if we know how much time this clock cycle runs at, and you multiply that by 141 steps, you get another idea of how much human labor was involved in this.

Dan: Fascinating.

Horace: And so I'm looking at this. I'm trying to get a clue from the videos as well. And there is no clear idea of how much this cycle time runs at. So you can do sensitivity analysis. You can say, "Well, what makes sense? Three minutes? Five minutes?" Probably five minutes is too long. Probably under a minute is too short because you can't do much. But we don't really know.

If you take a stab at it and say "three minutes per buzzer," you get about 7 hours in manufacturing. At that wage rate, again, $1.78 an hour—that comes to about $12.50.

So here is another data point. We had $8, we had $30, now we have $12. Which is it? Well, that's as far as I got today. Hopefully I'll get some feedback through the comments, but my assumption is that it's probably in that range. And if it is, it's certainly higher than what iSupply is suggesting. I think $8 is too low.

You can measure it as a percentage of the actual price of the product. We're looking at two to five percent, if you go $12 to $30. And I think that's in the right ballpark, but that's still a bit higher than what you'd expect for a cheap phone, or for an average phone, if you will.

It's also interesting to measure some of the other things they gave us, and this is where it gets a little bit difficult. Obviously, these 141 steps could be done in parallel. There would be one set of 141 people. There would be another set of 141 people. And all of these put together would allow you to produce a certain number of phones. It takes 24 hours, but if you have enough of these lines, then you can generate millions of these a month.

And in fact they did give another statistic. They interviewed a worker—she was working on the casing for the iPad—and they said that this person might actually handle this operation 6,000 times in a day.

That gives you an idea—up to 6,000. If you take that 6,000 and say, "Well, that means that she alone would be able to produce tens of millions in a month." But then it gets a little bit fuzzy because, first of all, she would be on a shift and there would be probably three people on a 24-hour-shift cycle. So there's a lot of questions around that number. I'm not convinced. It sounds way too high. The 6,000 number would imply that she does six of these a minute, given a certain number of hours a day. But I'm not certain of that. I don't know how many hours they work. We don't know because we don't know how much overtime. It may be that they have a regular eight-hour day, but maybe on that 6,000-unit rate they're actually working double shifts.

I put that in the footnote. I'm not comfortable saying that that's actually an indication of what the cycle time is. That would be way too fast. So, obviously, if you turn up the cycle time and you go beyond three minutes—you go two minutes or one minute per cycle—then obviously the price of labor or, the cost of manufacturing, I should say, goes down by the same amount, by the same factor.

It would be interesting for someone to take a run at this, given any fresh bit of data that they may have. Maybe someone knows, in fact, what's the typical time it takes for such a line to run. It also would be interesting to know if there are different lines in series. In other words, there's one line that we saw, but maybe there's another line that comes after it, sequentially, that would do more steps to the product.

Keep in mind that there are a lot of QA [quality assurance] steps, there's a lot of assembly steps, there's a lot of testing. And so we don't know for sure, but my initial run at this, given what we learned today, was that, firstly, I think the product is more expensive to manufacture. I think Apple has a lot of buffer available in which to actually spend that money because they do have this high gross margin. But strategically it's also interesting that it is so labor-intensive. Given that we have existence proof (my own personal experience) that you can automate this, they chose not to. One could argue cynically that it's cheaper. But I would argue that it's more than that. It's about flexibility. It's about being able to ramp up more quickly.

To get machines to do things, you've got to very carefully design the line, get the orders in for the equipment to have it all lined up, ready to go, tested, get it churning and churning and churning. And then you better hope that that line runs for a long time. I think if you want to get the ramp very quickly from zero to 30 million units a quarter, and then ramp it back down so that you can do another product next year, that is not a process today that's easy to do automatically. And that's why they're probably going to a labor-intensive process.

But we'll see. We'll see. This is the tug of war between all the constraints you have. Maybe you have economic constraints, you have flexibility, you have strategy, you have marketing and PR issues involving, obviously, the bad PR you can end up with from using labor. Sometimes people say they want jobs, sometimes people say they don't want bad jobs. So we'll see.

But that's one of the things I wanted to throw out there, in the sense that I'd like to get feedback and have people help move the ball forward and understand what's happening there.

Dan: Yeah. Fascinating, all that you were able to determine, though, from those numbers. And so, why is that so important knowing these numbers? I mean, it's neat to know them, sure. But what does it really tell us?

Horace: Keep in mind that this was a five-minute video with a bunch of slides and a bunch of numbers in the captions. And from that I am able to paint this picture. It's not a complete picture, but it's a lot more than what we had before. And you can see how important this is to a competitor, and how important this is to an understanding of what Apple is all about, and how they do things, and why they do things.

So a competitor might say, "We had been planning all along on doing this in an automated fashion. Now we see that Apple is doing this in a very crude sort of brute-force method. Maybe we ought to do brute force after all." So if you were a competitor, you would learn a lot from looking at this, which explains why companies don't like to share this information. And you're also getting these hard numbers, that you're able to calibrate your own production. So a competitor intelligence person would say, "We know our numbers. And now we can see that Apple might be…" And they might be able to fill in these blanks because they know their production system and they know roughly from contacts what Foxconn is using and so on. They might be able to say, "We're running over or under what Apple is doing." Then they go back to Foxconn and say, "Hey, are you giving Apple a better deal?"

Dan: Ah, right.

Horace: You see? All of these things can blow up. And I actually feel that Apple is opening a lot of cans of worms here because you never know what this is going to end up doing. But I think their hand was forced by the way the press is looking for a story here.

And I really never felt that there was a good story in the manufacturing business. It's sensationalized. There is a lot of fiction. People aren't calibrated to understand any of these things. They look at numbers like the wage of $1.78 an hour and they think this is somehow tragic, when in fact people are very delighted to have that income.

Ideally they would do better things later in life, and they are young [now]. But the alternative might be a lot worse. So, I don't want to get into that. It's a very political topic. It's a hot-button topic. It gets all blown way out of proportion. But to me, it's interesting more from the strategic angle and what's happening there.

I feel a little bit sorry for them because they had to do this, and I'm here prying the wound open a bit more, maybe by actually talking about it. But I feel that's my duty because the information is out there. Someone needs to look at it.

I don't know if [their performance] is good or bad right now. I don't think there is goodness or badness. This is about what they're able to do at this moment in time. And if there is one thing I would say that I was surprised at was that, indeed, there were that many steps involved. The human 141 steps seems like a lot. I would imagine even 10 percent of that, 14 steps, would probably be more what you would see in an average electronics product. That's what you normally would get a human involved in. But this is different, this is Apple. So they do it different, and I think this is an interesting story in itself.

Dan: Very interesting. So what else have you got here on a plate to talk about?

Horace: Well, the other data that I was able to run through some analysis on was with this notion from Tim Cook that $700 million was paid out to developers in the fourth quarter, and the fact that we're about to reach 25 billion downloads. Now, these points in and of themselves don't really ring much of a bell, and probably it's been weeks since the Tim Cook story. But he mentioned it, and nobody really picked it up as an interesting story.

But where it gets interesting is you take the 25 billion and then you realize that on October 4th of 2011, they gave another milestone, and that milestone subtracted from the current milestone gives you an idea of how many apps have been downloaded in the last quarter. And now we know how much developers got paid for that. And we know that Apple keeps 30 percent, pays out 70 percent. Then we know how much each app costs.

And if you know how much each app costs, you know how much a developer gets per app, and you know the number of units that were shipped over the lifetime of the product, then you can get an idea of how many dollars per device are paid out to developers. It's just two numbers you get, and then you build up this huge story. And the story I came up with was that since iOS began, 75 apps have been downloaded per device. That includes iPad.

And that number is rising. It's been steadily rising. You can draw the plot and show that going off into a straight line. And secondly, each app has an average price—or, I should say, there is an average income to developers and to Apple for each of these—and it's about 23 cents now. That includes all the free or zero-cost apps.

But then if you multiply the average revenue per app by the number of average apps per device, you get this interesting number of $17 of income for every iPhone sold. Seventeen dollars on top of what that product originally was priced at. So that's an interesting number. That means that you have a recurring revenue model. You sell an iPhone, it's $650 to Apple. And then on top of that, Apple collects another $17 in app income. And that $17 is paid out mostly to developers. About $12 is paid out to developers.

And so a developer can think about it as follows: "Every time I hear these numbers from Apple, that they sold 35 million iPhones, I can multiply that by $12 and say that over the life of those products the developers, of which I am one, are going to get this much money out of it."

Dan: Right.

Horace: So it's an interesting number. One other way to look at it is since it's $12 and the product lasts for two years, you can say that means $6 a year. By the way, that's rising. It just happens to be a snapshot of what it is today, about $6 a year. And that means about 50 cents a month. Fifty cents a month is being distributed for every iPhone that's ever sold, or iPad, or iPod touch. It's an interesting number, I think.

You don't know what percent you will get out of that pie. But that's the size of the pie. It will be interesting to know what the size of the pies are for different platforms. [Some] are suggesting that it's not Android that's number two, it's actually RIM, because RIM has made the claim already that they're number two. And they claim to be second most-profitable app platform.

Dan: Mm-hmm. Right.

Horace: They don't back that up, so I'm not going to really wave the flag very strongly on that number, but it's an interesting claim.

The other claim that's come in from sources is that Facebook is paying out better than Android. Android may be fourth on the list. And then some have said, "But Windows is still number one," which clearly I wouldn't doubt. But are we dealing with mobile? And are we dealing with social? Are we dealing with all of this as one big interchangeable pool of income? I don't know. That's a different discussion. But within the mobile platforms I wouldn't say Android right now is one of the highest performance.

Now, again, the big question is, it's a different kind of income that Android would provide you with, probably more of an advertising revenue model. But I would like to know what the numbers are. And we've never heard these things published. All we know is that Apple paid out $4 billion and that RIM claims to be number two. That's all we know right now, if you believe those two sources.

I would love to hear more about what it is. And, oh, Facebook also has revealed some numbers, I should say. So those three players have revealed something about the value they bring to developers.

But nothing as far as I know from Google, which is, again, the mystery of Google. It's the open company, supposedly the most friendly to developers in that sense, but it doesn't reveal any information that's actually materially useful to developers, like how many devices there are out there, and then how much money are they expected to make from them. I at least deliver one number that can be deduced from Apple's own information release. But I cannot do that for Google right now.

Dan: Yeah.

Horace: The other app-economy data point is that if you look at it on a yearly basis, together with songs [sold], over $10 billion was spent on iTunes. That's an amazing number to me. I mean, a $10 billion business. Now, some of that doesn't get accounted for by Apple. Apple does give out revenue numbers for what they call "music," an anachronism. It used to be a line item in their income statement, which was meant to reflect iTunes, and at the time it was about music. And now that line includes the App Store. But the way they account for app revenue—and this is where I apologize in advance, it's going to get ugly—but apps are not accounted for in the same way. In other words, if you pay $1 to Apple for an app, Apple doesn't say, "I just received $1 in revenue." They only declare the 30 percent that they keep as revenue within the music line.

However, for music, they do account for $1 of music income as revenue. So the problem is that you see the revenue of the so-called music business not grow as quickly as the iPhone business is growing. And some people cautioned and sounded an alarm, saying, "Look at the growth in device sales and look at the growth in the content sales. It's not keeping up." Well, that's because Apple decided on using an "agency model." The decision was made that with apps they act as a different type of seller, as a different type of retailer, than for music. This is an accounting decision. It's probably justified on a deeper level, that this is somehow the correct way of doing it. But they just talked about it very briefly during a conference call years ago, when they began accounting for that. It's buried in some quarterly announcement, probably back in 2008, where they said, "Going forward, sales of apps will be accounted for on an agency basis." And nobody knew what that meant until a couple of years later. When it's material enough, and the numbers are big enough, you can actually see that it doesn't really make an impact the way you would expect it [would], and so on.

But I backed out of that model, which is, I think, a bit obfuscating. What I said instead is, "If they accounted for the revenue as they did for music," meaning that they're going to count every dollar that they're paid for an app as a dollar of revenue, and then they pay out 70 cents out of that, and then they pay out to the music guys I don't know how much—probably 80 cents or something like that. Then, at the end, you get some gross margin, and then from that you have to subtract the operating costs. And then Apple says it's all breaking even. So you get an idea from all of that just how much the store costs to run.

But the big question is how much? What is the top line? How much money came in? What's the bottom line? And the answer is, right now, that they probably brought in $10 billion. They claimed that they really didn't make a profit, which means that they probably had to spend a lot on the infrastructure to keep these things running, and all the vetting of apps that they do. That's probably another interesting story. Someday we're going to get some data on how many people it takes to filter apps and do quality testing on them and all that, to approve them.

But nevertheless, [it's a] $10 billion economy. I think that number doesn't get talked about because it's mostly invisible or it's obfuscated. But if you were to think about a business that was $10 billion in income, it'd be a pretty substantial business. No doubt about it. It would be one of the largest—it would be Fortune 500 territory. And it is just iTunes itself.

The other story that's interesting in the data is that the apps are really growing so quickly that historically more apps have been sold than songs. If you accounted for them the same way, the revenue from apps is overtaking the revenue from songs. We're going to be looking increasingly—and the slope is so steep—we're going to be looking increasingly… I had this Freudian slip, I kept saying "App Store" when I meant "iTunes." But in fact that's what we're heading towards. The music business isn't going to grow that much going forward, especially in emerging markets, whereas I think apps are definitely going to go there.

So, that's what's happening there. And of course there are movies. There are a bunch of other things that could come on stream. TV shows and other things we might see with Apple TV that will change, once again, the dynamics. But right now, I think we're going to see an app story coming out of iTunes.

And again these anachronisms, like iTunes. Who cares about tunes now? But that's built-in legacy that we have to deal with.

They don't release how many apps or songs are downloaded on a regular schedule. They did it in October. It was because of the music event, I think. They do a product launch and they slip that into one of their introductory slides, to pat themselves on the back, "What a great job we did. Look at how big we are." They drop these hints that you can piece together, and you get a full picture. And in this case, they only mentioned the one data point: $4 billion paid to developers and, as an afterthought, $700 million in the last quarter. This is the crucial point because you can tie it in to the other data you have that was disjointed and out of phase. That gives you some idea of what the business looks like.

Dan: So a lot to think about. I mean, there really are so many moving pieces, and it really does require a lot of detective work to piece this whole thing together.

Horace: Once you get through that you can step back and think, "What is the big picture?" And normally I talk about big-picture stuff on the show, so I want to do that maybe a little bit now.

Someone noted—I think it was one of the big banks—that if you took Apple out of the S&P 500, or the NASDAQ, If you took Apple out, the economy wouldn't look as good. Which is an amazing thing to say.

But what struck me was that they were saying that this is reason for pessimism. This is a reason why you shouldn't be happy. You shouldn't be happy because Apple is the only thing doing well. And I had a visceral reaction to that. And my point is this: They talk about also, historically, that GM was in such a position, where it was a significant component of the S&P 500. Then there was an era when IBM was a significant component. And if you took those out, the economies would look different in the '50s, '60s, '70s and so on.

Fine. It would look like you do have some massively successful company that tends to blind us to what's happening behind the scenes. But my point is that those companies define the era they were in. They weren't just there doing great in order to make up for the failures of the others. They were there because they were the engines of growth. It was the GM era which caused a huge renaissance in the United States. Same with IBM. IBM changed the idea of productivity. IBM changed the idea of business processes. It changed a lot of retail. It changed a huge number of industries.

I saw recently they had the 100-year anniversary of IBM last year. And they had a couple of movies, and they showed the impact IBM had in the '50s, '60s, '70s. If it wasn't for IBM there wouldn't have been a space program. There wouldn't have been retail [bar code] scanners. Productivity at retail supermarkets and department stores and all these other things that we take for granted today. Also transportation—the Sabre system—which allows us to have ticketing of airlines. It's still in place in the way it was architected by IBM. And so a lot of these infrastructural things that we take for granted were things which improved the productivity for everybody.

And so credit where credit is due. I think those eras that are painted as saying, "There was a dominant player, and maybe everybody else was doing poorly." I think we're at the same point now where Apple is defining an era. And I think this is where we need to reverse this argument that Apple is really just an anomaly. It's an exception because they're doing so well. [The implication is that] it's a fad, and everything around Apple is a fad. Well, you could have argued that General Motors was a fad. The whole idea of General Motors was based on marketing, not so much engineering, right? That's what the innovation of GM was. They had all these brands. They had products which would change every three years, that they had these platforms. And all these innovations in automobiles that did away with what Ford came up with, which was very monotonic, and simplistic in terms of marketing. GM got a lot of negativity lately, even in the '70s that they had planned obsolescence, and that the engineering wasn't very good, and all these things.

And I concede that GM was a marketing concept. But nevertheless, it created enormous value. From GM's approach to markets, we had a lot of innovation happening in other industries, and they all copied what GM had done: the way the brands were done, the way the advertising was done. And so we have this effect of a company that seems to be a flash in the pan, but actually that the effect of that permeates throughout the industry. It permeates throughout the world. And everyone basically turns into a GM, and everyone turns into an IBM, in a way. And Walmart in many ways is like an IBM.

Dan: Right. That's an interesting comparison, Walmart-Mart and IBM.

Horace: If you applied IT to retail to such a degree, what you end up with is a Walmart.

And so the point is that you have to think about this era we're in, where Apple is teaching the world how to be a good company. And they're doing it in a spectacular way. It's almost blinding. And it's easy to say, "Once they fade we'll go back." But we'll never go back. What Apple teaches us today, everyone will do the same thing in a few years. And that includes what I talked about in terms of manufacturing, and that includes what I talked about in terms of ecosystems and how do you build brands. What we talked about in terms of innovation and the process of self-cannibalization. Everything we talk about in the podcast is really the lessons that Apple teaches us.

So the zeitgeist, if I may say so, today is that Apple is seen as the most prolific and obviously [successful formula] and now the market itself is catching on and saying, "Holy cow, this is actually affecting the whole economy, in a way, because the index itself is being so heavily weighted by this." You can't turn and not bump into an Apple idea.

And yet we shouldn't dismiss this as something that will fade. I think, in fact, the opposite will happen. It will become permanent, in that everybody will do the same thing.

And that's really my takeaway, the big takeaway from the last few days in thinking about what this impact... And it's still rippling now, this meme, that you should ignore Apple and see a better picture. Rather, ignore everything else and you will understand what the real picture is. Really, that's the story, it's that it's not that Apple is an exception to the rule, it's that Apple is redefining what the rule is.

I don't know if I could say it any more clearly, but that's how I see it, that's what's happening now. And just like there was a GM era, just like Ford in the '20s, '30s redefined transportation. GM redefined marketing. There are many other brands. You know, I'm not as good as I should be in this area [of] who defined what. But there were these eras, and even the '90s was probably the Microsoft era. And we redefined what it means to be an office worker. And now we're redefining what it means to have computers. And what it is that we do with our leisure time.

So all of that is, again, good news, in my opinion. And the Apple story is one of educating a lot of people about how to do things differently. And so that's what I see.

Supernova

Posted March 2nd, 2012 as The Critical Path Episode #27

We talk about iPads and what we'll hire them to do for us. We talk about how measurements of the market show an unprecedented growth in mobile computing and how that leads to a new context for computing along axes of non-consumption. That could mean that the devices will become powerful enough to allow most people to be creative and reach self-realization.

Horace: So, any thoughts of what you wanted to talk about? Or should I…

Dan: Well, obviously there is something that's going on next week, Apple is announcing a new iPad, which is being called, at least, by the general public and the media, the iPad 3. But that's going to be big.

Horace: Yeah, interesting. One thing I tweeted about was that I thought—and this is my first and only prediction for the year—that it's going to be called the iPad 2S. But, you know, that's… I'm sticking my neck out on that one.

The reason is because I think, from what we've seen leaked so far, that it's going to look very similar, almost indistinguishable, from the older model. So if you look at historically what Apple has done, when two products look the same they would be called the same. So they wouldn't create a completely new name for, or numbering scheme for, something. Because think of it from a consumer's point of view,. You look at someone's iPad and visually it says to you, "Well, I'm an iPad 2." And then the other person says, "No, no, it's really an iPad 3." "Let me see, let me check." That whole disconnect between the visual, what it is, what it looks like, and its specifications, if you will—I think that would cause some confusion. And Apple may not like that. But who knows?

They might also do something like HD, that's been a suggestion out there. But I think that, you know, this is part of the whole design philosophy, I think, in Apple, that everything—including the name, the price, the materials—everything is consistent to a particular brand, a particular positioning and a particular job it's hired to do. I think that that may make sense so far, to sort of stick to a certain name. But let's see how that goes.

I'm just skeptical that it's going to be called "3," given that it looks the same.

Dan: So is that what you believe is the differentiator, then, between the old version and the new version, is that it has to look different in order to get a full new number increment? So to go from a 2 to a 3, has to look different, otherwise it's an "S"?

Horace: I don't have any sort of rules in my mind. But if I look at patterns, and you observe what happened with the iPhone, if there was a significant change in the physical design, there was a new number. So actually the first one was called the iPhone. Then came iPhone 3G. Then 3GS. And 3G and 3GS looked very similar. Actually they looked identical.

Then came the 4 and the 4S, and they looked identical. Now, they didn't call the 4S [the] 5, because even though some people would have said it has significant improvements, but it was very similar.

Now, the counterargument to this is that if the iPad n+1—let's say the next version is an HD version, double resolution of what we have today, that is a significant departure, and it might be visible to someone who just glances at it. And I'll concede that that may happen, so they may call it iPad 3... but I think it's more likely it will be iPad 2HD, or iPad HD, or something. Well, not iPad HD. It will be something—I hope it's going to hold on to that number 2. But then you never know.

The other thing, of course, is you can look at iPods. You can see whether they introduced new numbering. In the case of the iPod, there were no numbers. It was simply the Shuffle, the mini, the nano. There was a nano, right? And the nano came after the mini. And then—and of course the Classic. And then the touch. And even though those products did change in their form factor, they maintained the name because the name identified the category of product, meaning in terms of price, in terms of positioning, and so on.

So you'd have to think through backwards in terms of how they would go about deciding this. And I'm not an expert, again, but I would think that this isn't a significant enough departure to give this a distinctive new number to it. It's a point release. And also, by the way, the other thing to notice is that with the iPhone they are on a two-year schedule. The fact—we talked about this in the show on manufacturing—that for purposes of optimization of your equipment purchases, of your engineering for process optimization, you want to have a longer lifespan for a product. And I think one reason for the 4S was that they were optimizing for production. And so I think the iPad itself, now we're in the the second version of the second generation, and they're going to try to amortize or, I should say, depreciate the equipment that was bought to manufacture the iPad 2 over the lifetime of two products, in two years, roughly speaking.

So, anyway, that's just a hypothesis. To me, that sounds more likely. I'm defending it here for like a solid ten minutes, but it doesn't deserve that much.

Dan: Do you want to make... I know you said you're limiting your number predictions and things like that. What about numbers? Do you want to throw out any total number?

Horace: The problem has been with the iPad 2 launch, we had a very slow quarter of the last quarter of the iPad 1. So there was this product transition, and we also had the same thing happen with the transition between the iPhone 4 to iPhone 4S. There are these last quarters. And management, in the past, has said that because of rumors the impending launch of a new product tends to slow down purchases, that they tend to blame that.

I think also that they proactively turn down the production lines because they do have the switchover that they need to plan for. And I think they probably would have begun production already a few weeks ago, maybe even in the last quarter, to begin production and ramp up the new product. And so I don't think it's entirely demand. I think there's demand and supply issues with respect to this transition period.

And over time you want to make that as smooth as possible. You want to also not get that speed bump, if you will.

Dan: Right.

Horace: But we'll have to wait and see. There was some "disappointment" about the launch, the pre-iPad 2 launch. So I'm not quite sure. It was very difficult during the first year of the iPad, or year and a half or so, to know how it would perform in the market. There was zero knowledge. This was a new category. We hadn't seen any pattern to the sales yet. People were measuring sequential growth when in fact it's probably seasonal, meaning that we should see the launch quarter be great, and then the next year's launch quarter also be great. And we didn't know if it would be launching in phase each year at the same time.

By the way, that brings this interesting dynamic that they're launching the iPad in the spring. They're launching the iPhone in what increasingly looks like fall. That fall period used to be allocated to the iPod. The iPod launch was September, usually because it fed into the Christmas period.

The launch windows for the Macs weren't particularly firm. But I'm curious because of what are they—what's the logic behind a spring launch of the iPad? Clearly it's still a giftable item, and it would make sense to have it in production and still in everyone's mind as a fresh product.

Dan: Right.

Horace: We're seeing a first-quarter launch. And there are considerations, for example, for education markets—their purchasing cycles. But, again, do they need to have the latest and the greatest? I'm not sure. Maybe they're also trying to optimize issues around production, issues around load balancing, issues around the financial performance of the company. You don't want to have breakneck speed one quarter and then doldrums the next. So you want to try to manage expectations.

There are so many constraints. Engineering is all about constraints. So this is an open problem. I don't have a solution, I'm just suggesting that we need to think through some of these things. And so that's what I'd like to get a handle on. The iPad 2 has sold very well. The growth rate has been actually faster than the original iPhone.

Dan: Mm-hmm.

Horace: Meaning that it's been ramping faster. It's sold more in the first year or two that we've seen it in the marketplace. It also is growing on a year-on-year basis above 100 percent. So even 180 percent.

I tend to use that figure as the dial I turn, in terms of modeling a product's launch and the product's growth. So if you look at this on the starting point on the same date, then it does look much, much steeper than the iPhone did. Of course, it's a different world than the one five years ago, but it's still a phenomenally successful product. So my expectation—minimum expectation—is around 100 percent growth. And that puts it about on par with the iPhone, knowing that it could even grow faster.

Today I published a model, or the results of a model, with which I try to forecast how the tablet market as a whole will grow, given the fact that we have also Android, we have Windows 8 coming up, and we had Amazon's version of Android with some estimates [of] what they did in the first quarter there.

I try to take that data—and actually it was prompted by a question from a reporter. And I won't name them because maybe they want to still publish or not publish the data, but the idea was to guess when there will be more tablets sold than traditional PCs. And the interesting thing there is that Tim Cook, in the last earnings call, did say that he firmly believes, and many of the people in the company believe, that the time will come when there will be more iPads—or, I should say, more tablets—sold than traditional PCs. And so the question was, "Well, when? When is that going to happen?"

And the modeling I did is exactly on this basis. How do you dial in a growth rate for each of the products that make up the combined tablet market? And as I said, that includes Windows 8, which we have no visibility into at this point. We may see them shipping at the end of this year. We just had great demos coming out this past week. But we don't know the mix. We don't know that first quarter. Will there be Windows 8 tablets launching on top of the traditional market, or will the HPs and Dells and Asus and all those PC vendors switch over their portfolio, increasingly because they're finding themselves losing marketshare, or constant volume overall, due to erosion from tablets coming from competitors like Apple and Samsung, which are not the giants of the PC world.

So an interesting question is—well, that's one of them… Again, given the time frame, only one quarter this year, we're not going to see a huge contribution from the Windows world in tablets. My assumption was the fourth quarter we'd be looking at about seven percent of all PCs, all Windows PCs, being in the tablet form.

Dan: Mm-hmm.

Horace: Then the next question would be Android. Now, Android, again we have very fragmentary data. Andy Rubin also this week mentioned that they had up till now shipped 12 million Android tablets. And that doesn't include Amazon. We have to be careful when Andy Rubin mentions a figure about Android, it's only Google-sanctioned versions of Android. So it doesn't include these variants that—there's Barnes and Noble and Amazon and perhaps some Chinese makers shipped without the Google services.

So we have fresh data from Google about the Android numbers, the Android tablets. But the challenge there is, how did those get distributed over time? We know roughly when they launched, about a year ago. So how did those spread out over the few quarters we have since? We have some data from other analysts that try to get market data, in terms of… They've sampled it and they've sort of given a figure for Samsung's volumes.

Anyway, I took all of the available data. I estimated, for example, that Android sold about half of their volumes in the fourth quarter, about six million. I estimated that Amazon sold about four [million]—could be four to five. Let's say a safe bet is four.

And so you put all these together and then you assign a growth rate. So the answer is that this market of tablets comprised of Amazon, Apple, Android, and even Windows will be bigger than the traditional desktop plus notebook plus netbook market by the fourth quarter of 2013.

Dan: Wow.

Horace: And again, given some of the growth rates we've seen… Now, the remarkable thing is that this market did not exist in 2009. Within four years it became bigger as a computing-device market than the Windows PC—traditional Windows PC plus Mac. Actually, I'm including the Mac as an incumbent platform that's being disrupted.

Dan: Okay.

Horace: So I'm trying to be fair and suggest that these tablets are going to be 50 percent by then. But keep in mind that the whole market is expected to grow. I published also the shared data, the growth data, but also the raw total number of units that are stacked by vendor. So we can see how each vendor will do. And essentially the picture would emerge that there was a significant increase in the total number of computers that will be sold. And these tablets are additive. They're not substitutive. They're not taking so much away.

If they are taking something away, it's most of the growth, most of the upside of the market, and then some. So this goes back to another post I wrote two days ago, which was that if you look at disruptive markets—the iPhone coming in, the iPad coming in, which this represents a disruption as well—is that they take the profits away from the incumbents, but they don't necessarily crush them in that they completely destroy the number of units sold of the incumbent technology.

We still have plenty of dumb phones sold, probably more than ever. We still have alternative platforms. And then when the PC came, it was decades before the incumbent platforms disappeared, meaning IBM mainframes. Some are still around. Or mini-computers. The PC took a long time before it became the dominant force in every area of computing.

Tim Cook also repeated this during the conference call: He did not see the tablet as going to destroy the PC market. There isn't this we win/they lose [idea]. It was more, "We come in, we double the market and thus we take half of it." And I think that makes a lot of sense. PCs in 2013 will still be selling by the tens and hundreds of millions, even. But the computing market would be much, much richer with this secondary format. And so people may have both. Quite a lot of people will have both. And quite a lot of people will only have tablets.

But you can't expect people to pull the plug on the PC in two years' time as so many enterprises depend upon them.

Dan: Right.

Horace: However, the profits available for those still in that market are already gone. We can't even have a debate about this because, literally, those numbers are so poor. I also published this week an article showing how the Mac itself is more profitable at four percent share than the whole of HP's PC division. The whole HP PSG, which is Personal Systems Group, is less profitable than the Mac business inside Apple. So it's not even about all of Apple. Obviously, all of Apple is enormously more profitable than HP is. But if you take the PC division versus Mac division, and try to do apples to apples, you see that the Mac with lower share is much more profitable.

The reason is that the Mac can charge a premium because it's the only product that runs OS X. And the people who want the Mac get it because it has OS X, and the Mac.

And this created a debate on the subject: Is the premium that we pay for Mac because of the fit and finish and quality and materials and attention to detail or [is it] the software?

Dan: Right.

Horace: And one way to settle that is [by asking], "How much would you pay for a Mac if it only ran Windows?" If you were absolutely incapable of running any other operating system than the same as an HP? You probably would pay a little bit more, but not three times more, which is what roughly the ASP of a Mac is vis-à-vis an HP PC.

And because you wouldn't be able to get that premium, as a manufacturer you couldn't make it as polished. You wouldn't have the incentives to create these aluminum unibodies. You wouldn't have the incentives to put [money] into the screens and the keyboards and the tactile feedback and the quality of all the components and the way it feels.

So even though the components that you might buy off the shelf are very similar, as a package you get this great-feeling piece of hardware. But it's the software, that's the magic that makes it all—the whole economic model—work. It's what allows you to charge more, and then it allows you therefore to reinvest a lot of that into a great experience and hardware as well.

So, anyway. Long story, but the bottom line is that the entry of the iPad into the marketplace is expanding the market. It is creating opportunity and also it's not necessarily destroying the volume business of PCs. But it is definitely creating—taking away some profit share, but creating a lot more. And again, historically, you can look at a lot of examples where technology and disruptive change allowed this rising tide to lift all boats. We can't assume that it's a zero-sum game. In fact, if we did, we'd all be still in the 19th century or earlier in terms of all the technologies we've had since—electrification, transportation, communications.

A hundred years' worth of improvements have just raised everyone's standard of living and everyone's essential feeling of wealth. And that is entirely surplus wealth, if you will, that didn't exist. And so that's the magic of innovation. I would just point out that people who are nervous, if you're looking at the stock price, for example, or if you're looking at questions about growth, and you say, "Well, it's reached this arbitrary limit we set, let's say $500 billion." It's just very rare, six companies in history have ever reached $500 billion in market cap or more. And the highest ever was Microsoft at something like 620. So people would naturally assume that there is a ceiling.

Well, I don't think there is any particular ceiling. It's an interesting historical footnote, but the question isn't, "Is there a sum of money that Apple can possibly become?" It's more that if there is value created, and if the value is infinitely higher, then the value they capture will be infinitely higher.

Not to suggest there is infinity out there as an option. I'm just suggesting that there is no necessary finiteness either. So it is all about analyzing it at a very fine granular level. Where is the innovation coming from? Is each product better than the market? Or is it good enough? And does the market value it? Does the market reward it? And so on. And if you answer on a micro-level that each component that makes up Apple is good, then you have to say the sum is good if not better.

So that all points in the direction of continuing growth. And that's all I can say. And the success, again—like we spoke in the last show—the success will depend on their ability to continue to execute on all of these innovations.

Another way to look at it is, imagine how many things are unsolved in the world, and how many problems we have, and how many ways we could fix things, and how inefficient things are. We talk about poor interfaces all over the place. We have lousy experiences with our TVs. We have lousy experiences with our cars.

Dan: Right.

Horace: I mean, think about the TV and the buttons on them, and we're going to laugh at them in a few years and say, "How did we ever tolerate this?" Just like how we ask ourselves, "How did we tolerate rotary dial telephones as the main interface to communicate with somebody?" Or even before then, just calling an operator and having to ask them to patch you through, and having them plug wires into a board to connect people.

And each of these things looks profoundly inefficient. But at the time, these were absolute marvels. So the thing is now, if you ask how could we possibly access communication or access entertainment in a better way—well, a child could tell you. A child could tell you how it could be better. We just are used to it so much that we don't imagine it possibly changing.

The other things that I said that I think are very poor, things like vehicles and the way we are transported. And car interfaces are archaic. Literally, do they still sell cars with CD players? I don't know, I haven't...

Dan: Yes, they do.

Horace: I think a few years ago you could have probably still bought one with a cassette player.

Dan: Probably. That's funny. No, they do. They do sell them. But typically now they rip the CD. You put the CD in, they rip it into the internal hard drive, and then you never have to put it in again.

Horace: Yeah, but the user interface?

Dan: It's horrible, I know.

Horace: We watched these old *Top Gear* episodes because my son is a big fan of the show. And this is the UK *Top Gear* that's been around for ten years.

Dan: Right.

Horace: And it's funny to look at the show from 2004 and '05, and they would talk about things like satellite navigation systems—"SAT-NAV," they call it. This was actually an option on the best luxury models, and if you had that option it was like you could brag about it, just like you could brag about having an 8-track player in the '70s, or a CB radio. So these technologies—I mean, come on. When you look at the quality of a 2004 or 2005 SATNAV system in a high-end car, it feels completely kludgy and really rough.

Dan: Right.

Horace: And the reason they are still that way to many—in many of the cars—is that they're still using an integrated approach. And remember we talk about integrated versus modular. In some cases, an integrated approach is better because you're trying to make the whole experience better, the whole car has to be better because... The engine has to be tuned to the transmission, which has to be tuned to the suspension, which has to be tuned to the overall type of car you need, whether it's a sporty car or whether it's a utility car. And so designers in a car have tended to be integrating things. But they've been integrating for over 120 years. And there are some points where you should actually modularize.

So one open question would be, for example, why can't you get an engine from one car company and then a body from another car company? Why are engines still produced by the same—if I may use the old phrase—"coach builder"? In the old days, when cars were new as a technology, you actually could order different engines and bodies by different coach builders, and then the engines would be provided by an engine builder.

Trucks are like that. If you spec out a large or commercial vehicle, you can specify a diesel from Cummins, then you can get a body from another company and have it spec'd this way, when you place your order. But somehow vehicles that we drive, consumer-grade vehicles, there is some collaboration that happens behind the scenes, where they certainly do engine development, sometimes in the collaborative fashion. And sometimes car owners... Firms are owned, brands are owned by different companies, so you may be driving what you think is a European car but in fact it may have a lot of parts in it that are American or Japanese.

But nonetheless, it's not quite modular enough. And forget about the mechanical stuff. Think about the electronics. There is no way for you to plug that much of an interface into your car's electronic system, which by now should be following Moore's Law, but it isn't. So the screens you use, the dials you use, all the user-interface elements, the knobs and the buttons and the layout, everything else, is designed on a car-by-car basis by the manufacturer. No one comes in from the software industry saying, "Just give me a blank spot where I can pop in a screen." And why wouldn't there be? There was a time when you could plug in your iPod and get music into your car stereo. And I think many cars still support this concept.

But that was an extraordinarily difficult sale for Apple to make, and you have to get in at the stage with the discussion with an automaker that you say, "Five years from now, when you finally ship this product, this car, it's going to have this interface and it will still work." Because they really work on a much longer time cycle.

So, anyway, transportation is another big area. But I'm just trying to point out that innovation is very, very hard to explain why in some cases it seems to be working extremely quickly—like we have in the smartphones and iPads—and in other industries like transportation it's extremely slow and we have this dissonance between the world we live in, where we have a wonderful experience in front of our computers and sitting with our devices in our hands. And then we look at the 1950s when we use our TVs [today], and we look at the 1970s when we use our cars.

Why this is... There's always a reason why. You have to be able to understand the dynamics of innovation theory to understand why things are happening this way, and then you try to explain it, and then you try to fix it, and you try to ask how can we overcome it.

So, that's my rant. But anyway, yeah, the iPad.

Dan: [laughs]

Horace: You know, when the iPad came out—here are a couple of personal anecdotes. One of the first things that got me excited about Apple... In 2005 they launched a couple of products which I thought were really exciting. And they're not anything anybody was excited about at the time. And that was the Mac mini and the iPod Shuffle.

It was then that I noticed something happened in the company that used to be known for these outrageously premium products: the Cube, and they had this thing going for a while with these clear acrylics, and they had these *objet d'art*-type of products. And here came these two rather low-end products. I mean, it wasn't totally cheap to get a mini, but it was stripped. I mean, it was really bare bones in that sense.

But it was small. And so was the Shuffle. In that sense I saw Apple coming in for the first time with what I thought were truly low-end products. And that's what woke me up to the potential, that they were able to tear themselves away from being a premium brand and being something, therefore, much more potentially low-end disruptive.

And they were doing stuff in new markets with the iPod, but nothing quite that spoke of mass market, like in the billions of consumers.

And one thing, by the way, that attracted me to the notion of the [Mac] mini was that this is actually small enough to become a module inside of something else. So, in retrospect, this is a silly idea. But I thought at the time that it would make sense, for example, to make small enough computers like the Mac fit inside a car dashboard. It almost fit in the same size.

Dan: Well, people have done exactly that, haven't they?

Horace: Yes, they have. And I was hoping to see more and more of it, that somehow Apple would make that happen, would be the catalyst. And the same thing with the Shuffle. The Shuffle was like a little bit too minimalist, but the idea was that they were thinking in the right direction.

So, as time went on, I kept looking for this kind of automotive integration with Apple, and the [iPod] was certainly doing very well. Ninety percent of cars could get an input from an iPod, although sometimes it was only analog, just the line out. But that meant something to me.

And then the second interesting thing is when the iPad shipped, a lot of people were saying, "Well, we could just put these in the dashboard of the car. Wouldn't that be great?" So people were playing with that. Again, this was in the aftermarket. People were putting them into seat backs. But here is why it didn't take off with the automakers: I think [it's] because they just work on different time cycles. So Apple would say, "We're working on iPad 3, in fact, because we'd better be, right now." They should be looking two, three years ahead. And the automakers are still right now working on a car that may come out five years from now. So they can't keep that space open in the dashboard. And the interfaces to that device open for five years. Apple cannot guarantee that they're going to be able to be compatible with that design. And for that reason, you don't get this kind of tight integration.

We'll see how it evolves. It would be nice to have some way of interfacing these products into more than a charger and line in—to have some kind of control function. And yes, there are, accessories and things like that. And they are really exciting, especially in medical sensors. If you can have sensors that help diabetics, sensors that help heart patients self-monitor, that's really disruptive. That really goes to the heart of being able to capture data, which is actually what I think most of the effort and money spent in healthcare is, diagnostics. It's really just capturing data that you need to have a facility with equipment and staff trained to do basic data capture, right? It's really fundamental.

And if we can package them in a way that consumers can self-diagnose, or at least capture the data and transmit it—I shouldn't say "self-diagnose." They should capture the data, allowing easy transmission to a person who can monitor it, at least make a first judgment on the data, therefore cutting down on the need to travel and the disruption that it has in people's lives—of traveling to healthcare providers, and sitting in waiting rooms, and being extremely unproductive.

All of that area of diagnostics is powerful, never mind transportation. We can do a lot with these devices if they get interfaces to other parts of our lives.

And as we'll see probably with the TV, the device conforms… Or, I should say, probably the medium of TV and the experience of TV needs to now conform to the controller, which might be a device, as again we might see the conforming happening with the other industries. Because we have this phenomenon of smartphones becoming such an important part of people's lives that other industries begin to conform to them, rather than vice versa. And this is where you get this tipping effect.

I could give some examples, maybe. If you think about communications, so many industries were built because we had a telephone network and we could communicate with each other. So you didn't have to build phones that worked in a specific way for a specific application. People just said, "We can build a whole industry, or we'll change the way we do sales, because now salesmen don't have to travel so much."

And on and on. So technology that gets important enough in people's lives causes transformational change in other industries that are not exactly touched by it. The Internet is another classic example, and how it changed the way companies operate, and industries make money. So, yeah, that's all part of the whole picture there, and the whole impact of the iPad.

Dan: So this is really interesting to speculate. Here is where the iPad is today. Here is all the things that it's changed and affected. And I was talking to John Gruber earlier in the week about this, and I asked him a similar question I'm going to ask you, which is: Obviously, the iPad is very much at the center of what Apple believes is the future of the company. Probably for most of the reasons that you just listed. It makes perfect sense. But what are we going to be looking at, not in a year from now, but in five years or ten years from now? Obviously, it's impossible to speculate on the look and feel of a device that doesn't even remotely exist yet. But more along the lines of the place that the device will have with the consumers, in the mind of the consumer.

You know, you talk about the telephone, and how that changed. I'm sure that when they were inventing the telephone they weren't saying, "This will affect how much salesmen have to travel," for example. That wasn't probably even slightly on their mind—maybe it was. But probably not. But so it's just as difficult, of course, to try and imagine how devices like the iPad might change all of these related industries, but specifically to technology—specifically in the computing industry. Where do you think things are going to be? What trend is this the start of?

Horace: Well, the thing is this. I think that the fact that it makes computing more accessible… And I think, by the way, there are two dimensions to that: more people and more places where they can use it. So, in other words, I think of the world as being a consumption map. And the consumption would be along these two dimensions, places and populations. And so there are vast empty spots in this map. Places where you don't think of using a computer. And lots and lots of people who find them too difficult to use, or they're using them for very basic tasks.

So what happened is, the PC revolution was all about actually bringing the PC power as it originally was a productivity tool, but it brought it to mass consumption, and it did it through offering communications, offering also email—and so messaging followed—and offering entertainment. And that came through not just music and YouTube, but even the whole notion of social media and most of the websites that people consume are entertainment in reality, as a job to be done.

So people latched onto this tool as much more of a leisure and social tool than just a productivity tool, and that allowed the consumer sector to overtake the corporate sector as the primary adopter, or early adopter, of new technology, even in the PC.

That's what people sometimes refer to as democratization: That the devices, the technologies that were for experts, are now in the hands of non-experts, amateurs, consumers.

So regarding your question, the answer I would see is that people will embed these things—call them iPads or iPhones or whatever variants will emerge...

Dan: Right.

Horace: But they'll embed them deeper into their lives in ways that we cannot anticipate. And I think that the most likely two areas are first, content creation. I think people will become much more creative and in many ways—not like they're going to all be artists, but they'll be able to repurpose media in many ways. So you see things like 80 percent of tweeting is relinking. It's linking stuff from other places.

Dan: Right.

Horace: So you look smart because you're essentially curating the Internet for your friends. A slightly different job than what we hire Facebook to do. Facebook is much more original content that people produce, in terms of what they think and feel.

But there are other areas. Like now we're seeing this Pinterest idea: You're not linking URLs. You're not sending people URLs to long pages to read and become intelligent. You're sending stuff you like. "Check this out." And it's just a picture, many times. So people begin to curate visual items. There's a whole new category now we're dealing with of creativity, if you will. And so more and more people will become a platform of their own. They become authors, become celebrities, become micro-nano-sized celebrities, in a way, among their peer group—among their friends, that they are the people who they turn to for opinions, for ideas. And that drives the ego of the individual to say, "Well, now I'm actually self-realizing through this new medium."

And when you trigger that in people, and enough people have the knack for it and get into it, then you'll have a completely new job to be done by these devices. The self-realization job. And you can't imagine the opportunities and the ways people will create—not just new experiences—but they'll be creating entirely new media types. The social medium itself.

So I see that the experiments that are going to happen are exactly along the lines of how many people can we get to do cool new things with these devices, which have ways of capturing stuff from the world outside—photos, links, videos, all these other things that right now are encapsulated in the Internet—and then can be captured with a device. All these things suddenly fuse and create this supernova of creativity. We've already mentioned YouTube as an example of that. I think it's still too hard to create video. But I'm thinking how quick and easy can you make the creation and amplification of these little clips of sensory perception?

Dan: It really sounds, Horace, to hear you describe this, it really sounds like what Apple has, in a very subtle way in some cases, expressed as being their focus. You know, the iOS devices and the camera. The fact that these devices, especially the iPhone, have a camera. I mean, if you combine the camera with Internet access and a really good user experience, you now have a device that allows you to really connect all of these different things that have traditionally always been separate. I mean, everybody loves the idea of, "I just took a picture, I'm going to share it with everybody that I know." Everybody's doing that. Everybody thinks that that's great.

But there's so much building around that. I like your term, "supernova," because it really seems like the integration of those three or four concepts, the notion that you can share an experience visually, instantaneously, from wherever that you've just captured... We've talked about this on some other shows, but if you remember when the Super Bowl that just happened a number of weeks ago, all of the players who were there that you saw, the shot of every single one of them with their iPhones videotaping—look at me with the old term "videotaping"—making videos of the event as it was happening, which no doubt they're saving, they're sending to their friends who weren't there.

Horace: I know. Isn't that amazing?

Dan: They don't even... It's not even a second thought to them. They're not thinking, "Huh, I wonder, how should we commemorate this?" No, they're just—their phones are already in their hand. They're already taking the video of it, you know?

Horace: Even though they're obviously...

Dan: Even though they're there.

Horace: ...the center of attention, they're the center of attention.

Dan: Right.

Horace: There's a thousand cameras on them already and they want to pull out their own just to capture it and say, "It's my version of the truth that I'm going to share with my friends."

Dan: Right. Right.

Horace: So that gives them a buzz because they say, "Well, look, I'm not just in the event, but I'm capturing it and sharing it." And I'm just saying, it's not just the video or the photo are the things, but it's all kinds of different things. Like this idea of the simplest thing you can do is just drag a link over, right? But that means that you've also created something new, whether it's in Twitter or in Pinterest or something like that. It's the idea that, "Look, I'm creating. I'm communicating. I'm speaking up. I'm making myself heard." These are very basic things. Everybody wants to say they're proud of that at some moment.

You know, when children go to school—and you have young kids, too—everybody is encouraged to draw pictures, right? And they draw all these wonderful pictures and put together all these arts and crafts, and do all these—like gluing things together and using fingerpainting. And teachers love to encourage them because the kids get a kick out of it, the parents get a kick out of it, and it turns on the brain. It does a lot of wonderful things. We just don't do that as much when we become adults. But that's a basic human need, right? Cave painters who painted caves in prehistory 50,000 years ago had the same impulse. We are a creative species.

So it's important, I think, that we allow as many people in as many places as much time of their existence to allow them to do these things. And that's what these devices ultimately will let you do. They will become pervasive enough—meaning, with you all the time, and with everybody all the time—that it will be very easy for everyone to actually say, "Here I am, look at me, I'm beautiful."

Dan: [laughs]

Horace: So, you know… No, I'm serious.

Dan: No, you're right, you're right.

Horace: In every way. It's not just physically beautiful.

Dan: No, I know what you mean, but it's funny. Okay, but this—and that's the core that I think—we can't say just Apple, although I think you and I are both of the opinion that Apple does it best. But there are other devices that do this also, or that try to do this. But it's exactly what you're describing. That thing that makes you think, like, imagine… I want all of our listeners to imagine this right now. You're going out for an evening with friends. You show up at the place that you're going to be, and you realize you left your iPhone at home—or your Android device. Let's be open-minded here. Your smartphone—it's at home. You're going to feel weird the whole night, most likely. If you're listening to this show, you're

343

probably going to feel really really weird. People right now are checking their pockets to make sure that they have it right now. You know, that—whatever it is that culminates to create that feeling, that I need to have this thing with me no matter what, no matter where I do...

Horace: Yeah, I had an episode like this. I went out to just clean off the car because it was snowed over, and I wanted to make sure that I didn't have to do that later when I needed to drive the car. So I only stepped out for a few minutes to brush it off. But I knew within about three minutes that I forgot my phone. And I was right next to my house.

Dan: Right.

Horace: There is no reason for me to have a phone. But I was thinking, "Hmm, what if I have an emergency right now? What if I drop the keys in the snow and I can't find them?" I then became extra conscious of everything I did, just to make sure that didn't happen, because the phone wasn't with me.

So it's just basic stuff like that. You're absolutely right. I think I was much more conscious, if I didn't have my phone than my wallet, or anything... You know, the wallet is practically obsolete now. But it's a nuisance to lose it. But it certainly isn't catastrophic, especially if you're not traveling.

Dan: Right. I mean, it's not like losing your phone, forget it.

Horace: Well, yeah. I mean, your phone, it's like—well, your phone can get you a new wallet. A new wallet—well, it can buy you a new phone, but it won't have any of the data in it, so it won't help you.

You're right. This device has elevated itself to a point of importance that's beyond any other device or any other technology, I think, historically. And the other thing this is the N x N matrix, because that dimension is multiplied by a second dimension, which is the actual ubiquity of it, so that enough people will have these things.

And again, another post I wrote is trying to put a number on how quickly Android—and I won't even get into iOS—but Android, how quickly it will get to a billion activations. And again, that happens to be, according to the data we have, and an extrapolation I did, it happens also to be by the end of next year.

And I had done in the past, things like the tipping point of smartphones. When will we have more than half of the adult population having smartphones? And now there is new data from the Pew Institute that it's already reached 50 percent of the United States. There are different methodologies we can get to. You know, Nielsen does it one way and comScore does it another way, and so on.

But it's going to happen this year for sure, if it hasn't already happened, that we're going to get that tipping point. And this was predictable a year or two ago.

Anyway, all these are happening and then China and then India and then Africa and then all of Asia. All of these places will all get saturated at some point in the near future with smart devices, with dual cores and touch screens, and beyond—whatever input method we'll have after that.

So all of that allows humanity to, I believe, prosper and go beyond what we think of as subsistence, as living, the notion of life having sufficient caloric intake to moving to the self-realization part of what we are. And these devices ultimately are going to solve part of that job. And to answer your question, this is why I don't find the limit, a visible limit, to the value created. Because this is such a powerful job and everybody has it, and it is getting solved. As long as that happens, people will find the ways of making it affordable—find the ways of acquiring it, or bringing the price down so that everybody can acquire it. It's just too important.

So that's about as optimistic as you can get.

Dan: It's very optimistic. And probably good. No, you've depressed us so often on this show.

Horace: Have I?

Dan: No, not really, but you know, when we've talked about RIM and Nokia and things, it's been—…

Horace: Oh, failure, yeah. Well, failure…

Dan: …some grim news that we've had to talk about. But this time, it's a very positive note for humanity, for all of humanity.

Horace: Well, but again, even the negative is positive, because in a way the negative is part of the process of creation, you know. It's as Jobs said, "Death is the best thing about life." It allows the new to emerge. And, yes, there will be victims along the way. If you want to call them that. But it's partly that they are all failures from which we have learned. And people move on, and we all benefit from that learning.

So it's a process you have to accept. Innovation isn't always positive in that there are many ways that people are hurt through it, and certainly we've seen that in the Industrial Revolution. We've seen that many innovations, technological innovations, have been used also for harm. But still, overall, you see a net positive. And a lot of the problems… I think one show we should dedicate also to this notion that we are hearing a lot of talk about limits to growth—especially because of energy issues—that there are certain physical limits that we cannot overcome, that Earth can only support so much consumption.

And I'd love to take a run at that because I think that, again, assumes a fixed view of what the world is. And there were previous such views which have been debunked. And so there are ways of thinking about sustaining growth, and not necessarily using the same variables to define that growth. So we need to go through and think that through.

I am fundamentally optimistic, and usually the answers come through weird things like technologies, like these which we think are toy-like, but ultimately they also solve these deeper problems of efficiency. And if people have the ability to be creative, they will be creative in very interesting ways that may solve problems that we don't anticipate are solvable. And that's another spin-off idea.

So, I think that's probably for another day.

The Consequences of Disruption
Posted March 14th, 2012 as The Critical Path Episode #29

We discuss the five characteristics of disruption: Net growth and value creation, inevitability, increased speed of change, necessity for macroeconomic growth, and historical consequences. This and much more will form the basis of discussion for Asymconf.

Horace: We're going to look at how Apple spends money on things that are assets—tangible assets, things which have a depreciable life, as well as real estate and buildings as well as their stores. And from that pattern, we can observe perhaps strategic intent and, furthermore, maybe even be able to predict a little bit medium term, given their budgeting, their expectations for units of production, for expansion plans and so on. Because they actually do tell you quite a bit in advance what the budgets are. We can get a lot of this interesting analysis done.

And this is actually quite a new topic because typically companies like Apple don't have large capital expenditures. Whether in software or whether you're even doing manufacturing, or you're a device maker, you tend to outsource a lot of things that require capital.

Dan: Why is that? Is that just the way they conserve cash?

Horace: No, it's actually because tying up capital in production equipment, buildings, land, what have you, tying up that capital has been considered inefficient. This has been something that's kind of been drummed into people's minds over the last few decades because, if you think about it, a company that is mostly driven by its intellectual property, or its creativity, or the process of orchestrating ecosystems—the Microsoft model or even predating them, even the IBM model—that a lot of the dirty work that goes into production, which is capital-intensive, was stuff from the industrial era. It was U.S. Steel, it was these Rust Belt companies that were considered obsolete in the post-industrial era.

And so a lot of that work ended up being outsourced because you still need to make these things, but it was outsourced usually to Asia, and sometimes to Mexico, depending on what era you were in. There was a lot of production that was going on in the '90s, for example, in Mexico. Not just for labor issues but, again, because you wanted to get rid of these assets that burned up capital and essentially tied up your capital in things which were not productive, by your definition of productivity.

So the problem was that we got into this mindset for a long time, and I think the renaissance that we're seeing right now with the device-driven model for wealth creation, vis-à-vis the pure services model or pure software model, is that we have to really pay attention to production. We have to really pay attention to how to optimize volume and speed of production. And that problem of optimization requires rethinking some of these old assumptions.

So here is the critical question—because the numbers we're dealing with, billions of units that need to be built and sold every year because that's the device economy—at billions of units, the economics change. And the innovation you need to get that volume built and delivered and on the shelf, and all the requirements of having a device business, these are things which I think people have to reevaluate and relearn how to do that profitably. And that's where I think Apple is, in a way, pioneering.

But there are so many dimensions we can take. We've already spoken to this topic: What is the labor. Here is the crucial question. Many conflate the idea of production and labor as bing the cost equation is predominantly labor, because a lot of people's minds are set in the 20th century, in that we had to have these giant factories to build the cars and other things, and we ended up having a giant labor force. And that labor force over time grew to also have lots of benefits, and have lots of costs associated with high-wage manufacturing. And all of those things... The debate has been, we needed those jobs back, or they'll never come back. But as it is right now, the labor component in an iPhone is really a tiny, tiny part. It's between $8 or $15, it depends a lot on how we measure it.

And we talked about this earlier. But what I'm discovering by looking at the data from the capital budgets is that once those monies are spent on equipment and machinery, Apple gets to depreciate that, which means that it becomes an expense that you can attach to a particular unit of production. So, in this case, an iPhone.

So an iPhone has associated with it, by my calculation, approximately $10 of depreciation. So essentially you're attaching the capital equipment that you've spent money on, you're attaching it to production of the iPhone and therefore you can attach this cost of that equipment to the unit of production, which means —depending again on a few assumptions—that depreciation on the equipment that's building an iPhone is about equal to or maybe slightly more than the cost of the labor that goes into that production.

In other words, *the cost of equipment is as important if not more so than the cost of the labor.* And this is where Apple right now, I think, is a little bit unique among all OEMs [original equipment manufacturers]. If you go and look at what Dell or HP are spending on capital equipment, it's negligible. And Apple, a few years ago, it was also negligible.

The only real, large CapEx spender out there in tech world, if we call it that, is actually Google. And Google doesn't buy production equipment, they buy servers, and they buy equipment that's used to maintain a service. That CapEx budget is also quite significant, and it goes up and down a little bit. It's volatile. But what Apple has spent has exceeded what Google is spending.

A lot of the people who analyze Google as a financial asset—or as a financial analysis, if you will—one of the big question marks out there is how much are they spending on CapEx? Now that discussion ought to be, how much is Apple spending on CapEx? It turns out that these are now comparable, although they're spending it on different things. Apple does spend on some servers, obviously. I don't know the exact amount, but they are spending perhaps 20 percent, perhaps 30 percent of their machinery and equipment budget on servers. And that's to fill the data centers that they're building.

But Google is about 100 percent [of its CapEx] spent on that, and there isn't any manufacturing equipment. But in the case of Apple, there certainly is. So now the question is, are they comparable? At the same time, you can't compare Apple strictly with Samsung, because Samsung is in the hardware-component business, and that's very capital intensive. They also manufacture all kinds of big items like ships. So it's not easy to really create a comparable to the way Apple is currently operating.

And then there is Asymconf, which is in about four weeks.

Dan: Yeah, getting closer and closer.

Horace: Yeah. And that one I've written two pieces, two of the case preparations for it, and maybe if we can talk a little bit about that.

To put a more specific point on this, the opening problem we want to address is that I wanted to introduce in a more broad sense what the notion of disruption is. And so the context that I've put out there is that disruption means, typically, that incumbents lose to entrants. And that's an extraordinary thing because the incumbents have all the advantages and the entrants have usually all the disadvantages. And it doesn't seem to be probable. And yet it happens. And not only that, but one of the consequences, or corollaries, of this idea that disruption happens is actually that is always happens. And so I put down a couple of thoughts on some of consequences of disruption theory. And so, I want to go over these maybe briefly.

Dan: Yeah.

Horace: And the idea is, like I said, we'll discuss a little bit the notion of what disruption means. But some of the corollaries, some of the consequences—the first one is that it sounds destructive. It sounds like when you have a disruption, people lose. Some win and some lose. But in reality, if you study it long term, there are typically more winners than losers, and the winners actually create a lot more value than the losers lose value.

In a way, it's like a rebirth. If an industry is destroyed a new one replaces it that's even bigger and more important. That doesn't excuse the fact that there are people who are going to lose their jobs or lose their livelihoods. But generally speaking, societies tend to benefit from it.

The problem is, typically policymakers will be very reluctant to allow it to happen because you do have this short-term pain. But the examples that we have are that disruption typically does create net growth.

So that's one thing that probably isn't on everyone's mind when they think about disruption, when they use this word.

The second thing is that it actually is quite common. We think of it as an anomaly. This is amazing! This is exceptional! This is unusual! But, in fact, history shows that every industry that's ever been has been disrupted. And what's interesting in that there are some cases where it seems like it's not happening, or that there are some industries that have remained rigid, unchanging, for a long, long time.

Clay Christensen has looked at a few of them. He's looked at healthcare and education, and these are close to his heart. Those are powerful industries. They're bedrocks of society. And yet they haven't really changed. Education is very much the way it was in agrarian societies. It hasn't—arguably, really—even entered into an industrial era. So it's 17th century concepts that are being used today.

And healthcare is more modern, but it's about 100 years old, out of date. So these are interesting studies. The other things you can study, for example—and we mentioned this on the blog, on the podcast also—is the transportation area. You have airlines and all of air transport, and many forms of road transport frozen in time. They cannot move, they cannot change. I exaggerate a little bit, but innovation has become illegal in these industries.

And so this is an interesting corollary. If you find an example where things haven't changed, then you should ask the question, "Why it hasn't changed?" Because, in fact, the force of disruption is a natural force that always is putting pressure. And I try to look at the entertainment industry, as well, as an example of something that is… It's a bit hybridized. Entertainment is not purely without disruption, but there are parts of it which have become extremely rigid.

And the other thing that's interesting when you study this stuff, is that the frequency of change is increasing. So historically you would expect an industry to undergo this changing of the guard every few decades. [The reason] it wasn't really all that exciting to study as a concept is because it just seemed like it took a lifetime for things to change, and who has the patience to actually do anything about it? You won't see the consequences of leading or of being an innovator.

However, we're finding that more and more the speed of change has increased. And this is an interesting topic because if you look at the mobile phone space, for example, it's taken five years for profits to transfer from incumbents to entrants, like Apple.

And what other industries can undergo this rapid change? I mean, will telecom itself, including local operators, go through this transition?

So this is important for the audience, to take this idea of speed of change and apply it to their own world, and apply it to their own industry, if you will, and see whether they're seeing evidence of that happening.

We in the software world were not only conscious of [disruption] but we're encouraging [it] all the time. The idea of being the professional developer meant different things a few years ago, that you would grow up and be a developer using a certain language, using a certain integrated-development environment.

Dan: Right. It was just like learning a specific trade. Even though you might share things in common with other people in a similar trade, it was separate. It was an individual thing, right?

Horace: Right. But it was also something you went to school to learn. And you became a professional at it, and then you expected to practice for a decade or so, when you knew that language and you were a professional in that language. The problem has been that nowadays the way you develop has changed. It used to be code, compile and run on a particular platform. Now with the web, you have multiple environments that you're working with simultaneously. You have interpreted code, you have binary code, you have, essentially, client/server-distributed systems. You have a lot of object-oriented programming and concepts. And you have constant evolution of these things. People debate one year, one language, and then the next year it seems to be already passé.

Last week I was in Stockholm, and it was an event sponsored and run by Facebook, where they were promoting their platform for developing apps, which is HTML5 today, and/or in the future as well. And they're really keen on this. But there aren't many people who are trained and there aren't that many tools available for you to do really spectacular work on this.

But I think that's one of the things, as a developer, you have to be conscious of, and realize that your skill set has to be constantly changing. And you are comfortable with the idea that you're coding in Java, but you're thinking maybe "Objective-C: I need to learn that. I need to move from being a Mac developer to being an iPhone developer. I'd like to learn how to be able to also develop for HTML5 because I see that changing." And you don't assume anymore that the languages you use today are going to be in use forever. And so we are comfortable in this dynamic environment. But it's a very uncomfortable notion for almost everyone else in the world that, whatever you're studying and training with and learning in life, is going to be obsolete in a few years.

And yet that's something I think is going to be more and more probable, and that's where I think it behooves everyone to understand this theory, so that they can see it happening to themselves. You will see this is another form of disruption. It's like the disruption of the professional tradesman, the idea that you used to know some trade and you yourself were disrupted, even if that trade was something extremely sophisticated.

Building buildings used to be a highly sophisticated skill, and the Masons were predicated on the basis that they knew how to make buildings stand up. And so the idea was that it was a secret society—that knowledge had to be very carefully maintained because the guild of people who knew that needed to make sure it doesn't leak out and then everybody will know how to make a building.

That idea has disappeared as the idea of protecting knowledge, crucial knowledge. And yet there are many skills today that aren't protected officially, but are regulated in such a way that it doesn't leak out.

Certainly, professionals in the healthcare world understand this. But there are parts of healthcare which are clearly disruptable because some under-skilled or non-skilled person can do some of the functions that only doctors are allowed to do today. And that's the basis of one of the disruption theories about how healthcare will change.

And they will be aided—these less-skilled individuals—by technology that will give them the data and information necessary to make diagnostic decisions that required a true expert.

And this gets into the whole question of, for example, how do we make decisions about allocating resources? As a side note, I wrote today a piece saying, "Why is it that we need to understand what a job for entertainers is? Or, specifically, the job to be done for the entertainment industry? You know, it's kind of a peculiar notion that we hire entertainment. It's a peculiar notion and many people will laugh at, that we hire art to do things.

But my point is that if it is commerce, it needs to be studied. If it's art that's done for art's sake, fine. But if you're going to be building a business on top of that, you have to necessarily think about how to allocate resources and how to understand what buyers need, and build for them. Otherwise, it's nothing more than an opportunistic building of something and hopefully someone might be interested enough in it to allow you to sustain your lifestyle.

But it's become much more than that. Art has become industrialized in the last century. So what we used to call the impact of art is now called entertainment, and that's an industry. And if it is an industry, it should be studied and understood. And the point is, then, that industry becomes democratized, because right now there is almost like central planning. You have these moguls who are making the decisions on what should and should not be produced, and where it could or could not be shown for all of the world. I mean, they really have a huge concentration of power right now. It's power that we gave to the industry, because of the technology that was needed to get the product consumed. And if that technology changes the concentration of power will shift. This is one of the things that you have to almost have faith in, but I think there is a huge amount of evidence building up that we will see a democratization of content creation and distribution. Therefore, if that's the case, everybody needs to learn how to decide what to do. You know, what to make, what to design, what to build, in order to meet the needs of an audience.

And understanding the needs of that audience is what jobs-to-be-done theory is all about. So the whole point of studying jobs theory for the purpose of an arts or craftsman is so that you can yourself make your destiny and not have to rely upon others to do this for you. And it's not a huge leap of faith to assume that this skill is something that can be obtained. With the right technology, by the way, with computers now we can manage a lot of things that used to require an organization. We used to have to have assistants. We had to have people who were trained in payroll to manage payroll. Now we have software to do that. You used to have to have people to help you write letters, called secretaries. Now you don't need them anymore.

As we are doing right now. We're actually creating content. And it's technology that makes it possible, tools that we have available, and suddenly we are broadcasters. And, yet again, there are millions of people who have very valuable talents that are unable to commercialize these talents, and are stuck in jobs that they don't enjoy, and they aren't being productive in. And if we give them the tools, and then the skills necessary, you learn a little bit of how to be an accountant if you have your own small business. You learn a little bit about how to sell, a little bit of this and a little bit of that. Just enough so you can stay alive doing the thing you love to do. And that skill, how does it get taught? How do you transfer that knowledge? That's what I'm trying to say.

Dan: Hmm.

Horace: I think it needs to be done. Basically, what I'm saying is that we need to teach. We need a new level of business training. Not book-keeping, but what is strategy to an individual? What is marketing for an individual? The things that we used to teach an MBA program in two years, we can probably package that and hand it off to someone who actually has something really useful to do, like creating beautiful things, like inventing new things. And they're busy doing those things and yet unrewarded because they're part of a huge machine today. We can try to make them independent creators and give them the skills to be able to analyze markets and analyze everything.

So all I'm saying is that this is my motivation. This is my motivation also for running shows and doing talks and things like that. To motivate people, other people, to do the same, but also to give them the tools and say, "If he can do it, I can do it." So there is this possibility to train people in all of this supposedly magical, analytical stuff. It's not that hard. And that's really probably one of the fundamental reasons why I'm doing a show at all, is to say, "Look, it's possible."

Dan: Right.

Horace: And so, we got off on that tangent because I was talking about entertainment as an industry that's going to get—if not disrupted, at least democratized to a certain degree that we'll probably be able to take away some of these middlemen who today add value because they know how to allocate resources in a way like a VC does or a banker does, that they take money from people who don't have any idea of how to use it, and give it to people who have an idea of how to use it. And they make that bet. And get paid for that bet.

But, increasingly, the bet should be made by the very person who actually is creating, and they need to apply that decision-making process to their own assets, their immediate circle of acquaintances so that they can say, "Okay, I can actually raise money from people. Like in Kickstarter or something like that. But how do I market myself? How do I define what my product is? How do I define my audience? How do I put my finger on this thing so that I can sell it to people who can give me resources?"

That's really what that this is about.

So just to finish up some of these consequences of disruption, when you step back enough and you look at the patterns—I have also hinted at this before—it affects industries. Obviously, it affects companies, but if you step back far enough you realize that companies tend to work—or get disrupted, or become powerful—in groups. They're all working almost in collusion. So the phenomenon is applied across an industry. It happens simultaneously. However, again, if you step back far enough, you realize that it actually probably affects economies. It affects the wealth of nations, if you will. And countries and nations and societies which allow disruption to happen tend to prosper more rapidly, at least. And societies which manage disruption, often inefficiently, tend to be themselves disrupted.

And what this gets a little bit into... A little bit stepping out on a branch here, but if you study economies—and we can look at, for example, Japan, China, the Soviet Union, United States, Great Britain (especially before and after the Industrial Revolution), and see what happens, what caused these changes—most historians look at these questions of the wealth of nations and the wealth of society through a set of causes which, in my opinion, they look at it as certain people did the right things or certain people did the wrong things. If you're lucky enough to have a good leader, then the country prospers. And if you're unlucky to have a bad leader, then the country may fail.

And sometimes it gets so bad that you lose freedoms. And sometimes it gets really good, and you have enlightenment. So, historically, I think a lot of the causality coming around this question of what is good governance and what is good government in general is really coming down to having enlightenment happen at the individual level, as a leader. And this is again very similar to what we observed in the leadership of companies, that we have enlightened management and stupid management, or the good management/bad management theory. And if only we had better managers, everybody would be happy and prosperous. And companies would succeed.

Again, I sense that this is not correct, that what actually is happening is forces acting upon nations which allow them to be prosperous and if you are putting the right perspective on the policy that it's independent of the people who are actually doing the leading and the managing of a nation.

It's an interesting idea, and I'd like to explore it. I don't have a lot of evidence for this. It's all anecdotal at this point, and you know I don't really like to make these proclamations without evidence. But there is interesting historical data—a little bit, I should say. I'll introduce some, hopefully, at the show. But I'd like to point out that you can apply this theory at a more macroeconomic level rather than microeconomic level, which is what we typically do.

At a macro level, it does look like you need an innovation policy, and that innovation management needs to happen at a national level, without necessarily being even guiding the principles—almost like sometimes the policy really would be more about taking a hands-off approach, although not entirely. There is always going to be a debate on how much government has a role to play or how much it doesn't. But I should say that the decision isn't simply yes or no, or you have it or don't have it. The decision ought to be, "What do we need to do to enable growth to happen through innovation?" Which, by the way, has some unfortunate consequences. How do we understand what those consequences are? And how do we manage so that we get an optimal solution for society in general?

So it's more about thinking about not just regulating on and off, but thinking about the whole picture as a disruption, as a positive thing, and as a growth enabler. Again, this is something that is just being nibbled around the corners right now when we discuss policy and when we discuss every aspect of government. And you know, certainly, there are deliberate attempts to enable innovation. But I think they often fail. And in fact it's something we should think about: What is the failure rate of deliberate innovation processes that governments enable? And do they really turn out to be something more like welfare for scientists?

Anyway, that's one more aspect, I think, that comes, or falls, out of this work.

Finally, the last thing is that if it is true that this theory has applications at a macroeconomic level, can we step back and ask: "Has our history actually been determined by this?" So if you step back even further and say, "That means that it may have affected who we are today because it may have affected what went on in history." What was going on with empires? What was going on with phases, and eras, in our history? Was disruption actually playing a role there?

Certainly, technology had a role. But was it just a random walk? Did the rise and fall of empires, was it all affected only because of complete randomness? There are plenty of examples. There are many explanations, but they seem to be very narrow. That this happened to this country, or this society, and that explains it. But it doesn't explain why, in another society, in very similar circumstances, it didn't happen that way.

So there is an interesting potential here to do a really deep review of history and what are the effects of what we call disruption today, and innovation. What did that actually... How did that actually cause civilization to change?

So it really gets quite deep, I think, if you get far back enough to applying this stuff.

Jet Lag
Posted March 21st, 2012 as The Critical Path Episode #30

We span a broad sweep of topics: The new iPad and the value of filling the gaps, trip report on the Apple Investor Summit, conversations with a TV show writer, Tim Cook's attack on the cash mountain, and an update on Asymconf. Horace also talks about his cure for jet lag.

Horace: We had breakfast with a wonderful lady who is a writer for the show *Nurse Jackie*. It's on Showtime. I don't know if I want to mention her name, I should have asked permission, but basically she gave me an interesting, fascinating I should say, overview of the writing process for TV shows. I had an idea already from Dan Abrams, of how that works, especially in comedy. But hers is a drama, although it's not her invention, the show is not her creation, she's a writer for someone who has designed the voices or the characters. But she is a creative individual on her own having been a play writer prior to getting into television. And she taught me not just her part of the contribution to a show, but how shows in general come together, how are they designed. Because in my contrast it is always, "What is that industry like vis-à-vis, let's say, software writing."

And I put it to her, as I do to my guests as well who are coming from professions—creative professions—that I ask, "What would this path be for you if you were in software," and "What would the path be of a software person in your world. Try to compare and contrast."

And it's interesting to see the level… One thing I learned, I think, and it's a pattern I'm observing, is that so much of the TV and show business in general is a collaborative process, meaning that's it art, but it is collaborative art. It's art where many people are involved, and there is no single author. And I talked about this before. There is the French theory called Auteur theory that implies that it isn't art unless there is a single mind [creating it]. But it is clear and obvious that this is art and that there are many people involved. And her point is that you cannot really make a show unless you have writers, producers, actors, and directors as creative talent. So in a sense there is many more, but this is at least a minimum needed to make a show happen. And one wonders if it is possible for one person to have all of that. Maybe you can have at least someone directing and producing or directing and acting, but to imagine one person doing all of those jobs and on the larger scale that is needed, it's quite a hard thing to imagine.

There is very much a division of labor and so we can imagine a division of creativity happening that makes it possible. So in that sense it's a challenge to be democratized in a way because you have to somehow

357

imagine it being reduced to the simplest and least-costly approach in order for the individual to take a role in this.

But, anyway, we will still try to think it through and imagine how this will evolve.

Many things were said about software, that also it required a division of labor. The devil's advocate view is that many years ago it was necessary to have a large team to create software. It was necessary during the mainframe era to have specialists, even to the point of optimizing certain parts of a program. And there would have to be a system administrator to manage the computer itself. There had to be a project manager. There had to be a systems analyst—which is, I think, a great job description. I think systems analysis is a wonderful idea in general, not just in computing— But all these jobs are required in order to "write software." And now the power of the software has increased tremendously and its complexity, in terms of interdependencies, has increased exponentially, and yet we have it at the fingertips of one individual to create.

So the productivity in that sense has exploded for software, and yet that did not happen in many of these arts-based industries or creative industries.

Again, there are some, like writing. Writing is an individual effort. Certainly visual arts are individual and some performing arts, but this ideas of cinema and TV are still collaborative and one wonders where that can go. I'd love to see a change there, but right now, I think the inside people don't see that as possible. So we have to take their opinion into account.

Dan: It's fascinating, though, that the technology is certainly there today for those thing to change. Maybe not as much TV, but certainly filmmaking. That whole process, what used to take dozens of people, might take a few people and maybe eventually one person.

Horace: That might be the case, and that's the thing, but technically you can see it happen, because the tools get easier and better. So mixing, editing, cinematography—even the process of directing—is becoming essentially easier due to technology. But the creative aspects, can you think through all of these angles on your own? Can you think through the story yourself? Can you then create characters, act those characters, direct those characters? Because the director has a completely different skill than a writer, and they are both trying to realize the concept of yet another person who may have thought of the voice of the show and had developed the essence of it.

For example, the people who are in charge of a show, they are called show runners, and they would hover in the background while actors did their work, and the director [did his work]. And sometimes these people come late in the process and are given the script that had been thought through by someone else. And they come and execute that. So I am not sure.

I mean theoretically, perhaps, it's possible for one person to go through all of that in their mind but, obviously, if you have any piece of work that requires more than one individual on stage, or performing, then it automatically requires collaboration, and that means coordination. And that type of storytelling requires, typically, more than one character.

So there is that question, what is the minimum input or minimum number of people because that is a proxy for the minimum cost of a production in order for you to imagine it being "democratized." So, again, I'm going back and forth. We are having conversations, we are thinking through the theory. Then we are thinking through the case studies, the examples. Then we are thinking through this idea of where are the limiting factors, what are the trend lines for technology, because we know technology is moving in exponential rates, whereas humans don't move in those rates. People don't change.

And I would, for example, propose, "What if you saw yourself doing this?" And many people have spent a lifetime getting to where they got, and now to suggest to them that it's all going to go upside down is not only uncomfortable but it's something they will resist. And the thing is, again, in contrast to our industries, we presume or assume that we are not going to see a lot of the stuff we are using now in a couple of years. We really adjust, and are so accustomed to turnover in not just the devices that we use, but the user experiences in terms of apps we use, in terms of everything. So everything is constantly changing.

You look at something from three years ago and it feels like it is from another universe. We couldn't imagine using a computer from four years ago, right?

Dan: Right. Unthinkable.

Horace: It's unthinkable. I mean, if the software hadn't changed, it would be. Many people do so in corporate environments, because they are still using software from the 1980s. But as far as personal computing, we've seen such rapid change that people say things are dated one year on.

But, anyway, that's the pace we are living through, and many industries are on different clock cycles, and if that's the case, what happens when these two worlds collide? That's what I'm saying. And the theory would say you can't fight exponential growth. And it's become so big and so rapidly overwhelms everything else that it is just an unstoppable force. And that's what you lean on sometimes, in terms of having faith that the future will change the world. But we will see.

And I'm constantly going back and forth on my thinking on this and getting great input from people.

Maybe we should touch a little bit on the iPad, too. I ended up getting one and we talked about it last time. I haven't used it.

Also the fact that we got this nice surprise from Mr. Cook on Monday, the cash deal.

Dan: Yeah, I really want to get your take on that, but I, as well as the audience, would probably love to hear about your experience with the new iPad.

Horace: Yes. I shy away from being a product reviewer. I feel that the average layman is far better than I am qualified to speak about this, and I think that anyone who is an expert is far worse qualified than any layman that I know. So my problem is I feel like I am somewhere in the middle between those two, so that disqualifies me.

But what I sensed was that it was definitely the same feeling and leap of experience that we had from 3GS to 4, and that you get used to it very quickly and it almost becomes, "Meh, not a bit deal." But then you go back, you're shaken because you are realizing how much it improved. And you go back one step and realize that can't use the old one anymore.

It is a screen that seems to, at first sight—again it's something you get used to—but at first sight it seems almost to be three-dimensional. I don't want to say that, it's a cliché. It just sucks you in visually and provides a depth that you don't think is possible, but you get used to it.

A lot of people will probably try to analyze the reason for that. Our minds are amazing. We adapt it, right? So we use all kinds of ways of interpolating things and massaging the data that our brains receive. But in this case it maybe frees up some of that processing, if you will. Then you can enjoy it differently.

You know, it's amazing. My son loves playing with Lego bricks. And if you think about it, that's a very pixelated experience. But our minds can create patterns so easily that you look at a very pixelated version of an object that he has built, and you very much believe that's exactly what it is. Even to the point of saying which airplane that is. And you know, it doesn't measure in any way proportionately or scale-wise or anything. It doesn't match what it should be, but our minds fill in the gaps. So in that sense our minds fill in a lot of gaps when we use certain tools. But when you take the gaps away and you fill them in correctly, then the mind is doing other things instead of filling gaps. So that's where I am wondering if there is this subconscious effect that it might have on people.

We filled gaps when we had gray scale and we moved to color. And we were comfortable. I was able to use computers like the original Macintosh, for example, that was black and white. Yet we could think in that world and express ourselves and do all kinds of things before we got color. But once we had color, we were suddenly expressing new things and going forward and forward. So it's the same progress.

I think, though, if it's reaching retina levels, resolution can't get any higher. What could get higher is maybe somewhere in the color perception, somewhere in terms of speed. And by the way, the other thing the UI of iOS did for us is, when it added a physics engine behind the movement of pages, you saw another lubrication, if you will, of our cognitive skills or our cognitive processes. The user experience that an iPhone or an iOS device first pioneered, in the sense that you used your finger to scroll and the faster you move your finger, the faster it scrolls. We have a direct connection with the information we are scanning that, again, it probably leads to a different sensation or a different mental process. I'm not an expert, but I have to assume this, and this is part of the addictive nature of these things, and why we also sense immediately when something doesn't have that nature. So if you go between an iOS device and an Android device that is jittery or scrolling is rough, you sense that right away, and the person who uses an iOS device says this is unacceptable, but the person who doesn't, who is accustomed to the Android scroll, they will say this is just fine without knowing that perhaps their brains are filling in the gaps that they shouldn't be.

But this is all part of the whole experience analysis, and I'm not an expert by any means, but I sort of try to think through these details. How much do we benefit from not having to fill in these gaps? I don't know. And maybe in some ways we lose some imagination because working with crude abstractions may force us to think differently in good ways. But who knows? Depends on what you are trying to do. If you are trying to be creative, sometimes abstractions are better. If you are trying to read the news, abstractions are not better.

So this is an interesting commentary. I would say if someone could write up something like this, [someone] who knows what they are talking about, that would be great. What is the benefit of more resolution? It can't be just, "It looks good." It has to be more than that. It has to give us more freedom in some way. Otherwise, why would we care, right? And so that's my thought on that.

And the other part of it, as far as the experience, I don't notice any difference: You get used to the weight and the thickness. In fact, I had a case for it that was sort of a snap case that allowed you to rotate the device.

Dan: It should still fit, right?

Horace: And it fit fine, yeah. Both the cover I was using—which was the standard one from Apple—works, and the back cover that I was testing for it, it was a desktop stand, that worked. And so I'm not yet finding any regression in any way of the experience. It's all been positive. The battery life is astonishing given what they've done. So I haven't tested it as thoroughly as I could have given the fact that I am writing stuff.

But anyway, yeah, great product, great price. I can't complain. I give it a thumbs up.

Dan: So one quick question that came up on a couple of my other shows earlier this week—maybe you have enough information to answer this now—do we know what percentage of iPads, especially this new iPad, what percentage is not necessarily activated on a wireless network but have the wireless potential in them? And the subset of that, which ones are actually...

Horace: You mean, cellular?

Dan: Cellular, I'm sorry, yes.

Horace: Generally, I don't have the data and I'm trying to recall if there was anything published to indicate it. I do remember some anecdote about it, but it's a minority, I think. There are less than 20 percent, I would guess, are activated, but more than that, much more than that, maybe more than half are actually purchased with that option. So in that sense I think this is like an option value in having the cellular capability.

And I remember myself—and maybe I told this story already—but I bought the first generation product as WiFi only, but I found that there were one or two occasions when I could have used it, so essentially I traded it in and got another one that had 3G on it just for those occasions. And, again, your mileage may vary, you may not ever take it out of your house or your office—wherever you are using it—but it in my particular circumstances, I do enjoy the flexibility and the options. We are so spoiled, we have the options of having desktops, laptops, even more than one of each. We're spoiled by choice, and I like being spoiled that way.

And to me, it's cheap insurance. It's $130 more. Again, I see it as: Use it once and it pays for itself. Like any tool.

I don't know if you know this story. I heard this many years ago. If you have to do work around the house and you need a tool, just go down to your local hardware store, buy it, use it and even if you'll never have to use it again it's paid for itself, because consumer products, tools especially in the consumer category, have become so cheap that they are way, way cheaper than the labor involved in bringing someone over and doing the job for you. So in almost all countries this is true now. That used to not be the case. You needed a repairman to come and fix just about anything in the house.

But I think of these things as tools. You have these computers and you put extra money in them, you put an extra hard drive in them, because on that occasion when you need it and you use it, it may save you that crucial moment in time.

Let me give you this example. When I was in London—and this will be a nice way to tie into the next topic—the news broke of the event with Tim Cook. It actually happened after I landed. And what I did was, since

I had many hours in London, I went and got myself one of these tiny hotel rooms. They are like little cubes, pods. It's a pod hotel they have in London. It's called YOTEL, and you could almost stretch your arms out and touch both sides. It's a little bit bigger than that, but it's nearly that much.

And this is such a cute little place, but the point being that I was able to plug in, take a nap, shower and do all those things, but I was able to be productive and write a post about what happened with the cash. And it was possible because I had the tools with me, because I had the computer that had all my data with me. It was possible because I had a large screen on the 17-inch laptop that I use that could bring in all the spreadsheet data I needed quickly. You have to understand that this could have been written on any computer, but in my setup, I was able to write it in half an hour. I may only have had half an hour at that particular moment in time and, to me, getting that article out in that time meant that I was able to get people to comment on it and read it while I was back in the air and wouldn't be back online again for probably 12 hours. And 12 hours later, the moment may have passed. There was that interesting opportunity I had.

I saw having the right tool at that moment pays for itself. Was that post worth it? Who knows. Businesses deal with this question all the time, and if they saddle their employees with shoddy equipment, they are robbing themselves more than anyone, because that employee, if it takes ten minutes to boot up a computer… You have all these software firewalls, restrictions and all of these issues that they have to deal with to get going.

I remember these because back in the day it took me almost twenty minutes… Actually I witnessed this. I was going through passport control, I forget which country, and a new line opened, a new officer sat down to open a new line, and I thought, "Yay, I get put into the new line and thus jump ahead." Instead of being fifth, I was second. A big win, right?

Well, the trouble is that that officer had to turn on his computer, and we just waited and waited and in every line around us everybody was flying through and I ended up getting penalized fifteen minutes while that computer booted.

That post was about the cash, so that we can talk about that now. If that's okay.

Dan: Yes.

Horace: Okay.

Dan: You've been building up to it for almost an hour.

Horace: Yes. Okay, we talked about this way back. I think it was a show called Cash is King or something to that effect.

Dan: Yes.

Horace: And back then the question was: What could [Apple] possibly do? And my answer was [that] the best thing they could do is use it for production. And since then we went through this analysis and we discovered the CapEx story. We discovered that they were spending on production equipment, and then I talked to that. That was my talk in L.A. Again a nice loop back into that. The idea was that they spend billions and billions of dollars already, not just financing the value chain or their supplier chain, but they are actually owning the equipment that goes into the production of their systems. And Tim Cook actually acknowledged that that's one of the large uses of cash. But it is still not large enough. It's still not possible to absorb the extra cash.

So two things, and each one must be analyzed separately. They did, first of all, a dividend. Now this is a fairly modest one as a percentage of the total amount of cash that's generated. Dividends, as I argued last time, are not efficient use because they are essentially subjecting profits—which is the value added of the whole enterprise—to double taxation, meaning that first they're taxed as a corporate tax which may vary, but I think Apple pays around 20 to 24 percent. If you get what's after the tax in your pocket, as a shareholder you will have to pay whatever the tax on dividends might be. Now this year I'm told it's a bit lower than—there's a dividend tax rate, but next year it will be taxed at your marginal income tax rate [in the U.S.].

So the thing is that at the end of the day, a hundred dollars in profit from Apple right before tax may end up really only being 55 in your pocket. So that's an effective tax rate of 40-some percent, and that's extraordinarily high given that it is value adding. [Meaning], it is not a tax on wealth, it's not a tax on consumption, it is a tax on productive work. You don't want to tax productive work highly because people will be deincentivized.

In fact, I think governments impose dividend taxes to discourage them because they'd rather have that money be reinvested by the company to create new things and be more productive, and that's as it should be. But, again, Apple's hand is a little bit forced here and they are distributing money in this way.

It isn't a large amount yet as a percent of total, and the yield—which is essentially the effective interest you are getting if you buy the shares at the current price—is less than 2 percent. If you bought the shares at $5 or $13 or whatever it was in 2003, you are going to get more than 100 percent on that money at this time per year.

So that's the dividend discussion. Not great news in my opinion, but it's a token.

By the way, one positive aspect of that will be that maybe institutions that may not want to own Apple because it doesn't pay a dividend, they may now get in, and as a result the share price will rise—and the share price has [already] been rising. Maybe that's one of the reasons. We don't know. But that also may benefit the current shareholders because they see an appreciation in the stock, not so much that the dividend is destroying value, but rather that the whole enterprise value goes up.

So that's the dividend issue. A lot of discussion you can have around it is a lot of theory, but it did happen.

The other thing though that is interesting is that they are also doing a share buyback which is the second method. So we've either talked about one or the other, but now we actually have both, which is a good idea, I guess. But the way they spun that is not like taking the shares out of use because we want to have somehow shareholder's value or share price go up. They did it specifically to address dilution that happens when they issue shares to employees as compensation, as non-wage compensation.

And so I did a short analysis just to see what that means. The amount that they pledged to that effort, to the share buyback, is $10 billion over three years, and that amount, if we assume that that money goes really towards paying for these employees' shares, then it amounts... I did an analysis of how much do they actually spend on employee wages, and I said this would imply about 25 percent of the wages, so there would be a 25 percent bonus. So let me walk you through that.

So back to this question of why would you do a share buyback in order to pay employees. The idea is that when you do give employees equity, usually that compensation is an incentive. It's not meant to be a wage, it's meant to be a bonus or a way to give extra motivation to the employee to get a performance. Of course, retention is another aspect, and of course it has become normative because everyone else is doing it. But theoretically, that's meant to be an incentive.

Now when you do that, what happens is that the number of shares outstanding increases by that amount. So Apple actually issues this number every quarter and it says the number of shares outstanding has gone up, and it was 920 million, let's say, and now it is 922 million. That means they issued 2 million shares, probably again offering them to employees. And in so doing, the existing shareholders are diluted because the earnings that are being earned are going to be spread over all those shares now. So you are getting this tiny little dilution every single quarter. And I showed how, in fact, from 2005 till present, the number of outstanding shares grew from like 860 million to 960, let's say. I don't recall exactly. But a hundred million shares, that's a lot...

Dan: Yeah.

Horace: ...considering you had only 800 to begin with. So one in eight shares essentially has just been created and diluted and anybody who owned shares in 2005 would have one-eighth less of the company than they had before. So that's bad. That's actually saying, "We're going to take equity from the existing shareholders and we are going to give it to new shareholders that happen to be employed by us." So that's not a good, equitable thing to do. And so what Apple did was to address this and they said ten billion dollars worth of shares, they are going to buy them back and thus retire them and essentially keep that number of outstanding shares more or less flat.

Of course, they could go beyond the 10 billion. They only said that they will reduce dilution. They didn't say they will eliminate it. So by doing this program, we will hopefully see that number of outstanding shares be more flat. Again, that's one of the issues with my analysis is that it doesn't mean that they've committed to ten billion dollars.

By the way, keep in mind, that really means it is ten billion dollars that they are going to also pay to employees as this bonus, right? A minimum of that. Because then those people might hold onto shares and they will go up in value. But still, that's a nice signal to give. They're signaling to their shareholders saying, "You are going to be compensated. We are not going to dilute you anymore." And to employees it is saying, "You are actually going to be getting at least this much." Of course, it's not so equitable either because it's skewed. There is a certain average, but the median is different. The median is going to be skewed because so many of the executive... There's always a non-linearity about the compensation, so you have many people who will be getting a lot of shares and that's not necessarily a good distribution. But that's how it is and that's the corporate structure.

Anyway, the point being that those employees therefore will be paid out of ongoing cash flow. They will not be paid out of what the shareholders already thought they had. That's interesting and that's good. And I think that's a good use of the cash.

Dan: You approve of this.

Horace: I think it's a good use. I mean, share buybacks have their problems. Dividends have their problems. Share buybacks typically don't create value and dividends destroy value. And so we've had both, but in this case I think the share buyback is actually a positive, at least psychologically, for multiple players, and a dividend might also be positive psychologically because you are going to get more buyers of the equity and therefore you are going to broaden the ownership pool, if you will. You are going to attract more owners and that may actually help existing owners. That is the theory at least.

A lot of these things we can't really put our finger on and that's why stock markets are unpredictable, because it's based on psychological factors, and here we see an example of that.

And again, if I may speculate, this might be a subtle shift in management theory that the company—that maybe a purist, like Jobs would not have agreed with. So in a way I'm channeling Steve Jobs and he'd say, "Why do this? This makes no sense. This doesn't create value, and to heck with it." But I think the pragmatist will say, "There are non-tangible benefits. Let's put theory aside, let's work out some of these issues." And maybe that's what Tim Cook brought to the table.

So one can be dogmatic or one can be pragmatic, and there we have it. But at the end of the day though, after all is said and done, what we are seeing here is not any way that Apple's cash mountain is going to decrease. If anything, the analysis I have also published is that the cash mountain will keep growing. Not as fast, however.

So the trajectory of the cash was actually parabolic. It was indeed growing in increasingly faster rates. Now we are going to see, perhaps, the trajectory go linear. So it is going to increase at a constant rate. And so we will still see a hundred and fifty [billion] dollars, perhaps, by the end of 12 months from now, and that would be an increase of $50 [billion]. It's amazing. Apple is generating a billion dollars in cash every week.

So that is the scale of the issue, and still we'll see probably a lot of agitation next year when we will see $150 [billion] on the balance sheet and all kinds of people will be saying, "This is too high," and "Let's do something about it. Let's put the brakes on that growth a little bit." But in many ways I see it also as, if I may use the expression, throwing us a bone, because Tim Cook here has essentially said, "Let's put this issue aside at least for the next year or two," and it is very much not solving the problem of cash use. Not that it's a big problem, but a lot of people would worry that this means they are stockpiled, they are cushioned, they are buffered—their ability, their flexibility, their leverage is decreasing. Not at all. It's still increasing but not as fast.

So there are positives and negatives to all these. You still shouldn't have too much, but then again, it's nice to have some. Much of capitalism, much of the business management, is filled with contradictions. There is not anything we can do about that. This is not a field that is axiomatic. I am always amused when I think about this fact that contradiction abounds.

I'd say it's not necessarily creative. It is a nice pragmatic approach. It is slightly, perhaps, value-negative, but on the other hand, we don't know the psychological factors that make it slightly positive. So on balance, I think it's probably a good decision, and longer term, we'll see. We will have to come back to it. It's only been deferred. What to do with the $150 billion that will be in the bank in the future?

Dan: So is this setting a precedent? Will we see this again in a number of years? Is this something that will continue.

Horace: If the growth continues, and I think the earnings and the sales have been something of a phenomenon lately, I think they are likely to continue. The other data point we have received, for example, is the iPad sold 3 million units in its launch weekend, and that number indicates that the iPad is on the trajectory of 150 percent growth. Now, that is my estimate because that's actually what it has been doing on the average for the last three quarters that we've had data, and I just wrote up a post today giving my forecast for this current quarter, what we will see for earnings and so on. And the assumption I am building into that is that it is 150 percent growth on the iPad.

And so the big question is, I think last year or the year before even, the big question was, "Is iPhone's growth sustainable?" The iPhone had grown at 100 percent in its first year. It had grown 100 percent in its second year. It had grown 100 percent in its third year. On average—there's been a lot of volatility due to the product launches and seasonality and all that. But if you smooth it out on a four-period average, you would get about 100 percent. And sure enough, last four quarters, if you look at 2011, you take the sum and divide by four, of the growth rates, you'd get 100 percent.

And so my assumption was, back in 2007, I predicted that the iPhone could sustain 100 percent at least for three years. Now we are into the fifth year of that.

The question that should be on everyone's lips now is: What growth rate is the iPad and can it be sustained?

And my initial assumption, it was 100 percent, because the iPhone could do it, I thought the iPad could do it. Well, the iPad is doing it at 150 percent. Will that be sustained? Again, we have to watch and see.

Now, the reason I was confident in 100 percent on the iPhone was because I knew the phone business. The phone business I knew as [having] limitless potential because it was a huge industry. It had billions of consumers. We knew a lot about smartphones at the time. Even though it was the first touch screen, there were all kinds of smartphones in the market place, and I knew something about that demand, and I was comfortable saying that if they double production, which I thought was scalable, they would get that 100 percent.

And I guess nobody else believed this because all the analysts were putting in numbers that would suggest 20 percent, which would actually be lower than the whole industry's growth rate. But somehow they thought that Apple would somehow underperform with this magical product. It would underperform even RIM, which had a track record of growing far faster than that.

But anyway, let's put aside this. The point is that 100 percent was reasonable. It seemed reasonable to me, and now the question is 150 percent. Now, again, like I said, the smartphone industry had a track record. What we don't have a track record for is the tablet industry. It was created out of thin air. There was no such thing before. So this is why it was very nerve-wracking to try to predict the business over the last year or two that the iPad has been in the market.

How do you tell? How do you know what they are going to ship in any one quarter? You have nothing to go on.

So that's why I was stating it clearly in every one of my posts about my forecasts: We don't know what the iPad is going to do. Nobody does. If anybody suggests they do, they don't.

So that's what I did for two years now, and now we've had three quarters of year-on-year growth. It has to be year-on-year because you are watching seasonality. And I said, it seems like 150 is the new benchmark, it is the new 100 percent. One hundred fifty is the new black. So if that's the case, can we dial that in and see what happens? And what data points can we get? What little crumbs can we see falling off the table of data here? And one of those crumbs that just fell was the 3 million on the launch weekend. Again, let's compare that, let's compare that to everything we can compare it to.

So what I did is pulled the data that showed what launch weekends were for all of the major products. Sometimes you don't get weekends, sometimes you get launch months. Sometimes you get days. But you put it altogether and you divide by the time duration involved. And I even took it a step further. I didn't publish this except on Twitter: I loaded up this graph where it shows the total divided by the number of countries because each product launched into different-sized markets. So what I did is, if you divide by time and markets, you get a very interesting pattern where essentially the current iPad looks to be on the par with the launch performance of the iPhone 4. Not iPhone 4S. 4S is way above. But that's because it is launching at a lower price point to the end user. It had a huge build-up in terms of demand and so there was a lot of anticipation. And they had a huge customer base. That counts for a lot, being able to upgrade.

A lot of the iPads that are going to be bought today are not going to be upgrades because the old ones are still perfectly good and they are not on contract in any way. So we don't have that dynamic. But we have new consumption. We have tremendous consumption. All of that said, the iPad 3 has reached 3 million, and so I put this chart together and the speed at which it is growing—again, it's a two-year-old product—and it is behaving as did the iPhone 4 which was, I think, a fourth-year product when it launched.

So, yes, I'm starting to believe now that maybe 150 is sustainable. We've got to get more data, obviously, but if you dial that in, you get 12 million units this quarter. The previous year-ago quarter was quite low because that was the launch quarter of the iPad 2, which was very weak because they had a terrible problem with the number of units they could deliver. That new form factor seems to have been difficult. In fact, for the iPad 2 they didn't even announce first weekend sales. It's the only data point that's missing right now.

So I only have [that data] to compare it to the original iPad, which was much much lower. In fact, the current iPad sales performance, or launch performance in terms of units per day, is 28 times higher.

Dan: Wow.

Horace: Again, if you divide it by country, the number of countries it launched to, the ratio becomes closer to three times higher.

So things are enormous here. The numbers are enormous, and yet you ask yourself, "Can they sustain that?" And you are looking at one after another, after another data point that confirmed that. And at some point you have to say, "Yeah, I think they can do this."

And, again, you've got to ask why. You have to become comfortable with the logic, why it is possible and the answer is always in production. We had the data coming in from China with the report from Foxconn that showed roughly how fast they were producing iPads. Just a glimpse. Again, another crumb fell off the table there. So we got that glimpse and we crunched the numbers and what did we get? We get, yes, they can sustain 12 million units a quarter. So they can sustain the production, it seems the demand is tripling, it seems that people are buying it, it seems the lines are there. All these indicators.

Lot's of people go and count people, how many people are in line. There's analysts who do this, and that's great, I think they should be doing it. But they get very limited samples. They get only, for example, a couple of stores in New York City because it happens to be where the analyst is working, so they send out an intern to go count people in line. Fine, it's not a great data set. I wouldn't count on it, but it does seem to add to the overall samples we have. And we have this nice number of 150 percent to put in there.

And I'm not alone. A lot of other analysts have been putting out 12 million unit figures, and they get it different ways. They'll get it through supply-chain samples, they'll get it through retail samples, they'll get it through intuition, what have you. But I'm comfortable with that number.

And now you put in all the other numbers that are also very much in line with what we've seen in the past, and you come out with this figure of earnings that I just published again today. I said, "I think $12 a share." Then the next step would be you add the 12 to the previous three quarters that we've already seen the data for. So we add that together, we get a whole year's worth, the trailing 12 months, and then you get $40 for that. And then you divide that by the price per share which we see today in the market, around 600. Then you get your P/E ratio. And then you ask the final question: Now that we see a P/E of 14, is this nuts or what?

So is this crazy, is this lunacy? In other words, it's a sanity check. All of those numbers boil into the 1P ratio, and you say, "Okay, that seems pretty much historically consistent. That seems like something that shareholders or investors are willing to pay for this. And so fine, it looks like a good number and we'll go with that." That's the process I use.

And the shocking thing is that a lot of people will put out numbers far, far lower than mine, and that's where I just don't get it. That's where I raise my arms to the heavens and ask why. But that's a topic for another day.

Dan: Yes. I'm glad you weighed in on this.

Horace: My pleasure. That's what I do.

Dan: I definitely would like to see how this plays out. I think this will be a great topic. We should revisit this.

The Futility of Machinations

Posted April 11, 2012 as The Critical Path Episode #33

Dan and Horace are back to discuss the latest news from Nokia, RIM, HTC and Sony, and what they have to do with each other. We touch on the distinction between market- and product-orientation and meander into the question of what is the value of the enterprise vis-à-vis the product it sells, and what management has meant and what it should mean. We even tackle the history (and future) of history.

Horace: I wanted to make sure we covered today a bit of news that's happened in the last few weeks with respect to some of the players we've been talking about over the last few months. Just today, in fact, was the announcement that Nokia is going to miss on its numbers in the quarter. This just came out a couple of hours ago, and I was actually called already to make statements about it from several news organizations. Bloomberg is one, and so I already kind of warmed-up by speaking to them.

Dan: Get rid of the small-time stuff first. Then you can come on your show.

Horace: Yeah, we can get into the meat of it. So I wanted to regurgitate some of what I said already. There's something almost—what's the right word—it's when you have serendipity, when things are happening at the same time. Not very positive things, though. We had also yesterday, or the day before, announcements from Sony, Sharp, Panasonic, HTC, essentially giving bad news. And we had RIM before that, about a week or two ago. And these are brand names that everybody is familiar with, and they are basically giving us really bad news.

Sony had the worst loss recorded in its history. Sharp also the worst in its 50-year history or so. Nokia just basically said they would lose money this quarter, that that they will lose money next quarter. They had given guidance that was higher than that and they are not going to meet it. They also announced what the volumes of units that they shipped are, and those volumes are significantly lower than most people expected. They gave numbers on the Windows Phone which they've never done before, not at least on a quarterly basis. They mentioned 2 million, a bit over 2 million Lumias had been shipped, which isn't necessarily a bad number. It isn't on the caliber of a competitor like Apple, but if you look at individual product lines, let's say from Samsung, it may have shipped in that volume in the first quarter of launch.

Now the [Samsung] Galaxy brand is much bigger today, but thinking back to when it launched, or the HTC products, one or two million is not a bad launch quarter. Nevertheless, the problem has been that the price they got for the product is 220 Euros on average. Two-hundred twenty

Euros is about $260 and that's not a great number. It's less than half what Apple obtains. And based on some teardown data, it looks like the margin on the Lumia is also in the 20s—25 percent at best (for the gross margin.)

So that means that the total revenue for Windows Phone from Nokia this quarter would be around 440 million Euros, and the margin on that would be whatever 25 percent of that is. Basically, not a large number compared to what Apple is getting, compared to what Samsung is getting.

But that's not the point. I mean we can talk about the end game or we can talk about some of the worst-case scenarios that Nokia is facing. But I think the real story here is the fact that we have these giant companies, these established companies—like I said, with Sony and some of the other Japanese and the RIM case—all of them failing roughly at the same time. If you'll recall back, one of the first episodes we had was called Conspiring to Fail or something to that effect. In fact, the subject at the time was Nokia and RIM hitting the proverbial rocks.

Dan: Yes, I think you were talking about synchronized failure.

Horace: Yes, synchronized failure, exactly.

Dan: Our second episode.

Horace: It describes the theory that companies tend to fail at the same time, meaning that there's something beyond the management of one company that's causing it. It's easy to blame, in this case, that RIM management screwed up, or in this case we'd say Sony management screwed up or Nokia management screwed up. But how did they all happen to screw up at the same time? Did they all coordinate their efforts?

So it's improbable and unlikely that "conspiracy to fail" is valid as an explanation. So what we have to think about is what's going on at an industry level. And I think the story here is disruption. The story has always been disruption, that you have these giant companies that were in the position of incumbency, were in the position of strength, missing the signals of the shift that was happening.

So there's a couple of blog posts I wrote recently highlighting some of these facts. For example, one was showing that the market capitalization gain for Apple in the last four years is roughly equal to the market capitalization losses of a group of companies that it competes with, including Microsoft, Sony, Nokia, RIM and others I just mentioned. And it's very interesting how you can almost see that there's been a transfer of wealth happening from shareholders of the incumbents to shareholders of the entrant. And although disruption doesn't necessarily say that, that's the whole story: It says that there will be winners, there will be losers, but the winner will actually obtain even more value, and the customers of the winner will obtain even more value than was lost by those who were victims.

What this tells us is this story of industry shifting the strength and the value proposition from one set of companies to another set, which, as the story goes, the set that enters doesn't have the advantages of the set that loses, and that's one of those magical things about disruption, is that it seems improbable until after the fact. So that's one story.

And the other story that I mentioned was actually tangential to this, and it was a story about how Microsoft was paying developers to write for its Windows Phone platform, and I weaved into that the story of how Toshiba paid a huge amount of money, $150 million, to studios in order to get exclusive content on its HD-DVD format as a competitor to Blu-ray. And my point was that this was happening five years ago—about 2006 or '07—that Toshiba was in a desperate attempt to promote its format as a platform. And the story is how they failed. The studios ended up keeping the $150 million, and they shipped on Blu-ray a couple of months later. Nine months after they got the money they were actually already shipping in Blu-ray because the deal fell through, but they got to keep the money.

So the point of that article was to take the money and run. If you were a developer and you were offered this opportunity to port into a platform and you were paid for it, by all means do it, but don't expect that to be a success.

What this has to do with Sony is that, interestingly, even though Sony won that battle with Blu-ray, the amazing story is that Sony is now in trouble and Sony is in trouble in spite of Blu-ray winning and in spite of its machinations essentially being successful. And you can see how Microsoft is, at the same time, doing similar types of maneuvering in the marketplace, making deals with participants like AT&T, making deals with Nokia and other vendors, getting royalties from Android, and doing all these power moves to try to create a position in the marketplace. And yet, there's no guarantee that that will work, even though they may check off their targets. "We've accumulated developers, we've accumulated apps, we've accumulated partners, we've done all these things that we think are necessary." You still don't necessarily get a success.

This is a long story, but what's interesting here is the power of the markets and the power of disruption isn't rooted in market mechanisms. These are sometimes necessary but never sufficient. What you need to have is great products that solve the jobs that people have and do so in a way that doesn't exceed the willingness of people to absorb these changes. And that's really, at the end of the day, why product orientation, rather than market orientation seems to be a better bet.

Very few companies are really focussed on the product as much as Apple, and yet they have a lot more energy put into trying to make sure they have distribution, make sure that they have partnerships. And somehow, that never is enough.

So that's a long story.

Dan: Isn't that, Horace, the old school, the old way of thinking ten years ago, even five years ago perhaps, that they were doing everything right?

Horace: A few years ago it was indeed almost unanimously believed that the way to be successful in the market was to control it, not to create great products, and this is one of the things that I, who started out in life as an engineer, found very difficult to accept even though I was presented with the evidence. When I was learning about business, I was presented with all this evidence that product doesn't matter. What matters is creating all of the other things, doing all the other things right: Doing marketing right, doing financing right, even, somehow, that somebody won because of some obscure mechanism of saving money on taxes or saving money on the way they finance their company.

It all seemed so far removed from where the value was. The value had to be the product at the end of the day, or the service or the customer. And we are talking maybe the '90s that that was the pervasive dogma, that product doesn't matter. But if you go back to the '60s or '50s, you go back to an era when product was the only thing and there weren't, as we might call today, a class of MBAs that were taught these new mechanisms, these new tricks of optimization. And product development was an engineering function, not a management function. And what management did was generally take care of operations. They made sure that things worked and were done and administered properly.

And we developed a culture, I think in the '70s and '80s, where management itself was thought to be value-adding. Management itself was the key to value creation. And so you would take the product and with marketing and other things you would make it successful regardless of how good it was, because you had distribution, because you had pricing, because you had value chains, because you had all these other things.

So, indeed, I think we are going back to the roots. Some people have even expressed this sort of distain for Apple saying that they are so old school—and not "old school" like in '90s, but "old school" like in the '60s. Old school, like in thinking about product and workshops and designers slaving away over a workbench trying to shave things to the right dimensions and sweating all these details which sound like what a craftsman would do, not so much as a true global entity who would sweat other things, who would sweat distribution. And so in that sense Apple has gone back, almost regressing all the way back to the industrial era. And many times these things are pointed out, but not contrasted properly.

You point out secrecy, but secrecy should not be seen as an anomaly. Well, secrecy was always important, and there is no need to tell people what you are doing. What happened with Microsoft in the '90s is that they would tell people five years in advance what they would be doing because they had to prepare their value chain saying, "We are going to develop this. This is our roadmap and please make sure you are on the right page as we go forward."

There was this notion that because you work as part of a team, as you worked as part of a consortium or value network, you have to share information and you have to be open about things, and that got taken to an extreme of opening everything. But that's not how business runs, or used to run in the old days.

So there is an interesting contrast, as you point out, between the fundamental question of what is the value of management and what is the value of the enterprise beyond the product. The product is the core and the enterprise is designed to serve the product. Whereas in many other cases, it's the other way around. The product serves the enterprise, meaning that the enterprise is built around markets and the definition of markets and customers and segments and access to markets and pipelines and all these other things that you push product into. So you make sure that that product fits into that pipe. That's how those companies were really built. And I would actually argue that that's how Nokia was built. You worry about distribution first, make sure you have partners, you have carriers, you have points of sale. Then you stuff the product into this end and it goes out to all those other end points.

And I think Apple thinks about it in exactly the opposite way. They first think about the product and then they worry about how to sell it. If they only thought that way, actually, it wouldn't always work because you do need the muscle. You need the skill and the art, but you also need the muscle because this is what we are seeing in the Tim Cook era is that the muscle becomes extremely important at Apple.

But that is not to lose sight of the product, the product which is the initial vision of the world. And with Tim Cook aboard, they now take it all the way by ensuring they have capacity and ensuring they have points of sale, and ensuring they have distribution.

And the tension within Apple in the long term would be: Can these two be kept in balance, these forces of greatness of product balanced with the greatness of distribution, and not to let one or the other take precedence. I think the failure of Apple in the early years was that there wasn't enough of the balancing of distribution, and I have it from sources who worked there in the '90s that their operations were a mess. Their operations and their ability to produce product were nearly catastrophically bad, and that didn't change again until, I think, the 2000s, and that's, again, credit to Tim Cook.

Anyway, it's a nuanced argument. I don't want to become dogmatic about it, but I think there has been this redefinition of what the value of the enterprise is. And, again, if you study enough of these companies that are struggling today, you tend to observe and you hear it in their language, like the words spoken by management at RIM. You get a sense by reading enough of these corporate-speak statements of where things are going.

I'll give you an example, and this is something I posted in my own blog initially. The CEO of RIM made a statement saying that they are going to refocus on the corporate customer and they are going to be very careful about what resources they put into other segments. And people took that and said that implies that they are backing off the consumer. And I wrote a blog post called "RIM gives up." It was actually a truncated headline from the post I was linking to which said, "RIM gives up on consumers." I just cut "on consumers" and left it at "RIM gives up," because I said if you give up on the consumer, you give up on everything.

Of course, after I published that, RIM issued a clarification from one of their VPs of marketing saying, "No, we are not giving up on consumers." And then you could argue that I should retract my story. But if you read carefully the statement from this VP, it isn't that they are categorically going to focus on consumers, he made it seem as if they were going to segment the consumers and then they are going to focus only on the most interesting segments of that market. And it's very hard to put your finger on this as a denial. It's a non-denial denial. Because the subtlety, again it's in corporate speak, but it is saying that they are going to focus, but they are going to think about customers essentially as a grid, as a segmentation problem, and they are going to cherry-pick the best customers to go after.

But that's, to me, even worse than saying you are not going to target consumers. What it is saying is basically that they don't worry about the job to be done, they're not going to solve the consumer's problem, they are going to find a consumer that meets their criteria in a way. That's almost as bad—or worse, I would say—than giving up because they are going to essentially engineer their markets and not worry too much about the product.

The answer I gave in my post was I said what matters in the end is solving the problem for the customer in a way that your competitors find difficult to match, or in ways that your competitors will find uneconomical. And in that sense, you will be extremely successful because you will be a monopolist, you will be the only one who solves that problem. And that's what Apple does. But when you talk about going to cherry-pick, going to engineer a solution for this and that, it's almost like I just saw the value evaporating in front of my eyes. It was classic compensation for failure to meet the job to be done with machinations, with optimization of these numeric models of consumers. And I can say that that's not going to be a success story there.

Dan: So again, you've brought up something where one industry, perhaps inadvertently, completely changes the entire foundation of another industry. Or one company really. They come in and make this kind of change. But it doesn't seem intentional. It doesn't seem like this is where anybody expected things to be. Why aren't these companies that you are describing—and you describe the old-school mentality—why can't they adapt? That's the question that I think people who observe this, when you see this—and again we've talked about it with tablets, one after another to come out, it's not even a joke that the tablets aren't going to sell well and yet they continue to make them. And they are like, "We didn't sell the way we thought we would." Of course you didn't. Everybody else knew it except you, right?

Horace: This is the thing. Of course, in retrospect, when cases are going to be written about this time in our lives, when we'll study the era we are in, all this will seem obvious. That clearly, here you had a changing of the game, and that people were slow on the uptake. But when you are in these companies, you realize just how hard it is to perceive this happening, and you also realize how hard it is to shift, even if you have observed or perceived the change happening. And this is something to do with organizational behavior. This is something to do with inertia. Again, I always stay away from saying things like "stupidity" or "human failings." I think it is very human what people do. It's very natural what people are doing. It's just not in our nature to do things which seem extreme, which seem unconventional, which seem destructive or break consensus. We are not the crazy ones. Most people are not the crazy ones. And as we know, only the crazy ones may change the world.

So in a way, although I do have faith that hopefully someday we will all be able to do this, and we'll be able to, not evolve, but at least become more conscious of a new way of doing business. It isn't something that many people have spent twenty, thirty years of their lives learning how to do. It does take that long.

People talk about athleticism and how muscle memory works and how to be a good athlete you need to start at an early age. Whether you want to be a race car driver or skier or something which requires skill, not just strength. These skills are developed at an early age. And so it is with our ability to manage and our ability to get stuff done at work. And we treasure certain things like being a team player. We treasure certain things like making sure you have your information with you, making sure that you defend your point of view. We train people in business school and in other schools to stand behind their data and so on. We don't train people, however, to be crazy. We don't train people to say, "Maybe the future doesn't look anything like the past ,therefore all our data is useless." We don't train people to say, "Before we devote all of our energy to one big project, maybe we should have many small projects that compete with one another in an inefficient manner in order to solve a puzzle which we don't know the answer to." We don't train people to say, "We don't know."

I mean, that's a very important statement to make right off the bat when you start on a business, when you start on a project. We are just completely clueless. It ought to be someone's mantra. It ought to be a vision statement "We don't have clue." If you start with that vision statement then you know that you are on the path of discovery. Then you know that you have to configure yourself into a learning institution. And these are the keys to creating really unprecedented stuff. And this is something we don't teach. And that's partly because... I don't know why. But I think that's because we can't measure [these] things.

One of the big problems in education, as you know, is that if you can't measure, you can't manage. If you can't manage, you don't know how well you are doing and you're not going to get funded. This is whether it is in education or it is in general management. There is this notion that you have to have metrics and a lot of the unknowables are immeasurable.

And just looking back we had the Instagram story as well. I don't want to dwell on its particulars except to say that if you thought back three years ago, this company did not exist. It wasn't even in someone's imagination. All we had were these toy-like apps. We had giants like Google and Facebook ascending, and who could have thought then there would be billion dollar valuations on essentially what amounts to an app. The devices which one could buy that could drive this kind of usage were a tiny percent.

So no one who could have proposed the Instagram business plan in 2008 could have possibly thought of saying... They would have been just completely ridiculed.

VCs were backing ideas and, as we know, there was the iFund that was trying to do start ups but I am sure most of the pitches were, "We're going to do a game." "We are going to do a social network." "We are going to do metrics." And those may be fine businesses, but it is unlikely that the things which end up being the home runs would have been envisioned three years earlier. And the thing that is amazing about the app ecosystem is how quickly things are happening. And the speed at which you go from nowhere to IPO, or to exit, is much faster than even a decade ago. And that's because they are built on top of massive, massive infrastructure—meaning, they are built on top of the fact that there is a Facebook universe, that there is an app universe, that there is an App Store, that there is an Apple, that there is an Internet, and the broadband, and all these other things which took decades to build. But once you are on top of that pinnacle you can absorb 30 million new users within a matter of weeks or months.

I think I tweeted this fact: AOL took nine years to reach a million users. It took Facebook, nine months, and it took Draw Something nine days.

Dan: Isn't that crazy.

Horace: So you can see the exponential increase in speed, the decrease in time it takes to reach critical mass, and that's amazing. That right there is disruption, and because things happen at exponential rates, you can't forecast. You can't. Modeling breaks down because it is so sensitive to the input that you make as an assumption. Being off by an infinitesimal amount causes an infinity of error. So you can't do [modeling] with any straight face.

So the way you approach things like this is you have to have a learning mentality, you have to have an experimental phase, you have a humble approach. "We don't know and we are going to learn and we are going to try and we may fail." That humility is not something anyone is given a lot of credit for these days.

So I don't know if that takes me off into another dimension in terms of how to speak about morality. But it's a simple fact. At the end of the day, this is what it all reduces to: You can't go about the process of creating things the way we used to, and I would argue it never really worked that way. We didn't realize, because of the length of gestation that was involved, we couldn't quite connect the causality. We didn't know what was happening because things seemed to be so far apart. But now with things happening on a monthly basis we can perceive what is causing things more quickly.

Dan: So this is our different perspective. And when do you think that... You talk about the future where we look back at this time period and study it. The implication there is that everybody's eyes have been opened and we now have a different model that we function in. You look at the smaller companies. Apparently the story behind the Draw Something guys is that this wasn't their first app. They had many apps. They figured something out, they launched it, nine days later they are where everybody else wishes they were after a year, two years, three years.

Horace: Yes, there's a saying that goes, "An overnight success that took a lifetime to build." And I fully believe that.

Even if you call what I do now success, it may seem like it. I just started two years ago in this business of blogging but I think the reason it is any good goes back to high school.

The other example is Angry Birds. I mean Rovio had 40 games before they finally launched Angry Birds.

But it is important to note how many failures there are, and that they were able to fail, that they were allowed to fail, and that they were learning every step of the way. And there's plenty of luck involved. I am not suggesting that this is all predictable. It is just that when you look at the actual case studies, if you line up all the hits in the world and whether they be movies or products or software or services, and ask those entrepreneurs who made them happen, "Did you anticipate the success," I am willing to bet 90 percent of them didn't anticipate the success, didn't know where they would end up, didn't start down that road, and ended up in a successful place because they changed course a dozen times.

And even Google. We know Google had five, six business plans before they hit upon the one that worked on how to monetize search. And they were just given enough latitude to fail, and investors trusted the founders' intelligence to let them figure it out. So that's the key. And then you take that data set of successes and then you take another data set of failures, especially ones which were involving large budgets...

When someone is given $300 million and told "Here, go succeed with that money," when you see the number of catastrophic failures, you could ask, "When you failed were you on the same plan as when you started?" And most often I would, again, say the vast majority of failures did not change course. They were on the same trajectory throughout. Why? Because had they changed, the money would have been withdrawn. The money was allocated for them to win. The money was allocated because they had a plan. You couldn't get that kind of money, not big money, unless you did have a great plan. Institutional money is all about making sure that those who grant the money are covering their decision with facts. They have to. Otherwise they get fired. Whether you are a VC or you are a corporate person who is allocating resources—hard-earned resources of your shareholders—you don't want to go with some harebrained scheme.

And governments are notoriously bad at funding great successes because everything in government has to be justified extremely rigidly. And so you don't get into a funding situation with a government unless you can prove almost categorically that you are trustworthy, that you've had a clear success record, that you are not going to blow the money. And you are not going to be given all the money at once, you are going to get it in stages. You get a little bit and then, "Have you met the targets? Have you met the milestones you set forth in your plan? All right, you did. Well, then here's more money."

And those milestones are not typically profitable. Those milestones are build X, Y and Z, and those are things that need to be built. And you build them up until the 20th milestone, and that's when you are supposed to actually make the service available and get customers. And then it doesn't happen.

So you could almost say that if you did this type of research where you try to find causality of success and failure and you said the variable you are testing is whether it was deliberate or it was accidental—I wouldn't say necessarily "accidental," but it was like a discovery-based process. When you see these two in contrast, it's pretty obvious, I think, that the thing that works is the learning process and the thing that doesn't work is the deliberate process.

This is not rocket science. This is not scientific by the highest standards, but the pattern is pretty clear, and it's amazing to me that the only people who really get this, I think, on that sort of intuitive level are VCs. Because that's typically how they at least try to operate on that basis. But they have a portfolio of potential failures, and they don't necessarily approve that any one of those is allowed to deviate from the plan. I think that they are basically placing a bunch of bets and saying that one of these will pay off. But they are not saying, "I'm going to fund a hundred learning experiences." In a way, the portfolio theory of the VC is not quite a learning algorithm appropriate to success. It just happens to allow a bunch of small bets to be made and that tends to be better than playing one large bet, which is what alternative financing would give you. So VCs are definitely a step up in terms of intelligent investing and better allocation of resources. But we can do a lot better than that, and I think it certainly doesn't need a VC, you can do this within a corporate setting by having your own company engage in this type of innovation funding.

Alternative methods have been proposed and there are many innovation gurus out there who will tell you… I think some of the phrases I've heard are "Let a thousand flowers bloom." "Create silicon valley inside your enterprise." And doing all these other things. They haven't been, I'd say, success stories. They have certainly sold plenty of books telling the story, but it hasn't quite caught on, otherwise everybody would be doing that.

Again, the answer is that it's almost like there is no answer. The answer is that it is within yourself. The answer is that you have to think about the world differently and approach your decision making day to day on a different basis. And that's, I think, the cultural paradigm.

I come from the disruption theory school, but I think the Jobsian theory has a huge overlap with that. I can't say for sure because we don't know what it is ultimately, how it is that Apple operates. We have all these wonderful books now that have made great strides in uncovering what's happening. Often, all they rely upon in evidence is oral evidence from people who have been there. But there is a lot more I'm sure we can find if we had data, if we could actually get a lot of the data that's locked up in the archives of Apple.

I hope Apple themselves have the data and they are able to leverage it. Many companies absolutely will not divulge, even to their own people, what their knowledge is. And so it is always lost. And it is lost in perpetuity. It's the job of the business historian… I think that's the most difficult historian job you can have because the objective of every company is destroy the history of itself. It destroys it in real time. It cannot allow that information to be shared internally because somehow it is material value, and rarely do business historians have access to data, and usually, it's very rare data from companies that have been forgetful of destroying it, like personal papers of people who worked there, et cetera. So it's a very hard type of research to do. And often historians also focus on the wrong thing. They tend to focus on the personality of the persons involved.

So I was struck by this question of how historians think because actually I was doing a bit of research for my conference and I wanted to have an opening statement about Amsterdam. You know, what's this [conference] about, why are we doing it here? So I am reading some history about the city and the country and I'm struck by the fact that Amsterdam and Holland were a very wealthy city/state at some point in time. That's what made their country so beautiful and made the city so beautiful, right? We go back in history and see these wonderful ancient cities, whether they be the great wall of China or Rome or London, and marvel at how these were places of great wealth at some point, because these things took money to build, especially at a time when everything around them was subsistence farming. There was no industry at the time. So how did these cities get built?

And when you start to read the history of anything, it's amazing how there is no causality ever discussed. It's like King So-And-So was in power between these years and he fought the following wars, and then there was a famine and then maybe there was a plague and then there was this. It's like a bunch of events that are all laid out and you may follow a thread of history and say, "There's the government thread," and then there's maybe the thread of epidemics, and then there is maybe natural disasters. And all these events happened.

So, then, what caused the wealth? What caused the prosperity? It's almost never answered by historians because they don't look at the problem from all these angles. And I think the disruption angle is one. Economics is another. I mean, they don't go into what was the interest rate. That would be a great story, right? Wouldn't you like to know whether interest rates had something to do with the success of a country. What was the trading pattern? What were the economic foundations?

By the way, I'm generalizing. Some historians are diving into this stuff. They are studying the mechanisms by which wealth was created in the particular moment, but it has not yet been woven into our consciousness and we don't think about what the financing mechanism of the Mayflower was. Who put the up the money for the American Revolutionary War? What are these links that we forget? We only think of battles, events, cataclysmic things, and not really the substance of daily life that made things happen.

So one thing I'll touch upon in this [conference] is perhaps this history of why Amsterdam turned out great, at least for a moment in time. But, again, whether the history is of cities or states or empires, or whether we are dealing with the history of a company, once you start with a hypothesis, you can either defend or deny the hypothesis, but maybe the cause is somewhere else completely. We are living through this history today. I think it is a very important time we are living through, and trying to piece it together is fascinating.

Dan: Very fascinating. But you know, this is exactly the kind of thing. It seems like there is time periods where history seems to be made and you could take the devil's advocate approach and say, "Well, any time you are making history, that's true." But there are certain time periods that we look back and say, "This was a big period of change. This was a big period of change." Would you say that the entire 20th and 21st century has been incredibly full of change?

Setting that aside for a minute, are we in a time period right now where fundamentally things are going to be different? Even if we shrink the scale down, and instead of saying across all history, if we say over the past fifty years we are in a time of extreme change?

Horace: I'm at that point where I am exactly asking myself this question because I'm fascinated by history. And even within the lifetime of people I know, we have an oral history. My grandmother was born in 1913, so she had lived through most of the 20th century, actually beyond it even, and she died at 96 years old, so it was a long life. And what's amazing to me, she lived through the 20th century and so she went from an agrarian society to an industrial society. She saw the birth of airplanes.

So my son was born was in 2005 and I'm wondering, "If he lives to be 96 will he see as much change in the same way?"

Now, here is the interesting thing. The question is what is the metric of change. In terms of a lot of this innovation that happened in the 20th century and a lot of the violence that happened, I think the violence and the warfare of that century is just unbelievable. People don't, I think, grasp it nowadays unless you are of that generation. The numbers are just enormous. And so we take life a lot more seriously now. And that's a very important thing. Because life was less precious, I think the changes that were happening were bigger. It was possible to do industrialization on a large scale because you could enslave the population, for example. It happened in the Soviet Union. Stalin went through a period of industrialization unprecedented in history, but it was at a great cost to civil society.

That is unlikely to happen again. So we are much more respectful now, and I think that's a good thing.

On the other hand, the question is, "Does that mean we won't have change?" There is a hypothesis that history will somehow cease to exist, that with the end of conflict on a global scale we won't have this kind of dramatic history anymore. I think the history we are moving into, though, is a different type of history. I think we won't be warfare driven. We won't be ideology driven. Great ideological conflicts we've had between isms—communism, socialism, fascism and so on. Those isms will not be clashing again. I'm not a believer in the clash of civilizations as a future.

What I think is happening is democratization in a sense of the ability of people who have certain power. They don't have the same kind of power they used to have. We will continue to regulate and increase regulation on some freedoms, but we will have increasingly more freedoms that we never had before. So people may argue that I can't do this and that anymore. "I'm being taxed out of doing this and I'm completely constrained. My life based on the 19th-century concept of freedom is less now than it used to be."

But at the same time, technology gives you new freedoms. Communication gives you completely new freedoms. Sometimes those are under constraint as well. And power will always be... There will always be a need to control it because it can be abused. But at the same time, I think the century we are in right now will see a change where we have seen people power affecting world events without as much violence. And I think that's a very important thing.

I think it is all positive in that sense and, yes, we may have potential for cyberwar, but I think the mechanism is in place as well for citizens to protect themselves as well. And it's going to require a lot of education. I think the power kids are going to have in this century when they grow up will be very different than the last century. People then were excited about the ability to travel. They were excited about the ability to read a newspaper, that these forms of communication were emerging. Forms of transportation were emerging that were unprecedented and gave more opportunity to billions of people. And now we are going to move into an era where we have vastly more computation, communication, storage, and ability to create for billions of people. It's a completely different game. You can't think of the new century in the same way that you thought of the old.

The problem comes when politicians or policymakers try to fit the new world into the old paradigm and the metrics they would apply in terms of standard of living. Even in terms of econometrics—whether we have GDP measures or whether we have measures of wealth or power or whatever influence you want to measure—they are all based on 19th-century concepts. The printing press or the automobile or the metrics of consumption. You are applying new methods to try to cram or slow down or fix them, and you have carbon taxes or carbon metrics and all these other things, applying them to valid concerns. But I think there's a whole new world, just as anyone who may have been born in 1900 could not have conceived of the late 20th century. And I think it's not quite possible for us to conceive the future.

We may be talking about flying cars, or we may be talking about extrapolating existing technology, but that's not interesting. What is interesting is having at your fingertips all of the knowledge in the world, or having the ability to communicate with millions of people even though it is just you in your bedroom.

So these are really magical things and I think the value, the wealth that will be created... Last century the value was in industrial enterprises. I think the value in this century will be around how to make people more powerful.

We touched on this when we talked about the iPad. What is the job to be done and what will it enable. And I think computing in general will enable this. We will be democratizing what was once only the dream of publishers, or only the dream of states: to control this kind of information. And now it is going to be available to five-year-olds. So on one hand we may feel that we lost some freedoms and, frankly, some freedoms are unsustainable when they scale to 5 billion people, but then we will get some new ones. We will be cyber people and we will live along those lines. And we have to deal with issues around energy.

We still need to talk about transportation someday. People talk about cars all the time and they love cars, and I do too, but maybe the future of transportation isn't better cars or flying cars. The future is in having no car at all. The future is having tele-presence. The future is having communication and not having to go to work and all these other things that will avoid the car altogether. So you don't disrupt the car by making a cheaper car or a better car or a flying car, it is just by not having a car at all.

So that's the sort of thing I'd like to think that, optimistically, we are going to have in the future. And I think the period we now are in is this transition period where not only do we need to change the processes we use but the metrics of success and performance we use.

Politically, by the way, I think there will be parties forming that will be essentially technology-based parties positioned around the notions of technological freedom, and it's actually catching on in Europe to some degree, the so-called pirate parties that basically are people who are saying... They are a bit rebellious, but all parties are in their early years. But the idea will be that people will grow up, as teenagers do today, assuming that their lives are so dependent upon the technology, and then you have old people trying to take it away from them. And then there will be a re-action and there will be political fighting. There will be all kinds of tensions but that's what we will be debating about.

So that's my hypothesis.

Climax and Anticlimax

Posted April 18th, 2012 as The Critical Path Episode #34

Horace describes the fascinating "lost tapes" of Steve Jobs and Nokia's latest anticlimactic results.

Dan: All right, so let's talk about the news here because this is critical.

Horace: There's one thing I want to talk about most of all, and that's an article that came out yesterday called "The Lost Steve Jobs Tapes." Now, I don't know if this is simmering in everyone's work pool right now as far as being something they are going to write about, because I haven't seen a lot written about this story, but to me this is the best story I've ever read about Jobs. And not just story, it gets down to really what I look for in an analysis of his career.

It's published by Fast Company. It's called "The Lost Steve Jobs Tapes" and the author is Brent Schlender, and he bases it on audio recordings that he made with Steve Jobs for a couple of years, during those times when he was in Pixar and NeXT. So his in-between years, in-between Apple 1.0 and Apple 2.0. And the reason I want to bring this up is because it hit on so many points that I wanted to explore in terms of what makes Apple great. And the basic point is that NeXT and Pixar were really the keys to the current Apple, that learnings from those two companies changed dramatically who Jobs was and therefore who the company that he essentially rebuilt became.

And the details are astonishing. Again, a lot of this stuff was in my mind because I felt that there are all these pieces of evidence out there that Pixar was influential, but I didn't have any hard evidence, and this is the first hard evidence we have of how influential.

So to that point... I mean, I remember I may have said this before, or you may remember I've said this, that to me Pixar is a company where there was the application of an engineering process to what essentially is a creative story-writing process. And in doing so, it became a blockbuster-manufacturing factory, and so the process of being able to repeatedly create great stories and great implementations of stories is what I think Pixar became.

At the same time I consider Apple to be an engineering company that got a huge dose of creativity process layered on top of it. So in the sense that creativity I mean to be the design process... and this again is touched on in the story, remarkably crystallizing what I had already envisioned. In other words, the symmetry is that Pixar is a creative company with an engineering process and Apple is an engineering company with a creative process. And these two things, the similarity and the symmetry

389

between them was too great for me to ignore or say its simply coincidence.

And he basically ties these two together through Steve Jobs. This story that Brent says is phenomenal, not to detract from the other research that's gone on, and the other biographers that have looked at both Apple and Jobs.

Multiple people have studied [this], but they don't study the process and the transformation in management theory that Steve Jobs had to embody, and to me that's where the magic lies: the self awareness, the ability to transform oneself. He has a great phrase in there, he says how Steve Jobs always got the vision right, but almost always got all the details wrong. And in a way, that's another wonderful thing I could probably frame as a very good thing to say, but basically a visionary is a person who always gets the vision right, and often gets the details wrong. A person who is not a leader, but is a great manager, gets all the details right but never has any vision, or at least their vision is always wrong. And so you have the contrast between these two types of skill sets.

The problem is, you still need the details. Even though Jobs made a lot of mistakes both with NeXT and with Pixar and with Apple, they were correctable because he was adaptable and he had great people to work with, and so those people essentially helped him see the light and fixed the details. But without the vision, it doesn't matter how right you are with the details, how well you execute. And the vision is something that always pulls you down if you have the wrong thing in the long term but you might survive in the short term. And so everything resonates around this philosophical foundation that I think is wonderfully tied together. It's a great story to read. I hope it gets developed further. Again, not to detract from the other work that has gone on.

I think many people will take this question as: How do I talk about Apple and frame the discussion? Well, it's about personalities. "Let's get a lot of people who were there to tell us their stories." That's a journalistic approach. That has its merits.

The biographical approach is, "Let's listen to the story of that one individual and try to weave into that story what was going on with the things that person touched." That's a different approach.

What I am saying is that what is missing—and what I think this approach helps with—is that it goes down to the bottom of what is it that the architecture, the infrastructure, the skeleton of the processes, the philosophies, the value systems. What are these things that bound together these different enterprises through the one individual?

And he has great anecdotes about Jobs' obsession with architecture, with foundations and how things are built, and that he would go around and look at buildings being built—in buildings like Pixar's building—and was really obsessed about making them work well, even when they were just nothing more than steel girders, and wanted to get the right design there. That's symptomatic, but to me it's a great story.

So I think that's the best thing that's come out in many months and I really appreciate the work that's been done there. And it's a gem.

I think the fact that these were captured on audio tape also is fascinating because here we have actually a first-hand account. And at the time maybe it wasn't that interesting. Maybe it was just a lot of rambling, but now we can step back and see how that affected the whole industry.

Dan: I was wondering if you were also going to, not to short-change your last topic, but comment about the new Nokia story in the news. That's what I thought. I mean, I like the Steve Jobs thing. I hadn't even heard about this thing yet. So I put that into the show notes.

Horace: Forgive me. To me this resonates strongly.

I think the Nokia story I could certainly talk about at length. To me it's not at the top of my mind because I think a lot of that is anti-climatic.

Dan: That's a good word for it.

Horace: Well, it simply isn't a surprise. If anything is a surprise it's the rate of things happening, but not what is happening.

So just to recap, what happened was Nokia issued a warning ahead of earnings saying that it will not make the target that they set for themselves, and they will lose money operationally and probably overall. And there will be a lot of structural changes coming essentially saying that, "We will crack the whip and fix a lot of these problems." And the stock took a huge dive afterwards and now is almost at the lowest point it's been for fifteen years.

Again, the thing is that I simply would link back to articles written about a year ago when the decision to stick the knife in Symbian—and to do so in a public way—was made. At the time, the post I wrote was "Who will buy the next 150 million Symbian devices" because they came out with a statement saying, "We are now committed exclusively to Windows Phone as our smartphone platform. Oh, and by the way, we are still going to sell 150 million Symbian [phones] and thus still be profitable." And people asked the question at the time, "Well, how can you be so sure?" They said, "Because people don't care what operating system is running on their phone." Or they said, "People value a nice phone and it's a good phone. There is nothing wrong with a Symbian phone. They'll still buy them."

So my concern wasn't that users were naïve or not, my concern was that the value network around Symbian was not naïve. If you've just been told that this is a lame duck, to put it nicely, then there would be an exodus of anyone who has any vested interest in this platform. And that doesn't mean just developers, but any distributors, operators, resellers, whoever is actually dealing. And support issues. The staff inside the firm will drop their pencils and stop work. When you make such a categorical end-of-life statement about a platform there are vast knock-on effects that you probably can't anticipate.

In fact, that was my question: Who will buy these 150? And that answer wasn't, "There are no users." But that there are no distributors of this. And that's what we are seeing. We are seeing an overall collapse in Symbian sales.

The Windows Phone, because when it was announced it wasn't anywhere near ready... Windows Phone—the Lumia line—did launch based on a hardware platform that had already been in the pipeline for a long time. In the summer they came out with an N9 which was the same hardware that the Lumia line uses. That hardware platform was used for Meego, which was Nokia's own operating system, a Linux-based operating system that was to be their future, post-Symbian. All they did was they switched it out to Windows Phone. So there wasn't a lot of engineering work needed on the hardware side to get this phone out, but it still took almost nine months to get the phone on the shelf.

So you have these massive delays to ramp up a new platform, even though you've got a lot of pieces on the shelf already. In the meantime, the Symbian business was submarine-ing. And what we see now is the financial consequences of that. Strategically, and even from the view of the product marketing, let's say, you can anticipate these things. But sometimes the financial consequences are harder to anticipate because we don't know exactly the numbers: How much price are they able to get? How many units can they ship? All these things. So now we are seeing those. We are seeing these things, and the other shoe is dropping.

The fundamentals are very poor. The bond rating, which means how much Nokia needs to pay if it wants to borrow money, the bond rating has collapsed. Their cost of borrowing will escalate if they can get any loans at all. Not that they need them yet, but they might. That's the problem with the cost of financial distress, once you get into a situation where you're seen as distressed, every cost you have goes up, and then you have people stampeding to get out. And so that drives your costs even more. And that's the problem. This is a slippery slope and there's a financial term, the cost of financial distress. There's actually a cost associated with being in distress.

Nobody knows when that happens. It's not like, "Oh, it's right here. This is the moment that the following conditions have to be met." No. The problem is it's a continuum, and this is where panic sets in.

Now, is Nokia there yet? We don't know. It is being valued on the stock market at book value, which means that there's no one really having faith right now in any upside. That's not uncommon. RIM has flirted with being at book value as well, and other companies have as well. But the history of the mobile-phone business is that anybody who gets into this state—making losses, being essentially value-free—hasn't recovered. There has never been a recovery. Out of fifteen companies I've looked at who have hit this point, not one has come back.

Dan: And they know that. For sure. And the analysts know that. Or are you saying that as they seem too oblivious in every other regard that they are oblivious to this, too? Really?

Horace: I don't know if anyone really does this sort of analysis, looking at all the possible failures in the past. But I'm just pointing it out. It's gotten some replay, some people have picked up on this theme, but we are not sure if this is actually becoming something people intuitively call upon as a rule of thumb. It's like you hit this point, that's it, the point of no return. I don't think we've seen that. There are still some people who think that there is recovery possible, even with RIM. And people will even point to Apple, that Apple has recovered. But my comments are specifically the mobile-phone business.

The key [difference] here is operators. Let's keep that in mind. You don't have the option to say, "I lost the faith of all my distributors. I lost the faith even of having customers, so I am going to reboot myself as a completely new entity and I'm going to refresh my brand and do all the things that turnarounds are all about." The problem is that you're a captive supplier to the network operators, and if they lose faith, why should they take a risk on you when they've got all these other guys lined up ready to take over your slot?

Dan: Right.

Horace: And that's really the key, I think, to why this doesn't happen in the mobile-phone business. It's very hard to recover because the amount of decline just becomes impossible.

So I think the hypothesis—the turnaround hypothesis—would be, "In our case it is different." That's always the hypothesis: "In our case it is different." Why? "Because we are big. Because we are the biggest."

And here is where it is undermined again. The other thing I wrote, "How did Samsung beat Nokia?" That was the headline. And by "beat Nokia," I meant, how did Samsung become the number one phone seller in the world. I think in Q1 we will see the numbers and we will see Samsung overtaking Nokia.

It might be close. It might be even maybe Nokia can hang on, but I doubt it. Nokia has already given us the numbers and we can just project. By the way, the problem will be that Samsung may not give us their numbers and we'll have to make a lot of estimates on that. There is a problem with Samsung, but a lot of analysts have already put forward their estimates and they are going to be a couple of million units higher than Nokia.

So that was headline. How did Samsung get to the point where they are actually number one, which has been the coveted spot that Nokia has had for fourteen years?

And the answer I gave is that, whereas there's been growth in Samsung's top line—the top number of units shipped—it hasn't been spectacular growth. What the real growth has been is that they've converted their dumb phones, their feature phones, to smartphones. Essentially, the mix was from like 3 percent to forty, fifty percent within a span of about a year and a half. Literally, from zero to more than half smartphone mix in your portfolio, whereas Nokia had 20 percent or so, and shrank down to about 12 percent of their portfolio. And the feature phone business did not grow. And so if the thing sitting on top of feature phones, the smartphone business, shrank, then the overall business was flat to down, and so Samsung ate up the volumes with the expansion of smartphone business.

So the question then is: How did Nokia allow itself to become "smart-free?" How did it allow itself to lose the—not only the number one spot in smartphones—but to lose the whole business? And this goes back to the original premise that they shot Symbian in the head in front of everybody. And that singular decision...

We know Symbian was on its last legs, but they could have managed that decline through a process of being public about it but stating, "We are supporting it and we are going to keep doing this because we feel that there are market segments where it serves."

In fact, that was my recommendation before the bombshell fell. My recommendation was that they have a balanced portfolio strategy where they have Windows Phone, for example, for North America, that they maintain Symbian, for example, in Asia, and perhaps emerging markets, and then they would put Meego, which was their own internal effort, a new OS, in Europe. A balanced approach to try to optimize platform-to-region as long as it fits certain criteria of cost and brand. But that didn't happen. It was "burning ships" scenario where they destroyed the life boats, [hoping] that the crew becomes more motivated.

And hindsight being 20/20 and all that, but I have to say that I did say at the time that it makes more sense to do a hedge approach than this "burning ships" approach. And I think that, clearly, it was a decision that was consciously made.

And so that's the story of Nokia today, and the discussion—private and public—is, "Will there be a way for them to recover still?" And let's talk a minute about the Lumia itself. The product line isn't bad. It's a decent piece of kit. I have nothing against the product. I've always said, though, that being good enough or being comparable to your competition is not enough when you are a challenger. And so the problem for Nokia would be—and many have said this on other tech blogs—it's not ten times better, which is what it needs to be. I would go a step further, that it is not even asymmetric. It needs to make money in new ways to truly be successful. It's not about being absolutely fantastic. That will work for an early-adopter crowd, but you have to have this phenomenal ability to draw huge numbers of non-consumers to this new platform. The non-consumers are becoming harder and harder to find because we are reaching saturation in most of the markets. So the way you should target it is through emerging markets, but then, again, you have to bring down the price point, and the footprint of the OS doesn't permit you to.

So a lot of constraints here, and when you add them all up and you say, "Well, this can't win as it is right now, regardless of the quality of the product." And it is not even about saying that it has a smoother experience or it is better than Android, or even the fact that you are promoting it with hundreds of millions of dollars, or even the fact that you have three CEOs up on stage, none of these are enough. They are not sufficient, and the challenges for an entrant are to be completely asymmetric, to make money in different ways, to be set up as an MVNO [Mobile Virtual Network Operator]. Do something crazy. Do something extraordinary. Something where you say, "We're going to provide a product as a service and appeal to people who are right now sitting on the fence or don't have a smartphone, or in regions where the prices are too high.

I'm not seeing any of these things from Nokia. Maybe they will. Maybe eventually. But the clock is running out. The burn rate of cash, if they don't make money, it's just going to get harder and harder. And so then what typically happens you have a rigidity of response. You have, within a few months, a crisis hitting like this—pressure from Wall Street, pressure from the board. You will have them divesting of certain assets. And the question will be: What do you get rid of?

Like Barnes & Noble may be under pressure for its bricks-and-mortar business being distressed, but what did they do? They will probably get rid of the Nook, actually the only growing business. They will spin-off the Nook in order for them to get some cash to sustain the business that's actually failing. So in many ways Nokia may actually get rid of assets that are valuable in order to save its core. And the question will be, what does it consider its core?

It may spin-off the low-end business. I think there are three main businesses. You could say three categories. Of course, there is also the network business which is Siemens, a joint venture, and I think that's a no-brainer. I think that should have been gone a long time ago.

But you've got low-end phones and smartphones as separate groups now, and then you have intellectual property in general. And I think these three assets might be in play if they need—in a few more months or quarter—if they need to do something about really drastic change.

There's one more thing by the way, and I mentioned this almost in passing, but it is an interesting hypothesis: If you do divide your phone business into smart and non-smart, it may actually lead to this core problem that we are talking about, that you couldn't transition your low-end business into a smartphone business.

Think of it this way: If you have a separate management and separate priorities and separate targets for these two divisions, what does each manager in each division think? They are not going to think, "My job is actually to destroy the other one." [Instead, they'll be thinking] "I'm trying to sustain my business; I'm trying to do the best I can." And in many ways, what that leads you to say is, "I want to make the smart business as smart as possible and I want to make the low-end business as low end as possible." But, in fact, the future that may make sense is actually for the low-end business to become the smart business, so going in the opposite direction. Or that the smart business ought to be less smart and become low end as Android is doing.

So if you have these two divisions, [you should] merge them or tell them to fight it out essentially. As it is right now, because of the way it is organized, Nokia probably never had that as a possibility, that they might end up with a portfolio-mix transition, which is what we saw in Samsung. The logic would be that every phone in the low-end business becomes a smartphone. "But that's not our division," that would be the answer to that. "That's not what we do." We have a very different strategy than the smart business does, and therefore…

That's one of the asterisks or footnotes to this whole story: Did the organization that Nokia put together actually commit them to a failure where they didn't move their portfolio to smart?

And that is an open question. I don't have the answer here. There are lot of other issues and a lot of moving pieces. But I think that's one piece of the puzzle.

So I think I've talked enough about Nokia there, but I don't have a lot of confidence that they will be able to turn around.

On the other hand, the only silver lining is that typically when a company reaches this point—which, by the way, is what Motorola reached, what Sony Ericsson reached, what RIM reached—is that they have to be reborn in some way. Rebuilt. And Nokia has already been rebuilt once before, or more than once in its history. So perhaps, as an institution, it might survive as a different business altogether. But right now it is looking very tough to continue as it has.

Being number one is what they were. Now that they are no longer number one, what are they going to be? That's the question: Can they survive as a brand, as an institution, as a cost structure or as a mid-player? There seems to be no room for middle players, right? It's either Apple, Samsung, and then the others. So will they be headed to where

Motorola ended up? Will they be headed where Sony Ericsson [ended up], which is now Sony? Taken over? Who knows?

Dan: Well, you may know.

Horace: I've stated my abilities. But the odds are not good, and getting worse. And I'm sad to say this. A year ago I was a bit more optimistic, but it hasn't turned out that way.

Dan: Well, on that sour note… As usual on this show, we always kind of end on a—well, not always but we frequently end on a—well, if you are Nokia fan, a depressing note.

Horace: It is, but as someone famous once said, "That is the best thing about life." So I think you just have to get through it and look beyond. It is normal, that things live and die. Things are born and things grow, and as I've said before, the world would be a much worse place, uninhabitable, if businesses didn't die. We'd still be dealing with kings as our rulers and with feudal empires as a business model. It died and it was disrupted. It was disrupted by technology, among other things.

By the way, that was another thing. Just as a bonus for the Asymconf, I opened with a monologue on what was disruptive about Amsterdam, which was our host city, and that will be in the video and you'll see it. So I won't give it away. But you can look at history through this lens, and you can see the change in the fortunes of nations.

Joys and Sorrows

Posted April 18th, 2012 as The Critical Path Episode #35

We review Apple's performance in the first calendar quarter. Covering the iPhone's predictability, greater China and international opportunity swamping the U.S. opportunity, the iPad surprise and what mobile means to Apple. Dan and Horace ponder what it means for the largest company in the world to also be the fastest growing company in the world. We discuss whether there is a mobile bubble and, as a bonus, Horace predicts the launch timing of the next iPhone.

Dan: Big day. Big day here.

Horace: ...we should get into some of the meat of the matter. I don't have a particular agenda I wanted to start thinking about what we just saw. And then can go through maybe some details of... Before I launch, what was your impression? Just, let's say, as an observer, a well-informed observer? Just how did you read the signals before, during and after the event? Did you feel excited, or was it boring?

Dan: No, it's not boring at all. But I don't know that I represent the typical person because this is, you know, this is a space that both of us—you more than me, certainly—but this is very exciting. And any time you have a company that does this kind of growth, it has to be. So how could you not get—if you care at all about any kind of business—how could you not get excited about this?

Horace: Yeah, I...

Dan: I mean, it's nuts. I was telling my wife—my wife could care less about this kind of thing—I was telling her today how... what they did. And she was shocked by it. You know, this is just not her cup of tea, caring about this kind of thing. But, I mean, and you highlight a lot of these numbers—and we'll put this into the show notes—but the iPhone grew units at nearly 90 percent, and revenue at 85 percent. What's shocking, and you add this—that's below the quarterly average of the last two years at 99 percent. And it's still nuts. Nobody—and again, you say that nobody can do this. Nobody can do this. And yet, here they are doing it.

Horace: Yeah. As a single company, I'm not sure I've ever seen anything like this. You know, platforms can grow a little bit faster. I mean, we've seen Android grow more than 100 percent. But that's the effort of dozens and dozens of companies, and potentially hundreds of products. To see one company, one product, do this sort of thing—it's hard to look to any example in the past. And so I think the headline is exactly what you picked up on, 94 percent earnings growth. Now, this is the bottom line. It is usually the most important line that you measure, how fast the company is creating value. Ninety-four percent while following a quarter in which it grew over 100 percent. And the whole year has been really four quarters—one quarter was a little bit low at 52 percent. And that was the transition quarter of Q3 last year. But if you look at the past four quarters, three of them have been above 100, or nearly 100 percent, let's say. Ninety-four was low, you know. But 120 was what happened in Q2 of last year.

So, it's fascinating to see these types of numbers—triple-digit growth—in something which is already considered the largest company in terms of market value in the world. And that's been the dilemma for a lot of observers and analysts to say… They cite this thing called the law of large numbers, which… Actually, there is no such law. But it is basically—the notion is a simple one—that big things can't continue getting bigger because the growth, exponential growth, reaches a point where you can't grow—you've consumed all available resources.

In a way, that is true, that exponential growth leads to saturation rather quickly. But what we haven't seen yet with Apple is saturation, because these markets that it's participating in are not nearly penetrated either from the smartphone as a whole or from its share of that market. So it's still dealing with fairly low market shares.

That's, I think, the headline. The headline is 94 percent growth from the largest company in the world. Growth, when you become the largest… The assumption is that growth slows down, that you become a boring cash cow, not a turbo-charged growth engine. And the growth we're seeing, again at 100 percent levels, is unheard of, not even if you're just the largest. But even if you're Fortune 500—just large period—would imply slow growth.

To be the largest and the fastest-growing…

Dan: Right.

Horace: …that's really what the story is. So how do they do it? I think that should be the next question: "What's going on here?" And my answer typically—if you want me to be terse—is, "Well, they're a disruptive company. That's what they do. That is not uncommon." What is uncommon is a disruptive company that is already mature, as Apple is, or having gone through several stages of life, as it has, to be doing these startup-like things.

When you start to look at the stack, I draw these area… stack area charts. And if you put this area in certain configurations, you can see patterns which you would not otherwise.

So, for example, if you put products in order of age, with the oldest at the bottom—so the Mac would go at the bottom…

Dan: Right.

Horace: …and then the iPod, and then iTunes on top of that, and then you put—there are very small lines also for what they call peripherals and software, which are small but still-growing business. But if you put those as the base business of Apple, they look pretty much as a healthy company growing in a steady way—not unlike Microsoft, for example, which has also its stack of Windows and business and server and entertainment divisions. They also tend to grow, but they're not growing at 100 percent. They're growing at four or five percent, individually, and sometimes ten percent, and that's considered a knockout.

Google, the same thing. Google actually grows through advertising, which is 94, 95 percent of its business. Advertising is growing again, some quarters faster than others, but it's getting 30 to 40 percent, let's say, on average.

Which is very good, by the way. But if you stack these things then Apple is pretty much in line. But the thing that strikes you is that when you layer on top the iPhone and then the iPad, the thing just goes off, like straight up. And that curve, this area chart, shows that five years ago, these business did not exist. Two years ago, the iPad did not exist and the iPhone just started five years ago.

So when you look at that, you realize that what Apple did isn't become big from what it used to be, it just grafted onto itself massive new businesses individually, one of which might be worth an entire Microsoft. In fact, the iPhone is bigger than Microsoft today. And that's the staggering thing, in terms of profitability. It's earning more than Microsoft is as a whole.

So you say, "Well, they've added a Microsoft plus maybe a Nokia on top of that, with a bunch of other things." It's hard to figure out just how... to give you just another metric that's kind of mind-blowing, after the numbers were announced the stock went up $50-plus. Fifty dollars multiplied by 950 million shares approximately gets you into the $40 billion range. So, $40 billion, the value of the company increased by that much, within seconds. When the numbers came out, after market close, you saw the line go straight up in terms of what the value of the company was. And to put that in perspective, $40 billion buys the whole mobile phone industry. I mean the whole industry. Think of it. Nokia is worth $13, $14 billion. RIM is worth seven. HTC, again, 12 maybe 13, maybe. Motorola got bought for 12. If you add those up, it's still under what happened in a couple of seconds with Apple. A couple of seconds.

Apple is changing value at the rate of $50 to $100 billion a week— and these are huge numbers. The whole company wasn't worth $50 to $100 billion a few years ago.

So the numbers are hard to get your head around because there are no comparables. You cannot compare these things to anything else. It looks like it's a whole economy, almost, can fit inside Apple. It might actually someday. If you believe some of the forecasts out there because some of the people are projecting numbers that would imply a trillion-dollar-plus valuation. And at a trillion dollars, one percent is [10 billion] dollars, right?

The numbers are so high that small inputs create gigantic outputs. And that's what we have to think about, what exactly are the inputs?

The inputs are the products. The products are iPhone, iPad and, as I said, a couple of legacy products. And the thing with the iPhone is that, to me, it's a little bit of an old story, and I said it's predictable. I forecast—my early forecast was 37. I took it down to about 35.4. I didn't publish that, that was my bad. I just forgot. The point being that that's not a particularly surprising thing, given that what happened was, for the last three years—this year included—we had sequential growth or very nearly the same iPhone units sold from Q4 to Q1. And the reason for that is China. Once the iPhone launched into that country, it's been very popular. And it sells into the holiday quarter for China. China's holiday quarter is Q1 [for Apple] because of Chinese New Year.

Dan: Right.

Horace: And it's something that surprises people to this day. And it shouldn't have been surprising. We can go back and see exactly how the quarter would go from Q4 to Q1. And the number of people—it's not just China. It's greater China. It's Taiwan, it's Hong Kong, it's Macao, it's everybody who is an expatriate Chinese person worldwide will probably be using this as a gifting opportunity.

So the number of people who are celebrating this particular holiday may be a significant portion, if not as big as the people who celebrate Christmas with a gift.

So the thing is that you have to think of Q1 now as Christmas 2.0, or the second gifting season that comes after. So it's no longer one quarter that's a holiday quarter, it's two quarters as the holiday quarters. So given that, you just have to think about what can we use as a guide to forecast the numbers? There are a couple of clues. They started selling with new operators in China. Next year, it will be probably China Mobile, which is the biggest in China, [that comes] on line because they're going to be delivering a product that works on their network. Thus far, that hasn't been the case. China Mobile uses a different technology than either CDMA or GSM. And so next year they're also going to migrate to a 4G network that's more standardized, and therefore I think we'll see something there from Apple. So it's possible, then, we'll continue to see this kind of roll out and increased distribution into China.

It's not a giant leap. The thing that was causing a lot of static and the reason the stock did fall 70 or so billion dollars is because there were some numbers leaked that suggested that operators may be either scaling back their investment or, in the case of AT&T and Verizon, that there was a sequential drop. And people are trying to extrapolate from that sequential drop what would happen globally. But, again, that's not taking into account the fact that there was massive expansion. I've done my own analysis. As soon as these [U.S.] numbers came out, I plugged them in and I looked at the data, and I said, "I don't need to change at all my prediction as far as the iPhone is concerned." Because I knew that globally it would kick in, 74 to 75 percent of all iPhones will come outside the U.S. So anyway, that turned out to be the right call.

Now, what's interesting, though, is what's going on with the iPad. I always said that this year, even last year, the really interesting story is the iPad. The iPhone is more predictable. The iPad, we've only had four quarters in which we can actually see growth, year on year. And so far, I remember I talked about this once before, and I said it looks like it's sustainable, then, that the iPad grows at 150 percent. The iPhone had been growing at 100 percent on average, so now we're going to have to see whether we dial in 100 or we dial in 150 on the iPad, and it looked like we could get away with 150, at least for the first three quarters of it. And sure enough, they came in at 151 percent.

I had a little bit higher, I believe, but because it was a launch quarter I wanted to see a little bit more. But they were very supply constrained. I think that the screens, they weren't able to get enough of them. And for that reason, they only came in at 151 percent growth.

I don't talk about the absolute numbers, I talk about growth numbers, because that's what you're going to plug in next quarter or the one after that. That's why for me that's what I'm dialing every time.

So, that's what we saw for the iPad. Now the interesting thing is, during the conference call, Tim Cook and Peter [Oppenheimer] were both very adamant that next quarter we're going to see some big numbers on the iPad. And they said we're finally able to get production. [Paraphrasing] "We believe we're going to get supply/demand balance on that product, and we're going to see substantial growth there." In fact, they said—they went so far—this is—they almost never do this. They actually said that they were going to see substantial sequential and year-on-year growth on the iPad.

Dan: Mm-hmm.

Horace: And so, again, what do you put in for a number? Now, if you put in the 150, which as I said has had a nice record—three, four—sequentially four quarters have shown that 150 is sustainable. Then you get an amazing number. And the amazing number isn't so much the units, it's actually going to be something like 22 million next quarter, if that's the case. But what's interesting is the price—you multiply that by the price and you get a revenue number. The revenue number of the iPad starts to be so big that it offsets any slowdown on the iPhone. And there will be a slowdown because next quarter is probably a transitional one for the iPhone.

I'll talk about that a little bit later. But the point being that whereas people might say, "Well, the iPhone is such a huge part of the business that if that ever goes down, then the business altogether goes down." Well, we're seeing already after two and a half years that the iPad can fill in any of the gaps from the seasonality of the iPhone. It is so big already, and it's coming up on being one year behind the iPhone, almost, in terms of tracking the volume and value. So I just put in some numbers just to pencil in something for the next quarter, and I was shocked to see that it's possible that they'll actually get almost the same EPS [earnings per share] number next quarter as they did this quarter, this recently ended quarter, because the iPad is growing so fast.

And again, they talked, and they keep talking about the iPad, saying it's going to be big in terms of numbers, units sold, because we believe it's going to outsell Macs or PCs. It already outsells Macs more than two to one.

Dan: Right.

Horace: But it's going to eventually be a bigger number than... The tablet market will be bigger than the PC number, and, maybe it might even catch up to the iPhone. It's possible, if it sustains 150 percent growth. That's the whole betting game. Can it sustain that? People didn't believe that the iPhone could sustain 100 percent growth for more than three years. I would have found it very hard to believe, but here we are, in the fifth year, at 100 percent.

So, again, the iPad, if it sustains 150, it actually could become as important, if not more, than the iPhone itself. Now, it doesn't get the same margins. The pricing of the product also isn't as high. One interesting thing: For the first year or so, or even longer, let's say nearly the first two years, the iPad pricing to the channel, meaning what Apple obtains... I shouldn't call it pricing, I should say revenue per unit, because inside of that unit there are licensing and accessories and a bunch of other revenue streams. Even revenue from Google, as far as whatever they pay for their traffic acquisition to that device is probably bundled into this price. It's only a few dollars, probably, per phone. But still, that number, the revenue per phone, has gone down from the launch iPad of about $650 down to about $550. And it's a big drop, because usually if you look at Apple's pricing, or these revenue per unit numbers, they've been very steady. There is some slowing, slight downward trend for the iPod and for the Mac, and even maybe sometimes it's seasonal, but for the iPhone as well. Very slight, very slight. You wouldn't be able to see with the naked eye when you looked at the graph over a five-year period. But you can see this decline in the iPad.

Now what's interesting is... What happened lately is that by leaving in an older generation, they've put this $399 price point, which I think that really is affecting the overall pricing. We haven't seen that effect when Apple puts out a low-end iPhone, or an older-generation iPhone, or the lower price, because I think many people buy—whoever buys the low-end product, there is also someone buying a higher-end version, even. You know, the 64-gig version that actually costs $800. And so you see the average price remained the same.

So my point being that I think there is something interesting happening there. You have to look at this revenue per unit on the iPad. I think this is a very aggressive strategy that they're allowing that price to come down, on average, because they're growing distribution. And this was into a launch quarter. Usually in a launch quarter you have much bigger numbers because you've got the early adopters buying the latest generation, and you're going to see a spike, a little bit of a bump in pricing. But here we saw a decline. And for some people that might ring alarm bells. I would set off fireworks because that means they're actually going to address a larger market. This is exactly what people have been complaining about, that they're vulnerable at the low end. I think by allowing the low end to essentially become an iPad, they're going to actually still maintain this 150 percent growth rate. And it's still a very healthy business because the margins are going up on these things.

Dan: Mm-hmm.

Horace: That's the other story. The margins, regardless of the price point, are very healthy.

So what we saw… Also, by the way, this is the other bombshell which I think maybe not many people will notice, or care much about: Their margins went up to something like 47 percent, way above everyone's expectations, including my own, but also something that is stratospheric, compared to what it has been historically. Something getting into the 50 percent range is something only software companies can dream of. Certainly a hardware company like Apple, although of course they're software as well and services, but where they capture value through hardware normally gets 30 percent at best. Thirty to forty percent. That would be if you have a really premium, high-end product. PCs get 5 percent or less, generally. Windows PCs don't make…

Dan: That's terrible.

Horace: Yeah, they hardly ever make over 10. And so you have this explosively high margin. Maybe again it's an anomaly, but I tweeted a chart showing the trend. The trend has been very steadily going up. Part of that is that they have more iPhones, and more devices in the mix, that are high margin. But even the iPad, I think, has to be 35 percent right now. Just plugging in the best numbers you could think of for everything else still doesn't drag it up high enough. So you've got to somehow tweak the iPad up. That's the way you play this game: You have more unknowns than you can solve for, so what you do is just try to make a lot of guesses and see what balances out. And the guesses are educated because you know roughly how much these things cost to make. You know roughly what comparable products from competitors might be going for. And so there is a lot of nuance you can add to your guess. And I have done this for a couple of years now, and I would say that the iPad seems to be holding, if not rising, in margin.

So it's a great business. I think it's extremely disruptive, unlike the iPhone. In many ways the iPhone is disrupting computing, but it has to still deal with the distribution network, which is not under Apple's control. And that means that they're still at the mercy, to a large degree, of the politics in the telecom sector. And Apple plays politics as well as anyone. But you can see how sometimes that may limit the way you package the product. If you remember way back when the iPhone launched, Apple didn't actually go for the subsidy model at all. They were rebels without a clue, and launched at $500-plus unsubsidized. They wanted to be creative about how to get some money back from the operator, and they used some model of getting commissions or royalty back from the carrier, which was AT&T. And they ran that program [for less than] one year, and then they completely ended it and went back to a default model of subsidy, which is now getting a lot of weird comments. But anyway, it works because that's what the operators want to have.

And [operators] would be the last people on the planet to want to cut that because that's the only way they can make sure that they get minimum churn and then they maximize the retention of their best customers. So what I'm saying is that the iPad doesn't follow that convention of having to deal with operators. The iPad is very much along the lines of a PC, or a Mac, in terms of being, in an unregulated way, sold to anybody who can [buy it]. It's liquid. It's unlocked. It's a completely open product in that sense.

And for that reason I think Apple really wants to see that grow as quickly as possible. In some ways, you might say that that's why they're pulling out all the plugs and making sure that that can really succeed. And then that's kind of the legacy, I would say, of Steve Jobs: Bringing computing to the masses.

Dan: Mm-hmm.

Horace: From way back, from the original Apple][, the idea was, "Let's make it affordable. Let's make it for everybody." It is in Apple's DNA to do so, and it is not an elitist company by any means. All they are elitist about is wanting to be the best. Their question is, "Why can't everybody have the best?"

So I think that's good. I like that about the iPad. It's a product that I think is going to increasingly catch people's attention, so in a few months or maybe a year from now it will be all over the news that the iPad is now the king of the hill within Apple. And that's what I'm looking forward to.

The other thing is that what I haven't done yet is dive into the CapEx. And here is where I'm going to make a prediction, if I may.

Dan: Yeah. But this is what we all wait for, your predictions.

Horace: Well, I think given what we've seen in the CapEx right now, it's unlikely we're going to see a June launch for the iPhone 5.

Dan: Really. So you're going to—You're saying no launch for the iPhone 5 at WWDC.

Horace: Oh, no, I don't think so. I definitely think it's unlikely for the simple reason that Apple hasn't ramped up CapEx to any degree that would indicate that. This is my hypothesis because I've observed the pattern. But we haven't seen this giant leap. As of October last year, they had forecast what their capital budget would be for the full year. So we know where they're targeting. But for two quarters now, they haven't been on the trajectory to meet that target. So we're waiting for the shoe to fall. We're waiting for that huge $5 billion dump of money that's going to be paid out to outfit the new factories that will build the components and the units that we need to see in a new iPhone launch. That's my hypothesis. Let's see what happens.

My expectation is that if you see it in one quarter, then it's likely you're going to see units coming out the next quarter. That's the whole premise, and since we didn't see it as of the end of March, that spending hasn't happened yet. I expect it will happen in this current quarter. It's happening right now as we speak. And then come June when they release their numbers, we'll see that in their books, and then that will imply a fall launch.

Unless, again, the game could change where they're able to spend the money and get everything done in the same quarter. That could be happening. That would imply massive ramp going on right now. It has to be happening right now in order to get the volumes they need for a launch of the iPhone 5, keeping in mind again that the next generation product has to be double the previous.

We had enormous numbers for the iPhone 4 in terms of ramp and the number of countries and everything else. We have to see that, more than that, next time. And if we don't see the signals in advance, I'm skeptical. So that's all the data tells me. That would be my guess, that we're going to see October launch rather than June launch.

Dan: You heard it here first, right?

Horace: That's my guess right now. It's not that that's a bad thing. I think they may be looking at that particular window as more logical. I talked about this before, but when they were launching the iPods, the iPod's music events were always in the fall…

Dan: Mm-hmm.

Horace: …targeting the holiday period. And now the holiday period happens to be, like I said, a six-month period, because if you're including Q1, would it not make sense to do it in October, so that people in China feel like they're getting a fresh product in January? [This is] Vis-à-vis launching in June, and a lot of people feeling, that's six months ago and now we're finally seeing it in our territory.

So I would say it's much more logical to do it all at the same time in October, and I think that's how they did it with the iPod. And I don't know why they may have moved some of the years where the iPhone launched in the summer. Summer is usually not a great shopping season.

Dan: Right.

Horace: Summer is vacation time. A lot of these things are constrained by many variables, and we don't know what they are. I don't see it as bad news that we see it in a consistent October launch. It may be that they couldn't ramp. It may be that in the early years of the iPhone they needed to launch in June because it was so hard to get the numbers. It took them three or four months to have the volume for Christmas. But now they're getting better and better at it, so they're able… if they launch in October, they've got the ramp. October/November, going into Western markets, and then January/February going into China and so on. And then we'll just have to see if they have to do something else if India… I don't know what festivals in India require gifting, but if they're ever going into India, maybe they will have to see an adjustment yet again.

Dan: And we've talked about that a little bit on a previous show. I can't remember the episode number. But you were very clear in saying that the next big frontier for Apple is India.

Horace: Yeah. I think it stands to reason, right? I mean, they can't go everywhere at once, immediately. And in these countries, they're taking a very… I think a holistic approach. I'm not sure if that's the right word, but a focused approach, where they're looking at each country and trying to optimize and understand that market. In fact, they used these very words in the conference call. They said, "We're learning. China is a huge opportunity for those who are willing to invest and understand that market." Implication being that they are doing just that. And it took years. It took years for them to get their feet on the ground in China, to put out points of sale. They also cited numbers. I forget them exactly, but they said "Well, we have X thousand iPhone points of sale. We have Y thousand iPad points of sale. And these are way under what we need." They're still building out the way of distributing in China for these core products.

Flagship stores are nothing compared to the vast expanse of that nation, and all the people who are distributed all around. I think it makes sense to have [distribution] in tens of thousands. They have fewer points of distribution in China than they do in the United States, and the population is a quarter of it. To me, it implies very careful thinking about how to optimize your business around that market. And I think in India it's completely different. I think in India the economics are different, and it's not just people having less disposable income. It's about how do you get things into the channel, who needs to handle the product on the way to market, how do you pay the taxes, how do you pay whoever needs to be paid. And there are a myriad of obstacles in that country. Maybe it's not possible, although, if it isn't, it would be a tragedy for not just Apple, but I think it's a market that needs to have access for all kinds of technologies to be able to be successful there.

To give you a point, there are obstacles everywhere. There are obstacles in Latin America, where you require local manufacturing sometimes. That's the case in Argentina and in Brazil. Unless you have local manufacturing, the taxes are extremely high. And so that's why they're putting up these satellite plants there to manufacture locally. That's how the law of the land is.

Anyway, I don't know, and I'm not an expert on India, but I do know that it's a huge opportunity, and that things are sold a bit differently there, that operator relationship is different with the consumer, and the retail channel is very different. There are very few mega-malls. Mom-and-pop-type shops are very prevalent. So, you don't have an easy plug-compatible model for an Apple Store, or an Apple certified reseller to plug into the way things are sold there. So that may be a showstopper. But they need to work that out. And I don't know whether they'll go with it. Also, I think the economics of it isn't just low price, but rather, how do they convince people to get a data package and a device that lets them do Internet on their phones, rather than just using removable storage to watch Bollywood movies.

So there are really different models of consumption of what the value of Internet is, what the value of content is, what the value of a phone is, that you almost need to reengineer the whole business around India in order to be successful there. But the smart people will do that. I think that's not an obstacle that's impossible to overcome. So, yeah. I'm very bullish on that, and I think India is a great market for them to go after. Maybe not next year, but it'll happen.

Dan: Well, very cool. We will have to see what happens there. It's fascinating because the infrastructure that is there, as you said, is so different. Seeing how a company like Apple adapts to it—and inevitably you have to imagine that they'll be successful there—will they have the same kind of success that... You've said this before: Apple's future is China. Apple's future is also India. Apple's future is not America, you know. We're English-speakers here. Apple comes from America, so that's generally what we tend to think about here a lot of the time on this show and other shows when we talk about carriers, and carrier results, we focus on the ones here in the U.S. But I would think that this is temporary, that the U.S. dominance in these kinds of conversations, that's going to change. That's a thing of the past, or very soon to be.

409

Horace: Just in the last quarter 74 to 75 percent of iPhones shipped outside the United States.

Dan: Amazing.

Horace: And so the U.S. is now essentially at 25 percent of the business. Overall I think that...

Dan: But is that, Horace, is that because we've already had the iPhone, we've had it for longer, and fewer new people are buying it? Or is that just an indication that really the audience for the iPhone is global?

Horace: Well, both, to some degree. First of all, you have to understand there is seasonality. Obviously, in the last... in the Christmas quarter there was a lot more U.S. But it still meant about 63 percent was non-U.S. But I actually headlined one post about it, saying the U.S. regains some relevance in Apple's overall marketshare. And the U.S. gets a boost once in a while because of launch events, because of seasonality. But again, over time, even those bumps are going to diminish in size because so much of the population of the world is—you know, we talked about saturation. Well, saturation in the U.S. will happen quite soon. I suspect smartphones are going to be 50 percent this year, or already are at 50 percent now, depending on who you ask and how you measure. But clearly it's going to go beyond 50 percent, which is probably a tipping point. And then we're going to have a slowing of adoption of smartphones—still probably reaching 80 percent. It has happened very quickly. And I've shown historic graphs also on my site where you can see what it looked it for various consumer technologies, how quickly they went from zero to saturation in the U.S. in terms of households, and then you can see phones, and then you can see cell phones, and then you can see smartphones.

And compared to everything else, from microwaves to cars to washing machines, smartphones is the fastest of all of them. But that's the U.S., and [saturation is] coming very soon. And at that point, the economics will also change in the sense that operators are going to have to fight a lot harder for incremental growth. We might see a lot of pricing competition at that point. It's happening already, by the way. The U.S. is not the first to reach that point. It happened already in parts of Europe, and when it does happen in these parts, what happens is typically there is a lot of price competition. And so data packages collapse. I mean, the pricing goes down to $20 or less a month. And unlimited everything, and all that. So that happens because of saturation.

It's not a pretty story for operators, I'm afraid, but it doesn't mean they stop buying phones. What people are buying the phones for is something completely different. They're their life companion. So all their apps and data and joys and sorrows are on their phones.

So that's definitely different. And you think of them as your computer, and your service, just like you might your laptop or your desktop and your ISP. That is the future, one which everybody has been nervous about in telecom, because it implies dumb pipes and so on. But that's where we are. And 4G isn't affecting much of that at all. I think maybe we are satisfied with 3G, and 4G is being only taken right now by early adopters who need to download whatever it is they download much more quickly.

Anyway, what I want to point out is that saturation begets price competition amongst operators, which might also imply reduced subsidies, which might hurt Apple... Well, a couple of things [first]. You have potentially reduced subsidies because you're not actually hiring the phone. The iPhone—many smartphones—are hired right now by the operator to sell services. They're essentially salesmen of mobile broadband.

So mobile broadband—the salesman comes knocking. He happens to be in the form of an iPhone. And if he gets the deal with you, then the iPhone gets a nice cut—a nice bonus. That's what the subsidy is. It's a kickback to the phone guy for having given me a customer that is going to pay me for two years, $100 a month. It's a wonderful proposition for everybody. It's a win/win. Tim Cook said it, and he's absolutely right. It's been a win/win from day one.

The problem might be that if everybody already has this—that the salesman has gone calling on everyone, and everybody has already bought a service plan, and it is locked in for two years, how do you deal with—where do you get the commission from? So at that point, the operator might slow down the commissioning process, but that doesn't mean that that's just the job that the operator hired the phone for. Now the question still is what did the consumer hire the phone for? The consumer always had been hiring it for something else. He hired it because, again, it was their joy and sorrow.

So in my way of thinking, then, at some point if the consumer says "I'll take the $20 plan," as he has already in the Nordic states, "I'll take the $20 a month plan and I'll still pay $600 to $800 for an iPhone because I value the iPhone for what it is." So the consumer then takes up the payment for that salesman's salary, and we will see a transfer of who pays the bill from the operator to the consumer. So we haven't seen—in countries where we've seen saturation—we haven't seen people abandoning iPhones. If you go to a country like Sweden or Denmark, iPhones are ubiquitous. And there are plenty of Android as well. I'm not suggesting that it's a dominant thing, but they are pretty much everywhere. It's not like they've become extinct.

If the nation is prosperous, people are feeling good about their prospects, then they will easily spend the money on the device. So I'm not worried about the impact of subsidy loss even if subsidy losses do come.

On the other hand, I still think there's a lot of cards to play in Apple's hand. I think that they could still do something about a subsidy-free model for the iPhone, changing it in some way to take some of the edge off the pricing, if they need to go there. And it doesn't necessarily mean lowering their own take of the product, but rather maybe they could come up with a creative way of packaging what they currently package, which is not just the phone but the services and everything else. I'm not going to make any speculation on how they will do it, but I think there are plenty of opportunities for them to modify the product line.

I've also said that even in emerging markets, it makes sense for Apple to introduce a new concept, both as a phone and perhaps as a device that isn't even called an iPhone anymore, because they may want to dress it a different way.

We can keep going on the iPhone. I want to make sure we touch on one or two other things. Two more things maybe I just want to touch on.

Dan: Yeah.

Horace: One is the cash—we come back to this often. It's now $110 billion. That's not much of a surprise again, but what's interesting about that is that having grown $12 billion, it actually grew more than what they're going to pay out in terms of dividend and share buyback. So it's interesting, because the prediction was that even though they're going to institute these cash distribution models, shareholder instruments, the cash will continue growing. We haven't seen the dividends yet, and we haven't seen the buyback yet. But just the rate of growth in this number is such that it's still an amazingly expanding cash pile. So it will lead to questions about how they might use that, and I think those questions will continue.

The other thing I want to point out is that on a unit basis, their Mac business didn't grow very fast. It was actually one of the slowest growth periods for the Mac, partly because a year ago there was a huge growth quarter. A year ago, they were at 32 percent, I think, revenue growth on the Mac, on the back of... I think it was the Air launch. And they haven't had a launch of any kind for some time. And so I think we're going to see—that's another easy-to-make prediction—we're going to see some significant growth quarters ahead for the Mac.

It was 4 million units. But in terms of growth, that was only about 7 percent growth in units. Even though they grew at 7 percent, that still outgrew the overall PC market, with them in it. I'm sure if we take—and we will, by the way, this is something I do regularly—take Apple out of that mix, and then we'll measure PC growth without Apple and PC growth of Apple, we'll see exactly how much more it is. Because when you fold it in, it increases the overall growth of the PC market with Apple in it.

So in that sense, I think they claim that they outgrew the PC market for 24 quarters in a row. That's still a very healthy business although, again, making up less and less of the overall numbers. Within the Mac business there are portables and desktops. The interesting thing is the mix of those two. Over time, it's not constantly diverging, but over time the portables have been reaching about 70 percent of all units sold. So think about that: Portable Macs are vastly more popular than the desktops. You might imagine that was the case, but to the degree they are, it's astonishing.

Now what I did further is, I took the portable Macs, assuming that they're "mobile devices," and added all the iOS devices to that total, and then I asked the question, "Of all the units that Apple sells, what is the percent of units that are mobile units?" In other words, is Apple a mobile-devices company? And to what degree?

I think we can agree it certainly is with the iPhone. But when you do this comparison, you reach the number of 98 percent of all units shipping out of Apple are meant to be used in a mobile way. Ninety-eight percent. So it's not even about being the majority or being a vast majority, it's actually pretty much all of the business that Apple has today is mobile.

And I point this out because if you look at Microsoft and Google, and try to tease out of their data just how much can you attribute their businesses to mobile—they don't publish anything. It's very, very hard to find any number at all. And if you did try to estimate it, it would come out to be very small. I think Google reports that they have a run rate of something like two and a half billion dollars from mobile, per year. But that's still a tiny fraction of their overall revenues. And in the case of Microsoft, it's far smaller. In fact, it's invisible, because all they really obtain from mobile is the licensing of the Windows Phone, and that right now is probably negative, because they're paying back almost everything they get as payments to Nokia to support the platform, which is $250 million a quarter now.

Dan: Mm-hmm.

Horace: So in fact, if anything, Microsoft has a negative revenue for mobility. So we have Apple, and people talk about the bubble. They talk about mobility being a bubble right now. They talk about the fact that you have huge valuations for companies like Instagram. Huge valuations. A few years ago [it was argued that] social was in the bubble, and yet somehow it hasn't popped. Facebook is about to go IPO. We have huge valuations for some of these mobile-oriented app companies. Rovio is rumored to be in the billion-dollar valuation already, and Instapaper has already been there. And there are a few others in the pipeline.

And yet, here is Apple with 98 percent of its product being a mobile product. Not to mention, of course, the apps. Not to mention of course the other businesses they have besides units of hardware. But just on the units of hardware, you have this overwhelming, almost-100 percent value coming from mobility. And what strikes me is that if you talk about mobility, the largest company in the world is positioned on mobility as its core business. And not just core, but it's essentially its only business. And I think that's a great testament to where we've come, both as what computing has become and what Apple has become. And the opportunities that exist.

And by the way, I want to deflate the bubble, not to puncture it. I would actually deflate the bubble, because if you think of Apple capturing the vast bulk of value in the computing universe, which it is—both in telecom and in personal computing hardware, at least—it towers above everybody in terms of these profitability measures and in terms of its revenue growth. But ultimately Apple is still very low priced because of it's multiple on those numbers. It's very low compared to those other non-mobile businesses.

So if you look at Google's P/E as 18, Apple's P/E's it's 15 to 16— Microsoft is a bit lower, not too far lower, I think in the teens. The point being that the biggest mobile player in this game is not being valued at hundreds of P/E. That's for Amazon. Amazon is 150 P/E. The big player in mobile today has a very, very reasonable—one would argue—even cheap valuation. So I don't see that as being bubble. Mobility isn't a bubble.

And I would add, again, the example of Apple's competitors in mobility from the phone space have all basically not been ballooning, as every dog was ballooning during the dot-com era. Every lousy idea was overvalued. Indeed, in mobility right now we have actually a crisis of value because we have companies like Nokia and RIM, and now HTC as well, suffering from a massive devaluation. So I don't buy the notion of a bubble forming around mobility. Some of it in the software space, I mean, I think those are fair numbers right now. I think a billion... If you divide by the actual number of users involved, and some of the data that's behind some of the values there, I think it's very reasonable pricing, actually.

So that's the last point I wanted to make. On this bubble talk.

Seeking Enlightenment

Posted May 9th, 2012 as The Critical Path Episode #38

Horace and Dan wade into Android economics, expanding on the series of posts on Asymco.

Horace: I wanted to jump in quickly because I think we have a little less time than usual. Last week I promised to publish this week an analysis or at least a straw-man proposal on how to analyze the Android business.

Dan: Right. People are eagerly waiting for that. You said you would do it, and you've done it.

Horace: I've done a couple of posts. It's not complete. You know, I try to do one a day, and four or five different posts could be made out of it. Even more, as I think of the different ways of framing it. But, yeah, I've sort of put the flag out there, planted something, and hopefully it will germinate. I think most of the discussion, if I may suggest this anecdotal evidence, is that most of the discussion around Android has been in the blogging community. It has been around whether it's good as an experience or whether it's growing as marketshare, or whether it's been a success story, if you will, winning versus not winning, open versus not open. I think those are interesting [topics] and they're all essentially moving the ball forward in terms of what it is. The understanding has been improving over the only few years since it launched.

But what has been missing is, I think, an economic analysis. And the reason for that is obvious. There is no data. There hasn't been anything from Google about how Android is performing. We barely have information from them about the activation rate, which is not a standard way of measuring sales. It's like an instantaneous derivative of sales, if you will.

Dan: Well, you hear this activation rate all the time, and this is the number that... I guess because those numbers are really good. Is that why they are always so willing to share activation rates, or what?

Horace: I'm not going to say that. What I would say is that it's the data that they have. It's because they're capturing that information from their servers. They're seeing activations, and that's a natural way to measure performance from *their* point of view. They could probably get [additional] data, but it would be taking some assumptions to go to the next step, which is asking how many people are actually using the devices. And to make that public would probably require them to make some assumptions. What they have is hard data and hard evidence—what they do publish—which is this activation data.

The problem is that they don't offer it regularly. They don't offer it continuously. They only give once in a while, a nice ballpark number.

415

Now, they're not the only company to give only nice ballpark numbers. Apple does it as well. They will do it about their apps, they will do it about their download numbers, like 25 billion apps, or something like that, when the time comes and they want to celebrate the fact. But Google—the whole ecosystem around Google and the number of devices involved is now the biggest such ecosystem, the biggest such platform. And it would be important, I think, for the world to know with a little bit more clarity.

The iOS environment is much easier to measure because Apple publishes these data points about their device sales, which we can add up and keep track of. So I'm not going to beat up on the fact that we have little evidence of what's happening. What I'm trying to point out is that we haven't even tried to get further than the number of units, or the activation rate, because there is even less data once you try to step forward from there.

So one of the questions has always been, what is the money... You know, "Follow the money" is one of the most important analytical techniques we have available. It gives us a clue, though not definitely an answer to where the motivation is for a company. So if we understand its economics, we understand something about what motivates the teams inside the company to do what they do.

And so that's been my question because on the one hand if we have units and marketshare data, is that really the driver for Google? I think it's one of the interesting inputs to a model. But it's not the only one. The next thing you should know is what is each one of those devices is worth to either Google or their partners. That's where I think the big unanswered question is. And Google has hinted in the past that they were targeting a certain number, like $10 per device per year. This was something Eric Schmidt mentioned, I think, last year. In their way of saying things, you don't know if it's wishful thinking, if it's far from that point, or how far we are from that, what's happened in the past, what's the pattern. We don't know. That just is one number.

So that's been one of the big debates: What is a user worth, and to whom? So let me just take you one step at a time. Once you establish how much a user is worth in terms of revenue, the next question is, how much of that user revenue is going to be shared with somebody else? In other words, what are the costs of that revenue? What are the costs of that sale?

And every business has costs of sale. In some businesses it's very small. Like at Microsoft, it's very small to measure costs of sales because each unit of software doesn't have a lot of cost associated with that particular unit. There is a lot of overhead costs of R&D, and sales and marketing, and those are taken out from the operating expenses.

But the interesting part of Google's business is that they do have costs of sales that are significant. It's not a software-company model where you simply get a software license paid for, and then you issue a thousand of them and it costs you just as much as selling one of them. In the case of Google, they actually transact in traffic. They don't transact in licensing agreements or in pieces of hardware. They license, essentially, *access* to consumers.

This traffic is what they try to purchase and monetize. And so they're paying somebody for that revenue. And this is where it gets interesting because you have to understand a bit... Again, Google isn't very clear about even this aspect of their business, how sales are acquired and how they're paid for. They have a term called "traffic acquisition costs," or TAC. This is a measure of a percent of sales that is paid back out to those sources of traffic.

It's an interesting thing to get your head around because we're talking about getting queries from users and then delivering to those queries results, and getting paid if users click or view those results. And that's the question: What are you paying for the traffic to come in the first place so that you can serve it back out?

And you can also sense in that that there is a vulnerability in Google's business that if somehow they stop getting access to end users, then the whole business would collapse. So how would they ensure, first of all, that they have access and, secondly, how can they make that access grow when the new devices and new experiences are coming on-stream.

So this has been the discussion any investor would have had with Google for a decade. How do you ensure you have access to customers, and how do you ensure that you grow if those access points change? And that is the second part. How do you grow? Is that what Android was originally designed to do for the company? Meaning, that they wanted to make sure that they have access to mobile consumers, which were threatened? The threat around 2005 was that Microsoft would succeed with Windows Mobile and thus block access to the Google search on their devices. And so by introducing a disruptive, free [zero-price] model of software for device makers, they would have a way to block Microsoft's hegemony in mobile?

It turned out that Microsoft was not the threat, the most imminent threat. It turned out that it was Apple, two years later, with the iPhone. Nevertheless, they tried to reposition the reaction of Android from one threat to another by going against Apple at a later point. By 2008 or '09 that transition was complete.

Now, my point is, then, can we put a number on these things? Here are the clues. We had some clues coming out from the Oracle trial. There are bits and pieces. It's fragmented, some of it is not trustworthy because it is leaked information or we don't know what the provenance of that information might be. But it's beginning to become clear. And you test these rumors or, let's say, these fragments against some other data which is public. So, for example, Google does publish overall that it obtains a certain amount of revenue every quarter, and that it pays out a certain amount in TAC, or traffic acquisition costs. And Android has exploded, right? In terms of users, what's been happening is that you can assume that the traffic has grown, but somehow the bottom line hasn't grown very much. So people are asking these questions in the Q&A with management: "Is your mobile TAC, or acquisition cost, higher? Because we're not seeing the trickle-down effect of all this new mobile usage." And so that's something that's indicated there. And their answer, by the way, was, "We fold it all in and it all comes out okay at the end." But they didn't really directly address that question. So I think there's a lot of investor skepticism already about mobile not paying off as a growth opportunity. Maybe it's a defensive strategy that's paying off, but it's not clear that it's an offensive or growth strategy that's paying off.

So there is some evidence that there might be something not yet there about mobile. And by the way, simultaneous with this discussion, we've had Facebook coming out also with a warning, that mobile hasn't yet been paying off with them either. This is a typical boiler-plate warning you give to investors prior to an IPO. You make a laundry list of all the possible things...

Dan: Everything you can possibly think of that this is already... We already know it's wrong. It's horrible. Don't expect anything good ever.

Horace: So far. I wouldn't read too much into a statement like that because saying that, suddenly this proves that Facebook is failing in mobile. But I would just point out that it is an open problem... You can also see the fact that the device-based interaction model and the visibility of ads in the device is very constrained for Facebook or anyone else, for Twitter as well.

But let's put that aside for a moment. I mean, mobile isn't monetizing the same way that the wide-screen experience on a portable or fixed computer would be. Clearly, there are some issues here. Now, again, I'm trying to just figure out what are the first numbers. So one of the numbers that's been leaked is that... Again, keeping in mind $10 a user was a target, that it was a data point that in 2010 they were looking at about $9.

Now, that was in 2010 when they had 50 to 70 million users, depending on when you measured. They didn't have quite even 100 million users. Now they have upwards of 300 million. So that's a huge change in two years. But at that time, they were looking at $9. Now, the question in my mind is, "Would they be able to preserve the $9, going from one to three hundred million [users]? Would the $9 go up to $10, going from one to three hundred million? Or would the number go down?" My guess is that it's going down because a lot of those hundreds of millions of users aren't in the United States, and there is certainly not that many either that can make the difference in Europe. So most of the growth has been in emerging markets and has been in China. And pretty much globally.

The problem with those users is that they're not targeted as much by advertisers, and I would imagine they're not paying. People aren't paying for those impressions or click-throughs as well. I don't have evidence of this, but this would be my guess, that commensurate with the GDP or per capita or whatever other economic metric you want to have—even to the point of measuring the average price of a device, the average price of a person's subscription to a data service, on and on. And also [there's] the fact that a lot of those users may not even have data services, that these are smartphones being used [largely] as voice products.

And we also see the indications from global figures of engagement on Android global figures of browser usage on Android vis-à-vis iOS. A lot of those factors aren't showing the kind of engagement that an advertiser would like to see, and therefore my assumption is it's gone down from $9, not up.

One other thing that they indicated in some of these filings was that they expected the market to grow less quickly than it did. So they had projections for 2011, 2012 and 2013 that were far below what we actually saw happening. Again, this is based on their activation numbers that we interpolate. And we figure out, based on activations, they must be looking at these hundreds of millions of users.

The idea was that they didn't see that growth as steep as possible, which is actually very important. I started my discussion with this point, saying Google itself seems to be surprised, or should have been surprised, by the growth in Android.

And it's an interesting point. On the one hand, it's a positive thing.

Dan: No, explain that. Why the surprise?

Horace: Well, again, it took off much more rapidly than anyone expected. I certainly was surprised by the growth in Android. I don't think many people who were analyzing the industry expected it to grow exponentially as it did. Now, you could potentially put a very aggressive curve on it, but it would have meant that this tripling in a short number of years is unprecedented. Nothing happened like this before in the platform game. And the reason for it, by the way, and I came to terms with it many months ago, is that Android was essentially of viral value to OEMs, and they really felt that they could get going much more quickly with it. It would allow them to increase revenues very quickly, and they took it and ran. It didn't require contracts, it didn't require a lot of engineering, it didn't require a lot of legal work.

There is a downside to that in terms of IP issues that they have to confront later. But it was fire now and deal with asking questions later.

And what happened is that everybody rushed into Android, and so essentially the world's non-smartphones, feature phones, were converted to Android as quickly as possible. And so we had this huge swap going on from feature to Android.

By the way, just one data point came out today. DoCoMo, which was number one in Japan, switched its entire portfolio of phones to Android. I mean, 100 percent Android. And they used to be 100 percent feature phones two years ago. There were a couple of Symbian phones that were actually acting as feature phones. You couldn't run apps on them or anything. It was using Symbian as embedded, so I wouldn't even count those as truly smartphones. But then they had a couple of Linux phones, again using Linux as an embedded OS.

So what they did is, they switched to 100 percent Android. Their competitors in Japan had been going with the iPhone, and thus woke up Docomo into the smartphone space and then they decided to retaliate with Android. And so you have this enormous flip, all of Japan going to smartphones within two years. And they were one of the laggards, again, because they hadn't gone with RIM at all. There was no RIM, there were hardly any iPhones or Windows Phones at all. So it was really like a switch going on.

So, we had this phenomenon in several countries, and as a result there was this viral growth of Android. And if you look at the data, you see that there was this hockey-stick effect of Android, where it ate into feature phones very, very rapidly. It also ate into Symbian, it ate into RIM. iPhone still grew, but not as quickly. So my point is simply that these new users weren't probably foreseen by Google itself, and once they did come on stream, they probably didn't return the revenues they expected.

There is one other small data point, and that is that they expected in 2010—just after the iPad launched—they did expect to also be in the tablet business. And tablet users were more lucrative in many ways. They paid more for apps. They engaged more. They paid more for content. All these things were already evident in 2010. And they probably would consume more ads, or search, on the device.

So Google was looking at this market and said, "We're going to take a significant proportion of the tablet growth and we're going to therefore keep this revenue per user high because of the tablet mix in the Android mix." And that didn't happen. So that's another interesting aspect. The tablet underperformed their expectations, but the handset overperformed their expectations, I think, in fact, by at least a factor of two. So to me, that speaks of, again, a great volume story, but not a great revenue story.

So I took these factors and came up with a figure that I felt was comfortable. And it can be changed, we can do a sensitivity analysis and tweak it, and move it up and down. But I chose $6.50. And then I chose an end-of-year figure to represent the whole year because we're looking at a polynomial or exponential growth. So I said, "Let's give the benefit of the doubt that the usage per year is roughly what it is at the end of the year." And I got beaten up on this, and I deserve it, but basically that was a simplifying assumption. Because then I'd have to make a second assumption, like, where do I pick as the average for the year, right? I'd have to make a model that's so complicated and then I'd have to explain myself on multiple levels, and I chose to just keep things simple and use this approach.

So I had a figure, let's say end-of-year 2011. Then I had a figure of $6.50, and it gives you the revenue number. Now the other thing is that we also know that Google splits this revenue into multiple pieces. They get search [revenue], but they also get AdSense, which is what affiliates pay for, they get traffic from affiliates. And then they have also AdMob revenue which is folded into the Android business.

And then of course there is apps, but apps are a tiny, tiny bit. Two to three percent of revenues that are booked.

That's in an agency model. So the gross revenue—again, like with Apple, gross revenues are off the books—what they're essentially reporting as revenues are only the leftover from having paid the developers and whatever else gets a piece of the action. Interestingly, operators get a piece of the action of app sales. And this is controversial, but it's true. Twenty-five percent, according to Google. Twenty-five percent of app revenues were expected to be paid to operators. It's a curious thing. When I tweeted that, a lot of people said, "Why did operators deserve anything?" And the answer is because you have operator billing. In operator billing, the operator takes the risk of clearing that transaction and making sure they collect the money. And many operators prior to the app ecosystem were handling content transactions. They were charging 45, even 50 percent. The operator line on this is, "There's a lot of risk associated with a billing statement from us, relative to a bill from a credit card because people many times don't pay their phone bills or they're slow." There is a greater penalty for screwing up with your credit card than there is with a phone bill. Anyway, that's the theory. In any case, they end up capturing a lot of [transaction value].

So on average, the theory goes that 25 percent goes to operators. That means that Google only keeps 5 percent of an app's value to book as its own revenue, which obviously cannot pay for much. One of the reasons the Android marketplace, now called "Play," is weak is because there's hardly any funds available. Apple keeps 30 percent from which they pay the credit card fees. But they have to keep some of that to maintain an army of people to check that the apps are not fraudulent, or whatever they do. There is all that checking that goes on, which Google doesn't do.

Secondly, they have to do the heavy lifting of updates and all these other things. And sure, Google does that as well, but I think the scale is a little bit smaller.

In any case, the bottom line is that there is a tiny bit of app revenue, then there is a whole lot of search. Then there is a big chunk of AdSense, and then there is sort of a smaller chunk of AdMob.

Now, how do you measure the cost of sales? That pile has to add up to what we call Android revenue.

And, by the way, there is another data point out there which you use to back into and check your assumptions, and that's the run rate of Android revenue. Andy Rubin mentioned that it's $2.5 billion, at some point this year. So, it was at 2.5 billion throughout 2011. It was at 1.1 billion, and now we know it's gone up to 2.5, so we don't know just how much came out for the whole of 2011, which is the time frame I'm testing here.

So let's say for a minute that these are the bounds, 1 to 2.5 [billion]. And so I did my 6.5 times the 200 million—whatever it was, users at the end of the year. I came up with a figure of about 1.5 billion for the whole of 2011. And from that now we start to cut it into pieces and decide how much came in via search, came in via these other components.

Dan: Right, right.

Horace: And again here, we get some other fragments of data, like the split is roughly—you know, I don't have it in front of me now, but it's like 35 percent for one, 45 percent for another, and so on. And there are ways to slice it up. And it makes sense also to look at the global picture for Google and seeing what its split is between search and affiliate income, and all of that. So there are some ways you can back into that. Probably direct, or their own search, is their own sites generate a bit more on mobile than through affiliates. But you put these numbers as an estimate, and you put them together, and then you start to figure out, "Okay, who gets paid for that?"

Here is where I think we have some really... You know, an opportunity to make a bold statement moving forward, and that is that operators get paid out of that revenue.

Dan: Right.

Horace: And OEMs get paid. That's interesting. That means the device makers themselves are paid. Now, why would I make such a statement, right? The answer is that Google actually let it be known that they pay OEMs and operators out of Android revenue. They did so at a conference call, again, in the last quarter. I cited this on my site, there's a quote there from an officer of the company.

So that means that we know that they're getting paid, but how much? And this is where it gets a little bit interesting. I would assume that search revenue gets a piece from the... There is a payment made from search to the carriers. Also because we know that carriers used to pay and, by the way, Apple is one of these beneficiaries of this sort of ecosystem because Apple gets a cut from searches originating on mobile Safari. And we don't know the structure of that deal. Someone posted—an analyst on Wall Street posted—that he thought it was 50 to 60 percent of search revenue originating from iOS was being paid back to Apple, which could be substantial. There were estimates, there was half a billion dollars a year.

By the way, all of that money ends up actually truly padding the revenue per phone because I think that's how Apple accounts for it. When you look at the $650 they capture per phone, they say that includes hardware revenue but also services revenue, and I think you might imagine what services does Apple offer? Right? And accessories too, by the way. So you add all these really lucrative pieces of revenue on top which have no costs at all to Apple, and that's why they're able to get a significantly higher average selling price for the device or, I should say, revenue per unit of each device.

And we don't know the amount again, I'm just pointing out that it's some measure of dollars on top of whatever the average price to operators is. Just closing that loop, basically, there is this money flowing from Google to Apple.

And so there is money flowing from Google, obviously, to Samsung, to HTC, and to whoever else is taking their phone. So, here is where I am trying to figure this out because my question is, how much? Because if that's really the business model of Google, right: Take a lot of money from—or not a lot, on a per-phone basis it's $6.50—and pay back out, my estimate is they pay back out about 40 percent of that. That's consistent also with their traffic acquisition costs on the regular business, right? Not the mobile, not the Android. So 40 percent is probably a feel-good number for Google, saying, "Okay, we'll share back 40 percent."

And they're sharing it with operators, they're sharing it with OEMs. And to some extent I think with AdMob they're sharing it with developers. In that sense, there is a sense that all of these ecosystem participants are getting a piece of the action. It encourages them to stick with the platform, it encourages them to stick with Google's version of that platform, and its services, because those are the services that generate their revenue, and so on.

The problem is, again, here is where we get to the question of the great idea. How much? Is it significant? And that's where I've been spending time putting it all in context, and showing the data. "Okay, this is the structure of the income statement. This is how much is paid out as a percent. This is roughly how big the stack is. And this is who gets what." And if you add it all up, you know, it starts to look pretty significant at 1.5 or 2.5 [billion] as we are running now. Maybe it's going to double again to $5 billion a year. And that 40 percent of that is going to go to these operators and these device makers, although there are many of them—there are many, many hundreds of them. Nevertheless, they each get a piece. So the question I would have, though—is that piece enough to keep you loyal to the Google ecosystem?

But when you take it in context and say, "Okay, that's…" Let's take this, for example: $6.50. Forty percent of $6.50 is how much? Let's see, I'm just going to punch this in here.

Dan: Okay.

Horace: I haven't done this, so I'm going to… It's 2.6 dollars. So, 2.6 dollars per Android device in the field is paid out to operators. Now, if operators—let's say operators and OEMs split it, although I think the operator would get a little bit more, but if we split—if they split that, and the operator gets 1.3 dollars, and the device maker gets 1.3 dollars, and that's on a yearly basis, and the lifetime of a phone is typically two years. So let's say again 2.6 over the life of a phone, that's 2.6 dollars out of $350 probably price to the channel for a Galaxy, or something like that. Or, if it was the iPhone, it would obviously be a lot more, but it would be, like, 2.6 dollars out of $600.

It isn't all that much. In fact, it's almost not worth discussing because also that operator—or, sorry, that OEM—is paying a significant penalty for that phone to Microsoft for being on the Android platform. So here is the economics from an OEM's point of view, which is what I should do next, look at it this way and say, "Okay, if I make a phone with Google, I'm going to be putting so much into R&D. I'm going to put so much into components and costs and so on. And I'm going to build this phone—I'm going to have a margin with it, which isn't going to be great, because there's a lot of competition. And then I have to pay off Microsoft, who has been suing me and everybody else because of IP issues. I've got to also pay for legal because probably I'm getting sued by Apple as well."

Dan: Right.

Horace: But that's just the running cost. But from the phone itself, I've got to take a piece out of that phone and give it to Microsoft. And then Google pays me back. But if they pay me back only $2.50 and I've got to pay $5 to $15 to Microsoft, it looks like I'm net negative on this thing, at least on the IP side of the software stack I'm running. What's in it for me? Yes, I'm not competitive without an OS. I need an OS, so I've got to have something to be in the game. But then you get into the strategic discussion. Maybe I'm better off throwing in with Microsoft, because even though Microsoft doesn't have the revenue from Bing to pay me, right? Maybe they will offer me something, you know. Maybe I'll get a dollar, you know, every two years or something out of Bing. But the discussion an OEM is going to have within a strategic sense with themselves will be, "What's the real value of this Android ecosystem?"

Putting aside the question of what is it worth to a Google share-holder, what's it worth to a Google developer or, I should say, an Android developer? I don't—you know, these numbers aren't that great so far. But let's put those aside and say that who's been really virally attracted to this thing has been the OEMs, and that's one of the key components of the puzzle as far as getting the volumes, right? So that's where I'm asking myself, "Is the payoff that an OEM is getting from search and AdSense enough to keep him loyal?"

And I think the promise was, and you can imagine when the deal was put forward to them two years ago—which is roughly about the cycle time to get a product out. [Google] said, "Look, you've come to us, to our ecosystem, we're going to do revenue share on search. Boy, that sounds great, doesn't it?"

Dan: Yeah.

Horace: A killer product that's going to be competitive with an iPhone, which we know is driving great margins, and I'm going to get a share of revenue from search. And that's where the whole model hinges on the question of the 6.5. Is it 6.5, is it 10? But even if it's 10, this is the real killer, right? Even if it's 10, the problem will be, is the 40 percent, which is now $4—let's say, even though we only get $2—is that really enough? And how much pain are you going to suffer from Microsoft attacking you, and Apple attacking you, to be on this platform?

I don't have the answer. I could still be missing a lot of pieces here. But I think this is the first step forward in understanding how the game is really played. And I'd like to sort of also put an underline here on this point: I think this is the gain. It's not about user experiences. It's not... It is partly about getting a marketshare and getting some profits as Samsung has accomplished. But HTC hasn't succeeded with this model. Sony Ericsson hasn't succeeded. We know that only Samsung is in the game right now making money with Android, on the core business. And all these other inducements, and all these questions: Is this ecosystem also actually spreading the wealth that Google is creating, from search? And is engagement there? Is that going to happen? Is it really going to take off as they expected?

And when you put all of these together—I added this, trying to visualize it by showing the size of the Android business as it is, right? All of Android, in terms of this 1.5 billion—what did it look like to be Apple relative to that? And I show this chart, and it's basically one-in-fifty scale. Apple's revenues... Actually, that's not even true. That one quarter of revenues, in the first quarter of 2011, was 50 times bigger than all of Android revenue for the whole of 2011. And so the portion that any of the Android OEMs gets, relative to the mountain of money that Apple is getting, must have felt pretty rotten, if that's what they were looking at.

And I would say it doesn't matters if it doubles or triples, it's not going to be there in terms of a real business, and a real inducement to business, for another couple of... You know, maybe even a decade. So I'm not yet convinced from this analysis. I'm impressed that Google is doing it, but I'm not impressed yet by the numbers involved in equality of the business so far. And the other thing I did today was to compare that chunk of money that's coming from Android to things like, what's Google's overall business? It turns out that Android would contribute significantly less than 5 percent of sales and about 5 percent of profits if we make a lot of assumption that their costs are under control. Again, that's not like earth-shattering news, that you've got hundreds and hundreds of millions of users somehow, and you're not contributing more than two to three percent. Google doesn't celebrate the fact to their shareholders and say, "Hey, look how well we're doing." They talk about these volumes, but they don't talk about the numbers in profitability, or the numbers in terms of revenues.

Dan: Right.

Horace: You would imagine that they would somehow break it out eventually in their statements, but they're completely silent about that.

So, relative to Google itself, it's not a lot of money. Relative to Apple, it's almost no money. Relative to Samsung's core business, it's not a lot of money. Relative to what Microsoft is charging them as penalty, it isn't enough to overcome that. So I'm still searching. And the last piece is, like, well, what about Motorola? Motorola was a 12.5 billion dollar acquisition, which hasn't closed, by the way. I'm talking all the time as if it did, but it hasn't, so there is a chance it won't. Nevertheless, if it is [a done deal], vis-à-vis that asset, right? 12.5 billion. Then you can ask yourself, well, this Google business—this Android business—revenues, earnings, growth rate. Take those three factors and ask yourself, "What is that business worth? Will it ever be worth $12.5 billion?"

You know, just as a benchmark. Is Android worth more than Motorola? And you would have to be extremely ambitious to think of a way to make those two actually equal from the numbers we have. And I'm sure that the market isn't putting that value on Android today. But the question then becomes, "If you have Android, why did you buy Motorola?" This is still an open question, and it's yet another roadblock on your way to finding enlightenment on Google.

I mean, I really seek enlightenment. I'd like to say at the end of the day, "I get it. I understand how Google is going to be like absolutely a winner here." And celebrate that, and sort of go buy their shares or something like that.

But I haven't found it yet. I'm still searching, and there might be still a magic formula I'm not aware of, that this is going to go to 1000 percent growth rates in profits. But I just don't see it. And I don't think the market does either, because Google's shares haven't gone anywhere for a long, long time.

So there is my long rant. But that's what I've been doing. And I've still…

Dan: That's what you work on. Well, I've put a bunch of the articles that you have written very recently into the show notes, so that people who would like to can read some of the more detailed analysis. This is a question that I've asked you before: Do you think that these things that you're experiencing right now, and going through as you analyze this, that discoveries that you're making, isn't this something that—I mean, it seems silly to say this—but aren't the companies themselves thinking the same way? Does it take an outsider like you to actually figure this out for him?

Horace: You know, my assumption is always that people have already figured all this stuff out, and just haven't told me yet. And I have to work on that assumption. But slowly, sometimes, you hear through comments that, "Hey, yes, we did see this. And by the way, check this out as well." But there is a lot of cases where people are so, let's say, impressed with this. But they come back and say "Can you tell us more? Because we —this is really interesting stuff." So whether it's CapEx discussion, which I've had a few times before, or what is the strategy of Apple in general? But I think in this case the Google stuff is—I feel like such a novice about it, because it isn't a company I follow closely. But when I uncover new things, there is a lot of people saying, "Yeah, that's fascinating. I didn't know that." So that kind of makes me think that there might be something new here. And I assume that there are analysts who follow Google who know all this. But I look through some of the data, I've looked through some of the commentary, and there hasn't been a moment yet that this has all been figured out, that there is a clear value proposition here that Android is really super-valuable. That I haven't come across yet, so I'm not trying to, again, find out that Google is not valuable. I'm trying to exactly define how valuable it is. But I haven't found that yet.

And the first cut I made to the whole problem was, "Why isn't the share price going up?" If you would have a business that was growing exponentially, in terms of usage, wouldn't you expect the stock price to follow? There are anomalies. Clearly, Apple is growing exponentially, but its stock price is growing, though now not as quickly as its profits. But it is growing. Well, Google's isn't. And from 2008 you can pretty much track every quarter and see: In 2008 they had zero Android users, and now they have 300 million Android users. Ad how much did their stock go up? Not anymore than their core business has grown up.

So I still struggle with the question all the time, self-doubt of, "Surely, I'm missing something. Surely, there is pieces of Google that I don't understand. Surely, those guys are far, far smarter than I am, and they know exactly what they're doing." And there are one or two clues. You know, obviously, this idea of sharing revenue is a very good idea. But again, it hasn't yet paid off. So, you know, we'll just... I'll just keep my head down and try to figure it out, and hopefully we'll get a lot of feedback. Unfortunately, a lot of people who do comment on Google, they tend to have a very antagonistic approach, which is kind of perplexing also if you're trying to do this type of work, that people—if you write a column, if you write the analysis as I did, and publish, "Okay, here is what the income statement looks like,"—you get a smattering of comments. Most people say, "Interesting," or whatever. But then there is—then you write another piece and say, "Well, by the way, that number that I published yesterday, this is what it looks like relative to Apple." People get all very religious at that point, and the idea is that, "Oh, you're comparing two unlike things, this is not fair." Or, "Android is really, really doing something completely different, this is not the point."

That's not what I'm trying to—I'm not trying to pick a fight on "My OS is better than your OS."

Dan: Mm-hmm.

Horace: The thing is that—do you have evidence? This is sort of my call to action here. Do you have evidence that Android is obscenely profitable and that its growth potential is far beyond what we can anticipate here economically speaking? I mean, units, yes. I understand that logic is easy to understand and embrace. But is it really going to completely change the economics of mobile?

If anything, it's disrupting, but it isn't creating value. And that is—as an observer and an advocate of disruption—I think there are probably a lot of disruptive elements here. But it isn't yet. All of the pieces aren't necessary to say, "The game is changing." There's a lot of moving pieces, and you've got to get them all aligned to succeed in this game.

Anyway, I'm just going to wait and see what we get back and, you know, shoot holes in it, by all means. That's the whole point.

Dan: Shooting holes. So where do we go from here? You have written these great pieces. You've come up with this analysis. People who are listening—who are thinking, "Hmm, interesting."—what do they do to actualize this? Should they change their own personal strategies, whether they're investing or just observing? Is this change what we should expect? How do they... What's the response to this?

Horace: Well, I don't know. You never know. There are all kinds of unintended consequences. But I would hope that we all become smarter as a result, that we all learn from each other and we know better how Google is operating. We understand the value proposition. We may even become more aware of the fact that what they're trading is not what we thought they were trading, that they're actually acquiring traffic and knowledge about us, and all these other things we talk about that we might...

Dan: The value, the inherent value of the invisible data.

Horace: Yes, they're creating value because they're indexing the world, but they're also sucking value because they're capturing information about us that we may not want shared, and so on.

So there is this moral tension about it, as well. But, fundamentally, all my core belief is that if the economics don't work, it doesn't matter how great your dream is, or how great your willingness to do good is. Ultimately, you run out of fuel and you can't execute those great things.

So that's the question: Is this Android ecosystem fueled by the money or is it fueled by a lot of other things which may or may not have value? Enthusiasm, hope, belief, whatever you want to call it. Nothing wrong with those things. But you better get some funding underneath them at some point in the future. And openness is not going to feed your family, right?

The Locus of Power

Posted May 23rd, 2012 as The Critical Path Episode #39

Dan and Horace take a nostalgic trip through the automotive industry. Horace asks why should a 20-year-old car (which he happens to own) be replaced? Why are cars built to be disposed of and why aren't they meaningfully improved based on new jobs to be done? In this episode we look at the auto industry as a proxy for other "network-based" industries which reach plateaus of innovation and can go no further. Plus, Horace challenges readers to guess what car he drives.

Dan: There was a study that came out from WPP's Millward Brown. It's called the BrandZ study. Did you get a chance to see this?

Horace: I think I saw that. Yes, I saw that.

Dan: So the top 100 most valuable brands. Apple is on top. Nokia is now gone from this list.

Horace: Yes. I see a lot of these, and everybody has a different list. It's kind of an interesting practice to try to put a dollar value or a ranking on brands, and it doesn't appeal to me as a solid method or way of valuing things.

For example, just to sort of give a simple sanity check, if you were to say a company's value of the brand is, let's say, $200 billion. I don't know what they put on Apple, maybe it was 180 or something like that. So does that mean that an investor owns twenty, thirty percent of the company's value is the brand. If that disappears then the share value should drop by 20 percent or 30 percent?

And conversely, you know, what if the company is worthless, and yet it seems to have a brand value that has a dollar amount. So how is that reflected in reality? There is no connection between the supposed brand value and the equity value. So I think that's problematic in my mind.

The other thing to note is that as companies are successful, their so-called brand value goes up, and as companies become unsuccessful, their brand value goes down. And is the value simply a reflection of the perception of its success in general?

I think it's more important—as we talked in previous shows about brands in general—I think it's more important to understand that brands are really reflective of meaning, not necessarily of value. That value is in everyone's mind who has a perception of that brand, and you can't put a dollar figure on it. It is, however, what compels you to make a purchase decision, and I think it is very subjective.

So, indeed, I've seen some brands or some brand metrics, that are simply a reflection of recognition. If you ask a random sample of people,

431

"What do you think of this particular name or icon," people will recognize it, and thus it becomes valuable simply because it is known. So I think that's not a particularly useful measure of willingness to buy.

I've said before, the most powerful brand probably in the world in terms of recognition and visibility is "Made in China." "Made in China" is a brand now in the sense that it is on almost every product you buy regardless of what the actual product is. In that sense, does that mean that if it's recognized by everybody—"I know what that means,"—does it mean that "Made in China" is worth more than "Made in Brazil" for example. I would argue, no. Maybe people would actually value that which is made in Brazil because it is more unique or it is something off the beaten path or distinctive in some way. So the brand value of "Made in Brazil" might be higher than the brand value "Made in China."

But I don't want to talk too long about this. I am just skeptical about these things because next month we might see a brand survey that suggests that Coca-Cola is far more valuable than Apple.

I remember one brand survey done out of the U.K. Similar to this, Apple was in the top three or so, but number one was Aston Martin, which is a car manufacturer. And you know, Aston was the cool brand that particular month or that particular season. And it doesn't mean that Aston is a particularly valuable company. Aston Martin is a very tiny company, in fact, that doesn't mean much to the automotive industry.

Speaking of which, I actually wanted to talk about the automotive industry today. I get tweets and reminders in the blog through comments that people try to relate what's happening to the automotive industry. It's one of the most interesting industries out there, and a lot of people can relate to it, so there is a lot of discussion like, "This is what happened in the auto industry," or "This is like that brand, and look at what happened to them," and so on. I thought it would be an interesting dialogue to have about cars in general and what happened to that industry, what's happening, what will happen to it, as a proxy to many other things.

And I think I've touched on it before, but is that something you want to talk about?

Dan: Yeah. Absolutely. I love it when you bring your analysis and insight to these different industries. We talk about Apple, we talk about mobile phones, things like that, but you know, we've also talked at length about television, about Hollywood, so, yeah, I mean, let's talk about this. This sounds really interesting.

Horace: When you do step out of your comfort zone and you step out of the analysis bubble you are in, sometimes looking at an industry that you are not an expert in, or the audience isn't an expert in, it helps you actually frame things a little bit better.

Clay Christensen, for example, would introduce, as one of the stock kind of basic descriptions of disruption, he would bring in a story from the steel industry. The steel industry is not well-known outside of the steel industry. You don't know the dynamics. But a technology company can still be persuaded of the value of this theory by explaining what happened to this completely abstract industry that you are not familiar with.

So in that sense I am not sufficiently competent to talk about something like the steel industry, but I think a lot of us, at least, have some recognition of the car industry and the car industry is sufficiently abstract, while being familiar at the same time.

First of all, I'm just curious. Are you sort of a car guy? Do you know about cars? Do you like cars?

Dan: In a past life I did like cars quite a bit. Now, for me it's more about safety and functionality for the family unit. Like, will this carry my family and my kids and all of our garbage around with us safely? If it will, then it is an adequate vehicle? And that's my main focus.

Jump back to when I was a younger man, I used to be very interested in cars. I used to really enjoy it. Definitely, I have a high level of appreciation for a nice car. In a past life, I had a nice car. But these days, no. I think I leave that to people like you and John Siracusa.

Horace: It's funny, because I had the same experience. I was much more of a car enthusiast earlier on. I think when men become fathers, I think it happens that you tend to lose that. And you can maybe get back into it later on when the kids grow up and then you start fondly—or maybe when your kids come to be of a driving age then you may want to reintroduce some of the enthusiasm around that part of your life.

Dan: Right. Right.

Horace: So I have gone though that myself. What I wanted to point out, for example, is that—and this is true, by the way, of a lot of men, is they go through a formative period. And this is for women too, not necessarily with the same passions though. The brand preferences get established early in life, pretty much from the teenage years up until mid-30s is when people's perception of what is good and what is not good in terms of product quality and so on. These perceptions are formed early.

For example, a man who enjoys a certain style of cars, a certain brand of car at a certain age, let's say in his late 20s, will probably be nostalgic about it in later life and will probably end up, if they reemerge into that hobby, then they will probably be buying up those cars twenty years later as memories of youth.

Dan: Right.

Horace: In fact, in many ways, also women will probably establish preferences for certain consumer products or certain brands in certain things early in life and they will stick with that for the rest of their lives as well. So from a marketer's point of view, that demographic, meaning the age group that you are targeting to form a brand image should be at that early stage in life.

And the trouble is if the medium that is being consumed is not attractive to those young people then brands cannot be targeting them through that medium. So to put that in perspective, if the average newspaper reader's age—the median age of a newspaper reader—if that extends to be in the 40s or 50s, then it is very inefficient for a brand to advertise in that newspaper medium because you won't be able to reach people who haven't already made up their minds. You won't be able to reach people who are in the formative phase of their life, and so you won't have the effect of formulating that image that then pays you back for the rest of that person's life.

And this is true right now. This is a serious problem with newspapers, with television, because the median age is shifting to higher and higher numbers, and so we are having a problem that the sort of things that are advertised on television and in newspapers are no longer the things that were advertised 20 years ago. For example, soft drinks and certain brands of consumer products, certain things for women and so on.

And that's an interesting dynamic. That's getting off the subject a little bit about cars, but I am pointing that out because I am interested in understanding how the car industry will evolve, because right now the car industry, I feel, not only has it been through a financial crises which exposed a lot of the vulnerabilities of the businesses, many of them were pretty much insolvent. But it's becoming harder and harder to see what improvements are being made in cars. And the way I've measured that through my own consumption. I have an old car, and in fact, this year it's going to be 20 years old.

Dan: Oh, wow.

Horace: Yeah, in July it's having it's 20th birthday.

Dan: This is your DeLorean, right?

Horace: No. Maybe we should have a little contest. People can guess what car I have. I'll give some clues. It is 20 years old, but it was actually originally developed even earlier than that. That happens to be the year of manufacture. Actually it's so old—the design is so old that it is in museums or it belongs in museums. And I was in a museum recently where I did find my car.

And in fact, what's interesting is that there were four instances of that car in that museum. And I can describe the four instances and people can then maybe guess what the car is. Does that sound interesting?

Dan: What do they win if they—we'll send them a free 5by5 T-shirt if they win.

Horace: Or the book. I don't know. Yeah, a T-shirt would be good.

Dan: Or both. A T-shirt and a book. They could win this.

Horace: Then I had better make it hard. There are four instances of the car. So it is interesting to see that, and this will tie into the discussion later. But basically the instances are that it was used by a celebrity. It was used in auto racing, and it was a record setter. I had set records that I think it still holds today. And it set certain new standards for safety and other breakthroughs, technological breakthroughs.

Dan: I think I could guess. I think I could guess. And John Siracusa, I want to mention, is not eligible to win this.

Horace: So these are the four instances, by the way. I mean, maybe it's has gotten other accolades or something, but these are the four instances that were actually represented in this museum.

Dan: Okay. So let's just go over these again. The four instances: Used by a celebrity; used in auto racing…

Horace: Used by a celebrity. I could name the celebrity but I don't know if that's actually giving too much information.

Dan: …record setter, and some of which are still had today; and it set new standards for safety.

Horace: New standards for safety, but there was a fourth. Oh, it was race car.

Dan: Got it.

Horace: It has a racing pedigree. And the other clue, obviously, is that my example of it is 20 years old, so you can kind of figure out what that means.

So I am driving around this old, you know, museum-quality car, and I ask myself every day I drive it, "Why don't I buy a new one?" And the answer usually is because I can't see any new cars being better than my car.

Now there are little things about new cars that are definitely better. Probably fuel consumption would be the best thing I would like to have. But when I bought it, I actually bought it because I wanted to hold onto it for a long time, because I felt that this was something that should last a long time. I didn't think cars should be disposable.

I was born in the '60s and I was born at a time in a place where there weren't many cars. Cars were luxury products and nobody would consider buying a car and then disposing of it three years later. And so it came to be over time I went to a society where that was acceptable, but I didn't change my point of view that I thought these things are, engineering-wise, very complicated, expensive and hard to make, and so on. Therefore, they should be… As an engineer, I also like to know how they work. You know, I think that it is fixable, and I think it is worth fixing and so on. Which, by the way, isn't what my parents feel at all. They've got onto the three-year cycle comfortably. I am not comfortable with that.

So I have this old car that I actually moved it with me from the U.S. to where I live now. I was so obsessed about it, you could say. I think it is not something you get rid of.

Anyway, the thing is, I do drive around and ask myself, "Why don't I get a new car," and "What is so great about new cars." And I drive new cars. I rent new cars. I check them out as much as I can. But they are expensive and in some ways they are not as good. They are somewhat more fragile. It seems like the components are designed to break in a way that they have a finite life. That used to be called planned obsolescence. But the idea was that Detroit wanted people to change cars frequently and so they would plan to obsolete the design.

The Japanese came in with a more intelligent approach to that by saying that they had a fixed life for all the components, but when the components would start to break, they all would break together. So the car basically was not worth repairing after a certain time.

Why is the industry doing this? Why is the industry not able to find compelling reasons to buy new things, because they are better, not because you engineer for them to fall apart.

So my question is: Why hasn't one car manufacturer put forward a brand, let's say, that says we have a brand for a car that lasts forty years? We expect this car to last a long time. And therefore the notion of luxury isn't something that is rich in features, but rather that it is rich in longevity. Or not that it is super fast, but it goes super far.

These are weird things. I mean, it seems like the industry is built on the notion of consumption and the more consumption the better, and I would say that something asymmetric to that would be, "Let's think of ways of making cars last a long time."

Now, people would argue that it's not environmentally good to have a long-lasting car because the engine would wear out and you would eventually be polluting and perhaps newer, more efficient engines should be used in newer cars. But why not make the engine a module that can be replaced? Why not make the parts that you think might end up being improved later be replaceable?

More and more, cars are made in an integrated fashion, even though the industry itself is so old that it should be modular today. It should make sense for you to swap out the engines and swap out even the electronics in a car, so that you should be able to pull out the motherboard and put in a new one if you wanted to support new technology in the dashboard.

None of these concepts exist. You used to be able to pull the radio out. You can't do that anymore. The radio has become something that is completely integrated into the dashboard and it cannot be removed. And there are fewer and fewer user-serviceable parts. And so in many ways the industry is integrating more than modularizing.

And I cannot see the reason because, again, these newer cars aren't necessarily better at getting you from point A to point B. They are trying to squeeze the vector of performance into a new dimension. But it isn't one that's particularly interesting, I think, to consumers.

So I am a little bit concerned about an industry which finds difficulty in finding new sources of innovation and growth. And you see the symptom of that when cars, during the '90s, became gigantic—the SUV concept—and you would try to sell those cars to people who lived in cities, these cars that would be good in the mountains. And that's a waste because you don't actually use it that way.

And then different things came and went as fashions. There are some improvements—like I said, in engines and efficiencies—but why throw away a car when you can just change the engine? So it puzzles me a little bit.

One reason industries like this don't seem to be able to innovate is because they have themselves constraints that are invisible and imperceptible. So one of the constraints is that once you are a large, incumbent manufacturer, you have invested in all the equipment and all the staff and all the distributors, your dealer network, and it's very hard for you to say, "We can change direction." And because you've grown to the point where you have stifled any entrant from being able to join into this industry, and also because regulators will say, "The minimum threshold for a newcomer to enter this business includes that you need to pass certain safety requirements. You need to pass certain regulations in terms of emissions and so on," a new manufacturer has to more or less work with an existing manufacturer and thus be compliant with their business logic in order to do anything new.

In fact, there are no new companies. Very, very few. Unless you are dealing with countries. Like in certain countries you have no local manufacturer. So a local manufacturer will emerge, like happened first in Japan, then in Korea, and now it is happening in some of the Pacific Rim countries, and in China, of course. Lots and lots of new manufacturers in China. But once they get established it's unlikely for someone to come in. There are some new ones also in India, I should mention.

So it is becoming a national asset that a car company is created, as if that is a better way of doing business, rather than importing the cars. And governments go along with that, and nurture these entrants, but these entrants don't have any asymmetries. The ambition of an entrant is to be just like an incumbent in another country. So the dream of a Korean manufacturer would be, "Someday, I will be like Toyota." Or the dream of an Indian manufacturer may be, "Someday, I will be like Hyundai."

And so this is a problem. Because there is no one trying to say, "I want to create a whole new concept of the vehicle. I want to create a whole new concept of how to manufacture that vehicle, how it should be fueled, how it should be maintained." Even innovation on concepts like, should it be owned, or should all car ownership be shared so that cars are a shared resource that you reserve online. We have experiments like city cars where a car is not really... It's a rented car in all cases and you just get it when you need it. And that's happening a little bit in Europe and the U.S.

You have innovations going on in power trains but, again, I'm concerned that these innovations are likely to be embraced and extended or... They should be, I should say, sustaining the core companies that are involved. And this is where I got into a debate online with some people. They would say, "What about electric cars? Electric cars are surely disruptive." You have companies like Tesla and perhaps a few others who are saying, "We are going to make a completely new vehicle concept, that it is actually completely different and better than what is available."

The way I would debate this question would be if you are an executive at an existing company. And let's say you are at Toyota, and you have perfect visibility into the roadmap of technologies out there for vehicles—surely you know about battery technology and you know about new ways of even using hydrogen, and you have new ways of dealing with materials used in manufacturing that will make the car better or lighter. So why wouldn't you accept that innovation when someone who takes a risk, like Tesla does, in proving a concept, and then you'd say, "Okay, we'll do that now because it seems to be working." And you could very easily out-spend someone like Tesla, billions of dollars in R&D, and get that technology in-house, and then run with it.

GM may be slower than others, but certainly Toyota may be quicker in getting technology in-house. And they have certainly done a lot with hybrid technology which actually was the smartest thing to do, rather than leap-frogging hybrid and going straight into electric from internal combustion. They took a halfway step and that's been successful.

So my concern for a Tesla-type model is that I see that as a potentially sustaining technology. A power plant is a sustaining technology. What an entrant needs to think about is, "Can I come up with a way of making cars that no incumbent on the planet, not even the ones in India, would be interested in doing—because it would somehow cause them to lose money, or it would somehow cause them to have lower margins than they have today, and would somehow be impossible for them to sell these products because it wouldn't fit into their distribution network?"

These are the checkmarks you need to have on your business plan. Now, that is not to say that Tesla won't be successful. Let's be clear: Tesla could be successful by building a great car and someday they might be acquired for their technology. Or they may still create a nice niche for themselves as a premium brand in an environmentally conscious market.

But being disruptive means—and this is very important—that in another decade or so, there will be no other car companies except yours. That's what that means. That means absolutely crushing everybody around you who is motivated to ignore you. That is the David-and-Goliath scenario that I talk about when I give presentations, that a disruption is about also causing failure in an existing market, from an existing incumbent, and then growing that market by an order of magnitude at the same time. So your objective as a car entrant would be, "I'm going to provide cars for ten times more people that have cars today. They will be at one-tenth the price, and by the way, in so doing, none of the car companies that are around today will be around anymore."

Now you don't have to make that third point your objective, but it is a consequence of being disruptive. It's like, "Oops, I'm sorry, I've destroyed 15 billion dollars worth of market value for you." So that's the question: Can that happen in the automotive industry?

And this is where I don't see the answer in anything that's coming down the pipe. Almost everything I see can be embraced and extended by the current car makers and they will say, "Yes, it is slightly better than before, and we are going to make a slight improvement, but overall, you are going to buy a car every three, four years; you're going to spend so much on insurance; you're going to spend so much on fuel; you're going to spend so much on depreciation. And these are the economics of car ownership. And by the way, we will pay so much in taxes, and thus the government will be happy. Also we'll make sure that as you use the car, you will pay so much in road taxes, you will pay so much in fuel taxes and everything else. Everybody else will get their share, as currently defined in this automotive industry. And that way, not only is the incumbent sustaining himself, but [also] sustaining all the value network and everything else that becomes the automobile industry.

This is why General Motors could not disappear. Because not only did they say, "Who wants a GM car?" "Nobody," that's not the point. The point is we have employees, we have pension plans, we have suppliers, we have the taxes that come along with all these externalities to our particular company, that that's why the government has to come in and support and sustain what is essentially an insolvent, dead brand. And that is not just in the U.S., it has happened in other countries with national flagship brands in the U.K., in France. Not so much in Germany. They've been successful there throughout their history.

Toyota is still a healthy company, but there are questions about how much they can sustain themselves given competition from the low end in Asia. So there have been low-end entrants, but they have been mostly localized and trying to expand slightly their footprint outside of their core markets. But these aren't disruptive in the same way.

There was a bit of disruption happening from Japan. And this is something, again, Clay [Christensen]would talk about. Japan came to the

439

United States and to the world with their car brands and essentially took a significant chunk, if not the majority of business, away from incumbents. But they didn't cause those incumbents to disappear, nor did they increase the value or the number of people driving. I think there would be the same number of people driving. If they didn't have the Japanese option, they'd be buying them from somewhere else.

But that's the problem. They came in, they got their fair share, if you will, but there were forces at play that essentially said, "We will make sure that the incumbents survive even though you guys came in." In fact, the pressure was so strong that the Japanese shifted business models to make sure that sustainability was ensured. They moved car plants to the United States, making sure that they employed American workers, making sure that the dealerships and everybody else would be satisfied with their entrance. They didn't come in with a "We will destroy you all" kind of mentality. They said, "We will work within the system." And that's fine.

At the end, I think it worked out. It was a pretty hairy time during the '80s when they were coming in and people didn't know what the impact would be, and there were a lot of angry people about the Japanese coming in with their cars. But now we've grown to be used to that, and somehow it reached an equilibrium and the domestic-versus-import debate is not that interesting anymore.

So I ask myself all the time these questions, because if I think again back to the fundamental question of why would I be fond of an old car, it is because I don't yet see this improvement. I would need to see a magical, huge improvement in what I hire cars to do. I hire the car to drive me around and, like you said, to have my family protected and cared for. And it doesn't break down and it carries all my stuff. That's the same job most people have, I think. But that can be accomplished in an old car. The only difference is most people just don't want to be bothered mentally or worry about maintaining an old car and it just feels like there is a hassle. Because they are hiring the car as a service. So they think, "I am going to have more service cost if I keep an old car. I have to worry about it and I don't want to worry about it." And so they tend to just upgrade the car or buy a new one. Not necessarily getting better, it just happens to be newer and I don't have to worry about it.

By the way, a lot of that is perception. Having lived in multiple countries, I can tell you that a lot of things in the U.S. are wrong perceptions of what makes cars good or not, or how to maintain things and how long you can stay between oil changes, and things like that.

Anyway, the point being that I still feel the car industry is an example of something a hundred years old—more than 100 years old—that probably became good enough in the job to be done twenty years ago.

Dan: But it's not like there hasn't been any innovation since then?

Horace: Yes, but the thing is the innovations have been tiny, incremental things. So again, the question is this:

Think back to this diagram where you have the trajectory of improvement in performance. Let's take a proxy for how you measure performance in a car. Let's take engine… Let's take not engine efficiency but let's say horsepower. Back in the 1930s cars had 20 horsepower. Then by the 1940s it probably had like 40, 50 horsepower. In the '70s they were probably reaching well over a 100 even though it was a big V8 engine. It probably only had like 150 horsepower. But then they got more efficient and you could get more and more out of those 8 cylinders, and the average 6-cylinder American car today probably has around 200 horsepower.

But that was true probably ten, fifteen years ago. So what they have been doing is either making those engines a little bit more efficient, or they have been trying to actually increase what people can absorb. You have car engines now that are sold as premium cars mostly, but basically way over 200 horsepower, some even going as high as 500 horsepower in some really exotic high-end cars. So if you were to think of… Every car maker has this premium branding, whether that is Cadillac in the U.S. or like a Mercedes.

What the Japanese did is they actually carved out a new brand. So if you have Toyota, you created a Lexus, and then Nissan created Infinity, just so that they could have a home for these improvements. So they would put these improvements as the luxury brand. Honda had Acura as well, and so on. And the measure of performance, one proxy would be the engine horsepower, and that's reached way beyond what people can consume. I would argue that based on the average speed limits globally, anything over 150 horsepower is excessive.

So you are building these enormous engines with all the costs associated with that and all the inefficiencies associated with that, and the weight, in order for you to sell the car, because you want to position it as being a high performance car, and somehow that is what makes a car better.

If you think about the microprocessor in your computer, there was a time when you did need more horsepower. There was a time when you did need more speed, but after a while you realized the marginal improvement to go from 2.5 to 2.7 gigahertz, I'm not going to be able to absorb that. Or if I am, it's not worth the impact it has on heat and battery life and maybe the size of the computer that that would imply. So you switch your buying behavior to de-emphasize the microprocessor speed.

So the thing with the car industry is that they've run up on all of these trajectories and they've run out of things that they could sell and position, that the vast majority of people could absorb. The thing I keep is mind is, what could they possibly improve?

441

They improved things like safety. Certainly that's an important thing to do. There were certainly safe cars twenty years ago, but they weren't as common or as safe as cars are today. They are improving weight, but mostly because increasing safety increases weight, so they have to cut down on the weight of other components in the car. So on average, cars are actually getting heavier, even though they are using lighter materials, because they are having to comply with more of these regulations.

And you are seeing again, in some ways, the right improvements in terms of efficiency, like we are seeing with the use of hybrids. But there are other things that they could have done that would have had an even higher impact than hybrids. For example, switching to diesel fuel, which is very common in Europe but almost impossible to find a good diesel car in the U.S. And I think there's zero chance of finding a diesel car in Japan.

Dan: What's the reason for that.

Horace: I think in Japan it's actually illegal to sell passenger cars with diesel engines.

In the U.S. some states have made it illegal. That may have changed recently but I know a few years ago that was the case. In Massachusetts and California you couldn't buy a new car that was a diesel. The reason for that is because regulators saw diesel smoke as a pollutant that was carcinogenic or was off the limits in terms of particulate or in terms of sulfur.

The funny thing, though, is that Europe is just as environmentally conscious as the U.S. More so in many cases. So how did they accept diesel as an option?

The answer turns out to be that in the U.S. refineries don't produce the same quality of diesel that they do in Europe. That is because diesel was [historically] only used in trucks and machinery. It didn't have to have a high standard of quality and as a result you had this issue in the U.S. that there wasn't production of the right quality of fuel to make a passenger car [clean enough], and that's what forced regulators to say, "Unless you change the fuel you are going to distribute to the pump, then I can't allow the car."

To changeover refineries is a much more difficult problem because they have their economies which are different than the auto economies, and so they are not going to completely redesign their processes and add costs to handle such a tiny market.

So it was this chicken-and-egg problem. I think that may have changed, and now the government can step in and say, "From now on all diesel has to be of a higher grade and everybody can then consume it. And, by the way, you state legislators need to change your laws to allow diesel cars because they are highly efficient and there will be a less [environmental] impact from a diesel car than presumably even from a hybrid car because a hybrid car is very expensive environmentally to manufacture."

And this is one of the other weird things about an economy which emphasizes replacement of old cars. Sometimes replacing an old car with a new car is vastly more polluting because manufacturing a new car takes an enormous amount of resources, far more than the old car would take if it kept running over the same lifetime. And this is where, again, governments come in and institutionalize the disposing of newly manufactured products.

They put in taxes for old cars because they are polluters, supposedly. They have these buyback schemes, so if things become difficult, "Just trade in your old car, we'll get you some money for that and you will stimulate the economy by buying a new car." And supposedly these are all positives. You will get these junk cars off the roads, you will reduce pollution, and you will have more efficient vehicles, et cetera. But in so doing you are just manufacturing millions more cars. And what is the cost of manufacturing? What is the cost of steel production? What is the cost of all of that supposed stimulus.

So there is always a cost associated with things.

Anyway, back to the diesel question. Systems analysis is what is missing here because you need to understand the whole system. You don't just try to optimize for the industry or optimize even for the pocketbook or for the treasury of the United States. You need to understand the whole breadth of impact here.

And the problem is that we have become modular as a society so you have different administrations or different bureaucracies thinking about optimization questions, and they are all doing their darndest. They are all doing the best job they can do given their mandate. And they think they are doing the right thing for the world because they have been educated about what is right and what is wrong and they are not fools.

At the same time, all these local optimizations may actually be a global sub-optimization. So that's where I am concerned about this lack of understanding of entire lifecycles. Some non-profits try to work these things out. Famously, probably infamously, someone actually posited that the Prius is more dangerous to the environment because of the cost of manufacturing —

Dan: Right. The cost of manufacturing and the toll that it takes to both manufacture and manage the battery later. I think there was some famous comparison at one point between it and the Hummer, right? Wasn't that what they were comparing it to?

Horace: Yes. I read that. It turns out that a lot of the assumptions that were underlying that study were flawed, and it is probably not true that the Prius is more hurtful than a Hummer. Nevertheless, what doesn't happen often enough, I think, is this type of breadth of analysis about the impact of things like stimuli or things like, "What is the right thing to do for the industry?"

So my vision, if I may think about what is the real future of transportation...

The 20th century was the century of transportation revolution. If you think the car, although it was invented 1886, it was really not in mass production until the early parts of the 20th century. The aircraft industry pretty much—well, the first aircraft was 1903 obviously, but we had phenomenal advances in aviation technology. If you were to say what was the most rapidly growing and most exciting industry in the first half of the 20th century it was definitely the aeronautics or aviation industry.

If you and I were geeks back in the 1920s, we would all want to be aircraft engineers, or maybe radio. But the idea would be that you were drawn to the most exciting technologically interesting and strategically important industry. Because in the wars—both wars were very largely determined by air power. And after the war—in fact, it was air power that determined also the cold war and almost all the R&D budgets that militaries had spent on that particular technology. It turned out to be the most important innovation in terms of war fighting.

But I would say it was definitely the century of transportation and, as a result, the century where fuel for transportation became the absolute most-strategic asset, which led to multiple wars and millions of deaths. So we are dealing with that century as the transportation century.

Let's not forget the electronics industry and the computer industry came so late in that century it would be like very much like talking about the internal combustion engine in the 19th century. Because the 1880s is when that began, but it didn't take off and become as important strategically and globally until the 20th century. And I believe that now we are feeling the final or real impact of the computer industry having started in the late 20th century. It is now the 21st and we are seeing it take root and become much more strategically interesting and important.

We are not contemplating warfare the same way we would have 50 years ago. Now we are thinking very much that information is the most important weapon you have. So in that sense, by reaching all the way to becoming a strategic asset—and the decision makers and the politicians and those who write laws begin to think consciously about those technologies—then that's when you reached maturity, in my opinion, and that did not happen in the 20th century with respect to computers.

It did happen in the 20th century with respect to transportation technologies. By the way, there was also transportation in the 19th century, the railroads changed everything as well, but they weren't personal transportation, they were long-distance transportation as aircraft made possible. But those are the innovations that I think determined history throughout the 20th century.

To me, though, that's what we are seeing. We are seeing the crisis situation of transportation in the 21st century because now it has reached its plateau in improvement. The same thing with aircraft. There isn't very much you can do to improve them without breaking the law. And the laws are written by sensible people who say, "This is what we need as a society."

So my only disruptive thinking about cars in general is that you shouldn't be thinking about the car anymore, you should be thinking about the roads. You should be thinking about filling stations and you should be thinking about what is the job to be done in general transportation.

I would say that the answer to the problem of how to improve the car, it's actually to not have the car at all, or to have a different means of transportation that doesn't depend on the road network.

There was the Segway concept which was interesting. The wall it ran into was legislation as well. It was illegal to drive it pretty much almost everywhere. It didn't fit on the sidewalk and it didn't fit on the street.

Dan: Well, it scared people in both situations because it wasn't anything that anybody was ever familiar with as far as how to get around. People on the sidewalk were worried that they'd get slammed into, and obviously dangers of those things being on the road. Really, the only people that you see driving it anywhere are like postal workers or, I've seen police officers with it, that kind of thing.

Horace: If you go to Amsterdam or Holland, in general you'll see how they redesigned the whole country around bicycles. I am not exaggerating at all. Every single street has a pedestrian area, bicycle area, car area. Sometimes the car isn't there, sometimes the bicycle isn't there, but basically most places have all three options. And so the whole country is built around it. They had to completely redesign everything in order to accommodate the bicycle. It didn't happen because they one day said, "Everybody can have a bicycle," they actually had to rebuild the road network. And it is an issue.

I mean it is a safety issue. You have sometimes too many bicycles, you have traffic jams, you have issues with pedestrians interfacing with bicycles sometimes. Construction areas cause problems when one of these three is blocked, and so on. But you could spend the whole day just staring at an intersection and seeing how it works. It is so so deeply embedded. And everybody there is conscious of it. The whole society is built around this third mode of transportation, and they've had to do it over probably a century to get that advanced level of transportation in the third medium.

So that's where you have to really think. By the way, it doesn't work elsewhere. Why? Not only because they don't have roads, but because Holland is very flat. It also has a good climate, so you don't have to deal with road conditions like salt and a lot of snow and ice and things like that. It's not very big so you don't have to deal with driving huge distances, so most people are close to where they need to go.

So these are some of the issues that come into play when you study the system and you realize that there are so many obstacles to innovation and, therefore, in order to untangle this mess and cut through it, you have to redesign from scratch, and hardly anybody wants to tear up the roads and tear up the systems that they built over a century.

So I don't have an answer, but someone needs to step up and think about the problem. What are the dependencies that exist right now? And exercising that thought process allows you probably to also apply that to your own industry and think, "How far up do I have to zoom out in order to see what I am doing, how that will change my industry, and how can I make the right improvements?"

So maybe, again, we ran out of time in terms of really hacking at this problem. I just want to plant some seeds of thought about transportation, not just the car.

And by the way, cars, airplanes, and electricity have one thing in common. They have a network. In the case of cars, roads. In the case of air travel, airports. In the case of electricity and power, the transmission network. And once you've built a network—these networks are extremely expensive to build. Just like a distribution network is for a company. And once you've built it, you think you're entitled to milk it for centuries. And you are absolutely not going to tolerate anyone interfering with that network. And you are going to lobby for legislation to make sure that that network is never, ever touched.

Furthermore, you are going to make sure that that becomes a strategic network that no one can alter or affect it. And *then* you realize why it is so hard to change anything. Because that network is so important.

So don't ask about cars, ask about roads. Don't ask about airplanes, ask about airports. And don't ask about efficiency or inefficiency of various power systems, but ask, "How did we get a network that allows everybody to have power, and how do we deal with reversing that."

When you discuss where is the actual locus of power in a business, you realize that the network that was established around the business—either the value network or distribution network—is usually much more important than the product. And when you get bogged down in managing that network, you realize that you are not focused on the product anymore, and that's where things start to go bad.

Dan: And just further to what you are saying, the transportation and electricity infrastructures, those are really what define us as a civilization. That's how this can be so different from something like we've talked about—disrupting mobile phones or disrupting entertainment. Those are things that most people, they might not like it, but they could do without

446

iTunes. They could do without fast distribution of their favorite TV shows and movies. But the two things that seem to really define a civilization—obviously communication is a big part of this and fits into that category—but transportation and the infrastructure that we have to power all of the devices and things that we use, which in turn define our modern style of living, those are the kinds of things that we rely on so much more. If all of us just thought for a minute how much we take for granted the fact that you flip that light switch and something turns on, or that you plug something in.

I mean all of these things. The phones that we love, you've got to charge them. All of these things. You look at modern transportation and how that is one of the most defining factors of the last hundred years. To somebody who was alive several hundred years ago, looking at how effortlessly we traverse the globe and get down the road... Where I go to drive to pick up dinner for my family once a week—you know, going down this hill that we live on and driving a ten-, fifteen- drive—that would have been a day trip to go and get some Austin Tacos for my family [back then]. You know what I mean?

Horace: You are absolutely right in emphasizing how important and valuable it is. And the network is what makes it possible.

And the challenge again, though, from an innovator's point of view, is that you have to understand and respect this network and realize that in order for you to truly change the world, you have to somehow either build a new network or do away with the existing network.

By the way, computers, even before the PC, were really a networked notion. You had a central computer with terminals hooked up to it. And so the idea was that in order for you to have computing power, you needed to have time sharing and you needed to have computer sharing going on, and that was the vision of the world. In order for it to become a power on the desktop and you have it isolated—in your own possession—in your own control... The thing was that it broke the monopoly of the network. It came back, however. Once the computers themselves, the PCs, were networked with each other, and then we had a different sort of network. It wasn't a centralized one, it was a decentralized one. But the power went to the edge and stayed there with PCs.

Now the problem is for power distribution: Power creation is centralized and consumption is distributed. In order for you to truly change the energy footprint of the planet, you have to have local production and central distribution. Completely the opposite. You can have that with solar, you can have that with various other forms of renewables, but you can't have renewables be centralized. This is one of the dichotomy problems we have. Renewables don't work well centralized because they are unreliable. You can't concentrate the power coming from the sun. The sun is distributed everywhere globally.

So fundamental questions about our future in terms of transportation, in terms of energy, you have to understand centralization, decentralization, modularity, and integration.

But the threads are very much intertwined, whether we are talking about the cars or the aircraft or the industries of computing—they have this common thread of, "How do you change things and the dependence you have on networks and dependence you have on incumbency?"

Awaiting the Big Bang

Posted May 30th, 2012 as The Critical Path Episode #40

Horace follows up on his discussion of automobiles and road infrastructure by talking about how road networks were rebuilt in European countries to accommodate cycling. That leads to hints about the challenge of rebuilding energy infrastructure to support new power-train technologies. Finally, he and Dan also analyze comments made by Tim Cook at the recent D10 conference about Apple TV and disruption of the entertainment industry.

Horace: So, I wanted to start today with following up from last week's chat about cars, actually, and…

Dan: A lot of… surprisingly, you know, of all the topics that we discuss on the show, the great things that you bring up, the one that I think has generated some of the most feedback has been guesses about what car you actually drive.

Horace: Mm-hmm. Not surprising, to be honest. I mean, generally I think cars are a topic that everybody likes to talk about.

Dan: Yeah.

Horace: You know, it's fun and these are objects we all use. And that we know how the business works, basically. So I'm sure it's a topic that can get a lot of debate.

But, yeah, so we actually did have someone who guessed correctly within minutes of when we had the post-show discussion, when I dropped another hint, and that hint was that the celebrity who owned the car, that was recognized in this museum as having owned the car, is Ringo Starr. So someone, I think, either knew that or Googled it, and found out quickly enough. And so that person will receive the gift. They tweeted the answer, so it came up on my screen very quickly. But there were many guesses. I won't For those who don't know yet, I'll mention it in a second, but we had guesses. You, Dan, you mentioned the Porsche 911.

Dan: Yes.

Horace: It was actually a very good guess.

Dan: But wrong.

Horace: Wrong, but it actually does meet all those criteria, and it's actually a car that I do fancy. But I don't own one. A lot of folks guessed, actually, Nordic cars like Saabs or Volvo.

Dan: Right.

Horace: I think that's another good guess because they do have these criteria that I listed. They do have museums. And they're nearby where I live, so presumably I would visit these museums.

And there were a few esoteric other options. Somebody guessed an Oldsmobile, I don't know why, but I don't think it has a particular racing pedigree that I'm unaware of.

Dan: Right.

Horace: Volkswagen Beetle came up. And although it does get used in racing, it's very historic as a product. Yeah, it's great, but it was not produced, except in Brazil, even 20 years ago. So, I wouldn't have been able to buy one new in 1992.

So, anyway, the car is a Mercedes-Benz 190E. And there are four examples of it in the Mercedes-Benz Museum in Stuttgart. I was actually there a few weeks ago. It was actually my third visit there, but it was my first with my son. And we went through that museum. We had hoped to also go to another museum in the same city, in a suburb, actually, the Porsche Museum, which actually I would love to go to. I have never been to it, but my son was a little bit under the weather and I also became sick as you might hear now still.

So we didn't make that second visit. But Stuttgart is an amazing place, highly recommended if you're a car fan. Not far is Munich, so you can go to a BMW museum as well there. So, almost every German car company has a museum, and they're very good. They're exceptionally good. I mean, they put a huge amount of resources into the building itself. They're aesthetically and architecturally astonishing buildings—highly, highly recommended.

So anyway, the car was there. It was interesting to me to see my own car there. When I had seen it—I'd been to that museum earlier—there was one instance of the car. Now there were four. It's not everyone's first option for a classic car, but it does have some qualities to it. In fact, *Top Gear*, which is one of the more popular car shows or car TV shows, if not just the most popular show in the world, actually, they claim 350 million viewers....

Dan: Wow.

Horace: But that show actually featured my car as a future classic. So, anyway, it has a lot of the things I like in cars. But I don't want to beat up on cars or talk too much about that, except to mention that follow-up.

Now, the other thing that came in my inbox was an email from a gentleman—let me just pull it up so I'm sure I'm doing it correctly. His name is Steve Crandall, and he gave a lot of reinforcement to the things I mentioned as far as the causes of the industry of automobiles not innovating.

What I concluded, basically, was that you don't look at cars for innovation. They have reached their zenith. What you need to see for a truly disruptive or a quantum leap in innovation in automobile transportation is actually looking at the road networks.

And so in the same way that any network-based technology—whether it's computers now or mobile phones—the network itself is as important as the device. And the network in this case, the road network, has become rigid and has not evolved. There have been very few innovations, notably it's been the interstate system in the U.S. or the Autobahn in Germany, but this is basically the idea of a divided highway that's already sixty, seventy years old as a concept, so not much has happened since.

But the reason networks are important is because they are very important to make the whole value of the system grow. But at the same time they're very hard to change once they're in place. So you don't have the ability to throw out the old network and put a new one in because they become part of the infrastructure. Same with rail networks: It's hard to go from a rail network that works with steam engines to one that works at the same time with high-speed rail. Steam engines and diesel locomotives are compatible, but to take that leap into high-speed rail, you need a completely new architecture, mostly because turns and grades and everything else has to be redesigned.

And so it is with automobiles. So the point is that he brought up an interesting paper that I linked to in Twitter, and I also put up some of the charts that are in that article. It's a paper highlighting why is it that in the Netherlands—which is what I mentioned also in the show last time—in the Netherlands we have enormous penetration of bicycles as the form of transportation. And I hypothesized, or guessed, that it had to do with the climate, it had to do with the fact that there is no hills. It had to do somewhat with culture. But this paper goes on to describe exactly how it happened and why it happened, and it wasn't all those reasons. There were no causal [reasons] to what happened. And they describe the Netherlands, Germany and Denmark, and they give statistics about other countries, western countries mostly, where cycling is a form of transport, and it happens in some countries and not in others.

And they conclude that it is [all about] the road network, even for bicycles. If you architect and if you design your network for transportation correctly, you will get people using bicycles. The problem in many countries is that the bicycle is not included in the discussion about how to accommodate traffic and how to accommodate different forms of transport. But in the Netherlands, it's a very important topic. And you'll see that if you visit, that every road has a provision for bicycles separate from pedestrians, separate from automobiles. And that, in itself, that decision was made quite late. It wasn't made until the '70s or so, and they completely rebuilt their road network. And as a result, that is what drives adoption of that particular mode of transport.

So you would have to think through these problems quite deeply, and there is a huge cost associated with that, which has to be borne by the public, typically because this is an infrastructure that is public-owned, and therefore the public has to agree to fund these products, which is very politically difficult, especially in a country where automobiles are an industry which has political clout. So rather than building more highways, you'd have to reallocate them to allowing for bicycle lanes.

It's not just lanes, it's actually separate roads. The paper is very thorough in explaining all the details that have to be addressed in order to make this comfortable. And safe as well. One data point which struck me, for example, is that the notion and the perception of bicycling in the Netherlands is such that it's not something that's done by people who are actually into bicycling. In the U.S., and many other countries, people [who cycle] are really hard-core cyclists. They're confrontational with automobiles in general.

Dan: You're right.

Horace: They are macho. In many ways they this is a rite of proof of their strength and.

Dan: That's very true.

Horace: It's amazing, right?

Dan: And terrifying. By the way, terrifying for drivers like me, who don't ever seem to know the right way to interpret what a bike rider is about to do.

Horace: Right. Sometimes they think that they have some right to the road. I'm not saying that they're wrong, but the point is that there is a confrontation. A lot of riders are risk-takers. You can see this in the data. You can see the percentage, for example, by age and by gender, of who consumes bicycling in, let's say, United States, U.K., Australia—which have very low penetration of bicycling—versus the Netherlands, Germany and perhaps Denmark. And even in Finland. In Finland about 11 percent of people bicycle versus 0.5 percent, I think, in the U.S.

But the statistic that struck me is that the number by gender—55 percent of women in the Netherlands bicycle. Fifty-five percent! More than half of bicycle trips are taken by women. Now, if you were to survey women in the United States, they consider cycling as a dangerous activity and it's not one that they're willing to risk. Of course there are many women cyclists.

The point is that, by far, the majority [of cyclists are] male in the United States. And this is interesting to me, because what it's saying is that [by fixing the roads] you've made the system work against non-consumption. You've made the system of roadways, and bicycling in general, acceptable to a non-consuming public. The job bicycling is hired to to do is *not* exercise. It is *not* to show machismo.

It's to actually get from point A to point B. And women have as much a need to do point A to point B as anyone else. They have a much lower interest in showing off their machismo, however. In that sense, you see

452

proof in the data that there is an equal split, and even slightly more favoring women as riders in these countries, which I think are highly developed in forms of alternative transportation.

So, these are interesting data points. And the other thing that struck me was—and also you see this when you travel to the Netherlands—that people don't have fancy bicycles. In fact, most bicycles look like they're heaps of junk. They're rusty, they're old, they look like they have one gear. They would be essentially scrap in most of the U.S. Whereas in the U.S., people like to spend $4,000 on a bicycle. That's very common now.

Dan: Right.

Horace: If you go into a bicycle shop in London or in San Francisco, what do you see? You don't see $10 bicycles. You see thousands of dollars per bicycle. Because that's the audience. Whereas I spoke with a Dutchman about the bicycle situation [in Amsterdam]—I said, there are heaps and heaps of rusty old bikes everywhere. And I was asking him, "Why?" And he said, "Well, a lot of these bikes are actually recovered from having been stolen." So the way it works is you park your bike and often it gets stolen. Like every other day, almost. So what do you do in that case? You don't worry about having a nice bike. I said, "Well, what happens if you get your bike stolen?" Well, you go to a shop and you buy another one for $10.

Dan: Wow.

Horace: Because that's been stolen too. And it's being sold again. So, not to say that this is actually common. I mean, maybe in Amsterdam it's more common. But the fact is that they've already created a market system to handle bicycles differently because they're not really objects of desire. They're just tools. And they are stolen by people who are desperate for money for whatever reason, but there is a way to handle that situation.

Also, they're building all kinds of bikes that are specialized, not just for carrying children but for carrying heavy objects, and you can go shopping with these bicycles. They've embedded them in their culture to such a degree. It's interesting to me to observe some of the economics behind this, and that's why I ask these questions sometimes about the degree to which they've changed the way they operate.

I asked one woman there, "Do you use a bicycle?" And she said, "Absolutely, every day. And that's how I get to work." "So how long is your journey?" "Oh, it's not very long [a few kilometers]." "And how many bicycles do you own?" She said, "Five." "Why do you have five?" She said: "Because I leave one in places where I may need it. You just have to sprinkle your bicycles around. So I have one at my friend's house."

Dan: This is like you with your safe houses around in every major city in the world.

Horace: Yeah, if you put all your assets into one giant palatial house, maybe it's one way to live. Another way might be to have five different small houses, right? You have a cottage here and maybe one that happens to be a boat somewhere that you can live on. Different lifestyle, different choices.

The thing is that the Dutch, all of them adopted this notion that you have multiple bicycles, you sprinkle them around and you don't think of ownership as something, that this is a prized object that I need to show to my peers as having achieved a certain status. It's a simple tool.

These are consequences of rewriting the rulebook on bicycle paths and how roads are built. The researchers that put this paper together say that if you do planning correctly, if you do these roads correctly, then you will invite people to bicycle and, what's more, someone tweeted that they actually pay for a lot of this [infrastructure through savings in healthcare]—the quality of health improves because people are bicycling. And there is better health preservation from bicycling. I'm not sure if that's actually linked that way, but it's interesting that you have all these unintended consequences—or intended consequences—that are so beneficial.

And yes, there are issues with weather, and there are issues with the grade, or how steep things are. But 65-year-old people bicycle regularly as a means of transport in some of these countries. And I'm just speaking from a perspective of having lived in Finland. People here bicycle in the snow. Not only do they bicycle in the snow, but deep snow. And they actually have—this is true, hard to believe—but they have winter tires for bicycles. They're studded bicycle tires. I didn't even think it's possible to stay upright on a bike in the snow, but not only do they do that, but they change their tires and they're ready to go for winter. And I've seen them in the deepest blizzards when you have winds blowing and howling, people bicycling to work.

It's not as common as in Holland, but it is something people do. So, it's a fascinating topic.

Now, what this has to do with cars and anything else, the bottom line is you work on the network and you get benefits in other ways. And in this sense, I think that if you want to plot the trajectory of transportation, you'll see these examples where people are redesigning the network and that's leading to new forms of transport.

By the way, the other thing that happens—I keep thinking of new topics—the other thing that happens is actually it's not just bicycles, but a certain grade of moped is allowed onto the bicycle path. So there are possibilities to have motorized transportation. Perhaps electric, perhaps very low-displacement engines available and allowed on these bicycle paths. And as a result, people will probably innovate on how to get the other half of the population also on that bicycle path, and that means some kind of electronics helping you to do that.

One other thing that came in as a feedback was, what about driverless cars as an innovation?

Partly I didn't mention it because I'm not well informed about it, but the other reason is that I think it's so early and the impact of this cannot be assessed until we see it as a market experiment. There is a lot of technology going on here, but it hasn't been proven as a market. The dream—and proposal from people who are doing this sort of thing—is that it's going to lead to an innovation where car ownership disappears, where cars are essentially hired to take you from point A to point B. You order one, and it's like a taxi, a driverless taxi.

There is a lot of Utopia in this thinking. And perhaps it will happen, but I just don't have any data to confirm that it's even feasible, technically, and also feasible as a market, because we saw the Segway, if you remember the Segway...

Dan: Yeah.

Horace: A lot of people were also extremely enthusiastic. They said cities will be redesigned around this product. That it will change the way we use transportation.

Dan: Very optimistic.

Horace: And it ran into several hard roadblocks, like legislation and accident rates. It was very smart but it wasn't smart enough. And in a sense, it didn't disrupt.

So I'm not saying that I don't believe in driverless cars. But I think it's just too early to make a judgment on it.

So, that was my segue into automobiles. And maybe we'll come back to it. I think another topic that will be great to talk about some time later would be air traffic and/or air travel...

Dan: Yeah.

Horace: ...and how that will or will not be disrupted. The other thing that comes up through Twitter conversations is that this will lead into a discussion about energy at some point. Because you'll realize that if you go into electric motors as a new power source, there are new, open questions. One other point raised by Steve Crandall was that auto manufacturers do see new power trains as sustaining. At the same time, however, dealerships may not find them sustaining enough, because a lot of the money they get from service may go away, because these are actually going to be much more reliable drivetrains, and there will be a lot less wear and tear on the product in general—on the car in general. For example, brakes won't wear out as fast, there will be less vibration, less heat, which will cause components to last longer, et cetera. And that might lead to [my] vision of a longer-lived car.

As a result, dealers may balk at the products and then it's possible that if dealers reject it, then car makers will stop making them. We don't know if there will be that reaction. The drivetrain is one thing, the dealer network is another thing.

The third thing is where will you get the energy for this? There is a wonderful diagram on Wikipedia I found, which is called a Sankey diagram—that shows where energy is coming from and where it's consumed in the United States. It's from the Department of Energy. It's a free resource, where they measure all the energy consumption in the U.S. And what's interesting is that petroleum is primarily used for transportation. There is a little bit that goes into industrial use, but predominantly transportation is not only depending on petroleum, but petroleum depends on transportation. So these two are interlinked.

Electrical power is coming from different types of fuel—coal, nuclear, hydro—a little bit renewable. The problem is that if you look at the size of the energy that's going in—converted from the raw chemical fuel to electrical power—where that's consumed today is mostly in residential use. Some of it is business, and some of it is industrial. None of it is transportation.

So the question is this, and this is where it gets interesting: If 20 percent of cars were to switch from petroleum to electrical power, is there enough capacity to drive that switch? If so, what are you going to burn or how are you going to generate the equivalent joules of energy?

Let's say one of the rules is that we don't burn coal instead of petroleum, right? We shouldn't have to switch from one fossil fuel to another fossil fuel. That's not ecological. So let's say that one of the stipulations of switching over to a new power train is that it should use clean fuel, and that means, renewables—maybe even hydro.

In those cases, though, there isn't enough capacity right now. So you have to ask yourself, well, how much capacity do you need to build? And then you realize that the numbers are astronomical, just to switch over 20 percent of your consumption.

It may not meet the goals of being ecological at all. You might get a bit more efficiency, you might get a bit more longevity and all these other good things, but you cannot claim that switching to electric power trains may necessarily cause less consumption of non-renewable fuel.

This is where I think you have to look at the big picture and ask the questions. Like, how much of the energy network we have, the energy production, and the energy sources available. How much of that can support this new technological shift? And so it's not just the roads, it's not just the fact that the automakers need to be incentivized. And not just that the dealer network has to be incentivized. But also you have to be able to sustain that source of clean fuel.

So then you say, "Well, let's do it. Let's build all the capacity we need with clean energy." And then you ask yourself, "Well, how am I going to do that?" That costs money, and that costs another load of fuel to actually build all the sources of energy you need in terms of machinery that's actually going to do the conversion process—the plant and equipment. A lot of people have ideas in that respect, but I'm not—we don't have time to dive into all of that. For example, what if we had better battery technology?

[…]

So all of that was follow-up. But new stuff has happened, right? Tim Cook went on stage again yesterday.

Dan: Right. This is the AllThingsD conference, I believe.

Horace: Right. So, AllThingsD, it's been a forum that Apple has participated in before. It's interesting because Apple execs don't usually get up in front of this kind of event, so we don't get a lot of chances to listen to them.

So the thing that I found interesting was some of the data about Apple TV. And he was asked point-blank about the TV, I think it was Walter Mossberg who asked, "Are you going to make a TV?" Even though he knew that there would be no answer.

Tim Cook said, "No, I'm not going to tell you that answer." It was interesting that the denial was like a non-denial. Basically, he didn't flat-out reject the notion, he just said there would be no answer to that.

But he did talk about Apple TV. Mossberg said, "[Apple TV] sucks. What are you doing to make it better?" And after getting past the defense of the product, saying that it does do a lot of good things, and it is much loved by consumers who use it, he went on to say that there are things it doesn't do.

And then he said that it's actually been not as unsuccessful as people think. He said that it's growing as well. The numbers he cited were that in fiscal 2011—and he didn't say "fiscal," he just said "last year." I'll explain why you can interpret that as fiscal. He said, "Last year we sold nearly 3 million. Actually, 2.8 million. In our year,"—he said the six months of *our* year—"the first six months of our year, we sold already 2.7." So nearly as much as last year.

Now, when he says "our year," he means fiscal because half the year has not gone by yet. So, he has to be talking about the fiscal year. So he's talking about the fourth quarter last year and the first quarter of this year together having sold 2.7 million, and the four quarters before that having sold 2.8.

So I went back in my spreadsheet, which I track all Apple data in, and I backfilled as much as I could all the facts or all the numbers that Apple revealed about the Apple TV, over many years. In fact, this product has been out five years. Can you believe it? It's been since 2007 it's been in the market.

Dan: Wow.

Horace: It's on its third generation. And they haven't given regular data about it, but they've given sporadically a few bits and pieces. For example, they would say "This quarter we sold three times as much as we did a year ago." They would say, "This version of the product has sold one million units as of now, and in the last quarter we sold 820,000." That's one data point.

So you put all these in, you have a lot of blank spots, and you try to fill in the blank spots so that all the statements are consistent. And that's what I did. There are a couple of assumptions in there, but once you put those in, you get a picture of what the product has done in terms of growth. And I've posted that data today.

What you can do once you get that data, though, is make a couple of interesting analyses. First, how many units total have shipped? That's about 10 million as of the end of last year. If it grows at the rate that it's been growing, which is doubling—this past two quarters, it says we're twice the speed. So presuming it's going to keep going like that for the rest of the year, then we might be looking at an additional 5 million for 2012, which would bring the total to 15.

Now, some of them will be put out of use. So let's say 12 to 13 million will be in use at any moment. That's a pretty decent number. Some people will object and say it's unlikely that 10 million were in use in 2011. But we've got to start with something.

So you know roughly the installed base. Then the next question is, do we know pricing? Sure we do. It's $99. In fact, with a little variance internationally, it's pretty much the same everywhere.

And I've analyzed this before as well, and they've been very aggressive about keeping the price consistent globally. That product is not used as a premium product to capture whatever brand value there might be out there. Now we can figure out how much the business is worth. Once you do that, you get some numbers that are interesting, like $330 million in all of 2011.

Now, this isn't a big number. It's essentially single-digit percentage of the iPod, for example, which is not a big business for Apple. It's not worth comparing to the iPhone because it would be a rounding error.

In that sense, it's not big. But at the same time, there is more to the Apple TV than the hardware sales. It's designed to be cheap to buy, but you probably make it up on other things. What other things? Well, obviously there is content. There is a lot of content that they sell for people to consume on this product. And so that brings up the question, "How do you account for that? How can you measure that?" My conclusion is, let's not quibble about what is the average revenue per user, whether it's $10 or $5 a month. But there is some dollar amount.

And the point is this: Here is Apple selling a hardware product at a very low price, probably a very low margin relative to what it's used to.

458

And yet it somehow uses this product to sell content. And look at its other businesses. The other devices they sell. Those are sold at a high premium price with a heavy margin, and they're using the content, whether it's apps or media, to sustain and create the value of that product, that allows them to charge a higher premium, plus subsidies, of course. But in general that's been the logic behind the iPod, behind the iPhone, and behind the iPad, is that the soft stuff is used to enhance—create a moat, protect, and create stickiness for a piece of hardware.

And here is the Apple TV—it's actually almost the exact opposite. A piece of hardware that's cheap in order for you to consume more content. Isn't that interesting? Isn't that interesting that Apple has within its walls these two very opposing, very orthogonal, asymmetric business models. And the other interesting thing is that everybody celebrates the products which are successful and then everybody says that this was a failure. And yet they persisted for five years, they call it a hobby.

It's interesting to me as an observer of business strategies, that this exactly fits the mold of the incubation of a disruptive opportunity within your own company. And you're doing it in a way that it's completely asymmetric, that it's patient for growth. It's profitable, by the way—it has to be. These numbers are small but they are actually probably making a profit on each one.

And it has this very patient, very asymmetric point of performance, and they keep talking about it in ways that make you think that they are thoughtful about it. That's interesting to me. And I left it open as a question: Isn't it curious that we see this phenomenon going on here? Note that content isn't high-margin. We're not talking about a perfect asymmetry, where you have cheap hardware and extremely valuable software, or media. The fact is that they still only get a percentage of the total value for themselves, it's not their media. They're acting as an agent for someone else. But it is very similar to the Amazon model, where Amazon also gives away a device as a player and essentially makes up for it in terms of volume of content sold, or as an Xbox, or a PlayStation, which the hardware is subsidized by the vendor and they make it up on the sale of games.

So we have an example right under our noses for five years of Apple experimenting with this. It has not taken off, but they haven't killed it either. And this is important. The importance here is that they haven't killed it. The importance is that they don't treat it with contempt.

And that is to me very heartening. It may not succeed, but it shows that they are willing to take internal risk of nurturing it.

Now, how will it go? Everybody is waiting for the big bang, and I've talked about this before. I had a post called "Hiding in plain sight." A lot of what's happening with Apple TV is that they're experimenting constantly. AirPlay is an example of a technology that's potentially very disruptive, and nobody knows about it. Apple doesn't tell anyone about it, even though they implemented it and they have extensions to it, which are extremely interesting from a developer's point of view. But they don't communicate it at all.

And famously the CEO of Time Warner doesn't know it exists. In a Twitter conversation I was having this morning with Benedict Evans— he's an analyst himself—and he said it's unlikely that Apple TV is used to sell a lot of content because probably people are using it for different things. And one of the things he pointed out was AirPlay. I had just thought that it's extremely unlikely that most people, who have Apple TV use AirPlay on it. It's extremely hard to discover as a feature. It doesn't show up on the UI anywhere. If you were to scour through every menu item, everything inside of Apple TV, you would not see AirPlay.

Dan: No, you'd never see a mention of it.

Horace: You'd never see it. So you won't discover it that way. You'd have to discover it through your device, and then you would have to discover that you have to set it up in a certain way. So it's hiding. All the time it's hiding there. Some people are using it for AirPlay. And it's very compelling. And it's extremely delightful to use as a feature. But I just don't think that Apple wants people to use it yet because they're not telling anyone yet. And they're not telling anyone because it's not yet good enough—it's got some rough edges. It's not intuitive enough, and they need to embed it in the device in a way that it just screams out at you and says, "This is something you've got to do."

It doesn't happen yet. So I think that these are building pieces. These are things lying around, Lego bricks lying around that are going to come together into an interesting product later. And that's been my hypothesis as far as Apple TV.

Now, is one of those bricks going to be a large screen actual piece of glass? It could happen. It could be one of the things they put out there, but there are many other pieces that are just as important: content deals, APIs, opening up AirPlay in a certain way, having apps available—all of these pieces, technically they're all do-able. The integration is where the magic happens.

To me it's interesting that Tim was able to talk to this point. He signaled that they are still going to be looking at it. They're still, as he put it, pulling on the string to see where that leads. And I'm cautiously optimistic about it. I think TV is the biggest open opportunity out there, bar none. After telecom, which is where Apple went and took the blue ribbon, the next big challenge is going to be television in general and video entertainment, and the placement of devices in that part of our lives. Devices conquered our pockets. They conquered our laps and the areas where we might place an iPad, which didn't have computing placed into them before.

And so they've conquered, decades ago, the desktop. They've conquered the operations room, the factory floor. They've conquered pretty much all communications. And yet, computers haven't conquered the entertainment piece of the map, of the roadmap or the area map of our consumption. And that will happen in the next few years, without a doubt.

One thing I also observed when I was in Amsterdam, I was at a conference on Mobilism. There was a great presentation by someone who went into television shops and he tested all of these big-screen TVs. Because you can't buy them all.

Dan: Right.

Horace: So he went into the stores and did this stuff. And it's shocking, it was shocking to him. One tidbit that I picked up was that he was trying to install apps. Some of these screens do have app stores. Samsung, for example, has smart-TV apps. And he said that whenever he loaded something, he got some notion about how much memory was left in the TV. So the TV, suddenly you realize it has memory, has storage. And yet no TV in the store had in its description the amount of memory available. Now that it becomes a computing product…

Dan: Right.

Horace: …it's still shown, and people are selling it and buying it as if it's a dumb product, because it's just the screen and you're looking for the most over-saturated screen to take home. The thing is that once it sinks in that this is a computing product, I don't think it will be sold the same way. I don't think it will be bought the same way. I don't think it will be positioned the same way. These things don't make sense anymore in that market. It's challenging if you're a Samsung. Or, let's say from Samsung's point of view they sell through "TV retail," whatever that might be, right? Discount stores, big-box stores, Amazon, whoever else will take inventory. And those guys will put it up and say, "Here it is. Click to buy or go to the cash register with it."

But the fact is that computers and phones are sold differently. There are sections of big stores that have these things, but the salespeople have to work differently to sell them. And so the buyer is also looking to evaluate product differently. That's where Apple has developed its stores in a way that is, I think, brilliant at selling a bunch of its own products. I think it was Ron Johnson who once said that when the iPad shipped, he said, "It's as if the Apple Stores were designed for this product." It's the perfect place to try it out, to understand it, to discover what it is, and to buy it. And you have the people and the infrastructure to allow you to actually use it, and that's not easy to do if it's a new product that needs explaining in a Best Buy environment or any other major retailer.

So TVs again will have to be sold—if these are smart TVs; if they're going to be used in different ways; if they're going to be expected to be for making calls, like talking to your grandmother through a webcam; if they're going to be used as an app repository or an app server, or an app—not just games, but all kinds of clever new apps that are something to do with families using it together, or having some shared environment that the whole family can relate to. This is where we're going to see innovation because app developers are going to look at this thing and say, "I have a great idea." And it's not that I'm going to take Angry Birds and port it to a TV. That's obvious. But the next big idea will be like Instagram. "I'm going to create a new way for people to have fun and be cool," or whatever it is, the job to be done, on this new huge piece of glass that's sitting in a common area.

And so people will just create new stuff that not even Apple can envision—no one can envision.

Dan: Right.

Horace: This will be coming out of the genius of millions of people who only see the world through their own personal circumstances, which no one else can see. That's how innovation happens. They see the need, they see the way to execute. And no one else can. And so they are going to be enabled by the context of the tool and the product becoming available. And that magic happens once the product is in the hands of many.

I really think that there is a huge opportunity and I think Apple knows that too, because they're doing all these interesting things and signaling all these interesting signals. And I think the Apple TV is, from a business-model point of view, interesting enough, but also technologically and in many ways… The way they're going to package it and sell it, and build an ecosystem—all these things—it seems almost like there is a checklist out there and someone needs to go through it.

That's what I picked up from a few words from Tim Cook.

Dan: Yeah, a few words.

Horace: I just try to find these little nuggets because the other stuff is… The CEOs have a difficult time being entertaining because they can't reveal any material information. There are laws against it. You can't reveal anything that competitors can benefit from. You can't say bad things about your own stuff because you're supposed to be marketing stuff all the time, as if you're selling it.

So the fact is that nothing interesting gets said, usually. It's always basically a rephrasing of what's already known.

So in that sense there is little out there to be happy about as an analyst. But this was one bit of data that I thought was worth exploiting.

Dan: Ferreting out.

Horace: I guess there is one more piece of news that came in which was that the news from RIM just gets worse and worse every day. First, there was speculation from an analyst that they might do a huge write-down on inventory again, for the third time. That things aren't selling. I wrote a post about that, and I talked about the longevity of a company that has hit a crisis. I called it a trauma. What is the lifetime post a traumatic event? If there is a huge trauma to a company in the phone space, usually there is no recovery. But they don't go, they don't all exit at the same time. There is a variance in the lifetime, or the life expectancy, post this traumatic event.

And so I try to measure that, and I gave a couple of data points where we know how long it took for some people to exit, and the question I was struggling with was, is RIM—or Nokia, but mostly RIM—how long do they have?

And the post assumes that they will exit because no one has recovered yet. There have been 15 failures. We have data for about five or six of them.

And so, these companies that exited, how long did it take? If you start on that basis, how long do they have… By the way, the exit is not necessarily that. It just means that you might lose independence, you might be acquired, you might become part of something else. So certainly Sony now has the remnants of what used to be Ericsson's phone business. And Motorola is now a part of Google. But the thing is that these brands used to be independent and they're not anymore. So RIM and BlackBerry will probably survive as a brand once they change ownership.

But I'm saying that the period when that company may be independent, will probably not be much longer.

So measuring that is interesting, and the question is: Is there a pattern? And my conclusion was that if a company has a phone division, they're actually much more willing to get rid of it if it's performing badly and preserve other divisions. So that's what Ericsson did. They got rid of the phone business, but they kept the networks business. And LG has also been in distress, they've had a trauma, by my definition—which is a period of loss-making. So if I were to analyze it by those measures, LG would be more likely to spin-off this division.

There might be reasons it won't, and then there are all kinds of complications, but I think they would like to get rid of it as soon as possible. But what do you do with RIM? Because RIM has nothing else but its core business. This is the core. And those guys will fight longer. That's what Motorola had to do. They split off, first of all, Motorola—but it still remained as an independent business. It became Motorola Mobility. That itself held on as long as it could until finally it was taken out. And so that took a long time.

RIM is cornered. They have no way out. So they'll fight as long as they can, and nobody wants to take an exit which is humiliating. So these are the two questions: How long do they have, in terms of the clock running out, in terms of money running out? And then, is the spirit willing to continue, because there is no other alternative?

These are interesting questions. And just last night, after closing [of the stock market], the RIM CEO issued a press release saying that they will again make losses, that they hired an investment bank to look for exits. My post predated this other shoe falling by a couple of hours, and, if anything, it confirmed that they're looking for an exit.

And the stock went down another nine to ten percent as a result, to a new low for the year—and for the decade, probably. Things are really quite ugly there.

And speaking of stock dropping, Facebook is another story, isn't it? I don't think we have time for it. Maybe we should talk about social as a topic.

Dan: That would be... I would love to. I was going to say, that would be something I would love to hear your thoughts on because this whole IPO thing, a lot of people don't understand it. A lot of people don't know exactly what it meant: Was the price too high? What does it mean when they talk about it topping? And all of this other nonsense, in technical terms.

Horace: Let me give you a three-minute summary of what I think there.

Dan: Right.

Horace: Facebook is a company that used to be private and Facebook is a company that's public now. It's the same company, right? What's changed is that when it was private, there were a few people who decided what it's worth. And now there are a lot of people who decide what it's worth. So the question in this transition through an IPO is not that the company changes. The company doesn't change. It's not even a question of its value changing. Its question is, how many people are voting on what its value is?

So prior to the IPO, there were hundreds of people, perhaps, involved in thinking about what it's worth, and they were either people who had shares who could trade them, privately. Maybe there was a little bit of trading going on, I don't know. There are some mechanisms for that. But mostly it was bankers, it was executives, who were thinking about it and debating amongst themselves what it's worth, right?

Dan: Right.

Horace: So they set a price based on their own internal consultation. And what happened is, you have a bunch of people who are in the middle, who take this company from private to public, by buying up a bunch of these shares and then selling them to the public. There has to be this quantum shift, if you will, in ownership, and therefore somebody has to take a bit of risk while the transaction is actually initiated. And so the mistake, if there is a failure of an IPO, is that a lot of the guessing that went on prior to the IPO about what it's worth may have been wrong. That's the whole problem. It's the job of those bankers, the underwriters, to figure out what it's worth. Because not only do they have to think about the fundamentals, but they also have to turn around and say, "Let me look at the demand out there, let me look at how eager people are, the psychology of the market." So then they have to go back and refigure it out. Perhaps they sense there's a huge demand, that people are really rabid about this product, this equity. "We've got to give it a higher price"—because their job is to optimize the price, right? The sellers want to get the best deal.

So what happened, if there is a failure of an IPO, is that they all guess wrong. The voting that gets done by the millions of people who want to get their hands on the shares is what the real price is. Now, we're seeing what it's really worth in the eyes of a mass market. And that's why you see potentially this downdraft happen.

It doesn't mean anything, however, about whether Facebook is a good business or not. It's all about what you think it's worth at this given time.

Dan: Yeah.

Horace: And, you know, $30 is a lot. When you add it up, it's $60 billion, it's ridiculously, hugely expensive as a property. It's 100-plus times earnings. It's by no means cheap. And so they decided that that's what it's worth, and they said, "Okay, we'll offer it at this price." But buyers said, "I'm not willing to pay for that," twenty-four hours later. So a lot of people get hurt, especially those who were trying to time it. I'm not going to get into the mechanics of the market, but what we should talk about is what is a business like that really worth. And why does Facebook get a 100 P/E, Amazon gets a 150 P/E, or whatever it is today, and Apple gets a 12? On a good day—it's phenomenal. And why does Microsoft get, like, a 7? Or an 8, or whatever it is.